TRADING WITH THE ENEM

TRADING
WITH THE
ENEMY

John Shovlin

YALE UNIVERSITY PRESS
NEW HAVEN AND LONDON

Published with assistance from the Annie Burr Lewis Fund.

For information about this and other Yale University Press publications, please contact:
U.S. Office: sales.press@yale.edu   yalebooks.com
Europe Office: sales@yaleup.co.uk   yalebooks.co.uk

Set in Adobe Garamond by IDSUK (DataConnection) Ltd
Printed in Great Britain by TJ Books, Padstow, Cornwall

Library of Congress Control Number: 2020949791

ISBN 978-0-300-25356-6

A catalogue record for this book is available from the British Library.

10 9 8 7 6 5 4 3 2 1

CONTENTS

ILLUSTRATIONS

PLATES

ILLUSTRATIONS

MAPS

BIOGRAPHICAL SKETCHES

AIGUILLON, EMMANUEL-ARMAND DE RICHELIEU, DUC D' (1720–88). French foreign minister from June 1771 to May 1774, he sought to recast the French relationship with Britain on the basis of a new commercial treaty and an entente in India.

ANISSON, JEAN (1642–1721). Deputy to the Council of Commerce from Lyon, he saw the advantages of a freer foreign trade. Along with his fellow merchant-deputy, Jean-Baptiste Fenellon, he was sent on missions to London in 1713 and 1714 where he gathered information on British trade laws and taxation that decisively changed the French perspective on the Franco-British commercial treaty of 1713.

BARING, SIR FRANCIS (1740–1810). An English merchant banker and leading shareholder in the East India Company, Baring was approached for advice on commercial questions by William Pitt the Younger, Henry Dundas, and Lord Shelburne. He supported freer trade in the 1780s and a partnership between the new French India company founded in 1785 and its British rival.

BARNARD, SIR JOHN (c. 1685–1764). Patriot Whig politician, MP, and Lord Mayor of London (1737–38), Barnard was a merchant with interests in marine insurance. He opposed Walpole's Excise Scheme, supported war with Spain in 1739, and campaigned unsuccessfully to reduce the interest on the national debt in 1737. Reflecting the interests of his mercantile constituency, Barnard favoured a freer trade with France, which, he argued, would tame smuggling and increase tax revenues.

BEDFORD, JOHN RUSSELL, DUKE OF (1710–71). A politician who supported the Patriot-inspired Anglo-Spanish war of 1739, and a proposed invasion of Quebec in 1746, Bedford served as Southern secretary from 1748 to 1751 in the administration of Henry Pelham, settling the outstanding claims of the

South Sea Company on Spain for the nominal sum of £100,000. He proposed reactivating elements of the commercial treaty of Utrecht, hoping to win a share of the French carrying trade for British shipping. In the cabinet he pushed for a compromise peace with France during the Seven Years' War in opposition to William Pitt, rejecting Pitt's objective to permanently break French commercial and naval power. He was the British signatory to the 1763 peace of Paris.

BOLINGBROKE, HENRY ST JOHN, VISCOUNT (1678–1751). Created Viscount Bolingbroke in 1712 (the name by which he is generally known), he was Robert Harley's partner and rival in the Tory government that signed the treaty of Utrecht in 1713. He took the lead in negotiating both the Franco-British commercial treaty of 1713 and the Asiento provisions of the Anglo-Spanish treaty. After the accession of George I in 1714, Bolingbroke came under scrutiny for intrigues with the Jacobite Pretender and fled to France where he lived until 1725, occasionally attending the Club de l'Entresol. After securing a pardon he helped form the Patriot parliamentary opposition to Walpole, denouncing the prime minister's supineness in the face of growing French power, while secretly accepting a pension from French foreign minister Chauvelin. Bolingbroke left for France again in 1735 when Walpole threatened to expose his corruption. Always a fierce critic of public borrowing, in the last years of his life he worried that the burden of public debt would crush Britain.

BOURDIEU, JAMES (1714–1804). A London merchant banker, Bourdieu was a tobacco-buying agent in Britain for the French Farmers General, and as the London correspondent of Thellusson & Necker in Paris raised money to finance the trade of the Compagnie des Indes. Bourdieu was d'Aiguillon's go-between to Lord North when the French foreign minister sought to negotiate a new commercial treaty in 1772. That same year, Bourdieu failed to interest the East India Company in financing the commerce of a proposed new French Indies company. At the end of the American War, he offered his services as a peace negotiator to Lord Shelburne but was rebuffed. In the mid-1780s, Bourdieu helped broker a partnership between a new French East India Company and its British rival, though the deal was subsequently rejected by foreign minister Vergennes.

BURKE, EDMUND (1729–97). An Irish-born British politician, parliamentarian, and writer, Burke began his parliamentary career as secretary to Charles Watson-Wentworth, marquess of Rockingham. He was a leading advocate for

Caribbean free ports in 1766 and contemplated a more comprehensive revision of the trade laws. Burke opposed the coercion of the Thirteen Colonies in the mid-1770s, arguing that Parliament should use American commerce to increase tax revenues at home rather than tax Americans directly. From 1781 to 1784 he led a parliamentary select committee looking into abuses of the East India Company in Bengal, and from 1788 to 1795 led the impeachment of former governor-general Warren Hastings. Like most Whigs, Burke opposed the Franco-British commercial treaty of 1786.

Bute, John Stuart, earl of (1713–92). Bute was tutor to the young George III and, after the prince's accession to the throne in 1760, became the leading minister in his government. Identified with Patriot positions, Bute nonetheless broke with William Pitt over the latter's desire to continue and expand the Seven Years' War. Bute and the king were anxious about the burden of public debt and this dictated a policy of peace. The principal British architect of the 1763 treaty, Bute retired from office after it received parliamentary assent, driven out by furious criticism of his personal influence over the king.

Calonne, Charles-Alexandre de (1734–1802). Appointed contrôleur général in November 1783, Calonne was an ally of foreign minister Vergennes. Calonne supported a deal between the new French East India Company established in 1785 and its much larger British rival. He was a principal architect of the 1786 commercial treaty with Britain, which, he hoped, would make French manufacturing more competitive. He envisioned further reforms to improve state finances which were in desperate condition at the end of the American War. Calonne was unable to control the Assembly of Notables he convened in 1787 to approve his reform programme, and went into exile in Britain later that year, having lit the fuse that would touch off the French Revolution.

Chauvelin, Germain-Louis, marquis de Grosbois (1685–1762). French foreign minister and *garde des sceaux* (Keeper of the Seals) from 1727, Chauvelin was Cardinal Fleury's chief lieutenant and presumed successor until his mysterious disgrace in 1737. Chauvelin embodied the contradictions of French foreign policy in this period, being both intensely concerned about Austrian power and anxious to check Britain's ascent. Believed to be open to financial innovation in the spirit of John Law's 'System', Chauvelin was the recipient of proposals in the 1730s to consolidate the royal debt and expand the money supply. In the comtesse de Verrue he shared a patron with the political economist Jean-François Melon, and some of the latter's ideas resonated with views Chauvelin expressed as minister.

CHOISEUL, ÉTIENNE-FRANÇOIS DE STAINVILLE, DUC DE (1719–85). Louis XV's leading minister from 1759 until his disgrace late in 1770, Choiseul occupied at one time or another the portfolios of foreign affairs, the navy and colonies, and war. He helped negotiate the novel French alliance with Austria in 1756 and after the Seven Years' War planned for a Bourbon naval war to cut Britain down to size. Choiseul was advised by the political economist François Véron de Forbonnais, and some of the policies he favoured resonated with those proposed by the Gournay circle. As minister, he presided over the cession of Canada in 1763, preferring an empire with minimal territory and strong commercial prospects, protected by strategic strong points. He disapproved of empire-building in India and looked to a league of friendly Indian powers to protect French trade there. In the Caribbean he favoured a limited relaxation of the Exclusif, and appointed the Martiniquan planter Jean-Baptiste Dubuc as head of the Bureau of Colonies. He was removed by Louis XV in 1770, when, in the midst of a financial crisis, he nearly allowed a war to break out between Spain and Britain over the Falkland Islands. His cousin and ministerial ally, César-Gabriel de Choiseul, duc de Praslin, shared his disgrace.

CLIVE, ROBERT, BARON (1725–74). One of the most effective officers serving in the forces of the East India Company in the 1750s, Clive engineered a revolution in Bengal in 1757 where the company and its Indian allies overthrew Nawab Siraj ud-Daulah. Clive subsequently won a battle in the company to determine whether it would govern a territorial empire in Bengal. In 1765 he accepted the *diwani* (the right to gather taxes in Bengal), initiating an effective transfer of sovereignty. Clive spent the rest of his life defending the enormous perquisites he had acquired in India from critics who blamed him for the plunder and corruption increasingly associated with company rule.

COLBERT, JEAN-BAPTISTE (1619–83). Serving as Louis XIV's contrôleur général from 1665 until his death, Colbert established the framework under which French commerce was governed in the eighteenth century. He is known for raising tariffs to foster import-substituting industries in France – a policy that sparked a trade war with the Dutch Republic. Often represented as aggressive and bellicose, in fact Colbert's hope was to make France the dominant state in Europe by peacefully expanding its commerce.

COLBERT, JEAN-BAPTISTE, MARQUIS DE TORCY (1665–1746). The nephew of Jean-Baptiste Colbert, Torcy was foreign minister from 1696 to 1715, favouring a relaxation of tensions with the Dutch. He sent Nicolas Mesnager to Spain in 1705 and again in 1708 with a view to opening Spanish America to French merchants, and subsequently European merchants in general. Torcy directed Mesnager's negotiations with Bolingbroke in 1711 over the privileges of the South Sea Company, insisting that no Pacific ports be conceded to British control, but making no objection to the company's acquisition of the Asiento.

DAVENANT, CHARLES (1656–1714). The foremost British political economist of his day, he built on the 'political arithmetic' elaborated in the seventeenth century by William Petty. Davenant was also a Tory MP and leading journalistic spokesman for Tory causes. As inspector-general of the Exports and Imports from 1712, he helped elaborate a Tory case for freer trade with France. Davenant's writings continued to be cited down to the end of the century.

DECKER, SIR MATTHEW (1679–1749). An Anglo-Dutch merchant, Decker had been an early backer of Robert Harley's South Sea Company. With the Tories in the wilderness after 1714, he made his peace with the Hanoverian regime and was raised to a baronetcy in 1716. Decker was a long-standing director and twice chairman of the East India Company, and was close to Gerard van Neck, another leading shareholder and director. In his retirement, Decker penned two oft-republished tracts, *Serious Considerations on the Several High Duties Which the Nation . . . Labours Under* (1743) and *An Essay on the Causes of the Decline of the Foreign Trade* (1744). Both made a case against high taxes on trade, while the latter called for freer foreign trade, representing the abandonment of the commercial treaty of 1713 as a mistake. Decker's works continued to be reprinted and cited through the 1780s.

DESMARETZ, NICOLAS, MARQUIS DE MAILLEBOIS (1643–1715). A nephew of Jean-Baptiste Colbert, Desmaretz was contrôleur général from 1708 to 1715. He believed commercial openness was necessary to market French products abroad and supported a reopening of trade with Britain in 1713. He belatedly came to see how unbalanced the commercial treaty was in Britain's favour and vainly sought to renegotiate it.

DUBUC, JEAN-BAPTISTE (1717–95). A Martiniquan planter whom Choiseul appointed as head of the Bureau of Colonies in 1764, Dubuc pushed for a greater measure of free trade for the French Caribbean colonies.

DUNDAS, HENRY, LATER VISCOUNT MELVILLE (1742–1811). The most powerful Scottish politician of his day, after serving Grenville and then North Dundas became William Pitt the Younger's trusted lieutenant. He presided over the Board of Control established under the 1784 India Act, using his influence to try to curb the expansionism of the East India Company and get its financial house in order. He strongly supported conciliation with the French in the mid-1780s, seeking an arrangement that would permanently pacify Franco-British relations in India. He also supported the commercial treaty with France in 1786.

DUPLEIX, JOSEPH-FRANÇOIS (1697–1763). Appointed governor-general of the French settlements in India in 1742 after a career in the service of the Compagnie des Indes, Dupleix's policies got the company embroiled in succession struggles in the Carnatic region, and in military conflicts with the East India Company. He came to believe that the French company would need to extract substantial tax revenues in India to cover its defence and administrative costs. He was removed in 1754 as part of the company's search for an accommodation with its British rival.

DUPONT DE NEMOURS, PIERRE-SAMUEL (1739–1817). Drawn as a young man to the Physiocratic political economy of François Quesnay and the marquis de Mirabeau, Dupont subsequently became the friend and protégé of Jacques Turgot, contrôleur général from 1774–76. In the controversy over the relaxation of the Exclusif in the 1760s, he supported greater freedom of trade for the Caribbean colonies. Having secured a position working for the contrôle général, he came to the notice of foreign minister Vergennes. Dupont became his trusted aide and helped design and promote the 1786 commercial treaty with Britain. A legislator during the French Revolution, Dupont immigrated to America in 1799 where his descendants established what would become the DuPont chemical company.

EDEN, WILLIAM, LATER BARON AUCKLAND (1745–1814). A lieutenant of Grenville and then North, Eden was selected by William Pitt the Younger to negotiate the Franco-British commercial treaty of 1786. Well-read in political economy, he came to the conclusion in the late 1770s that Britain faced a competitiveness crisis partly due to its monopoly position in American trade. He opposed the establishment of full free trade with the United States in 1783 because he wished to reserve the carrying trade to and from the Caribbean for

British vessels. After his successful negotiation of the commerce treaty in 1786, Dundas employed Eden to negotiate a convention signed in 1787 regulating French commercial access to Bengal. He was created Baron Auckland in 1789.

FENELLON, JEAN-BAPTISTE (*c.* 1650–1720?). Deputy to the Council of Commerce from Bordeaux, Fenellon vocally supported freer trade and a commercial treaty with Britain to restore French wine markets there. Along with fellow merchant-deputy Jean Anisson, he travelled in 1713 and 1714 on missions to London, where he admired Robert Harley's South Sea Company. He subsequently supported John Law's founding of a similar company in France and served as inspector-general of Law's Banque Générale.

FÉNELON, FRANÇOIS DE SALIGNAC DE LA MOTHE, ARCHBISHOP OF CAMBRAI (1651–1715). The leading critic of Louis XIV's foreign policy, Fénelon called for a retreat from expansionist and Colbertist policies that had embroiled France with its neighbours. His *Adventures of Telemachus* (1699), a utopian epic, was one of the most widely read books of the eighteenth century.

FLEURY, ANDRÉ-HERCULE DE, CARDINAL (1653–1743). Louis XV's childhood tutor and his principal minister in all but name from 1726 until his death in 1743, Fleury consistently pursued a policy of avoiding war with Britain and the Dutch Republic, abandoning this commitment only in 1740 in the face of a large-scale British invasion of Spanish possessions in the Caribbean.

FORBONNAIS, FRANÇOIS VÉRON DE (1722–1800). The most prolific and influential of the circle of writers around Jacques Vincent de Gournay, Forbonnais hailed from a family of textile manufacturers and sought to use his political economic expertise to win government office. He was appointed inspector-general of the coinage in 1756, and informally served as an adviser to Étienne de Silhouette on the American boundary commission and when Silhouette was contrôleur général in 1759. He was subsequently consulted by Choiseul. Forbonnais emerged as one of the earliest and most important critics of Physiocracy in the 1760s.

FOURNIER (OR FORNIER), FRANÇOIS (1698–1784). A merchant based in Nîmes but with interests in the Spanish-American trade from Cádiz, Fournier was part of the circle of *négociants* who advised the comte de Maurepas, naval minister during the War of the Austrian Succession, and pressed him to expand the navy.

FOURNIER, JEAN-BAPTISTE (?–1782). Director of the tobacco department of the General Farms in 1745 when he travelled to England on a mission to end the War of the Austrian Succession, Fournier would go on to become a Farmer General in 1755.

FRANCIS, PHILIP (1740–1818). An Irish-born British politician and secretary to William Pitt the Elder in the early 1760s, Francis is thought to have been the author of the anonymous *Letters of Junius* which excoriated leading politicians from 1769 to early 1772. He also translated Isaac de Pinto's *Essay on Circulation and Credit* (1774). In 1773, Francis was appointed one of the councillors to the Supreme Council of Bengal, intended to advise the new governor-general, Warren Hastings. Francis criticised the wars Hastings conducted in India and, when he returned to Britain following a duel with Hastings in 1780, he seconded Burke's efforts to impeach him. A Whig, Francis opposed the 1786 commercial treaty with France.

GEE, JOSHUA (1667–1730). A merchant consulted by the Board of Trade, Gee wrote a widely read political economic tract, *Trade and Navigation of Great-Britain Considered* (1729). He admired France's Colbertist administration of trade and worried that Britain's commerce was in relative decline. It might improve its balance of trade, he argued, if it imported from its American colonies goods currently bought in Europe. He rejected freer trade on the grounds that it must bring British manufacturing into competition with lower-wage continental rivals. His work was translated into French in 1750 by Jean-Baptiste Secondat de Montesquieu, a protégé of Vincent de Gournay.

GLOVER, RICHARD (*c.* 1712–85). An MP and London merchant specialising in the import of linens from Central Europe, Glover favoured a limited free trade in such goods, arguing that it benefited Britain more than developing a domestic linen industry. A Patriot Whig, he had joined in the opposition to Walpole in the 1730s, supporting war with Spain, but later proved a friend of peace, arguing in Parliament in 1762 'that our trade had suffered by war'. Glover was selected to conduct informal negotiations with Lord North on the possibilities for a new Franco-British commercial treaty in 1772.

GOURNAY, JACQUES-CLAUDE-MARIE VINCENT, MARQUIS DE (1712–59). Born Jacques Vincent in the Breton port of Saint-Malo, he spent fifteen years in Cádiz as a merchant in the Spanish American trade. In the mid-1740s he came to the attention of Maurepas, the naval minister, and undertook fact-finding missions on his behalf to Britain and parts of northern Europe. Vincent gave up trade definitively in 1747 and was ennobled as the marquis de Gournay. He bought the office of intendant of commerce, which gave him a seat on the Bureau of Commerce, and encouraged a circle of writers to translate and compose works on political economy. Gournay pressed for a strategic reorientation of France towards the Atlantic and commerce. He valued peace as the condition for French aggrandisement and called for a navigation act to enhance the strength of the French fleet. He supported the opening of the French East India trade to all French merchants, but opposed a wider measure of free trade.

HARLEY, ROBERT, EARL OF OXFORD (1661–1724). A former Whig who became the leader of the ascendant Tory party during the War of the Spanish Succession, Harley (ennobled in 1711 as earl of Oxford) was Lord High Treasurer from 1711 to 1714. In 1711, he founded the South Sea Company, using it to consolidate unfunded government debt. In the negotiations for the treaty of Utrecht, he sought to carve out a privileged place for the company in the trade to Spanish America.

HOLDERNESS, ROBERT DARCY, EARL OF (1718–78). Southern secretary from 1751 to 1754 in the administration of Henry Pelham, Holderness sought a greater measure of free trade with France, and supervised negotiations to resolve Franco-British boundary disputes in America, and to end the wars between the British and French East India companies in India. In 1772, now as a confidant of George III rather than a minister, he proposed a new Franco-British commercial treaty to the French ambassador.

HUME, ALEXANDER (1693–1765). A major shareholder and, for a time, director of the East India Company, Hume steered the company's negotiations with its French counterpart from 1753 to 1755 as the two bodies sought to end their wars in India and to neutralise the region in case of future wars in Europe. Having begun his career in the less militarised Ostend Company, Hume saw no advantage to acquiring territory in India and hoped the French company might be prevented from using such acquisitions to exclude British trade. As an MP, he was associated with Henry Pelham, providing assistance to the government in the management of public credit.

HUME, DAVID (1711–76). A Scottish philosopher who published a series of essays on political economy under the title *Political Discourses* (1752), Hume sought a more peaceful relationship between Britain and France and favoured a freer trade as a means to achieve it. Fiercely opposed to the expansion of

Britain's empire under William Pitt, Hume feared that the weight of public debt would eventually destroy Britain's constitution and its ability to intervene when necessary in Europe. He served the British government on minor military and diplomatic missions during the War of the Austrian Succession, was secretary to Francis Seymour-Conway, earl of Hertford, British ambassador to France from 1763 to 1765, and subsequently served as undersecretary in the Northern department under Hertford's brother, Henry, from 1767 to 1768.

HUSKE, JOHN (1724–73). A Boston-born merchant and MP, Huske was a principal architect of the free ports established in the Caribbean by the Rockingham administration in 1766, though he had a far more expansive vision of free ports in the Americas, advocating their extension to all the major trading cities of North America. He regarded free ports as a means to peacefully penetrate the French and Spanish colonies and to draw off their trade to British advantage.

LAW, JOHN (1671–1729). The son of an Edinburgh goldsmith-banker, Law killed a man in a duel in 1693 and was forced to flee England. He would spend much of the rest of his life on the continent where he speculated in financial markets and theorised on money and banking. In 1716 he persuaded the French regent to allow him to establish a bank issuing paper currency in Paris. He subsequently founded the Compagnie d'Occident in imitation of Harley's South Sea Company, and in 1719 the Compagnie des Indes, which he planned to use to consolidate the whole public debt. Law claimed that his bank and companies would preserve the peace of Europe by turning France into a benign commercial colossus, uninterested in Spanish-American silver or in conquering its neighbours. His 'System' collapsed in 1720 when the speculation it encouraged gave way to financial panic, and Law fled France, dying nine years later in Venice.

MAUREPAS, JEAN-FRÉDÉRIC PHÉLYPEAUX, COMTE DE (1701–81). The son of Jérôme Phélypeaux, comte de Pontchartrain (1674–1747) and naval minister from 1699 to 1715. In 1723 Maurepas was appointed to his father's former office and served as naval and colonial minister until 1749, when he was disgraced at the behest of Madame de Pompadour. Maurepas came to see France's Caribbean colonies as its principal commercial asset and he pushed from 1745 to build a larger navy to protect French trade. After decades in the political wilderness, Maurepas was recalled in 1774 to serve Louis XVI as senior councillor and minister without portfolio, remaining in this role until his death in 1781.

MELON, JEAN-FRANÇOIS (1675–1738). The most widely read French political economist of the 1730s, Melon had been employed as John Law's secretary under the 'System', and campaigned in the 1720s for Law's return to France. His *Essai politique sur le commerce* (1734, revised edn 1736) argued that France could exit the brutal competition for global markets by fostering the prosperity of its own population and tapping this potentially huge market to support an expansive manufacturing industry. His work sparked a lively debate inside and outside the French administration.

MESNAGER, NICOLAS (1658–1714). A merchant and diplomat, Mesnager represented Rouen on the Council of Commerce, and in 1708 designed French plans to open Spanish America to a freer European trade. He helped negotiate the Franco-British commercial treaty of Utrecht in 1713 and the provisions of the peace that accorded the Asiento to the South Sea Company. Once active himself in the Spanish-American trade from Cádiz, he was representative of a new social type in France, the *négociants*, major overseas merchants whose interests and expertise were to play an increasing role in the formation of French policy.

MIRABEAU, VICTOR RIQUETI, MARQUIS DE (1715–89). He became a literary celebrity with the publication of his *L'ami des hommes* (1756–58), where he advocated major changes in French political economy, including freer trade, a retreat from Colbertist promotion of manufacturing in favour of agricultural development, and the abandonment of slavery. He was recruited by François Quesnay, and the two men elaborated the foundations of Physiocracy together, while pressing the principal Physiocratic policy recommendation: complete freedom of the grain trade.

NECKER, JACQUES (1732–1804). A Genevan with a successful Paris banking practice, Necker became a leader of the Compagnie des Indes in the 1760s by using contacts in London to fund the company's trade in India. He pressed it to stay out of geopolitical conflicts and focus exclusively on trade. In 1769, when the monarchy suspended the company's monopoly, he was its most influential defender. In 1777 Necker would become director of finances – effectively finance minister – in the government of Louis XVI (as a Protestant, he could not be contrôleur général). Necker was sceptical that war would secure any advantage for France and made peace overtures to Lord North during the American War. He resigned in 1781 but hoped to return to office, promoting reforms that would renovate royal finances without major changes to taxation or the economy. He returned to power in 1788 in the early stages of the French Revolution.

NEWCASTLE, THOMAS PELHAM-HOLLES, DUKE OF (1693–1768). Serving as Southern secretary in Walpole's administration, Newcastle had responsibility for relations with France and Spain. He became increasingly uncomfortable with the prime minister's war-avoidant strategy and supported Patriot positions leading to the war with Spain in 1739. After Walpole's fall, he continued to play a key role in government under his brother, Henry Pelham, and succeeded him as prime minister in 1754. In coalition with William Pitt, he helped lead Britain during the Seven Years' War, focusing on financing the conflict and managing Parliament while Pitt directed the war effort.

NORTH, FREDERICK, KNOWN AS LORD NORTH (1732–92). British prime minister from 1770 to 1782, he averted conflict over the Falklands in 1770 but led Britain into war with its rebellious colonies in America. North appeared briefly open to an entente with France in 1772 but did not decisively embrace the offer of a commercial treaty. He resigned in 1782 after the battle of Yorktown, but continued to play an important role in politics until the mid-1780s.

PATERSON, WILLIAM (1658–1719). A Scottish merchant involved in Caribbean trade, Paterson was one of the architects of the Bank of England, established in 1694, and subsequently helped establish a Scottish company to found a colony at Darien on the Isthmus of Panama. The venture failed disastrously in 1698–99, but Paterson continued to see Darien as the strategic key to world trade – the site from which Britain might dominate the commerce of the Americas. He proposed to William III in 1701 that free ports be established there, and at Havana, to channel the commerce of Spanish America and give Britain the means to check Bourbon power and foster a permanent peace.

PELHAM, HENRY (1694–1754). Having served in various roles under Walpole, he emerged as his political heir in the 1740s, succeeding the earl of Wilmington as prime minister in 1743, a position he held until his death in 1754. Like his political mentor, Pelham had a consistent preference for peace. He favoured ending the War of the Austrian Succession as early as 1745, and in the postwar period fostered a warming of relations with France by moving to roll back restrictions on French trade.

PITT, THOMAS, FROM 1719 BARON OF LONDONDERRY (c. 1688–1729). The son of Thomas Pitt Sr, chief of the Madras presidency of the East India Company, and the uncle of William Pitt the Elder. Thomas Pitt was cultivated by John Law, who saw him as a conduit to Pitt's brother-in-law, James Stanhope. Pitt ventured £6,000 in Law's Compagnie d'Occident, losing most of it in the 1720 crash.

PITT, WILLIAM, THE ELDER, EARL OF CHATHAM (1708–78). A leader of the Patriot opposition to Walpole, Pitt built his political career arguing that French commerce and the naval power it sustained was the principal threat to Britain's security. As Southern secretary he played a leading role in managing the British war effort during the Seven Years' War in coalition with the duke of Newcastle. Late in the war, he saw the opportunity to permanently cripple French power by seizing much of its empire, but those who took a more moderate view forced him to resign in 1761. He would return to office as prime minister from 1766 to 1768 but poor health limited his participation in government. Pitt was well disposed towards the American colonists, but rejected American independence, seeing Britain's wealth and power as depending on the American connection.

PITT, WILLIAM, THE YOUNGER (1759–1806). Son of the elder Pitt, as prime minister in the mid-1780s he backed away from his father's attempts to crush French commerce and naval power militarily. He was chancellor of the Exchequer in the Shelburne administration and introduced the failed American Intercourse Bill to Parliament in 1783. As prime minister from the end of 1783 he backed free trade with Ireland, supported negotiations for a commercial treaty with France, and pursued separate trade talks with Spain, Portugal, and Russia, intended to revitalise British commerce.

QUESNAY, FRANÇOIS (1694–1774). Physician to the royal favourite, Madame de Pompadour, Quesnay used his position at court to attract followers to the Physiocratic political economy he developed from the 1750s. Quesnay early recruited the marquis de Mirabeau, who proved an indefatigable collaborator. The two men argued that land alone is the source of wealth, promoted free trade domestically and in the French colonies, and recruited many younger men to promote and elaborate their doctrines.

RAYNAL, GUILLAUME-THOMAS, ABBÉ (1713–96). The lead author of the *Histoire des deux Indes*, first published in 1770 and destined to be a bestseller, Raynal managed a team of writers, most prominently Denis Diderot. He drew a pension from the foreign ministry, and some of the positions he took echo Choiseul's, but the multi-volume work, produced in three expanding editions, was truly 'polyphonic', mapping the history of European colonisation and trade, advocating changes in policy, and occasionally launching impassioned attacks on the cruelty and destructiveness of European expansion.

RAYNEVAL, JOSEPH MATTHIAS GÉRARD DE (1736–1812). A key aide to Vergennes in the foreign ministry, Rayneval negotiated preliminaries for the 1783 peace of Paris in informal discussions with Lord Shelburne, and subsequently negotiated the Franco-British commercial treaty of 1786. He is to be distinguished from his brother Conrad Alexandre Gérard, who negotiated the treaty of amity and commerce between France and the United States in 1778.

ROCHFORD, WILLIAM HENRY VAN NASSAU VAN ZUYLESTEIN, EARL OF (1717–81). After a career in which he served as ambassador in a string of major posts, including Madrid and Versailles, and a spell as Northern secretary from 1768 to 1770, Rochford was Southern secretary from December 1770 to November 1775, a role in which he showed a disposition to warmer relations with France. In 1772, when French foreign minister d'Aiguillon sought a commercial treaty and an entente in India, Rochford proved open at first. However, fearing that he would be perceived as a dupe of the French, he backtracked, threatening to mobilise a British naval squadron against a French expedition bound for Sweden.

SAINT-PIERRE, CHARLES-IRÉNÉE CASTEL, ABBÉ DE (1658–1743). French cleric and man of letters, Saint-Pierre argued in his *Projet pour rendre la paix perpétuelle en Europe* (1713) that only a European confederation could end war in Europe. As a member of the regent's household, he would have known John Law. Remaining well connected politically in the 1720s and 1730s, Saint-Pierre participated in the Club de l'Entresol and continued to promote his projects for perpetual peace.

SHELBURNE, WILLIAM PETTY, EARL OF (LATER MARQUESS OF LANSDOWNE) (1737–1805). An Irish-born British politician, Shelburne began his career with a spell as president of the Board of Trade in 1763. He gravitated thereafter into the orbit of William Pitt the Elder, and became the latter's chief lieutenant in Parliament, serving as Southern secretary in Pitt's administration from 1766 to 1768. As a minister and a major shareholder in the East India Company, Shelburne backed Laurence Sulivan in the political battles that roiled the company in the 1760s. In the 1770s, he sought conciliation with the American rebels but opposed American independence, which he thought must be disastrous to Britain's commercial well-being and future power. Shelburne became prime minister in 1782 and personally conducted the key negotiations ending the American War, in which he told his French interlocutor Rayneval that Franco-British enmity should give way to partnership, sealed by a new commercial treaty. Yet he resolutely opposed the extension of French empire in India, conceding only a token rounding out of territories near French settlements. Shelburne's political-economic views are usually assumed to derive from those of Adam Smith, Josiah Tucker, or the abbé André Morellet – men of letters whom he occasionally consulted. But his emergence as a supporter of free trade with America and with France in the early 1780s is better understood as a reaction to the geopolitical shifts initiated by the American War. He resigned as prime minister early in 1783, unable to command a majority in Parliament, and went on, from the political sidelines, to support freer trade and more amicable relations with France.

SILHOUETTE, ÉTIENNE DE (1709–67). Resident in London as a tobacco buyer for the Farmers General in the 1730s, Silhouette came to know British Patriot leaders and was impressed with the strategic importance they placed on America. After writing a celebrated memorandum exploring the foundations of British power in 1747, Silhouette came to be seen as an expert on Britain and sat on the commission to settle boundaries in America while also serving as royal commissioner in the Compagnie des Indes. Committed to averting war in India and America, which he believed would undermine French commerce, he hastened it by his ham-fisted diplomacy. Silhouette briefly served as contrôleur général in 1759, raising money for an abortive raid on Britain intended to cause a financial panic. Silhouette resigned following the temporary collapse of royal credit in 1759.

SMITH, ADAM (1723–90). A professor of moral philosophy who began to explore political economic subjects in the 1760s, Smith is celebrated as the author of the *Inquiry into the Nature and Causes of the Wealth of Nations* (1776). He advised officials such as Alexander Wedderburn, William Eden, and Henry Dundas, who played a leading role in the management of British affairs with America and France. Smith welcomed the prospect of a reopening of trade with France but saw little reason to extend commercial advantages to the United States in 1783. His ideas acquired a new authority when leading British politicians, including Shelburne and Pitt, began to look to freer trade to vitalise British commerce after the American War.

STANHOPE, JAMES, LATER EARL STANHOPE (1673–1721). Commander of the English forces sent to Spain to support the campaign of Archduke Charles of Habsburg to win the Spanish throne, Stanhope negotiated the treaty of Barcelona with Charles in 1707 which guaranteed British merchants privileged access to the trade of Spanish America should the archduke become king. Subsequently, as George I's Southern secretary, Stanhope negotiated additional privileges for the South Sea Company, including a yearly 'permission ship' to trade in Spain's American empire. A fierce critic of the commercial treaty of Utrecht in 1713, Stanhope subsequently negotiated an alliance between France and Britain which was supported at first by John Law. He became increasingly alarmed about Law's 'System' as it became clear that the Scot was turning from an ally into an enemy of Britain.

SULIVAN, LAURENCE (1713–86). An Irish-born merchant, Sulivan was the dominant figure in the East India Company in the early 1760s and remained influential through the following decades. He vainly opposed Robert Clive's drive to acquire a large territorial empire for the company in Bengal. An MP in the interest of Lord Shelburne, Sulivan was an important link between the British government and the company.

TUCKER, JOSIAH (1713–99). Anglican dean of Gloucester, and a prolific political economist, Tucker was a fierce critic of Britain's 'jealousy of trade'. He privately opposed Britain's war against France in America from 1756 which he derided as 'ye Pittian madness'. Tucker admired the foreign policy of Robert Walpole, which he praised as 'truly patriotical'. He believed that Britain could prevail peacefully against France by developing its commerce and manufactures, which would have little to fear from the low-wage challenge of European competitors.

TURGOT, ANNE-ROBERT-JACQUES, BARON DE L'AULNE (1727–81). A disciple of Vincent de Gournay as a young man, Turgot served as provincial intendant at Limoges from 1761 to 1774. He was appointed naval minister briefly in 1774 on the accession of Louis XVI and then contrôleur général from 1774 to 1776, a position in which he undertook major reforms of the grain trade and the guilds. Turgot opposed French intervention in the American War, which made his position in the ministry untenable.

VAN NECK, GERARD (1692–1750). Gerard and his brother Joshua, members of a politically influential Dutch family, settled in London and became major shareholders in the East India Company, and tobacco-buying agents for the French Farmers General. Gerard was a go-between in a major peace initiative undertaken in the midst of the War of the Austrian Succession, when Jean-Baptiste Fournier was sent to London by the Farmers in 1745 to make contact with a peace party in the cabinet led by Henry Pelham.

VAN NECK, SIR JOSHUA, BARONET (1702–1777). After his brother's death in 1750, Joshua remained the principal tobacco buyer for the French in London, and launched an abortive peace overture to avert the Seven Years' War in concert with his son-in-law Thomas Walpole.

VERGENNES, CHARLES GRAVIER, COMTE DE (1719–87). French foreign minister under Louis XVI from 1774 until his death in 1787, Vergennes led France into the American War, which he anticipated would reduce British power – based on privileged trade with America – and lay the foundations for an equilibrium that would facilitate a Franco-British peace. He strongly supported a commercial treaty to reopen a freer trade with Britain in 1786. He also wanted an accord between the new French East India Company and its British rival, though he vetoed the deal signed in 1785 as too advantageous to Britain.

WALPOLE, HORATIO (1678–1757). The brother of Sir Robert Walpole, Horatio was his loyal lieutenant, serving on key diplomatic missions to The Hague, Paris, and the congress of Soissons. He strongly supported his brother's policy of maintaining peace with France in the interests of Britain's commerce.

WALPOLE, SIR ROBERT (1676–1745). A leading Whig politician already in the 1710s, Walpole was a fierce critic of the Tory treaty of commerce with France in 1713. He came to power in 1721 through his astute handling of the political and financial fallout from the South Sea Bubble and was appointed first lord of the Treasury in April 1721. Regarded as Britain's first prime minister, Walpole dominated British politics for the next two decades. He favoured keeping Britain out of wars with the Bourbon powers, arguing that peace best served the interests of a trading state. He was fiercely criticised for this pacific stance from the late 1720s by a parliamentary opposition styling itself 'Patriot' and mobilising both Whigs critical of Walpole and some Tories. The Patriots turned sporadic Spanish interdiction of British shipping in the Caribbean into a political crisis in 1738–39 in a successful effort to force Walpole into a war with Spain. They subsequently used his management of the war to oust him in 1742.

WALPOLE, THOMAS (1727–1803). The son of Horatio Walpole and nephew of Sir Robert Walpole, Thomas married a daughter of Sir Joshua van Neck, who took him as a partner in 1750, and he helped manage the tobacco buying business for the French General Farms. He was a director of the East India Company in 1753–54 when it negotiated with its French rival to reach an accommodation in India. Together with his father-in-law, Walpole engaged in informal peace overtures attempting to avert the Seven Years' War, and in 1780 offered his services to Lord North as a peace negotiator during the American War.

NOTE ON THE CALENDAR, MONEY, AND TRANSLATIONS

From 1700 until 1752, Britain's Julian calendar ran eleven days behind the Gregorian system used in France and much of the rest of western Europe. Moreover, in Britain, the start of the year was often dated from 25 March. Britain switched to the Gregorian calendar in 1752, skipping the eleven days between 2 and 14 September, and simultaneously adopted 1 January as the start of the year. I have cited all dates as they appear in original sources, but to avoid confusion, I alter the year where necessary to conform to the Gregorian style.

In the eighteenth century, monetary sums in both France and Britain were denominated in monies of account known as the *livre tournois* in France and the pound sterling in Britain. The actual coins in circulation, which varied widely in metallic content, and were often foreign in origin, did not conform to the livres, sols, and deniers, or the pounds, shillings, and pence of the monies of account. But the value of the latter in terms of silver or gold was strictly regulated in law, and prices and contracts were designated in these monies of account.

From the late 1720s through the mid-1780s, the exchange rate of the livre tournois to sterling hovered around twenty-one livres to the pound. Before the stabilisation of the French currency in the late 1720s, frequent official manipulation of the silver value of the livre led to widely ranging exchange rates, making cross-Channel equivalents difficult to specify without attention to exchange rate listings in the contemporary commercial press.

While the modern reader might wish to see direct equivalents for the many sums mentioned in the book in connection with trade and public borrowing, such equivalents would generally be misleading. They would have to account not only for changes in the buying power of money but vast differences in the size and structure of economies. Instead of offering direct equivalents in the text, I have tried, where possible, to indicate contemporary scales of value.

As a very rough indicator of the value of eighteenth-century sums of money, a yearly income of £50 in the early eighteenth century would have placed a family comfortably in the top 20 per cent of earners in Britain. A century later, £100 might have been necessary to achieve the same status. In 1734, Jacob Vanderlint suggested that £500 per annum was necessary to live as a 'gentleman' in London.[1] Far less would have been adequate in France, especially in the provinces, where the cost of living was lower than in Britain. A noble family in France could live gently for less than 5,000 livres a year. The labouring poor, meanwhile, might have eked out a living in France on 200–300 livres a year.[2]

All translations are my own unless otherwise indicated.

TIMELINE

1664	Colbert reorganises French tariffs
1667	Colbert raises French tariffs sharply, initiating trade wars
1672	Louis XIV invades the Dutch Republic
1678	Franco-Dutch war concludes with the Treaty of Nijmegen
1683	Death of Colbert
1688	Glorious Revolution in Britain
1689	Outbreak of the War of the League of Augsburg (Nine Years' War)
1697	Treaty of Ryswick, ending the War of the League of Augsburg
1698	Scottish expedition to establish a colony at Darien on the Isthmus of Panama
1699	Franco-Dutch commercial treaty initiating lower tariffs and exemption from French port taxes for Dutch shipping
1700	Grandson of Louis XIV declared king of Spain as Philip V
1701	Start of the War of the Spanish Succession
1707	Act of Union between England and Scotland
	In treaty of Barcelona, Archduke Charles concedes postwar commercial privileges to Britain in Spanish America
1708	Philip V provisionally approves Nicolas Mesnager's scheme to open Spanish-American trade
1709	Louis XIV withdraws most troops and advisers from Spain
1710	Tory government comes to power in Britain
1713	Treaty of Utrecht ends the War of the Spanish Succession for France, Britain, and Spain
	Franco-British commercial treaty invalidated by House of Commons
	Publication of Saint-Pierre's *Projet pour rendre la paix perpétuelle*

1714   Treaties of Rastatt and Baden conclude the War of the Spanish Succession in Central Europe and Italy
Queen Anne dies and is succeeded by George I

1715   Death of Louis XIV; Philippe d'Orléans becomes regent

1716   Orléans grants John Law permission to establish a bank in Paris
Alliance negotiated between France and Britain
Stanhope secures 'permission ship' privilege from Spain for the South Sea Company

1717   Law establishes the Compagnie d'Occident (Mississippi Company)

1719   Law establishes the Compagnie des Indes

1720   South Sea Bubble begins in London
Law's 'System' and South Sea Bubble collapse

1721   Sir Robert Walpole comes to power in Britain

1726   Cardinal Fleury takes the reins of government in France

1727   Death of George I and accession of George II

1731   End of the Franco-British alliance initiated in 1716

1733   War of the Polish Succession begins

1734   Publication of Melon's *Essai politique sur le commerce*

1735   Truce concludes fighting in the War of the Polish Succession

1739   Britain declares war on Spain
Admiral Edward Vernon captures Portobello

1740   Prussian invasion of Silesia begins the War of the Austrian Succession

1742   Sir Robert Walpole falls from power

1743   Death of Cardinal Fleury

1744   France and Britain formally declare war during the War of the Austrian Succession

1745   Fall of French fortress of Louisbourg on Cape Breton Island
Jean-Baptiste Fournier's peace mission to London

1746   Fall of Madras to French forces

1748   Treaty of Aix-la-Chapelle concludes the War of the Austrian Succession
Publication of Montesquieu's *De l'Esprit des loix*

1749   Passage of Henry Pelham's reduction of interest scheme
Franco-British commission established to adjudicate boundary disputes in America

1766	Repeal of the Stamp Act
	Free Ports Act establishes free ports in the British Caribbean
	Rockingham administration falls and William Pitt (now earl of Chatham) returns to power
1767	Free ports established in the French Caribbean
1769	Monopoly of the Compagnie des Indes is suspended
1770	Lord North becomes prime minister
	Britain, Spain, and France come to brink of war over Falkland Islands
	The duc de Choiseul is disgraced by Louis XV
1771	D'Aiguillon and Bourgeois de Boynes enter the French ministry as foreign minister and naval minister respectively
1772	D'Aiguillon proposes a new commercial treaty to Lord North; Bourgeois de Boynes backs the establishment of a new French East India company and proposes an entente with the British in India
1773	East India Company receives a financial bailout and accepts a Regulating Act intended to create more government oversight
1774	Death of Louis XV and accession of Louis XVI
	The comte de Vergennes and Jacques Turgot are appointed ministers
1775	Outbreak of the American Revolution
1776	American Declaration of Independence
	Turgot pushed out of the ministry after contesting French support for the American revolutionaries
	Publication of Adam Smith's *Wealth of Nations*
1777	Jacques Necker appointed director of French finances (effectively finance minister)
1778	Treaty of amity and commerce between France and the United States
	France enters the American War
	Carlisle peace commission travels to America
1781	Necker resigns as finance minister
1782	Lord North steps down as prime minister
	Rockingham takes over as prime minister and peace negotiations begin with America and France
	Rockingham dies and is replaced by Lord Shelburne
1783	Treaty of Paris secures the independence of the United States
	Shelburne steps down

Shelburne's effort to open full free trade with the United States fails

William Pitt the Younger appointed prime minister

1784   India Act establishes a Board of Control to give the British government more influence over the East India Company

1785   New French East India company agrees to partnership with its British rival but the deal is vetoed by Vergennes

1786   Franco-British treaty of commerce signed on 26 September

1787   Vergennes dies and is succeeded as foreign minister by Montmorin

Calonne calls the Assembly of Notables, fails to control it, and goes into exile in Britain

Franco-British convention signed regulating French trade in Bengal

PREFACE

Rivalry between Britain and France was a perennial feature of eighteenth-century global politics. Their antagonism not only roiled Europe in repeated wars, but extended through their empires to the Americas, West Africa, India, and the oceans of the world. This book explores the actions and ideas of the British and French officials, merchants, and writers who sought to direct the rivalry of these Leviathans into a more peaceful channel – towards commerce rather than war. They looked to free trade to thaw frosty relations and lay a foundation for a less belligerent relationship in Europe. They negotiated to share or divide resources or markets, and to demilitarise their competition overseas. It was not enlightened cosmopolitanism that drove these efforts, but a self-seeking quest for power through trade. Today, in the twilight of the liberal order that emerged in the decades after 1945, we can more readily see the eighteenth century for what it was. And it is illuminating to do so, for it offers parallels with the present, and can orient us in a world at once new and rooted in the past.

Certain features of geopolitics today have analogues in the eighteenth century. By fostering growth at home and building opportunities abroad, a succession of trading states – China, most recently – have emerged since 1945 as economic powers on the world stage. While capturing global markets, and investing overseas, they seek to avoid confrontation with other powers. Such an aggrandising, but war-avoidant, strategy would serve them too, many eighteenth-century officials believed. Though the commercial realpolitik of the eighteenth century appears bellicose, the ministers and politicians who embraced it were anxious to avoid wars because the costs would likely outrun the gains, while the legacy of debt and taxes threatened to strangle commercial dynamism. States bent on security and power, they argued, should pursue trade and eschew war.

Yet their efforts to avoid conflict derailed. It is instructive to consider why aggrandisement by peaceful commercial means proved so difficult to sustain in the past. We may find here an augury of our future. The peaceful rise of trading states since 1945 was only possible in a context of US hegemony. Increases in the wealth and economic reach of these nations had little consequence for the balance of power. But can this strategy be sustained as US dominance erodes – an erosion that has been occurring for decades as economic power has been redistributed? We are moving towards a world where success in the market-place will translate increasingly into power, and in such an environment geoeconomic competition will slip towards geopolitical rivalry.

Policies adopted today and in the near future will slow or accelerate this slippage, and, in this respect, the outlook currently appears gloomy. The institutional framework for global trade has been more contested in recent years than for several decades past. States in the Global South have long, and rightly, questioned the equity of the institutions that govern their integration into the world economy. What distinguishes the current moment is the sense of grievance among privileged states. Some of the powers that have benefited most from the order built since the Second World War seek to renegotiate their place in the global trading system, if necessary, by breaking out of it altogether. The United Kingdom has left the European Union, and further breakaways seem possible. The United States seesaws between forging new trade pacts and repudiating co-operation, pursuing trade wars, and obstructing the WTO.

At such a moment, we can benefit by looking back upon the earliest stumbling efforts to institutionalise a stable and peaceful global trading order. These endeavours were driven in the eighteenth century by the desire to contain the costly conflicts that arose when trading states separately and competitively forged institutional frameworks to advantage their commerce overseas. Attempts to create more consensual arrangements mostly failed, and conflict followed. In a self-help system where economic might underpins the balance of power, the agreements necessary to exit political struggles over trade and investment are difficult to make or keep. The eighteenth century should serve as a reminder of how destabilising capitalism can be for geopolitics. Whatever the costs of the current order, they are likely lower than those we will face in a world without a collectively agreed institutional framework for global commerce and investment, whatever its frustrations and inequities.

The other feature of the present paralleled in the eighteenth-century past is the hitching of free trade to commercial realpolitik. States embrace free trade and protection as allied strategies, not opposing principles, regarding free trade as a tool appropriate in certain contexts but not others. Arguably, this has always been true and is simply more evident today. It was certainly so when free-trade thinking emerged in the eighteenth century and states sought to institutionalise it selectively. Some suppose that political economy became modern during the Enlightenment, when philosophers grasped that politics and economics ought to be separate – that commerce should be governed not by the state but by self-regulating markets. But this was never the position of the eighteenth-century officials who managed the global trading order. They always understood free trade as a strategy to be deployed selectively – an instrument in the struggle for wealth and security. It is illusory to think that the spread of free trade equates to the spread of liberal values.

To have a realistic sense of the past is to have a map that can orient us in the present and the future. We live in a world that imagines itself to be in a constant churn of novelty. Bombarded from moment to moment with messages that what is happening right now is transformative, even revolutionary, we sometimes conceive ourselves to be free of the past. History is uncongenial to this view. Much of what is crucial in shaping our daily lives and our near future is an inheritance from before – often from long ago. Of course, real change is happening all around us too. But how can we see it clearly if we cannot distinguish true change from pretended transformation? In this work of discrimination, history is vital – the cold dose of reality we need.

INTRODUCTION

That France and Britain were bitter rivals is one of the commonplaces of eighteenth-century European history. Memorably dubbed a 'Second Hundred Years' War' by the English historian John Seeley, their antagonism provoked war eight times between 1688 and 1815, running from the climactic European struggles to contain Louis XIV's France to the wars of the French Revolution and Napoleon. The competition of these dominant powers formed a major axis of eighteenth-century global politics too. French and British forces clashed not only in Europe, but in North America and the Caribbean, India, and West Africa, in the Mediterranean, and on the sea lanes of the Atlantic and Indian Oceans.[1] Alliance politics drew the French and the British East India companies into power struggles within and among the successor states to the Mughal Empire, while American Indian nations exploited and suffered through Franco-British imperial collisions. Often deemed 'natural enemies' in their day, the mutual hostility of these neighbours can seem inescapable – preordained by religious suspicion, ideological antagonism, balance-of-power politics, and commercial and colonial jealousy.[2]

Yet when we look more closely there is much that this utterly familiar history of persistent conflict cannot explain. British and French officials, sometimes allied with prominent merchants, laboured fitfully between the 1710s and the 1780s to reduce or avoid conflict over commerce and empire. Periodically, they sought to remove from geopolitical contention some of the world's key commercial resources: to open these to the trade of all European nations, to partition them between the rival powers, or to declare them neutral ground in case of future Franco-British wars. By these means, they hoped to limit the jealousy and suspicion the powers harboured of each other's economic success, and to diminish conflict over trade. An early and signal instance saw diplomats serving Louis XIV work to convince their British and Dutch counterparts during the War of the Spanish Succession (1701–14) to open Spanish America – chief source of the world's silver, and a key market for European manufacturers – to the goods of all European nations on the same terms.

Later in the century, merchants and officials repeatedly tried to end conflict over European commercial access to India. In the mid-1750s, the French and British East India companies bargained to end proxy wars that embroiled them in the Carnatic region of southern India, to share access to the areas they controlled, and to make common cause against Indian powers. They pressed their governments to establish a vast neutral zone in which the European trade to Asia could be carried on free from geopolitical encroachment. These negotiations foundered when the Seven Years' War (1756–63) broke out in North America. But officials returned to the idea in the early 1770s when the French colonial ministry proposed a treaty to permanently pacify Franco-British relations in India. Twelve years later, a newly established French East India Company and its British counterpart negotiated a cartel to supply Bengal goods to the French market. Versailles blocked the deal. But the governments subsequently signed a convention to ease access for French merchants in territories controlled by the British company. They hoped it would seal a permanent peace in Asia. Common themes arose repeatedly in these negotiations: officials imagined a Franco-British concert in India; they aspired to disentangle the Asian world of trade from European geopolitical competition; they talked of establishing open-access commercial empires. How can we reconcile these ambitions with the conventional story of Franco-British enmity?

Also anomalous is the history of efforts to reopen cross-Channel trade. British and French officials intermittently proposed to loosen or eliminate the high tariffs and trade prohibitions that each side had used since the seventeenth century to enhance its own position and strike at its rival. In 1713, again during the early 1750s, the 1770s, and the 1780s, ministers intent on fostering a better relationship tried to re-establish freer trade. They signed commercial treaties to this effect in 1713 and 1786, though the House of Commons nullified key provisions of the former. Normalising commercial relations might lay the foundations of a more pacific future, officials believed, by giving each nation an economic interest in maintaining peace with the other, though they also feared that freer trade would expose domestic producers to dangerous competition. The appeal of freedom of trade was as much geo-political as economic, and Europeans recognised its promise to stabilise inter-state relations not just in the period of the high Enlightenment but earlier, during the wars of the late seventeenth and early eighteenth centuries.

To complete the picture of this more pacific pattern of behaviour, consider two other key moments: first, the episode during the Regency of Philippe II, duc d'Orléans (1715–23), when the Scottish financier John Law launched a state bank in France which, he claimed, would settle the peace of Europe, and diminish competition among states for trade and empire. Using paper money, Law promised to revolutionise the French economy while freeing it from dependence on American silver, the basis of its money supply. A world in which the great powers no longer competed for this strategic resource would be one conducive to European peace. Law's scheme collapsed in 1720, partly as a result of financial warfare waged by Britain's South Sea Company – underlining the role of non-state actors and networks in international politics. But the Scot's defeat did not end hopes for Franco-British rapprochement. A more conven-tional and lasting effort to preserve stability and avoid war followed. The long Franco-British peace presided over by Sir Robert Walpole and Cardinal Fleury was inspired by a conviction on both sides that peaceful commercial develop-ment would best serve the power-political interests of each nation. The long peace of the 1720s and 1730s deserves renewed attention as part of a series of efforts to stabilise and pacify the Franco-British relationship.[3]

To understand this history requires that we recognise the realities of conflict and war but also account for the efforts to forge an alternative, more pacific, future. Both the pattern of clashes and efforts to deflect them, I will show, derive from the ways rivalries between states became entwined with commer-cial competition in an emergent capitalist order. Grasping the character and significance of the specific events explored here, then, requires us to move beyond the histories of eighteenth-century France and Britain to wrestle with a larger question: the repercussions of capitalism for global political order.

This is not a simply academic problem. Most scholarly efforts to grapple with the relationship between capitalism and geopolitics derive from long-standing political debates. Dispute on the connections between trade and war first emerged during the Enlightenment and has been constantly renewed in the shadow of major shifts in world politics. A nineteenth-century liberal tradition held that commercial competition, when distorted by mercantilist policies, produced endless wars for trade and scrambles for colonies. An economic order built on free trade, by contrast, would lead to international harmony. Britons in the Victorian age viewed free trade as a way to secure not only cheap bread but international peace.[4] The return of protectionism and imperialism in the late nineteenth century elicited dark warnings about the renewal of great-power conflict – presentiments seemingly borne out by the two world wars.

Building upon but diverging from the liberal tradition, radicals and Marxists argued that capitalism drove imperialism and incited great-power conflict.[5] Only international socialism could deliver peace. American policy-makers sought to prove the contrary after 1918 and again after 1945, and create a world where interstate competition for markets and resources would never again lead to massive violence. But they succeeded only by displacing the threat of war to the borderlands between capitalism and the opposing communist world. Moreover, the institutions they forged drew the ire of postcolonial leaders, who charged that a Western-dominated order enforced unequal relations of trade and a dependency that hollowed out the sovereignty of new states.[6] The oil crises, stagflation, and the waning of American power in the 1970s produced new questions. Was a hegemon needed to stabilise an international order agitated by capitalist instability?[7] The renewal of American power at the end of the Cold War brought a brief, giddy return of optimism. The dream of a capitalist peace seemed finally on the verge of being realised. In fact, the neoliberal moment proved one of nearly constant American wars which critics denounced as a new imperialism.[8]

This book explores the nature of geopolitics at a time when the capitalist order had recently emerged. To consider Franco-British conflict over trade and colonies, and the efforts to contain it, engages some of the big questions perennially posed about capitalism and geopolitics. Does mercantilism necessarily lead to war? If so, by what mechanisms? Is free trade inherently pacific? Is capitalism intrinsically imperialist? More precisely, what kind of political framework for overseas commerce and investment does a capitalist order require or favour? What forms of hierarchy or dependency can a capitalist system produce between independent, sovereign states? Are there logics inherent in capitalism that restrain war? What is the place of hegemony, and the drive for commercial pre-eminence, in stabilising or unsettling a capitalist interstate order? Final answers to these questions are unlikely to be forthcoming based on a history of just two powers over a single century. But because we are dealing with structures, or at least recurrent logics, that are stable or iterative, it is possible to say much about the problem of capitalism and geopolitics in general by looking at eighteenth-century Britain and France in particular.

The first point to grasp is that the history of capitalism and that of states has always been intertwined. Viewed as an economic system based on private property, competitive markets, and free enterprise, capitalism and states can seem separate, even opposing structures. But this familiar perspective captures only one side of a binary relationship. In fact, sovereignty is both the greatest threat to capital and the source of its fullest flourishing. Political authorities have the power to block profitable activities or to appropriate the wealth of capitalists in the name of social harmony, religious scruple, economic justice, or political necessity. Rulers have always had incentives to prey on capitalists, especially at moments of communal emergency. But the benefits to capital of sovereign power outweigh the risks. Indeed, we should understand capitalism as an order in which ruling elites deploy state power to support capital accumulation. Capitalists prosper when they enjoy security to trade and invest, when laws safeguard their property rights, when courts enforce contracts, and when owners can call on the state to discipline rebellious workers. States regulate or limit competition, manage the money supply, and stabilise the financial order. In Nancy Fraser's words, the use of sovereign power to create the political framework for accumulation is part of capitalism's 'background conditions of possibility'.[9]

States favoured capital accumulation because they were locked in rivalry with other states. Sovereigns in parts of early modern Eurasia limited exactions on merchants and promoted the flourishing of commercial capital because trade augmented their ability to compete militarily with other sovereigns.[10] The priorities of states shaped the resultant capitalist order; on the Atlantic littoral it assumed a highly 'extroverted' form.[11] The most dynamic sectors of the commercial economy, and those most favoured by the eighteenth-century French and British states, were seagoing trade, manufacturing for export, and colonial commodity production, along with the slave trade that sustained it.[12]

5

Historians have debated how important international and colonial trade were to stimulating European economic growth in the eighteenth century. As a direct contribution to the total product of European economies, their place was relatively small. Vastly more important was agriculture and the production of goods and services for the domestic economy. It has been argued that it was the *indirect* consequences of foreign trade for economic growth that were really significant – its effects on wages, institutions, or incentives.[13] But growth as such was not what eighteenth-century officials were after. While they certainly cared about the employment of the poor, and in this sense about general prosperity, the word growth was not part of their vocabulary; it is tied to a later way of imagining the economy.[14]

It was less the aggregate production of goods and services that interested early modern policymakers than what they called 'circulation'. Trade facilitated public borrowing, augmented the money supply, and stimulated domestic economic exchanges, expanding the tax base. These specific effects of foreign trade enhanced state capacity. No eighteenth-century state could sustain a war for long without massive loans, and overseas commerce created the pools of capital that governments borrowed. States faced chronic monetary scarcity, but foreign trade drew in bullion to augment the money supply.[15] It stimulated port economies and their hinterlands, generated taxable flows of goods, trained sailors who could be drafted into wartime navies, and built trade balances to be tapped to remit money abroad to pay armies and subsidise allies.[16] In short, overseas commerce underwrote the power of the French and British states.

Competition between states, in turn, galvanised commercial expansion. In early modernity European capital expanded across the globe in large measure because states proved willing to protect merchant enterprise, and to secure the commodity frontiers opened by colonial planters and the men and women they enslaved. In these ways, states (and companies, to which we will return below) served as accelerants for the dynamism intrinsic to early modern modes of production. A key source of such vitality was rural manufacturing (or protoindustrialisation). Using ties of credit and debt, merchant entrepreneurs mobilised and exploited independent artisans, many located in the European countryside, to spin yarn and weave cloth. They co-ordinated the production process, acquired and distributed raw materials, had them worked up and finished in forms sensitive to fashion and market opportunity, and sold the

6

product hundreds, or even thousands, of miles from home. This was not the capitalism of the nineteenth-century factory. Instead of being fixed in buildings and machinery, capital circulated. Most labourers were, formally, subcontractors – independent producers rather than wage labourers. This system of production produced profits less through the application of technology than via improvements in skill, deft marketing, and by mobilising the cheap labour of women and children.[17]

The sale of protoindustrial goods drove an increase of trade both within and between regions and continents that, in turn, fostered the division of labour and the higher productivity that specialisation encourages.[18] The seventeenth and eighteenth centuries saw an expansion in commercial intermediation that brought advances in shipping, warehousing, insurance, currency trading, and banking. As the sources of the circulating capital – the credit – on which a capitalist world economy was built, merchants benefited most, and increasingly organised this early modern global economic expansion.

The opening of commodity frontiers in the Americas to extract minerals or to cultivate cash crops such as sugar, tobacco, and coffee both augmented trade and created a colonial capitalism that expanded rapidly across space. Planters and miners aggressively pushed the frontier of production, chasing virgin soil or unworked mineral seams, imagined to be free or at least cheap, and quickly worked out or discarded in favour of fresh pickings.[19] The labour of enslaved or bonded people produced colonial commodities for sale on world markets, while many of these labourers were themselves commodified and sold, driving another thriving intercontinental commerce. Slavery has appeared incompatible with capitalism for scholars who identify wage labour as that system's signature. Others see it as a component of a 'primitive, hybrid capitalism'.[20] But plantation slavery can also be read as a 'hypercapitalist' institution in which the capital embodied in enslaved human beings replaced free labour as a factor of production.[21] Exotic commodities produced by unfree labourers helped in turn to stimulate an 'industrious revolution' in Europe whereby workers, many involved in protoindustry, were induced to work harder and longer, and to produce more goods for markets so they could participate in those same markets as consumers of commodities.[22]

Similar kinds of commercial dynamism characterised parts of early modern East and South Asia too, where protoindustrialisation, monetisation, and the spread of market relations were either long established or in full swing.[23] Asian states sought to harness capital as an essential support of political power in zones of intense interstate competition.[24] Yet the kind and degree of political support given to commercial capitalists by European states helped Europeans, over the long run, to extract wealth from other world regions, to foster their own manufactures in the face of Asian competition, and to dominate intercontinental commercial networks. Activist state policies were a key factor propelling the Great Divergence – the leap in economic growth achieved by certain regions in eighteenth- and early nineteenth-century Europe compared to the most affluent and vibrant parts of Asia.[25] State support and protection has never ceased to be critical to economic dynamism – witness the rise in the nineteenth century of imperial Germany or the arch-protectionist United States. Activist states continued to drive development in the twentieth and twenty-first centuries, steering postwar East Asian economic miracles, capped in recent decades by the explosive growth of China. State action is now a critical factor in the Great Convergence that is ending the one-time lead of the West.

The principal means by which European states fostered commerce beyond their own borders in the eighteenth century was by forging political frameworks to extend protection to merchants and planters overseas.[26] Governments encouraged merchants and investors to found colonies, and projected their sovereignty to defend colonists from the indigenous peoples they displaced, from the men and women they enslaved, or from rival European powers. Empire created the legal regime to secure the claims to property of merchants and planters against interlopers from home, and to attract new investment.[27] New institutions evolved to supplement states in the form of chartered trading companies, which provided security for distant trade by hiring troops, arming ships, fortifying settlements, and negotiating diplomatic arrangements with local sovereigns to protect trade from what Europeans regarded as predatory exactions. The company form allowed European merchants to mobilise large concentrations of capital to exploit tempting commercial opportunities in distant places by projecting sovereignty in new forms. States permitted these ventures because, at minimum cost to the exchequer, they promised to expand taxable trade, reduce that of European rivals, and capture transnational capital and expertise to harness it for national ends. Companies extended the capacities of states, and states in turn provided the monopolies, diplomatic cover, and, in extremis, military aid, that companies needed to thrive.[28]

Yet companies and colonies do not exhaust the means deployed to extend a protective framework for trade beyond the territory of the home state. In Europe, sovereigns tried to induce rival rulers to supply the legal order and checks on predation necessary to safeguard the foreign trade of their subjects – something rival sovereigns were often reluctant to do, wishing to favour their own subjects. States used commercial treaties to oblige foreign powers to provide such protections, and pushed for such treaties at moments when they enjoyed leverage (in return for an alliance, or at the end of major wars).[29] States with the capacity to do so used naval power to protect trade at sea, and sometimes in foreign ports. Loosely speaking, these arrangements corresponded to different geographical zones: colonies predominated in the Americas; companies often prevailed where European merchants encountered powerful polities outside the European diplomatic system, on the West African coast and especially east of the Cape of Good Hope; in Europe, states typically depended on foreign sovereigns to govern and protect trade when they could be induced to do so; and on the oceans, where ship captains carried the sovereignty of their home polities with them, navies protected trade and fisheries.

Admittedly, officials often overestimated their power to shape the contours of global trade. Virtually all of the commercial activities with which we are concerned were sustained by self-organising mercantile networks, which states might seek to regulate or encourage but which they could never fully control. The project of early modern mercantilism, especially in its British and French variants, was to capture and mobilise intrinsically transnational phenomena for national ends. When states established juridically closed commercial empires, smuggling was endemic, and often large in scale.[30] But this does not mean that statist efforts were in vain. Livorno would have remained a fishing village if the Medici grand dukes had not established a free port there and offered protection to the Western Sephardic diaspora, whose expertise and capital helped turn it into a principal port for Mediterranean trade.[31] Without the British navigation acts or the French Exclusif (trade laws that reserved commerce with the colonies to French merchants), cheaper Dutch shipping would have continued to dominate the Atlantic carrying trade.[32] States and self-organising mercantile networks conflicted in the sense that merchants often sought to evade mercantilist strictures but, viewed at a structural level, they were symbiotic – the mercantile networks supplying the capital and expertise states could not; states selectively supplying the protection merchants often needed to flourish.

Understood as a political-economic order, then, capitalism was not separate from the interstate system but inextricably interwoven with it. States struggled for advantage by trying to shape political frameworks for economic activity both within their own borders and beyond them – frameworks intended to advantage their 'own' capitalists at the expense of foreign rivals, or to harness and territorialise transnational capital and expertise for national ends. This is a structural feature of capitalism, as salient today as it was three centuries ago. A critical consequence, then as now, was that while sovereign power promised to protect capital at home, the potential threat of predation it embodied could return redoubled in relations between states.

Strategies states used to protect their own trade turned sovereignty into the nemesis of foreign capital. Where states established colonies, they typically excluded the merchants of other nations. Sovereignty protected one group of capitalists but preyed on or obstructed others. Companies sheltered the monopoly trade of one group but exploited political relations with local rulers, where possible, to exclude or disadvantage competing enterprises. Where commercial treaties did not prevent it, merchandise from one European polity often faced prohibitions and discriminatory taxes in others – such as the tariffs British goods encountered in France and vice versa. Naval power that protected merchants of one nation harried those of others. If the problem of sovereign predation on capital was checked, at least to a degree, at home by each state's need to foster capital accumulation, it returned with a vengeance abroad.

This world of competing protection-suppliers was theorised by the pioneering economic historian Frederic C. Lane in the 1940s and 1950s.[33] Lane underlined forms of mercantile competition mediated by political rather than strictly economic means, a competition between protection-producing enterprises (states and chartered companies) aimed at maximising the take of 'their' merchants by manipulating political barriers to the free flow of goods and people, or by protecting trade more efficiently and cheaply than competitors. Lane argued that such protection was often a more fundamental driver of commercial success for early modern merchants than economic factors such as the quality or price of their goods. This perspective offers a starting point for understanding the history explored in this book, a history of efforts to contain conflict over trade and empire between Europe's two most powerful commercial states.

Protection was expensive, and eighteenth-century officials and directors of chartered companies were highly attuned to the balance between its costs and its benefits. They grasped that the costs of sustaining a political framework to protect trade – be it in the form of empire, company sovereignty, or a tax regime that excluded foreign goods – might outrun benefits from the trade protected. One solution might lie in agreements with rival states or companies that promised to lower these costs – agreements to share or partition markets or resources, or to reduce political barriers to trade.

Wars fought to secure trade generated powerful counter-pressures to limit conflict. Officials struggled to balance the costs of defending distant commerce against the profits it was supposed to yield. They worried especially about the public debt run up during wars. France and Britain borrowed to fund their militaries to a degree that would not be matched until the world wars of the twentieth century. Neither power was able to reduce the burden of debt much between wars, and so it ratcheted up to ever higher levels. Growing debt threatened the very survival of political regimes, critics warned – a presentiment that proved far-sighted in the case of the French absolute monarchy.[34] But long before debt could precipitate a cataclysm, officials believed, it would sap the capacity to produce future wealth. When governments borrowed, they permanently raised the tax burden that merchants, manufacturers, and consumers had to bear. Taxes threatened to stifle investment at home and render a nation's goods uncompetitive abroad. Perpetual debt fostered a torpid rentier culture, raised interest rates, and inhibited enterprise. In a negative feedback loop, debt run up in wars for trade and empire strangled the commercial dynamism these wars were fought to secure. Officials who saw that the costs of protecting distant commerce fed back to destroy future capital accumulation looked for ways to avoid war, pacify the Franco-British relationship, and remake the international order.

A similar dynamic pushed the chartered companies to avert or end military clashes. In the case of these corporations, investors rather than the public shouldered protection costs. Thus companies were even more exposed when the expense of war consumed the profits of trade. The French and British East India companies were drawn into military conflict with one another in the 1740s and early 1750s in support of Indian princes competing to instal themselves as rulers of successor states to the Mughal Empire. Victory promised commercial privileges, perhaps the exclusion of the rival, and the prospect of tax revenues from territories assigned to company fiscal control by Indian allies. But when the companies had to rely on force to achieve these ends, this drove up costs, dried up trade, and increased future geopolitical risk. Intended to improve balance sheets, military action could threaten the solvency of the companies. Financial pressures intermittently pushed them towards an accommodation with one another. Such pressures also reshaped the balance between corporations and states as bearers of sovereignty – in some cases pushing companies to become more like states, and in others forcing companies to shift sovereignty to their home governments.

I put states and companies, rather than trade as such, at the centre of my story because these protection-suppliers, rather more than merchants, bore the heaviest costs of geopolitical instability. While war was quite disruptive of commerce, merchants evolved means to manage its ill effects and continue to pursue a profit. For some, war could even bring lucrative new opportunities in privateering, military contracting, and war finance. States and companies, on the other hand, always saw costs explode in wartime while revenues declined; they inevitably carried a crippling legacy of debt away from every conflict. Officials, company leaders, and the writers and thinkers in their orbits, therefore, tended to be most fertile in generating schemes to limit geopolitical conflict.

The problem of protection costs outrunning profits made such actors question whether empires paid, embrace schemes to remake them, and even imagine alternatives to empire. Leagues of allied states, confederations of former colonies, or international trade regimes built on multilateral agreements between states might protect trade as well as existing arrangements, and at far lower cost. Following mid-century wars, some critics charged that colonies cost more to protect than they could ever repay in the form of commercial profit, prosperity, or tax revenues. Leading officials imagined an alternative political framework to secure French trade in India: a league of friendly Indian powers, perhaps a reinvigorated Mughal Empire. Later, the French finance minister Jacques Turgot and likeminded officials called for the French Caribbean colonies to be reconstituted as a confederation of sovereign trading partners.

The American War of Independence, in particular, promised to remake the political framework for Atlantic trade. Louis XVI signed a treaty of amity and commerce with Britain's rebellious Thirteen Colonies in 1778, intended to be the central node of a future network of commercial treaties to replace Britain's closed commercial empire with an independent United States open to the trade of all Europe. In response, Lord North's government appeared ready to remake the British Empire on a confederal basis as a union for commerce and defence. Radical Whigs seeking conciliation with America proposed a league of European maritime states to manage a joint free-trade area in the Americas. The ideal scenario, from the perspective of many critics of existing imperial arrangements, was to reap the benefits of trade without incurring the costs of sovereignty.

For the most part, these schemes did not constitute a rejection of European rule as such. Typically, it was the *form* rather than the fact of European imperium over people and places far from Europe that was at issue. This history does not point towards a post-imperial world of sovereign states, then, so much as towards a geopolitics in which Europeans accommodated one another in the collective exploitation of the non-European world. It anticipates efforts to avoid great-power war over colonial empire in the nineteenth century by reaching agreements to partition parts of the world among European powers, or to keep China open to the commercial exploitation of all. We might also see these eighteenth-century designs as harbingers of the framework of international institutions that emerged in the decades since 1945 to prevent interstate competition for resources and markets from poisoning relations between states. Under these arrangements, states gradually agreed to mutual commercial disarmament, setting aside or limiting the use of many of the political weapons so long deployed to advantage their own capitalists by undercutting the profits of foreign competitors.

The proponents of the various partition schemes, neutrality proposals, freetrade deals, and peace pacts analysed here framed their initiatives in the language of political economy. Recovering their political-economic ideas, and thinking about the implications of these for the broader history of political economy in the eighteenth century, is one of the objectives of the book. Political economy was a branch of statecraft that emerged in early modern Europe as commerce became an interest of state. It guided officials in the economic management of polities locked in competition for wealth and power with rival states.[35] While some historians privilege the writings of political economists who wrote for an enlightened public, especially the most sophisticated and original among them, others focus on the institutional contexts in which political economy was forged – to show that ideas were anchored in social and political contexts, and that officials were producers not just consumers of political-economic ideas.[36] I draw on both intellectual history and institutional approaches, using the insights of each to enrich the other. This book centres on state and company officials who made foreign policy, directed the chartered companies, and governed the French and British empires.[37] But it also draws on many published works of political economy that were part of the policy conversation or that illuminate its contours.

The world of officials and that of men of letters were close. Writers engaged by political economy did not speculate in a rarefied philosophical sphere. In search of favour, position, or influence, they often articulated official views, or grappled with problems that were important to ministers. Officials contributed to public debate or sought to mould opinion by publishing their own views, while prominent political-economic writers were frequently recruited to official positions. The border between the two realms was porous, to both ideas and people. Varieties of political economy that took an independent and philosophical tone, critical of existing policies, such as Physiocracy in France, or the works of David Hume and Adam Smith in Britain, orbited the official world at a greater distance from its centre than works written or commissioned by officials. But they too sought to engage policymakers. Whether as echoes or as criticisms of official positions, many works in print illuminate the serial efforts to remake the Franco-British relationship on which this book concentrates.

Officials, ministers, and politicians were often conversant with published works, and took them seriously. But I am sceptical that such works constituted a major, independent influence on their thinking. As Keith Baker has observed, it is important 'to avoid treating ideas as if they were causal, individual agents of motivation and determination'. To understand the place of the political-economic doctrines published in France and Britain on the thinking and action of officials, we need to grasp that 'texts, if read, are understood, and hence rein-terpreted, by their readers in con-*texts* that may transform their significance; ideas, if received, take on meaning only in relation to others in the set of ideas into which they are incorporated'.[38] The institutions in which they worked, and the problem of managing geopolitical competition between states, shaped the way officials understood and used ideas drawn from the public sphere. If published works, or their authors, were often a part of the official conversation, they never dictated its terms. Officials appropriated ideas from the world of print selectively, integrating them into frameworks derived from the practical business of governing trade and framing foreign and imperial policy.

From the perspective of officials, political economy could never be solely a reflection upon what Istvan Hont fittingly called 'the economic limits to national politics'.[39] Political economists, be they inside or outside government, emphasised that commerce had a logic of its own, recalcitrant, to some degree, to political manipulation. John Robertson is surely right that part of the thrust of eighteenth-century political economy was to explain why 'the powers of poli-ticians and statesmen over society were by no means as great as they supposed'.[40] But if they recognised the limits of political will to manipulate economic life, few imagined that markets existed outside a political framework or that the contours of this framework did not matter to market success. Officials knew that competitiveness in the price and quality of goods, low labour costs, or high productivity could be key factors in commercial success, but they also under-stood that commercial treaties, navigation acts, imperial monopolies, tariff regimes, and chartered trading companies could advantage a state's merchants, check the superiority of a rival, or block it from competing altogether.

The use of such strategies did not become less important over time, but neither were they always deployed for invidious purposes. If political actors could manipulate institutional frameworks for trade to secure exclusive advan-tages, they could also use them to reduce international conflict over resources and markets, or to ensure that the gains of trade would not be engrossed by any overmighty commercial state. When the costs of conflict rose high enough, such means to mute 'jealousy of trade' appealed to officials. A central problem in European political economy, especially viewed from the perspective of the official realm, was how to reconfigure the political frameworks for global commerce to create a more stable and peaceful world.

I challenge the enduring notion that what is often called mercantilism was essentially aggressive and bellicose. In fact, early modern political-economic ideas were Janus-faced, serving both to stir up conflict and to inspire efforts to limit it. Mercantilism acquired its dark reputation for aggression in part because the idea assumed its modern form between the 1880s and the 1930s, when liberals feared that moves away from free trade would trigger new scrambles for economic resources and unleash global conflict – forebodings they saw realised in the two world wars.[41] Mercantilism gave rise to 'endless commercial wars', argued its most distinguished analyst, the Swedish liberal economist Eli Heckscher, in 1931. His younger contemporary, Edmund Silberner, concurred: mercantilism 'led fatally toward war'.[42] While not wrong, these classic arguments obscure a second dimension of seventeenth- and eighteenth-century political-economic thought that is just as important. By exploring the political-economic ideas that eighteenth-century officials used at moments when they worked to make a more peaceful world, this book shows that the outlook we associate with mercantilists often inspired efforts to stabilise and pacify global politics.

For Heckscher, mercantilism's inherent bellicosity followed from the belief that the quantum of wealth in the world is fixed. This is an error. Early moderns did not tend to have a zero-sum understanding of trade because they thought there was a fixed pie of wealth.[43] Some may have believed this, but it is both unnecessary and insufficient to explain the invidiousness of their outlook. Many seventeenth-century commentators whose outlook Heckscher would unhesitatingly have classified as mercantilist were convinced that wealth could be expanded in unlimited fashion through 'improvement' – the application of human labour to natural resources. Yet they were no less apprehensive about the economic advance of rival nations. This was because they understood that commerce underpinned the power of states, and that in the logic of power-balancing it is not the size of the pie that matters but how the slices are apportioned. Whether the pie is fixed or growing is irrelevant, because power is a positional good. One party's gain is necessarily another's loss.

Seventeenth-century language lends itself to the interpretation that early modern political economy was bellicose because of the recurring equation of trade with war. Louis XIV's celebrated finance minister, Jean-Baptiste Colbert, described trade as 'a perpetual and peaceful war of wits and industry between all nations'.[44] The aphorism captures the agonistic way the minister thought about commerce, but the phrase 'peaceful war' is also worth dwelling on. For most of its political-economic proponents, commercial competition offered less a rationale for war than a *substitute* – a means to aggrandisement, or security, that avoided the hazards, and above all the expense, of military confrontation. Many claimed that commerce would bolster the power of nations without resort to war, indeed that war might undermine the foundations of power by sapping the commercial vitality that sustained the power of states.

This perception was grounded in the history of the preceding centuries and in recent experience. The commercial Dutch Republic had broken the power of the martial Spanish monarchy, suggesting that new forms of power based on trade were displacing traditional forms founded on territory, population, and a warrior ethos. The Spanish seemed to teach another object lesson in the colonial realm, where their model of empire, supposedly based on conquest, depopulating violence, and extraction, appeared less and less viable against an Anglo-Dutch style of imperialism based on trade, improvement, and plantation slavery. In Asia, the experience of the British and French East India companies indicated that the costs of coercion and protection must be contained if trade was to be profitable. Finally, the fate of Louis XIV's France confirmed the truth that commerce sustained the power of states but that war could undermine it. The Sun King loved war too much, and its costs and dislocations sapped the wealth of his kingdom and derailed Colbert's aggrandising, but peaceful, project to make France Europe's pre-eminent state by expanding its trade and manufactures. Commerce, not conquest, appeared the high road to power and security.

This preference for commerce over conquest was commonplace in eighteenth-century political-economic reasoning and was ubiquitous in the thinking of officials and merchants who sought to stabilise Franco-British relations. It is on a spectrum with the familiar notion of *doux commerce*, part of the same broad Enlightenment effort to weigh the political and cultural consequences of the rise of commercial society. But this spectrum accommodated a wide range of positions. Some Enlightenment-era writers argued that commerce was naturally gentle (*doux*). Commercial exchange fostered civility and refinement, produced sociable dispositions that substituted for the lost public virtue of the ancient republics, and conduced to amity between peoples.[45] Those who held this view celebrated the idea that an age of conquest was giving way to a more peaceful, humane, and enlightened age of commerce – at least if outdated prejudices could be set aside. At the other end of the range were officials and writers on trade interested in assessing the consequences for power politics of the fact that an age of commerce was replacing an age of conquest – and positioning their nation to secure or aggrandise itself accordingly.[46] Though part of the same broad body of ideas, their views had different implications in practice. They continued to see commerce as a field of struggle between states, in the mould of Colbert. While they agreed that an increased density of commercial relations between nations tended to foster peace, this would be a peace that sapped the wealth and power of some parties unless reciprocity were negotiated and preserved by an active state. They deplored war not principally as a vestige of barbarism, or as a scourge of humanity, but because the debt and taxes it drove up threatened to strangle the commercial vitality that underpinned power.

The two emphases were not necessarily incompatible. Enlightened French men of letters – *philosophes*, such as Voltaire, Diderot, and Raynal – deplored the costs of conflict and warned of its debilitating consequences for wealth creation while also decrying the inhumanity of war or celebrating the moderating potential of trade in international relations.[47] Indeed, part of what they meant in describing commerce as civilising was that its increasing role in generating power shifted the power-political calculus of rulers against war, making violence seem less profitable and attractive. The celebrated Enlightenment authors tended to assume a deliberately cosmopolitan stance in their published writings rather than the more Machiavellian outlook of officials, but again we should not draw too sharp a distinction. *Philosophes* hoped that cosmopolitan ends could be achieved by the exertions of great powers, while officials understood that their own objectives might readily be advanced under the banner of humanity.

We can see something similar at work in talk of perpetual peace. The idea is indelibly associated with Charles-Irénée Castel, abbé de Saint-Pierre, who used it in the title of a famous book he published in 1713 calling for the establishment of a European confederation to end permanently the scourge of war. It was later taken up and married with republican ideas by Rousseau and Kant in their own celebrated musings on the possibilities of escaping armed conflict.[48] But we now know that these views were much more variegated than once believed, and that Saint-Pierre, Rousseau, and Kant were by no means typical exponents.[49] Talk of perpetual peace was not necessarily quixotic. The term referred to a peace without a specified end, and was widely used in treaties.[50] The most politically influential strand of thinking about how a stable European peace might be achieved, I will show, envisioned a remaking of the political framework for international and colonial commerce to mitigate the effects of jealousy of trade. Many of the official efforts I examine in this book can be read in such terms. None of these actors were pacifists – a label applicable in the eighteenth century only to religious sects such as the Quakers.[51] The interest of officials in peace was often inconsistent and opportunistic, the fruit of a particular moment, a particular set of geopolitical pressures, not a durable commitment.

Those officials who worried that war would undermine commercial prosperity never imagined that organised violence had no role in trade. The chartered companies, for example, generally enjoined 'peaceful measures' on their employees in India because war was costly and disrupted trade, and conquests must entail additional expenses to govern and defend. But the directors in London and Paris did not think they could pursue profits in India without troops, fortifications, and a capacity to confront local rulers when necessary. Likewise, European trade in the Americas rested on empire and on an ongoing coercive capacity to keep rival powers, indigenous nations, and enslaved people in check. The preference for commerce over coercion rested on an opposition between expensive, extractive imperium, and commercial empires that were cheap and profitable. The commerce-versus-conquest opposition constituted an unresolvable antinomy: the prospects for trade were dim without protection, and this meant coercion, or the capacity to coerce; but an excess of violence threatened to undermine the very trade it was deployed to secure. It was never a question of choosing commerce outright over coercion, then, but of negotiating an equilibrium between the two.[52]

Within the terms of this antinomy, there were situations where war could appear the most reasonable choice despite its huge cost. These were cases where a single power threatened to acquire a lasting, even a permanent, pre-eminence founded on commerce. Underneath the ordinary balance of power, officials distinguished a balance of commercial power, or wealth, that had to be preserved if the hegemony of any single state was to be avoided.[53] Just as a polity might threaten the security of its neighbours by amassing too much military capacity, it might also do so by engrossing too much commerce. Europeans feared the prospect of a 'universal monarchy of trade', a new form of geopolitical dominance predicated on a massive concentration of commercial capacity. The drive to prevent the emergence of a commercial superpower was a key impetus to war between France and Britain. Britons worried that this was Louis XIV's design or, less plausibly, that his successor aimed at such domination. French officials warned of a British aspiration to a universal monarchy of trade even before British victories in the Seven Years' War seemed definitively to upset the balance. The effort to restore equilibrium justified French action to prise the Thirteen Colonies out of Britain's hands once the American independence struggle had begun.

Indeed, the idea of a balance of wealth, understood in the bipolar sense that was common in French and British thinking, proved to be a major stumbling block to a more pacific relationship. (When they imagined other states to be key components of the balance – the Dutch in 1713, or Central and Eastern European powers in the 1770s and 1780s – French and British officials were more inclined to compromise.) It is striking how few of the many efforts to reach an accord between the two powers resulted in a lasting accommodation. The obstacle that emerged repeatedly was fear that compromise would leave one side better off commercially than the other, if not immediately then in the future, with ramifying and eventually disastrous consequences for the balance of wealth. A kind of discounting in reverse prevailed whereby the future, even the distant future, appeared more valuable than the present. An understanding was likely only when both sides believed they stood to benefit as much as or more than the other, and this proved a rare alignment. Balance-of-power thinking, in the domain of commerce, was inhospitable to stability, even while other political-economic logics conduced to make or keep the peace. Hence the pattern of repeated, and repeatedly failed, initiatives to change the pattern of Franco-British relations.

From this perspective one can better understand why nineteenth-century British preponderance in commercial and financial power might have fostered stability. The British economic lead over France was substantial by 1815 and continued to grow until the 1860s; there could be no question of a balance of economic power in the century after Waterloo. In this period, Franco-British relations were still characterised by remorseless rivalry, but never again by war. Franco-British military conflict over trade and colonies ceased to be a structural feature of the international order, though of course French and British imperial violence continued to be directed against non-European peoples.[54]

The story I tell both affirms and complicates the view that the hegemony of a leading state is necessary to provide a stable global environment for capitalist accumulation. Hegemony once established was stabilising; hegemony in prospect could loose tremendous violence. The Dutch Republic triggered international instability when it demonstrated the immense power states could generate from trade, unleashing a scramble in which France and Britain struggled to emulate its success and usurp its position.[55] This produced the three Anglo-Dutch naval wars of the seventeenth century and the 1672 Franco-Dutch war. The great Franco-British power struggle of the long eighteenth century was the sequel to the Dutch breakthrough. After 1815, the British Empire achieved a position of unchallengeable pre-eminence in the sphere of commerce and colonies, and presided over a long period of relative European peace and economic expansion, while after 1945 the baton passed to the United States.[56] Preponderance once achieved stabilises, because power-balancing by commercial means makes little sense in the face of hegemony; bandwagoning becomes the more rational strategy. But states will fight tooth and nail to prevent the emergence of an economic hegemon.

Admittedly, a few eighteenth-century figures held that only a benign hegemon could pacify the conflict-prone international order. Yet no French or British official imagined that the overwhelming predominance of the *rival* state could spell anything but disaster for their own. The struggle to check the emergence of a commercial hegemon was a principal source of the violence that characterised Franco-British relations from 1688 to 1815. In the nineteenth century, once Britain's economic preponderance began to ebb, the possibility of great-power wars for markets, resources, and colonies re-emerged, while from the late nineteenth, arguably, the prospect of American economic preponderance spawned further instability.[57]

In nearly all efforts to stabilise the conflict-prone Franco-British relationship, officials looked to free trade as a strategy. Put aside for a moment the free trade of textbook economics. Freedom of trade meant above all freedom *to* trade – the relaxation of politically imposed barriers that prevent the movement of merchants, ships, and goods, be these the prohibitions and high duties that hedged most national economies in Europe, or the national monopolies states imposed on their colonial empires. As a growing body of scholarship has shown, the push to lift trade barriers need not imply any special faith in the virtues of free markets, nor any attachment to economic efficiency, natural rights, or the interests of consumers.[58] Nor were the free-trade ideas entertained by eighteenth-century officials centred on the idea of absolute or comparative advantage.

Officials saw freedom of trade mostly as a means to mitigate problems created by a necessary protection. Protection is to be understood here, broadly, as the full spectrum of measures adopted to secure the property of capitalists and to foster accumulation. This includes protectionism in the narrow sense, but also the extension of sovereignty overseas in the form of colonies, the chartering of companies, the use of force to secure trade – all the means states used to establish a protective framework for commercial activity on or beyond national territories. Protection in these varied forms created frictions and feedbacks, especially when other states deployed similar measures, locking the whole system into a disadvantageous equilibrium. Consider the case of manufacturing protectionism. When Nation A closed its markets to Nation B, a series of negative feedbacks followed: retaliation by Nation B, leading to the loss of export markets for producers in Nation A; diminished tax revenue for both, as international flows of goods dried up; increased smuggling, as international trade was diverted into the black economy; and loss of commercial vitality, as producers sheltered from foreign competition failed to innovate while others lost access to cheap raw materials. The economic advantages of freer trade lay in mitigating these unintended consequences of protection: in ending trade wars and reopening closed export markets; checking smuggling and increasing taxes on trade; and making domestic producers more competitive.

Freedom of trade and protection were never antitheses. Policymakers and merchants understood that commerce required liberty *and* protection, but a tension existed between these desiderata that could never be fully resolved.[59] Merchants, manufacturers, and planters wanted freedom to make the most advantageous individual choices. They criticised state regulation in matters of trade, and denounced monopolies (though only the ones from which they did not benefit).[60] They also relentlessly demanded protection. Merchants and planters wanted an interventionist state, quick to shield them from foreign or domestic rivals, privateers and pirates, foreign sovereigns, or their own labour force. Protection bore the additional sense of favour or patronage. The state's protection was supposed to actively foster the good of trade. But protection for one set of merchants always meant restraints on liberty for others. Consider the example of French colonial trade under the Exclusif. The *négociants* of Bordeaux and Nantes were protected, but at the expense of the planters' liberty to trade with whom they wished. Protection in its many forms produced a persistent hum of complaint from merchants, colonists, and manufacturers. The point of such cavilling was never to do away with protection as such, but to maximise its benefits or to reduce its costs for one group at the expense of another. For their part, officials were often sympathetic to calls for greater liberty. The trick was to strike a balance that would produce the largest aggregate gain for the state.

Some may object that what I describe as free trade here is not free trade at all, but a modified protectionism. This critique substitutes an imaginary and idealised free trade for the real thing – theory for history. In the words of James Livesey, 'If we approach free trade in an ahistorical manner or as an element in a timeless model of economic liberalism, we run the risk of completely misunderstanding what was at stake in arguments about trade in the eighteenth century.'[61] Free trade (or 'freedom of trade', or 'freedom to trade', or the 'liberty of a free trade', or '*liberté de commerce*') was part of the everyday vocabulary of eighteenth-century actors, and as historians we would do well to understand what they meant. There is little that resembles free trade in the textbook economics sense – not in the wild. Real-world free-trade agreements take years to negotiate and run to thousands of pages because they are riddled with exceptions, special arrangements, and horse-trading intended to advantage privileged sectors, protect national security, and create reciprocity. Arguably, eighteenth-century officials and merchants simply saw free trade more clearly than we do. In a world of competing sovereigns there is no freedom of trade outside a protective politico-legal framework. In this sense, free trade is never fully separable from protection.

The weightiest problems created by protection in this broad sense were international conflicts generated by competing efforts to foster and secure trade. Freedom of trade promised to alleviate these. In Europe, Britain and

France were locked in a commercial cold war from the 1690s to the 1780s based on the prohibitions and high duties they used to exclude the goods of the rival from their national markets. Freer trade promised warmer relations by dismantling these barriers, creating economic constituencies with an interest in preserving peace, and offering incentives for the two states to avoid coming to blows. But embracing greater freedom of trade never meant abandoning protection. It was always a question of balancing the gains of liberty against those of securing the nation's merchants and producers.

Beyond Europe, the efforts of British and French officials to protect their own trade and colonies constantly threatened to embroil the two powers in war – at an expense that might outrun any benefit from the commerce protected. Freedom of trade offered a solution to the most intractable source of conflict – the threat that one power would gain an unbridgeable commercial lead, overthrowing the balance of power. While systems of closure and prohibition might allow a single state to monopolise key resources and markets, universal access promised to distribute gains from trade broadly. An all-embracing regime of free trade could prevent commercial power from being engrossed by any one state. It could create and sustain a balance of wealth.

But freedom of trade might also favour one power at the expense of others and, when it entailed access for a single state at the expense of others, conduce not to balance but to hegemony. Thus, when a grandson of Louis XIV acceded to the throne of Spain in 1700, this raised the prospect that France would gain exclusive access to the markets of Spain's vast empire in America – a freedom benefiting French merchants alone that threatened the liberties of all Europe. The English and the Dutch would not stand by and allow the emergence of a Bourbon common market that excluded them. Through the rest of the century, the threat that one or other of the great commercial states would use an exclusive free-trade arrangement to engross the wealth of critical trading zones was a cause of major wars. Free trade could be the source of instability as well as a foundation for peace.

The inspiration for official visions of freer trade in the eighteenth century came partly from smugglers and neutral traders operating in the interstices of the mercantilist trading world. But the freedom they enjoyed was never the ideal, because it was insecure. The norms of this realm were the reverse of the official sphere: smugglers, neutrals, and small chartered companies plied an open, but relatively unprotected, trade in the spaces between empires. Great powers sought to shut each other's commerce down in wartime. Commercial networks took advantage of such conflicts to profit from neutral trade. The dominant commercial states built colonial empires; the mercantile networks of the shadow order built none of their own but penetrated those of the great powers and profited from them in defiance of national monopolies. In the Asian world of trade, the great India companies built fortifications, armed ships, and fought wars. The smaller players – the Danish, Swedish, Prussian, and Ostend companies – never became 'company-states'. Taking their cues from Asian traders, they hired few soldiers, seldom built expensive fortifications, and waged no wars.[62] Though it was the bugbear of officialdom, the realm of the 'unfair trader', the smuggler, and the interloper also exerted a pull on the official world, an attraction at its greatest when the costs of war and empire were most apparent. Freedom of trade as envisioned in the official sphere was akin to the trade in the informal realm – it connected empires, penetrated closed spaces, flourished during wartime, took advantage of neutrality – but with one great difference: it enjoyed a full measure of official protection.

In the world of French and British officials, initiatives to open a balanced freedom of trade that would foster peace rather than trigger conflict waxed and waned to the pulse of the great wars that repeatedly roiled Europe and its global outposts. These initiatives unfolded in two waves, the first from the 1690s through to the 1710s, culminating in the final years of the War of the Spanish Succession, when diplomats discussed opening Spanish America to the goods of all nations, and negotiated commercial treaties intended to re-establish a freer trade between France and Britain, and between France and the Dutch Republic. The second wave came a generation later, starting in the late 1740s and climaxing in the 1780s with the birth of the United States as a free-trading nation, the 1786 Eden–Rayneval commercial treaty, and efforts to end Franco-British conflict over commercial access to Bengal. Both moments were responses to a generation of system-wide wars in which trade had been a major stake of conflict.

The more familiar story of efforts to promote free trade by Adam Smith and the Physiocrats, political economists who came to prominence in France during the 1760s, has a place in this narrative, but a subordinate one. Smith and his French progenitors worked in the shadow of renewed wars for trade and colonies too. They, no less than officials, hoped to pacify the international order by ending the secular struggle between France and Britain. Officials and writers together were participants in an Enlightenment project to ameliorate the social world. To be sure, the textual form of the new political economy was different from the memoranda of the official world – more systematic, more self-conscious about first principles. *Philosophes* often presented their ideas as a critique of the official world. They located the balance between liberty and protection in a different place than officials. Yet in practice, if not in theory, official and philosophical projects became entangled and hybridised as *philosophes* tried to shape policy, and officials ransacked their work for serviceable ideas.

These appropriations were selective: Smith's political economy never *structured* the thinking of Shelburne or Pitt, any more than the agriculture-focused Physiocrats determined the outlook of Vergennes or Calonne. Officials set aside much of what was distinctive, indeed essential, about the new political economies – the moral philosophy that underpinned them; the concern for the welfare of the consumer; the principled rejection of monopoly. Notwithstanding this selectivity, the embrace of freer trade by officials gave new weight to philosophical political economy, especially Smith's. The *Wealth of Nations* seemed destined for relative obscurity on its publication in 1776, but this changed when politicians began to draw on Smith's work for strategies to solve the new geopolitical challenges they faced.

I focus in this book on the place of political competition for commercial wealth in Franco-British relations, and the efforts to rein this in, but this was just one factor in international politics. Others often proved more important. Tending the balance of power in the ordinary sense, by building and sustaining alliances, whether with European powers or indigenous peoples in the Americas, was central to the management of foreign affairs. Dynasticism, too, remained a factor in European politics, while religious alignments could be significant, as could ideological affinity or antipathy. The point I insist on is not that commercial interests were consistently more important than other factors in policy-making, but that they were strategic. Historians sometimes distinguish too sharply between political and commercial interests in interstate relations, with the latter implicitly categorised as private and the former as public. To assess the weight of commercial interests in foreign affairs, in this logic, is to weigh the influence of merchant lobbying on policymakers. Officials were wary of or even hostile to such special pleading, scholars rightly insist.[63] Yet it would be a mistake to conclude that commerce mattered less than 'political' concerns. Commerce was a strategic interest because it generated the resources that underpinned power. If officials sometimes had little time for *particular* mercantile interests, what they conceived to be the *general* interest of commerce could never be a merely private concern. In the same vein, the sharp distinction some historians draw between European balance-of-power politics and a distinct realm of commerce and colonies is overdrawn.[64] If it was true that Britain's geopolitical priorities were often centred in Europe, wars and alliances there could only be sustained with the wealth that poured in from foreign and colonial trade. The balance of power was inseparable from the balance of wealth.

It was the need to discern the public interest in matters of trade (or to reframe private interests as matters of public concern) that gave rise to the language of political economy. Classic studies of eighteenth-century foreign policy attributed little importance to ideas, seeing these as the province of intellectuals, while policy was the affair of more practical beings.[65] But this has changed. Following what David Armitage describes as a 'fifty-year rift' between the history of ideas and the history of international affairs, a burst of new scholarship on international and imperial political thought has appeared in recent years.[66] The history of political economy, read as reflections on a world of clashing commercial states, has been one focus of interest.[67] I hope to convince the reader that political-economic ideas were as central to the world of foreign and imperial policy in the eighteenth century as they plainly were to domestic politics – ideas understood here not as rigid philosophical principles emanating from outside, but as flexible heuristics created and constantly reworked by practitioners in living administrative traditions, or selectively appropriated from more formal works of political economy to meet the practical challenges and contingencies of politics.

Specialised institutions designed to discern the public interest in matters of trade developed on both sides of the Channel. In France the Council of Commerce, founded in 1700, served as a central site for the Chambers of Commerce of the major commercial cities to press their claims on the royal administration. In Britain, the Board of Trade, which managed the Atlantic trading system, regularly entertained expert advice from merchants and petitions from planters and colonial commercial interests. There was no equivalent body to manage Britain's trade with Europe, while commerce east of the Cape of Good Hope was governed by the East India Company, which came under close public regulation only in 1784 with the establishment of Pitt's Board of Control. The French India Company, by contrast, had always been more tightly supervised by the Contrôle Général. In both nations, ministries were important avenues for lobbying, with responsibility for various aspects of foreign trade divided in France between the naval and foreign ministries and the Contrôle Général, and in Britain among the secretaries of state, the lords of trade, the Admiralty, and the Treasury.

The most fundamental difference in institutional architecture between the two countries lay in the emergence of Parliament in Britain as the central clearing house for the adjudication of all major political-economic questions.[68] The primacy of Parliament entailed a range of other institutional differences. Parties and factions sought to mobilise merchants behind partisan political causes, as Tories and Whigs did around the commercial treaty of Utrecht in 1713, or opposition Whigs did in favour of war with Spain in 1739, and as the Rockinghamites would again in the mid-1760s in favour of free ports and against the Stamp Act. It is sometimes difficult to discern in these campaigns where political manipulation leaves off and genuine merchant groundswell begins. That said, organised pressure groups representing major industries developed in the British public sphere especially from the 1760s, and with growing organisational coherence and weight from the 1780s. French merchant interests were much less likely to resort to press campaigns or petitions to advance their interests. In the absence of a national representative body, mercantile interests in France sometimes turned to the regional *parlements*, bodies with both judicial and administrative functions, but generally focused on lobbying the ministries.

A further fundamental institutional difference between the two nations lay in the structure and vigour of their public finance systems. British arrangements gave great City merchants, the directors of the Bank of England and the chartered companies direct access to and considerable informal influence over ministers, because of the role they played in arranging credit for the government. Merchants did not enjoy the same stature in France. There, a specialised class of financiers managed the tax system, supplied the monarchy with short-term credit, and through their social networks held a significant share of the long-term debt. Not only did the French system give merchants less political weight, it proved less robust than British public credit, subjecting the French monarchy to greater financial strain in wartime, despite its larger tax base. The differences between the systems elicited French 'jealousy of credit', manifest in numerous schemes floated over the decades to transform the French system into something more like Britain's. These I examine in Chapter 3. The point I want to stress here is that French financial weakness put it at a structural disadvantage in geopolitical struggles with Britain between the 1690s and the 1780s, and this was reflected in the greater activity and creativity of French officials, allied merchants, and political economists in dreaming up schemes to pacify global politics and drive rivalry into safer commercial forms.

I put states and chartered companies, and the officials who managed them, at the centre of my story, and this, perhaps, requires some justification. Many historians of empire and global trade in the eighteenth century downplay the role of states. States, they argue, lacked the capacity to police flows of people, goods, and ideas; real agency lay with men and women on the ground who operated through self-organising networks. In the realms of trade and empire, especially, the boundedness and centralisation of states yielded to cross-imperial entanglement and local initiative. Atlantic history emphasises the interpenetration of empires in the Americas, and the agency of smugglers, migrants, indigenous peoples, and the enslaved. From this perspective, to focus on the action and thinking of metropolitan elites might appear a step backwards. This network turn in historical thinking represents a major advance. It is true that the reach of eighteenth-century states regularly exceeded their grasp. Yet, in certain domains, states, or the people who managed them, exercised decisive agency: in the choice for war and peace at scale; in framing treaties; borrowing money in the name of nations or kings; and shaping the regulatory environment, even if evasion was pervasive. States could never fully control mercantile networks, but they were the final arbiters of the political framework for global trade and, through their exercise of this power, they shaped an emergent capitalist order.

Writing about states as if they were unitary actors is a shorthand for a more complex reality. States are structures, not agents – bundles of powers and rights that politicians, courtiers, and officials operated to achieve their own or their superiors' ends, those of factions or parties, or the good of the public, as they saw it. Eighteenth-century states were only partially bureaucratised. They were 'familial states' – loose agglomerations of elite families, organised in networks, or corporations, competing and collaborating for the spoils of power.[69] Officials and their equivalents in the chartered companies are the central actors in my story because theirs were the hands on the levers of state and company power. They bore corporate responsibility, and stood to gain or lose with the success or failure of the bodies they managed. This position gave them a strong collective outlook and imposed significant constraints on their thinking and behaviour. Yet they remained embedded in the family and factional coalitions of which they were a part, and open to the same ideological influences as other members of their class.

In what follows, I organise chapters topically rather than chronologically, each investigating a problem or theme and tracing its unfolding over time. Some cover the whole century from the 1690s to the eve of the French Revolution. Others focus on just a few decades. Though they can be read singly, the full argument emerges only when they are taken together. Writing in this mode can elide the links between what was happening at the same time across diverse policy areas. I try to draw attention to these links where relevant. The advantages of this model appeared to me to outweigh the drawbacks. Familiar understandings are woven into the narrative form in ways difficult to disentangle. Narrative makes sense of events by relating what occurred to earlier happenings, usually squeezing out paths not taken, which can be ignored or minimised because they had no issue. To break with narrative allows us to assemble and analyse these alternate paths, and to grasp them as structure.

1

TRADE TALKS

Peace, Protection, and the Rise of Free Trade

In the second half of the seventeenth century, and especially during the two great wars that followed the Glorious Revolution, the French and British governments adopted trade prohibitions and high duties that greatly restricted licit commerce between the two countries. French wine producers lost much of what had been their largest export market, priced out by Portuguese and Spanish wines admitted to Britain at a lower duty. Conversely, England's staple woollen manufacture found French markets closed. Enacted to undermine a rival, to fund wars by raising new revenues, and to protect infant industries, these trade barriers became quasi-permanent parts of the political-economic armature of the French and British states. Such measures institutionalised a struggle in which market success was mediated by political, not just economic, means – a competition between the two states aimed at maximising the take of their subjects and fostering the development of strategic economic sectors by establishing fiscal and legal barriers to the free flow of goods and ships. Commercial competition mediated by political means is a structural feature of a capitalist order where commerce is entwined with, and made to serve, the interests of contending sovereigns. States protect and encourage the economic activities of their own subjects at the expense of foreign rivals, especially in sectors regarded as crucial to power and security. In this case, however, such competition took an especially invidious form: the two nations fought a commercial cold war during the century after 1688.[1]

Yet at certain moments French and British officials tried to roll back barriers, to establish a freer trade, and to institutionalise greater openness under the aegis of commercial treaties. In 1713, officials negotiated a treaty of commerce promising to do away with prohibitions and to lower duties as part of the broader peace of Utrecht (though the House of Commons refused to legislate

31

key provisions, rendering it a dead letter). Four decades later, during a thaw in relations after the War of the Austrian Succession (1740–48), British ministers talked of reviving portions of the 1713 treaty, and introduced legislation to lift a ban on fine French linens with the hope that France would admit British hardware and clocks. The issue arose again in 1772 when Versailles proposed a trade treaty as part of a design to create a common Franco-British front in Europe and an entente in India. Finally, in 1786, the two kingdoms reached a new commercial accord, the Eden–Rayneval treaty, intended by the French foreign minister, Charles Gravier, comte de Vergennes, to lay a foundation for Franco-British concord, perhaps even future partnership.

Commercial treaties were not the only means to establish a freer Franco-British trade, and Chapters 2, 5, and 6 will explore other initiatives in the Americas and India. But in a world without multilateral institutions to establish the ground rules, bilateral commercial treaties were key instruments to shape the political terrain on which the game of international commercial competition would be played.[2] Such treaties played a critical part both in efforts to transform the Franco-British relationship, and in the eighteenth-century history of free trade.

All of the commercial treaty initiatives from 1713 onwards were driven as much by geopolitical as by economic logics. Officials often sought treaties of commerce at the end of, or shortly after, major wars, when they were acutely conscious of the costs of conflict in the form of ballooning public debt, and often anxious to avert future clashes. Officials envisioned that a freer trade, if it could be made genuinely reciprocal, would reduce tensions, and create a mutual interest in better relations. It would tend to erode long-held national prejudices, and cause leaders to hesitate before the prospect of renewed warfare. This would allow France and Britain respectively to break out of a cycle of ever-expanding public debt, which threatened to undermine social hierarchy, to erode the political foundations of the polity, and above all to destroy the basis for future prosperity (and thus power) by driving up taxes and interest rates and sapping economic dynamism. It was the rising costs of conflict that pushed French and British officials recurrently towards an understanding based on freer trade.

Relative freedom of trade would simultaneously alleviate some of the costs of protectionism – the loss of export markets, customs revenues, and competitiveness that barriers to trade entailed. The economic arguments that underpinned all proposals for a commercial treaty emphasised the high costs of protection. Prohibitions and exorbitant duties provoked neighbours to retaliate, and led to the loss of export markets. These might be recovered by restoring some measure of free trade. A diminished volume of commerce, whatever the provenance of the goods, damaged the carrying trade. For the British and the Dutch, with their huge investment in shipping, this was an argument in favour of openness. Shutting down trade flows decreased tax revenues from customs. The ideal equilibrium from a fiscal point of view was to set lower duties on a higher volume of trade. Trade barriers also fostered smuggling, which gave rise to serious public order problems.[3] Some observers grasped that closure could undermine competitiveness: a policy that excluded low-cost imports, such as the cheap French linens worn by the seventeenth-century English labouring poor, inflated the cost of living because working people had to buy more expensive domestic substitutes. Wages might have to rise accordingly, driving up the cost of a nation's exports – a particular problem for a high-wage economy like England's.[4] Moreover, producers unexposed to foreign competitors might fail to perfect their product, and never make the leap to international markets where they could contribute to a positive balance of trade.

Given the disadvantages of closure and the potential benefits of openness, a commercial treaty that offered benefits to both sides could be envisioned. The difficulty lay in achieving a balance of gains and losses between the two parties such that the benefits of the treaty were reciprocal. A key problem eighteenth-century officials faced was to make sure that their nation gained more than its rivals in the aggregate of international exchanges, or at least gained no less. Absolute gains from trade were less important than how the benefits were distributed between nations. Because commerce underpinned the power of states, the problem officials cared about most was less economic scarcity (though they lived in a far poorer world than ours), than how much states acquired relative to their politico-military rivals. This was the calculus that produced a zero-sum attitude to trade, not a belief that the world contained a fixed quantum of wealth. Many English Whigs in the late seventeenth century, like the merchant writer John Cary, believed wealth was infinitely expansible because it was created by applying labour to nature. This made him no less apprehensive of any French commercial advantage.[5] Such thinking was a major obstacle to free international trade except in cases where the gains from exchange were distributed evenly.

There was a second objection to surmount. If a nation adopted freer trade, this might check its ability to build up or sustain the most important economic sectors, locking it into a status it is tempting to describe as 'underdeveloped'. Officials typically held that nations did not prosper by sticking to economic activities where they had a natural advantage but by breaking into, or maintaining an edge, in strategic sectors – textile manufacturing for export; the production and re-export of colonial commodities; or the carrying trade.[6] To promote these, they believed it necessary to erect barriers to the entry of foreign competitors, such as Britain's navigation laws, which reserved the carrying trade of the empire to British subjects, or the tariffs Colbert adopted to protect French manufacturing. Indeed, modern critics of unlimited free trade echo such wariness about commercial openness. To specialise in agriculture, even if this is where one's natural advantages lie, may be tantamount to specialising in being poor. If a nation wishes to alter its capabilities over time so as to move up the value chain, it may be rational to create protective barriers until new industries are strong enough to face global competition.[7] A kind of under-development linked to an excessive openness had been the fate of Spain, many Europeans believed. Because it was relatively accessible to foreign merchants under treaties signed in the seventeenth century, it was difficult for the Spanish to develop their own manufacturing sector. Given such assumptions, the exchange of French wines and brandies for British textiles could not alone form the basis for an acceptable treaty. A balanced freedom of trade would have to allow French manufacturing and colonial trade to flourish or it would be a recipe for British aggrandisement and French subordination.

In the eighteenth century, most people thought about free trade as patchy and uneven; they regarded it as a strategy not a precept, a complement to protection, not its antithesis. Since the previous century, officials and merchants had advocated greater openness in some contexts but not in others, and this without any sense of contradiction. From the 1680s, Whig critics of the monopolies exercised by the Royal African and East India companies pressed under the banner of 'free trade' for the admission of broader groups of merchants into the slave trade and English commerce with Asia.[8] But such anti-monopoly sentiment did not translate into rejection of broad imperial monopolies, such as the navigation acts, or into support for freer trade with France. Henry Martyn penned a brilliant endorsement of freedom of trade with Asia in his *Considerations upon the East India Trade* (1701) but bitterly criticised the commercial treaty of 1713, helping to write the *British Merchant*, which became the gospel of Whig protectionism.[9]

French officials and merchants questioned the use of monopoly and protection to foster particular economic sectors, but this did not extend to a critique of monopoly or privilege as such.[10] Across the eighteenth century, officials established free ports, suspended monopolies, and granted exemptions to regulations for the entrepreneurs and innovations they wished to foster, all within the context of a general embrace of privilege and regulation.[11] The 'dichotomy between free trade and protectionism as more or less absolute categories', as Lars Magnusson has observed, developed only from the 1840s.[12] For officials and merchants, commercial liberty was not a principle or an ideology but a strategy to achieve specific goals. Nor do we see any radical change in this outlook across the century.

To be sure, new political-economic thinking emerged beginning in the 1740s and 1750s with Montesquieu, the Gournay circle and Physiocracy in France and the Scottish Enlightenment in Britain. These novel intellectual developments are a part of our story, though not as a primary inspiration for official moves towards a freer international trade. The new political economies were often articulated as critiques of the status quo, and in some cases drew on philosophical traditions alien to the power-maximising stance of officials. But they grappled with the same problems that propelled policymakers to seek a freer trade, and this made it possible to find common ground. Physiocracy and the writings of the Scots eventually attracted a respectful audience among officials. David Hume, Adam Smith, and the Physiocrats enjoyed, or developed, close links with the administrative world. Pierre-Samuel Dupont de Nemours, a Physiocrat, helped design the Eden–Rayneval treaty.

But when their ideas entered into policy conversations, they did so on the terms of the officials. Policymakers borrowed their ideas and integrated them into an ideological framework in which states rather than firms or individuals were imagined to be the crucial competitors for trade, where the idea of a natural harmony of interests between commercial nations was little credited, where only the constant vigilance of states could ensure that gains from trade were reciprocal. Philosophical political economy got a foothold in the world of commercial treaty-making entangled with, and subordinated to, official projects aiming to make peace in the service of power.

THE FRANCO-BRITISH COMMERCIAL TREATY OF 1713

The Franco-British treaty of commerce officials signed on 11 April 1713 at Utrecht was part of the peace negotiations ending the War of the Spanish Succession (1701–14), in which Britain had allied with the Dutch and the Habsburgs to remove a grandson of Louis XIV from the Spanish throne. The war initially went the way of the allies, but despite the exhaustion of France, Louis XIV refused draconian peace terms offered in 1709. The British broke the deadlock two years later when a newly elected Tory government agreed to accept the French claimant to the Spanish throne in return for a partition of the Spanish monarchy and other concessions. A commercial treaty under which French and British goods were to be treated on the most-favoured-nation (MFN) principle was one provision of the peace settlement. The treaty is sometimes seen as a piece of predatory commercial diplomacy – the price France had to pay for peace.[13] The English and the Dutch had used commercial treaties since the seventeenth century to establish unbalanced, non-reciprocal privileges for their merchants in the territories of economically less advanced polities, notably Spain and Portugal. Indeed, a key dynamic of international relations in this period was a commercial imperialism by which leading states exploited other European powers.[14] But in fact the architects of the 1713 commercial treaty intended it originally to offer benefits to both sides. It represented an implicit alliance between French Colbertists and British Tories over the merits of cutting the Dutch down to size and reopening cross-Channel markets long closed by war and hostility.

The treaty was part of an effort to lay a basis for better relations between the two countries which would permit an escape from the quarter-century of conflict that followed the Glorious Revolution. It needs to be seen alongside initiatives to resolve geopolitical tensions over commercial access to Spanish America in which many of the same officials were involved (to be examined in the following chapter).[15] Yet there is no doubt that the fear that former enemies would use trade to achieve an ascendancy that eluded them in war haunted the negotiations. Many French officials worried their kingdom would be the victim of an excessive openness to British goods. By contrast, British Whigs and some Tories ultimately rejected the deal in Parliament on the grounds that it was too favourable to France. Proponents of the treaty drew on ideas about the economic advantages of a freer trade that had been developing since the previous century and that emphasised the downsides of the protectionist policies each nation had embraced. The commercial treaty of 1713 was an expression of this logic.

French officials and merchants grasped both the advantages and the potential dangers of a Franco-British commercial treaty within a way of thinking about freedom of trade that had evolved within Colbertism – the seventeenth-century French regulatory tradition associated with Jean-Baptiste Colbert, Louis XIV's contrôleur général des finances from the mid-1660s until his death in 1683. (The Contrôle Général was the ministry with responsibility for finance and economic development.) Colbert's name is a byword for protectionism – though this term did not exist in French before the nineteenth century, emerging then alongside its modern opposite, *libre-échange*.[16] In the late seventeenth century, *protection* and *liberté* were viewed as complementary, not antithetical, and the term *liberté de commerce* was used to denote the freedom to trade. Historians have long viewed Colbert's tariff of 1667 as the first move in an aggressive campaign to expand French manufacturing at the expense of other countries, and the trigger for a wave of trade wars.[17] But the minister and those who came after him also understood the drawbacks to commercial closure, and grasped how a more open trade – always envisioned tactically and selectively – might solve these problems.[18]

Colbertist advocates for a freer trade claimed it would augment French exports by removing political blockages to commerce. It was the chance to unload larger volumes of French goods, not to acquire foreign wares more cheaply, that seemed the key payoff. To be sure, officials understood that competition could stimulate domestic producers to innovate, and they sometimes acknowledged that buying cheaper foreign goods would benefit producers and consumers. But this was not the priority. Most importantly, greater exports and the positive trade balance they made possible would draw in specie and enlarge the money stock.[19] Conversely, high tariffs could reduce the outlet for exports by cutting foreign traffic in French ports, and by provoking trade wars. From this perspective, greater commercial openness had its attractions.

The first major test of these ideas came at the end of the War of the League of Augsburg (1688–97), when Louis XIV agreed to make trade concessions to the Dutch in the treaty of Ryswick. Under the ensuing tariff of 1699, the French monarchy slashed duties on thirty of the principal items imported from the Dutch Republic and exempted Dutch shipping from port taxes imposed on foreign vessels.[20] Some officials worried that Dutch competition would ruin French fisheries, strangle navigation and colonies, and undercut manufacturing. Others embraced the Ryswick trade deal because they saw the Amsterdam entrepôt and Dutch commercial networks and shipping as essential to sustain export markets for French goods, particularly wines and brandies. Both the supporters and the critics of a more open trade regime were Colbertists, each emphasising different elements of the minister's legacy. Colbert understood both the damage the Dutch could do the French economy and the constructive role they played in marketing French exports. The second generation of the Colbert clan, from positions in the ministries and at court, lined up on both sides of this divide. Colbert's son, the marquis de Seignelay, naval minister from 1683 to 1690, took an anti-Dutch position. Colbert's sons-in-law, the duc de Beauvillier and the duc de Chevreuse, led the charge to reconcile with the Dutch. Colbert's nephews, Jean-Baptiste Colbert de Torcy, foreign minister from 1696 to 1715, and Nicolas Desmaretz, contrôleur général from 1708 to 1715, also took a softer line.[21] Desmaretz in particular believed commercial openness was necessary to market French products abroad, as we will see.

The key published statement of this free-trade Colbertism was a book by the cleric and scholar Pierre-Daniel Huet which circulated in manuscript from 1694 and was used to support the change in policy at Ryswick. It appeared in at least four French editions between 1712 and 1714, implicitly to make the case for a further freeing of French trade at Utrecht, and again under a different title in 1717 and 1718, before its translation into English and Spanish.[22] The French goal had been 'to sell lots of things to our neighbours and to buy nothing from them' – a fine plan, conceded Huet, if it had been practicable. New manufactures were established to substitute for products formerly imported from the Dutch Republic. But predictably the Dutch retaliated, damaging established French exports. Ultimately the aggressive trade policy led to war, 'properly speaking a war of trade'. The resulting losses were the more galling because excluding the Dutch was misconceived: 'as long as those Republicans had the freedom to come to our ports and harbours, the sale of our commodities . . . was always very great'. France did not need to exclude foreign goods to assure a positive balance of trade. Its neighbours would always need its products more than it would need theirs. Huet's prescription for French commercial success was to imitate the Dutch, which meant embracing commercial liberty. Dutch merchants traded with their enemies in wartime because they understood that 'commerce once rerouted never returns to its original course', something Colbert had also appreciated. They were 'protected without being constrained'.[23]

Summing up this attitude was the dictum that commerce required 'liberty and protection'. This catchphrase, invoked endlessly by French merchants and officials down to the nineteenth century, underscores the inadequacy of attempts to understand eighteenth-century French political economy in terms of a dichotomy between protectionism and laissez-faire. Liberty and protection were not key words of opposing regulatory philosophies: they were complements, not opposites.[24]

A strain of Colbertist thinking on freedom of trade found a home in the Council of Commerce, established in 1700 to institutionalise consultation between policymakers and merchants. (This was renamed the Bureau of Commerce in 1722: for more on the Council's role, see below, pp. 90–1).[25] It is evident in a series of memoranda prepared by the thirteen merchant-deputies for the opening sessions of the body. French trade policy since the 1680s had been ruinous, most complained, sparking trade wars and drying up export markets. The wine-producing provinces had particularly suffered.[26] The deputies criticised protection of infant manufactures, which elicited retaliatory duties and spurred foreigners to establish import-substituting imitators in place of goods made in France. Under freer trade, French manufacturers would quickly stamp out these 'counterfeits'. But foreigners could be induced to lower duties on French goods only by reciprocal treatment of their own exports. Some deputies made arguments for freer trade on the basis of absolute advantage. The deputy from Bordeaux, Jean-Baptiste Fenellon, argued that France should specialise in those branches of commerce it excelled in and leave to others those they did best.[27] France benefited when it imported goods foreigners could manufacture better and more cheaply. He particularly doubted the value of the woollen manufactures established to compete with English producers: French woollens were uncompetitive outside the kingdom, he claimed, and to keep the industry alive, high duties were imposed on imports to the general prejudice of trade.

These position papers are at the centre of an old controversy about whether a liberal current of thought had emerged in merchant circles by the 1690s – a debate that underlines the distorting effects of the conventional contrast between freedom of trade and Colbertism.[28] The memoranda of the deputies are both Colbertist and critical of Colbert. Colbertism was not a dogma but a living administrative tradition responsive to the challenges generated by governing commerce. The deputies made a strong case for freer trade, but they did not do so within the terms of a laissez-faire vision: they believed that only state action could align merchant interests with the public welfare; the monarchy ought to foster some trades while discouraging others. Infant manufactures should not be sustained by protective duties, which distorted foreign trade, but the use of privileges or subsidies to this end would be perfectly acceptable. Preserving a positive balance of trade to draw specie into the country and augment the money supply was critical. The deputies' commitment to commercial liberty was limited and instrumental. France could expect other nations to buy its goods only if it bought theirs, argued the Lyon deputy, Jean Anisson. Still, the goal was to buy fewer foreign goods than one sold, and to import raw materials, not high-value-added goods which should be produced at home. But this objective could not be achieved under conditions of trade war, the deputies insisted; gentler methods were required. This was not a rejection of Colbertism but a tactical reworking of its premises.[29]

Also playing into the making of the 1713 trade treaty with Britain were tensions over the place of the Dutch in the political economy of the French kingdom. France banned trade with the republic in 1703 but permitted Dutch ships and commodities to enter under passports.[30] Most of the deputies argued that the Dutch enemy was indispensable; French manufacturers needed the raw materials they carried and the outlet for exports they provided, especially to the Baltic and Germany. The trade might be lost permanently if it were interrupted. There were initiatives to divert French trade to neutral shippers such as Denmark and Sweden, yet down to 1710 the deputies held that neutral shipping was not enough. Finally, in November of that year, they were persuaded that a definitive trade ban might bring the Dutch to the peace table.[31] To compensate for the shortfall in shipping – and to threaten the Dutch with the permanent loss of the traffic – they proposed to eliminate port duties on all other shippers, even the British, a proposal Desmaretz adopted. In effect, they threw open French ports to freedom of trade but left the Dutch out in the cold.

Both the urge to check Dutch economic power and the impulse to reopen lost British markets for French exports framed the design for a commercial treaty with Britain. There was a strong implicit case in the deputies' memoranda of 1700 for such a treaty, and some had called for it openly.[32] Such thinking was still in evidence a decade later and shaped the advice the Council gave Desmaretz, Colbert de Torcy, and the naval minister, Jérôme Phélypeaux, comte de Pontchartrain. Deputies Anisson, Fenellon, and Nicolas Mesnager (who represented Rouen) played key roles in negotiating the commercial treaty. The Council envisioned an accord based on the principle of reciprocity, suggesting mutual concession of MFN status as its foundation. The key was to maintain a rough equality, a balance of advantages for French exporters and damage to industries like woollens which would face competition from British imports. The blanket re-establishment of the relatively low tariff of 1664 demanded in Britain's favour would be ruinous, they agreed. France needed to exclude East India goods and sugars, to prohibit British *cabotage* (port-to-port shipping in France), and to maintain barriers against the products of British fishing and whaling. These goods should be admitted only under the higher tariff of 1699, which applied to equivalent Dutch products.[33]

Desmaretz, in particular, felt that a broad measure of free trade was necessary to guarantee export markets. 'I do not think bad consequences for French trade are to be feared in granting to all nations a reciprocal equality,' the contrôleur général told Mesnager. 'My opinion is that the easier we make it for foreigners to communicate their merchandise and the productions of their countries to us, the more we will facilitate the sale of our own.' The quality of French products would assure their sale so long as the necessary access was maintained: 'because France abounds in commodities and merchandise of a quality superior to other countries, and foreigners, finding an easy entry into France, will the more willingly carry away our merchandise and commodities'. Thus, he concluded, 'Uniformity and liberty in matters of trade always make for the wealth of the country where they are established.'[34]

A treaty according MFN status to Britain also offered an opportunity to limit concessions to Dutch traders, and to balance Dutch economic might, especially in the carrying trade. The Dutch Republic was pressing for a return to the low tariff of 1664 as a condition of peace.[35] This would be disastrous, Mesnager warned: the French herring fisheries would be wiped out, as would French whaling; the Dutch would import sugar more cheaply than it could be carried from the French colonies; the Levant trade would be undercut. Mesnager envisioned the commercial colonisation of France as Dutch trading houses displaced native French merchants. France risked being pushed altogether out of navigation and fisheries, with dire consequences for the navy, which depended on these branches of commerce to train sailors who could be drafted in wartime. The deputy raised the spectre of mass unemployment and depopulation, indeed, of 'a nullity of the State such as we see in Spain'.[36]

But a commercial treaty with Britain might be a means to limit concessions to the Dutch. 'I am truly persuaded,' he told Colbert de Torcy, 'that the treaty of commerce proposed by the English in the preliminary articles of the peace will offer means to . . . remedy the evil.'[37] By playing the British off against the Dutch, Mesnager hoped to secure concessions from both sides – from the Dutch, exemptions for certain goods from the tariff of 1664; from Britain, fishing rights in Newfoundland. For the same reasons, Jérôme de Pontchartrain favoured a commercial treaty with the British: it would be a means to evade subordination to the Dutch. If British shipping could enter French ports on the same terms as the Dutch, the near monopoly of the latter on the French carrying trade would be broken. In matters of trade, the naval minister argued, France and Britain had 'a common enemy which can subsist only at their expense and enrich itself only by fleecing them'.[38]

British Tories shared this view, and it constituted a principal ground for a Franco-British accord. For Tories, it was the Dutch, not the French, who were the true threat to Britain's commercial future. Certain Tory politicians, financial projectors, and writers had come to regard foreign trade, shipping, and commercial services – the lucrative activities of the port and City of London – as the keys to national wealth and power.[39] Indeed, a revolution had occurred in this sector since the Restoration. Between 1660 and 1700, English imports grew by about a third and exports by half. A particular darling of Tory political economy was the re-export business, which had expanded from negligible proportions before the Civil War to compose more than 40 per cent of English exports by 1700. Two-fifths of these were plantation products, mostly tobacco and sugar, while East India goods accounted for another two-fifths. Burgeoning long-distance trade stimulated merchant shipping, with tonnage increasing by 70 per cent in the quarter-century after 1660.[40] Enthusiasm for shipping and long-distance trade fit with Tory proclivities in foreign policy, which exalted the navy as the nation's defender and the most effective means to project British power.[41]

The development of this Tory perspective was facilitated by ties to some of the great joint-stock companies.[42] Two of the leading Tory architects of the 1713 commercial treaty – Charles Davenant and Arthur Moore – were closely tied to the East India Company and the Royal African Company. The foremost political economist of his day and a prominent Tory journalist, Davenant consistently supported the East India and African companies in his published writings. Moore, the principal government spokesman on the commercial treaty in the House of Commons, served on the direction of the old East India Company from 1698 to 1704 and from 1705 to 1709. In 1709 he was elected a director of the Royal African Company.[43] To Tories like Davenant and Moore, the Dutch, with their dominant position in the carrying trade, the thriving East India traffic, and the teeming Amsterdam entrepôt, seemed a far more dangerous rival than the French.[44] Moreover, Davenant argued, the French 'constitution' placed it at a great disadvantage. Here, as in political economy generally in this period, 'constitution' referred to more than formal political arrangements, and embraced social mores and political culture.[45] In the long run, commerce flourished among free peoples, Davenant asserted, while the Colbertist model, in which trade was 'forc'd and onely Artificial', was unsustainable. Moreover, Britain had geographical advantages and a natural bent for trade the French lacked.[46] Given the emphasis Tories placed on navigation, the comparative insignificance of French shipping almost ruled them out as serious rivals.

The same commercial access to French ports and markets as the Dutch was what Tory leaders wanted from the commercial treaty with France. For Henry St John (from 1712, Viscount Bolingbroke), the position the Dutch acquired at Ryswick in 1697 was a huge commercial advantage from which Britain had been excluded.[47] This is why he insisted so strongly on the MFN clause in the trade deal with France, for 'certain it is that we should make a bad bargain for

G. Brittain, if the Dutch were allowed all the advantages of the Tarrif of 1664, whilst these advantages were denied to us, or at least Suspended till we could come into a proportionate Regulation of Dutys'. His attitude was tied to a broader suspicion of the Dutch, whom he regarded as a parasitic and selfish ally which profited from the war while trying to deny Britain any commercial gains.[48]

But balancing the Dutch was not all that was at stake. Bolingbroke welcomed the idea of closer relations with France and believed that freer trade would facilitate this, while it would also shake the pernicious hold of Whig ideology at home. Of the Utrecht Peace he wrote that it was 'the only solid foundation whereupon we could erect a tory system'.[49] There were domestic and international dimensions to this claim. Reopening trade would weaken British francophobia which Bolingbroke rightly viewed as an emotional linchpin of the Whig outlook. The commercial treaty was 'calculated to hinder those prejudices, which our people have been possessed with against France', he noted, by promoting 'an open and advantageous commerce between the two kingdoms'. Freer trade would reduce future conflict too because 'nothing unites like interest, and when once our people have felt the sweet of carrying on a trade to France, under reasonable regulations, the artifices of Whiggism will have the less effect amongst them'.[50] A Tory system at home had its parallel abroad. If Whigs counted on coalition with the Dutch and the Habsburgs, a Tory system required independence from these troublesome allies and better relations with Spain and France. Indeed, Bolingbroke foresaw an eventual alliance with the Bourbon powers.[51]

Peace with France would make possible a retreat from Britain's disastrous embrace of public debt. The two great wars that followed the Glorious Revolution had initiated a financial revolution in Britain. Public borrowing rose from negligible proportions in 1688 to roughly £36 million by the end of the War of the Spanish Succession. Taxes increased sharply too, leaving British taxpayers roughly twice as heavily taxed in the postwar period as their French counterparts.[52] Tories objected to high taxation and to massive public borrowing, which transferred wealth from the taxpaying landed interest to Whig financiers and merchants. These 'Undertakers and Projectors of Loans and Funds', complained the Tory propagandist Jonathan Swift, formed a 'Money'd-Interest, that might in time vie with the Landed'.[53] 'Twenty years of the most expensive wars Europe ever saw,' complained Bolingbroke, had produced 'a sort of property which was not known twenty years ago, [and] is now increased to be almost equal to the *Terra Firma* of our island.'[54] A long peace was necessary to prevent such novelties from subverting the constitution. By 1709 most Tories believed the war was no longer necessary. Louis XIV had been chastened, and continued fighting was unnecessary to preserve a balance of power. Victory in the election of 1710 brought a Tory-dominated ministry under Robert Harley (from 1711, earl of Oxford), which moved quickly to sign peace preliminaries with France.[55] The Tory peace envisioned partition of the Spanish monarchy, leaving Spain and its American dominions to Louis XIV's grandson, Philip V, while conceding the Low Countries and Spain's Italian provinces to the Habsburg claimant.

The leading economic rationale for trade with France came from Davenant, who articulated powerful arguments in favour of targeted forms of freer trade. As inspector-general of the Exports and Imports, he published a report in 1712 defending the idea of trade with France. He denied that England had generally suffered a negative trade balance with the French in the seventeenth century, as Whigs claimed.[56] Attacking the 'Scheme of Trade' often touted by Whigs, he argued there had been a large and mutually beneficial Anglo-French trade before it was destroyed by prohibitions. British advantages would 'at all times render us superior in an open Trade with France'.[57] Reopening commerce with France would restore a market for English woollens and for colonial and East India re-exports. But this would require reciprocity: 'we must treat others no worse than they treat us. We must buy as well as sell'.[58] Davenant authored a ministerial journal, the *Mercator*, to promote the treaty after it was first signed. It claimed that under the relatively modest tariff of 1699 markets in France would be reopened for woollens.[59] The treaty would allow Britain to stamp out the competing French woollen industry. And by exempting British merchants from paying shipping taxes imposed on foreigners, the treaty would break the lock the Dutch had achieved on the French carrying trade.[60]

Davenant's vindication of the commercial treaty reflected arguments for freedom of trade he had developed in the 1690s to defend the import of Asian textiles by the East India Company. He argued then that England could drive down its high wages by importing cheap fabrics from India to clothe the common people, while focusing on producing high quality woollens for export. If this argument applied to Indian cottons it spoke implicitly to French linens – once the garb of the English poor.[61] Moreover France, with its twenty million consumers, was by far the largest potential market for English broadcloth. To re-establish trade, however, import substitution would have to be sacrificed. Small loss, in Davenant's view. The silk and linen industries would never be internationally competitive because England lacked the cheap labour necessary in these sectors. These industries absorbed labour and capital better employed in manufactures 'wherein we cannot be undersold by other Countries'. Leaving linens and silks to the French would generate income for them to buy English woollens.[62] But, for Davenant, arguments about industrial grand strategy were subsidiary to another claim – that manufacturers should not be favoured over the shipping and re-export sectors. Long distance and colonial trade, he argued, were the source of three quarters of the annual addition to national wealth in peacetime, and the foundations of English naval power.[63] Commercial liberty was best for these sectors.

If Tory proponents of freer trade with France argued that it would reverse Dutch gains and recover export markets for British goods in France, Whigs raised the spectre of French products flooding into Britain, ruining branches of its manufacturing, and locking in a negative balance of trade. They claimed that the commercial treaty failed to protect the interests of manufacturing, a sector they privileged as the fount of national wealth. If Tories particularly valued the carrying trade, and the re-export business, and therefore saw the Dutch as Britain's main rivals, Whigs like John Cary, the foremost merchant writer of his day, saw France as the threat because it was a potential manufacturing dynamo.[64]

Whigs argued that trade with France generated a negative balance of trade and disadvantaged Britain. Historically, they claimed, more French goods were imported into England than were exported, many of them luxuries such as wines and silks. The balance eventually had to be covered by the export of specie, draining the English money supply. A 'Scheme of Trade' drawn up by London merchants in 1674, and later used by Whigs, put the imbalance at £965,000.[65] This way of thinking about foreign trade had been challenged from the 1680s by political economists such as Nicholas Barbon and John Houghton, who argued that the stimulus to consumption and innovation supplied by foreign luxuries outweighed any disadvantages, and that the money supply would take care of itself.[66] Authorities such as East India Company chairman Josiah Child asserted that what mattered was not bilateral trade balances but the *general* balance, the aggregate of imports and exports with *all* trade partners rather than with one.[67]

Despite these criticisms, Whigs succeeded in framing the commercial treaty of 1713 as a threat to the balance of trade. In the words of one historian, 'Tory and Whig calculators spent month after month trading computational blows over the value of one number: England's *balance of trade* with France.'[68] Rather than focusing on the export of specie, Whigs emphasised the vitality of the all-important manufacturing sector. When a nation's trade was healthy, it exported manufactured goods in exchange for raw materials, and forwent the purchase of high-value foreign goods when domestic substitutes were available. One approach among others to understanding the balance of trade before 1713, its utility for Whig critics of trade with France helped make this the leading version of the balance of trade doctrine in subsequent decades.[69]

Though making and signing the treaty was the exclusive prerogative of the Crown, to enact the key articles Parliament would have to abrogate legislation discriminating against French imports. Bolingbroke placed a bill to this effect before the House of Commons in June 1713. However, with an election in the offing, the ministry had chosen an inauspicious moment to push the bill through the Commons. Manufacturing and commercial interests mobilised by the Whigs sent nearly fifty petitions to Parliament opposing the treaty.[70] No major commercial interest supported it. A sense that the treaty was a Trojan horse for Tory designs to forge a closer relationship with France further undermined its chances. For Whigs it was an emblem of Tory flirtation with the Bourbons and betrayal of Britain's wartime allies.[71] The measure was defeated on 18 June by a margin of nine votes, with close to eighty Tories voting against it.[72]

Opposition to the treaty is typically viewed as protectionist, and the triumph of the 'no' vote as a defeat for freedom of trade, but this imperfectly captures the stakes of the debate. It was principally the perceived failure to establish reciprocity that critics attacked – that is, the failure of the treaty to deliver the benefits of free trade. Certainly, protectionist arguments had a place, adduced, predictably, in favour of industries such as silk- and linen-weaving, paper-making, and distilling, that faced competition from France.[73] These industries would be wiped out by French competition, Whigs charged. But worse, there would be no countervailing advantage to British industry – the treaty would not actually open foreign markets as it promised. Faced with the tariffs agreed in the treaty, Whigs argued, British woollens would not sell in France.[74] The French could compete on both quality and price and would thus, in Whig politician Sir Robert Walpole's words, 'admit none of ours under these Tariffs'.[75] In short, while Britain would be opened to French wines, brandies, and silks, there would be no reciprocal opening of France to Britain's principal manufacture, woollens.

Moreover, critics claimed, expanded trade with France would damage established commercial relationships that were more beneficial because based on an exchange of British manufactured goods for foreign primary commodities. *The British Merchant, or Commerce Preserv'd*, which began publication in August 1713 to counter the Tory *Mercator*, charged that French competition in silks would undermine British capacity to buy Ottoman and Italian raw silk, which would in turn destroy the market for English woollens in the Mediterranean.[76] Britain must weigh the benefits of expanded trade with France against the prospect of disruption of its relationships with other trading partners. A key relationship threatened was with Portugal. The French treaty would abrogate the Methuen treaty (1703), which guaranteed Portuguese wines a one-third duty preference in the English market, and this would ruin the Portuguese and Brazilian market for English woollens.[77] Whigs in 1713 depicted the Anglo-Portuguese accord as a monument to wise commercial policy.[78] Again, the logic of these arguments was not protectionist as such. The claim, rather, was that the new treaty would sink a more advantageous trade deal with Portugal.

The official *Mercator* reversed the claims of the Whig critics, claiming that there was indeed a lack of reciprocity – but in Britain's favour. The treaty would secure markets for British goods in France without corresponding commercial concessions to the French. British industries would continue to be protected, Davenant argued, because, while the treaty had secured relatively free British trade to France, it did not offer reciprocal tariff treatment to French goods. The French would continue to face high tariff barriers because they were entitled only to the same treatment as the most favoured nation – not to reciprocity with the rates faced by British goods entering France.[79] The arguments of the *Mercator* were intended to appeal to independents, sceptical Tories, and Whigs. This was the logic of entrusting the journal to Daniel Defoe from the autumn of 1713 after Davenant fell ill. As Harley's propagandist, and editor of the *Review* from 1703, he often supported Tory positions using Whig language.[80]

By this time, French officials had also come to the conclusion that the treaty lacked reciprocity and was fundamentally unbalanced in Britain's favour. Mesnager had always been wary that too much openness would render France vulnerable – as he thought the Ryswick trade treaty had already done.[81] Desmaretz sent Anisson and Fenellon to London in January 1713 to study British trade law. This mission was decisive, as the commissioners 'discovered the size of the duties which weigh on the merchandise of other nations', and concluded that under the treaty France would 'meet the same treatment without having the right to complain'.[82] By 1713 French officials preferred no treaty at all to the treaty then on offer, which lacked reciprocity. This lack of equivalence became the basis for a long rearguard action to replace the MFN clause with concrete agreements on tariffs that would equalise French and British duties.[83] In the end, however, facing a British ultimatum on other matters, Louis XIV yielded. The commercial treaty concluded at Utrecht was constructed on the MFN principle which the French had belatedly come to see as a trap.

But it had not been Bolingbroke's intention to make a treaty that would benefit Britain exclusively. He no doubt welcomed the ways it would advantage Britain disproportionately, but to serve the political ends he envisioned for it, it had to be mutually beneficial. Far from wishing to extort the maximum advantage, he proposed during the negotiations that 'we ought rather to reduce our demands as low as the expectations of our trading people will allow us'.[84] To be sure, he would insist on MFN status, knowing that the arrangement was unbalanced in Britain's favour. But parity with the Dutch could not be achieved without this. Bolingbroke admitted that the MFN clause would not produce reciprocity but promised in time to settle 'a system of commerce, still more reasonable than that which will be in force at first'.[85]

This lack of reciprocity proved a key factor in the final undoing of the treaty, which had not been killed definitively by the Commons vote in June. Bolingbroke hoped to reintroduce the bill after the Tory electoral landslide of 1713.[86] Most of the works debating the treaty were published after the June vote; the circulation of the Whig *British Merchant* did not peak until April 1714. But the Tory leader felt he needed new concessions to facilitate its passage through Parliament, especially better terms for the classes of goods to enter under the tariff of 1699 (rather than the lower tariff of 1664 which applied to all other goods).[87] Louis XIV wanted to support the Tories, whom he saw as partners, and to deny Whigs a victory, so he agreed to act provisionally as if the other treaty clauses had gone into effect, including the lifting of taxes on British shipping.[88] He sent Anisson and Fenellon back to London, but more as a goodwill gesture than with any intention of conceding more when France had already given so much.[89] The death of Queen Anne on 1 August 1714, and the replacement in October of the Tory ministry by a Whig one more to the taste of her successor, George I, finally ended negotiations.

Thus the Franco-British commercial treaty of 1713 never came into effect; the commercial cold war begun in the seventeenth century would continue down to the 1780s. Yet the treaty remained a touchstone for later generations of officials interested in using a freer trade to improve Franco-British relations. They continued to imagine commercial openness principally as a tool to re-engineer the international relationship; it would give both nations an interest in the prosperity of the other, and diminish interstate jealousies over commerce. Officials proposed to revive the treaty, or to negotiate a new one on the same model in the 1750s, the 1770s, and the 1780s, always at moments when one or both sides sought a better relationship. The kinds of economic arguments officials and writers made in favour of freer trade in 1713 continued to structure official thinking on commercial treaties down to the 1780s. Such proposals continued to arouse suspicions that the benefits would be non-reciprocal and unbalanced. Indeed, in the short term, scepticism that a fair and advantageous trade was possible between France and Britain was the principal legacy of the 1713 treaty.

FREE TRADE AFTER UTRECHT

The prospects of freer Franco-British trade dimmed in the following generation.[90] New elections triggered by the accession of George I in 1714 brought a Whig majority, and for decades thereafter Tories were proscribed at court, banned from office, and reduced to a rump in Parliament.[91] One of the great critics of Bolingbroke's treaty, Sir Robert Walpole, dominated British politics for most of the 1720s and 1730s. To the degree freer international trade enjoyed popular appeal in this period, it was in the form of free port schemes.

It was not until after Walpole's exit from the political stage that British ministers would pursue a relaxation of trade barriers with France again amidst a warming of relations following the War of the Austrian Succession (1740–48). It was in this context too that the Scottish philosopher David Hume entered the debate about freedom of trade, arguing that it might be the basis for a more peaceful British relationship with France, which would in turn permit a retreat from public debt.

Indeed, from mid-century, an important new current of thinking on free trade began to develop on both sides of the Channel, beyond the administrative realm, and sometimes sharply critical of official attitudes. The new political economy nevertheless shared the ambition to direct Franco-British competition into less dangerous and expensive channels. Whether in Scottish Enlightenment accents or in the guise of French Physiocracy, new thinking about freedom of trade continued to centre on the problem of Franco-British rivalry and the distorting consequences of this conflict for the political-economic evolution of the two kingdoms. Hume and the Physiocrats promoted Franco-British accommodation, imagining an essential harmony between French and British economic interests. But they did not think international rivalry could be wished away, and their political economies laid out strategies for national success in a world of competing commercial states.

With a French commercial treaty effectively off the table after 1714, talk of free trade in Walpole's Britain mostly turned on transforming Britain into a 'general free port' by lowering or removing the taxes on trade that increased the cost and inconvenience of all foreign commerce. Free ports had long flourished in the Mediterranean as means to attract a larger share of international commerce to particular harbours, such as Livorno in Tuscany (which became a free port in 1591), by exempting merchants from the kinds of commercial restrictions that typically burdened trade and by keeping customs duties low.[92] Such freedoms might be extended to British ports in general, merchants argued, and with the same consequences. A British general free port would attract much of the entrepôt trade of Europe. The point was to supplant Amsterdam, which levied low taxes on trade, and to secure British dominance of the carrying trade and the services that went along with it – warehousing, insurance, and banking. A general free port would also strangle the smuggling that high customs duties fostered. Smuggling was the particular bane of the

East India Company, which reckoned that well over half the tea drunk in Britain was smuggled. Arguments for a general free port were widespread enough by 1729 that Joshua Gee, perhaps the most widely read political economist of the Walpole years, felt the need specifically to combat this scheme. Even the low-tax Dutch entrepôt was not a true free port, he pointed out, and their tax structure was commanded by their situation. If they raised customs duties, they would lose their role as intermediaries for the trade of Central Europe. But as a nation dependent for its prosperity on manufacturing, England's situation was different. High duties kept out imports from low-wage nations like France and Italy and could not be forgone.[93]

Walpole flirted (with what seriousness it is hard to say) with the general free port idea – a reminder that freedom of trade was not a unified principle, but a basket of different proposals to be chosen or rejected according to their perceived benefits. He favoured shifting from reliance on customs duties to excise, both to foster an entrepôt trade and to increase tax revenue – excise being more difficult to evade. The Excise Scheme he set before Parliament in 1733 was intended to reassign wine and tobacco, two of the most important commodities from a revenue perspective, from customs to excise. The importer would avoid all the hassles of paying duties on imports, only to have to turn around and seek drawbacks of these taxes on re-export. In the words of a ministerial pamphleteer, this would allow England to compete with Holland as the 'storehouse of Europe'.[94] Indeed, Walpole declared in Parliament, a move towards excise 'would tend to make London a Free Port, and by consequence, the market of the world'.[95] But the prime minister had to shelve such ideas when the Excise Scheme triggered a wave of opposition, notably from London merchants who benefited from fraud in the payment of customs and from smuggling the goods that Walpole wanted to excise.[96]

After Walpole's fall in 1742, the idea of a general free port, and even of free trade with France, was put back on the agenda by Sir Matthew Decker, the most widely read political-economic writer of the 1740s. Decker was an old Tory, a former client of Robert Harley and a leading backer of the minister's South Sea Company (see pp. 97–8). He made his peace with the new Whig regime and was created a baronet in 1716, going on to serve as chairman of the East India Company from 1730 to 1733. His position on freedom of trade was shaped by the company's position that high taxes on trade encouraged smuggling and denied revenue to the state. He was also representative of a broader merchant protest against the way the national debt had come to be funded – that is, increasingly in the form of taxes on trade. His *Serious Considerations on the Several High Duties the Nation Labours Under* (1743) went through at least nine editions before 1757, while his more substantial *Essay on the Causes of the Decline of the Foreign Trade* (1744), which identified a competitiveness crisis caused by high taxes, went through at least seven. Decker argued that a freer trade was simply the best means to enrich Britain and thereby to reduce the relative power of France. Given the context of the War of the Austrian Succession in which he published, the implicit claim was that Britain would be better served by fighting France on the terrain of commerce than in Flanders. The failure to ratify the 1713 commercial treaty had been a mistake, Decker held. The British could have replaced the Dutch as international carriers of French goods, and benefited from low-priced French goods, notably linens. The nation would have no trouble winning an economic struggle with France if the price of labour were contained. But the customs and excise taxes increasingly used to fund the public debt were driving up the cost of labour, and pricing British goods out of foreign markets.

Here was a classic instance of negative feedbacks from war. Wars fought in part to extend or secure trade and attack that of the enemy generated public debt, which drove up taxes, which now threatened to strangle commerce. Decker called for radical reform of the tax system and the transformation of Britain into a general free port. This differed from Walpole's proposal, which had aimed to replace customs with excise. Decker wanted to see taxes lifted off trade and manufacturing altogether and shifted onto houses or luxuries such as wine and brandy. The middling sort rather than the rich would bear the increased burden, while the labouring poor would see their taxes fall.[97] Lowering labour costs would be a far more effective mode of protecting British industries than high duties, which encouraged smuggling.[98] While Decker's call for a radical overhaul of the tax system went nowhere, his arguments were widely respected and would be cited in debates on freedom of trade down to the 1780s.

Moreover, some of the arguments Decker adduced in favour of a freer trade resonated with an official initiative in the wake of the War of the Austrian Succession to revive provisions of the commercial treaty of 1713. In 1749, John Russell, duke of Bedford, then serving as Southern secretary (with responsibility for British relations with Catholic Europe), argued that those elements of the 1713 treaty not thrown out by the House of Commons ought still to govern trading relations between Britain and France.[99] Reviving the ambition of Bolingbroke, he hoped to capture for British shipping the carriage of French goods in Europe – a trade still dominated by the Dutch. The British unilaterally abrogated the duty imposed on French ships in British ports, and pushed the French to reciprocate. French officials rejected the argument that provisions of the treaty remained in force, but showed an interest in lowering shipping duties, recognising these as 'an obstacle to the English coming to France to load merchandise the export of which it is important to facilitate'.[100]

In the same spirit, Robert Darcy, earl of Holderness, (who replaced Bedford in 1751), sought to open French markets to British hardware and clocks. This design for a freer trade occurred in the context of a warming of relations in the early 1750s, when British and French officials sought to resolve ongoing sources of Franco-British tension in India, North America, and the Caribbean (initiatives examined in subsequent chapters). Again, some in the French administration were open to a measure of freer trade.[101] But the British would first have to abrogate an act passed in 1745 banning the importation of the fine French linens known in Britain as cambrics. Prime Minister Henry Pelham introduced a bill to repeal the exclusion in 1753, but gave it only luke-warm support when it came before the Commons, where the measure was anathema to some of the government's own supporters. The only prominent member of Parliament who spoke in its favour was Sir John Barnard, a merchant and former lord mayor of London, representing mercantile interests in London, Westminster, and Southwark. Barnard drew on some of the classic arguments in favour of freer trade, stating that 'he was and would always be opposed to the act prohibiting French cambrics . . . and against all steps of that nature by which smuggling received greater encouragement, the merchant acting in good faith was reduced to greater difficulty, and the king's revenue diminished'.[102] The bill failed to pass and even elicited a counterproposal (eventually shelved) to tighten smuggling enforcement. It represented a renewal of the politics that underpinned the 1713 commercial treaty and suffered a similar fate.

A product of the same moment, but different in emphasis and framing, are the arguments in favour of freer trade with France made by the philosopher

David Hume in his *Political Discourses* (1752), a volume of essays mostly on political-economic subjects.[103] Hume sought to rise above party prejudice and the lobbying of special interests to develop an impartial and philosophical account of political economy, while gleefully exploding many of the shibboleths dear to politicians, among them the Whig nostrum that trade with France could not be beneficial.[104] 'Our jealousy and our hatred of France . . . ,' he chided, 'have occasioned innumerable barriers and obstructions upon commerce . . . But what have we gain'd by the bargain? We lost the French market for our woollen manufactures, and transferr'd the commerce of wine to Spain and Portugal, where we buy much worse liquor at a higher price.' This was a barely veiled critique of Whig opposition to the 1713 commercial treaty, which would have allowed the French to recover markets for their wine, which had become the preserve of Portugal and Spain. Hume rejected the old apprehension that through a negative trade balance the French drained Britain of money. All measures taken artificially to preserve or increase the money stock were pointless, he argued, because they simply served to make British goods more expensive, obstructing exports and making imports cheaper.[105]

Hume's case for freer trade with France contained an implicit critique of Decker and Gee's ideas, but diverged little from long-established arguments emphasising the disadvantages of closure. He rejected the notion that there was a competitiveness crisis caused by indirect taxation, and implicitly dismissed the general free port idea, favouring customs duties as a particularly convenient mode of taxation. Duties should be calibrated to maximise revenue, which meant that prohibiting foreign goods altogether, or setting tariffs so high they depressed trade, made no sense – a critique of Gee. Yet Hume was quite prepared to acknowledge the good done by tariffs when set to give a preference to home manufactures, so long as they did not actually exclude foreign wares which were necessary to spark emulation and improvement.[106] He did not suggest that when goods could be produced at lower cost abroad it always made sense to import them rather than to produce them at home.[107]

Hume's essays appear disconnected from the politics of the moment, except in his Olympian disdain for them. But the stance is itself political. Hume pushed in 1752 for a fundamental rethinking of relations with France. He criticised British strategy in the War of the Austrian Succession, which had not been driven by a prudent attention to the balance of power, in his view, but by a reflexive hatred of the French that drew Britain early and passionately to the Austrian side – emboldening Empress Maria-Theresa and thereby fomenting a general war. Once it had begun, Britain might have achieved as good a peace in 1743 as in 1748, and avoided the vast debts taken on in the latter years of the conflict.[108] Hume believed Britain was on an unsustainable path with its public borrowing – that the rise of public debt threatened the integrity of its constitution, its security, and its ability to intervene in Europe when this was actually necessary.[109] The best prospect to escape this disastrous course was to abandon the 'imprudent vehemence' many British leaders had shown since the 1690s where France was concerned – to adopt the detachment Hume modelled in his essays. A moderately protective trade with France, without any prohibitions, from which both nations might benefit, could be a means to place Franco-British relations on a better footing, while an expanded commerce would be a first dividend of this happier connection.

While implicitly criticising Pelhamite policy, there was actually a good deal of resonance between Hume's positions and those of the prime minister and the Walpolean parts of the coalition he led. Pelham too thought the war should have ended long before 1748 (he had pressed for peace in 1745), that public debt had grown excessive, that prohibitions on French commerce might be eased, and a warming of relations cautiously welcomed. Though protective of his political independence, Hume was well connected politically, indeed had served the Pelhamite regime in small ways. In 1746 he joined a distant kinsman, General James St Clair, on an expedition slated to invade Quebec, later diverted to raid the Breton port of Lorient. In 1748 Hume accompanied St Clair on a diplomatic mission to Vienna and Turin. Among his friends were three men who sat for Scottish constituencies in the House of Commons: Gilbert Elliot of Minto, William Mure of Caldwell, and James Oswald of Dunnikier (the last an important sounding board for Hume's political-economic ideas, and from 1752 a member of the Board of Trade).[110] Hume's arguments did not evolve in a realm remote from the British governing elite or its concerns.

In his hope for improved relations with France, however, Hume was to be sorely disappointed. Within a few years, Britain and its rival were at war again, with empire in America and India at the heart of the conflict. For Britain, the Seven Years' War (1756–63) was the negation of almost everything Hume stood for politically. The leadership of William Pitt the Elder epitomised the anti-French zealotry he condemned. Public debt exploded, driven by the enormous costs of subsidising Britain's Prussian ally in Central Europe while simultaneously conducting military and naval operations in North America, West Africa, the Mediterranean, and India. The war left a bloated British Empire in its wake, absorbing French Canada, and the trans-Appalachian west to the Mississippi, while the East India Company laid the foundation for territorial sovereignty in Bengal. In the midst of the war, Hume published his famous attack on the 'jealousy of trade', asserting that 'not only as a man, but as a BRITISH subject, I pray for the flourishing commerce of GERMANY, SPAIN, ITALY, and even FRANCE itself'.[111] This was Hume at his most overtly political, rejecting the stance of Pitt, 'that wicked madman', who sought to smash France once and for all as a commercial and naval power.[112] Hume's political economy was no less a reflection of the global struggle between Britain and France than was Pitt's, or that of the intellectual predecessors from whom he distanced himself. But rather than using free trade to win this struggle, as Decker advised, he regarded it as one of the gains to be hoped for from a better relationship with France, and one of the ties that would benefit both nations as peaceful neighbours. He would work to improve the relationship further as embassy secretary in Paris in the 1760s.

It was in France above all that Hume found an avid readership for his *Political Discourses*, but here they were read through the lens of French debates.[113] It was Hume's arguments about luxury, public debt, and money that drew most attention.[114] His views on freedom of trade excited little comment, probably because they failed to resonate with any major camp in French political economy. To be sure, the most widely read political economist of the 1730s, Jean-François Melon, had declared it an open question whether an exchange of French wines for English woollens would not have been more advantageous to the two nations than mutual prohibitions. Yet he accepted, as a general rule, that only raw materials should be admitted freely in international trade, while manufactured goods should be prohibited. International free trade, in any case, was not central to his thinking.[115] The same can be said of the group of political economists associated in the early 1750s with the intendant of commerce, Jacques Vincent de Gournay. While sometimes viewed as liberal because of the stance they took against guilds and against the French monarchy's ban on cotton printing, most of the writers close to Gournay rejected international freedom of commerce.[116] When French and British officials were negotiating a possible loosening of restrictions on commerce in the early 1750s, Gournay's most prominent acolyte, François Véron de Forbonnais, published a translation of the *British Merchant* with virtually a second work appended in the form of editorial commentaries to warn against the snares of any commercial treaty with Britain.[117]

As Forbonnais was publishing his translation, the first writings of the Physiocrats began to appear in print, offering a new rationale for free trade among nations. Physiocracy was the most ambitious of a range of visions promoting agriculture as the key to French prosperity and power that erupted in the 1750s.[118] Part of its appeal was as a peace project which doubled as a programme to regenerate French power.[119] Physiocrats held that by transforming the political economy of the French monarchy the foundations of the international system itself could be changed, and placed on a more peaceful basis. Physiocracy emerged in the mid-1750s and took off in the midst of the Seven Years' War because it offered an exit from wars for trade and empire, vocalised the disgruntlement of the landed interest which had hardened into a campaign of resistance to further taxation in the last years of the war, and offered a new way to think about the economic foundations of power.[120]

François Quesnay, a court doctor, founded Physiocracy alongside Victor Riqueti, marquis de Mirabeau, a literary celebrity after the publication of the first volume of his *L'ami des hommes* (1756). The Physiocrats argued that only land produced real additions to national wealth.[121] France might have avoided war had it properly understood its political-economic interests, which lay less in trade with America or India than in exporting the products of its own fields and vineyards. Conflict with Britain for a dominant position in global trade was unnecessary: far from being the key source of national wealth, the profits of trade were simply transaction costs that siphoned wealth from farmers to merchants. Since Colbert, France had pursued a perverse strategy. It interdicted the export of grain, and artificially lowered the cash value of its commodities, all to foster a manufacturing sector producing goods which the French ought to buy from abroad. Mirabeau invented the term '*système mercantile*' to decry this fetishisation of manufacturing and foreign trade. In 1762, the colonial administrator Paul-Pierre Le Mercier de La Rivière (who had begun to correspond with Mirabeau and Quesnay) told the colonial and naval minister,

Étienne-François de Stainville, duc de Choiseul, that free trade with Britain, exchanging French agricultural productions for East India goods, would have better served French interests than breaking off commercial relations in the previous century. It would have reflected the natural advantages of the two empires and might have so aligned their interests as to avoid the clashes that triggered the Seven Years' War.[122]

If there were no commercial grounds for Franco-British animosity, this did not mean that the Physiocrats thought it would be easy to achieve peace or that it was unimportant to check British power. Quesnay argued that France 'must prevent other powers gaining the dominion of the seas and commercial advantages and becoming through these means the dominant powers of Europe'.[123] For his part, Mirabeau was sceptical that Britain could be brought peacefully to accept freedom of trade with its European neighbours. In *L'ami des hommes* (1756–58) he had envisioned an eventual war to be fought by a French-led free-trade league to force the British to give up their navigation act and other prohibitions on the free movement of goods.[124]

Physiocracy was not the immediate inspiration for the major official free-trade initiatives to be explored in this or subsequent chapters, but it was an important part of the free-trade debate in France. Moreover, as journalists, pamphleteers, or officials, Physiocrats played a role in promoting or even designing initiatives like the Eden–Rayneval treaty of 1786. Here, though, we need to distinguish Physiocracy as a doctrine from its messier, less doctrinaire, political reality. Physiocracy evolved. The actions and thinking of Physiocrats as participants in politics, or as officials in service to the monarchy, cannot simply be read off from the founders' ideas.[125] In the 1760s, when Choiseul was Louis XV's leading minister, there was little appetite for freer trade with Britain, which the minister planned to humble in a future war. It was in the Caribbean that the greatest possibilities seemed to present themselves, and this is where the Physiocrats concentrated their efforts, as we will see in Chapter 5. The next effort to use a commercial treaty to open a freer trade between France and Britain in Europe would have to wait until 1772, after the disgrace of Choiseul, whom Louis XV removed at the end of 1770 when his policies seemed to threaten war with Britain. Under the succeeding ministry, a proposal for a trade deal emerged as part of an ambitious initiative to transform the international relationship between the two powers.

THE COMMERCIAL TREATY PROPOSAL OF 1772

It was geopolitical pressures that put freedom of trade back on the official agenda. In 1772, Emmanuel-Armand de Richelieu, duc d'Aiguillon, then French foreign minister, presided over the most overt effort since 1713 to reconstitute the European and global relationship between France and Britain on a new political-economic basis. The centrepieces of this failed initiative were to be a reopening of trade between the two nations on a freer basis and an accord to end Franco-British rivalry in India. The proposed India deal will be explored in Chapter 6. Suffice to say for now that it was intended both to help launch a new French India Company by assuring a more secure and advantageous trade there for French merchants, and to address what had seemed in the late 1760s one of the most likely flashpoints for the next Franco-British war over access to globally sought-after commercial resources.

In d'Aiguillon's eyes, a new commercial treaty would create incentives for the British to accept a long-term peace with France and might ideally form the basis for an entente that would allow both states to pivot towards Eastern Europe.[126] He came into office in the wake of an international crisis in 1770 over the Falkland Islands that narrowly averted war and brought the dismissal of the anti-British Choiseul. D'Aiguillon did not aim to repeat Choiseul's mistakes. A second context for his initiatives was chaos in public finances. Under the contrôleur général, the abbé Joseph-Marie Terray, the French monarchy underwent a partial bankruptcy, forcibly renegotiating its obligations and slashing interest rates on parts of the debt.[127] More than ever, France needed peace, yet tensions in Eastern Europe and the Baltic threatened war. The traditional allies of the French monarchy – Sweden, Poland, and the Ottoman Empire – faced a threat from growing Russian power.[128] In 1772 Russia, Prussia, and Austria secretly agreed to partition sections of Poland, while Tsarina Catherine II threatened intervention to overturn the new French-backed regime of Gustav III in Sweden. If Louis XV sent a naval force into the Baltic to support him, the British would likely arm their own squadron and clashes might ensue.[129] Russian naval incursions into the Mediterranean also posed a threat to French trade. The commercial independence of the Ottoman Empire was vital to the continued flourishing of French industry because trade privileges conferred by Constantinople helped the woollens of Languedoc to dominate Levantine markets.[130] An expansion of Russian power in the region potentially posed a threat to continued French commercial pre-eminence there.

In London, there was some receptivity to an understanding with France, though a parliamentary opposition liable to spring on any perceived lenity towards the hereditary enemy limited the North administration's scope for action. George III was open for a time even to a French alliance. 'The antient animosity would appear absurd,' he argued, 'if Britain and France would with temper examine their respective situations.'[131] The competition between the two powers had weakened them while aggrandising their Eastern neighbours, the king feared.[132] The monarch and his government were disturbed at what seemed increasingly aggressive actions by Russia and Prussia. According to the French ambassador, the Southern secretary, William Henry van Nassau van Zuylestein, earl of Rochford, favoured an entente with France, while North, who had intervened decisively to prevent war over the Falklands, might warm to it because of the financial implications. Peace was positively commanded, thought the ambassador, by Britain's financial overextension, its dearth of allies, and its need to keep a grip on its rebellious subjects in America while stabilising the finances of the East India Company.[133] Indeed, the initial proposal for a commercial treaty came from the British – but unofficially, and from the king rather than the cabinet, through the mediation of Lord Holderness, a royal confidant who had been one of the doves in the Pelham administration of the 1750s.[134]

Pleased to hear of these dispositions, d'Aiguillon moved to draft a trade treaty, which he hoped would disarm old hatreds and cement a permanent peace. 'It seems that if the English found advantage in [the trade] they did with us,' he told Terray, this might 'insensibly weaken the animosity they bear toward us, and form a tie that would make the continuation of peace as valuable to them as it is to us.'[135] Lukewarm, Terray admitted the potential advantages of moderate duties on the import of French wines to Britain. France might also seek the 'free introduction' of its linens. But, in his view, there was a lack of equivalence between French and British trade policy that would make reciprocity difficult to attain. Britain had imposed high duties on French wines, not to protect any industry of its own, but out of 'jealousy of French trade'. French prohibition of British goods was a different story. They struck goods also made in France – a legitimate protection of domestic producers. In return for concessions on wines, however, Terray was prepared to admit English hardware, at the risk of wiping out the small French industry. He was unwilling to consider a blanket admission of English woollens, but would permit the least threatening varieties under the same duties paid by similar foreign imports.[136] Ultimately, d'Aiguillon resolved to proceed on the basis that France receive MFN treatment for its wines and brandies, and that British prohibitions on fine French linens be lifted. In return France would admit English hardware and selected woollens at the 30-per-cent duty levied on equivalent foreign wares.[137] Such thinking would not have been out of place in negotiations for the commercial treaty of Utrecht sixty years earlier.

The absence of Physiocratic arguments from the official discussion is striking but unsurprising: the Physiocratic movement was at a particularly low ebb, and the leading Physiocrats were *personae non gratae* with d'Aiguillon and Terray, who had clashed with them repeatedly over the liberalisation of the grain trade. The monarchy moved to lift regulations on the grain trade in the 1760s, permitting interprovincial circulation and even freedom to export, with a view to stimulating the agricultural economy, easing tax collection, and appealing to the landed interest. Physiocrats became closely identified with this policy, all the more so as it ran into popular opposition in the late 1760s. A series of poor harvests, combined with problems of hoarding and speculation, produced steep price rises and shortages, giving rise to grain riots in many regions. The policy was attacked by critics in some of the kingdom's *parlements*, and the first serious critiques of the intellectual foundations of Physiocracy began to appear.[138] The policy of liberalising grain markets was abandoned by Terray after he became contrôleur général.[139] Opposing the freeing of the grain trade, the ministry nevertheless entertained the idea of freer international trade with Britain, underlining once again the fragmented quality of thinking on freedom of trade, which might yield benefits in certain contexts but not others.

French officials feared that the entrenched British prejudice against trade with France would be an obstacle to a successful treaty. In this context, a replay of 1713 appeared likely. A commercial treaty, because it would require parliamentary assent to lift discriminatory taxes, would raise objections – minimally, the old problem of the special treatment of Portuguese wines. The opposition might even seize on the occasion to raise new barriers to French imports.[140] The French ambassador to London, Adrien-Louis de Bonnières, comte de Guînes, believed an entente between the two nations to be impossible because the British ministry was afraid to be seen as soft on France.[141] To tackle this problem, one adviser recommended a public relations campaign: the ministry should 'cause to be insinuated into the public papers the advantages that will follow from letting go of those principles of jealousy'. In this way a 'national discussion' might be initiated 'which would prepare minds for the propositions of the ministry'. The British public would be more open to such an initiative, others assured d'Aiguillon, than it might have been in the past.[142]

Certainly, the views advanced by David Hume in the 1750s had come to be taken up by a wider range of writers. In a pamphlet published at the end of the Seven Years' War, Josiah Tucker, the irascible dean of Gloucester, and a widely read writer on trade, had excoriated the jealousy of trade that induced Britons to believe that commerce with France could be of no benefit. 'Do you envy the Wealth, or repine at the Prosperity of the Nations around you?' Tucker asked. 'If you do, consider what is the Consequence, viz. that you wish to keep a Shop, but hope to have only Beggars for your Customers.'[143] And in lectures delivered at the University of Glasgow in the early 1760s, Adam Smith, too, deplored the prohibition of trade with France. 'It were happy, therefore, both for this country and for France,' he argued, 'that all national prejudices were rooted out, and a free and uninterrupted commerce established.'[144] With his extensive political connections in the Chatham and North administrations, no doubt Smith had opportunity to share such views.[145]

Yet in public discourse traditional Whig shibboleths continued to reign, even among the well-informed. In his *New and Complete Dictionary of Trade and Commerce* (1766), Thomas Mortimer rehearsed the old Whig line that trade with France was harmful because it always entailed a negative trade balance. He cited the usual authorities, including the *British Merchant*, and adduced new statistics to show that because of successful import substitution in both nations there was little potential market for British goods in France.[146] (Lord Shelburne would present his French interlocutor with a copy of the *British Merchant* in 1782, telling him that the book 'has formed the principles of nine tenths of the public since it was first written'.[147]) Arthur Young, perhaps the most widely read contemporary writer on economic matters, took Hume to task in 1772 for arguing that trade with France could profit Britain.[148]

In was probably not in terms of any advanced political-economic thinking that a commercial treaty with France was presented to Lord North that same year. D'Aiguillon tapped James Bourdieu, an international banker with ties to the Compagnie des Indes, to approach North, and Bourdieu engaged Richard Glover to manage the discussions.[149] A London merchant in the Hamburg trade, Glover had made a name for himself as an advocate for a freer trade in the tradition of Sir John Barnard, with whom he had been linked in the early 1740s in the opposition to Walpole. Though an enthusiastic proponent of war with Spain in 1739, he gravitated into the peace camp of Lord Bute during the Seven Years' War and in 1762 argued forcefully that British trade 'had suffered by war'.[150] He opposed protective duties for the Scottish and Irish linen industries, arguing that importing linens from Germany and the Dutch Republic benefited Britain more than any expansion of the domestic linen manufacture. Raising duties drove such foreign goods into illegal channels, as it had cambrics, and proved a boon to smugglers, while the 'fair trader', and tax revenues, suffered. Even if smuggling could be stopped, protecting the home industry could be counter-productive when it raised the cost of living and the price of labour by forcing the poor to buy more expensive domestic substitutes. Moreover, keeping home and American markets open for foreign goods made possible a substantial reciprocal export of English woollens to the continent, which would be jeopardised by reprisals if new duties were raised on the import of foreign products.[151] These were the kinds of arguments Glover would have made to Lord North in favour of a freer trade with France, one must assume. What was good for Britain in its commerce with Germany and the Dutch Republic might be equally good for it in a reopened trade with France.

But it was not to be. The hope for a commercial treaty evaporated in the spring of 1773 in the face of renewed political tensions and misgivings on both sides about the intentions of the other. D'Aiguillon's prospects for an entente, or even an alliance, with Britain collapsed when Rochford, worried that he had exposed himself politically by an excessive openness to French overtures, threatened to mobilise a British naval squadron to prevent French action against Russia.[152] D'Aiguillon never formally proposed to North the terms for a commercial treaty he discussed with Terray. He wanted certainty that Britain was serious about a negotiation before making any concrete propositions.[153] The British had to make the running if a repetition of 1713 were to be avoided.[154] But North temporised, asking Bourdieu to specify what France was offering and what it would demand.[155] Facing this impasse, the talks fizzled out before they had acquired any momentum. In truth d'Aiguillon was not offering the British anything very alluring. When the proposal for a commercial treaty was renewed in the 1780s by the comte de Vergennes, his successor, it would be on a far more generous basis, and would be welcomed by the government of William Pitt the Younger. In the intervening years, of course, the American War of Independence had erupted and transformed the context in which free trade would be understood and debated.

THE EDEN–RAYNEVAL TREATY OF 1786

The commercial treaty signed by William Eden and Joseph Matthias Gérard de Rayneval on 26 September 1786 pledged France and Britain to remove many of the prohibitions and high duties that had choked off licit commerce between them since the 1680s, replacing these with moderate imposts.[156] As in the past, the move to a freer trade should be understood in the first place as an effort to re-engineer the Franco-British relationship, and with it the international order. Both sides regarded it as more than a commercial accord. Vergennes and his allies intended it to preserve peace between the two powers and prepare the ground for a broader entente. After some hesitation, Prime Minister William Pitt also embraced the treaty, seeing it as a potential basis for a more stable relationship with France. As in the past, this move appealed because the costs of conflict and protection had risen to dangerous levels. Both states faced a crushing burden of public debt, a financial crisis that would soon push France towards revolution.

The 1786 treaty and its 1713 predecessor are rarely considered as parts of a whole, but Utrecht was ever-present in discussions of the Eden–Rayneval treaty; much of the text of the new accord was copied verbatim from the 1713 original. The framework of ideas in which officials made sense of what they were doing in 1786 was substantially the same as in 1713. To be sure, there were novel elements drawn from the new political economies of the 1760s and 1770s: in Britain, proponents of the treaty drew selectively on the arguments of Adam Smith, giving these a new authority, while in France one can discern the stamp of a modified Physiocracy. But these new ideas were grafted onto the older framework, rather than displacing it.

The decisive differences between 1786 and 1713 were less ideological than economic and geopolitical. The independence of the United States, secured in

1783, was a key factor. In a world where America was open to the commerce of all Europe, competitiveness would matter more. Faced with the threat of lost business in America, British manufacturers sought new markets in Europe, which would require reciprocal concessions to foreign producers. With Britain apparently weakened by the loss of America, a balance of commercial power appeared to the French to be within reach, and a freer trade might actually help France to achieve economic parity. A key problem for the French officials who made the treaty in 1786 was the burgeoning British industrial revolution; if vulnerable French industries were to remain competitive, they would have to be exposed to a measure of British competition.[157] If, in 1713, economic openness threatened prospects for future development, by 1786 exposure to foreign rivals seemed necessary to sustain it. Conversely, technological advances made many British producers confident they would be the gainers from freedom of trade with France.

The entente Vergennes sought with Britain originated in discussions in the autumn of 1782 between his deputy, Rayneval, and William Petty, earl of Shelburne, the prime minister who oversaw the negotiations ending the American War. Shelburne and Rayneval agreed that France and Britain should move beyond their historic pattern of conflict and combine to pacify Europe.[158] The two nations were 'not natural enemies, as has been thought up to now', Shelburne told his interlocutor, and 'have common interests which ought to bring them together'. Rayneval, speaking for Vergennes, assured him that Louis XVI desired 'a sincere and permanent rapprochement', so that the two nations might be 'arbiters of the European peace'.[159] George III's position in 1782 was strikingly similar to the one he had taken a decade earlier. 'France and Britain were made to be friends,' he told Rayneval; 'their union convened perfectly to their interests . . . they would prevent war not only between the two powers but also between the other sovereigns of Europe'. 'We have had . . . a first partition of Poland,' he reminded the Frenchman, and 'we don't need a second one.'[160] Shelburne concurred. 'Let us unite, let us be in accord, and we will give the law to the rest of Europe,' he told Rayneval. 'Formerly, no one dared fire a cannon shot in Europe without the consent of France and of England. And today the Powers of the North wish to be something by themselves.'[161]

Vergennes too had been troubled by the partition of Poland; he wanted to check expansive Russian power and shield its next likely victim, the Ottoman

Empire, to which he had once served as French ambassador.[162] The Levant was a key market for French goods – not just the woollens of Languedoc, but Caribbean coffee and sugar – and French merchants carried on this trade under favourable treaties with Constantinople. Should the Turks be pushed out of Europe, Rayneval speculated, the seventeenth-century shift of Europe's commercial centre from the Mediterranean to the Atlantic might even be reversed to the advantage of Russia. France and Britain had a joint interest in preserving the existing global order, predicated on European exploitation of the Americas and India, but if they wanted to preserve their pre-eminence, they must reorganise it on new free-trade lines.[163]

For Vergennes and his political allies, the future Franco-British commercial treaty promised in the 1783 peace of Paris was to establish a basis for long-term harmony.[164] Ideally, it would make possible a dual hegemony to keep the peace in Europe. If a profitable cross-Channel trade could be re-established, the minister believed, it would give the British incentives to accept the postwar status quo and avoid future conflict.[165] In the commercial treaty negotiations, also conducted by Rayneval, the French diplomat 'dwelt much on the effect which this approach of the two empires to a more amicable intercourse and connexion must have, in preserving them from such frequent wars, and also in maintaining an irresistible influence, for the same salutary purposes, over the rest of the world'.[166] This idea was restated by Pierre-Samuel Dupont de Nemours, a Physiocrat who had been close to Turgot (contrôleur général from 1774 to 1776), but was now a trusted aide to Vergennes. Dupont laid out more fully the political-economic logic for remaking the relationship with Britain.[167] The wars they fought had weakened both nations, he claimed, and permitted the rise of Russia and Prussia.

The Physiocrat underlined the tendency of wars for trade and colonies to sap the economic foundations of power because of the debt and taxes they left in their wake. War 'necessitates borrowing which absorbs public revenues and requires the multiplication of taxes', Dupont argued, 'so that even conquests are never worth what they cost, and leave the nations which have made them less powerful'. As bankers to other powers, Britain and France held the keys to peace. Echoing Shelburne's words, he claimed that 'Nobody would dare fire a cannon shot without their permission because nobody can do so for a year's length without their assistance.' The two powers should 'unite with one another to command the world'.[168] Here was the old Physiocratic dream of establishing peace on the basis of free trade, but now in a new guise. Instead of the earlier project of transforming France into an agricultural dynamo and withdrawing from the race to dominate international trade, peace might be achieved by Franco-British partnership, and peaceful competition in trade and manufacturing, without a reorientation of the French economy towards agriculture.

The fall of Shelburne in 1783, in the face of a hostile Parliament, did not end Vergennes's hopes for an accord based on freedom of trade. He came to see that Pitt, Shelburne's eventual successor, could also be a partner in his design to remake the international political and commercial order. France must take advantage of the free-trade orientation of the new administration evident in the plan Pitt had unveiled to open a freer trade to Ireland in 1785. 'If Mr Pitt's system prevails,' Vergennes told his ambassador in London, 'England will shortly be led toward a new system of navigation and commerce, and we can only gain from that change.'[169]

Indeed, there was some openness in Britain after the American War to remaking the Franco-British relationship. Britain was financially overstretched and needed peace to recover; this was Pitt's highest priority. The nation was diplomatically isolated in Europe, and the degree to which the loss of America had weakened it was not yet clear. Pitt was initially suspicious of French intentions, but once engaged he recognised both the commercial and political benefits of what Vergennes offered.[170] He supervised the treaty negotiations personally, and recruited Eden to conduct them, knowing that his foreign minister, Francis Godolphin Osborne, marquess of Carmarthen, was unshakably mistrustful of French designs. In the Commons debate on the treaty, Pitt represented it as a French quest for an 'amicable connexion'. He rejected as 'weak and childish' opposition insistence that France and Britain were 'naturally and invariably rivals'. The treaty would invigorate Britain while promoting peace through 'habits of friendly intercourse, and of mutual benefit'.[171] Opponents understood that the treaty implied a rapprochement. The 'constant language' of the French, the Whig Philip Francis carped, is invariably 'let France and England unite, and let us govern the world', but France wished to be the 'husband' in this 'marriage'.[172]

Ministerial propaganda took a more expansive view still of the possibilities for burying the old animosity. Pamphleteers reappraised the whole history of

Franco-British relations, asking why it was 'a duty incumbent on every sensible Englishman to persecute the French nation in every corner of the Globe?'[173] To some Tories especially, past enmities appeared in a new light after the loss of America. They wondered if the rivalry with the French had not simply played into American hands. 'We have been long the dupes of our own prejudices,' claimed William Knox, a former undersecretary in the American department. 'If France has been hostile to us in her negociations since the peace of Utrecht, it was we who made her so, by treating her as our enemy.' Knox questioned the justice and prudence of British entry into the Seven Years' War: 'Who will now be hardy enough to assert,' he asked, 'that we had any business to interrupt the French in establishing a communication by water between their provinces of Canada and Louisiana?' Britain had been manipulated into the war by Americans bent on removing the only obstacle to their independence.[174] This was hardly the official view, but Knox's efforts to support the treaty neverthe-less earned him an offer of a knighthood.[175]

The champions of the treaty hinted that it laid the foundations for lasting peace and Franco-British unity. For one such exponent, the 'enlarged system of universal commerce' of which it was a part was 'a system of universal peace'.[176] According to another, the commerce treaty would 'lay the foundation of a perpetual peace between the two greatest nations on the earth, and who have it in their power, whenever they have the inclination, to impose silence on all the world'.[177] This suggestion of an alliance to restrain the restless powers of Eastern Europe was taken up by Knox, who thought it would check the mach-inations of the 'unstable' Habsburg Emperor, Joseph II, and the 'wily' tsarina, Catherine II.[178] Such talk was taken up by Shelburne (now marquess of Lansdowne), rather more than the cautious Pitt. 'If to-morrow the Imperial Courts and Prussia should join to give laws to govern Europe, would any man say that the liberty of Europe would not depend on the junction of France and England?' the former prime minister asked. The British prejudice against France was absurd in the age of Louis XVI, who was as mild and peace-loving as Louis XIV had been ambitious and warlike.[179]

Never far from the minds of either proponents or critics of the Eden–Rayneval accord was the 1713 commercial treaty of Utrecht. French officials worried that the new treaty risked succumbing to the fate of the old.[180] In Britain, critics revived arguments mustered in 1713, notably the canard that

Britain would inevitably suffer a negative balance in trade with France.[181] Proponents of the treaty pointed out that Britain's present situation was totally different than in 1713; they debunked the statistics once used to prove a negative balance, and claimed that the earlier treaty would have profited Britain had Whig demagogues not killed it.[182] The Whig leader Charles James Fox claimed that the deal would wreck the Methuen treaty with Portugal, 'the commercial idol of England'. Edmund Burke and other Whigs returned relentlessly to the same point.[183] But these arguments were easier to dismiss in the 1780s because – hypersensitive about this issue – the French allowed continuing British discrimination against their wines in Portugal's favour, and because the Portuguese trade with Britain, which had spawned numerous commercial disputes since the 1760s, no longer seemed so advantageous.[184] Adam Smith had long argued that the French trade given up in 1713 was a hundred times more valuable than that to Portugal.[185]

The treaty-makers were still in the world of 1713 in the deeper sense that the way they thought about freer trade hearkened back to old ideas. The principal arguments in its favour, as we have seen, were that it would help forge a lasting peace and extricate the respective nations from cycles of military spending and debt. As in 1713, the principal economic arguments hinged on undoing the negative effects of protection: the 1786 treaty would recover export markets lost through retaliation; it would drive smuggling into licit channels and increase customs revenues; it would foster competitiveness. To be sure, there were changes in emphasis. The carrying trade was less important to the British in 1786, the interests of manufacturing even more so. The French were concerned with competitiveness in 1786 to a far greater degree than in 1713. But they were still in the world of 1713 to the degree that the power of states remained the focus; officials assumed that a reciprocal trade was only possible if created by careful negotiation and a balancing of gains and losses. No policymaker imagined that international trade should be governed by market forces, that states should refrain from regulating trade flows, or that the interests of consumers should come first, much less that natural rights ought to be respected.

Freer trade would help meet the revenue needs of both states by driving smuggling into licit and taxable channels, and in so doing it would create a symbiosis between the fiscal well-being of each state and the commercial prosperity of the other. As we have seen, both governments were facing difficult conditions in their public finances. Smuggling of French linens, wines, and brandies into Britain was endemic. Conversely, huge quantities of English hardware and woollens passed illicitly into France. Slashing duty, Pitt emphasised, would 'crush the contraband by legalising the market'.[186] The expansion of the volume of trade would increase tax revenue from French wines and brandies even at much lower duties, he assured Parliament.[187] The treaty would be less advantageous to France in this respect than to Britain, Pitt insisted, but this was disingenuous since he expected a significant expansion of British markets in France, which would entail a corresponding boost to French customs revenues.

A freer trade with Britain, together with other reforms, might actually preserve the French monarchy from bankruptcy, which threatened in 1786. In France, the treaty was part of a programme of tax reform, pushed by the contrôleur général Charles-Alexandre de Calonne and backed by Vergennes, intended to resolve the financial crisis caused by the war. Competing reform parties struggled for dominance. The former finance minister Jacques Necker represented one of these, arguing that reforms to introduce economies in pensions and tax collection would be enough, together with a rationalised system of public borrowing, to meet the deficits faced by the monarchy. His successors – Jean-François Joly de Fleury, Henri Lefèvre d'Ormesson, and Calonne – believed, in the tradition of Jacques Turgot, reforming minister from 1774 to 1776, that deeper change was necessary, particularly taxing the wealth of the privileged, and reforms to dynamise the French economy.[188] Calonne saw the commercial treaty as part of a package that included tax reform, the abolition of forced labour (*corvée*) and militia service, the clearing away of the tolls and customs frontiers that choked internal communication (the 'single duty' project), and the lifting of civil disabilities for Protestants. France would be a keener competitor once these disadvantages were shed.[189]

What was different in 1786 from in 1713 was less ideology than economics. If policymakers in 1786 still had one foot in the world of 1713, in economic terms that world was no more. A gamut of British industries now welcomed an open French trade. Manufacturers, organised in a General Chamber in 1785 to resist Pitt's Irish trade proposals, had to be handled carefully, and the Board of Trade made a show of consulting industrial leaders like Josiah Wedgwood, Robert Peel, and James Boulton about the treaty with France, inviting delegations from manufacturing centres to testify in London. A few were opposed to a commercial accord – hatters, wallpaper-makers, some manufacturers of superfine white cloth and cloths dyed in the piece. Manchester calico manufacturers and printers wanted to be secured against the import of Indian calicoes printed in France. But more typical were the Sheffield cutlers who declared themselves 'not afraid of the Rivalship'. Manchester cotton interests declared that they had 'great advantages at present in skill and machines which reduce the price of labour below that which the French now pay'. Wedgwood, who had resisted free trade with Ireland, came out in favour of a treaty with France.[190] Indeed, many manufacturers maintained that new outlets needed to be opened for goods driven out of traditional European markets by protective duties recently adopted in Spain, the Habsburg Hereditary Lands, and Portugal.[191]

Geopolitical shifts are also essential to explaining the Eden–Rayneval treaty – in the first place the defeat of Britain in the American War. For the French, with victory in the American War the threat diminished that Britain would achieve a permanent lead as a commercial power. The chief obstacle to a balance of wealth had been removed, allowing French officials to hope that they might achieve parity by peaceful commercial means. The perception that Britain was significantly weakened also opened a space to renegotiate long-standing trading relationships in Europe. Vergennes worked on as many as fifteen commercial treaties and conventions intended to foster French trade, most aiming to loosen Britain's grip over its commercial sphere of influence in Europe and create a more even playing field for French merchants. He sought concessions in Portugal, Spain, and Russia, intended to match British privileges.[192] These traditional British commercial partners hoped to take advantage of Albion's weakness to recast the arrangements that had long governed their commercial relations. Responding to these pressures, Pitt pursued eight separate negotiations in the 1780s or early 1790s, including new commercial treaties with Spain, Portugal, and Russia. If the impetus for these came initially from foreign powers, Pitt hoped to turn them to British account by demanding reciprocal concessions to maintain or expand access to continental markets.[193]

The loss of America also impelled Britons towards greater commercial openness with France. The late stages of the American War produced a debate about what free trade might mean for Britain that will be examined in

Chapter 5. It pitted proponents of a postwar freedom of trade with America against Tory politicians like Eden who looked to revived commercial ties with continental Europe to stimulate postwar prosperity. The Tories defeated the American free traders, with whom Pitt was aligned in 1783, and the same forces worked to block his search for a freer trade with Ireland in 1785. In pursuing the commercial treaty with France, Pitt allied himself with these elements – as the choice of Eden suggests. The core of the prime minister's case for the treaty in the Commons was that commercial access to France would open new markets for British manufactured goods – replacing lost American outlets. 'A market of so many millions of people – a market so near and prompt – a market of expeditious and certain return – of necessary and extensive consumption, thus added to the manufactures and commerce of Britain,' Pitt argued, 'was an object which we ought to look up to with eager and satisfied ambition.'[194] This was virtually a quotation from the third edition of the *Wealth of Nations* (1784), to which Adam Smith had added a passage – no doubt anticipating the commercial treaty promised in the 1783 peace – arguing that opening a trade with France would more than compensate for the loss of American commerce. France offered a market 'at least eight times more extensive, and, on account of the superior frequency of the returns, four and twenty times more advantageous, than that which our North American colonies ever afforded'.[195]

But it was hardly an embrace of Smithian ideas that turned British officials into free traders. The idea that Smith was an important influence on the treaty-makers is not compelling. That they should borrow from Smith is not surprising. He had been an informal consultant to government, mostly on tax questions, since the mid-1760s.[196] His opinions were sought after by Eden, Henry Dundas, and Alexander Wedderburn – all former North men, now lieutenants of Pitt. The question is what to make of these borrowings. Generally, where we speak of the *influence* of intellectuals on policy what is actually at issue is an *appropriation* of ideas by policymakers, usually in ways that do not respect the integrity of the ideas in question. British officials grafted Smithian ideas onto older ones in ways that deformed Smith's arguments, leaving behind much of the substance of his political economy.[197]

Smith's perspective certainly did not *structure* the views of either Pitt or Eden. The prime minister never argued that British consumers would benefit from access to lower-cost French imports, or that Britain's own surplus might be exchanged for a larger complement of foreign goods under conditions of free trade. Instead, he reiterated the old imperative to expand export markets. Britain would enjoy a favourable trade balance under the deal, he assured MPs. Some supporters even emphasised the continued protection it would confer.[198] Eden's position was more Smithian than Pitt's in that he believed there was a competitiveness crisis and that freer trade would stimulate innovation and lower costs. But if he borrowed ideas from Smith about the ways freer trade might increase competitiveness, he took on board neither the ethical underpinnings of the Scot's political economy nor Smith's concern for the welfare of the consumer. Moreover, he rejected Smith's root-and-branch critique of Britain's commercial system – the status quo required some adjustments, in his view, not a complete overhaul. Eden harnessed Smithian ideas to the task of checking the French rival by commercial means.[199] His intellectual borrowings suggest as much: Smith and Hume took their place alongside Davenant and Decker. Where there is a deeper resonance between the treaty and Smith's thinking (or that of Hume) is in its politics. Eden and Pitt had, by a different route, arrived at a similar conclusion about the Franco-British rivalry to the Scottish political economists: that Britain would be best served by viewing France with less passion, and that freer trade might be both a means to, and a reward for, better relations.

The imprint of the Physiocrats on French choices is greater, though this was a Physiocracy that had evolved far from the positions of the 1760s and become entangled with the kind of Colbertist thinking it was originally elaborated to criticise. Some of the earliest historians of the treaty believed that French officials had been inspired by Physiocratic principles to sacrifice French manufactures for the good of agriculture, especially viticulture.[200] Despite scattered references to the primacy of land over industry in the documents, there are no grounds for understanding the treaty in these terms.[201] Certainly, officials hoped to give a boost to the wine and brandy industries, especially to ordinary wines, long excluded from Britain by swingeing duties of £99 a tun. They permitted British hardware entry to French markets on a favourable basis in exchange for better treatment of French wines and spirits. But British hardware already dominated the French market, so in legalising this contraband traffic negotiators gave away little, while the treaty halved duties on French wine.[202]

The chief Physiocratic influence on the treaty came via Dupont, but he did not push the original Physiocratic position that France ought to specialise in agricultural production and cease protecting manufacturing and trade. Instead he embraced the vision of his ministerial superiors, focused on enhancing French manufacturing.

Far from favouring agriculture over industry, the treaty was supposed to increase the competitiveness of French manufacturing sectors threatened by Britain's advancing industrial revolution. Calonne was convinced that France could catch up to Britain in mechanisation if the government assisted with the transfer of technology, and exposed manufacturers, in a measured way, to the shock of competition.[203] He never intended to abandon protection.[204] While overseeing the reopening of a freer trade with Britain, he took steps to protect the sugar-refining industry from British competition by adopting bounties for the export of refined sugar.[205] Indeed, in key respects, protection and free trade were not opposed. If a high duty encouraged massive smuggling of British wares, it offered little real protection. A lower duty on a legal commerce would cushion French producers more effectively. Moreover, in the long run, the only way to compete would be to lower manufacturing costs, and only competition would force French producers to adapt. Dupont accepted this position and continued to articulate it even after Vergennes had died and Calonne went into exile – an early casualty of the French Revolution.[206] In practice, sharp distinctions collapse between a Physiocracy that supposedly aimed to force France back onto an agricultural path and a Smithian political economy that had come to terms with the 'unnatural' development path of commercial states and sought to reform them on their own terms.[207]

There is a larger point worth making here. When *philosophes* became officials, as many did, they could rarely simply enact their theories in office. While political economists were clearly regarded as having something useful to contribute to policy discussions, abstract arguments had little purchase in a milieu where the tried and true had greater weight than novelty, where solving problems was more important than forging intellectual coherence, and where options were always limited by political constraints. Subordinate officials had to accept the agendas of their superiors and couch arguments in language meaningful to them. The shape of abstract political-economic ideas simply did not conform to the problems with which policymakers grappled – they were square pegs that had to be transformed (or deformed) to fit round holes. As an official, Dupont had to accept the priorities and limitations of the official world, constraints he may not have felt as a writer and journalist. His many memoranda on the treaty resorted in only limited ways to Physiocratic theory.[208] Even in his public defence of the accord during the pre-revolution, he cited Quesnay only once while giving equal weight to Montesquieu's *De l'Esprit des lois* (1748), which Quesnay had once sharply criticised.[209]

Where Physiocracy may have marked the treaty most significantly was in encouraging the belief that, over the long run, freer trade would weigh more to the advantage of France than Britain. This idea hinged on a distinction between permanent, natural, agricultural wealth, and more transient manufacturing success. The benefits France would enjoy under the deal, Dupont argued – especially markets for its wines and brandies in Britain – were less precarious than those Britain would acquire, because they were based on territorial and climatic factors, which were permanent, while the technological advantages Britain would have at first might in future be attained by France. Technological parity combined with lower French labour costs would swing the balance of advantage sharply in French favour. Physiocracy was not strictly necessary to make such an argument. This was a version of an older, and widely shared, view that Britain's economic advantages must be fleeting because based only on wise policy, not natural endowments. Some of the British critics of the treaty also took this position: the deal was not truly reciprocal because Britain had no equivalent for French viticulture. The French advantages would be permanent, while Britain's might only be fleeting.[210] But in the French context it is nonetheless true that Physiocracy, with its strong distinction between natural and artificial advantages, encouraged this belief among French officials.

Considered as an intellectual dogma, Physiocracy was a sharp critique of Colbertism, but as it was drawn into the policy realm it became enmeshed with its nominal opposite. The same might be said of Scottish political economy in Britain. The new political economies were bent to the logic of power, or selectively appropriated and hybridised to perspectives still rooted in the kind of thinking that produced the commercial treaty of 1713. Both French and British officials who championed the treaty referred to their positions on international trade as 'liberal', in the eighteenth-century sense of 'generous', or 'unselfish' – in contrast to the invidious logic inherent in prohibitions and high duties. This is the moment at which the adjective liberal became firmly linked to free trade. But this did not betoken the adoption of a laissez-faire outlook. Officials did not argue as a justification for the treaty that markets should be left to their own devices to dispose efficiently of resources, or that nations should stick to what they did best and import the specialities of others, or that the interests of consumers ought to have preference over those of states.[211] On both sides, officials continued to subordinate trade to political objectives. A few may have imagined that international commercial harmony could be spontaneous, but most thought it would have to be painstakingly constructed. To the degree that this is a story about the new prominence of liberal ideas, these remained subordinate to a political-economic project that went back to Colbert.

By restoring a measure of free trade, the Eden–Rayneval treaty was supposed to end the post-1688 Franco-British commercial cold war. There was an economic case for freer trade made recurrently across the century, but it was secondary to a geopolitical rationale. At each of the moments when officials considered a more open trade, they aspired to change the international relationship. They acted during thaws in hostilities and with the hope of avoiding future clashes. At moments, some thought freer Franco-British trade might cement a European peace. If they normalised trade it might remove some of the grounds for animosity and give each nation a stake in the prosperity of its rival. In 1713, 1772, and 1786, certain officials foresaw that freer trade might even prove a foundation for future partnership.

When we examine these efforts, a distinct way of thinking about free trade emerges. Officials identified polities rather than firms or individuals as the principal prospective beneficiaries of freer trade; they imagined power and security more than increased consumption as the final end of economic activity; they tended not to justify commercial openness in terms of the virtues of markets, but assumed that states must continue to police commerce; they focused more on relative than absolute national gains, and insisted that the advantages of freer trade would outweigh the drawbacks only if states negotiated reciprocity and balance. Officials hoped freer trade would recover export markets closed by the retaliation of rival states. They believed it would favour navigation, an advantage with special attraction in Britain but which appealed in France too, because when foreign ships visited French ports, they carried away French goods. Freer trade would stifle smuggling and make formerly illicit trade flows taxable, to the benefit of exchequers. It would stimulate competitiveness by reducing workers' cost of living or by forcing domestic producers to emulate foreign rivals. These had been the core economic arguments for freer trade since the late seventeenth century, they underpinned the 1713 treaty, and remained the chief advantages adduced for the 1786 accord.

None of this implies that the new political economies of the 1750s and 1760s (sometimes taken to be synonymous with free-trade thought as such) are irrelevant to our story. Physiocrats, and Scottish political economists too, hoped to remake the Franco-British relationship, and with it the international order, and they looked to freedom of trade as one means to do so. Common concerns drew many of them towards the official world, formally or informally, and their ideas enjoyed serious attention from some of the officials who played a key role in the search for a freer trade. But it is not helpful to think of the new political economy as a decisive influence on official thought. Officials borrowed ideas eclectically, and mobilised them instrumentally in line with their own priorities. It was their usefulness for the ends of power politics and the successful government of commerce that advanced them in a context transformed by revolutions in America and British manufacturing.

In eighteenth-century debates over freer Franco-British trade, we can discern something perennial – a tension recurrent in the history of capitalism. In a capitalist system, sovereignty is bent to serve the accumulation of private capital, and private capital harnessed to bolster sovereignty. This involves an implicit alliance between two different varieties of power: one grounded in mercantile networks, intrinsically borderless, and oriented to the pursuit of profit; the other centrally controlled, territorial, and oriented to security. There is an inherent tension between these logics. The network-based, mercantile variety thrives to the degree that economic actors are free to pursue the main chance. However, the state must limit this freedom to protect other capitalists from losses or to check the danger that whole industries die, move elsewhere, or are never born. Absolute free trade is the undoing of sovereignty. Yet when sovereigns act to protect 'their' capitalists at home or overseas, negative feedbacks are common. Protection untempered by liberty threatens the dynamism inherent in the networked, mercantile form of power. States may weaken relative to other states that strike a better balance between liberty and protection.

This was a central problem in the governance of commerce in eighteenth-century Europe, and it remains a central problem for rival states in the global capitalist system today.

The story of Franco-British free trade cannot be told on the basis of commercial treaties alone. This was just one of several sites where freer trade was imagined and enacted. At each of the moments I have discussed, some of the same officials were involved in separate talks to transform the Franco-British relationship and stabilise interstate politics by recasting the political framework for trade outside Europe. In the last years of the War of the Spanish Succession, officials talked of opening Spanish America to a freer trade so as to balance the gains from trade and to prevent any one power from monopolising them. In the 1750s, the same officials who hoped to reopen cross-Channel trade participated in talks between the French and British East India companies to end the military struggles between the two in southern India, and perhaps to establish a political partnership there. In the 1760s, a measure of interimperial free trade was created between the French and British empires with the establishment of free ports in the Caribbean, a network extended in 1784. In the early 1770s, d'Aiguillon sought not only a commercial treaty with Lord North but an entente in India. And in 1785, French and British officials and chartered companies again worked to build a less contentious relationship in Asia. It is to these other efforts to stabilise and pacify the Franco-British relationship that we turn in the following chapters.

2

A SYSTEM OF COLLECTIVE RESTRAINT
Spanish America, Freedom of Trade,
and the Problem of the South Sea Company

On 2 May 1738, Thomas Pelham-Holles, duke of Newcastle, went before the House of Lords to defend the foreign policy of the Walpole administration. Aggravated by smuggling from Jamaica to the Spanish colonies in America, Spanish *guardacostas* boarded and confiscated British ships. These 'depredations', the parliamentary opposition howled, required a forceful response from Britain – a war to be carried on against Spanish settlements in the Caribbean, ideally to secure new footholds for British trade. The prime minister, Sir Robert Walpole, resisted these calls. Though unhappy with Walpole's stance, as the minister with responsibility for relations with Spain, Newcastle defended the government's policy. War must destabilise the present balance of power, he argued, because of the great importance of the trade of Spanish America – a key market for European goods, and the source of most of the world's silver. If Britain struck at Spain in the Caribbean, he pointed out, other nations would believe 'we designed to force the Spaniards to allow us a free trade in all its branches to their settlements in America'. Such commercial access the French would surely oppose, for the Spanish monopoly on the trade, and the exclusion of more advanced commercial nations, 'has always been looked upon as a necessary step toward preventing any one nation in Europe from becoming too rich and too powerful for the rest'.[1]

In Newcastle's telling, the Spanish commercial system in America, excluding all but the king of Spain's subjects, underpinned a system of collective restraint, written into the treaty of Utrecht (1713), which was intended to create and stabilise a balance of commercial power among the other European states. The closure of the Spanish trade 'was not the effect so much of the Spanish policy, as of the jealousy which the powers of Europe entertained among themselves, lest any other should acquire too great a property in that valuable branch of commerce'. So long as the treasures of the Indies were channelled through Spanish hands, every nation in Europe could expect to get its part through trade. 'Whereas, should too large a share of them come into the hands of any other nation in Europe, whose situation, power or trade, render them perhaps already formidable to their neighbours, they might be employed to purposes inconsistent with the peace of Europe, and which might one day prove fatal to the balance of power.'[2] If Britain fought a war to force a broader freedom of trade on Spain in the Caribbean, it would overturn one of the mainstays of the international order – a foundation of the quarter-century of peace that had reigned between itself and its major commercial rival since the War of the Spanish Succession.

The problem Newcastle outlined in 1738 had overshadowed European politics since the turn of the century. As the duke suggested, the Spanish commercial system – from one perspective, a closed mercantilist empire – constituted, from another point of view, a kind of international regime, enshrined in treaty, and imposed by the principal commercial states to preserve the balance of power.[3] Closed to non-Spaniards *de jure*, since the seventeenth century the trade was operated *de facto* by Dutch, French, and British merchants as an informal international condominium. If any of these commercial nations came to engross them, the riches of Spanish America would quickly make it a threat to the security of its neighbours. If either France or Britain were to achieve a free commerce there, exclusive of the other – access unmediated by the regular, official trade through Spain – it threatened to erect a universal monarchy of trade.

This was the menace that had mobilised the commercial powers in 1700 when a grandson of Louis XIV inherited the whole of the vast Spanish monarchy, the kingdoms and provinces of which sprawled from the Low Countries to Italy, and from South America to the distant Philippines.[4] To prevent Spain becoming a satellite of Versailles, and to stop France monopolising the Spanish-American trade, the Dutch and the English allied with the Habsburgs to wrest the Spanish crown from the new Bourbon king, Philip V, and to give it instead to Charles of Habsburg. In the eyes of British critics, the French had achieved a kind of freedom of trade to Spain and its empire, or threatened to do so as they won new commercial liberties. Some worried that the whole Spanish empire would be integrated into a Franco-Spanish economic union – a common market of the Catholic world – that would exclude or discriminate against British merchants and goods. Free trade and monopoly are not the categorical opposites they are imagined to be: a customs union offers freedom of trade to the nations on the inside while prejudicing goods coming from without. One nation's free trade may be a monopoly from the perspective of others.

The ultimate stake of these early eighteenth-century struggles over freedom of trade was the balance of power among the leading commercial states. Subtending the balance of power in the ordinary sense, Europeans recognised a balance of wealth that checked the ascendancy of any one state. If Louis XIV's France were to win a dominating position in what was widely regarded as the most valuable European trade, the consequence must be an enormous aggrandisement of French might at the expense of the British and the Dutch. These powers fought to preserve the balance, or to tip it in their own favour.

Of course, commerce was not the only factor driving conflict in the War of the Spanish Succession – far from it. For Leopold I, the ruler of the Austrian Hereditary Lands and the Holy Roman Emperor, dynastic considerations were primary, while they were also important for Louis XIV. Notwithstanding their alliance with the Catholic emperor, concern to secure the liberties of Protestant Europe shaped British and Dutch efforts to check Bourbon power. Preventing the Spanish Low Countries from falling into French hands and threatening Britain's security was no small factor either. In no eighteenth-century war was commerce the sole consideration, and in some, such as the later War of the Polish Succession (1733–35), it was relatively insignificant. Yet because, for Britain and France, wars were sustained by the commerce that made it possible to borrow money and raise taxes, trade must always be a strategic consideration. Given the role of commerce in the balance of power, it makes little sense to insist on a hard distinction between the struggle for power in Europe and the pursuit of commercial aggrandisement overseas.[5] Conversely, military successes on the continent could deliver commercial gains both in Europe and overseas.[6]

If a commercial opening of Spanish America that benefited just one nation threatened the balance of power, a broader freedom of trade, which advantaged all, might secure that balance by distributing the profits of the trade more evenly. Indeed, such a balancing free trade promised to affirm peace by reducing international conflict over commerce. Officials talked of re-founding the Spanish-American trade on such an arrangement. In 1708, French officials proposed that Spain open its American viceroyalties to all European goods on the same terms. The Spanish Crown provisionally accepted this scheme, and French diplomats subsequently used this promise as a centrepiece of their efforts to end the conflict. Employing a different means to assure the same end, officials serving Philip V proposed to internationalise the trade in the form of a multinational company with Spanish, French, British, and Dutch participation. Britain's Tory government pushed a third vision of a balancing trade from 1711, demanding that Spain admit the newly formed South Sea Company to trade directly with its American empire, while the French (but not the Dutch) would enjoy access on similar terms. It was the governance regime for postwar trade that was at issue here: officials assumed that this was not a merely Spanish matter but one that the leading commercial powers would have to resolve among themselves.

Free trade is sometimes viewed unreflectively as commerce unhampered by the interference of states. But in a world of competing nations, it always implies a political framework – an agreement between states, implicit or express. Europeans could observe an open commerce carried on by smugglers in the spaces between empires, sometimes with the connivance of states. But free trade meant more than *de facto* access; it was a juridical status – a liberty.[7] It implied a protective structure to secure merchants from the predations of foreign sovereigns, to incline sovereignty in places far from home to respect their property and persons. All of the competing schemes for freedom of trade that officials proposed or pursued during and after the war entailed changes to the political framework for European trade in Spanish America. French and British officials did not, for the most part, contest the sovereignty of Spain over its American empire or the populations that lived there. They did not want to bear the costs of American rule themselves – better that Spain continue to do so, as long as the profits of commerce could be channelled into their hands. The point was not to acquire sovereignty but to limit its use in the hands of others.

In the end, the commercial regime the European powers created under the treaty of Utrecht pleased no one. While the treaty is notable for its attention to the balance of political and military power in Europe, in the eyes of its critics it failed to establish or preserve a true equilibrium of commercial power, leaving a legacy of instability.[8] The signatories adopted none of the schemes for a balancing free trade proposed in the latter years of the war. Instead, they restored the prewar system of informal joint exploitation under nominal Spanish control, while allowing special privileges to Britain's South Sea Company which gave it direct access to American markets. French and Spanish officials and merchants saw these advantages as a violation of the spirit of the treaty and as a threat to the balance of commercial power.[9] Idealisations of the treaty as the foundation of a 'Utrecht Enlightenment' thus carry a peculiarly British inflection.[10] Newcastle's account in 1738 was fair only to the degree that the treaty foreclosed an even more unbalanced distribution of commercial power.

From the mid-1720s, French and Spanish officials worked to remove the imbalance in the Utrecht regime either by abrogating the privileges of the South Sea Company or by buying them out – an idea that appealed to many of the company's shareholders, and to some British officials. But these efforts were unavailing and, ultimately, wrangling over the company's privileges helped trigger the Anglo-Spanish naval war of 1739, which quickly evolved into a new effort to force a free trade on Spain to Britain's benefit. The power that had done most to craft the Utrecht system, and which, in the eyes of others, benefited most from it, sought to remodel it in its own interest.

OPENING SPANISH AMERICA TO FREE TRADE

In a memorandum prepared in 1701 for William III and shared with the speaker of the House of Commons, Robert Harley, William Paterson, a Scottish merchant, presented a daring scheme to block the fatal consequences of a Franco-Spanish commercial union – a union that threatened to overthrow the balance of commercial power and establish a universal monarchy of trade. For two centuries, Spain had held in its hands 'the most easy and natural means of becoming masters of the world' by dominating American trade. It had bungled this opportunity, adopting monopolistic policies that stifled the growth of its colonies, and allowing foreigners to infiltrate its commercial empire. But a Bourbon takeover in Spain raised the threat anew. Philip V would reform Spain's commercial system. He and his French allies would shut down English and Dutch smuggling hubs at Jamaica and Curaçao. Louis XIV might establish a customs union of Catholic Europe to 'join the industry of the popish world to the Indies', and this vast new Bourbon free-trade zone would engross the trade of America and shut Britain out of key markets.[11]

Paterson was one of the most influential financial and commercial projectors of his day – a leading example of the type of merchant who used commercial knowledge to make a place for himself as a counsellor or 'calculator' for politicians and officials.[12] In 1694, under the patronage of chancellor of the Exchequer, Charles Montagu (later earl of Halifax), he had been a principal architect of the Bank of England. A few years later he was the prime mover behind the Company of Scotland Trading to Africa and the Indies, launched to establish a trading entrepôt at Darien on the Isthmus of Panama.[13] Following its failure – a failure that led in part to the 1707 Act of Union which joined England and Wales to Scotland – Paterson moved in the early years of the new century into the orbit of Harley, an erstwhile Whig, leader of an alliance of Whigs and Tories in Parliament, and soon to emerge as the head of the ascendant Tory party. Harley used Paterson to help negotiate the Union, where he helped devise the 'Equivalent' – a payment compensating Scots for assuming a portion of the English national debt, and making up losses sustained by Scottish elites in the Darien venture (whose collapse many blamed on lack of support from the Crown and the hostility of the East India Company).[14] It was with a new Darien venture in mind that Paterson approached the king in 1701.

To avert the threat of Bourbon domination of American trade, Paterson recommended that England charter a company to seize commercial choke points in the Caribbean – notably Darien and Havana – and through them to channel the commerce of the Americas. Instead of founding a closed English commercial empire on the ruins of the Spanish system, Paterson proposed to establish freedom of trade. Free ports should be opened in the conquered enclaves where merchants of all nations would be allowed to trade. As a merchant in the Caribbean in the 1680s, Paterson would have observed the operation of the Dutch free port established in 1675 at Curaçao.[15] Adopted in the Mediterranean since the sixteenth century, free ports attracted a larger share of international commerce by relaxing commercial regulations and by keeping taxes low.[16] Paterson hoped the success of his scheme in America would stimulate a free-trade revolution in Europe – encouraging Europeans to 'root out all those pernicious restraints, prohibitions, pre-emptions, and exclusions now in these nations, not only in respect to foreigners, but even in respect to one another'.[17] His ideas about freedom of trade were grounded in a Whig critique of monopoly that flourished in the 1680s and 1690s in opposition to the exclusive privileges of the East India Company and the slaving monopoly of the Royal African Company.[18]

By establishing a free-trade system in the Americas, Paterson hoped to avert future contention over American trade. The traffic to and from the Caribbean entrepôts, 'of what nation or quality soever', should remain inviolably neutral in wartime, he insisted. Though Paterson did not say so, there was a precedent for such neutrality in the free port of Livorno, which in 1646 its Medici grand dukes had declared perpetually neutral in all international conflicts, exempting it from blockades and the ordinary disruptions to wartime commerce.[19] The free port system should not inspire the kind of rivalry among states generated by closed commercial empires, because every nation stood to gain in proportion to its exports, navigation, and enterprise. No nation would acquire a dominant position – as the Bourbon powers now threatened to do. Indeed, the success of the design would force those powers to 'such a peace as it shall never more be in their power to break', for to do so would cut them out of the benefits of American commerce. As for 'the rest of America', excluded from the commerce of the free ports, it could 'never after be worth the expense of keeping'.[20]

The freedom of trade at the centre of Paterson's vision required a political framework. Force would be necessary to seize the enclaves in the first place – he reckoned 8,000 to 10,000 soldiers would be needed, a huge force to transport so far in the age of sail. To enforce and preserve the system demanded naval power. England was the natural choice to be the guardian of free trade. Modest duties levied on the traffic of the free ports would fund the Royal Navy and give it unshakeable command of the seas. But Paterson's was a vision of hegemony rather than empire. He proposed that Britain seize a globally commanding position by offering a public good to the rest of the world – freedom of trade as a substitute for the clashing empires of the Americas. He expected the Protestant maritime nations of Northern Europe – Denmark, Sweden, Prussia, and the Dutch – to rally quickly to the idea, but he did not mean to exclude France and Spain. Their own interests would force them to join this British-led league, which would double as a system of permanent peace.[21]

Paterson was unable to win the king's support for his new Darien venture. His views though are worth dwelling on, because he articulated so starkly the problem the accession of a Bourbon to the Spanish throne represented for competing commercial states, the way some Europeans looked to freedom of trade to solve this problem, and how calls for free trade in America could catalyse a radical reimagining of the political framework for global trade. In the last years of the War of the Spanish Succession, many Europeans envisioned that the formally closed Spanish commercial empire in America would be opened to the trade of foreign nations. Ministers, diplomats, and merchant projectors in France, Britain, Spain, and the Low Countries designed competing schemes for the postwar imperial trade of Spain, and jockeyed to get them adopted by the British or French, the powers expected to shape the peace. They generally envisioned one or another form of free trade as the basis for the postwar system – a legal opening of Spain's American traffic to one of the combatants exclusively, to several, or to all the commercial nations of Europe. To the degree they envisioned a trade that was to exclude major powers, their ideas gave rise to conflict; to the extent they imagined access as universal, this might serve to cement a peace. Talk of free trade inevitably entailed debate over the appropriate political framework for commerce. Formal Spanish sovereignty in the viceroyalties of America was not, for the most part, in question. Though some believed foreign enclaves might be required to secure a freedom of trade, they hoped to combine a minimum of sovereignty with a maximum of commerce. Schemes for companies, free ports, and neutralities proliferated as mechanisms to reorder and internationalise the governance of commerce in the Spanish monarchy's American possessions.

The accession of Philip V to the Spanish throne threatened to create a French monopoly of the American trade, which the leading commercial nations informally shared before the war – for while the viceroyalties of Spain in America were organised juridically as a closed commercial empire, the traffic had been financed and largely controlled by French, Dutch, and English merchants. A merchant guild, the Consulado de Cargadores of Seville, nominally controlled Spain's American trade (subject to the oversight of the Casa de la Contratación, or 'House of Trade', which registered and licensed all

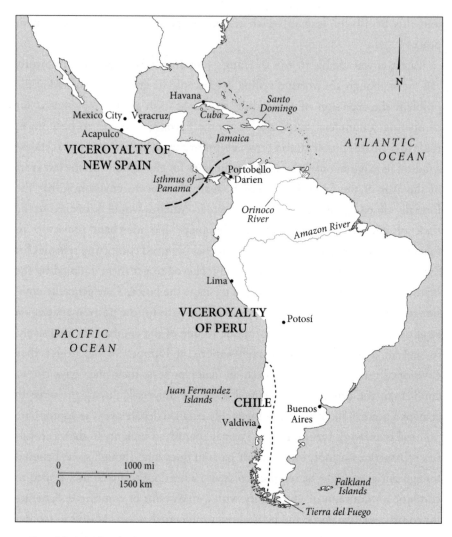

1. Spanish America *c.* 1700

shipping, passengers, and goods). This official trade was carried in periodic convoys – *flotas* and *galeones* – from Cádiz (downriver from Seville) to fairs in Portobello, on the Isthmus of Panama, or Veracruz in Mexico. But in the second half of the seventeenth century, Spain had been opened to foreign traders under a series of treaties signed by the Spanish Crown which conferred privileges that facilitated the trade of foreigners and secured their property. Although France had no commercial treaty with Spain, under a clause of the treaty of the Pyrenees (1659), which granted it most-favoured-nation (MFN) status, French merchants could claim the same liberties allowed the Dutch under the treaty of Münster (1648), or the English in treaties of 1645, 1667, and 1670. In the words of one French consul, these rights amounted to a kind of 'freedom of trade'.[22]

The trade to Spanish America was the most strategically important branch of European overseas commerce. By the 1680s, Dutch, French, and English merchants supplied over 90 per cent of the goods exported from Cádiz.[23] The Spanish Indies was a key export market for the manufacturers of Northwest Europe.[24] Prices for imports of linens, fine woollens, and silks were high in the viceroyalties of Peru and New Spain, sustained by official restrictions on trade, which limited supply, and high wages in mining centres, which allowed even workers to consume such luxuries.[25] Rendering the trade even more advantageous was the fact that returns came in silver, the region's most important export. Although production had declined from the highs of the 1620s, nearly 85 per cent of the world's silver emanated from Peru and Mexico.[26] Silver was not only the basis for the European money supply, but the chief lubricant of Europe's commerce with Asia – there being little market for European manufactured goods but endless demand for Spanish piasters.[27] The Spanish-American trade appeared to be the engine that made the global trading world turn.

Given the importance of this commerce, some merchants devoted great efforts to circumventing the official Cádiz trade. A flourishing contraband traffic developed in the Caribbean between the English and Dutch colonies of Jamaica and Curaçao and the Spanish mainland. The French were latecomers to this interloping commerce, acquiring a suitable base in Saint-Domingue only at the treaty of Ryswick (1697). Spanish authorities in America often winked at this commerce, or collaborated in it. Cover for further illegal trade, much of it English, was provided by the Asiento, a contract to supply enslaved Africans to Spanish America held by Portuguese and Dutch syndicates during the last decades of the seventeenth century.[28] The trade of the Spanish viceroyalties had thus been thoroughly infiltrated by foreign capital before the war. Yet its illegality, or semi-legality in the case of the Cádiz traffic, rendered it structurally insecure.

France might seize a dominant position in this trade, and exclude the Dutch and the English – this was the challenge that Philip's accession to the

Spanish throne presented.[29] The treaty allying the Maritime Powers – the Dutch and the English – with Habsburg Emperor Leopold I underlined the danger that the 'free intercourse of navigation and commerce' they enjoyed in the Mediterranean and in the Spanish Indies would be destroyed. The French must never be permitted to control Spanish trade.[30] But they appeared already to be moving in this direction. A first coup was French acquisition of the Asiento by the hastily formed Guinea Company in August 1701. Philip authorised it to trade directly with Spanish America, without having to pass through Cádiz. While its monopoly extended only to slaving, the privilege would screen a more expansive contraband traffic. Indeed the Guinea Company was built around the same syndicate that launched the Compagnie de Saint-Domingue in 1698 to turn the new French colony into another Curaçao.[31] French merchants took advantage of Spanish naval weakness to expand illicit trade in the first years of the war. Better they should have the profit than allow these riches to fund the enemy's war effort.[32]

The French monarchy also tried to open Spanish markets by securing commercial liberties for French merchants in Spain. Like other foreigners, the French could not operate as open participants in the Cádiz trade. Spanish strawmen had to serve as merchants of record and the trade operated in a legal grey zone. Foreigners were vulnerable to harassment and were forbidden to export bullion – a *sine qua non* of the trade. The transhipment of silver before it could be registered and dutied siphoned off half or more of the specie crossing the Atlantic in the 1680s. Some of this lost revenue was recaptured for the Spanish Crown through *indultos* – periodic levies made on precious metals imported from America. Arbitrary and often heavy exactions, these excited bitter complaint from foreign merchants.[33] French officials hoped to change all this. Responsibility for negotiation devolved on Michel-Jean Amelot de Gournay, Louis XIV's ambassador to Spain (1705–9), and a leading commercial policy-maker, who served from 1699 as director of commerce and manufactures, and sat on the Council of Commerce. His effort to negotiate a 'union' in Franco-Spanish trade was a priority for the council. In 1705 one of its leading members, the one-time Cádiz merchant Nicolas Mesnager, joined the ambassador in Spain to second his efforts.[34] The two pushed for direct French trade to America.[35]

This attention to trade, and the leading role officials from the Council of Commerce played in negotiations with Spain, underlines not only how significant commercial questions had become in the strategic calculus of the French monarchy but the fact that elite merchants had acquired new weight in the king's councils.[36] The establishment of the Council of Commerce in 1700 signals both shifts. Created to co-ordinate commercial policy between the Contrôle Général and the naval ministry (which had responsibility for colonies and the protection of foreign trade), and to institutionalise consultation between policymakers and merchants, the Council was composed initially of four royal commissioners, including Amelot, and thirteen merchant-deputies, most of whom came from the world of large-scale international trade. We have encountered several of the deputies already, notably Mesnager, Jean Anisson, and Jean-Baptiste Fenellon, all of whom played key roles in the negotiation of the Franco-British commercial treaty of Utrecht (see above, pp. 41–2). While the organisation of the Council formally subordinated merchants to royal officials (deputies could speak only if called upon, and could not vote), informally those deputies most trusted by ministers exercised a great deal of influence.[37] The elite of great wholesale merchants that the Council represented were coming to a new sense of their own worth at the end of the seventeenth century, and had begun to use the term *négociants* to distinguish themselves from lowly retail traders (*marchands*). The new label suggested a quasi-public role, extensive interests, and wide views, and inverted stereotypes of merchants as incapable of placing the public good before private interest.[38]

This social and political ascent of merchants marked the advent of capitalism – not in the sense that merchants became fully integrated into the French ruling class, but in that the monarchy was becoming increasingly committed to fostering commerce. From a social-structural point of view, the *ancien régime* was a polity organised around the extraction of rents, seigneurial dues, and taxes from the peasantry by a coalition of mostly noble landowners led by the king. The monarchy functioned as an engine, pumping resources out of the agricultural economy and redistributing them to the landed elite in the form of salaries (*gages*) for venal office holders, commissions in the army and navy, pensions for long-serving or high-ranking royal servants and courtiers, and interest payments to bondholders.[39] This system was shaken over the course of the eighteenth century by the monarchy's need to tap the wealth of the privileged, but it was not fundamentally restructured until the French Revolution.[40] Seen from this point of view, France was not a capitalist society.[41] However, these social arrangements proved compatible with a high degree of commercialisation, manifested in increasing market dependence, protoindustrialisation, and a consumer revolution.[42] Hitched to the seigneurial society was a commercial sector which was to show considerable dynamism in the eighteenth century, especially in international and colonial trade.[43] Merchants remained largely outside the ruling coalition through the 1780s, but the strategic need of the monarchy to foster commerce – to harness the wealth, credit, and monetary abundance it created – meant that the state must nonetheless favour the interests of merchants and seek better to integrate them into its deliberations.[44] The state's drive to compete internationally, especially against Britain, led it to adopt policies that favoured capital accumulation, especially in the vital sectors of export manufacturing, long-distance trade and colonial agriculture. This is the sense in which eighteenth-century France was capitalist. It was already moving fast in this direction from the days of Colbert, but the renewal of general war after 1688 proved decisive, and the establishment of the Council of Commerce and efforts to foster French trade in the Spanish monarchy were key moments in this trajectory.

As it happened, however, it was not an officially sponsored initiative in Spain, but a new branch of interloping commerce on the Pacific coast, that proved the most significant breakthrough in the wartime French commercial penetration of the Spanish Empire. Merchants from the Breton port of Saint-Malo opened a new trade route to Chile and Peru.[45] By one estimate, they carried nearly 70 per cent of Peru's wartime foreign trade. Assessments of the value of the silver imported from the so-called South Sea range from 55 million piasters to nearly 100 million.[46] This was a significant addition to the total French money stock, depleted by wartime export, and was regarded in France and abroad as a signal contribution to the French war effort.[47] Tightness in the money supply made tax collection and public borrowing difficult, especially in wartime. While contractors could generally be paid in government paper, soldiers required cash, and large sums were transferred abroad to pay subsidies to foreign governments or to supply armies.[48] Falling money stocks had a deflationary effect on the economy which influxes of American silver eased.

To balance French designs on the trade of Spanish America, some Britons argued that enclaves be conquered there to anchor and protect a competing British commerce. The treaty allying the English and the Dutch to the

Habsburg Emperor conceded the right to keep Spanish-American conquests, though Leopold soon had qualms about this clause, proposing instead that the Maritime Powers 'be recompensed with a free liberty of trade into all those parts'. The English secretary of state allowed the advantages of a free trade, but noted that, for his countrymen, conquests in Spain's empire seemed the best security for it.[49] Echoing William Paterson's schemes, Darien was often mentioned as a candidate for annexation, it being the 'undoubted Interest of England to take care that no other European Nation become Masters of that Neck of Land'.[50] Indeed, Paterson envisioned Darien as the gateway to the wealth of the South Sea, and as a potential transit point for European trade with Asia, an idea echoed by others. 'Allow us but one Town on the Isthmus, and our Trade may exceed the return of the Spanish Galleons,' wrote John Le Wright. 'Was a free Port settled there, it would inevitably draw all the Trade of Europe to it self, which other Parts of the World now hold in America.'[51]

But an altogether different project to counter French domination of the Spanish trade was embraced by Britain's Whig-dominated government. A free British trade was to be organised under the auspices of an Anglo-Spanish monopoly company, once Charles of Habsburg was installed as king of Spain. Such was the tenor of the commercial treaty James Stanhope, envoy to the archduke and commander of English forces in Spain, negotiated at Barcelona in 1707. Stanhope was a rising Whig star, a future minister of George I. The original project for a commercial treaty envisioned carving out a privileged position for English merchants in the Cádiz trade, along with acquiring the Asiento. Stanhope pressed for more, winning from Charles the promise of direct British participation in the trade to America.[52] A secret article specified that an Anglo-Spanish Indies company would be formed after the war to monopolise the commerce. In the event it could not be established, the archduke promised to accord to Britons 'the same privileges and liberties of a free trade to the Indies enjoyed by Spanish subjects'. Moreover, from the day peace was made until the foundation of the new company, the king would permit British subjects 'to traffic freely in all the ports and cities of the said Indies', paying the same duties as Spaniards, so long as the total shipping did not exceed 5,000 tuns. The French would be excluded altogether.[53]

In theory, Whigs were hostile to monopoly companies, and Stanhope's preference may have been the broader freedom of trade promised in default of a company. The proposal for an Anglo-Spanish Indies company likely emerged from the Spanish side, where merchants and officials had sporadically proposed a company to structure the American trade, in imitation of the Dutch East India Company, since the 1680s.[54] The merchants of Barcelona, where the treaty was negotiated, hoped to use the accord to break what was effectively an Andalusian monopoly and seize a place for themselves in future commerce with America. Yet Whigs, too, were willing enough to employ monopoly privileges when these served their ends – witness the Bank of England and the New East India Company founded in 1698. As zealous a Whig as Paterson had used a company to launch his Darien venture in 1695, and proposed another such company to William III in 1701.

Europeans looked to chartered companies to institutionalise the postwar American trade in part because companies appeared to offer unique advantages as a political framework for trade in this region. A narrow understanding construes companies only as a form of rent-seeking.[55] But part of what was special about these bodies was that the costs of protecting trade – in the form of soldiers, armed ships, fortifications, diplomatic gifts, and payoffs to foreign officials – were borne not by hard-pressed states, or their taxpayers, but by wealthy shareholders. The bearers of monopoly privileges justified them on these grounds – extraordinary profits being required to offset these additional heavy costs.[56] By selling shares, companies made it possible to mobilise large capitals for vast and risky commercial projects. They allowed the costs to govern and protect distant trade to be borne by its most direct beneficiaries: merchants.

Companies typically separated sovereignty over territory from the governance of trade – a further benefit when considering the trade of Spanish America. The East India Company, for example, ruled small enclaves in Asia, but its trade extended over vast zones where Indian states, not the company, were sovereign. Company merchants – its 'subjects' – carried the protections and privileges negotiated by the company wherever they went, enjoying exemptions from taxes imposed on regular traders, for example. It was this quality of sovereignty over trade without sovereignty over territory (enclaves aside) that explained part of the appeal of the company model in Spanish America. The commercial powers were not interested in controlling large territorial swathes of the continent: there was near-universal agreement that territorial empire had not benefited Spain; it seemed impractical for Protestant powers to govern a Catholic population; and there was little reason to do so, because control over production (mines and plantations) was unnecessary for control over trade – whence the super profits of European rule could be extracted.[57] The same advantages of sovereignty over trade without sovereignty over production were manifest in the free ports Paterson proposed, and in the Franco-Spanish customs union he and other Britons feared.

A further peculiarity of the company model which also flies in the face of the ordinary way we think about monopolies was that, because of the way they facilitated joint ownership, companies could appear vehicles for cross-national exploitation of trade. Paterson envisioned his new Darien company as an English, Irish, and Scottish joint venture (an advantage over the Company of Scotland, which suffered from the hostility of English officials and merchants). Stanhope saw a company as a means to divide the trade between Britain and Spain (though Britain, with its superior commercial resources, would predominate). The clearest instance was a company proposed in 1708 to internationalise this trade. In response to the treaty of Barcelona, and seeking a means to end the war by tempting the Dutch to make a separate peace, Philip V called for a new monopoly company to carry on the Indies trade in which Dutch, British, French, and Spanish merchants would all have shares. The architect of this proposal, Jan van Brouchoven, count of Bergeyck, a senior official in the Spanish Low Countries, even suggested that the seat of the company rotate between Cádiz, Brest, Amsterdam, and London to reassure foreign merchants.[58] Counterintuitive as it might seem, monopoly companies could serve as a vehicle for the internationalisation of Spain's monopoly trade.

What the treaty of Barcelona offered was commercial access to the British from which France, and implicitly the Dutch, would be excluded – a recipe for British commercial aggrandisement. For their part, and for equally selfish reasons, the French were coming to envision a universal freedom of trade in Spanish America as an alternative to the virtual French monopoly that was their initial objective. Years of negotiation had failed to persuade the Spanish to open America on the basis the French desired. The incursion of French merchants into the Pacific was a boon for a specie-strapped French state in wartime, but it envenomed relations with Madrid, and would not be politically sustainable in the long run. Prospects for preferential treatment narrowed further when Louis XIV withdrew support from his grandson in 1709 and pulled most French troops and advisers out of Spain. The situation for French merchants deteriorated sharply, and from the spring of 1710 there was a growing tide of complaints from traders who felt themselves mistreated.[59] Moreover, the interloping of the Saint-Malo merchants undermined both the profits of the Cádiz trade and those of the slave-trading holders of the Asiento.[60]

More importantly, by 1708 Louis XIV was desperate for peace, and understood that suspicions over the Spanish trade were a major continuing cause of conflict. A means had to be found to neutralise the issue without simply ceding the commerce to the British and the Dutch. The author of the new French vision of universal freedom of trade to Spanish America was Nicolas Mesnager. He came to see that an exclusive position in the Spanish trade would have to be jettisoned for the sake of peace. France needed to 'show the whole world that it claimed no exclusivity on the treasures of America'.[61] Moreover, an arrangement that set the trade on a multilateral basis might be more acceptable to Madrid, which fiercely resisted becoming a French economic satellite.[62] With the support of foreign minister Colbert de Torcy and the king, Mesnager returned to Spain in the summer of 1708 to seek consent for a reform of the Cádiz trade.[63]

What he proposed, and convinced the Spanish to accept, was nothing less than an internationalisation of the commerce. America being 'a common *patria*', Spain should be the trustee of its resources for the rest of Europe. While it was to remain the monopoly of Cádiz, and would be carried in Spanish ships, every European nation was to be admitted into the liberty of the Spanish-American trade. Foreigners henceforth could embark their merchandise on the same terms as Spaniards. Merchants would pay modest duties on the goods they shipped, payable on export from Spain and arrival in America. Especially in the later versions of the plan, Cádiz was to be a kind of international city, a free port with a multinational consular jurisdiction. At one point, Mesnager even proposed that the town be occupied by a garrison of Swiss Catholics – the UN peacekeepers of the eighteenth century. Moreover, the city was to be neutral ground in any future conflict. The merchants of every country could remain there in wartime 'and continue to trade as in times of general peace'. Any nation that disturbed the tranquillity of the trade would be ejected from participating. This was a vision of a balancing free trade intended – by opening the trade to all – to check the possibility that any of the principal powers should acquire a dominant position. As such it might form the basis for peace and for an easing of tensions over trade in the postwar world.

Mesnager's scheme embodied what might be called the Cádiz view – that of the city's foreign merchant community, which embraced the proposal.[64] The deal offered every protection foreign merchants had long sought. In Amelot's words, its object was 'to give liberty to the French, the English and the Dutch to export their merchandise in their own names, without being obliged to pass through the hands of Spanish merchants'.[65] *Indultos* were to be abolished. On import to Cádiz, a modest duty would be paid on specie, which could then be freely exported. Mesnager's scheme constituted the juridical recognition of the Cádiz trade as it had developed in the late seventeenth century. Even better, from the perspective of Cádiz, it promised to shut down the traffic of the interlopers, removing the principal competition. The contraband trade was to be closed by international agreement, and the navigation of the South Sea in particular punished as piracy.

Mesnager's plan was not immediately implemented, but became central to the French strategy to end the war. Following approval by Philip V in July 1708, Louis XIV dangled it before the Dutch as an inducement to make peace. From the Spanish perspective, its formal adoption was contingent on shutting down the smuggling trade, while the French wanted to reserve a ban on South Sea commerce as a further incentive to their enemies to enter into peace talks.[66] It was attractive to the Dutch, but not until late in the war were they prepared to accept Philip's accession to the Spanish throne. Moreover they rightly saw the scheme as a lever to prise them from their alliance with Britain. As a result nothing had been resolved when, in 1711, Britain's new Tory ministry elaborated its own vision of the postwar trade.

THE SOUTH SEA COMPANY, THE ASIENTO, AND THE PEACE OF UTRECHT

In May 1711, the lord high treasurer, Robert Harley, chief minister of Queen Anne, introduced a bill to charter a 'Company of Merchants of Great Britain Trading to the South-Seas'. He had designed the company to shore up public credit by consolidating over £9.5 million in floating debt. Holders of depreciated Exchequer bills, navy debentures, and other short-term government paper could exchange these for shares, with Parliament to guarantee a 6-per-cent dividend on the stock, to be supplemented by profits from the company's trade.[67] From 1713, the South Sea Company came to exercise the Asiento, but slaving was not the original business Harley envisioned for it. This was a consolation prize for the loss of more valuable commercial opportunities. As first conceived, the company was to seize a portion of the lucrative South Sea trade which the French had virtually monopolised during the war. Parliament granted the company a monopoly on British trade from the Orinoco River south to Tierra del Fuego and thence northward up the whole Pacific coast.[68] The company was to carry on a South Sea trade from new settlements which Harley planned to demand from Spain – echoes of Paterson's Darien project but without the free ports.[69] He asked for Gibraltar and Minorca as securities for Britain's Mediterranean trade, along with unspecified settlements in Pacific waters.[70]

Some historians argue that the Tories saw the South Sea Company as a means to establish a territorial empire in South America.[71] But viewed in the context of wartime debates about how to organise the Spanish trade, the company appears less a bid for empire than a move to shape the postwar trade regime. Harley endeavoured to institutionalise British commercial access to America in ways Spain and France would accept. Unlike the previous Whig-dominated administration, leading Tories consented to partition the Spanish monarchy, leaving Spain and America to Philip V. For Whigs, only a Habsburg Spain would offer any real guarantee for a free British trade. In response to the Tory peace plan, they reiterated that a Bourbon on the Spanish throne would herald a French universal monarchy of trade and relegate Britain to poverty and impotence. Francis Hare, chaplain-general to the duke of Marlborough, worried that France would establish a customs union between itself and Spain; Portugal too would soon be absorbed into this Catholic common market, and France would monopolise all the silver and gold of the New World.[72] The Whig MP Arthur Maynwaring agreed: 'Does any Man imagine that the Liberty of Trading which France has obtain'd, will not be exclusive of all other Nations?' he asked. The freedom of Europe would be precarious 'when the Navy and Troops of France shall be paid with the Riches of Peru'. Stanhope had already laid the groundwork for a free British trade to Spanish America after the war, but the treaty of Barcelona would come to fruition only with Archduke Charles on the Spanish throne.[73] To win that throne for Charles, however, might prolong the war indefinitely; Harley sought a different means to secure British trade with Spanish America, this time with a Bourbon monarch. He hoped that, with the intercession of Louis XIV, Philip V would grant the South Sea Company the right to trade with the viceroy-alty of Peru from Pacific bases. What the minister's journalistic proxy, Daniel Defoe, envisioned was 'Quiet possession . . . of Four Ports . . . in the Kingdoms of Chili and Peru, with sufficient Extent of the Country round, and Freedom of Commerce to all the Spanish Dominions, South of the Equinox on the Western Coast of America.' Together with 'a Free Trade to and from Old Spain', he promised, this would guarantee the future flourishing of British commerce.[74]

As first conceived, the South Sea Company was to carry on a balancing trade against French rivals, already well established in the Pacific. The Tory ministry envisioned sharing commercial access with France – an idea the Tory MP and writer Matthew Prior floated when he travelled to Fontainebleau at the behest of Harley in 1711 to discuss British peace demands with Colbert de Torcy. When the French minister rejected initial British demands, claiming that if Britain alone received Pacific trading enclaves this would overturn the balance of commercial power and make them 'masters of the whole trade of the world', Prior insisted that such bases were rather intended to produce 'a more equal distribution of traffic'. Britain would not object if Louis XIV sought equivalent enclaves to harbour French trade.[75] Tory publicity surrounding the South Sea Company took for granted that the French would remain commercial competitors in the Pacific – and indeed this must have seemed a reasonable assumption in 1711.[76] In this vision of a balancing trade, the Dutch were to be excluded; as we have seen, Tories regarded them as far more dangerous commercial rivals than the French.

If a trade to the South Sea shared by Britain and France and enshrined in international treaties did not materialise, it was because the French rejected it. 'If France, for its part, formed the same pretention [to Pacific settlements] in order to maintain a kind of balance in America,' Colbert de Torcy observed, 'the King of Spain would no longer be able to call himself master of the Indies.'[77] This concern for Spanish sovereignty was unfeigned – the war had been fought, from a Spanish perspective, to keep the monarchy intact, and breach of this principle would create major difficulties for Philip V. Yet some of Philip's French advisers were already preparing him for the sacrifice of American settlements. The duc de Vendôme, anticipating that the British would demand ports in Spanish America, had already suggested that Louis XIV ask for equivalent concessions.[78]

Ultimately, French refusal to consider the version of free trade the Tories offered was less about solicitude for Philip than fear of British competition. The stakes of the Pacific trade were far higher than those in the Caribbean. Britain annually carried on a contraband traffic worth 10 million livres from Jamaica, argued Antoine Pecquet, Colbert de Torcy's principal aide, but if they were to become masters of the whole American trade – which a South Sea base would make possible – the yearly commerce could be worth 60 million. Pecquet envisioned the British using the Juan Fernández Islands as a trading station to market Asian goods in Mexico and Peru, smashing French competition in silks and luxury items. Better to fight on than concede an advantage that would give Britain a dominant position in American trade.[79]

Without French co-operation, Harley had little prospect of winning Spanish assent to carry on a licit British trade in the viceroyalties, so from this point the South Sea Company project began to evolve away from its original conception. First envisioned to carry on a balancing trade, it turned into a vehicle for an exclusive British commerce; originally a means to exercise a legitimate commerce, it became a new kind of interloper; designed to penetrate the Pacific, it finished by exploiting the Asiento in the Caribbean. It was a question of what Bourbon Spain, and especially France, would accept. Against Prior's proposal for French and British exploitation of the South Sea trade, Colbert de Torcy countered with Mesnager's design for universal commercial access to Spanish America via Cádiz. Prior brought the veteran commercial diplomat back to London where Mesnager offered Harley and Bolingbroke a version of the plan modified to make it more attractive to the British: Cádiz would have a Swiss garrison; Britain would be allowed to supply the naval escorts for biannual *flotas*; and British goods would enter Spain with a 15-per-cent duty preference.[80] Mesnager was told he might concede Puerto Rico or Trinidad to Britain in extremis. He was to make no difficulty about other commercial concessions Britain sought, including the Asiento. But he was to hold firm against any British settlements in the Pacific.[81]

For their part, the British ministers were uninterested in Mesnager's plan, and with this refusal ended the possibility for any radical reorganisation of the Spanish trade by international agreement. Presumably, even with the guarantees

Louis XIV offered, Harley and Bolingbroke believed the Cádiz traffic would remain a hostage to Bourbon power. Moreover, Mesnager's scheme benefited the Dutch equally – another drawback. While they found appealing the preferential access to Spain that Mesnager offered, British negotiators held out for some compensation for giving up American settlements. Harley floated the idea of allowing Britons to reside in two towns in America, to sell British goods transported in Spanish vessels – another vision for a licit British commerce.[82] But this too proved unacceptable. Bolingbroke broke the deadlock with a proposal for a thirty-year Asiento (three times the ordinary duration of such a contract), plus factories in Spanish America to 'refresh' enslaved captives. Everyone understood that slaving would permit a lucrative contraband trade on the side, but from a Bourbon point of view this was a transfer from the right hand into the left: Britain already carried on an interloping commerce in the Caribbean. Louis XIV accepted this bargain with alacrity, and Mesnager signed the preliminaries on 8 October 1711.[83] The various balancing visions of a free European trade to Spanish America had been relinquished in favour of a model that advantaged Britain exclusively, if in smaller ways than first proposed.

Not only was the Asiento far less dangerous than the South Sea concessions Britain originally demanded, French officials hoped to participate in the profits. The naval minister Jérôme de Pontchartrain even imagined that Britain might share the Asiento with France – in effect that the measure of open trade it represented might be operated as a Franco-British cartel. He instructed French plenipotentiaries at the peace talks in Utrecht to propose that Louis XIV be assigned a share in the venture, in addition to the quarter share assigned to Philip V. The French *assientistes* would contribute their knowledge and facilities, lowering start-up costs, while French involvement would smooth potential future frictions between Spain and Britain.[84] That such a proposal would even occur to them suggests the degree to which the ministers of Louis XIV had come to see Tory leaders as potential partners. This has to be placed in the same context as the Franco-British commercial treaty of Utrecht, under negotiation at the same time by the same officials. But having given up the project of Pacific settlements, Harley and Bolingbroke did not intend to share their consolation prize with France. The project for a multinational trading company to carry on a free trade to Spanish America, even in this attenuated form, was not to be realised. Yet even without a cartel the French might hope to profit,

Mesnager suggested. The reopening to France of markets in Britain, guaranteed under the prospective commercial treaty, should allow French producers to piggy-back on the contraband trade of the South Sea Company – a hope that the failure of the commercial treaty rendered unavailing.[85]

The treaty of Utrecht institutionalised a new regime for European trade in Spanish America entailing a set of collective constraints on commerce, and limitations on Spanish sovereignty. The signatories restored the place of the official Cádiz trade to its prewar status: 'the exercise of navigation and commerce to the Spanish West Indies' was to 'remain in the same state it was' before the accession of Philip V, this 'by common consent established as a chief and fundamental rule'. Offering informally a measure of balance, this was the arrangement for sharing the profits of the trade that aroused the least suspicion among the leading commercial powers. But contrary to the ethos that informed this element of the treaty, it also granted Britain special privileges – the thirty-year Asiento, and other advantages to be specified in an Anglo-Spanish commercial treaty to follow. Under this convention, overseen by Stanhope, now a minister of George I, Spain granted the South Sea Company the right to send an annual vessel of 500-tuns' burden – the so-called 'permission ship' – to carry British wares directly to Central America, establishing on a smaller scale the direct and exclusive trade that Stanhope had earlier sought at Barcelona. Spain undertook at Utrecht to grant no other trade privileges to any other power, particularly France. Finally, neither Philip V nor his successors were permitted to 'alienate from them and the crown of Spain, to the French, or to any other nations whatever, any lands, dominions, or territories, or any part thereof, belonging to Spain in America'.[86] The further quest for trading enclaves in the American viceroyalties was banned by formal treaty. These provisions of the Utrecht negotiations did not constitute an inevitable outcome. They represented a sort of third-best result of the negotiations to end the war, as more ambitious projects to establish a freer trade met the veto of one or other of the leading states.

THE CONTINUING STRUGGLE OVER THE SPANISH TRADE

Though the privileges of the South Sea Company were modest compared to the advantages British and French ministers, merchants, and envoys aspired to in the course of the War of the Spanish Succession, they would trouble international relations for a generation. For many, they breached the spirit of the treaty, which in other respects strove to establish a balance of power. The privileges of the company betrayed the hopes raised in the last years of the war that, in the interests of future peace, the powers would concert a mechanism to share access to the vital markets and silver of Spanish America, and eliminate these as sources of conflict in international politics. For the next three decades, French and Spanish merchants and officials sought ways to overcome this perceived imbalance of the Utrecht order. During the Regency that followed the death of Louis XIV, the French monarchy embarked on a bold experiment to liberate the kingdom from dependence on Spanish silver by shifting to a paper currency designed by the Scottish financier and monetary theorist John Law – an effort to unilaterally and peacefully change the very foundations of the postwar order. But this bid failed (as the next chapter will explain), leaving the Utrecht order unchanged. In the 1720s, an exaggerated concern that South Sea Company privileges would unbalance the international order by giving Britain the lion's share of the Spanish trade gripped French officials (a fear ably stoked by the Cádiz mercantile community). 'In vain will we believe we have established a balance in Europe so long as that nation enjoys such prerogatives,' lamented the French trade commissioner in Cádiz.[87] But the French monarchy recoiled from attacking the Utrecht order directly. Fear of the Habsburg menace demanded that it preserve British goodwill.

Merchants and officials instead sought an accommodation acceptable to all parties to break out of the baneful legacies of Utrecht. They renewed Mesnager's call for the internationalisation of the trade, and called for a buy-out of the rights of the South Sea Company – a solution proposed by the Cádiz merchant community that also resonated with some British officials and even shareholders. The Walpole administration did not regard the company's trading privileges as especially valuable, seeing the British trade to Spain itself as far more important. The prime minister regretted the recurrent frictions, and threat of war, that the company's behaviour incited. War would be far more costly than any possible benefits it might secure for British trade. But the leaders of the company, who benefited from smuggling, were resistant to a Spanish buy-out of its rights. When in the late 1730s, the self-styled Patriot Whig parliamentary opposition sought to thrust war on Walpole in response to Spanish interdiction of British shipping in the Caribbean, the unresolved question of a payoff to the South Sea Company proved a major stumbling block to peace.

The considerable instability of international politics in the 1720s was linked to the perceived imbalances left by the Utrecht settlement. It was Spanish ministers and officials above all who resented the privileges of the South Sea Company, and the illicit trade in which the company participated.[88] They launched the first major challenge to the Utrecht order, together with an unlikely ally, the erstwhile Archduke Charles, now reigning as Charles VI of Austria. He and his former rival, Philip V, equally resented the way the Utrecht order constrained them. American trade might renew the Spanish monarchy, Spanish officials believed, if they could reverse its penetration by foreigners. For his part, Charles had chartered a new venture, the so-called Ostend Company, to realise some of the commercial potential of the formerly Spanish Low Countries (modern-day Belgium), which had passed under Habsburg sovereignty in 1713. The Company consolidated a private trade from Ostend to India and China, and aroused bitter opposition from the British and Dutch India companies. By allying with Spain, Austria might secure new privileges for the Ostenders to ship East India goods to Spanish America. An undeclared Anglo-Spanish naval war erupted in 1726 as British squadrons cruised the Spanish coast, and blockaded Portobello while Spain besieged Gibraltar and seized the permission ship *Prince Frederick* in Veracruz. This threatened to drag in France, which had moved into closer alignment with Britain in response to Austria's apparent willingness to undermine the 1713 settlement in coalition with Spain. But Louis XV's new leading minister, Cardinal André-Hercule de Fleury, was determined to avoid a war that would be ruinous for French trade, and that might allow the British to make new inroads in Spain's empire. He succeeded in forging a preliminary deal in 1727 to end hostilities, restore the commercial rights of the major commercial powers in Spain, and suspend the privileges of the Ostend Company, pushing remaining questions to a congress held the following year at Soissons.[89]

The first major diplomatic gathering since 1713, the congress seemed to Bourbon officials to offer a chance to renegotiate the political framework for trade in Spanish America, which had left a structural imbalance in the international system. Spanish diplomats complained of the way the South Sea Company used its privileges to cover a contraband trade.[90] Politically connected French merchants assailed both British smuggling and the company. In the words of one memorialist, 'All the power of the English comes from a fraudulent trade that they ply to the Spanish Indies for the past sixty years.'[91] What France needed was 'an equal balance', and the only way to achieve it was to use the congress to revoke the privileges of the South Sea Company and to check their contraband trade.[92] 'Nothing would be better for the kingdom than the abrogation of the Asiento,' concurred a memorandum produced in the naval ministry, because the Spanish trade was 'the most advantageous trade in the world'.[93] Fleury's principal deputy, the minister of foreign affairs Germain-Louis Chauvelin, and his aide, Antoine Pecquet (son of Colbert de Torcy's adjunct), shared the view that British commercial penetration of Spanish America upset the balance of commercial wealth on which the regular balance of power rested. Just as states were not permitted to extend their frontiers beyond a certain limit, Pecquet grumbled, nations should not be allowed to overextend their trade, as doing so threatened the interests and the security of all.[94] Such balance was impossible under the terms of Utrecht.

Yet the constraints of alliance politics left the French monarchy little choice but to put up with the status quo. An alliance with Britain, begun under the Regency and persisting to 1731, was predicated from the French perspective on containing Austria. This was less a question of the old dynastic Bourbon–Habsburg rivalry, which Fleury, and later Louis XV, were prepared to suspend, than the perception that Austria was a rising power, and one ready to disturb the peace.[95] The tension between continental security and preserving a balance with Britain in the realm of trade and colonies would prove a recurrent problem for French foreign policymakers.[96] Chauvelin epitomised the tensions in the regime's strategic outlook: intensely anti-Austrian, he also felt keenly the strategic importance of trade, but the need to check the old enemy to the East meant Britain had to be appeased.[97] In these circumstances, progress on trade questions was impossible. Neither the congress of Soissons nor the treaty of Seville to which it eventually led in November 1729 resolved grievances over the South Sea Company or British smuggling. The signatories deferred these thorny issues to a commission that did not meet until 1732, and that broke up over two years later without resolving anything. Even after the end of the Franco-British alliance in 1731 and a new French alignment with Spain in 1733, Louis XV had to avoid threatening British interests because he needed to keep Britain and the Dutch neutral in the War of the Polish Succession (1733–35), which France and Spain undertook against Austria.[98]

These circumstances produced a string of proposals from French officials to revive schemes set aside in 1713 to open the Spanish-American trade on equal terms to all European goods. Gérard Lévesque de Champeaux, French trade commissioner in Cádiz, and later commercial attaché in Madrid, tried to revive Mesnager's 1708 plan in anticipation of the congress of Soissons. Cádiz should become a free port, he argued; the Spanish trade should be opened on reasonable terms to all of Europe, and an international agreement hammered out to ban the contraband trade. The silver of South America was a common European good of which Spain was the trustee, but unless all European states could access it on equal terms, there could never be 'a balance in Europe'.[99] Lévesque de Champeaux was no isolated figure, but a member of the influential Club de l'Entresol, a kind of salon which met from 1724 to 1731 and where men with backgrounds or ambitions in foreign policy discussed European affairs.[100] The abbé de Saint-Pierre was a member and the British ambassador, Horatio Walpole (Sir Robert's brother), visited occasionally, as did Lord Bolingbroke, the architect of the Utrecht Peace, and twice an exile in France.

Out of step with the peace preliminaries of 1727, Lévesque de Champeaux's suggestion received no support from Chauvelin, but it was renewed a few years later by a senior official in the Contrôle Général, Jean-Roland Malet, on the eve of the first meetings of the international commission established under the treaty of Seville to resolve differences over the Spanish trade.[101] Malet summarised all the schemes for the internationalisation and neutralisation of the trade devised in Mesnager's day, and modelled his own proposal on a plan providing for all nations friendly to Spain to be allowed to participate in the trade, but for Spanish ships alone to carry the goods. Cádiz should be a free port for merchandise traded within Europe; moderate duties would be levied on the American trade alone. All the old Spanish vexations – indultos, visitation of vessels or warehouses – must end. As in Mesnager's original proposal, the traffic was to be neutralised in wartime. While there was no question of taking the Asiento or the permission ship away from the British, the latter would have to be inspected in Cádiz and sail with the rest of the fleet. To control competition, each nation would have an annual quota of goods (not to exceed 8,000 tuns in aggregate). Malet envisioned allowing the emperor 1,000 (against 1,200 each for France and the Dutch, and 900 for Britain, not including the additional 500 tuns of the permission ship) – a bid to compensate Charles VI for the loss of the Ostend trade. It would also serve to draw Austria into a balancing coalition against British naval and commercial power, and thus to keep Britain and Austria apart – a proposal also mooted by Lévesque de Champeaux, who suggested recruiting Austria and the Dutch into a league of commercial states to check British power.[102] In short, Malet's was an ambitious and creative design to meet the problem of imbalance created by the trade privileges accorded to Britain in 1713 and 1716.

As obvious non-starters with the British, these proposals received no official backing. But another idea that aimed to neutralise the problem of the Spanish trade was to have much greater influence – that of buying out the South Sea Company's privileges. The remaining years of the Asiento might be purchased by the payment of 200,000 piasters annually to be levied on the Cádiz trade – an expedient far less ruinous than the status quo, suggested one French merchant on the eve of the congress of Soissons.[103] This was a scheme with more appeal in Britain. Walpole's brother-in-law and political partner until 1730, Charles Townshend, the Northern secretary, raised the possibility that 'if Spain w^d give to the S. Sea Comp. a sum of money, by way of Equivalent . . . and faithfully restore all the effects of that Comp. or their value, which were seized in the former war . . . the Company may upon those Terms relinquish the Assiento Contract'.[104] He had discussed the idea with Walpole, who hated the wrangling associated with the Asiento.[105] At Soissons, the Spanish would 'certainly push us vigorously upon ye head of our S. Sea Trade, and the Annual Ship of 500 Tun wch the Assiento allows to be sent thither', Townshend told Horatio Walpole, 'endeavouring to cramp us in that particular, so as to make that Trade impracticable'.[106]

The idea of an Equivalent had more promise as the basis for an entente: many South Sea Company shareholders would have accepted it. The British ministers expected resistance to the idea of a buy-out of the company's privileges from some of the directors but not from shareholders, who benefited little from the contraband trade. A leading director, Richard Rigby, was 'violently bent upon carrying on that Trade to the utmost extent', Townshend noted. Rigby and Sir John Eyles, the subgovernor of the company, opposed a buy-out, while admitting that the 'greater part of the Court of Directors would with joy close with it'.[107] A significant fraction of shareholders was interested in withdrawing altogether from the trade and turning the South Sea Company into a simple annuity company. Ordinary proprietors benefited little from the commerce. The nominal trading capital, used to consolidate a part of the national debt during the South Sea Bubble, was so large that, even in good years, there was no prospect of a large dividend. Many were 'rich merchants who believed that the Asiento commerce was ruining their trade with the Spanish peninsula', claimed Matthew Plowes, the company's secretary.[108] Only the company's factors, who managed the contraband trade, and the directors, who winked at their activities, were truly in a position to profit. Thus Townshend concluded, 'tho' some of the Managers of the S. Sea Trade might perhaps not like it, I am fully persuaded that the Bulk of the Comp. & of ye Nation would; and I am sure it w^d be for the Publick Service'.[109] If the project of an Equivalent was not pursued at this point, it may have been because the British ministers were not pushed hard enough by the Spanish and the French.

But the proposal did not die. It accorded too well not only with the interests of South Sea Company shareholders but with those of the Spanish government and the Cádiz mercantile community whose profits the contraband trade eroded. In March 1732, William Tyrry, a politically connected Cádiz trader, proposed on behalf of his fellow merchants to buy out the permission ship privilege, 'a Commerce so pernicious to all Europe', in return either for a fixed percentage of the profits of the *flotas* and *galleones*, or for a preferential duty on British goods imported to Spain.[110] That autumn Don Tomás Geraldino, the official representative of Philip V to the South Sea Company, renewed the proposal for an Equivalent.[111] Eyles and his fellow directors sought to shelve the matter, but the body representing the shareholders, the General Court, expressed interest. When the Eyles faction was ousted from the leadership of the company early in 1733, the new direction under Sir Richard Hopkins made it a priority to convert most of the stock into annuities and to rein in the illicit traffic, which was a source of endless friction with Spain. Over the next two years, they reduced the number of factories, cut back the Asiento trade, and sent no more permission ships.[112] The question of an Equivalent was deferred for a time, but returned to centre stage in April 1734 when renewed by Geraldino, inducing the General Court to petition George II for permission to treat with the Spanish king.[113] At this point the question of a buy-out of the trading privileges became linked to company demands for compensation for Spanish seizure of its property during previous crises, a tactic intended less to wreck talks than to increase the potential payout.[114]

Had the question of an Equivalent been resolved there would have been one less factor inciting the Anglo-Spanish naval war of 1739 (later known as the War of Jenkins' Ear, or in Spain as the War of the Asiento). The occasion for the conflict was Spanish confiscations of British ships supposedly engaged in illicit trade, which the Patriot opposition to Walpole seized upon to push the ministry towards a war it did not want (with the additional goal of rendering Walpole's position untenable). Because of Spanish attacks, claimed the Patriot George Lyttelton, 'this most beneficial commerce will be utterly lost'.[115] Walpole was not indifferent to the trade of Spanish America but believed that peace and negotiation, more surely than any war, would secure it for Britain. Spanish confiscations were a nuisance, in his view, not a real threat to British trade. A ministry pamphleteer estimated the total losses at £5,000 a year – just a fortieth of the value of the illegal commerce.[116]

Conflict with Spain would jeopardise a far more valuable commerce through Iberia, the ministry argued. The trade to peninsular Spain was much greater throughout the 1720s and 1730s than the trade with Spanish America.[117] In the words of Horatio Walpole, 'War is particularly disadvantageous to a trading Nation; and of all Wars, a War with Spain is most so to the British Nation, as it deprives us of our most valuable Commerce, as our Trade with Spain is by all confess'd to be.'[118] The trade with Spain was subject to brutal plunges during wars, as John Crookshanks explained to Sir Robert Walpole. He drafted a chart plotting total British exports to Spain and imports from it against 'melancholly events' and 'favourable events' in European politics from 1697 to 1729. Trade soared in peacetime and plunged in war.[119] Another cessation of trade might permanently displace British exports from these traditional channels. The sale of a single ship load of French woollens in Spain did England more harm than ever the Spanish *guardacostas* had, claimed one ministerial pamphleteer.[120] With such concerns foremost, in 1739 Robert Walpole concluded a compromise agreement, the Convention of El Pardo, with Madrid to avert conflict, but the South Sea Company refused to accept the compensation offered for its prior losses and the agreement collapsed.[121]

Walpole's Patriot opponents rejected the political framework for the trade to Spanish America embodied in the treaty of Utrecht, seeing in it not a structural advantage for Britain but a source of British decline and French commercial advancement. These ideas will be explored at greater length in Chapter 4, but suffice to say that the Patriots were in many respects the inheritors of Whig positions from 1713 opposing the Tory peace. They had a realistic assessment of how limited in value the privileges of the South Sea Company were. They assumed that a growing closeness in Franco-Spanish relations signalled by the first Bourbon Family Compact in 1733 meant that the old French project of a commercial 'union' with Spain was again on the cards. Indeed, Fleury was busy in 1738 using growing Anglo-Spanish tensions to press for a commercial treaty between France and Spain that would remove once and for all the obstacles to a thriving French trade in Spain, and through Cádiz to America.[122] France seemed more commercially dynamic than ever, given the rapid growth of its plantation colonies in the Caribbean, while a French monopoly of the Spanish trade would certainly launch Louis XV on a bid for universal monarchy, Patriots supposed.

The war of 1739 saw a recrudescence of many of the old dreams, nurtured during the War of the Spanish Succession, of laying open Spanish-American markets to British merchants. War was needed, Patriots argued, not just to punish Spanish attacks and defend British honour, but to preserve, and ideally expand, Britain's access to American markets. They revived designs to establish trading enclaves in the Caribbean and the Pacific. For William Pulteney, perhaps the most influential Patriot leader, such acquisitions would 'put the trade and navigation of this nation beyond all future violation'.[123] It was through conquests, concurred John Carteret, a leader of the Patriot opposition in the Lords, that 'we can most effectively enlarge our commerce and navigation'.[124] 'A Harbour, a Settlement, a Colony can alone conclude our Disputes with Spain and assert and preserve the rights of Great Britain,' argued the Scottish Patriot Lord Polwarth.[125] Again, it was sovereignty over trade, not over territory or production, that was at issue. Dreams of Darien, access to the South Sea, and free ports also revived. Jamaican interests invested in contraband trade with Spanish America wanted to take Panama and establish a trading station there to trade directly to the Pacific. Martin Bladen, a key commercial adviser to Walpole, and a leading figure on the Board of Trade, favoured this scheme. The seizure of Darien would allow the British to 'prevent great part of the riches of Peru and Lima from being exported to Old Spain, or to make them our own'.[126] In September 1740, the Admiralty sent a naval expedition under Commodore George Anson to explore and maraud in the Pacific, and to establish a permanent base there if possible.

Here was a frankly bellicose political-economic position intent on using force to improve Britain's commercial position. Just as during the War of the Spanish Succession, it was the threat of a French universal monarchy of trade that justified this resort to war to transform the political framework for foreign trade. Patriots were acutely conscious of the costs of conflict. They had long harangued Walpole on his failure to pay down the national debt, which, they argued, tended to strangle British commercial dynamism because of the taxes on trade needed to fund it. Military intervention was justified in this case because of the enormous stakes: only war could arrest the ascent of France to a position of overwhelming commercial dominance. 'The French are our most dangerous and our most inveterate enemies,' Admiral Edward Vernon reminded his officers before the Spanish-American port of Cartagena.[127] It was the long-standing French design to penetrate and monopolise the commerce of Spanish America that the war would check. This was also a war for free trade. Having taken Portobello in November 1739, Vernon opened a kind of free port there, publishing a proclamation encouraging Spanish subjects to come and trade freely, indeed allowing merchants of any nation to do so.[128]

The results of this assault on the Utrecht order by the power perceived to benefit most from it were predictable. As Newcastle had warned in 1738, the greater the success Britain enjoyed in this venture, 'the greater will be the jealousy of our neighbours', especially France. A balancing coalition would be formed to check Britain's bid, and after a long and expensive war it was likely that the old equilibrium would be the best result Britain could attain.[129] This prediction was doubly farsighted (though Newcastle himself promptly ignored it and threw in his lot with the Patriots). In the summer of 1740, Louis XV responded to Britain's assembly of a large naval expedition to attack Spain in America by sending much of the French fleet to the Caribbean with orders to defend the Spanish colonies.[130] When Britain and Spain finally resolved their differences a decade later in the October 1750 treaty of Madrid, Whitehall proved ready to close this ugly chapter in Anglo-Spanish relations in return for the modest payment of £100,000 to the South Sea Company to settle all its outstanding claims. What the British now wanted above all was to revive the trade to Spain itself (and onwards through Cádiz to Spanish America). John Russell, duke of Bedford, the Southern secretary, secretly contemplated suppressing the contraband trade altogether if the Iberian commerce Walpole had favoured could be reopened on an advantageous basis, and if Spain would renounce actions against British shipping in the Caribbean.[131] In effect, the pre-1713 framework for the trade to Spanish America was restored, and the worst elements of the Utrecht peace undone.

Struggles to shape the political framework for global trade persistently drove conflict in eighteenth-century Europe as sovereigns deployed closed colonial empires, navigation acts, high duties, monopoly companies, and commercial treaties to advantage their own merchants at the expense of rivals. Frictions over trade could lead to war, especially when one state threatened to acquire an insurmountable advantage over rivals. But the desire to limit the costs of conflict also prompted officials to craft frameworks to reduce or eliminate jealousy of trade. The trade to Spanish America was a persistent source of strife because of the commercial importance of its markets and its vital role in global silver production. It was also a recurrent site for proposed accommodations between the two leading commercial powers, France and Britain. The French bid for commercial 'union' with Spain from 1700 both helped to start and to prolong the War of the Spanish Succession, while efforts to allay British and Dutch concerns about commercial access to American markets became central to the peacemaking process from 1708 to 1713. Freedom of trade in the guise of a Catholic common market threatened the balance of power, and the French and Spanish in turn offered schemes for a more universal free trade through Cádiz that would distribute the profits of the American trade widely and prevent any one state from monopolising them. Even Britain's South Sea Company was first conceived as a vehicle to share the Spanish-American trade with the French, though it quickly evolved into an exclusive means to exercise the Asiento and carry on a smuggling traffic. In its failure to offer a commercial balance acceptable to all, the peace of Utrecht miscarried, and bore the seeds of future conflict. The perceived disequilibrium that was the legacy of the treaty led to new clashes culminating in the Anglo-Spanish war of 1739, but also in designs for an entente between the Bourbon powers and Britain to undo South Sea Company privileges.

These efforts to reach accommodation betoken a pacific political-economic stance shared by an assortment of officials and merchants in both France and Britain. When they worked to eliminate the Spanish-American trade as an incitement to war, it was to limit the costs of future conflict, to establish a balance of power, and to check the commercial expansion of rivals. The same drivers gave rise to a host of schemes to rework the form of European empire in the Americas. William Paterson dreamed of a free-trade system based on free ports in the Caribbean under British guarantee that would render traditional commercial empires in America 'never after . . . worth the expense of keeping'. Schemes for new monopoly companies anchored in Spanish-American enclaves promised sovereignty over trade without the expense of sovereignty over people or production. French officials envisioned Cádiz as an international city where Spanish sovereignty would be merely nominal, and represented Spain as the trustee rather than the outright owner of its empire in America. The treaty of Utrecht established an international regime in the Spanish-American trade, a system of collective restraint, to formalise a condominium of the trade among French, Dutch, and British merchants that had emerged in the latter decades of the seventeenth century.

The negotiations bearing on the future of the Spanish trade and those for a Franco-British commercial treaty at Utrecht were entangled in certain respects. The same officials were involved in both sets of talks – Bolingbroke, Colbert de Torcy, Mesnager and, behind the scenes, the French Council of Commerce. The assumption that a relatively free cross-Channel trade would be inaugurated after the war temporarily altered the French attitude to a British Asiento because offi-cials hoped to piggy-back on the South Sea Company to sell French wares in America. Freedom of trade was at the centre of both negotiations, but imagined in different ways. Between France and Britain, it would be institutionalised by a bilateral commercial treaty, while the trade to the Spanish viceroyalties was to be organised under a multilateral agreement to establish Cádiz as a free port, to set up an international company, or in the form of an informal partition of the trade by competing French and British merchants. The threat represented by an unchecked free trade was different in the two cases. In Europe excessive openness threatened strategic economic sectors, especially manufacturing; in the case of the Spanish trade, the threat was that a state benefiting exclusively from commercial openness would achieve overwhelming commercial dominance. But in both instances, freer trade, constructed in a balanced fashion, would diminish tensions by limiting or eliminating trade as a source of future conflict.

As with the Franco-British commercial treaty, we are dealing with a vision of free trade distant from textbook assumptions. In this paradigm, states were the chief competitors for commercial resources, merchants only their instruments. It was relative not absolute gains from trade that counted. The good of American consumers was never considered, and there was no talk of the advantages of competition. Officials even imagined that monopoly companies might serve as vehicles for a freer trade. The geopolitical advantages of free trade were paramount. The harmony between states it might foster was not a natural thing based on absolute or comparative advantage, but something laboriously built by political action. In a capitalist world where commerce was deformed to meet the purposes of competing states and sovereignty bent to enrich merchants, a prize like the markets and silver of Spanish America must naturally be a source of conflict unless that trade was placed in a political framework designed to prevent any one state acquiring too much of the benefit.

The officials and merchants who strove to regulate access to the trade of Spanish America, or to transform the existing governance regime, were unexceptional. The search for such arrangements, in fact, punctuated the history of the European states system in the century after 1688. As we will see in Chapter 6, French and British officials negotiated repeatedly from the 1750s through the 1780s to establish an equivalent framework for European trade in India. France entered the American independence struggle in the 1770s not just to wrench the Thirteen Colonies out of the British orbit, but to set up an international commercial regime to protect trade to North America, and to keep it open in future to all of Europe. These efforts were impelled by the search for a balance of commercial power, and frequently also to contain the costs of conflict over trade. Strife came at a high price both to merchants and to states, in the form of damage to commerce and the upward spiral of public debt. The urge to avoid these costs periodically drove officials and companies to seek a less antagonistic equilibrium. This pacific impulse is a structural feature of a capitalist system in which states compete for the economic sources of power, security, and advantage. It is the unrefined ancestor of our own global politics, where international institutions mediate or inhibit conflict over trade, and developed states league under the banner of the West to limit the economic sovereignty of the less powerful.

3

TO KEEP THE EUROPEAN PEACE
John Law's Financial Revolution and Its Legacy

'There are events that affect the interests of great powers to which inadequate attention is paid,' John Law told the French regent, Philippe d'Orléans in 1715. He singled out two such events: 'the discovery of the Indies', which swelled the power of commercial states, and the 'introduction of credit', which had empowered only a few of them. Before the conquest of America, Law pointed out, silver had been scarce in Europe. The ensuing expansion of trade enlarged the money stock of all nations, but 'the commercial states benefited more than the rest, and by this means greatly augmented their power'. The second break, 'not less considerable than the first', was the adoption by the Dutch and the British of modern institutions of public credit – what scholars now refer to as the financial revolution.[1] Governments began to market long-term funded debt to a broad investing public, to borrow cheaply through proxies such as the East India Company and the Bank of England, and to consolidate unfunded debt by converting it into share capital in specially designed joint-stock ventures such as the South Sea Company. The development of European public finance exemplifies the way interstate competition was entwined with the evolution of capitalism. The new financial practices allowed England – later Britain – to expand its capacity to borrow and service debt.[2] They propelled it from the status of a second-rate power into the first rank of European states during the two great wars that followed the Glorious Revolution. In fact, Law claimed, credit had boosted British power more than if it had conquered Spanish America.[3]

If France was to compete, argued the Scottish monetary theorist, it must emulate its rival or continue to be overmatched in the struggle for power and security, as it had been during the War of the Spanish Succession, and as it seemed likely to be in the new international order that had emerged from the treaty of Utrecht. What was at issue was the balance of commercial power – power based on national wealth and the capacity to mobilise it for politico-military purposes. If Orléans embraced a modern system of public credit, Law urged, the French monarchy would soon redress the imbalance. His arguments eventually persuaded the regent. An exile since 1693, when he had killed a man in a duel, Law entered the regent's service and became one of his closest advisers. With his support, and that of a diverse coalition of French merchants, courtiers, and men of letters who brought their own ideas to the table, the Scot founded a bank in Paris in 1716 to issue paper money and, in 1717, a joint-stock enterprise on the model of Britain's South Sea Company to recolonise Louisiana and absorb part of the unfunded public debt.[4] Two years later he created the Compagnie des Indes, a huge conglomerate with a monopoly over all the kingdom's extra-European trade, which absorbed existing commercial companies. Law also took over the royal mint and some of the tax farms, arrangements under which the French monarchy outsourced the collection of certain taxes to syndicates of private businessmen. In 1719, he took steps to convert the whole public debt into shares in his company in a vast debt-consolidation scheme.[5]

We have read the financial revolution too narrowly as an institutional trans-formation of public credit when its early architects strove to bring about more sweeping economic, social, and cultural transformations.[6] The Scot claimed that the institutions he was building would transform relations among the states of Europe. Wealth underpinned power. This had been the lesson of the two great wars that marked the last decades of Louis XIV's reign. Britain seemed to have a structural advantage in the Utrecht order. Above all, the thirty-year Asiento secured for the South Sea Company, and the contraband traffic it would shelter in Spanish America, threatened an uneven playing field. But Law offered a radically different reading of the sources of Britain's geopo-litical advantage, and in so doing promised an escape from the constraints of Utrecht. He believed that Britain's financial institutions had transformed the nature of its money supply, giving an enormous stimulus to commerce. France might profit from the same vitality and realise thereby its own enormous potential. In the medium term, Law's revolution would redress the balance of commercial power and re-establish the French monarchy as an equal to its British rival. In the long run, he argued, the kingdom would emerge as Europe's dominant commercial state – a benign colossus that would lead its neighbours into an age of peace.

Law's 'System', as it was known, requires that we think about the place of public credit in early modern European politics differently than we typically do. Generally, systems of public credit were extensions of warmaking capacity – part of the machinery of fiscal-military states. Unlike their modern equivalents, states spent the great bulk of their revenues on the armed forces, and on servicing debt borrowed to fight wars.[7] Taxation and borrowing served essentially to shore up power and security. But Law presented his financial revolution in radically different terms – not as a preparation for war but as the key to a more peaceful world. He saw that twenty-five years of warfare had ravaged the French economy, bequeathed a public debt that sapped the vitality of commerce and enterprise, and nurtured a class of financiers that checked its prospects for future recovery. He predicted that his financial revolution would create monetary abundance, reverse deflation, displace the financiers, and drive commercial growth. Paper money would free France from the necessity to compete with the British and the Dutch for Spanish-American silver, and decrease the tensions over extra-European trade that poisoned relations. France would grow peacefully back to a position of power and security, and recover its natural position as the arbiter of European politics without threatening the security of its neighbours.

Consistent with these bold geopolitical ambitions, Law contrived to shape French foreign policy. He formed a partnership with the abbé Guillaume Dubois, broker of an alliance between the regent and George I that promised to shore up each ruler's fragile hold on power. Law made himself a mainstay of the connection. Later, however, he reversed direction in a bid to protect the System from a new threat. In 1720 London financiers launched a scheme in emulation of Law to consolidate a large part the public debt as equity in the South Sea Company. Law saw this as an attack on his own financial project. To block the competing South Sea scheme, he shook the Franco-British alliance, tried to have Dubois disgraced, and even threatened to fund a Jacobite invasion of Britain. His stance, which was to have a long afterlife in Franco-British relations, I describe as 'jealousy of credit'. It entailed wary scrutiny of a rival's public credit with a view either to imitating its innovations or undermining its successes. With his bank and companies, Law emulated the British model and, by manipulating French foreign policy, he set out to frustrate the South Sea Company's competing debt-consolidation scheme. Jealousy of credit extended into the realm of finance the kinds of rivalries over trade that marked the international order. A state enjoyed good credit at the expense of its rivals, it was assumed, either because all states vied for the same pool of mobile international capital, or because, in a balance-of-power system, the financial gain of each struck at the relative power of the rest.

Though Law's enemies pushed him out of office and exiled him from France in 1720, jealousy of credit continued to mark the French relationship with Britain. The final section of this chapter sketches the legacies of Law's System and the competing South Sea Bubble, and examines how these events shaped thought and action down to the 1780s. One sequel of the episode was the belief some Britons harboured that their system of public credit was exposed to foreign interference – a weakness French officials and projectors hoped to exploit. Even without French action, British officials worried, the funding system adopted in the 1690s might eventually crush the nation beneath the weight of accumulated debt. In France, Law's geopolitical ideas continued to appeal, if only to a minority of merchants, officials, and men of letters, who aspired to a financial revolution that would renew French power. Competition for mobile international capital would return, climaxing during the American War when the French administration diverted Dutch investment from London markets and drew it into the French debt. But as in the case of Law's thinking, these later schemes are better understood as strategies to unleash commercial growth by expanding the money supply than simply as means to expand the fiscal-military capacity of the state.

PAPER MONEY AND PERPETUAL PEACE

If his System had endured, Law told one admirer, it 'would have kept the peace of Europe'.[8] To understand the logic of this statement, we need to grapple with Law's views on money. If France could move from a silver-based currency to a credit money, it would be freed from the need to compete with the British and the Dutch for the trade of Spanish America, with all the conflict this entailed. It would be less reliant on foreign trade for its prosperity, because it would no longer depend on securing an influx of specie from a positive trade balance, further reducing international contention for commercial and colonial resources. Eventually, by mobilising its great internal resources, stimulated by manufacturing and a healthy trade, and tapping the consumption of its huge population, France would realise dividends from its greater size, and emerge as the dominant commercial power in Europe. But it would be a benevolent hegemon. Invulnerable to the assaults of its neighbours, it would have no incentive to conquer them. Law diverged from conventional thinking in viewing hegemony rather than balance as the key to ending jealousy of trade. Only the emergence of a state unchallengeable in its economic dominance, yet uninterested in crushing its neighbours, would end conflict over trade.

For Law, as for many of his contemporaries, an adequate money supply was the key to economic development. Neither he nor they conflated money with wealth – this is a persistent myth about the age of mercantilism.[9] Rather, they believed that a tight money supply checked economic expansion. Modern scholars affirm this view. The small size of the monetary stock in the eighteenth century stymied the unlimited anonymous transactions with strangers that constitute the lifeblood of modern commercial economies.[10] One consequence of monetary scarcity was that merchants transacted most business on credit. But credit was subject to periodic crises, triggered by rumours of war or major private bankruptcies. Traders periodically lost confidence in commercial paper, and it temporarily lost its capacity to mediate transactions. Liquidity scrambles ensued when hard money was sought after, hoarded, and disappeared from circulation.[11] Instability aside, there were monetary needs credit could not meet: urban wages were paid in coin; regular cash settlements had to be made with creditors; above all, quarterly payments of rent and tax payments typically had to be settled in cash. From the perspective of certain modern monetary theories, this scarcity of money should not have mattered. Prices should have adjusted to the limits of the money supply without effects on the volume of transactions. Whatever its merits, this view was alien to the thinking of early eighteenth-century officials and merchants. They assumed an inadequate monetary medium would diminish 'circulation', leading to depressed conditions in trade and unemployment.[12]

Under such conditions, Law argued, if the money supply could be increased interest rates would fall and unexploited resources and labour would be set in motion.[13] Foreign trade stimulated prosperity, in this way of thinking, by augmenting the monetary stock of flourishing commercial states. By exporting more by value than they imported, they forced trading partners to pay them the balance in specie, which went to swell the money supply. Law saw in credit an alternate way to boost the money stock. As Carl Wennerlind has shown, similar assumptions, originally derived from the seventeenth-century Hartlib circle, underpinned many of the schemes to establish a credit currency in England, culminating in the foundation of the Bank of England.[14] The notes of the Bank expanded Britain's money supply. Because of their relative liquidity, Law argued, the shares of chartered companies too served as a money equivalent, being used both to settle debts and to store value. By borrowing through chartered companies, which financed their lending to government through selling shares to the public, Britain had transformed its public debts into money, stimulating the British economy. If it were forced to depend on silver exclusively, Law held, 'manufactures and trade would diminish by more than half'.[15] To solve France's problems of deflation and recession, Law proposed to emulate the British model – to establish a bank issuing paper currency to supplement the money supply, and joint-stock companies whose shares would serve a parallel purpose.

But there was a second predicament the French kingdom faced – a hangover from the quarter-century of warfare after 1688 – which called for a different remedy. The Crown's huge debt was locked up in annuities (*rentes*), which were difficult to trade and thus illiquid. In Law's view, the proliferation of such instruments had bred a society of rentiers inimical to commerce. When one could invest money in stolid annuities, why take a chance on riskier ventures? Here was another case of feedback from war strangling commercial vibrancy. French investment culture had become sclerotic and deleterious to trade.[16]

This sclerosis was exacerbated by the place of a class of financiers in France, whose power Law wanted to root out. The Crown depended on these contractors to collect taxes and to make payments, often in the form of advances. They borrowed money from the public on their own credit, and loaned it to the Crown, often at high interest, meeting short-term borrowing needs. In Britain, by contrast, the Bank of England facilitated unfunded borrowing at lower rates of interest. In Law's view, the financiers sapped commercial vitality by drawing capital and talent away from trade, keeping interest rates high, and fostering a deflationary regime. In the long run, he anticipated, his revolution would sweep this class away.[17]

Unfunded war debt to the tune of 250 million livres, which languished at deep discounts on secondary markets, also burdened the kingdom. When the regent had tried to reduce it using a special financial tribunal – a *chambre de justice* – intended to claw back some of the wartime gains of the financiers, this triggered a crisis in royal credit and made an already deep recession worse. Taking a leaf from Robert Harley's book, Law established his Compagnie d'Occident in 1717, permitting investors to exchange 100 million livres' worth of unfunded debt in exchange for shares. Two years later he took on the problem of the *rentes*. The Compagnie des Indes he established doubled as a debt-consolidation scheme. It would convert the illiquid *rentes* into company shares that would serve to augment the money supply.[18]

The creation of a credit money would release France from some of the chief constraints of the international order – the need to secure a substantial share of the silver of Spanish America to sustain its money supply, and thus to compete fiercely with rival commercial states. Public credit would augment the money supply more effectively than a positive trade balance. During the War of the Spanish Succession, Law pointed out, France dominated the trade to Spanish America – especially the critical South Sea trade – yet it was Britain, with its superior financial institutions, that prevailed. Its national bank had propped up Britain 'without the trade of the Indies, and . . . the trade of the Indies without a bank was not able to sustain France'.[19] If new forms of paper credit were launched in France, Law argued, they 'would augment the quantity of money more in a year that an advantageous commerce could in ten'.[20]

Once his System was established, Law argued, France would no longer need Spanish America and its silver. 'By my work,' he claimed, 'I will render the Indies superfluous, and France will no longer need other powers.'[21] It is striking in this light that not a single director of the old Asiento company subscribed to Law's Compagnie d'Occident. The same is true for the Compagnie de Saint-Domingue, established to run an interloping trade to the Spanish Empire and draw out its silver.[22] Of course, France would not be able to do without American silver entirely. It would be needed, at a minimum, to subsidise foreign allies and to fund trade to Asia. But silver would no longer be the lifeblood of the kingdom.

Struggles with other powers for distant colonies played little role in Law's vision of French prosperity and power, though the same cannot be said of some of Law's partners in France. As Arnaud Orain has shown, Law collaborated with networks of French merchants, financiers, scientists, and journalists who sometimes had very different ideas about how the System might be used to renew the kingdom's wealth and power.[23] To the degree that future profits in Louisiana were represented as a major asset of the Compagnie d'Occident, this was not Law's doing but the work of some of his associates. When the creation of the company was first proposed, the Scot said almost nothing about Louisiana's commercial or agricultural prospects, focusing instead on the capacity of the new enterprise to absorb unfunded public debt in the manner of the South Sea Company. The chief asset of the Compagnie d'Occident was not undeveloped land in North America, or the fur trade, much less undiscovered mineral deposits, but the dividend the monarchy guaranteed stockholders, secured on tax farms in France.[24] The initiative to revivify Louisiana came not from Law but from financiers and merchants associated with Antoine Crozat, who had held the monopoly on the trade to Louisiana until 1716. Jean-Baptiste Duché saw in the colony a future source of tobacco. He speculated that gold and silver might be mined in the Illinois country, and envisioned an interloping trade with Mexico.[25] Such a fixation on precious metals and on the Spanish trade were foreign to Law's thinking. He arrived late to negotiations to establish the so-called 'Mississippi Company'. (The nickname would later be applied to the Compagnie des Indes too.) His decisive contribution was to argue that it could be used to soak up a larger share of the unfunded debt.[26]

There was certainly a place for foreign trade in Law's vision of a prosperous France, and he likely played this up to attract the support of the French mercantile community. An adequate supply of money 'would put France in a position to do all the trade of Europe, and would render this great kingdom cultivated like Holland, full of towns, villages and people; it would restore navigation and the navy . . . the lands of France would be brought to produce double what they do at present. This product would be worked up in the country and transported abroad on French vessels'.[27] Here was a design to displace the Dutch as carriers of French goods – one of the dearest aspirations of many Colbertist officials. Law foresaw a recovery of markets for French staples, especially wines. The mercantile interests he hoped to recruit as investors in his bank and companies must surely find such a vision appealing. He recruited the directors and subscribers to the Compagnie d'Occident, for example, heavily among western port interests that had suffered from the disruptions of trade with Britain and the Dutch Republic caused by Colbertist policies and wartime disruptions. Three western deputies to the Council of Commerce were original company directors – François Mouchard of La Rochelle, René Moreau of Saint-Malo, and Jean Piou of Nantes. The last named had also been an early supporter of Law's banking projects.[28] The deputies Jean Anisson and Jean-Baptiste Fenellon had admired Harley's South Sea Company and proposed that the ministry establish a similar institution in France.[29] Fenellon subsequently served as an inspector of Law's bank.[30]

Paper money would liberate France from the need to compete fiercely with the British and the Dutch for the silver of Spanish America. This was one foundation of Law's claims that his System would assure the peace of Europe. More fundamentally, a reinvigorated France would transform the structure of the international order by rendering war essentially pointless. Once it was able to tap its own vast domestic resources, France would have little to gain from war, while its former rivals would be utterly incapable of crushing it. It would become 'the arbiter of Europe without having to use force'.[31] Law rejected the idea that such a preponderant France would contend for universal monarchy; it would 'command other nations without dominating them and give them the law without usurping anything of their rights . . . qualities . . . much more glorious than the vain title of a universal monarchy which having grown beyond its just limits collapses finally of its own weight'.[32]

For Law, universal monarchy was an aggressive political order tied to conquest, but he regarded the feedback effects from war as ruinous for the foundations of power, and the pursuit of universal monarchy as self-undermining. Conquest enervated the state even when it was victorious: 'The title of unjust conqueror is not only odious in itself but ruinous for a State,' he held; 'everything conspires to ruin a prince who wishes to extend his empire against the right of peoples and nations; agriculture, the arts, and commerce are neglected; while he occupies his subjects in war, the homeland is exhausted of men and money'. Not conquest, but economic expansion was the royal road to power and security: 'A fertile, extensive, well-peopled and well-situated kingdom has surer means of augmenting its power in cultivating manufactures, land and trade; it finds by this multiplication of riches an increase of power deterring its neighbours from daring to attack it.'[33]

There are echoes here of Archbishop François Fénelon, who had been among the most highly placed critics of Louis XIV's foreign policy. But there is also an implicit critique of the archbishop's views. Territorial expansionism of the kind indulged in by the Sun King ought to be avoided, Fénelon urged. Instead power could be husbanded, and the security of the kingdom assured peacefully, by the careful management of economic resources.[34] In *The Adventures of Telemachus* (1699), the epic tale he composed for the instruction of the king's grandson, the duc de Berry, Fénelon celebrated a simple agrarian economy, without luxury, in which external trade, conducted reciprocally, played a modest role.[35] Such a system would conduce to peace between nations. Like the archbishop, Law believed France could be secure and powerful, and live in peace with its neighbours, mostly on the basis of its domestic resources – its vast agricultural wealth and its huge population. Where he differed from Fénelon was in looking to manufacturing and high domestic consumption as a foundation of French prosperity. Law also rejected Fénelon's view that balance alone could form the basis of a stable and healthy international order.[36]

In this respect, Law's project can be compared to the abbé de Saint-Pierre's vision for perpetual peace published in 1713.[37] Saint-Pierre was part of the household of the regent, and Law would certainly have known him. The abbé rejected balance-of-power politics as a suitable foundation for the European states system, arguing that it gave rise to never-ending wars. His perspective on war was similar to Law's. War was disadvantageous even to the victorious power because it cost more to prosecute than any possible gain. His alternative – European confederation – differed radically from Law's, but underlines that not everyone thought balance was the key to peace in the aftermath of Utrecht.[38]

Law hoped to build a new kind of international system, one in which empire and international trade would count for less, where France's demographic and territorial lead would be translated into supremacy in wealth and power. This would only be possible with a credit-based currency to unleash domestic economic activity and to demote American silver to a secondary role. Peace would follow eventually from the benign hegemony of an economic superpower invulnerable to assault by its neighbours and with no interest in conquering them. But all this lay in the future. For the time being, Law had to accommodate the mercantile interests and other partners he hoped to enlist, and theirs was a more conventional vision of international competition based on reviving foreign trade, expanding navigation, and developing the colonies. He made further compromises to get his System off the ground, as we will see in the following section, when he embraced the diplomacy of the abbé Dubois and the regent, not to overthrow the Utrecht order but to run it as a Franco-British duopoly.

LAW'S BATTLE WITH THE SOUTH SEA COMPANY

Law expected foreign rivals to launch an attack on his financial operations in Paris – hardly surprising, given his belief that the System would recast the balance of power. He complained that the 'ministers of England and the English bankers appear to be leagued against the bank of France and make efforts to destroy it and discredit it'.[39] Cross-border campaigns to disrupt the credit of a geopolitical rival had been a feature of international affairs at least since the late seventeenth century. The British government acted during the War of the Spanish Succession to block French bankers from circulating bills in London and Amsterdam used to finance Louis XIV's armies.[40] Law would surely have known of these endeavours. He certainly knew of the Darien Company's travails – its admission to London capital markets obstructed by order of the Westminster Parliament under the influence of the East India Company.[41] Law's fear that foreigners would intervene to check France's rising credit moved him to support the abbé Dubois, who with James Stanhope had built an unconventional alliance between France and Britain. From Law's perspective, the alliance would have to serve his financial objectives; his support would be provisional only.

Stanhope and Dubois made common cause to stabilise the European order to the benefit of the regent and George I, and to bolster the Utrecht settlement. Britain's new king would benefit from French backing to counter the claim to the throne of the exiled James Stuart, while the agreement also guaranteed Orléans's succession to the French Crown in the event of Louis XV's death. The child king's uncle, Philip V of Spain, had a stronger claim, which the peace of Utrecht had forced him to renounce. The regent, Dubois, and their British partners intended the alliance, concluded in 1716, to confront international crises by agreement among the major powers. To begin with, they hoped to arbitrate ongoing conflicts: the Great Northern War (1700–21) between Sweden and Russia in the Baltic, and the war launched by Philip V in the Mediterranean to reclaim Spain's Italian possessions ceded at Utrecht. In that theatre, the Royal Navy and French troops pressured Spain to accede to an accommodation.[42]

If France co-operated with the British to check the Spanish threat to the peace, Law grasped, London might be induced to favour his System, or at least to mount no attack on it. The Scot worked with Dubois and Stanhope to sustain the novel alliance, which faced the hostility of the 'old court', grandees from the days of Louis XIV who supported the Jacobites and for whom French partnership with Spain was the natural state of affairs. 'I know how much he was concerned in the treaty that was to affirm our union,' Stanhope would remark later to Dubois, 'and that he regarded the union of the two crowns as the foundation of his schemes.'[43] According to a well-placed Jacobite in France, Law was 'in strict union and a fast friend to *Dubois*' at this time, while he and the British ambassador, John Dalrymple, earl of Stair, were 'very often shut up with *the Regent* for whole hours . . . these two with *Dubois* govern all *foreign affairs*, and especially such as regard *England*'.[44]

Stanhope and other British officials were initially untroubled by Law's financial schemes. If France remained financially insolvent, it could be of little use as an ally. By relieving the credit of the regent, Law's System might serve the ends of George I – to obstruct Spain and protect the Utrecht order. Ambassador Stair grumbled in 1718 that the 'derangement of the finances' ensured that the French ruler would 'never dare take a vigorous step, and those who serve him will ever go a trembling'. Law's bank might remedy French financial disarray, Stanhope saw, and he urged Stair to unite Law and Dubois.[45] Law's bank soon proved itself as a remitter of international payments for the French monarchy, arranging subsidies to Sweden as early as 1716.[46]

Law enhanced his position as a broker of good Franco-British relations by offering attractive financial opportunities to British officials, a practice also indispensable to his success in France. He invited Stair, and the embassy secretary, Thomas Crawfurd, to invest in his System with generous offers of credit.[47] 'I did not think it became the King's Ambassador to give countenance to such a thing,' Stair protested.[48] Law's most important coup came in establishing indirect financial ties with Stanhope. He cultivated the minister's in-laws, the Pitts, notably Stanhope's brother-in-law, Thomas Pitt (from 1719, Lord Londonderry, and the uncle of William Pitt the Elder). Soon Pitt owned 200,000 livres in shares of Law's Compagnie d'Occident, likely purchased on credit.[49] Law initiated the relationship in 1717 when he negotiated the sale of a 140-carat diamond owned by Thomas Pitt Sr (former East India Company president in Madras), who could not find a buyer rich enough to purchase it. Law's bank financed the acquisition of what would later be known as the Regent Diamond on behalf of the French Crown for 2 million livres (or £125,000; the diamond is worth approximately £50 million today).[50] The Pitts used the initial instalment to help Stanhope purchase a great landed estate in Kent.[51]

Alarm bells began to ring for British officials when Law moved to convert the *rentes* into company shares – the boldest stage of his financial revolution. In the summer of 1719, he proposed to lend the French Crown 1.2 billion livres to consolidate almost the whole French debt, an operation to be financed by the sale of company shares. In effect, he would convert the *rentes* into equity in the company. Law hoped to attract investors by guaranteeing them a 3-per-cent return on their shares to be paid by the Crown. The company would supplement this interest payment with dividends generated from the profits it would make in its financial and commercial operations. Law modelled this venture on what Robert Harley had achieved in 1711 when he launched the South Sea Company, though Law's scheme was to be on a vastly larger scale. In the early autumn, the Compagnie des Indes issued 324,000 new shares. The bank primed the pump by offering credit for the purchase of shares which could be acquired on instalment. Investors, grasping that these operations were supported by the Crown, were not slow to sense an opportunity.[52] The new stock was easily sold, and soon its price was rising fast. With Law seemingly on the verge of consolidating the whole French debt at a very advantageous interest rate, Stair grew alarmed. 'By the success of Mr. Law's project the public debts of France are paid off at a stroke,' he exaggerated, 'and the French king remains master of an immense revenue and credit without bounds.' Law seemed on the brink of shifting the balance of power. Britain had to respond, the ambassador warned, or suffer an immediate decline in relative standing.[53]

A British counterattack, launched by the South Sea Company, was not slow in coming. In imitation of Law's recent operations, the company proposed to issue new stock early in 1720 to exchange for public debt valued at £31 million. Law viewed the design as an assault on his System which he was determined to repel.[54] A battle ensued in which Law's Compagnie des Indes and the South Sea Company competed to attract the same pool of mobile capital, which investors could move quickly from one financial centre to another using a network of bankers and correspondents. The managers of the French and British public credit systems fought one another in a battle to consolidate debt. Law manipulated diplomatic ties in an effort to protect his System. Abandoning his previous support for the Franco-British alliance, he threatened to throw in his lot with Dubois's enemies if the British ministry did not reign in his financial competitors. His rivals in London deployed tested tactics of financial warfare against him, and Law struck back in kind once it became clear that his strategy of shaking the alliance had failed to deliver results.

The South Sea scheme underlined the vulnerability of Law's System, threatening to draw capital away towards the London market. Law's position was tenuous because of the speculative fever he had helped stoke. He had driven up the value of shares in 1719 to finance his takeover of existing chartered trading companies and the royal mint, and then to raise capital to consolidate the public debt as equity in the Compagnie des Indes.[55] He depended in part on money from other financial centres, including London, Amsterdam, and Geneva, attracted to Paris by the enormous speculative gains to be made there. The London press carried stories about the opportunities for enrichment in Paris.[56] A few major British speculators set up shop in Paris, though most British investment in Law's System was handled by correspondents – individuals such as Richard Cantillon, James Colebrooke, and John Drummond, who managed stock professionally for others.[57]

Once even more attractive speculative opportunities appeared in London with the beginnings of the South Sea Bubble, Law's System came under pressure. One of the first great capitalist speculative bubbles, frenzied trading of South Sea shares would develop on London markets over the first half of 1720, only for prices to collapse spectacularly in the autumn. London markets threatened to draw British funds back across the Channel, and to pull foreign capital – including French money – in its wake. There was evidence as early as December 1719 of massive transfers of capital from Paris to London. Law's System wobbled, seeing a short-term drop of 25 per cent in share prices.[58]

Large capital transfers continued in January to the expanding London bull market.[59] Coinciding with this movement of money, Law's bank suffered a run which he believed had been co-ordinated between his enemies in France and foreign financial interests. He accused Stair of being involved, claiming the ambassador had the backing of the British ministry.[60] According to one source, 'the publick stocks here fell mightily of a sudden and there was a great run upon the Bank, it was believ'd here that it proceeded from a combination chiefly in England with some people in Holland and some here'. It was said that 'the two Mr. L—s [Law and his brother] were convinced it was so, and that England had a main hand in it, and even that Ld. S—rs [Stair] had concurr'd a good dale [deal] in it'.[61] In making his financial revolution, Law had elbowed aside leading elements of France's established financial class – men such as Samuel Bernard and Antoine Crozat. These financiers might be expected to participate in an attack on his bank. Moreover, Bernard had friendly relations with Stair, and close ties with financial circles in the Dutch Republic and Britain.[62] Orchestrated runs on banks were not uncommon in the cut and thrust of financial politics in this period, so it is not unrealistic to think that Law's bank was the target of such an attack.[63]

Certainly, hostility to Law was growing in Britain, where a press campaign had been launched against him late the previous year. Dubois was told that the Compagnie des Indes inspired 'an incredible jealousy in this country'. The East India Company, it was said, would petition parliament to make it illegal for Britons to invest in its French rival – an echo of the Darien scheme a generation before. Late in 1719 Law complained that an English newspaper had represented his company as 'Chimerical'.[64] Daniel Defoe attacked Law's System early the next year in *The Chimera, or, The French Way of Paying National Debts Laid Open*, which ruthlessly exposed the poor prospects of the Compagnie des Indes, and predicted that it would soon collapse.[65] Law felt it necessary to defend himself in *A Full and Impartial Account of the Company of Mississippi* (1720), suggesting the continued importance of London capital in the health of the System.[66] He continued to complain of his treatment by the London press.[67]

Law hoped to demonstrate to George I's ministers that they would pay a high political price if they permitted the South Sea scheme to continue. He sabotaged talks to resolve disputes over the boundaries of French and British possession in America (a problem that would come back to haunt

Franco-British relations after 1748). The British commissioner sent by the Board of Trade, Daniel Pulteney (cousin of the later Patriot leader, William Pulteney), claimed that Law had scuttled the negotiations.[68] The Scot told Pulteney that he planned 'to improve as much as possible the French sugar Plantations, & to beat us entirely out of the sugar trade'.[69] Law exploited tensions over the future of Gibraltar in an effort to destabilise the position of Dubois, Britain's key diplomatic partner in France.[70] He even plotted with Jacobites, who hoped that the Scot would supply money for a Russian invasion of Britain to restore the exiled James Stuart.[71] Stair told his political masters that Law had switched sides, and that instead of supporting the Franco-British alliance he now embraced a pro-Spanish, pro-Jacobite, and anti-Hanoverian stance.[72]

Once forced to see Law as an enemy rather than an ally, officials in Britain began to grasp what a threat the System represented. Stanhope told a correspondent in April 1720 that if Law's financial revolution 'came to be established and to take root . . . the Emperor, England and Holland united will not be in a position to oppose France'.[73] Embracing the logic of jealousy of credit, he saw that if Law were successful in France this would check any coalition of other European powers to resist French aggression. The System threatened to overthrow the balance of power.

But if Law destroyed the alliance it might lead to the collapse of his own System. Were France once again to embrace Spain the position of the South Sea Company would have been shaken, as its profits depended on good relations with Madrid. Yet investors in the System would surely have been unnerved by a break with Britain. Law is unlikely to have risked the possible fallout. George I thought as much. 'It seems to me that it is he who ought most to hope for a perfect union,' he told an agent of Dubois; 'Does he think that peace does not suit his System?'[74] In fact, Law quickly backed away from a rupture with Britain, and gave up his previous efforts to jeopardise good relations. He told Crawfurd that 'his intention never was to advise a rupture with Great Britain, nor would he ever doe it'.[75] Stair's successor, Sir Robert Sutton, had 'cause to be satisfy'd with the Conversations I have had with him, in which with the greatest air of Sincerity he hath professed all the Respect and Veneration imaginable for His Majesty's Person, & his extreme Desire to be well in the opinion of His Maj[ty] & His Ministers'.[76]

Law had changed tack, but Stair and Pulteney for some time feared that he planned a different form of aggression – an attack on London financial markets meant to scuttle the South Sea Bubble.[77] Convinced that the Scot had acquired huge holdings of South Sea Company shares, Pulteney believed he planned to 'make such a strong and sudden push on our stocks as we may not be able to stand'.[78] Stair reported that Law and his cronies hoped to trigger a financial panic by suddenly selling off their shares. Rumours circulated, perhaps spread by Law and his supporters, of vast acquisitions of South Sea Company stock.[79] If he could take down the South Sea Company, Stair surmised, Law would shore up his own position in France. The ambassador implored his bosses in London to consult City men 'to prevent ourselves being destroyed by our enemies with our own arms'.[80] For his part, Pulteney believed Law's prospective raid on British stocks was meant to suck money out of London capital markets and back into the System: 'Mr. Law certainly intends to make a run on our Funds, and . . . he will at the same time declare a higher dividend on his stocks to engage those whom He can frighten out of our stocks to place their mony here.'[81]

Law certainly talked about a raid on London markets, and there is some evidence that he tried to orchestrate one. He boasted that 'the jealousy of neighbouring nations' would be unable to ruin his System. If his enemies sought to do so, he could 'ruin their credit' by forcing French shareholders to repatriate their money.[82] In June 1720 Pulteney suggested that 'something will soon be done to oblige all French subjects to withdraw their effects out of foreign funds'.[83] An edict to this effect was issued commanding subjects of Louis XV with funds in foreign companies to remit them home within two months.[84] But, Pulteney notes, it had still to be published.[85] His political credit falling in France in parallel with the stock of his company, Law may have lacked the authority to force through the measure. Rumours circulated in July of another attempt to get French subjects to withdraw their money from Britain.[86] The South Sea Bubble popped a few months later without any help from Law, the victim of a liquidity crisis in London markets apparently caused by the enforcement of the 'Bubble Act', passed, ironically, to shore up the value of South Sea stock by suppressing competing, unauthorised joint-stock companies.[87]

Law's System did not long survive its rival. He fled France in December 1720, eventually finding refuge in Venice, where he died in 1729. The South Sea Bubble did not prove the critical factor in sinking the prospects for Law's companies; his schemes were overly ambitious, he made major errors, and he had powerful enemies in France.[88] However, it was not misguided to view the rival debt-consolidation scheme as a menace. When speculative capital began to move in volume from Paris to London, drawn by the South Sea scheme, the implications were damaging for Law's System. In response to this attack from abroad he had so long feared, Law shook the alliance with Britain he had initially helped construct. When these tactics failed, he fell back on the same strategy as the financiers behind the South Sea scheme, and tried to orchestrate a market panic in London as a last-ditch means to rescue his own fortunes, though this too proved futile.

THE AFTERLIFE OF JEALOUSY OF CREDIT

The Scot's dream of bringing about a financial revolution that would turn France into an economic powerhouse remained unrealised, but down to the 1780s continued to inspire French financial projectors, political economists, and officials. Like Law, they generally favoured peace. International rivalries should be fought out on an economic plane, they argued – a terrain on which France might expect to triumph if it modernised its public credit. Jealousy of credit persisted. Projectors proposed schemes to emulate Britain's financial institutions, but also to attack and destroy them. Stratagems of this sort proliferated in the 1720s and 1730s, as during all the subsequent wars of the century. Indeed, during the American War, French officials worked to draw Dutch investment into the French public debt, and to bankrupt Britain. The continuing attraction of public credit schemes in the mould of Law's tends to undercut the idea that the French were simply too traumatised by the System to contemplate financial revolution again before the 1790s. Rather, the British model may have seemed too susceptible to foreign interference, too exposed to external shocks, too unstable to justify imitation.

For their part, British officials observed the progress of French credit warily; they worried periodically that France would seek to launch an assault on British public credit, or to draw foreign money into the French funds. Some British politicians regarded their own funding system as a vulnerability, and envied French financial arrangements which appeared more stable. We are prone to think of public credit as a facilitator of war in the eighteenth century.

And rightly so. Wars could not have continued so long, and might not in some cases have been started in the first place if credit had not been available to cover the gap between what states could raise in taxation and what they needed to keep armies on campaign and fleets at sea. But there is another side to this story: at some point in every major war, concerns about public credit drove the warring parties to the conference table. The use of public credit to fund wars entailed risks and carried heavy costs – constitutional, fiscal, and commercial. Officials understood the dangers of credit and would have appreciated David Hume's witticism that 'princes and states fighting and quarrelling, amidst their debts, funds, and public mortgages', were like 'a match of cudgel-playing fought in a China shop'.[89]

After 1720 Law's ideas continued to enjoy a real appeal in France. While the regent lived, the Scot aspired to return to France and to revive his System, albeit on a less grandiose basis.[90] He would not trouble the alliance with Britain, he promised, but by reviving French credit would render the monarchy less dependent on its partner.[91] This was not to be, yet champions of Law's ideas called, in his absence, for a new system of public credit to reverse the deflation and recession of the mid-1720s. Banks or paper money would reinvigorate commerce, they claimed. Some called once again for the monarchy's debt to be consolidated as equity in the Compagnie des Indes. Law's views on finance and international politics found a home in the company, which though reduced by his enemies, remained the institutional nexus of the great Mississippians – the investors whom the System had enriched, and who continued, in some cases, to champion Law's ideas.[92]

In the early 1730s, projectors launched a new wave of paper-money proposals, bank schemes, and debt-consolidation projects. They directed many of these to the French foreign minister, Germain-Louis Chauvelin, regarded as well-disposed to innovation and apparently set to assume power as first minister if the aged Cardinal Fleury died. The problem of financing the War of the Polish Succession (1733–35) further stimulated such designs.[93] While jealousy of credit marks some of this material (one proposal to turn the Compagnie des Indes into a bank concludes that 'this public credit will give us a superiority over our neighbours that will make them tremble'), the pacific hopes associated with Law's System also found an echo.[94] Jean-François Melon, the Scot's one-time secretary, developed a peace project in his *Essai politique sur le commerce* (1734).

An expansion of the money supply might help renew the wealth and power of the French kingdom. Like his former patron, Melon looked to manufacturing for a domestic market to renovate the French economy, and relegated foreign trade to a secondary role.[95] Another of Law's former lieutenants, the political economist Nicolas Dutot, echoed Law's commerce-versus-conquest theme, but with a different emphasis to Melon's. Picking up on the Scot's efforts to win over French port interests, Dutot held that foreign trade and shipping would prove the key to expanding French prosperity and power. This had been Law's true objective, he argued. France must avoid war, however, which would tend only to enervate the kingdom, as it had under Louis XIV.[96]

In Britain, Patriot critics of Robert Walpole identified the public debt as Britain's Achilles heel and regularly lambasted the prime minister for failing to discharge it.[97] The taxes that funded public borrowing made Britain uncompetitive, they claimed – a critique of Walpole's reliance on customs and excise, and his aspiration to do away with the land tax in peacetime.[98] Indirect taxes, Patriots complained, drove up the cost of living, increased the cost of labour, and priced British goods out of foreign markets.[99] Too much of the interest was paid to foreigners, transferring money out of the country. Shocks to investor confidence exposed the entire system to breakdown and capital flight.[100] Walpole remained unconcerned.[101] He had been in the political wilderness when his compatriots Stair, Stanhope, and Pulteney were struggling to manage Law. Walpole's archenemy, erstwhile Patriot leader Henry St John, Viscount Bolingbroke, took the gloomiest position. The nation would be vulnerable until a considerable portion of the debt was paid off, he warned in 1749 after the War of the Austrian Succession. France too was financially depleted, but not as severely as Britain, and it had in place a mechanism for liberating itself from debt in the form of the self-retiring life annuities (*rentes viagères*) which the French monarchy relied upon to raise loans. 'They, who get first out of a distress common to us and our neighbours,' Bolingbroke warned, 'will give the law to the rest.'[102]

After the war, the administration of Henry Pelham pressed to lower the burden of the debt by refinancing it at a lower rate of interest. With the support of Sir John Barnard, whose own debt-consolidation scheme failed to receive parliamentary assent in 1737, Pelham introduced a bill to reduce the interest rate on government stock immediately from 4 per cent to 3.5 per cent, and subsequently to 3 per cent by 1758. The measure threatened to reimburse creditors their principal if they did not accept the reduction, and the vast majority grudgingly assented.[103] In his analysis of the scheme, the French political economist François Véron de Forbonnais presented it as a response to a competitiveness crisis. In his reading, investments in risk-free securities paying a high rate of return raised the rate of profit required to compensate merchants for the greater risks run in commercial ventures, making them uncompetitive with their Dutch peers.[104] For most of Pelham's colleagues, the reduction of interest served rather to shore up Britain's international standing by demonstrating that it was not a spent force financially. Pelham had substantially reduced the weight of the debt relative to taxation, and therefore demonstrated the state's capacity to borrow more without immediate tax increases. 'You cannot conceive how much Weight, Credit, & Solidity It is universally thought abroad to give to the King, & his Government,' exulted his brother, the duke of Newcastle.[105] William Bentinck, duke of Portland, congratulated Pelham on 'the great weight this affair will give to England on the continent'.[106]

But not everyone thought the reduction of interest adequate to deliver the nation from the threat the national debt represented. The kingdom had to compete more effectively with France, which had adopted a sinking fund (*caisse d'amortissement*) to reduce its debt, warned one pamphleteer: 'that Nation which first eases itself of its Burthen will be enabled to give the Law to the other, and to the rest of Europe'. Within fifteen years the French would have discharged 30 million sterling; if Britain failed to keep pace it would be powerless to block their bid for universal monarchy.[107] Complaints about public borrowing in a similar vein continued through the following two decades.[108] In a 1752 essay, David Hume reiterated in the starkest terms the constitutional dangers of public debt. Left unchecked, the debt would mount until it collapsed under the weight of some new emergency, or some daring effort to reduce its weight. Hume supposed that debt must incapacitate Britain, in time, from maintaining the balance of power – a failure which might even lead to its conquest by an enemy. The ultimate remedy was voluntary bankruptcy: 'either the nation must destroy public credit, or public credit will destroy the nation'.[109]

City financiers warned that the reduction of interest might backfire and cause mobile capital to flood back across the Channel into the French funds.

Much higher interest could now be earned in Paris, warned John Page, Newcastle's trusted financial adviser, and 'many both Dutch and English, being dissatisfied with the then late reduction of their Interest, had been drawing their Money out of ours to Invest it in the French Funds'. According to Page, this capital flight had been the underlying cause of a credit crisis in London during the summer of 1753.[110] The problem was not simply the reduction in interest: 'confidence in French Faith, respecting their Public Credit, grows every day; and has been growing with very little Interruption, ever since the commencement of Fleury's administration'. Page represented the improvement of French credit as part of a strategy to achieve universal monarchy by peaceful, commercial means. 'France now seems to be pushing as strongly for Universal Commerce as Lewis the 14th for what we call Universal Power,' cautioned Page. 'I own myself more afraid, at this hour, of French Credit and French Commerce than of French Fleets and French Armys.'[111]

As these remarks suggest, jealousy of credit endured in part because France and Britain continued to compete for international capital. In 1740, on the eve of the War of the Austrian Succession, foreigners owned perhaps 20 per cent of Britain's debt, and perhaps 12 per cent of France's.[112] While the French monarchy eschewed the British path, the pressures of geopolitical competition induced France to embrace some of the procedures that reassured creditors and allowed Britain to borrow more cheaply. The contrôleur général, Jean-Baptiste de Machault d'Arnouville, set up the *caisse d'amortissement* (sinking fund), alluded to above, after the war, which quickly turned French debt into a more appealing option for foreign capitalists. 'The bare creation of a sinking fund,' claimed Isaac de Pinto, a Dutch-Jewish financier and political economist, 'subdued the old prejudices, by which credit had been destroyed.'[113] Growing confidence among creditors drove down interest rates on French debt in secondary markets in the early 1750s.[114] Anecdotal evidence suggests that French annuities appealed increasingly to foreigners. The British diplomat William Mildmay reported from Paris that the French, because of the 'great Interest they offer', were able to 'allure over vast sums of money', large enough to alter the exchange rate between sterling and the livre.[115] Such investment continued even after the start of the Seven Years' War in 1756. Late in 1757, the Anglo-Dutch financier Joshua van Neck and his son-in-law Thomas Walpole (a nephew of Sir Robert) placed orders for a total of £84,000 in *rentes viagères*.[116] The generous interest rates available on French annuities were simply too tempting for some Britons to pass up.

Predictably, the renewal of conflict in the mid-1750s elicited new French schemes to attack British public credit. On the eve of the Seven Years' War, Forbonnais proposed to the contrôleur général, Jean Moreau de Séchelles, to set up a bank modelled on the Bank of England which he claimed would sap British credit and draw mobile European capital back across the Channel.[117] During the war, projectors barraged the finance ministry with schemes to revolutionise public credit.[118] According to Jacques Vincent de Gournay, the eminent intendant of commerce, a system of public credit like Britain's was 'necessary if we wish to maintain the balance of wealth, of men, and of power in Europe'.[119] Like Law before him, Gournay regarded the monarchy's financial system as a drag on enterprise and commercial vitality. Leading ministers appeared open to financial innovation.[120] The future cardinal de Bernis, then minister of foreign affairs, claimed France would have to adopt a public credit model emulating Britain's or lose the war.[121] It was said when Étienne de Silhouette was made contrôleur général in 1759 that he planned to remodel French credit in a revival of Law's System.[122]

In fact, Silhouette was sceptical of the British model, seeing it as too insecure – a sentiment he absorbed, in part, from the Patriot opposition to Walpole in Britain, where he had lived in the 1730s.[123] He threw his energies into planning a French invasion of England intended to incite panic in London capital markets.[124] His opposite numbers in Britain worried about such a prospect. 'I cannot help thinking,' wrote Philip Yorke, earl of Hardwicke, 'that even such an attempt, made in a formidable manner, by the effect it would have on our Funds and public Credit, would do more towards disabling England from carrying on the War, than all the Interruptions such a Plan can give to our Trade.'[125] 'We stand in Danger of being seized with a General Pannick, no less Destructive to Public Credit than to an Army,' warned Page.[126] In every succeeding war, French schemes to land an army in Britain aimed less to conquer the country than to strike at its credit.[127]

Taking such views into account, one can better understand by French officials were so reticent about adopting a British-style financial revolution. When it came to raising and funding debt, Britain succeeded admirably, but its funding model appeared exposed to external shocks and vulnerable to capital flight. The long-established French financiers had one great merit, comparatively speaking. The mutual dependence of the monarchy and this moneyed class served to territorialise what would otherwise have been a mobile capital capable of flowing to opportunities in other markets. If the financiers were parasitic, they were also a captive class of capitalists – their fortunes entirely dependent on their service to the monarchy. Thus, the temporary collapse of French public credit in 1759, when news of the conquest of Quebec reached Europe, meant only a partial capital flight to other markets.[128] The monarchy was quickly able to assemble a new coalition of financiers, led by the court banker Jean-Joseph de Laborde, to meet its needs for short-term funding.

Despite the remarkable success of its public credit system, fears about debt haunted the politicians who led Britain out of the Seven Years' War – indeed, impelled their search for peace. The young George III and his favourite and former tutor, John Stuart, earl of Bute, had fully absorbed the horror of public debt that haunted many Patriots.[129] The enormous increase in the magnitude of public borrowing over the war appeared to them to leave the nation vulnerable to a brutal credit crisis. An incisive analysis of the financial situation by Bute's lieutenant, Charles Jenkinson, identified an impending catastrophe. The costs of public borrowing had almost doubled between 1755 and 1762. Taxes raised during the war to fund loans would stop the Exchequer from paying down the debt using the sinking fund. There would be no surplus from ordinary taxation to pay into the fund because new taxes adopted during the war had so reduced the yield on existing levies. Jenkinson was most disturbed by the huge overhang of unfunded debt, equivalent to more than a year of public revenues. The government would have to borrow the entire sum necessary to cover debt service, the civil list (the annual sum, granted by Parliament in 1760, paid to the monarchy to cover official expenses), and military spending in 1763. In a serious credit crunch, Jenkinson warned, unfunded debt threatened to become 'meer waste paper'. Prospective creditors understood this, he emphasised, as also did 'the Enemy, who is to take the Advantage of the Situation'.[130]

Those who held out for a continuation of the war and a Carthaginian peace with France conceded that the conflict had been enormously expensive, but argued that the debt would easily be paid if Britain held onto all its conquests.[131] Their critics worried that new colonial acquisitions would only drive up costs. Weighing the gains of the war against its expenses, the Whig politician George

Bubb Dodington, an occasional adviser to Bute, fretted that 'if the account were made up in a mercantile way, I am not sure that the balance would appear in our favour'.[132]

From this perspective, British financial strength and French weakness after 1759, paradoxically, redounded to the benefit of the French because they could not load themselves with vast new debts. 'France already feels its full distress; ours is not yet come,' argued the literary hack Edward Richardson in one of the most successful products of Bute's pro-peace propaganda. 'France supports the Expence of this War by an immediate and cruel Taxation; we borrow immense Sums, the Burden of which we shall feel hereafter.'[133] It was French strategy to hold out long enough to overstrain Britain's credit, claimed another pamphleteer.[134] Bute shared these fears. Through Jenkinson, he sought 'as exact accounts as possible of the present state of the French finances'. Richard Neville, secretary to the duke of Bedford, who was in Paris negotiating the final details of the peace, assured the prime minister of French financial capacity to continue fighting.[135]

Debt hawks feared that increased taxation would push up the cost of labour and price British goods out of foreign markets. Bubb looked with foreboding to a postwar future where 'you will find yourselves loaded with the additional interest of £50,000,000 . . . far the greatest part of which will ultimately fall upon the labour or the materials of your manufactures'.[136] Thomas Whately, who advised George Grenville, Bute's successor as prime minister in 1763, analysed the problem in a pamphlet serialised in the *Gentleman's Magazine* and translated into French under Grenville's name. He foresaw an impending crisis of competitiveness. Taxes that drove up the cost of everyday items, such as excises on beer and malt, were a particular burden. 'Rival Nations who were not before, may now be able in many articles to undersell us at Foreign Markets,' he warned, 'and even become Competitors at our own.'[137] This kind of pessimism about public debt and its consequences for taxation, prices, and competitiveness created pressures to make and keep the peace with France. Here was a classic case of negative feedback. A war fought to protect British commerce had generated costs that threatened, in the long run, to strangle the prosperity it was supposed to secure.

Apprehensions about debt had also played a key role in bringing peace in 1713 and 1748, as they would again in 1782. In the 1710s, the concerns were partly constitutional. Tories, as we have seen (above, pp. 44–5), objected to the explosion of public debt sustained by taxes on land which undercut the landed interest and raised up Whig financiers and merchants to positions of new eminence. This constitutional perspective was not shared by the Whig government that led Britain out of the War of the Austrian Succession a generation later, but Prime Minister Henry Pelham's concerns about the overextension of public credit certainly hastened the war's end. 'Credit was sinking, & the Stocks falling,' Pelham remarked, 'upon hearing nothing from Aix[-la-Chapelle], that look'd like a Finishing.'[138] During the American War, the British debt soared from £127 million to £243 million, leaving nearly 60 per cent of government revenue mortgaged.[139] William Petty, earl of Shelburne had long worried that the debt would undercut competitiveness, and subvert the constitution.[140] Almost the entirety of the state's borrowings had been run up in wars with France, the only other power that could mobilise financial resources sufficient to compete with it. Only through an accord with the French could Britain wind down its baneful addiction to public credit.

Following the Seven Years' War, both France and Britain focused on financial retrenchment; the overhang of debt from the war made them wary of further conflict despite the French desire for revenge. Paris could not compete for mobile international capital in the aftermath of the 1759 partial bankruptcy. Indeed it was not until the 1770s that the finance ministry seriously explored this option again when the contrôleur général, the abbé Joseph-Marie Terray opened a French loan on the Amsterdam bourse.[141] Only when Jacques Necker, a Genevan with international banking connections, assumed direction of French finances on the eve of French entry into the American War did international capital again make up an important proportion of French borrowing. Investment from Geneva and other Swiss financial centres flowed towards Paris, as British officials were well aware.[142] Necker's successors relied on Dutch capital for the massive loans necessary to sustain the war effort, with more new Dutch money pouring into the French debt than into Britain's.[143]

During the American War, rival reform factions pursued French aggrandisement by trying to renovate the French financial system. Again, it was a question of replacing irrational military struggles with a surer – and safer – means to assure security and power. Necker believed that French entry into the American War had been a mistake, and once in power he reached out to Lord

North to try to find a negotiated settlement.[144] In his postwar writings, he rejected the notion that war could ever deliver benefits commensurate with its costs. Wars for trade or colonies were especially irrational: the high interest rates and heavy taxation conflict brought in its wake would always overbalance any gains. In Necker's view, France should try to secure itself instead by peacefully stewarding and augmenting its economic resources.[145] His vision of financial revolution was not as radical as Law's, but as his critics liked to emphasise, many of his practices in office recalled his Scottish predecessor. He worked to attract international capital into the French funds, especially from his native Geneva. He publicised public accounts to create confidence, most famously in the *Compte rendu au roi* (1781), intended to show that France remained a good credit risk despite heavy wartime borrowing. And he struck at the position of the financiers, seeking to move the funds of public money they controlled into a centralised treasury. For Necker, paper money might prove a useful supplement to hard currency, but he did not see it as the key to unleashing the potential of the French economy. He permitted the *caisse d'escompte*, a bank established in Paris in 1776 to discount commercial paper, to expand its issue of notes, but only modestly.[146]

The *caisse* had been set up by a rival reform faction led by Isaac Panchaud, a British stockjobber with Swiss roots who had made and lost a fortune speculating on the shares of the British and French East India companies in the late 1760s and early 1770s.[147] For Panchaud, the *caisse* was to be the vehicle for a financial revolution on very much the same lines envisioned by Law. If the bank was allowed to expand its note issue, and if the Crown would accept these in payment of taxes, they would quickly become a national paper money, supplementing the monetary stock, pushing down interest rates, and stimulating the agricultural and commercial economy.[148] Joined with a revamped sinking fund, Panchaud argued, the *caisse d'escompte* would put French credit on a firmer footing than Britain's. It might even drive Britain into bankruptcy by drawing mobile European capital away from London and back to Paris. (Concerned, Shelburne kept a close eye on Panchaud's activities.[149]) Notwithstanding his rather shady past, Panchaud became a key councillor to the contrôleur général Jean-François Joly de Fleury. From this position, he steered a French strategy to direct new Dutch investment into the French public debt rather than into Britain's. This strategy continued under Charles-Alexandre de Calonne. The minister planned to extend to the *caisse* the privileges of a national bank in 1787 under the reforms he presented to the Assembly of Notables.[150] As in 1720, the kingdom appeared to be on the brink of a financial revolution, though the revolution that actually transpired was not the one planned by the minister, who was an early political casualty of the prerevolutionary crisis.

If capitalism is a system in which sovereign power is bent to serve private capital accumulation, and accumulation in turn serves the ends of sovereignty, if it is predicated on an implicit alliance between transnational-commercial and territorial-military forms of power, then public debt would appear the exemplary manifestation of a capitalist logic. In no form was the early modern alliance between sovereignty and capital clearer. Unable to tax the liquid wealth of merchants, which could easily be moved abroad or hidden, and unwilling to risk destroying the mercantile goose that laid the golden egg of commercial wealth, states created a new form of property, a promise to divert to the hands of the bearer future flows of taxation in the form of interest payments on public debt.[151] Historians have not considered how this complex shaped the international behaviour of eighteenth-century polities. The fact that debt was the lifeblood of the fiscal-military state made foreign trade strategically central, I suggest, and protecting this sector generated endemic conflict. The ability to borrow on a massive scale in turn facilitated wars fought to secure this trade by easing financial constraints on military mobilisation. In these ways public credit seems a structural source of geopolitical conflict in the capitalist inter-state order – so much so that Kant called for its proscription in the interests of perpetual peace.[152]

Yet it also created incentives to avoid or limit war, and even to find ways to transform the international system. Public debt is a classic instance of a negative feedback from war. Fought in part to secure the benefits of trade, debt threatened to sap the sources of future commercial vitality. France after the War of the Spanish Succession is an exemplary case. The enormous debts piled up during the conflict weighed on the prospects for future growth. The export of specie to supply armies and subsidise allies had depleted the money stock. Private capital accumulation had materialised in the guise of the *rentes*, but these became a further obstacle to commercial dynamism as they were illiquid and encouraged a deflationary policy to protect bondholders. The easy profits of financiers servicing the monarchy's fiscal and credit needs sucked money and enterprise out of the commercial sector and tended to orient policy to fiscalism rather than commercial development. Law's read on Britain was that it had turned this negative feedback into a virtuous circle by transforming public debt into a supplement to the money supply – a trick he hoped to emulate.

But Law aspired less to beat Britain at its own game than to transform the ground rules of capitalist geopolitics and to break France and its rivals out of an unfavourable equilibrium. If public credit was generally an extension of warmaking in the eighteenth century, his vision underscores a different potential. Though French officials planned attacks on British credit in wartime, schemes for a financial revolution to check British power were generally an extension of that 'perpetual and peaceful war of wits and industry' envisioned by Colbert. Law and his subsequent admirers viewed financial revolution less as a means to prepare for war than as a substitute for it. Paper money would be a vehicle to move from monetary scarcity to monetary abundance, and to stimulate an expansion of economic activity. According to Law, financial revolution would turn France into a benign commercial colossus – invulnerable to attack by its neighbours, liberated from the need for Spanish silver, and therefore peaceful and satisfied. He never suggested that paper money or debt consolidation were meant to ready the kingdom for new conquests; indeed, he rejected this objective outright. Law saw commerce rather than conquest as the key to power and security – a characteristic feature of political-economic thought in this period, and one to which we will return in the following chapters.

Law's view may have been naive. If the French monarchy had suddenly been released from financial constraint, what would have prevented it from returning to the warlike ways of the Sun King? But before we dismiss his vision, let us remember that public finance and an expansive monetary policy promote peaceful economic development today in almost every industrialised, capitalist nation. Modern public borrowing serves to sustain full employment, prop up aggregate demand, and build infrastructure. The point is not that Law was ahead of his time – a meaningless notion. Rather, the possibility that public credit might serve purposes beyond facilitating war was obvious from the beginning. Indeed, the Hartlib theorists who helped inspire Law saw an open-ended process of economic improvement as the chief point of the expansion of public credit.[153] Such an economic revolution might be channelled into expanded funding for war and conquest, but it also opened a road to prosperity and security without the need to struggle against other nations – potentially driving international rivalries into less destructive and hazardous forms.

Through peaceful development of its existing resources, Law argued, France could transform the international order, greatly reduce jealousy of trade and 'keep the peace of Europe'. When compared to the designs explored in the two preceding chapters, this is a strikingly unilateral vision for the stabilisation of global politics. I have focused so far mostly on strategies to remake the international order based on agreements between states. Through deals to establish freer trade, or to neutralise key commercial activities in case of future war, the most powerful commercial states could build a more stable and peaceful international environment. Law's scheme depended only on remaking the political economy of the French monarchy. The alliance with Britain that he at first supported seems merely an expedient to keep the System safe from outside attack while in its infancy. Such a partnership would be unnecessary once his financial revolution was complete. The same unilateralism marked William Paterson's vision. A fellow Scot and also a theorist of financial revolution, influenced like Law by the writings of the Hartlib circle, Paterson too dreamed of a world of peaceful commerce achieved through the establishment of a benign hegemony – in this case Britain's. But the means adopted could not have been more different. Paterson looked to free trade in the Americas, enforced by a muscular British navy, as the solution to jealousy of trade. Law proposed a qualified withdrawal from competition for global markets and the development of French resources at home.

It was mostly in France that unilateral visions flourished. Admittedly, there were echoes of Paterson's schemes in later British thought, notably in designs to forge a freer trade in the Caribbean in the late 1730s and again in the 1760s (analysed in Chapters 2 and 5). But the idea that one nation, by transforming its own political economy, could change the whole international order enjoyed peculiar appeal in France. A repeated refrain was that, following some major reordering of its political economy, the French monarchy would lead its European neighbours into a more pacific future where jealousy of trade was transcended (and where France would recapture its natural status as the arbiter of European politics). Law's former secretary, Jean-François Melon, gave the idea a new lease of life in the 1730s, as we will see in the next chapter. In a different vein, the Physiocrats argued from the 1750s that if France abandoned the Colbertist political-economic model it had pursued since Louis XIV, and embraced agriculture as the foundation of national wealth, it could escape the destructive race to dominate world trade and by so doing draw the rest of Europe into a new order where jealousy of trade might be a thing of the past. These were political-economic ideas that appealed in a nation anxious about its own place in the world, and facing an assertive Britain, whose leaders were only sporadically open to joint measures that might extricate both kingdoms from costly wars. Such projects were unrealistic, perhaps, in their aspiration for revolutionary economic transformation, and no less so in their geopolitical utopianism. For on its way to becoming an economic superpower, France must appear a dire threat to its neighbours' security. The kind of rapid economic development that these models envisioned is destabilising in a capitalist inter-state system – as the history of the 1720s and 1730s would show. It is to this story we turn next.

4

AN ELUSIVE BALANCE
The Long Peace and the Problem of Uneven Development

For more than a quarter of a century after 1713, peace prevailed between France and Britain – the most protracted period of relative harmony over the long century from the Glorious Revolution to the fall of Napoleon. Ill-assorted allies since the days of John Law and the abbé Dubois, the two kingdoms went their separate ways in 1731, only to preserve a wary détente down to the end of the decade. Favouring this policy of peace were the dominant political figures of the era, Sir Robert Walpole, Britain's prime minister from 1721 to 1742, and Cardinal André-Hercule de Fleury, Louis XV's chief minister in all but name from 1726 to 1743. Yet before either lost his grip on power, the long peace broke down. A state of undeclared war had developed by 1740, as Britain launched a military expedition to force open markets in Spanish America, and Louis XV sent the French navy to defend Spanish colonies. The old problem, not fully resolved in 1713, of the place of the Spanish monarchy and its New World resources in the geopolitical order had exploded anew. This conflict was soon subsumed by the larger War of the Austrian Succession (1740–48), the first general conflagration in Europe since 1713, and a prelude to the still more destructive Seven Years' War (1756–63).

In the 1720s, after the failure of Law's System and the bursting of the South Sea Bubble, France and Britain found a *modus vivendi* on a mix of strategic and political-economic grounds. To some degree, the long peace was an extended reaction against the rapid development of a fiscal-military state in both countries between 1689 and 1713. Fleury's preference for peace derived in part from the desire to avoid the erosion of fiscal privilege that had been a hallmark of Louis XIV's reign, when, to pay for war, the monarchy had introduced universal taxes falling on the nobility and privileged office holders. One of the cardinal's first acts on coming to power was to abandon the *cinquantième*, a new tax to be used to establish a sinking fund adopted by his predecessor, and destined to fall on all landed wealth, including that of the church.[1] Across the Channel, Walpole sought to lift the tax burden from landowners, on whose votes he depended in Parliament, and to expand the efficiency and range of excise.[2] These fiscal priorities reinforced his commitment to avoid war, which must immediately lead to raising the land tax.

Though French officials worried about the privileges Britain had acquired in the Spanish-American trade, seeing these as a threat to the balance of commercial power, they had to tolerate the Utrecht settlement as long as they needed British goodwill to keep Austria in check. Indeed, in certain respects, the Fleury administration proved willing to foster Britain's empire at the expense of its own, allowing the French tobacco monopoly to buy nearly all its product from British merchants who imported it from the Chesapeake. Yet the ministry quietly fostered colonial trade, which grew quickly in this period, propelled by the expansion of sugar production in the Caribbean. Louis XV declined to build the kind of navy that a growing commercial empire might require for its security. Naval funding under Fleury was a fraction of what it had once been under Louis XIV, or what it would be again after 1748.[3] A policy adopted to appease Britain, keeping the fleet small also required the kingdom to avoid war with the Maritime Powers.

An intellectual framework that affirmed the value of peace as a condition for commercial flourishing, and underscoring the ruinous costs of war, was one of the ideological foundations of the long peace. Walpole loudly and repeatedly affirmed that peace was the best strategy for a trading state – none more so than Britain. French officials said the same thing, but assumed France would be the chief gainer by avoiding war. Political-economic thinking based on this assumption flourished in both kingdoms. In Britain, veteran analysts such as Daniel Defoe lauded Walpole's peace policy. The publication of Jean-François Melon's *Essai politique sur le commerce* in 1734 sparked a wide-ranging exchange of views in France about how the kingdom might compete with Britain commercially while keeping the peace. Historians have typed both Melon and Defoe as apostles for the idea that trade naturally conduces to peace between nations. But it would be more accurate to classify their thinking as a pacific commercial realpolitik. They regarded trade as a terrain of struggle between states; peace fostered the commercial aggrandisement of those best placed to take advantage of it. The same general outlook could favour war when only military action seemed likely to preserve a balance of commercial power.

Peace itself could seem a threat to security when it fostered the rapid ascension of one power at the expense of its rivals. In Britain, the Patriot opposition to Walpole began to suspect that Fleury was trying to seize a position of supremacy in Europe by fostering French commerce and colonies, achieving by stealth what Louis XIV had failed to win by intimidation and conquest. The long peace had fostered the rapid growth of French trade and colonies, while Britain's commerce appeared comparatively stagnant. French trade was indeed growing quickly – more quickly than Britain's – a trend sustained down to the 1780s, when France would surpass its rival as Europe's greatest trading state in absolute terms.[4] Patriots peddled an 'adulterated mercantilism', construing war as a means to secure Britain's commercial future, and favouring British colonial expansion at French and Spanish expense.[5] They mobilised the mercantile classes of London and other commercial cities behind this bellicose policy – not the mercantile elite tied to the chartered companies and Walpole's coalition, but middling merchants, especially those trading in the Atlantic economy.[6] They rallied to a war with Spain, as we saw in Chapter 2 (pp. 110–11), as a way to break into the Spanish Empire in America and rebalance an international system France threatened to dominate. William Pitt the Elder rode a similar wave of sentiment to power in the Seven Years' War, seeking to expand the British Empire and smash France as a serious contender for commerce and colonies. The end of the long peace highlights a structural instability in a capitalist order where commerce is an underpinning of power: the problem of uneven development. Peace itself can come to seem a threat to security when it fosters the rapid economic growth of one power at the expense of others.

The War of the Austrian Succession prompted a peace initiative in 1745 mounted by parts of the old Fleury and Walpole coalitions. Major business interests – the Farmers General in France, who collected many of the kingdom's taxes and operated the royal tobacco monopoly, and British commercial interests tied to the tobacco trade, which benefited from re-export markets in France – mobilised to broker a settlement. Though unsuccessful, this peace overture underlines another political-economic element sustaining the long peace, and is suggestive of the potential a normalisation of trade relations from 1713 might have held for limiting conflict between the two nations. Exploring this incident also permits a fuller assessment of the ways Britain's fiscal-military state co-opted mercantile interests that might otherwise have been disposed to peace.

Though it ultimately failed to secure Patriot objectives, the British expedition to the Caribbean, which ended the long peace, affirmed what many French officials and merchants had long claimed – that the British sought universal monarchy based on engrossing the commerce of the New World. Without its colonies and the Atlantic commerce they sustained, France would be locked permanently into a second-class status. In this light, the small navy maintained under Fleury came to seem a strategic blunder; France needed a larger fleet to guard its colonies and trade, increasingly the foundations of its power. Its naval weakness had exposed it and its Spanish ally to British predation. After the War of the Austrian Succession, officials committed to this perspective sought to persuade the political nation that France's geopolitical future lay in the Atlantic, not Central Europe. In the 1750s, the Cádiz merchant turned intendant of commerce, Jacques Vincent de Gournay, fostered the translation of British works of political economy into French, and encouraged a circle of protégés to publish writings of their own in the same vein. Yet while calling for a larger navy, these commentators affirmed that French commerce required peace to flourish. The monarchy scrambled to rebuild a substantial French fleet after 1748, and the security of New France emerged as a key problem in Franco-British relations – laying the ground for the Seven Years' War, which erupted on the American borderlands between the French and British empires.

COMMERCE VERSUS CONQUEST: POLITICAL ECONOMY IN WALPOLE'S BRITAIN

One of the foundations of the long Franco-British peace of the 1720s and 1730s was Walpole's position that peace best fostered British commercial prosperity. This was also the view of the principal British writers on trade of the 1720s and 1730s. But this stance contained a contradiction. If pacific commercial development was the path to power and security, might not Britain's enemies take advantage of the long peace to threaten the balance of power by fostering rapid commercial growth? The Patriot Whigs who opposed Walpole suspected that peace had, in fact, fostered the disproportionate expansion of French trade, and that France was again on the path to universal monarchy. Peace itself had become a menace to the balance of commercial power. Patriots saw in Spain's interdiction of British shipping in the Caribbean an incitement to war that would not only protect British navigation and punish an aggressor, but permit the nation to break out of a cycle of relative decline by seizing new commercial opportunities in Spanish America. Walpole's reluctance to engage Spain in war might be used to oust him and establish a Patriot regime more favourable to the future expansion of British trade and capable of checking the French menace.

Peace offered the best means for a trading nation to build wealth and sustain power, while war undermined trade and thereby sapped the foundations of power. So maintained Walpole. During the War of the Polish Succession (1733–35), Britain remained neutral, a decision the prime minister would defend as 'the safest and the wisest conduct for the general interest of a trading people'. 'I have seen how destructive the effects, even of a successful war, have been,' Walpole observed, and 'I always have been, and always will be, an advocate for peace.'[7] The logic of this view emerges most clearly in the position Walpole took against war with Spain in the late 1730s, as we saw in Chapter 2 (p. 109). Peace and diplomacy, more effectively than war, would secure the wealth of Spanish America, he believed. Military action would cost Britain a more valuable trade with peninsular Spain, which the French would be quick to engross. Moreover, the British had more to lose in a Caribbean war than the Spanish – colonies, shipping, and the property of the South Sea Company. Having little navigation of its own, Spain was relatively invulnerable.[8] Finally, there was the question of the expense of war: all efforts to pay down the national debt since Utrecht would be set at naught; indeed a war with Spain would add millions to the debt, and if the conflict became general, strain public credit.[9]

That Britain could augment its wealth and power most effectively by using well-contrived policies to pursue commercial development peacefully was the message of much of the most widely read public commentary on trade of the Walpole years. Nowhere are the assumptions – and ambiguities – of this line of thinking more evident than in the writing of Daniel Defoe. We have encountered Defoe before as a journalist working for Robert Harley, editing the principal government journal calling for freer trade with France in 1713 (see above, p. 48). By the late 1720s Defoe was still making a living from his pen, producing an enormous volume of writings focused on the challenges and potential of British commerce and manufacturing. In the *Advantages of Peace and Commerce* (1729), he argued that commerce rather than military might constituted the road to power. 'Peace and Trade have so far got the Start of War and the Sword,' he affirmed, 'that the *Trading Nations* of the World are now become infinitely superior in Wealth and Power, to those who might properly be call'd the *Fighting Nations*, and whose Grandure depended on the Extent of their Dominions, and number of conquer'd Countries.'[10]

At the most basic level, this argument reflected what appeared a fundamental shift in the nature and foundations of power that had emerged in the previous century. It evoked the emergence of the Dutch Republic as a great power on the basis of commerce, allowing the Dutch to defeat the militaristic and commercially backward Spanish monarchy. This theme was not new for Defoe. Notably in debates over the Anglo-Scottish Union in 1707, he had argued that the spirit of commerce was more important to the power of modern nations than the martial spirit.[11] The theme re-emerged in his writing in the late 1720s against the background of the war scares of that period. Defoe praised the forbearance of the Walpole ministry: 'I cannot but pay a great Deference to the Endeavours of those Ministers,' he wrote, 'who, notwithstanding the Murmurs of the People, apply themselves to preserving the Peace of *Europe*, and preventing a war.'[12] The policy was wise, because peace fostered the growth of trade while war injured it, and Britain with its great navigation had the most to lose.[13] Here emerged a second dimension of the commerce-versus-conquest trope: peace rather than war best fostered the power-political interests of trading states. This claim too found confirmation in the Dutch example. The financial overstretch of fighting a series of great wars to check and contain Louis XIV's France had undermined Dutch power and reduced the republic to the second rank of states.

This preference for peace, however, did not imply a conceptual separation of commerce and violence, or that Defoe saw no role for coercion in pursuing profits. Indeed he implicitly saw violence, when deployed by merchants, as an aspect of trade. The empire of the Dutch East India Company in the East Indies, he noted admiringly, was 'raised by Commerce, without the least

Assistance from the Government'. The greatness of the British nation was all owing to trade, none of it to conquest, he also affirmed. Trade built an empire in America, in colonies settled by Britons who had subjected nobody – excepting, he had immediately to acknowledge, the slaves they had brought there to work, and the indigenous peoples they had 'destroyed and cut off'. Commerce for Defoe evidently could embrace massive violence against non-Europeans. His preference for commerce over conquest meant not eschewing violence, but building the political framework for a thriving extra-European trade without burdening taxpayers with the costs of state-driven empire-building. In other remarks, he allows for conquests directed against Europeans for commercial ends. Defoe credited Tsar Peter I's wars against Sweden, by which Russia gained access to the Baltic, with giving it a chance of 'launching thus out into Trade'.[14] Here there could be no commerce without prior conquest, because the Swedish Empire blocked it.

But Defoe rejected the idea that war served the ends of commercial competition among established trading states. Louis XIV's wars had impoverished his merchants, overburdened the kingdom with taxes, forced damaging manipulations of the coinage, and sunk the public credit. Instead of fighting one another, he recommended that the British, French, Dutch, and Spanish co-operate against common threats like Barbary pirates. Following a joint expedition against this menace, he proposed, the trading states might colonise the coast of North Africa, taking a share in proportion to their contribution to the venture.[15] Conquest, again in the service of commerce, but now imagined as a European consortium displacing the Islamic sovereignties of the southern Mediterranean.

In yet another layer of ambiguity, Defoe acknowledged that the peaceful power of trade represented a new kind of threat to the security of all – commercial ascendancy a new form of conquest. Louis XIV understood that the way to make France 'the Terror of the World', was not by success in arms but by 'encouraging the Commerce of his own Country'.[16] Even global empire might be possible on a commercial basis for 'if any one nation could govern trade, that Nation would govern the World'.[17] Defoe's writings on trade in this period have been described by his biographer as a plan for British world domination.[18] Yet we are not to imagine a traditional territorial empire. Defoe seems rather to have envisioned an unchallengeable economic supremacy based on industry and improvement, extended geographically to 'unimproved' parts of the non-European world by the kinds of free-enterprise imperialism that had built the British Atlantic colonies.

If a nation sought to achieve power by such means, might not war be a necessary and legitimate check on its designs? Defoe never says so, and it seems far from his preoccupations in the late 1720s, when he thought it was Britain that had the potential to achieve such dominance. But this had been an essential element of British involvement in the War of the Spanish Succession – fought in part to check the emergence of a French universal monarchy of trade – a struggle of which Defoe approved, while deploring its economic costs. In the post-Utrecht context, he believed, like Walpole, that peace served Britain's commercial interests more than those of any other state.[19] But if one held, as many Patriot Whigs came to do, that France was growing much faster than Britain under the aegis of the Pax Walpoliana, then war might be justified as a means to arrest its dangerous progress.

In the late 1730s, Patriot supporters of a warlike foreign policy argued that Fleury's peaceful strategy had fostered an unprecedented French commercial expansion.[20] The French monarchy's 'Treasures are no longer wasted in wild and expensive Projects to alarm her Neighbours; they are laid out in mending Highways, and in repairing Fortifications, cutting Canals, [and] promoting Commerce,' claimed the Patriot journal *Common Sense*.[21] 'The French have, by attention to trade . . . laid a foundation for their future greatness,' argued the author of an essay in the *Gentleman's Magazine*.[22] The pacific policy of the cardinal had augmented the power of France more than any war, Newcastle argued.[23] In the *Craftsman*, Pulteney noted that Fleury 'hath omitted no means of increasing' French 'riches, power and dominions'. He quoted a statement from the French political economist Nicolas Dutot, whose *Réflexions politiques sur les finances et le commerce* appeared in 1738. 'To make peace in order to reap all the advantages of a great trade is to make war on our enemies,' Dutot argued. Pulteney repeated the assertion as the epitome of Cardinal Fleury's strategy for French aggrandisement.[24] In the words of Robert Harris, 'There was a sense that the Bourbon powers were winning the peace.'[25]

The impressive growth of French trade had come at the direct expense of Britain, many believed. The French 'have run away with the best part of our trade, and are daily growing great on the basis of our ruin', claimed Walpole's critic, John Campbell, duke of Argyll.[26] The traditional British staple, the manufacture of woollen cloth, was stagnant, if not declining.[27] Critics were quick to point to France as the culprit. The French had pioneered the use of protective duties to foster a home manufacture, and other nations had followed suit. The French woollen industry had reached a level of technical proficiency that, combined with lower labour costs, and commercial privileges won from Constantinople, had pushed the English product out of its traditional Levantine markets.[28] Worse, they had done so using smuggled wool from Ireland on which their woollen manufacture now depended.[29] Even Horatio Walpole held that 'our neighbours are industrious to strip us of our woollen manufacture', calling for reprisals on French linen.[30]

Patriots feared that French efforts to expand their trade and political influence with indigenous peoples in America struck at the security of the new Georgia Colony founded in 1732 by Patriot darling James Oglethorpe. Such fears seem overwrought in light of French weakness in the region. British merchants engrossed most of the huge trade in deerskins with the Creek, the dominant regional power, exporting nearly ten times more than the French. French traders from Louisiana simply could not match British merchants in the quality, quantity, or price of the goods favoured by the Creek and other American Indian nations involved in the trade. Commerce was the key to alliances, with the result that the French enjoyed little success in this respect either. French–Indian relations had further deteriorated by the late 1730s after an inconclusive and expensive war against the British-allied Chickasaw.[31]

The French challenge was real, however, in the sugar trade. The British Caribbean colonies were the leading producers of sugar for Europe in 1700, but in the following decades lost this supremacy to the French Antilles. The growth of the French sugar industry, concentrated on Saint-Domingue, was vertiginous in the first third of the century, expanding from just a few dozen plantations in 1700, to 138 in 1713, and 339 by 1730.[32] The French advantage was mostly geographical – they had about twice as much land available for sugar cane cultivation as their British rivals, and the soil was not yet exhausted as was the case in parts of Barbados. France was the beneficiary of a shifting capitalist commodity frontier that moved from island to island as planters sought richer returns from as-yet-unexploited land.[33] An additional edge was provided by Saint-Domingue's superior system of irrigation, which also furnished waterpower for milling.[34] Domestic sugar consumption was low in

France, prompting the re-export of three quarters of its product, sustaining a large positive balance of trade with the Baltic and Central Europe. The late 1730s were a crisis point for the British sugar islands (from which they would later recover), with especially depressed prices.[35]

The French surge had been assisted, sugar planters charged, by the sale of lumber, horses, and provisions to the French islands from British North America, and the market the latter provided for French molasses. There was a fierce legislative fight in the early 1730s to shut down this interimperial trade in the hope that this would increase costs to French producers while lowering those of Jamaican planters. By this means the global competitiveness of the sugar islands might be restored, to 'enable them to supply foreign Markets with Sugar as cheap as the French'.[36] To be sure, British North America would be the loser by the imposition of such regulation, but 'the least Sugar Island we have, is of ten Times more Consequence to Great-Britain, than all Rhode Island and New England put together', claimed the partisans of Jamaica.[37] Rather than subsidising French sugar production by buying their molasses and provisioning their plantations, New Englanders should concentrate on producing cheap naval stores for the home country. For the Whig political economist and former Jamaica merchant William Wood, the function of the northern colonies of New England was essentially as a magazine to supply the sugar colonies with flour, fish, and lumber.[38] Sugar had another tribune in Martin Bladen, the most active figure on Walpole's Board of Trade.[39] He helped push through the Molasses Act of 1733 which aimed to prevent the American colonies from provisioning the French islands by laying a heavy duty on French molasses.

Nobody was more a doomsayer than Joshua Gee, perhaps the most widely read writer on trade of the 1730s, and reflexively disposed to view France as the source of British commercial decline. First published in 1729, his *Trade and Navigation of Great Britain Considered* was in its fourth edition by 1738. Gee's aim was 'to shew the Wounds our Trade and Manufactories have received', and to explain how Britain's slide could be reversed. He admired the French monarchy's Colbertist economic management. Far from believing that trade 'will never become considerable anywhere but in Republicks', he regarded the more centralised French regime with its comprehensive commercial policy as a major advantage. The steps taken to foster the linen and silk industries in particular 'must make them the richest Nation in Europe'. Gee regretted the loss to France of sugar re-export markets, suggesting that an expansion of sugar production into South Carolina could reverse the trend. Recognising that the prospects for recapturing woollen export markets in Europe were poor in the face of continental protection, he focused on reducing British dependence on foreign linens, silks, and naval stores, and by this means tilting the balance of trade back in Britain's favour. He valued the North American colonies as producers of raw materials to be worked up by import-substituting industries at home. Some of these would in turn be exported to colonial populations, which he hoped would expand if government encouraged emigration from continental Europe.

As these examples suggest, the means to compete against France commercially lay in better regulation, and the careful management of the British economy, especially imperial resources. Not once in Gee's writings is there a hint that military means might reverse the trend in France's favour. Indeed, nobody argued that fighting a war against France would be good for British trade. The war Patriots wanted was with Spain, as we saw in Chapter 2 (pp. 110–11), and it aimed not just at curbing Spanish actions against British shipping, but at opening up grand new possibilities for British trade in the Spanish Empire. From a Patriot perspective, Britain had to find a way out of the trap by which a peaceful France would continue to expand its trade faster than Britain could, eventually overturning the balance of wealth. This required a means to break out of the constraints of the existing order, a way to reshuffle the cards of commercial power. If France declared war to prevent Britain from seizing this opportunity in the Spanish Caribbean, this was a war the Patriots were willing to fight, even if they did not seek war with the French as an end in itself.

COMMERCE VERSUS CONQUEST: THE POLITICAL ECONOMY OF THE FLEURY REGIME

The French monarchy was in a thorny geopolitical predicament in the late 1720s and 1730s. As we saw in Chapter 2 (pp. 105–6), leading officials including the foreign minister Germain-Louis Chauvelin believed that the position the South Sea Company had acquired in the trade to Spanish America threatened the balance of commercial power by giving Britain an outsize share

LIBERTÉ DE COMMERCE
AVEC L'ANGLETERRE.

DE PAR LE ROI,
ET MONSEIGNEUR
L'AMIRAL DE FRANCE,
OU
MONSIEUR LE LIEUTENANT GENERAL
de l'Amirauté de Roüen.

ON FAIT SAVOIR à tous qu'il apartiendra, qu'en exécution des Ordres du Roi, portez en la Lettre de Monsieur le Comte de Pontchartrain, du vingt-unième de ce mois; SA MAJESTE' est convenuë avec la REINE D'ANGLETERRE, d'une Liberté réciproque de Commerce; au moïen de laquelle, les VAISSEAUX FRANC,OIS & ANGLOIS, peuvent deformais Commercer dans les Ports de France & d'Angleterre sans Passeports, en y portant des Marchandises permises de part & d'autre par les derniers Arrêts & Réglemens, même d'aporter des Bleds en France; & qu'il sera libre aux Vaisseaux armez en Course, de relâcher dans les Ports des deux Nations, pourvû néanmoins que les Armateurs & Vaisseaux armez en Guerre, n'y conduisent point de Prises : Et que les VAISSEAUX FRANC,OIS seront bien reçûs en Angleterre, comme les VAISSEAUX ANGLOIS seront pareillement bien tráitez dans les Ports de France. Enjoint à tous Marchands, Négocians, Armateurs, & tous autres, de se conformer au Present, à peine de desobéïssance. FAIT à Roüen, audit Siége Général, le vingt-quatriéme jour de Septembre mil sept cens douze. Signé, PIGOU, PERCHEL, & LE SORT.

La lecture & publication du contenu ci-dessus, a été faite par moi Michel Mullot Huissier du Roi au Siége Général de l'Amirauté, ce jourd'hui 25. jour de Septembre 1712. sur les Quays, Place de la Bourse, & autres lieux publics, à ce qu'aucunes personnes n'en prétendent cause d'ignorance, pour être exécuté dans sa forme & teneur. Signé, MULLOT.

Par JACQUES BESONGNE & ANTOINE MAURRY
Imprimeurs ordinaires du Roi, au coin de la Fontaine S. Lo.

1. Proclamation posted by the French Admiralty in Rouen in 1712, late in the War of the Spanish Succession, declaring 'freedom of trade' with England – the general readmission of English shipping into French ports. In the early eighteenth century, free trade, always selectively applied, promised to moderate the worst drawbacks of protection and prohibitions, to foster a balance of wealth among nations, and to make possible more amicable Franco-British relations.

2. Darien may have been one of the places Robert Harley hoped Spain would cede to the control of the South Sea Company to allow it to compete for the South Sea trade. The site of an ill-fated Scottish colony in the 1690s, William Paterson touted its strategic importance, urging that a free port be established there.

3. Nicolas Mesnager (1658–1714), merchant and diplomat, helped negotiate the Franco-British commercial treaty of Utrecht in 1713. In 1708 he had been the leading architect of French plans to open Spanish America to a freer European trade. Mesnager was representative of a new social type: the *négociant*. The interests and expertise of these great merchants carried increasing weight in French foreign and imperial policy from the foundation of the Council of Commerce in 1700.

4. John Law (1671–1729), the Scottish monetary theorist and speculator authorised by the French regent to found a bank issuing paper money in Paris in 1716. He subsequently created the Compagnie des Indes which he planned to use, in the manner of the South Sea Company, to consolidate much of the public debt. He fled France late in 1720 after the collapse of his 'System', which he had argued would preserve the peace of Europe.

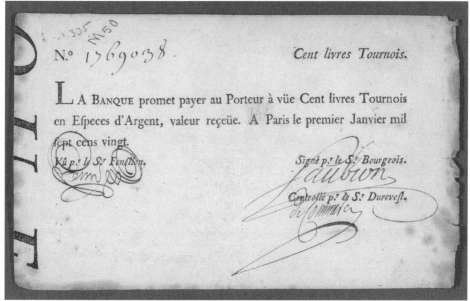

5. A 100-livre banknote issued by Law's bank in 1720, carrying the name of the bank's inspector-general, Jean-Baptiste Fenellon. A deputy to the Council of Commerce from Bordeaux, Fenellon had travelled to London in 1714 with fellow deputy Jean Anisson on missions connected to the Franco-British commercial treaty of 1713. Impressed by the South Sea Company, he became an early supporter of Law's 'System' in France.

The Stature of a

Great Man or the English Colossus.

Why Man, he doth bestride y narrow World | Men at some times are Masters of their fates
like a Colossus, and we petty Men | The fault, dear B—y is not in our Stars,
Walk under his huge Legs, & peep about | But in ourselves, that we are Underlings—
To find our selves, dishonourable Graves. | Shakespear.

Description.

The Colossus at Rhodes, a Stature of y Sun 70 Cubits high, placed at y Mouth of y Harbour, one Man could not grasp its
Thumb with both his Arms. Its thighs were stretchd out to such a Distance, that a large Ship Sailing might easily pass
into y Port betwixt them. It was Twelve Years a making, & cost 300 Talents (a Rhodian Talent is worth 322 Pounds 18
Shillings & 4 Pence in English Money) It stood 56 Years, & at last was thrown down in an Earth-quake. And from this
Colofs y People of Rhodes were named Colofsenfes, & every Stature since of an unusual Magnitude is called Colofsus.

6. Satire of British prime minister Sir Robert Walpole as the Colossus of Rhodes, alluding to his
'extreme reluctance to engage in war . . . to resist the aggressions of Spain and France'. Walpole's
sword hilt is inscribed 'for peace'.

7. Gerard van Neck (1692–1750), an Anglo-Dutch merchant and leading figure in the East India Company. Van Neck was also the principal buying agent of the French tobacco monopoly in Britain. He brokered informal peace talks in 1745 between an employee of the monopoly, Jean-Baptiste Fournier, and a peace party in the British cabinet led by Prime Minister Henry Pelham.

8. Gerard's brother, Sir Joshua van Neck (1702–77) (far left), and his family at their home in Putney. Sir Joshua carried on his brother's role as tobacco-buying agent for the French and sought to maintain peace between France and Britain. He and his son-in-law, Thomas Walpole (far right) – Sir Robert Walpole's nephew – worked unsuccessfully to avert the Seven Years' War.

9 and 10. The capture of Portobello by Admiral Edward Vernon on 22 November 1739. The only British victory of any significance in the course of the Anglo-Spanish naval war launched that year, the capture of Portobello was celebrated enthusiastically by British 'Patriots' – opposition Whigs who derided Sir Robert Walpole's policy of preserving peace with Spain and France. They hoped to use the campaign to create footholds for an expanded British trade in Spanish America and to check French efforts to become Europe's dominant commercial power.

11. A victory for Patriot Whigs during the War of the Austrian Succession (1740–48), the taking of Louisbourg convinced French officials that Britain was bent on conquering French colonies in the Americas and erecting on this basis a 'universal monarchy of trade'.

12. Action between HMS *Nottingham* and French naval ship *Mars*, 11 October 1746, during the War of the Austrian Succession. The inability of France to defend its seaborne trade in the face of British naval superiority persuaded French officials to invest in naval expansion after the conflict.

13. The costs of protecting trade in India, partly in the form of fortifications and war ships, drove a series of efforts from the 1750s through the 1780s to reach an entente between the French and British India companies.

14. *Shah 'Alam Conveying the Grant of the Diwani to Lord Clive in 1765* by Benjamin West retrospectively dramatises the shift of sovereignty over Bengal to the East India Company. By seizing a territorial empire, the company hoped tax revenues would cover its protection costs, but these still regularly threatened its profits, pushing it towards accommodation with the French.

Lond. March of 1788 by S.W. Fores DUN-SHAW. "One Foot in Leadenhall Street & the other in the Province of Bengal."

15. This caricature of Henry Dundas (1742–1811) satirises the key figure behind Pitt's India Act of 1784, intended to check the expansionism of the East India Company and stabilise its finances. Dundas hoped by an understanding with the French to bring about a 'permanent peace' between the two nations in Asia.

16. The port of Roseau, Dominica, site of one of the free ports established by the Rockingham administration in the Caribbean in 1766 to open a freer trade between the British and French empires. In the words of one supporter of the free ports, they would allow Britain to 'reap the advantages' of the French and Spanish colonies in America 'without conquering them'.

17. Depicting Louis XVI with Benjamin Franklin, this statuette commemorates the treaties allying France and the United States in 1778. Inscribed 'Liberté des mers, 1778', it emphasises that the alliance was intended to secure freedom of the seas for ships trading between America and Europe and, by prising America out of the British Empire, to turn it into a great neutral trading power.

18. William Eden (1745–1814) served as the British negotiator of the Franco-British commercial treaty of 1786, which re-established a measure of free trade between the two nations. In 1787, he negotiated a second compact to protect French commerce in Bengal. Eden was a proponent of freer trade with Europe rather than the United States in debates following the American War.

19. Charles Gravier, comte de Vergennes (1719–87), served as foreign minister to Louis XVI. He was the architect of the French alliance with the American revolutionaries, calculated to dismember Britain's empire and draw America into a free trading system. He pressed for the Franco-British commercial treaty of 1786, which he believed would make peace or even partnership possible with Britain while strengthening France and preserving the balance of power.

20. *Mercury Uniting the Hands of Britain and France* shows Britain and France shaking hands under the auspices of the Roman god of commerce, and commemorates the Franco-British commercial treaty signed on 26 September 1786. Josiah Wedgwood, a supporter of the treaty, commissioned this bas-relief. 'As they are meant to be conciliatory,' he noted, the figures 'should be scrupulously impartial . . . and Mercury should not perhaps seem more inclined to one than the other.'

in the markets of the viceroyalties. But Louis XV could not challenge Britain directly while the Habsburgs remained a serious threat in Central Europe. Britain had swapped its French alliance for an Austrian one in 1731. If its commitment to its ally was weak, as British neutrality in the War of the Polish Succession demonstrated, it was still vital to French interests to mollify the British. This entailed keeping the navy small so as not to threaten British trade or security. But without a larger navy France could not hope to protect the international and colonial trade on which it increasingly staked its prosperity and power. Moreover, as we have seen, French successes in these domains would inevitably excite British jealousy, raising the prospect of future conflict. The political-economic path on which the regime had embarked was contradictory and unsustainable.

These contradictions were reflected – and, at a conjectural level, resolved – in the rich political-economic debate sparked by the publication in 1734 of Jean-François Melon's *Essai politique sur le commerce*.[40] For the first time since the Regency, political-economic debate spilled beyond the bounds of the official world and flourished in the public sphere. Debate evolved not in a philosophical space abstracted from the realities of politics, but in quite direct engagement with them. Melon's work, and the responses it elicited, must be read in the political context of the Fleury–Walpole peace. These works serve in turn as a mirror that reflects the challenges and the choices French policymakers faced in negotiating the competition for wealth and power with European rivals.

Melon offered a bold exit from the contradictions of the Fleury regime. Drawing on the thinking of John Law, whose secretary he had once been, he proposed that France shift away from direct competition with the Maritime Powers for colonies and global markets and focus on manufacturing for domestic consumers. Transformed by this reorientation, France would draw the whole international system towards a more stable equilibrium than was possible under the Utrecht order – and this without a naval build-up, without challenging the privileges of the South Sea Company, and without confronting Britain. The *Essai politique* was a peace plan. Others rejected Melon's vision, arguing that commercial flourishing and long-term security were possible only with a stronger navy that would protect a burgeoning international and colonial trade, but for a third group this raised the spectre of war, which all agreed would undermine the rapid commercial growth France had enjoyed under Louis XV.

Melon has been viewed as a proponent of *doux commerce*, and this is correct so long as the *doux commerce* thesis is not understood too narrowly. Albert Hirschman read Melon to exemplify a shift away from the Colbertism of the seventeenth century, when commerce was seen in agonistic terms, to the more pacific idea of trade manifest in the claim of Melon's friend, Charles-Louis de Secondat, baron de Montesquieu, that 'the natural effect of commerce is to lead to peace'.[41] Whether Montesquieu was in fact so optimistic about the effects of trade has been questioned. If its *natural* effect was to lead to peace, it was obviously the case that under prevailing political conditions commercial jealousies incited war, and commerce could double as a form of conquest.[42] Melon's adage that 'the spirit of conquest and the spirit of commerce are mutually exclusive in a nation' was, in any case, less an anticipation of Montesquieu's famous assertion about commerce than a restatement of Law's claim that 'everything conspires to ruin a prince who wishes to extend his empire . . . agriculture, the arts, and commerce are neglected while he occupies his subjects in war'.[43] For Melon, the point was not that commerce promotes peace but that war damages trade, sapping the foundations of future prosperity and power.

Montesquieu made a parallel argument in his 'Reflections on Universal Monarchy', completed but withheld from publication in 1734. At one time, he argued, conquest had been the high road to wealth; the sack of a city could pay for an army and a successful campaign enrich a conqueror. But modern warfare entailed negative feedbacks that made it economically disastrous even for the victor. Modern armies had to carry provisions and money with them into the field, impoverishing their own country and enriching only conquered lands. Debt financing drove up taxes and exhausted the people. Countries were so interdependent that a state trying to augment its power by beggaring its neighbours generally impoverished and weakened itself.[44]

In the framework of the commerce-versus-conquest tradition in European political economy, Melon's views are best understood as a form of pacific Colbertism. The idea that trade ought naturally to be a peaceful tie between peoples was widely shared (indeed, it is quite ancient). But most commentators understood that commerce would foster peace only if it were uncoupled from the competition of states for power – an unrealistic prospect given the ineluctable links between trade and state capacity. Melon recognised the ideal of a commerce that could be free, reciprocal, and conducive to the happiness of peoples but, in the conditions of rivalry prevailing in contemporary Europe, he argued, commerce served to destabilise international order not to pacify it. The relative economic success of one polity threatened to 'give laws' to the others, inciting these to defend themselves and giving rise to war.[45] Melon believed France had the capacity to play and win the same game as Britain – the race to acquire commercial empire and to dominate world trade – but it was not the option he advocated. Instead he outlined the political-economic framework in which a beneficent commerce might be possible.

Melon sketched a more 'introverted' development path that would contain jealousy of trade and render the French kingdom secure without threatening its neighbours. Manufacturing offered the prospect of nearly unlimited economic expansion through technological improvement and the boundless human capacity to develop new needs – by no means a novel insight in European political economy. But unlike the British Whigs, who looked to imperial markets for the sale of British goods, Melon envisioned French goods being consumed domestically. One of the outstanding features of his political economy was his valorisation of consumption, and his promotion of democratic luxury. His work can be read as a reflection on the possibilities of the 'industrious revolution', an intensification of labour and a deepening of market relations across Northwest Europe in the late seventeenth and eighteenth centuries as families participated in new modes of consumption – dressing fashionably, buying commercially produced food and drink, and consuming exotic commodities such as tobacco and sugar.[46] This secular shift in the European economy might allow France to turn its huge demographic resources into a trump card. But this depended on diffusing a broad prosperity among ordinary French consumers, a strategy that required the monarchy to foster agricultural wealth and expand the money supply. To be sure, there was a role for colonial production in Melon's vision, but this need not entail rivalry with the Dutch and the British. He emphasised, for example, that the advantage the French had in the East India trade was their large domestic market – they need not compete in the re-export trade.[47]

For Melon, it was critical to prosperity and power for the nation to have an adequate quantity of money, and following Law he argued that a credit currency could best meet this need.[48] The 1734 edition of the *Essai politique* contained a veiled apology for Law's System which he developed openly in the expanded 1736 edition. However, Melon reluctantly set aside his preference for fiat currency because of the strong prejudices of ordinary people against paper money.[49] In situations of real scarcity of coin, he held, the legislator should instead resort to manipulations of the coinage so that a fixed quantity of specie could serve to mediate a larger number of transactions. This was an aspect of Melon's thinking totally at odds with the political-economic commitments of the Fleury administration, where there was near consensus that currency manipulation always produced more ill than good. It was also the principle objection to Melon's argument made by Nicolas Dutot in the most important published response to the *Essai politique*. However, in a broader sense, Dutot's work should be seen as a sympathetic critique.[50] Both men were admirers of Law, and had worked for him, and Dutot's *Reflexions politiques* also contained an enthusiastic apology for Law's System.

The same cannot be said of the marquis d'Argenson's response to Melon. A future foreign minister and in the mid-1730s a close associate of Chauvelin, René-Louis de Voyer de Paulmy d'Argenson knew that the minister was interested in projects to boost public credit, and had toyed with using the Compagnie des Indes as a vehicle to help pay for the War of the Polish Succession.[51] He wrote a critique of such ideas in the form of a letter to Melon, hoping to inoculate Chauvelin against such misguided thinking. D'Argenson attacked all the schemes to boost the money supply or to lower interest rates. The French had learned the wrong lessons from the English and Dutch experience, he complained; circulation was an *effect* of abundance, not a cause.[52] This attack should not obscure the ways d'Argenson's thinking overlapped with Melon's. His too was an 'introverted' system of political economy, one calculated to disengage France from bitter competition for global markets. The marquis sought to foster the domestic development of the French economy, especially agriculture, rejecting Melon's emphasis on manufacturing and the high consumption required to foster it.[53] Like Melon, Law, and the marquis's mentor, the abbé de Saint-Pierre, d'Argenson hoped to re-establish the peace of Europe, back-stopped by a benign French hegemony.[54]

Melon offered a recipe to break out of the constraints of the Utrecht system without disturbing the peace of Europe. He squared the circle of the Fleury regime's political economy: France could have power based on economic flourishing without a larger navy (and the heavier taxation it would require), without ousting the British from the Spanish Empire, indeed without threatening the economic foundations of Britain's security – the maritime trade that sustained its navy. Naval power is virtually absent from the *Essai politique*, while the chapter on colonies ends with a call to colonise wasteland at home, where wealth was acquired without the dangers of war and without attracting the jealousy of neighbours. Melon had a positive attitude towards colonies, if managed correctly. But they appear inessential to his strategy. He does not mention colonial demand for manufactured goods, nor does he argue that colonies are a vital source of raw materials for manufacture or re-export, though there was a place for exotic goods in his vision of democratic luxury. There is ambiguity in his handling of the Asiento. He describes it as a real advantage to Britain yet points to the failure of the South Sea Company to make a profit.

Melon took the unusual step of publishing the *Essai politique*, challenging the convention that economic policy was a matter for the royal government alone, and implicitly claiming independence from the officials he had lobbied behind closed doors in the 1720s.[55] Yet it is obvious that the *Essai politique* was also meant precisely for these officials, especially Chauvelin, who shared a patron with Melon in Jeanne-Baptiste d'Albert de Luynes, comtesse de Verrue, the centre of a circle of great Mississippians who continued to invest in the Compagnie des Indes and who remained sympathetic to the projects of Law. Chauvelin owned a copy of Melon's work and of the two major published responses to him – part of the minister's wider engagement with published political economy.[56] Melon's proposals resonated, in certain respects, with Chauvelin's own recommendation to the Council of State (Conseil d'État) during the War of the Polish Succession that France preserve the balance of power by building up its strength through a programme of economic reform – establishing 'its own greatness by its interior administration and by the wisdom of its policy'. By such a strategy, he argued, the monarchy would 'make itself respected without making itself feared'.[57] While the first edition of the *Essai politique* was not widely disseminated, the second circulated widely and was treated with implicit approbation by the authorities, signalled by the long, highly favourable review it received in the quasi-official *Journal des sçavans*.[58]

Melon's work sparked a broader debate that occurred partly in print, and partly in manuscript. The principal response, as previously noted, was Dutot's

Réflexions politiques (1738), a work widely and favourably reviewed, which brought its author to the attention of leading officials.[59] If Melon sought to withdraw from or transform the Utrecht order, Dutot accepted it as it was and laid out a strategy to augment French power within it. Foreign trade and navigation were the keys to expanding national wealth. Dutot claimed that Law had established his bank and companies with a view to reviving French trade and shipping and creating the foundation for a powerful French navy – the critical condition for the renewal of French power. Criticised for underestimating the cost of a larger navy, Dutot retorted that, whatever the price, it was necessary to command British respect and the peace this would assure.[60] In 1739 when he travelled to London to supervise the translation of his book, he was invited to reside with the French ambassador, Louis-Dominique de Cambis, who recommended the author's work to the minister of foreign affairs, Jean-Jacques Amelot de Chaillou.[61] Dutot corresponded with Marc-Pierre de Voyer de Paulmy, comte d'Argenson (the younger brother of Melon's critic), who was regarded as a candidate for the ministry at the time, and who served as minister of war from 1743 to 1757.[62] While in London, Dutot gathered works on political economy and wrote an analysis in a political-arithmetical vein of Britain's financial capacity to sustain a general war which he made available to the younger d'Argenson.[63] The future minister owned manuscript copies of the unpublished third volume of Dutot's *Réflexions politiques*, and also of his history of Law's System.[64] This is in line with a broader interest in political arithmetic manifest in the comte's papers.[65]

In the first edition of the *Essai politique*, Melon had virtually nothing to say about foreign trade. Responding to Dutot, most of the new chapters added in 1736 develop a vision of international commerce in which foreign trade could serve to 'contribute equally to the happiness of all'.[66] The export of agricultural commodities is at the heart of this vision. Trade was necessary to carry off the surplus of French agriculture: 'Our interior commerce could be so great that we would barely need foreigners,' Melon claims, 'were it not for the superfluous abundance of our commodities [*denrées*].'[67] Melon saw agriculture as a foundation for the rest of the economy. The land had to generate an adequate surplus to feed an expanding industrial workforce, and a prosperous agriculture would foster a growing population. But agricultural prosperity was threatened by the prospect of glut, which drove down prices. Freedom to export was the solution to this problem. In such an exchange, free trade would be the ideal, but this was unattainable in current circumstances. For the present, imports of raw materials should be encouraged and manufactured goods excluded.[68]

A problem Melon raised that was explored by other commentators was whether universal monarchy could be achieved by commercial means and, if it could, whether this power would be permanent. Melon claimed it was possible for one state to overthrow permanently the balance of wealth.[69] In the 1730s the threat was that Britain would do so, reducing France perpetually to a second-class position. Herein lay the urgency of Melon's message. France needed to transform itself or suffer the consequences. His interlocutor, Montesquieu, took the opposite view: a modern universal monarchy was impossible.[70] Where the distribution of power depended on commerce, it must shift constantly. The expansion of the money supply brought about by a successful foreign trade would drive up the cost of living and allow lower-cost producers to undersell the affected nation. An extreme case was the Spanish monarchy, which had declined almost from the moment of its enrichment by the conquest of America. But Montesquieu conceded that the effects of wealth acquired through trade were less immediately destructive.[71] This is an argument likely borrowed from Richard Cantillon, the Irish banker and one-time associate of Law whose *Essai sur la nature du commerce en général* circulated in manuscript in the 1730s and 1740s. A critic of Law's System, Cantillon claimed that increasing the money supply raised the cost of labour, eventually pricing the goods of the affected country out of international markets. In the case of a gradual increase via a positive balance of trade, however, the ill effects could long be deferred. The implications of this argument were reassuring in a French context. Britain with its banks and paper currency, its expanding trade and wealth, was on an unsustainable path. Sooner or later its own prosperity would be self-limiting, and lower-wage nations following a more conservative monetary policy would have their place in the sun.[72]

If Melon's *Essai politique* had sparked a range of contrary positions on certain issues, consensus reigned on one question: France was better off pursuing power and security through peaceful commerce than via war or foreign adventures. This insight was basic to Melon's political economy. It was also central to Dutot's thinking. For him pacific commerce was a substitute for war. 'To make peace in order to reap all the advantages of a great trade is to make war on our enemies,' he wrote – a line that had alarmed the Patriot Whig William Pulteney. The irrationalities of actual war were to be avoided in favour of the commerce that would more surely and effortlessly deliver power. 'An end to those victories won by ruinous efforts,' exhorted Dutot; 'Let glory lie still! It is in the bosom of our countryside that industry will open to us easy roads to greater conquests . . . France, superior by the advantages of her commerce will make known to neighbouring states that she is as capable of increasing her power by peace as by war.'[73] A future minister, Étienne de Silhouette, who met Dutot in London in 1739, recommended his work – and particularly this precept – to Cardinal Fleury. 'It is in fact *more by the arts of peace than by those of war*,' he told the cardinal, 'that France is in a position to ruin that rival and enemy nation.' Enumerating the major branches of British trade, Silhouette wrote: 'these, my lord, are the kingdoms and provinces it would be necessary to conquer from these island dwellers; every branch of commerce is for them a fort, a citadel – impregnable by storm and by armies, easy to take by industry and economy'.[74]

Reading these lines, it is clear that Patriot Whig concerns about France, however exaggerated, were not entirely unfounded. Many French officials had in fact embraced a strategy of French aggrandisement based on peaceful commercial development – a plan of action theorised by French political economists. The Patriots' war against Spain on which Britain embarked in 1739 was intended to renew the nation's commercial vitality by establishing additional advantages for its trade in Spanish America. When Britain sent a major naval expedition to attack strategic Spanish ports in the Caribbean, even the cautious Fleury had to respond, exposing the contradictions at the heart of the French strategy. In August 1740, Louis XV dispatched much of the French fleet to the Western Atlantic with instructions to attack British ships if it had superiority in numbers and, if possible, to reconquer Jamaica for Spain. By sheer chance, the two sides did not clash before Admiral d'Antin ran out of supplies and brought the fleet home in 1741. By this time, a general war was brewing in Europe triggered by the death of Emperor Charles VI, the accession of his daughter, Maria-Theresa, as sovereign of the Habsburg Hereditary Lands, and Prussia's opportunistic invasion of Austrian Silesia at the end of 1740. Some French leaders saw an opportunity here to deal a final blow to Habsburg power.[75] Louis XV backed Prussia, while Britain entered what would come to be called the

War of the Austrian Succession in 1742 on the Austrian side, seeking to check French expansionism. The rivals formally declared war on one another in the spring of 1744 as the French prepared an invasion of Britain.

The Patriots got their war with France, ostensibly to preserve the balance of power, but this was not really the war they had wanted to fight. The naval conflict in the Caribbean became little more than an expensive sideshow, stymied by the failure to achieve an early breakthrough, tropical disease, and by the diversion of men and money to the European theatre. One bright spot for Patriots was the 1745 conquest of the French fortress town of Louisbourg on Cape Breton Island, which stood sentinel over the sea lanes leading to French Canada and the Newfoundland fisheries. The capture of Louisbourg fired Patriot ambitions to push the French out of North America altogether, setting the stage for new rounds of conflict in the 1750s.[76] But for officials who had come up under Fleury and Walpole, and who had entered the war reluctantly in the first place, it was the prospect of an early and durable peace that most appealed.

BUSINESS, PUBLIC FINANCE, AND THE SEARCH FOR PEACE IN 1745

In April 1745, Jean-Baptiste Fournier arrived in London on a secret mission, nominally as an employee of the General Farms, the chief French tax-farming syndicate, but in fact to sound out the British ministry on the possibility of peace.[77] His principal interlocutor was Gerard van Neck, a prominent merchant and financier – and a tobacco-buying agent of the General Farms in Britain.[78] Fournier stayed in London for over six months, assured by van Neck that key figures in the ministry wanted an end to the war. He met informally with cabinet members but, with the Jacobite rising underway in the north, in November he returned to France. Peace would have to wait two more years. Though the back-channel talks failed, they shed light on forces that had served to keep the peace in the 1730s, and that now worked to return Franco-British relations to the uneasy harmony of the Fleury–Walpole years. The peace parties on both sides were mostly veterans of the Walpole and Fleury ministries. The respective finance ministers, Henry Pelham, first lord of the Treasury, and the contrôleur général Philibert Orry, were the chief supporters of peace – wary of the fiscal and public credit burdens of the war. They found allies and intermediaries among some of the great business interests in their circles that wanted to end the uncertainty and commercial disruptions attendant on the war. Fournier and van Neck were proxies of these forces; the conversations they had represent the efforts of these lobbies to achieve a cross-Channel understanding.

The peace initiative of 1745 opens a window onto structural features of the Franco-British relationship. Though a special case, the tobacco trade offers a kind of natural experiment in the potential effects of normalised trade on the Franco-British international relationship – the kind of open commerce Bolingbroke had tried and failed to establish in 1713. British tobacco was imported into France on a vast scale in the 1720s and 1730s. Around this lucrative business grew up a thicket of powerful special interests who fought for its continuation, who worked to end the war that threatened their profits, and would work again to avert future Franco-British clashes. These efforts failed to renew or keep the peace: the interests concerned were too narrow; too much of the British mercantile community had no direct interest in peace. But the case of tobacco suggests that a trade organised on a broader basis, engaging a wider range of commercial interests, might indeed have helped check conflict.

We should not imagine that the middling British merchants who rallied behind the Patriot Whigs were incurably bellicose. It might not have required a vast Franco-British trade to weaken the Patriot siren call of popular imperialism and anti-Bourbon fervour. To be sure, war could bring benefits to well-placed merchants.[79] But for many others the losses would exceed the gains. For all the thrilling promises of new markets, disruption to the enemy's trade, and prizes for those who took up privateering, war could also entail high costs for merchants. They stood to lose traditional markets, as in Spain, during periods of wartime embargo. These might never be recovered if competitors became securely installed. Though merchants usually diversified into multiple trading voyages, and insurance would cover much of the damage, thousands of ships were lost in eighteenth-century wars. Between 1689 and 1697, roughly 4,000 British merchant ships were sunk or captured; the War of the Spanish Succession saw 3,250 such losses, and the War of the Austrian Succession another 3,238.[80] Impressment into the navy left the carrying trade short of seamen. Ships that put to sea had to pay higher wages and higher insurance costs. The costs of private credit rose, as merchants had to compete with the state, which was forced to pay higher real rates of interest.[81] Another inevitable consequence of heavy government borrowing was increased taxation, and in Britain these taxes fell substantially on trade, as Sir Matthew Decker and other critics bitterly complained in the 1740s.[82] New taxes, used to fund the public debt, would be a permanent legacy of war, increasing the price of many goods and driving up the cost of labour. Traders could be fickle in their support for war, depending on how they were affected.[83] If the balance of advantage had been shifted by the 1713 commercial treaty, if British manufacturers had developed important export markets in France, for example, there might have been less mercantile enthusiasm for war.

The case of the tobacco trade is certainly suggestive in this respect. The manufacture and sale of snuff and pipe tobacco was organised as a monopoly in France, held from 1730 by the General Farms, which sourced up to 90 per cent of its tobacco in Britain, virtually all of it imported from Virginia and Maryland. This was the best way to organise the trade from a fiscal point of view. The principal threat to the profitability of the tobacco monopoly was smuggling, and to help limit contraband, the monarchy banned tobacco cultivation in all but a few frontier zones. The Farmers General deployed an army of guards and bureaucrats to keep smuggling in check, but their most effective tool was to keep official tobacco prices low and quality reasonably high, and to this end they bought the cheapest tobacco available – produced in British North America. Tobacco was Britain's largest import from the Thirteen Colonies, and France, which bought up to a quarter of the British product, its most important re-export market. Thus an element of the Fleury–Walpole equilibrium was a symbiosis between the fiscal needs of the French state and Britain's interest in fostering the growth of its colonies. (Though this was a mixed blessing for planters, the farmers being such a large-scale buyer that they were able to depress the market price.)[84]

The tobacco monopoly was one of the most stable and lucrative income streams of the General Farms, and the farmers in turn assured the monarchy a regular and substantial flow of payments. In addition, the General Farms served as a rudimentary state bank, making short-term credit available to the administration, while offering a mechanism to make payments in the provinces. If the tax farmer needed extra money to cover his obligations, he could borrow from the public through *billets des fermes* – effectively a disguised form of short-term government borrowing through the corporate intermediation of the tax farmers. The Farmers General also extended long-term loans to the monarchy at low interest in the guise of the bonds they paid to secure their places. Prospective farmers raised the capital by tapping broad credit networks among the richest strata of French society.[85] The tobacco monopoly helped sustain this whole financial architecture. Thus an implicit alliance existed between the French monarchy, the financiers who served it, the planters of the Chesapeake who produced the tobacco sold in France, and buying agents such as Gerard van Neck who assured its delivery.

The elite merchants who were part of Walpole's coalition were generally disposed towards his pacific line. Closer to ministers and officials than middling merchants, moreover, they were better placed to exert an influence on policy. Great merchants like van Neck knew ministers personally. Two of his nieces (daughters of Gerard's brother, Joshua van Neck) married sons of Horatio Walpole, Sir Robert Walpole's brother. The van Necks were also linked to leading Dutch politicians; one van Neck brother was pensionary of Rotterdam while another was attorney general of Holland. During wartime, governments depended on elite merchants to organise subscriptions to public loans. These were the 'gentlemanly capitalists' who integrated relatively easily into a clubby world dominated by landowners and noblemen.[86] Broadly speaking, this mercantile elite did not share the popular imperialism attributed to middling merchants.[87]

However, in wartime the largest, best-connected merchants stood to make a fortune in military contracting, the remittance of funds abroad, or organising subscriptions for government loans, and this must have tended to dispel whatever mercantile objections they had to a bellicose foreign policy. The van Neck firm is a case in point. Their investment in the tobacco business aside, Gerard and his brother Joshua must have been rather the gainers than the losers by war. Gerard was a major underwriter of government loans, serving notably as a conduit for Dutch money buying into the British public debt.[88] Joshua would play the same role on an even larger scale during the Seven Years' War.[89] Gerard was also part of a syndicate of London houses that had loaned money to the Habsburg monarchy.[90] Their specifically *commercial* incentives may have inclined them towards peace – as Gerard's role as peace intermediary shows. But whatever losses war might entail for politically connected British merchants, many stood to make over in their role as financiers, bankers, and military suppliers. Such side-payments must have tended to neutralise what hesitation they had about conflict, and prevented them from emerging as a major lobby against war.

French merchants did not enjoy the same range of opportunities as their British counterparts, and their aversion to war tended to be less mixed. The elite *négociants* were not involved in arranging subscriptions for French public loans, the credit of the monarchy being supported principally by the financiers. Merchants had some scope for war contracting, but the major players in this domain were the *tresoriers généraux* and court bankers (when it was a question of remitting funds abroad). To be sure, merchants could profit from privateering, and the disruptions of war sometimes offered new opportunities that would never have opened in peacetime. Think of Saint-Malo's trade to Peru during the War of the Spanish Succession (see above, p. 92).[91] Moreover, commerce could be diverted in wartime to neutral carriers, or placed under neutral flags, limiting damage to profits, while wartime losses would be partially recovered in the booms that always came with peace. But generally speaking, there was no broad French mercantile constituency in favour of any of the century's wars.

War had even more depressive consequences for planters in the French colonies. They scrambled to feed their slaves and to keep their creditors at bay in wartime. Moreover, the ill-effects of war weighed on the peacetime plantation system, as Paul Cheney shows. While it paid to specialise in cash crops and to invest in machinery, many planters instead bought more slaves whose labour could be diverted to produce scarce foodstuffs in wartime during which new mills would sit idle or turn out larger quantities of unmarketable sugar.[92]

The commercial and financial incentives of the Farmers General, for whom Fournier worked, were complex, but in the context of 1745 their interest was rather to see an end to the war than its continuation. War imposed strains on the General Farms, especially on the tobacco monopoly. The tax farmers leased the right to farm taxes for a fixed annual sum: when receipts shrank due to depressed economic activity, they had to absorb the loss. The royal administration's ordinary practice of drawing on the farmers for short-term credit increased from 1742, forcing the company to issue larger volumes of short-term paper.[93] The monarchy also squeezed the farmers for loans. More than 15 per cent of total French non-tax revenue raised during the war was extracted from them.[94] This opened new prospects for profit, certainly, but combined with significantly increased risk; if the war went on for too long, it might threaten the farmers' solvency or their credit with the public. No tax farmer was unaware that the War of the Spanish Succession had driven an earlier syndicate into bankruptcy. The tobacco monopoly presented particular challenges. If the British cut off the supply, or raised its price by ending drawbacks paid when tobacco was re-exported, the monopoly would be at the mercy of smugglers.[95] The most immediate problem in 1745 was a shortfall in the quantity of tobacco reaching France. English tobacco exports fell off from an average of £11.6 million a year before the declaration of war to £2.7 million in 1745. A new pass system established at the behest of the van Necks in September 1745 led to a restoration of virtually normal tobacco trading in 1746, but nobody could foresee this when Fournier went to London.[96]

If he carried with him the knowledge that the tobacco monopoly in particular, and the tax farmers, more generally, would benefit from peace, he was also a proxy for the contrôleur général, who had opposed the war at almost every step, citing the financial burden and the likely overextension of public credit.[97] At the outset of the conflict, the marquis d'Argenson complained that Orry raised financial obstacles at every turn to war planning; the chief architect of the war strategy, Charles Louis Auguste Fouquet, duc de Belle-Isle, demanded that he be removed.[98] In the following years, Orry did battle over funding for the army with the comte d'Argenson (the war minister) and Adrien-Maurice, duc de Noailles, a key strategist.[99] In 1745 he vetoed a funding increase for the navy.

Orry's equivalent in Britain, Prime Minister Henry Pelham, was the leading figure in a peace party that had emerged by the latter half of 1745.[100] Pelham had support from the earl of Chesterfield, lord lieutenant of Ireland, and Lord Harrington, the Northern secretary.[101] His brother, the duke of Newcastle, sympathised with the peace party in 1745, but soon changed his position.[102]

Newcastle quickly concluded that peace was impossible given the strength of parliamentary opposition to an accommodation with France. He cited in particular the weight of Patriot interests calling for the war effort to be continued but redirected to achieve colonial gains at French expense. Pelham observed that the desire to hold onto the French fortress of Louisbourg on Cape Breton Island, captured in June 1745, would be an obstacle to a necessary peace. 'The generality . . . look upon it as a most valuable possession for this country; as indeed it is, if it did not endanger the quiet possession of what is more valuable,' he complained. 'Gibraltar and Minorca have kept us, for thirty years, at variance with Spain; I am of opinion. Cape Breton will do the same with France; and to speak as a financier, the balance of that account is much against us.'[103]

A peace deal turned out to be impossible in 1745. In December, Orry was pushed out of office by a coalition of forces seeking to capitalise on French military advantage in the Austrian Low Countries – ousted for having said too often 'that the state of the king's finances would not permit him to continue the war much longer'.[104] With Orry gone, immediate peace had lost its strongest advocate. But some of the same pressures weighing in the balance for a 1745 accord were critical in bringing the war to an end two years later. Pelham pushed again for peace in 1747, citing the overextension of public credit and the potential difficulty of financing another year of war. This time, with Dutch exhaustion apparent, and the French at the walls of Maastricht, he succeeded. Louis XV was advised by his leading financier, Joseph Pâris-Duverney, to abandon any ambition for territorial gains in the Low Countries in favour of ending a war that had pushed public credit to the breaking point.[105]

The idea that France was best served by peace was powerfully reinforced by the expensive, stalemated War of the Austrian Succession. For their part, Britons drew divergent lessons from the war. Its principal legacy was a ballooning national debt, Britain having been forced to return Louisbourg at the peace. The conflict had renewed the conviction that France was Britain's most dangerous rival but left unresolved how the British might best respond to the French challenge. Some Patriots looked with equanimity on the prospect of a new war – this time to be concentrated against French naval power and colonies. Others, reflecting on the futility of the preceding struggle, and alarmed by the augmentation of public debt, sought more peaceful ways to contain France.[106] Yet the growing conviction in both nations that America was the principal stake of the Franco-British rivalry would make it difficult for the powerful peace parties in London and Versailles to prevent colonial clashes in 1754 from spiralling into a major war.

THE STAKES OF AMERICAN EMPIRE

The late stages of the War of the Austrian Succession saw a major shift in strategic thinking in France fateful for the subsequent history of Franco-British relations. Highly placed French officials and politically connected merchants came to see British naval power, and the menace it represented to French and Spanish colonies, as the decisive threat to the balance of power and to the future status and security of the French monarchy. They argued that France would not be able to grow peacefully back to a position of power and security if Britain used its navy to engross the trade of America. The small navy policy of the Fleury regime came to seem a mistake – an invitation to war rather than a means to keep the peace. To prevent the erosion of the French position in North America became a priority it had not been before. Louis XV embraced an alliance with France's old Austrian nemesis, weakened by war, to keep the peace in Central Europe and to allow France to turn westward. Combined with Patriot attachment to America as the key to Britain's commercial future, the stage was set for a generation of conflict between the two nations in which continental North America and its trade would be the principal stake.[107]

Yet there is an irony here. Many of those in France who most ardently touted the value of the navy and the strategic importance of America were committed to avoiding war with Britain because they believed that peaceful trade best served the growth of French power. This position was elaborated in dozens of works of political economy written for a broader public in the 1750s by a circle of writers linked with the intendant of commerce, Jacques Vincent de Gournay. Gournay and his protégés are sometimes read as apostles of *doux commerce*, a position that can be sustained only if this idea is stretched to encompass those who sought to win the game of power politics by peaceful commercial means.[108] The tensions in this political economy were brought out by the international crisis out of which the Seven Years' War emerged – a crisis over the fate of the Ohio Country, and other borderlands between the French and British empires in America. It reminds us that there were limits to the claim that commerce could substitute for war. When one power seemed bent upon using political or military means to permanently overthrow the balance of wealth – to establish itself as a hegemon – war might have to be embraced as the only means to check this prospect.

In the latter years of the War of the Austrian Succession, starting in 1745, the minister of the navy and colonies, Jean-Frédéric Phélypeaux, comte de Maurepas, campaigned to abandon the small navy policy of the Fleury regime, backed by a network of shipowners and merchants who served him as informal advisers and besieged him as lobbyists. While Fleury was alive, Maurepas had not contested the policy and even entertained the idea that a naval war would damage Britain more than France.[109] The experience of fighting the Royal Navy convinced him otherwise. Late in 1745, he took advantage of Orry's depleted political capital to push for a larger fleet. He traced the history of naval decline: from a force of 120 ships of the line in the heyday of Louis XIV, the fleet had slipped to just forty-nine in total from 1719, not all fit to serve. Naval spending was set at a modest 9 million livres in 1725, permitting a maximum fleet size of fifty-four vessels in the first six grades.[110] (The Royal Navy, by contrast, boasted roughly 170 ships of equivalent size.[111]) Matters had deteriorated further since 1744 when, despite having only thirty seaworthy ships of the line, Orry slashed naval funding.[112] Maurepas denounced the small navy policy as a strategy that had failed to avert the jealousy of the Maritime Powers. Appeasement had revealed its bankruptcy when Britain attacked Spain in 1739, and its crippling consequences could be read in the 150 million livres in French prizes taken by British warships or privateers. Only a stronger navy would deter Britain and protect French trade.

Maurepas did not press for a return to the battle fleets of the age of Colbert: his demand was for sixty ships of the line, a commerce-protection force, not a fleet capable of contesting for naval supremacy.[113] The navy must secure the colonial commerce that had become a key underpinning of French power. The British were bent on a universal monarchy of trade, the Anglo-Spanish war only the latest step in a series of efforts to master the trade of America. For Maurepas, colonial re-exports had become the key to a positive balance of trade. France need not draw in specie directly from Spanish America if it could continue to sustain a large positive balance by marketing its sugar in Hamburg and Amsterdam and its cod in the Mediterranean. Colonial commerce had overtaken the Spanish trade as the kingdom's leading commercial interest. The minister reckoned its value at 140 million livres annually before the war – three times the sum he had estimated fifteen years earlier, and far more than the 80 million at which he rated the Spanish trade.[114]

In stressing the costs of naval weakness, Maurepas echoed the complaints of the *négociants*, the elite merchants who were his principal link to the world of trade. Two years of naval warfare had decimated French maritime commerce, complained François Fournier, a partner in a prominent Cádiz house, and brother-in-law of the deputy of commerce Simon Gilly.[115] Since the declaration of war, merchants had lost shipping worth 190 million livres, Fournier claimed. The Compagnie des Indes alone had given up 16 million livres in prizes to the enemy, while Atlantic colonial trade had lost 90 million and dropped to half its prewar level. The Newfoundland fishery had collapsed, and slaving voyages had ceased. A vicious circle had been established, Fournier argued: the weak navy led to the ruin of trade, while collapsing trade deprived the king of the revenues needed to build and outfit ships.[116] A dozen vessels in America might have averted the losses in Atlantic trade, he argued, while four or five would have protected the Compagnie des Indes.[117] Other ship-owners in the minister's circle mirrored this bleak assessment. Pierre-André d'Héguerty complained that France had neglected its navy for forty years – an invitation to British aggression in America. The war might never have started if Louis XV had eighty ships of the line.[118] A governor of the Île de Bourbon (now La Réunion) with interests in Caribbean plantations and privateering, d'Héguerty's views carried weight.

In the short run, Maurepas's Atlantic and navalist vision was contested in the Council of State and he was unable to secure an immediate increase in funds for the fleet. The war minister, the comte d'Argenson, was not insensible to the British threat (recall his association with Dutot; see above, p. 162), but he could reasonably argue that only conquests in Europe would balance colonial losses such as Louisbourg. Maurepas's enemy, Cardinal de Tencin, also pushed a continental strategy. Tencin's secretary, the abbé Gabriel Bonnot de Mably, while conceding the economic importance of America, argued that a universal monarchy of trade was impossible. Global in scale, modern commerce was simply too extensive to be taken over by any monopolist. Moreover, naval power never proved decisive in modern wars, where sieges were always conclusive; in fact, the empire of the sea would follow from dominance on land.[119] With the armies of Maurice de Saxe, Louis XV's leading general, preparing a surprise winter attack on Brussels, this was not an ideal moment to make the case for naval power. But the argument for a stronger navy would only grow more compelling in the last year of the conflict when Britain achieved total mastery of the seas, French trade suffered brutal losses, and the whole Atlantic empire appeared threatened.[120]

Once peace was concluded, the monarchy launched a major naval rebuilding effort, if not quite on the scale Maurepas hoped. The navy constructed thirty-seven ships of the line between 1749 and 1755.[121] In his last full year as minister, Maurepas was accorded an extraordinary budget of over 15 million livres, while ordinary naval spending was raised to 15 million livres annually in the 1750s. He managed to secure this increase before his disgrace in April 1749 (having fallen afoul of the king's mistress, Madame de Pompadour, who was to play an increasingly powerful role at court in the following decade).[122] Some observers would see the naval building programme retrospectively as the root cause of the Franco-British war that erupted in 1755.[123] Certainly, the French effort was observed 'with considerable anxiety in Britain, provoking frequent comment in the press'.[124] But the strategic goal of the new navy was defensive: nearly all the new ships were seventy-four-gun cruisers suitable for commerce protection but not for fleet actions.[125] Louis XV looked to safeguard the tap root of the monarchy's wealth, not for command of the sea.

The revaluation of the navy came along with a new emphasis on the importance of the French colonies in North America – Cape Breton, Île Saint-Jean (now Prince Edward Island), Canada, and Louisiana. Like the move away from a small navy, this was a reaction against the events of the recent war, when Louisbourg had fallen and Quebec had been threatened, but it was also a consequence of French readings of British political economy, which accorded North America a new importance from the 1730s. British commentators concerned about competitiveness, and barriers to trade in Europe, came to see the American colonies as key sources of raw materials and vital markets for British manufactured goods. The political economist Joshua Gee hoped to tap the colonies for naval stores that would break British dependence on the Baltic, and for raw materials to feed import-substituting industries in Britain, especially linen, silk, and iron-founding. (Gee invested in the Principio Company, alongside George Washington's father, a venture that promised to produce semi-processed iron for the British market.[126]) By such means Britain could reverse a balance of trade that had supposedly become increasingly unfavourable.

In the ranks of the Patriots, especially, many saw Britain's commercial future in protected imperial markets in North America. 'Of all the branches of our commerce that to our colonies is the most valuable,' wrote George Lyttelton, 'Foreign Markets may be lost or spoilt by various Accidents. Other Nations . . . by working cheaper, may be able perhaps to undersell us there. And by these means I am afraid we have found our Trade decline considerably in many parts

2. Eastern North America in the era of the Seven Years' War

of the World. But in our own Plantations nothing of this can happen'.[127] It was not just a question of protected markets. We must grasp the exceptional qualities many contemporaries projected onto economic life in America. Because of its high wages, and access to almost unlimited supplies of cheap land, it was argued, British North America could not soon develop a manufacturing sector of its own. Rather, it would be a privileged market for British industry, which enjoyed the special access conferred by its trade laws. As Steve Pincus has argued, Patriots emphasised American empire primarily as a site of consumption – a market for British manufactured goods rather than a source of raw materials.[128]

The Thirteen Colonies were, in fact, an important and fast-growing market for Britain. British exports to continental Europe largely stagnated after the beginning of the century, due to import substitution in competing nations, and increased competition from France. North America absorbed about 6 per cent of British exports in 1700, rising to 26 per cent of a much larger aggregate by the early 1770s. Colonial needs had permitted a tremendous diversification of British production, especially in the metal trades. Indeed, England's industrialisation 'was to an important extent a response to colonial demands for nails, axes, firearms, buckets, coaches, clocks, saddles, handkerchiefs, buttons, cordage and a thousand other things'.[129] Given the vast spaces west of the Appalachians, and its fast growing population (increasing nearly ninefold between 1700 and the eve of the American Revolution), North America would remain a growing market for a century to come. Already valuable, its true significance lay in the future.[130]

Two figures are essential for understanding French efforts to grapple with British ideas and policies in the late 1740s and 1750s: Étienne de Silhouette and Jacques Vincent de Gournay. Silhouette we have encountered in the political-economic debates of the 1730s, propounding Dutot's view that France could grow its way to security and power by peaceful commercial expansion (see above, p. 164). He entered royal service as an observer of British politics from London in the late 1730s, having spent the previous five years there, much of it as a buyer for the tobacco monopoly. While in England, he developed links with the Patriots – Bolingbroke pre-eminently, but also Sir William Wyndham, William Pulteney, Lord Chesterfield, and John Carteret.[131] He published a translation of Bolingbroke's *Dissertation upon Parties* in 1739, the same year he became an agent of the French ministry of foreign affairs.[132] Interacting with these men, reading the opposition press, and watching the course of the war, Silhouette came to believe that American trade would be the decisive theatre of future geopolitical struggle. He was repeatedly struck during the conflict by the British focus on American gains. They were not interested in Germany but in America, he reported in the summer of 1741, their goal being to produce a 'general revolution' there, to prise it 'from submission to the Spanish', and 'to take over the exclusive trade of all of America'.[133]

In the late 1740s, Silhouette would make a place for himself in the royal administration as an authority on British politics and economics, a status signalled by his appointment in 1750 as commissioner (alongside Roland-Michel Barrin, marquis de La Galissonière) to negotiate boundary disputes between the French and British colonies in America.[134] At issue was sovereignty over the so-called neutral islands, Tobago, Saint Lucia, Saint Vincent, and Dominica; the limits of the province of Acadia, or Nova Scotia, ceded to Britain in 1713; and rights to trade and build forts in the Ohio Country, between the French and British colonies. In 1751, Silhouette was also named royal commissioner of the Compagnie des Indes, which was locked in military conflict with its British counterpart in India. As François Ternat has shown, in the early 1750s the French monarchy sought to resolve sources of tensions with Britain globally.[135] Silhouette's twin positions put him at the centre of these efforts. His name would be mentioned as a prospective foreign minister in 1754, and he finished his career with a brief stint as contrôleur général in 1759.[136]

It is unclear precisely when Silhouette came to be linked with Jacques Vincent (ennobled as marquis de Gournay in 1747), a partner in a Cádiz merchant house, who by 1746 enjoyed a semi-official status as a counsellor to Maurepas. Vincent attended peace negotiations in the Dutch Republic in 1746, and travelled to Britain to report to the naval minister on the sources of British commercial vitality. He weathered his patron's disgrace, impressed other powerful men, notably the contrôleur général Jean-Baptiste de Machault d'Arnouville, and entered the royal administration in 1751 by purchasing the office of intendant of commerce, which gave him a seat on the Bureau of Commerce.[137] From this position, with the help of likeminded officials, he embarked on a campaign to disseminate knowledge of the 'science of commerce' by encouraging a circle of budding political economists to translate foreign, predominantly British, works of political economy and to compose works in a similar vein.[138] Roughly fifty such works were published before Vincent de Gournay's death in 1759, many written by men still in trade, or from families making the move from the mercantile world to royal service. The works of the Gournay circle broadened and publicised conversations that had begun in Maurepas's milieu in the 1740s. (Pierre-André d'Heguerty was an early recruit.) Gournay sought to convince those who mattered that France's geopolitical destiny lay in the Atlantic, in America, and above all in the peaceful development of its own considerable economic resources.

This was precisely Silhouette's view, and he became rather a patron of the Gournay circle than a mere participant. He employed several of Gournay's protégés, notably Georges-Marie Butel-Dumont, whom he appointed secretary to the American boundary commission, and François Véron de Forbonnais, who worked behind the scenes for the commission and advised Silhouette when he became contrôleur général.[139] Silhouette himself wrote only one important text in this period, exploring the foundations of British power and prosperity, which was not published until 1760 but which circulated widely in manuscript within the royal administration.[140] Here he argued that Britain's dynamism derived principally from its advantageous position in American trade.[141] It was the continental American colonies he emphasised, but not for the same reasons as his Patriot friends. He stressed the importance of American re-exports, especially the tobacco with which he was familiar. He had relatively less regard for the British Caribbean colonies because the sugar they produced was mostly consumed in Britain itself. This emphasis Butel-Dumont faithfully reproduced in his *Histoire et commerce des colonies angloises, dans l'Amérique septentrionale*, which declared that 'The colonies that the English possess on the continent of North America are the principal source of their strength and of their wealth.'[142] Above all, Silhouette valued the navigation that carried colonial commodities to Europe, while also seeing the continental colonies as an important source of naval stores and centres for shipbuilding. In short, what impressed him about Britain's American trade was its capacity to sustain naval power.

This was one of two keys to Silhouette's vision. Dual logics promised to shape the geopolitical future, he believed, and between them to decide the contest between France and Britain. Much of Britain's advantage in wealth was artificial, a product of good policy rather than natural endowments, Silhouette assumed. Its head start would disappear once France adopted what was best in the British model. Britain was actually quite vulnerable commercially, he argued: its tobacco re-exports would collapse if the French developed their own sources of production, which Silhouette advocated; its sugar islands were becoming exhausted, while production surged in Saint-Domingue.[143] Moreover, Britain had the burden of high wages, which in time would render its manufactures uncompetitive. In a power struggle played on the terrain of peaceful commercial competition, Silhouette believed, France would win.

However, a different logic threatened to derail this rosy scenario. If Britain could secure a monopoly on American trade by seizing French and Spanish colonies, it would acquire a position of commercial supremacy that would likely be permanent. Atlantic trade and naval power sustained one another because merchant shipping trained the sailors who were drafted into wartime navies. If France were excluded from commerce with the Americas, it could never hope to marshal the navy necessary to reconquer lost colonies; the chief foundation for its merchant marine would have disappeared. Silhouette emphasised American trade so heavily because it was the one site where military power could be used decisively to set aside the regular economic underpinnings of the game, and to secure for Britain a lead France could never close. Familiar with the French debates about whether a universal monarchy of trade was possible, Silhouette believed that it would be if Britain gained a chokehold over American commerce. America had become the key to the balance of power.

It may be illusory to search for doctrinal unity among members of the Gournay circle; they constituted a network rather than a school, and Gournay deliberately cultivated debate.[144] But Silhouette's position clearly resonated – not least with Gournay himself. Echoing the political economy of the late 1730s, nearly all of Gournay's disciples held that geopolitical rivalries were better fought out in the economic realm than on the battlefield, an outlook that underpinned a strong preference for peace over war. They carried forward Melon's call to foster a democratic luxury among ordinary people, and to relax restraints on the grain trade, including prohibitions on export, in order to dynamise agriculture. Like Dutot, they held that France's principal strategic interests lay in trade rather than in managing the politics of Central Europe, that Britain therefore constituted France's most dangerous rival, and that there existed a perilous imbalance of naval power.[145] The question was how to address this problem, and here Gournay's associates and allies offered a range of views.

For Silhouette, France simply could not compete in naval terms with Britain in the short run, and therefore needed a substitute for an adequate fleet.[146] He found this in Canada. He and La Galissonière drew up a memorandum arguing for the strategic centrality of Canada as a safeguard for the rest of the French colonies. Canada would protect the commercially valuable Caribbean colonies from invasion by serving as a perpetual threat to the security of British North America, diverting British power and preventing the mobilisation of the

Thirteen Colonies to conquer the French Caribbean.[147] Silhouette reiterated the argument that commerce had become the foundation of power, and that the chief British geopolitical objective was to take over the trade of America and thereby to win superiority in Europe. If Canada ever fell to the British, the days of France's empire in America would be numbered. The most important prescription of Silhouette and La Galissonière was to build forts in the Ohio Country to defend the marchlands of New France and its communications with Louisiana, and to exclude British establishments from the region, by force if necessary.[148] The French imperial presence in the Ohio, secured solely by trade and alliances with American Indian peoples, was rapidly eroding from the late 1740s as Miamis and Shawnees increasingly gravitated towards British trade circuits. The French and British empires were drawn into a struggle precipitated by the actions of traders and Indian allies over whom they had little control.[149]

This 'fortress Canada' strategy can be contrasted with other proposals to counterbalance superior British naval power. An alternative Maurepas had raised in the 1740s was to create a league of smaller naval powers such as Denmark, Sweden, and the Dutch to check British naval strength. After his disgrace, this proposal was taken up by François-Dominique de Barberie, marquis de Saint-Contest, foreign minister from 1751 to 1754.[150] Silhouette and Gournay rejected such modes of maritime balancing as inconsistent with the long-term development of French naval power. Silhouette called for a navigation act by which all vessels carrying the national flag would be built in France and have two thirds of their crew French. This would only be feasible once the colonial potential for naval stores and shipbuilding was realised, but a second provision might be adopted sooner: to push the Dutch out of the French carrying trade by eliminating the favourable tax treatment accorded to Dutch vessels in French ports since 1699 (and renewed in 1713). There would be significant short-term prejudice to commerce in such a measure, he conceded, but the eventual payoff for the French merchant marine and navy would make it worthwhile.[151]

Navigation acts are often perceived as aggressive, but they were widely regarded as necessary in the eighteenth century to create a balance of commercial power. If every maritime nation adopted such laws, this would produce a rough equilibrium in merchant shipping, rather than the overwhelming predominance of one or two nations. Melon had praised the seventeenth-century English navigation acts as necessary to curtail Dutch control of the carrying trade, and implied that it might be proper for France to deny the Dutch renewal of the privileged position they held in French shipping, which had been extended for twenty-five years at Utrecht. Gournay agreed. Only by expanding merchant shipping would France ever have enough seamen to mount a larger navy, and to this end Dutch privileges would have to be curbed.[152] He pressed the same point in remarks on a translation of Josiah Child's *Discourse Concerning Trade* (first published in 1689), but was forced to strip these from the translation before its publication in 1754.[153] His anti-Dutch attitude clashed with the policy of the monarchy on the eve of a new war with Britain, which was to encourage neutral powers – pre-eminently the Dutch – to supply the shipping needs of the colonies.[154] Forbonnais, who opposed a navigation act, spelled out the rationale for the policy of favouring neutral shipping in a 1756 pamphlet.[155] His cousin, the political economist Louis-Joseph Plumard de Dangeul, called on the Dutch to remain neutral and for the formation of a league of neutral naval powers including the Dutch Republic, Sweden, and Denmark.[156]

The policy of confrontation with the British in the Ohio Country proposed by Silhouette was a trigger for the war that broke out in America in 1754. Clashes between Virginia militia troops led by George Washington, and French colonial regulars and their indigenous allies developed into a wider war after reinforcements arrived from Britain. But Silhouette's goal was to deter a British attack, not to court one. His work on the boundary commission convinced him of the aggressiveness of British intentions. William Shirley, one of the two British commissioners, had organised the capture of Cape Breton in 1745 as governor of Massachusetts, and aspired to annex all of Canada. He insisted on George II's claims to all of the neutral islands and to an extended Acadia encompassing everything south of the Saint Lawrence River.[157] This greater Acadia would soon permit Britain to regain Cape Breton and 'to make themselves masters of Canada whenever that should be thought proper'.[158] Indeed, Shirley hoped, an expanded British Empire, stretching to the Mississippi, growing in population and consuming British manufactured goods would one day allow Britain to dominate European politics.[159]

Silhouette failed to appreciate the differences between Shirley and his fellow commissioner, William Mildmay, and squandered the best chance for a deal between the peace parties in both governments. Mildmay's views reflected the pacific attitude of Walpole and his political heirs, especially Pelham and Robert

Darcy, earl of Holderness, who, while committed to checking French expansion in America and India, were anxious to avoid war.[160] A keen student of political economy who published several works in the 1760s, Mildmay believed British trade needed peace to prosper.[161] Remarking from Paris on the progress of simultaneous negotiations to avert further conflict between the French and British India companies, he noted that 'All sensible people in this Country, as well as in ours, are convinced that a flourishing Commerce cannot be carried on by either Side without a mutual agreement to keep Peace with one another.'[162] Among these sensible people was Daniel Trudaine, whom Mildmay had befriended.[163] Trudaine was director of commerce, Gournay's superior on the Bureau of Commerce, and a patron of the Gournay circle. Mildmay was convinced that Britain would prevail in commercial competition with France because its 'constitution' was more conducive to commercial success than the French.[164] He rejected the idea that France was preparing for war: French finances remained weak; raising taxes was impossible because of conflicts between the monarchy and the *parlements*; the French navy was unprepared, and few ships were being outfitted.[165]

When Shirley's commission was revoked in April 1752, Mildmay sought to push the negotiation in a more constructive direction. He proposed that the question of each power's rights be put aside in favour of a pragmatic partition of territories, and the creation of unsettled buffer zones between French and British possessions.[166] Pelham was enthusiastic.[167] But little progress was made, and the commission spent much of 1753 bogged down in procedural issues. Once a rupture appeared imminent, following clashes between French and British forces in the Ohio Country, Silhouette moved quickly to restart negotiations. He resurrected the idea of buffer zones and was prepared to accept withdrawal from French-held territory in return for similar British concessions. This was also the preferred solution of Forbonnais, whom Silhouette consulted.[168] Silhouette reached out directly to the peace party in Britain in hopes of an accommodation. (Joshua van Neck was involved in a separate back-channel peace overture at the same moment.[169]) Silhouette suggested that his old protector, the duc de Noailles, lead a peace embassy.[170] But Noailles now endorsed confrontation. Echoing Silhouette's own words, the elder statesman fretted that 'however chimerical the project of universal monarchy might be, that of a universal influence by means of wealth would cease to be a chimera if a nation succeeded in making itself sole mistress of the trade of America'.[171] The position Silhouette had outlined in 1747 had proven all too persuasive. He was caught in the contradictions of his own political economy, which emphasised that peaceful commercial growth was the best means to renew French power, but that British dominance in America would close the door to this strategy by shutting down French Atlantic trade.

Such fears were not unfounded. During the Seven Years' War the extraordinary successes of British arms under William Pitt's leadership seemed to put the prospect of British hegemony within reach. In 1758 a British expedition seized the French factories at Gorée and Saint-Louis in West Africa. The following year, British forces took Guadeloupe and Quebec; the rest of Canada would fall in 1760. Martinique was taken in 1762. The East India Company completed the conquest of French settlements in India in 1761. These successes were aided by the diversion of French forces to Central Europe, where a new Austro-Prussian war dragged in France, this time on Austria's side. The new alliance had the perverse consequence of entangling France in Europe rather than liberating it to fight in the Atlantic. The radical strain of London opinion linked to Pitt envisioned using war to smash the French threat once and for all by driving France out of its American colonies and the fisheries that helped sustain its navy.[172] The *Monitor*, founded by a brother of Pitt's closest city ally, William Beckford, called for the total exclusion of the French from the Newfoundland fisheries, the fur trade, and sugar production – that is, for the annexation of Newfoundland, Canada, and the French Caribbean islands. Hoping this was the intention of 'our patriot minister', the *Monitor* held that such would be 'the only secure method to reduce the naval power of our enemy to a state of impotency, and to carry our own to such a height, as to put it out of the power of all Europe to contend with us, for the sovereignty of the seas'.[173] In place of the French universal monarchy Louis XV threatened to foist on Europe, Pitt and his supporters would establish an empire of liberty. A British hegemony built on unshakeable commercial and naval supremacy would guarantee the liberties of Europe and extend British freedom to the former colonies of France and Spain, integrating them into the British Empire.

The Pittite programme of imperial expansion elicited a powerful pushback from several of his fellow ministers, including both former Walpole allies like Lord Hardwicke and erstwhile Patriots like Lord Bute and the duke of Bedford. 'It is possible for England to be overloaded with foreign colonies,' Hardwicke told Newcastle.[174] Was Britain 'to wage eternal war and run in debt fifty millions more,' he asked, 'upon wild imaginary schemes of conquest?'[175] 'We have too much already,' Bedford told Bute in 1761, 'more than we know what to do with; and I very much fear, that, if we retain the greatest part of our conquests out of Europe, we shall be in danger of over-colonising and undoing ourselves by them, as the Spaniards have done.'[176] Hardwicke's client Josiah Tucker, then the most widely read English writer on trade, privately bemoaned 'yᵉ Pittian Madness' that pushed Britain to ever more extensive conquests.[177] Tucker rejected the idea that the French constituted a real threat in America.[178] A bloody and expensive war was being fought there for a useless wilderness. He was no more enthusiastic about Britain's acquisitions in the Caribbean in the 1763 peace of Paris, the islands of Grenada, Saint Vincent, Dominica, and Tobago. 'I hardly thought these Islands, or any other Acquisitions . . . worth the Costs of both Men and Money, which had been, and would be, bestowed on them,' he told Shelburne, then president of the Board of Trade.[179] Above all, Tucker's target was the notion beloved of the Patriot press that successful war could enrich a people. He deplored such thinking, 'for of all Absurdities, that of going to War for the Sake of getting Trade is the most absurd'. Tucker implicitly contrasted Pitt with Walpole whose 'Endeavours to prevent an infatuated People from quarrelling with their best Customers, were truly patriotical'.[180]

In the war aims debate that played out in the press from 1760 through 1763, the *Monitor* demanded that Britain retain all its conquests, because only by so doing could French and Spanish power be permanently crippled. To reduce for good the French threat to British security, the Bourbon enemy would have to be stripped of the colonial resources that sustained its trade and naval power. Guadeloupe and Martinique should be annexed. Havana, captured from Spain in August 1762, should also be kept because thereby Britain could open a 'free trade' to Mexico, and break for good the French scheme 'of engrossing the riches of that vast empire subject to the Crown of Spain in South America'.[181] Pitt may or may not have subscribed to this radical vision in its particulars, but he inclined towards a maximalist vision of an acceptable peace.[182] Ultimately he was overruled and pushed out of the cabinet by one-time allies like Bute and Bedford who thought it unrealistic to expect France to 'give up its Existence as a Trading State and a Maritime Power'.[183] Pitt subsequently criticised the peace treaty on the grounds that the peacemakers had 'lost sight of the great fundamental principle that France is chiefly if not solely to be dreaded by us in the light of a maritime and commercial power' but had been given the means 'of recovering her prodigious losses'.[184]

The peace of 1763 closed a long moment in British politics extending back to the end of the 1730s, when Patriot fears that France was seeking to aggrandise itself on the basis of an expanding commerce largely prevailed against the Walpolean claim that peace was most advantageous to British trade and power. The latter position, rooted in the Fleury–Walpole détente of the 1720s and 1730s, had never ceased to appeal to many officials, merchants, and political economists. We see it above all in the call of Henry Pelham to end the War of the Austrian Succession, and later in the efforts of Pelham, Holderness, and Mildmay to hold the line against a renewal of war over territorial disputes in North America. The writings of Josiah Tucker represent its clearest expression among writers on trade. Even one-time Patriot Whigs like Bute and Bedford were partially won over to this view by the excesses of Pittian imperialism and the explosion of public debt. Despite Britain's sweeping victory, there was a certain disillusion with the aggressive expansionism of the Patriot stance.

Yet there could be no return to the Pax Walpoliana after 1763. The French monarchy would never again be willing to appease Britain by neglecting its navy. French officials and merchants learned the lesson that a small navy was incompatible with a strategy of exploiting colonies and building up colonial and international trade. Even if France had the potential to outcompete Britain on the terrain of global commerce, as some French officials and writers held, Britain could block a purely commercial strategy by seizing French colonies in America. A larger fleet might deter British aggression, but a modest one seemed to invite it. Moreover, in allying with Austria in 1756, Louis XV meant to end the strategic tug-of-war in which French resources needed to prosecute the struggle against Britain had been diverted to continental defence. The Franco-Austrian alliance would never be an easy one, but it would hold until the French Revolution, permitting an Atlantic-facing strategic orientation. This could not be a recipe for an untroubled Franco-British relationship. Indeed, the duc de Choiseul, Louis XV's leading minister in the 1760s, was committed to a Bourbon war of revenge to redress the balance of power and check the British bid to establish a universal monarchy of trade.

The breakdown of the long peace confronts us with the Janus-faced character of the political economy that prevailed in official circles in France and

Britain in the age of Walpole and Fleury: political-economic understandings anchored a strong peace preference, but the same frameworks rationalised the march to war at first in the Caribbean in 1739 and later in America in the mid-1750s. For Patriots, peace itself had become a threat to the balance of commercial power and to Britain's security. The kind of uneven economic development that is typical of capitalism – the rapid growth of economically less-developed states – could quickly inflate the power of the beneficiaries and thereby jeopardise the security of longer-established rivals. Walpole's opponents could see no exit from this predicament short of a bold stroke to change the underpinnings of the global commercial order in Britain's favour.

Similarly, in America during the 1750s, French policy was trapped in an unresolvable contradiction between the desire to preserve peace and the imperative to confront militarily what was perceived as a British bid to oust France from its colonies and permanently tilt the balance of wealth in its favour. Empire in America would remain the principal stake of Franco-British struggle in the twenty years following 1763. But with Canada having failed in its designated role of diverting British power from the more valuable Caribbean colonies, Choiseul relinquished it at the peace, and new means had to be found to balance British power in the Americas. The French monarchy would find these in the American Revolution.

5

MADE IN AMERICA

Free Trade and the Crisis of Empire

A free-trade revolution occurred in the Americas between the 1760s and the 1780s. Territories long held in closed commercial empires were opened up to a greater measure of interimperial and international trade. In 1750 the French colonies in the Americas, which still included Canada and the vast Louisiana Territory, were governed under the terms of the Exclusif, which prohibited trade with competing empires. The navigation laws regulated Britain's colonies in North America and the Caribbean. With few exceptions they channelled commerce through British ports and on British ships. By 1785, a much freer trade characterised commercial relations in the Western Hemisphere. An independent United States welcomed ships from all nations to its harbours. French free ports established in the Caribbean in 1767 had expanded into a wider network in 1784 and legalised a thriving trade between North America and the French sugar islands. The British Empire had welcomed French and Spanish planters and merchants to free ports in the Caribbean since 1766. After the American War, it permitted a mostly free trade with its former colonial subjects in North America, though insisting that only British ships carry provisions from the United States to the British colonies in the Caribbean.

Freedom of trade in the Americas was a weapon in struggles for commercial advantage, a means to re-establish a balance of power, and a strategy to reduce the relative burdens of empire. The Whigs led in Parliament by Charles Watson-Wentworth, marquess of Rockingham hoped in the 1760s to draw the French and Spanish colonies into a British commercial orbit by encouraging smuggling between the British and Bourbon empires, and to deprive France and Spain of the economic benefit of these possessions. In adopting its own free ports, the French monarchy hoped to parry this thrust while expanding North American markets for the molasses and rum produced in its sugar islands, thereby stimulating their prosperity. At later moments French officials envisioned that a freer trade between their colonies and British North America might destabilise Britain's political hold there. When rebellion erupted in the Thirteen Colonies, certain officials saw that they could use it to open North America to a universal commerce, taking an enormous weight out of the scale of wealth and power to Britain's loss, redistributing the gains of American trade broadly, and thereby improving permanently the French position in the balance of power. For his part, in sponsoring legislation to reopen trade with America on a free-trade basis in 1783, the British prime minister, Lord Shelburne, hoped to reverse the outcome of the American War by recovering the lion's share of Britain's markets in its former colonies.

By mid-century, America had emerged as a flashpoint of the Franco-British rivalry because of its perceived economic and strategic value. Many French officials, as we have seen, believed that Britain intended to construct a universal monarchy of trade by using naval dominance to engross the commerce of the Americas. Patriot Whigs in Britain, conversely, held that the nation's commercial future depended on expanding markets in the Thirteen Colonies. After the Seven Years' War, British concerns about competitiveness further augmented America's importance because the colonies could be viewed as a remedy for a British economy running into the limits of its own success. Britain's high wages would make its manufactures increasingly uncompetitive, some argued. In 1779, the merchant writer Thomas Tod recognised the fear (though he did not share it) that competing European nations 'have the materials of many manufactures cheaper; and as they have less money, less luxury, less paper credit, less public debt, and fewer taxes, their labourers will work for less wages, and consequently can bring goods to America much cheaper than the British'.[1] Without the privileged access to America secured by its trade laws, the concern was that Britain could not remain a dominant exporter. The projected expansion of American markets in the future, buoyed by rapid population growth, would guarantee Britain's prosperity indefinitely, boosters claimed.[2]

As we have seen, in a capitalist interstate order even peaceful economic expansion could be a destabilising threat to the balance of power. From the French perspective, it was not only that America was growing fast and seemed to anchor British prosperity, but that it must be the launching pad for any prospective British attempt to conquer French or Spanish colonies. Conversely, if Britain's hold on America could be broken, balance might be restored, creating the basis for a more stable and peaceful future. The French attempt to force free trade on Britain in America by recognising the independence of the Thirteen Colonies might ultimately decrease tensions between Europe's two dominant commercial states by re-establishing a balance of wealth that the Seven Years' War and the explosive growth of American markets had overturned.

Freedom of trade also promised a new and better kind of commercial empire – cheaper, more dynamic, and more acceptable to disgruntled colonists. From the British perspective, freer trade in the Caribbean would conciliate Americans, expand trade flows (which might be taxed without offending anyone), and, by enriching the American colonies, increase their capacity to absorb goods manufactured in Britain. The Seven Years' War had underlined the immense costs of empire. Public debt ballooned, eliciting the reaction against Pittite imperialism that prompted Lord Bute to make peace in 1762, and raising fears that the higher peacetime taxes necessary to service the debt would undermine British competitiveness and sap the vigour of the British economy. Intended to secure commerce, war threatened to devour its benefits. Proponents of the new British free ports in 1766, who aspired to penetrate the French and Spanish colonies commercially, viewed this as an alternative to Pitt's destabilising and appallingly expensive conquests. It would pull the French and Spanish settlements into British commercial circuits, delivering profits without the burdens of sovereignty.

At Versailles new thinking about increasing the value of colonies without augmenting protection costs ran along similar lines, indeed, at certain moments, involved a still more fundamental reimagining of empire. After relinquishing Canada and Louisiana in 1763, the French monarchy embraced a largely de-territorialised empire of sugar islands, enclaves, and bases, which promised to be cheaper to govern and defend without any loss of commercial advantages. The drive to lower costs elicited still more radical revisioning. Might France not be better off depending on the sovereignty of others to secure its trade – at least in some parts of the world – rather than paying for an empire of its own? Some officials suggested replacing formal French Empire in the Caribbean with a loose confederation of ex-colonies, henceforth to be independent and tied to the mother country only by trade. Others hoped to establish a league of allied regional states in India to protect French trade there – a governance structure that would cost French taxpayers nothing while allowing an expanded commerce (see pp. 249–50). The same idea could readily be translated to the

American context when, with the American Revolution, the prospect opened of replacing the British Empire with a confederation of small, independent republics, obliged by a network of treaties with European polities to keep their markets open to all. Britain's imperial framework for trade in America might be replaced with an international regime that opened America to joint European exploitation.

Though the chief inspiration for freer trade did not come from the new political economies elaborated in this period, such as Physiocracy in France or the work of David Hume and Adam Smith in Britain, officials and politicians mobilised these to make the case for change. Part of the impetus behind Physiocracy came from efforts to reform the French Empire in the 1760s, and Physiocrats promoted the relaxation of the Exclusif in 1767.[3] The leading advocate for remaking French empire as a loose free-trade confederation in the 1770s was Jacques Turgot, a former acolyte of Gournay and a Physiocratic fellow-traveller. He was also the principal critic of French intervention in the American War, implicitly rejecting the argument that a free-trading America would restore a balance of wealth between France and Britain. Turning to the British side, officials there consulted Adam Smith in the 1770s and 1780s on how to remake the economic and political relationship between Britain and America. The debates on American free trade at the war's end transformed the reception of Smith's ideas, giving them greater currency and prominence than they had before, as both Shelburne and his critics invoked Smith's authority. For all that, Smith's thinking was never the foundation for the political economy either of the Whig prime minister or his Tory critics. These early stirrings in the sphere of international commercial policy of what is retrospectively viewed as economic liberalism emerged in complex entanglement with a long-standing project to remake the political foundations of global trade in the name of national power, stability, and security.

RETHINKING COMMERCIAL EMPIRE IN THE AMERICAS: THE FREE PORTS OF THE 1760S

The British and French governments established free ports in the Caribbean in 1766 and 1767, respectively, to permit interimperial trade in a range of commodities. The near simultaneity of these openings was no coincidence.

The French correctly understood Britain to aim at penetrating their empire by fostering illicit trade – to draw French sugar, coffee, cotton, and indigo into the circuits of British imperial commerce, and to deprive France and Spain of the benefits of their own colonies. The French free ports were partly a defensive measure intended to limit the impact of the British initiative. Yet for all the aggressiveness of the British free ports, their proponents rejected the agenda of conquest pursued under Pitt and the burdensome imperial sovereignty it implied. The commercial advantages of the French and Spanish empires could be engrossed without war or annexations, and would channel the Franco-British power struggle in the Americas into more peaceful competition. The free ports were vehicles for a less expensive, commercial imperialism. For their part, officials in the French naval and colonial ministry looked to the ports to win larger markets for French molasses and rum in North America, and to stimulate the growth of the plantation economy. Britons could not draw off part of the French colonies' production without also contributing to their prosperity. If carefully managed, a more open French empire might be a more vibrant one. The move to a freer trade in the Caribbean drew on long-standing practices of extending commercial liberty selectively, on novel political-economic reasoning, and above all on a burgeoning demand for freer trade from French and British colonists.

Free ports had long sought to bend smuggling traffic to the advantage of states. Louis XIV had granted Dunkirk free-port status after he acquired it from England in 1662, and it became a centre for smuggling contraband goods into Britain – notably, in the 1760s and 1770s, the foreign teas that created such problems for the East India Company in the home market. Such strategic resort to freedom of trade was consistent with the Colbertist traditions examined in Chapter 1 (see pp. 37–40). The French monarchy, as Jeff Horn has shown, had long adopted measures of free trade where these had seemed advantageous.[4] There was an established British tradition of thinking about how free ports might draw a greater share of foreign trade into British ports. The inspiration for their adoption in the Caribbean lay also in the parallel world of trade that occupied the interstices between closed mercantilist empires. Smuggling had always been a major feature of life in the Caribbean, but it exploded during the Seven Years' War, particularly between British North America and the French islands.[5] Officials sought to appropriate some of the dynamism and flexibility of the realm of smugglers and wartime neutral traders to surmount the deficits of colonial empires. Free ports in the Western Hemisphere were modelled on smuggling hubs that developed spontaneously in harbours far from imperial control.[6] Pioneered by the Dutch in the Caribbean, official free ports extended an umbrella of legality, and some limited protection, over an otherwise precarious trade, making it serve the interests of states.

A relaxation of the Exclusif was part of a broader design to foster colonial prosperity and to secure the French Empire that Louis XV's dominant minister, Étienne-François de Stainville, duc de Choiseul, came to embrace. Serially, and at times concurrently, minister of foreign affairs, war, and of the navy and colonies, and assisted by his cousin, César-Gabriel de Choiseul, duc de Praslin, from 1758 until 1770 Choiseul superintended the French Empire and its relations with rival states. His imperial priorities were shaped by the failure of Canada to serve the strategic purpose envisioned for it of diverting British strength from the Caribbean. By 1761, when the first serious peace overtures began, he had decided to relinquish it. In 1763 he presided over the cession of much of the trans-Appalachian West to Britain. The concession of the rest of Louisiana to Spain at the same time was not just compensation to an ally, François-Joseph Ruggiu argues, but a deliberate rejection of extended land empire with all its expense and potential for boundary conflicts.[7] Choiseul was far from indifferent to arguments for strategic possessions. He would have liked to retain Louisbourg as a strong point to protect the all-important Newfoundland fisheries. He embraced the idea of a colony of soldier-farmers in Guiana to protect Martinique and Guadeloupe – sponsoring the disastrous Kourou expedition in 1763, which failed with great loss of life.[8] He came to see Mauritius as a key strong point to protect French commerce in the Indian Ocean.[9] But, in general, he believed, colonies must generate economic benefits adequate to justify the cost of their administration and defence. The right kind of possessions were commercially differentiated from the metropole and exchanged exotic commodities for its provisions and manufactured goods.[10] Guadeloupe, Martinique, and Saint-Domingue fitted the bill. Canada did not.[11]

Though he advanced an aggressive programme to tighten the administrative links between Versailles and what remained of the empire, the most alluring possibility, from Choiseul's perspective, was overseas trade without the burdens of empire – the promise of a commerce protected by allies rather than at the expense of the French monarchy. Sovereignty might be necessary to create the legal and security framework required to foster profit in distant trade, but that sovereignty need not be French. Choiseul revived the ambition to turn the Spanish Empire into a zone of French commercial exploitation. In echoes of the early years of the century, he and his principal agents in Spain, the ambassador Pierre-Paul d'Ossun and the consul general, the abbé Béliardi, aspired to a kind of commercial union of the French and Spanish empires.[12] At its most grandiose, they imagined a semi-exclusive Bourbon trading zone stretching from the Mascarenes to the Philippines, encompassing the Mediterranean and Spanish America. Béliardi dreamed of a Bourbon navigation act integrating the smaller Italian states and Venice.[13]

But nothing like this could be achieved for the same reasons that it had been impossible during the War of the Spanish Succession: the Spanish did not want to become a commercial satellite of France. Indeed, French merchants complained of continued mistreatment in Spain, despite article 24 of the 1761 Franco-Spanish alliance, which promised conditions for French merchants akin to native Spaniards. Instead, the Spanish monarchy hoped to vitalise its own empire, in part by relaxing the monopoly of Cádiz in 1765, allowing certain other ports to ship goods to and from destinations in the Caribbean. Eventually, Choiseul sought a commercial treaty with Spain to extend to France the liberties already accorded British merchants – a pale shadow of the privileges he originally hoped to secure, and little more than an affirmation of the international regime that had emerged by 1750.

Choiseul planned a new war against Britain in partnership with Spain, to be undertaken once the Bourbon monarchies regained strength. To this end, he tried to rebuild the French fleet and encouraged Spain to do the same. However, as Bourbon naval readiness remained a distant prospect, avoiding conflict, which had initially been tactical, became a more enduring feature of Choiseul's stance. He sought not merely revenge, as is often asserted, but to check a growing imbalance of commercial power in Britain's favour that threatened the security and status of France and the peace of Europe. He viewed Britain in terms similar to Silhouette, his former colleague. The rival threatened to construct a universal monarchy of trade by using naval power to monopolise Atlantic commerce. If peaceful commercial competition were to create balance with Britain, this rogue nation would first have to be cut down to size. Short of financial collapse, or rebellion in America – uncertain and distant prospects – only war might avert the danger Britain incarnated.[14]

Choiseul's policy of relaxing the Exclusif has to be seen, at least in part, as an effort to mollify planters, the better to secure the French Empire in case of future conflicts with Britain. Never had the trade laws appeared more burdensome to the colonists in the French Caribbean. The cession of Canada, the end of the British occupation of Guadeloupe and Martinique (conquered during the Seven Years' War), and the economic hangover from war gave rise to high prices and acute shortages of slaves, foodstuffs, and construction materials.[15] French merchants could not meet demand, especially in the Lesser Antilles. The only licit sources of wood and corn had been lost, while the Newfoundland fisheries, dislocated by war, could not meet colonial needs for cod. Planters were accustomed to marketing molasses and rum on a large scale to North Americans, and there were no alternate outlets. For these by-products of the sugar industry to lie worthlessly on the hands of planters in the face of growing American demand constituted a real grievance.[16]

If the war had left planters with a new sense of resentment – and of commercial possibility – it taught equally important lessons at Versailles. To prevent the kind of wartime defections that facilitated the British conquest of Guadeloupe and Martinique, the colonists needed to be appeased. Moreover, there might be major benefits to the colonial economy from greater openness. Production burgeoned on Guadeloupe during the years of British occupation (1759–63) thanks to easy access to slaves, provisions, and markets. British traders imported nearly 24,000 slaves into the island between 1759 and 1763 (in contrast to just 3,000 legally imported between 1713 and 1755), allowing the number of sugar plantations to increase from 185 before the war to 447 at its conclusion.[17] Choiseul could not but be impressed at the stimulus the colony received from its integration into the circuits of British trade.

As minister of the navy and colonies, Choiseul entrusted the Bureau of Colonies to Jean-Baptiste Dubuc, a Martiniquan planter and committed supporter of an opening to foreign trade in the Caribbean. Two of Dubuc's brothers sat in Martinique's *chambre d'agriculture*, a hotbed of planter resentment at the subordination of colonial to metropolitan interests. Another sat on the Bureau of Commerce representing Martinique. However, as Pernille Røge has shown, Dubuc was forced to incline to the will of Choiseul, whose views on the measure of free trade permissible were more limited than his own.[18] It was in a Colbertist spirit that Dubuc articulated the official position on the reform of the Exclusif, and the eventual establishment of free ports.

Neither merchants nor planters, but the state alone, had the perspective to discern the true interest of commerce, argued Dubuc. He did not question the principle that colonial trade ought to be a metropolitan monopoly. But the Exclusif must be relaxed so as to maximise colonial prosperity and thus the capacity of the islands to consume French goods and to send tropical commodities to French ports for re-export to Northern and Central Europe. French trade could not absorb molasses and rum; it raised the costs of cultivation by failing to deliver enough slaves; and it procured none of the livestock, timber, barrel staves and hoops required. Dubuc pushed to make permanent and general three liberties already extended provisionally to parts of the French Caribbean in response to the dislocations of war: the freedom to buy slaves from foreigners, to sell rum and molasses to them, and to purchase cod and other provisions from them when French merchants could not provide them. Stiff duties on such imports, he promised, would give French traders the preference and limit the gains of foreigners.[19] In the spring of 1765, the Bureau of Commerce, which represented pre-eminently the interests of the French ports, rejected these recommendations. The Council of State would have the final word, but it shelved debate for a time.

Even among officials sympathetic to the planters and to commercial liberty there were doubts about the prudence of allowing foreigners to trade in the colonies. Consulted by Choiseul in 1762, Paul-Pierre Le Mercier de La Rivière, a once and future intendant of Martinique, had opposed as 'impracticable and dangerous' the freedom to import slaves sold by foreigners. If such liberty were accorded, French merchants would soon be pushed out of the slave trade. Moreover, to pay for 10,000 captives, 10 million livres' worth of sugar and coffee would have to be traded into British hands, giving British merchants the power to rival France in re-export markets. A better solution would be 'an entire liberty of trade on the African coast,' that is, the abrogation of taxes on the slave trade and the admission of slaving ships from the Caribbean. Most importantly, the metropole must lower costs for provisions and freight. Le Mercier de La Rivière, who cultivated ties to the marquis de Mirabeau and François Quesnay, recommended the Physiocratic cure-all of freedom to export grain, which would unleash a virtuous cycle of higher investment in agriculture, expansion in production, and lower prices. Only for provisions like wood, which the metropole could not supply, should the colonists be allowed to trade with North Americans.[20]

Yet it was among the Physiocrats that French ministerial reformers most readily found allies. As Røge has shown, this group of political-economic thinkers and writers engaged deeply with problems of colonial reform. The founder of Physiocracy, François Quesnay, had some initial hesitation about the value of colonies. A nation with undeveloped lands at home had little business establishing colonies, he argued, in a remark that found its way into *La Philosophie rurale* (1763). Yet he acknowledged that, in theory, plantation colonies could generate wealth in the same fashion as any other agricultural enterprise.[21] Mirabeau's brother had served as governor of Guadeloupe in the early 1750s, and through an extensive correspondence the marquis developed an interest in colonial reform. In his bestselling *L'ami des hommes* (1756–58), Mirabeau condemned plantation slavery and argued that planters should enjoy freedom of trade. Later Physiocrats and Physiocratic sympathisers would differ on the value of colonies. Nicolas Baudeau, Pierre-Joseph-André Roubaud, and Pierre-Samuel Dupont extended Physiocratic imperial thought, developed abolitionist schemes, and called for new colonies in Africa based on free labour.[22] Yet those Physiocrats or Physiocratic sympathisers who focused on the costs of sovereignty, rather than purely commercial questions, took a more sceptical view. Louis-Paul Abeille and Jacques Turgot held that the sugar islands were expensive to administer and ruinous to defend. Turgot argued that they benefited the metropole no more than they did any other European nation that imported their productions. Both Turgot and Abeille supported independence for the colonies, as we will see (below, p. 206), and their integration with the mother country only through ties of trade and culture.

There were profound differences between the Physiocrats' positions and those embraced by Choiseul, or even Dubuc, with whom they had more in common. Physiocrats argued that colonies ought to be treated like provinces, not managed under a regime of exception.[23] This meant that colonists should enjoy the same rights as metropolitan subjects, and some Physiocrats held this argument should extend to an abandonment of slavery. Choiseul rejected this understanding of colonies totally. Successful colonies were entirely unlike the metropole, did not compete with it, but specialised in producing goods unavailable there and exchanged them for the product of French cultivation and manufacturing. For Dubuc, too, it was colonial difference that mattered. Colonies served as mechanisms to exchange French products for exotic commodities more highly sought-after on European markets. Unlike the Physiocrats, he saw labour, not land, as the principal source of wealth. Perhaps the starkest divergence between Physiocratic and official thinking lay in the Physiocratic argument that France would be best served by specialising in agricultural production. From Choiseul's basically Colbertist perspective, this meant specialising in being poor.

Despite these differences, on the question of the Exclusif Dubuc formed an informal partnership with the Physiocrats. His personal vision of free trade as it applied to the colonies was closer to theirs than to Choiseul's, though in his official capacity he had to toe the ministerial line.[24] For the Physiocrats, nothing so typified the irrationality of the existing order as mercantilist empires set up to maximise the monopoly profits of metropolitan merchants. Any merchant gains, they argued, were overbalanced by the losses to planters and French farmers who provisioned the colonies. Colonists should be allowed to trade their sugar and coffee to the highest bidder, while exporters of provisions to the Caribbean ought to be able to use the cheapest carrier. In this way the prosperity of the colony, that of French producers of goods for colonial markets, and the monarchy's tax yield would all be maximised.[25]

After the Council of State deferred a decision, debate on the Exclusif moved into the salons and the press, encouraged by Dubuc, who participated in the enlightened sociability of the French capital.[26] While there was sympathy in these circles for the planters, and a tendency to see varieties of commercial liberty as a solution to problems of the imperial economy, no consensus emerged on the advisability of allowing the colonists to trade with foreigners. Dubuc leaked his own proposal for a relaxation of the Exclusif to the *Journal de l'agriculture, du commerce et des finances*, a semi-official periodical whose editorship had recently passed to the Physiocrat Dupont. The latter published it, and followed up with other materials tending to support Dubuc's view, while also pressing home a Physiocratic critique of the whole system of official favour for French overseas trade.[27] Though Dubuc was also the source of many of the materials used in the monumental *Histoire des deux Indes* (see below, p. 251), written by the abbé Guillaume-Thomas Raynal in collaboration with others, most prominently Denis Diderot, the book's first edition in 1770 rejected the relaxation of the Exclusif.[28] To allow British Americans to trade in the colonies risked their loss. Free trade between the French islands and North America would stimulate the latter's growth, and prepare the absorption of the French colonies into the British Empire. Instead, Raynal proposed an alternate free-trade scheme. The metropole must admit colonial rum and permit the direct shipment by French carriers of colonial produce to foreign markets. This would lower costs, increase the consumption of colonial goods, and thereby stimulate production.[29]

If nothing came of his initiative in 1765, Dubuc had not given up hope. A more propitious moment to introduce a measure of free trade arrived in response to the British Free Port Act of May 1766, which created two free ports in Dominica, an island acquired from France in 1763, and four in Jamaica. The Rockingham administration intended the free ports to foster a smuggling commerce between the British islands and the possessions of France and Spain by welcoming foreign traders to exchange their goods with British and American buyers and sellers.[30] The Dominica free ports, Prince Rupert's Bay and Roseau, situated between Guadeloupe and Martinique, would facilitate an interloping trade with the French. Those on Jamaica – Kingston, Montego Bay, Santa Lucea, and Savanna-la-Mar – were intended to boost the once valuable, but now flagging, contraband trade to Spanish America. (By some accounts it diminished tenfold between the 1740s and the mid-1770s.[31]) In part this was a reaction against the policies of the preceding Grenville administration, which enforced the trade laws strictly, especially those regulating the traffic between the French islands and America.[32] This general tightening of enforcement was applied for a time to the trade between Jamaica and Spanish America, leading to complaints that this misconceived policy was destroying a useful commerce.[33]

The short-lived administration of the marquess of Rockingham (1765–66) took a sharply different view of imperial political economy.[34] Rockingham helped to direct, and benefited in turn from, a campaign against Grenville's legislation led by a Committee of North American Merchants formed at the end of 1765 under the chairmanship of Barlow Trecothick, a substantial London trader and provincial agent for New Hampshire.[35] The repeal of these

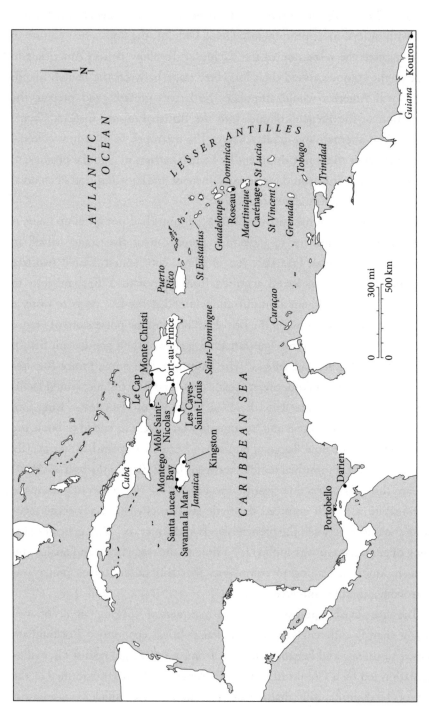

3. The Caribbean in the 1760s

measures, including the Stamp Act, in 1766 marked a moment of heightened influence for organised trade in British politics.[36] Rockingham's supporters, including his secretary and key Commons spokesman, Edmund Burke, held that Grenville's policies threatened to kill the goose that laid the golden egg. America was valuable to Britain principally as a consumer of its manufactured wares; Grenville's measures undermined the ability of Americans to consume, and indirectly damaged British production through the American boycotts of British goods they elicited in retaliation. The best way to harness America to British revenue needs was to foster American economic growth, and to tax the flows of trade this generated.[37] Instead of setting a relatively high molasses duty to maximise revenue, as Grenville had done, the Rockinghamites cut the duty to a penny a gallon, seeking to push as large a trade as possible into legitimate channels, and to skim from these flows as high a revenue as was practicable without arousing the ire of American consumers. By taxing an expanded, legal American trade, one key supporter argued, 'you may have a sufficient revenue to pay all Great Britain's expense for her colonies'.[38]

The free ports represented only part of a much more ambitious programme of commercial reform. The most expansive vision was that of John Huske MP, a merchant with Boston roots who called for the creation of a dozen free ports in the Americas, including New York, and was for 'extending our trade with foreign colonies in America far beyond whatever it was in its most flourishing state'. Linked originally to the former chancellor of the Exchequer, Charles Townshend, Huske supported Rockingham's initiatives on trade and the Stamp Act, and was considered a contender for a cabinet position if the administration had survived.[39] He envisioned a zone of relatively free interimperial trade in the Americas as a branch of a broader British commercial-imperial system. He wanted foreign shipping to have liberty to carry the produce of the French and Spanish colonies to North America, in exchange for slaves, provisions, and British manufactured goods. Relative American freedom of trade would be compatible, at least in spirit, with the navigation acts because British shipping would still carry all American goods to Europe, be they of British or foreign provenance, while all raw materials necessary for industry would be channelled to the British market.[40]

Leading Rockingham Whigs aspired to renovate the whole of Britain's commercial system, 'a complete revision of all the Commercial Laws, which regard our own or the foreign Plantations, from the act of Navigation downwards', as Burke put it.[41] They wanted to remove restraints on American trade with foreigners unnecessary for the protection of British commerce. Without giving the fullest possible rein to their trade, Huske argued, Americans could not buy British goods. Trade with foreigners enabled them to afford the products of the mother country. 'Many of the colonies were so situated as to have very few means to traffick with this country,' Burke agreed. 'It became therefore our object to let them into as much foreign trade as could be given them without interfering with our own.'[42] Trecothick's committee hinted that these measures might be 'but as the great Out Lines of a plan to extend the National Commerce'.[43] As Burke noted of the intra-Caribbean trade, 'we have the advantage in every essential article of it', such that 'almost every restriction on our communication with our neighbours there, is a restriction unfavourable to ourselves'.[44] The planter interest, though favourable to the Jamaican free ports, blocked a wider extension of free trade. Planters worried that a more ambitious measure of the sort Huske called for would stimulate French sugar production, and that through leakages from the new system foreign sugar would compete with their product in imperial markets.[45]

Within the broader history of free-trade ideas explored in this book, how should Rockinghamite ideas be understood? They represented not an outright attack on the navigation acts, which Burke would later defend, but a significant modulation of their rigour where freer trade seemed certain to yield greater benefits to the mother country. There were precedents for such a move, for example in the 1730 bill allowing South Carolina to export rice directly to Southern Europe, bypassing British ports, because, as Joshua Gee wrote, 'it will not bear the charge of bringing home and Re-shipping'.[46]

For Burke the free ports marked a prioritisation of the needs of British manufacturers. There had been complaints of high prices in the postwar years for sugar and cotton from refiners and cotton manufacturers respectively. The French islands might expand the supply of both, especially raw cotton, of which they were an exporter second in importance only to the Ottoman Empire. Interimperial freedom of trade in the Caribbean would secure the cotton producers of Lancashire raw materials at a lower price, and, by allowing American merchants to trade provisions for French molasses, give American consumers greater buying power to purchase the wares of Manchester and other industrial centres.[47] The free trade in question was thus to be piecemeal and strategic in the way typical of contemporary understandings. There was certainly little hint here of laissez-faire ideas – of self-organising markets, or the need for government to step back from the governance of trade.

Viewed in the broadest geopolitical terms, the free ports initiative expanded and strengthened the British commercial empire at Bourbon expense without war or conquest. It offered an implicit reply to a more aggressive Pittite demand for freedom of trade during the war – to be based on the annexation of key parts of the Spanish and French empires.[48] Free ports were first proposed by Campbell Dalrymple, a past client of Pitt who hoped to win a new patron in Bute. As wartime governor of conquered Guadeloupe, he remarked on the success of the Dutch free port at Sint Eustatius (founded in 1737), which drew a great deal of foreign commerce into Dutch channels.[49] He proposed that by the establishment of a free port on Dominica to channel slaves, East India goods, British manufactured wares, and American provisions to the French islands, Britain might 'reap the advantages of all their Islands without conquering them'.[50] Huske echoed this message in 1766: 'does not the supplying foreign Colonies with what they want & taking from them what they produce', he asked, 'make them the Colonies of Gr. Britain, & this too without the expense of supporting or defending them?'[51] The free ports represented a low-cost commercial imperialism that would harness smuggling to knit the empires of rival powers into British commercial circuits without the expense of conquest or administration.

The Free Port Act marked an inflexion point in British commercial relations with Spanish America. Instead of seeking coerced access by commercial treaty, a new Asiento, or the exertion of naval power, Britain strove to ease commercial access to its Caribbean colonies for Spanish colonists willing to trade for British goods. Huske suggested that Jamaica might in time convey the whole of Spain's American trade into British hands, and this without exciting the kind of tensions that led to war in 1739, because it was Spanish subjects that would carry on the trade.[52] There were echoes here, no doubt unintended, of William Paterson's proposal for Caribbean free ports sixty years earlier, which were to channel the trade of Spain's empire, and serve as foundations of a benign and pacific hegemony (see above, pp. 85–7).

The architects of the Dominica free ports intended them to expand the British slave trade by selling enslaved Africans to the French colonies, though in Britain the passage of the Act was the occasion for some early anti-slavery talk. Between 1766 and 1770, British slavers brought 17,353 enslaved labourers to Dominica, the majority to be sold to French planters.[53] While Burke did not allow his own reservations about the slave trade to interfere with his schemes to expand interimperial trade in the Caribbean, his Grenvillite opponent, William Knox, though himself a slaveowner, complained that while the act 'for opening free ports in the West-Indies declares Negroes a *lawful commodity*', this had not aroused 'a single protest in abhorrence of that trade, or *of treating rational creatures as property*'.[54] The postwar moment, as Christopher L. Brown has shown, fostered new thinking about how emancipation might be bent to the purposes of empire-building. Maurice Morgann, secretary to Lord Shelburne, the president of the Board of Trade, developed a plan to settle a colony of free Africans in West Florida. He held that the advantages of free labour would eventually push the older colonies to emancipate bondsmen. For Morgann, emancipation would strengthen the empire and raise Britain 'to the seat of unenvied and unlimited dominion'.[55] Despite their radically different implications for the enslaved, we might situate such schemes alongside the free ports of 1766 as designs to extend British imperial power peacefully after the Seven Years' War.

In France, some of the Physiocrats criticised plantation slavery and proposed schemes for new colonies based on free labour in West Africa intended to renovate the French Empire. The marquis de Mirabeau had attacked slavery on both moral and economic grounds in his *L'ami des hommes* (1756–58) but these ideas barely found a place in the *Philosophie rurale* (1763), the first full statement of the Physiocratic doctrine. It fell to younger Physiocrats to elaborate the critique. Before he turned to Physiocracy, the abbé Nicolas Baudeau had proposed to renew French power in the Indian Ocean by establishing a free port in the Mascarene Islands and to build up an agricultural workforce by importing and emancipating enslaved Africans and Asians.[56] In the pages of the journal he founded, and later repurposed for Physiocratic ends, Baudeau attacked slavery as contrary to the laws of nature.[57] But it was only after the fall of Choiseul at the end of 1770 that Physiocrats concertedly attacked slavery. As in Britain, it was difficult to mount a critique until reformers could show that colonies could survive – even thrive – without slavery. This was the thrust of Pierre-Joseph-André Roubaud's call to develop plantations in West Africa on a free-labour basis, eventually to replace French colonies in America which were likely to become independent with the assistance of their rebellious British neighbours.[58]

The French government had grasped immediately that the Dominica free ports made a weapon of freer trade and directed it against France. As the translation of an English newspaper in the archives of the naval and colonial ministry put it, 'It is true that we have returned to France by the last peace treaty our principal conquests in the sugar islands: but a free port will put Great Britain again in possession of their trade.'[59] The establishment of rival French free ports might keep traffic away from these British competitors and limit trade to those goods in which the ministry favoured a more open commerce. In the summer of 1767, the Council of State ordered the creation of two free ports, one at Carénage on Saint Lucia, the other at Môle-Saint-Nicolas on Saint-Domingue. Formally, this opening to trade with foreigners was narrow. Only a handful of imports was permitted, notably wood, hides, and livestock; only molasses and rum, or European goods, could be exported. But as Jean Tarrade points out, this constituted a major rupture with the Exclusif. For the first time, a permanent foreign trade was authorised to supply needs which, the Crown officially acknowledged, French commerce could not fulfil. This principle once admitted would serve to legitimate a wider toleration of foreign trade by officials in the islands with the tacit consent of the ministry.[60] In the following years, despite a loosening of some of the original restrictions placed on its trade, Carénage proved a failure – unable to compete with the contraband traffic that continued through Guadeloupe and Martinique. Môle-Saint-Nicolas boomed. One British naval officer identified it as a threat to Britain's commercial empire in the Americas. 'In time of Peace it inveigles the whole North American Trade to them,' he warned, 'which supplies them lumber and Provisions at a low sale and drains us of Cash, and at the same time supplies North America with Sugar, Molasses and Rum, to the great distress of our West India Islands.'[61]

In 1769, Choiseul considered a further relaxation of the Exclusif to strike a blow at the British Empire. The protests in North America inspired by opposition to the Stamp Act (1765), which imposed direct taxes on Americans, led the minister and other French officials to weigh for the first time the possibility of eventual American separation from Britain.[62] American reaction to the Townshend duties – a further attempt to tax Americans, imposed in 1767

– prompted Choiseul to send an agent to report on political sentiment in America.[63] That same year, the comte du Châtelet, ambassador in London, proposed that the French monarchy open its colonies to a freer trade with British North America as a means to foment trouble between the mother country and its American subjects. A further relaxation of the Exclusif might also serve to introduce French manufactured goods in place of the British wares subject to American non-importation agreements. The greatest blow that could be struck against Britain, argued Châtelet, would be to deprive it of this critical market. Choiseul was intrigued, floated the idea in the Council of State and even asked the ambassador to Spain, the marquis d'Ossun, to propose it to the Spanish government. But Madrid feared that new American republics would be a more dangerous threat to its empire than Britain itself, and Choiseul dropped the plan.[64]

A still more radical suggestion was made later the same year by Louis-Paul Abeille, secretary to the Bureau of Commerce, formerly a member of Gournay's circle, and later a Physiocrat. Abeille proposed that the French colonies be granted independence. The monarchy could not secure them, he argued, and would exhaust itself in their defence, as it had exhausted itself to retain Canada only to relinquish it finally to British power. The regime of the Exclusif required too much of the colonists: that they sell cheaply and buy dearly and do without when they could not be supplied by the metropole. In the state of commercial freedom their independence would entail, they would function as a weapon pointed at the heart of British power, destabilising further the relationship between the British metropole and its American colonies, perhaps even occasioning 'a total and durable rupture'. The colonies of all European states would sooner or later throw off the metropolitan yoke, Abeille predicted, so why not seize this moment and strike a blow against the British enemy?[65] This anticipated the proposals of Turgot on the prospect of French entry into the American War, to which we will turn in the next section (see below, p. 210). Freedom of trade figures in these arguments as a means to prise open Britain's closed empire in America, and as a wished-for end state in which this vital zone would be open to commerce with all nations while Britain was stripped of its exclusive benefit. These officials imagined a world of independent sovereign nations around the Atlantic rim, open to a universal commerce – a vision that seemed more favourable to French power and security than the existing world of empires.

THE PROMISE AND CHALLENGE OF AMERICAN INDEPENDENCE

Louis XVI recognised American sovereignty formally in February 1778 when he concluded a treaty of amity and commerce with the United States. Under its terms, Versailles hoped to deny Britain a chance to renegotiate preferential trade with its now independent colonies. Adopting an MFN arrangement, France and the American Republic undertook 'not to grant any particular Favour to other Nations in respect of Commerce and Navigation, which shall not immediately become common to the other Party'. The treaty reserved to each side 'the Liberty of admitting at its pleasure other Nations to a participation of the same Advantages'. Versailles accepted that the United States would make similar agreements with other European states, extending the bilateral accord into a network of trade treaties. The 1778 pact thereby created the template for an international regime that would not only keep America commercially open but guarantee rights to neutral trade in wartime. Accordingly, the treaty gave no special preference to France. Negotiators signed it along with a secret treaty of alliance to come into effect once war broke out between France and Britain, intended to secure the independence of the United States 'in matters of Government as of commerce'.[66]

Why did the government of Louis XVI accept a United States open to free trade rather than a zone of preferential French commercial access? Versailles was certainly in a position to demand commercial concessions in return for its support. Congress in turn was willing to extend special privileges. As early as the summer of 1775, Benjamin Franklin had talked of offering the commerce of America to a foreign power in return for its friendship.[67] From late in 1776 the committee of Congress handling foreign relations had come to believe that trade privileges would be necessary to buy French intervention. Instead, the French foreign minister, Charles Gravier de Vergennes, accepted an American trade open to all comers.[68] The direct commercial advantages to France of such an arrangement would be limited, he recognised. 'American trade, thrown open as it is to be henceforth to the avidity of all nations,' he remarked, 'will be for France a very minor consideration.'[69] This being the case, why not negotiate a better deal for France when the Americans had nothing else to offer?

The American commissioners sent to Paris wanted a treaty permitting the United States to trade with all nations on the same basis. Although for tactical reasons leaders in the Continental Congress had played down grievances against the navigation acts, and largely omitted them from the Declaration of Independence, economic sovereignty, including the right to trade with all nations, was a key objective of many in New England and the South. This did not mean that American leaders were committed to a United States open in the future to free trade; the American Republic would adopt measures of protection after the ratification of the Constitution.[70] They wished simply to be able to choose whom to trade with and under what conditions. In America, as in Europe, liberty and protection were not opposites but complements. In 1775, moreover, throwing the ports open to all nations except Britain was a strategic necessity if the United States was to acquire arms and sell the goods necessary to pay for them. Yet if the initiative was American, it was the logic of the geopolitical conjuncture that convinced Versailles.

An America open to a universal trade would help restore the balance of power and check Britain's march towards universal monarchy, just as in 1708 when French commercial diplomats concluded that opening Spanish America to all European goods would tend to produce a balance of commercial power (see above, p. 96). Britain's advantageous colonial position had been essential to its ascent – of this French officials were convinced.[71] An America free of Britain's trade laws, Vergennes believed, would entail a great and irreparable loss of markets for British manufactures, and a partial loss of the American carrying trade for British shipping – the collapse, that is, of two of the pillars of British commercial power.[72] Britain's dominant commercial position in these sectors, French officials assumed, followed from the navigation acts, which either excluded a broader European competition entirely or raised costs so as to advantage British producers. But American commerce 'if it is free', Vergennes wrote, 'will circumvent England'.[73] French merchants acting alone, however, would be incapable of breaking the British stranglehold on American commerce – they would need the concurrence of the rest of commercial Europe. This would entail the added advantage of investing all Europe in a future of American independence. France would gain in proportion to Britain's loss, but not because French merchants would take over Britain's formerly privileged position. In the calculus of power politics, as opposed to a merely commercial accounting, any loss of trade to Britain constituted an equivalent gain for France.

While the freedom of trade embodied in the treaty of amity and commerce was broad in the way European trade to America was conceived, in other respects it was restricted and uneven. To grant the United States MFN status in France meant no more than that its trade would face the same thicket of commercial regulations and taxes as competing states. To be sure, the free ports adopted in 1767 in the Caribbean to facilitate the American trade in provisions would be maintained in America's favour, and Louis XVI promised to open one or more new free ports in metropolitan France to facilitate direct American trade. Still, this was a far cry from throwing French markets open to American goods on the most generous terms.

An elaboration of the idea of free trade adopted in the treaty of amity and commerce was the principle that neutral nations should be allowed to trade with the enemy in wartime. One of the objects of the war, Vergennes noted in retrospect, had been 'the freedom of the seas and consequently that of trade'.[74] This principle had an important place in the treaty. The French position on neutral rights had evolved by the time of the Seven Years' War away from a prior hostility. In wartime, French merchants and planters relied on neutral carriers and neutral flags to provision the French colonies – to circumvent the blockade imposed by enemy privateering and naval predation.[75] The utility of neutral trade might be institutionalised through a network of trade treaties, building protections for neutrality into the fabric of the international legal regime, and thereby shielding the French colonial empire from future British naval pressure in wartime. The 1778 treaty marked a new milestone as it defined neutral rights essentially in terms of the principle of 'free ships, free goods', permitting subjects and citizens of the signatories to engage in wartime trade with the enemy in all goods not defined as contraband. And contraband was narrowly circumscribed, excluding most naval stores (articles 15–16, 25–6). This provision could hardly have much effect until it came to be accepted by Britain, and it was partly with a view to establishing it, eventually, as a principle of relations between states that Vergennes agreed to build it into the treaty.[76] The principle was provisionally applied to French relations with all neutral powers later that year.[77]

French sponsorship of neutral rights partook of the same logic as the support for American commercial independence. A major power imbalance in the Franco-British relationship followed from the larger size of the Royal Navy and its capacity to hamper French trade in wartime, which impeded the dynamic French colonial trade of the western ports (though it was never able to choke it off). France looked to neutrals to carry on its wartime trade – to the Danes, the Swedes, the Dutch, and, in the future, the Americans.[78] France had long pushed the smaller maritime European states to insist on their trading rights in the face of British efforts to blockade French trade. Louis XVI later welcomed the formation of the First League of Armed Neutrality in 1780, based on much the same principles as those he had endorsed in 1778.[79] When the Dutch Republic broke with Britain on the issue of neutral rights and entered the war in 1780, this seemed like a major victory for the policy, and inaugurated an informal Franco-Dutch alliance.

Such strategic visions, not any conception of free trade derived from Physiocracy, or other new currents of political economy, influenced the decision to enter the American conflict. But Physiocratic ideas were quite central to the debate within the administration on the wisdom of helping the Americans. The one member of the government strongly opposed to French entry into the conflict – the contrôleur général, Jacques Turgot – sympathised with Physiocratic ideas, and was an important and original political economist in his own right. Rather than supporting the American revolutionaries, he argued, France should anticipate the inevitable tendency of geopolitics in the Americas and declare its colonies independent, tying them to the mother country in a loose union based on freedom of trade both with the former metropole and with the Thirteen Colonies. Turgot argued that the implications for world politics of a free-trading America would be very different from those Vergennes imagined. With a commercially independent America, it would be impossible to preserve closed European colonial empires, as nothing would stop American merchants from trafficking with the colonies of all nations. They would draw these territories towards independence by integrating them into American commercial circuits. Thus the free-trade revolution centred on the Thirteen Colonies would inevitably spread to the rest of the Americas, smashing the French empire there.[80]

Turgot's critique tapped a well of French suspicion that an independent America might spell danger for the Caribbean colonies. Vergennes claimed that the war between Britain and its colonists threatened the security of the French islands because Britain might seek compensation there for losses in

America, or reconcile with the rebels by allying with them to conquer the empires of the Bourbon powers. Turgot turned this logic on its head: an independent America must necessarily entail the breakup of the French Empire. Vergennes preferred to think, as Manuel Covo has noted, that a friendly and allied America would help secure Saint-Domingue from British power. This small territory was rapidly becoming the richest, most productive, and most valuable colony in the world on the backs of half a million slaves who produced sugar, coffee, and indigo in brutal conditions. In the words of the London *chargé d'affaires*, the security of the French colonies depended 'essentially on the alliance or the neutrality of the continent which neighbours them'.[81] A friendly United States would be a bulwark against British attempts against Saint-Domingue in a way analogous to Canada before its cession in 1763.

Turgot attacked the notion that the independence of America would produce a balance of commercial power – an idea based, in his view, on false political-economic premises. Britain's exclusive empire in America could not be the source of its wealth, he implied. Hence the loss of this privileged position would not leave it any weaker. Nations with an exclusive colonial commerce profited not a whit more from it, Turgot argued, than their neighbours who possessed no colonies of their own. More was spent on the defence and administration of the Caribbean colonies in peacetime than they ever paid in taxes, while in wartime they cost France vast sums to defend. Colonial trade flows could be taxed just as effectively if these goods arrived as imports from other countries. For Turgot, the real sources of wealth and power were domestic – they lay in employing land and labour in the most advantageous ways possible, and this could be achieved by legislating greater commercial liberty at home. The clash between Turgot and Vergennes pitted a version of the new, land-focused political economy articulated during the Seven Years' War against an official perspective privileging foreign trade as the leading source of wealth and power.

The real advantage the American Revolution entailed for France, Turgot argued, was to absorb British energies and resources for a time. Holding down its colonists would strain British finances, making it incapable of any mischief against the Bourbon powers. Indeed, France stood to gain more from a British victory than an American one, because this would bog Britain down militarily in America for a generation. The monarchy should use the breathing space provided by Britain's war to undertake vital internal reform, especially to get its own financial house in order by consolidating the royal debt at a lower interest rate. If France intervened in America, these necessary reforms would be delayed, perhaps indefinitely, and this opportunity squandered.[82]

In the short run, Turgot lost the debate, and was pushed out of the ministry. But he would be posthumously vindicated when the costs of fighting the American War left the monarchy so financially crippled that it was unable to capitalise on its victory. He would be further justified when his old opponent, Vergennes, took up plans to restore the finances of the state substantially modelled on Turgot's.[83] The foreign minister's wager that Britain's loss of economic sovereignty in America would handicap British merchants and goods, and distribute the benefits of American markets widely, proved unfounded. By the early 1790s, more British goods were selling in America than ever before, and without the costs of administering and defending a continent.[84] But all this lay in the future. Many British officials facing the prospect of an independent United States thought this presented just the kind of danger to future British prosperity and power that Vergennes assumed. Some looked to freedom of trade with the United States to restore Britain's commercial fortunes and recover the advantages that had underpinned the nation's rise to greatness.

THE BRITISH DEBATE ON FREE TRADE WITH AMERICA

The signing of the treaty of amity and commerce, with the greatly increased prospect of American independence it implied, catalysed a reimagining of Britain's empire and its commercial system in the later war years. British officials, parliamentarians, and men of letters grappled with what a free-trading America would mean for British trade.[85] They groped towards the idea that free trade itself might be part of the solution to the problems that American commercial independence would create. Two major opposing perspectives emerged by the end of the war. Some mostly Whig politicians and officials, and much of the merchant community, argued that Britain could restore the substance of its prewar commercial system by opening a free trade with the newly independent United States. A group of Tory legislators, by contrast, doubted that full freedom of trade with America would be either necessary or beneficial. Both sides looked to an augmentation of Britain's trade with Europe via greater openness as a means to recover commercial vitality. This official embrace of free-trade policies transformed the reception of Adam Smith's arguments. The prospect of American economic independence gave some of the ideas he explored in the *Wealth of Nations* (1776) a new pertinence, and launched the selective reading of Smith (which would prevail in the nineteenth century), as the leading apostle of free trade.

Smith's principal concern in 1778 was not with freedom of trade or access to American markets, but with protection costs and who would pay them. He was approached by an old friend, Alexander Wedderburn, Lord North's solicitor general, for advice on how Britain ought now to proceed with the Americans. Smith had written eloquently about the American quarrel in the *Wealth of Nations*; Wedderburn had consulted him before on American questions, and his advice had been sought in 1777 and 1778 on the budget. As he had two years earlier, Smith proposed that the best resolution of the war would be an incorporating union of the kind that joined England and Scotland in 1707, with the Americans to receive parliamentary representation and the rights to trade enjoyed by all Britons, with the obligation to pay taxes on the same basis.[86] This last point was crucial. So long as Britain had to bear the costs of defending America, its empire must be regarded as an albatross.[87] Smith rejected the argument of Edmund Burke and other Rockingham Whigs that America paid for itself in the taxes generated on a greater economic output at home – that it need not be taxed directly. Indeed he rejected the whole thesis of American economic exceptionalism, arguing that trade with the colonies had drawn capital away from alternative investments at home that might have delivered a better return. The second-best option after a union would be American independence, a free-trade treaty, and perhaps in the future, when tempers had softened, a federal union. At least under such an arrangement Britain would not pay the costs of sovereignty in America. The outcome of the war 'likely to prove most destructive to Great Britain', in Smith's view – and most likely – would be a victory or partial victory by which it held onto all or part of the colonies, requiring 'a much greater military force than all the taxes which could be raised upon it could maintain'.[88]

Smith did not expect his views to get much traction – and they did not – but facing the prospect of a treaty between France and the American rebels, the North administration was prepared to rethink its position. In 1778 it led with a major peace initiative, the Carlisle Commission, which offered Americans autonomy within the British Empire and greater commercial freedom. The king authorised the commissioners, led by Frederick Howard, earl of Carlisle, to propose a federation between the metropole and its American colonies, with Americans to enjoy some representation in Westminster and to exercise home rule through their assemblies.[89] The commission was permitted to concede a loosening of the trade laws to allow Americans to carry a wider range of articles directly to European markets, and to import European goods in return. But North hoped an effective British monopoly on American markets might be preserved by encouraging the colonists to lay duties on goods imported directly from Europe.[90] Proposed ten years earlier, such arrangements might have won support, but they were out of step with events by 1778, and the peace embassy went nowhere.

The parliamentary opposition was divided early in 1778, with Lord Rockingham calling for immediate recognition of American independence to keep the United States out of the French camp, but the followers of William Pitt the Elder, now earl of Chatham, taking a less compromising line. Pittites believed that Britain's commercial future lay in trade with North America. Despite sympathy for the American patriots on constitutional grounds, Pitt opposed independence, arguing that it would be strategically and economically ruinous for the mother country.[91] His chief lieutenant, Lord Shelburne, concurred, claiming that 'The sun of Great-Britain is set, and we shall no longer be a powerful and respectable people the moment that the independency of America is agreed to by our government.' He approved a measure of American self-rule so long as a commercial union was preserved. A trade treaty with an independent United States would not be adequate for this purpose; Britain's trade laws, in some form, had to be preserved.[92] John Almon, a leading Pittite journalist and publisher, argued that America was worth holding only as a market for manufactures with 'the almost certain prospect of a vast extension'. Questions of where sovereignty lay were comparatively unimportant. Under Almon's plan, Americans would have the right to trade directly with any European power, and to import whatever they liked so long as foreign goods paid 20-per-cent-higher duties than equivalent wares from inside the empire. Almon described this as a scheme of 'free trade' – a common market integrating the British Empire with a quasi-independent United States.[93]

The failure of the peace initiative, and the growing prospect of American economic independence, elicited new rounds of reflection on how Britain might compete in a world where America was open to the trade of other nations. It drove William Eden, an architect of the Carlisle Commission, and one of its members, to reflections on the freedom of trade that would shape British commercial politics after the war. A former follower of Grenville, Eden had become a lieutenant of North, appointed undersecretary in the Northern Department and a member of the Board of Trade. His hawkishness on American affairs moderated once he realised that a treaty was imminent between France and America. French entry into the war altered its stakes. A Bourbon victory would threaten the whole system on which British power had developed since the peace of Utrecht: 'our Colonies, our Islands, all our commercial establishments and distant possessions, our navy, our foreign garrisons, the free entrance and use of the different seas, and all the various parts of that complicated machine of trade, credit and taxation, which forms our position among the states of the world'.[94]

In his *Letters to the Earl of Carlisle* (1779–80), Eden sketched a programme for the renewal of British power in a more competitive world by adopting a measure of free trade. He recommended that the nation replace prohibitions and high duties on imports with moderate tariffs to maximise revenue and drive smuggling into licit channels. He embraced the virtues of competition with foreign producers, which would catalyse improvements in manufacturing. He implied that merchant and shipping interests had been victims of Britain's Byzantine trade taxes, established to favour a manufacturing interest that sought the easy profits of monopoly. A freer commerce would give a boost to the carrying trade, spur emulation of foreign best practices, make Britain a keener competitor, destroy smuggling, and above all raise substantial revenues when every penny was needed to fight the Bourbons. Eden's programme anticipates in detail William Pitt the Younger's agenda of postwar revenue reform and freer trade, which, as we have seen (above, p. 68), Eden helped enact.[95]

Eden's *Letters* are important for the light they shed on the ways published political-economic writings were appropriated by politicians. He drew synthetically on a wide range of sources, including the writings of Hume (an intimate of his father-in-law), Charles Davenant, Sir Matthew Decker, and 'our friend Mr. Adam Smith'. Eden corresponded with Smith while writing the letters, and received advice that found its way almost verbatim into the fifth and last.[96] What particularly attracted him to Smith was the latter's argument that the American monopoly was a source not of strength but of weakness. Privileged access to American markets had allowed British manufacturers to become uncompetitive. Freedom of trade would force them to lower prices, cut the cost of living, and restore competitiveness. But Eden's appropriations were selective. While largely accepting the views of the Scottish political economists on taxation, money, and competition, he rejected Hume's pessimism about public credit, and integrated his borrowings into a political and ethical framework that Smith and Hume did not share.[97] The British commercial system was based on sound principles of political economy, he argued; it required modest adjustments, not radical reform. With such fine-tuning the nation would prevail in its commercial and financial contest with the Bourbons.

In Eden's post-Carlisle reflections, we see an emerging realisation that the solution to the challenge of American free trade might lie in more free trade. The same insight, in many competing forms, arose repeatedly in these years. Britain might counter-balance American commercial independence with a yet wider freedom of trade to be won by prising the French and Spanish colonies out of Bourbon hands, some argued. Once Mexico had been assisted 'to throw off the Spanish yoke', and Havana was back in British hands, one Patriot argued, Britain should open the trade of the Americas to all friendly states. The shipping of the Baltic powers and Russia might thus be fostered – these could never be a danger to Britain, but might one day support it in a naval league.[98] Here was an old Whig dream given a new spin. Eden's brother-in-law, Hugh Elliot, serving as envoy to Berlin, told him that Britain should concede American independence and compensate itself by making the French and Spanish colonies independent too – establishing a great free-trade zone in the Americas. 'Let our fleets and armies evacuate North America,' he urged, and 'fall upon St Domingo, Martinico, Cuba, and force a free trade in the Gulph of Mexico, the straight road to . . . the revolt of the Spanish settlements.'[99] The suggestion illuminates the British predicament in 1778. An America open to the trade of all would shift the balance of commercial power, long favourable to Britain, in an ominous direction. If it could not coerce the colonies back under its tutelage, why not strip the Bourbon powers of their own exclusive commercial assets and open these to freedom of trade?

Some hoped to achieve the same ends by agreement rather than conquest. The Whig political economist James Anderson, backing away from an earlier commitment to the war, called for peace based on the establishment of a free-trade zone in the Americas by a league of maritime states, potentially including the Bourbon monarchies. The colonies of all of the parties would be open to the trade of the other confederates, and non-members would be excluded. America would be removed as a bone of contention in international affairs, and neutralised in time of war so as to 'fix the general tranquillity of Europe on a firmer basis'. Anderson hoped that the commercial opening of the Americas would lead to a free-trade revolution in Europe – another striking restatement of Paterson's vision of a free-trading world from the opening years of the century.[100]

Anderson is interesting for his thoroughgoing scepticism about the value of traditional empire – a view increasingly sounded towards the end of the war, more often by Tories. Far from America being the secret to Britain's commercial success, he held, it had been a millstone weighing down the development of the British economy. Anderson agreed with Smith that empire in America was at the root of a competitiveness crisis in British manufacturing. Easy profits in colonial markets had allowed high prices and poor quality to prevail in British industry so that British goods could no longer 'stand a competition with the manufactures of other nations in foreign markets'. It followed that the loss of that monopoly might actually be a boon. But Anderson went further, under-lining the immense burden America had actually been to British economic development. If all the people who had emigrated there had remained at home, and all the money spent on colonial wars had been saved, Britain would be far more prosperous.[101] As an alternative to empire, Anderson proposed domestic colonisation – agricultural improvement in the Highlands of Scotland and the establishment of commercial fishing settlements there.[102]

Some Tories agreed that the American monopoly had diverted capital from domestic improvement, where it might have been more productively employed. According to George Chalmers, an exile from Maryland who would later serve as secretary of Pitt the Younger's Board of Trade, Britain had actually benefited from the American War because by turning 'additional capitals into domestic employments, [it] necessarily contributed to improve the agriculture, to augment the manufactures, and to increase the wealth of the country, by yielding a greater quantity of productive labour'.[103] The most influential exponent of this view was John Baker Holroyd, earl of Sheffield, a close ally of Eden, who emerged in 1783 as a leading opponent of Shelburne's plans to open a free trade with the United States. Sheffield argued that 'Britain will be highly benefited by the separation from the American States'. He couched this argument in terms of a general critique of colonies: 'Nothing can be more impolitic, at least in a commercial nation,' he argued, 'than a fondness for foreign dominions, and a propensity to encourage distant colonisation, rather than to promote domestic industry and population at home.' Britain's domestic economy was far more important than its external trade. The costs of defending and expanding its empire exceeded any possible gains. To the degree American commerce was worth having, Sheffield held, Britain would preserve it after the war without any colonial monopoly or any special commercial privileges, but simply by virtue of the quality and price of its products.[104] Such claims would be central to the battle for Britain's political economy in the postwar world, a battle initiated when Shelburne, now prime minister, turned to establish a free-trade union between Britain and the United States.

I have already noted (see above, p. 67) Shelburne's acceptance of freer trade with France, which he discussed in conferences with Vergennes's deputy in 1782. To understand his embrace of freedom of trade, historians usually point to the minister's personal ties to celebrated political economists – Josiah Tucker, Adam Smith, and especially André Morellet.[105] Shelburne met Smith as a young man, and as a minister in the 1760s occasionally consulted him and Tucker. He met Morellet in Paris in 1771, and a return visit and correspondence ensued.[106] Shelburne later credited Gournay's former disciple with teaching him the benefits of free trade. Yet as a general account of Shelburne's stance in 1782, this is hardly satisfactory.[107] As late as 1778, he regarded the trade laws as vital to Britain's commercial relationship with America. The very idea that men of letters influence politicians has to be handled with care, as what is invariably involved is a selective appropriation of ideas by politicians, who often graft them onto new and alien agendas. Shelburne's espousal of freedom of trade with America and Europe in 1782 is best viewed as the extension in new geopolitical circumstances of long-held and widely shared views – especially the idea of America as an economic space of exceptional value. Shelburne was not an outlier in thinking that free trade with America was necessary in 1783, or that a wider freedom of trade in Europe might benefit Britain. His assumption of these positions is better understood as part of a broader shift in the political culture than in terms of a personal intellectual epiphany.

To understand the shift, it is helpful to compare Shelburne to the colonial administrator and MP Thomas Pownall, whose ideas on trade also changed in this period, and whose intellectual starting point was similar to Shelburne's. Pownall's changing vision offers a natural experiment in what could happen to a broadly Pittite political-economic perspective when confronted with the prospect of an independent and free-trading America.[108] A former governor of Massachusetts and South Carolina, Pownall shared the view that America was a key to Britain's commercial and political ascendancy. In 1776 he published a sophisticated critique of the *Wealth of Nations* (the only substantial published review) in which he allowed that greater commercial freedom could be used selectively to address inefficiencies in Britain's commercial system. But he defended the monopoly on American trade as the chief source of the nation's opulence and power.[109] By 1780, faced with the near certainty of American independence, Pownall's view shifted.

He now argued both that Britain needed freedom of trade with America, and that an independent America would drive a free-trade revolution in Europe, forcing European powers to embrace commercial liberty in their turn – and not just with America, but with one another. The interest of the United States, Pownall saw, was to be 'a FREE PORT to all Europe at large; and that all Europe at large should be THE COMMON MARKET for American exports'. America would demand such treatment from European commercial partners as the price for the entry of their manufactured goods into its markets – markets from which no nation would wish to be excluded given their nearly endless prospects for growth. Moreover, as Americans took a commanding position in the global carrying trade, which Pownall regarded as inevitable given their advantages in shipbuilding, they would demand freedom not just for their own staples but for the goods of all nations they carried. Once one state conceded this, competition would force others to follow. Finally, European nations would have to accord the same treatment to one another or risk American domination of international commerce. The nation that adapted most successfully to this new order would become the leading power in Europe. So far, with great foresight, Pownall admitted, France had seized this opportunity. Yet it was Britain, if it understood its interests, that might have the most natural connection with America. Ideally, he argued, the commercial states of Europe would work out the rules of a new global trading order adapted to the emergence of a free-trading America in a congress of all nations, and establish permanent institutions to govern their commercial relations. In this case, instead of being a source of discord, commerce might help assure peace.[110]

Here were all the key elements of Shelburne's position in 1782: the idea that it was imperative for Britain to recover her dominant trading position in America, no longer through political union but on the same juridical basis as other European nations; that European countries would benefit from opening a freedom of trade with one another; that commerce could be turned thereby into a source of amity rather than discord. What Pownall's case suggests is that it was not contact with philosophical free-trade ideas that turned people into free traders. Rather, it was the logic of the new situation created by the commercial independence of America.

America's exceptionalism as a site of expected future growth produced in one of the best-informed observers of Britain's commercial system a defence of colonial monopoly as long as it still seemed possible to continue it. Once all hope had been lost of doing so, the same exceptionalism translated into an expansive vision of a global free-trade order centred on America, and a call for Britain to seize a leading place within it. There is no way to be sure if Shelburne ever read Pownall's work (though it seems likely given the theme, Pownall's network, and the broad diffusion of the text). The point, in any case, is not to substitute one claim of influence for another. Pownall's intellectual trajectory shows how a subtle defender of Britain's commercial system – like Shelburne in 1778 – could be turned into an ardent kind of free trader merely by the changed context of American commercial independence.[111]

To foster the revival of trade with America in anticipation of a more permanent commercial settlement, Shelburne had John Pownall (brother of Thomas) draw up a bill that his chancellor of the Exchequer, William Pitt the Younger, presented to Parliament in March 1783. (Shelburne had by now resigned the premiership after losing key parliamentary votes.) The American Intercourse Bill proposed to treat American goods imported to Britain in American vessels as if they had been carried in British ships. It promised to allow American ships, carrying American staples, to engage in direct trade to the British Caribbean, and to be treated there in the same manner as British vessels. It even proposed to re-establish the drawbacks and bounties formerly offered on British exports to America, and still paid on the like goods exported to the remaining American colonies. In effect the bill promised to treat the American trade as if the Revolution had never happened, and as if the United States were not now an independent nation.

If the bill exemplified the faith that Britain's commercial future lay in America, it also reflected the demands of the London merchant community and the Caribbean planter interest for a restoration of the prewar trade with America. Merchants urged that Britain treat American goods such as whale oil, furs, pig iron and lumber not as alien goods, but as raw materials necessary for British manufacturers that should be imported duty-free, as they had been before the war. If Britain fostered these imports this would also make it possible for Americans to purchase British manufactured goods. Merchants wanted to recover Britain's former position as the entrepôt for American trade with Europe. Unless 'every difficulty' were removed on this intermediary trade, they warned, the ships of other nations would carry American merchandise directly to Europe and 'the Navigation of this Country will receive a most essential Injury'.[112] Planters claimed the Caribbean colonies would be ruined unless the government re-established the provisions trade with America on the traditional basis. American ships must be admitted into Caribbean ports on the same terms as before the war.[113]

For some merchants, these restorationist ideas broadened into an expansive vision of freedom of trade. To recapture the prewar trade and to exploit the advantages of a fast-growing America, the Bristol merchant and manufacturer Richard Champion argued, Britain should follow the example of the Dutch, 'whose immense riches shew the advantages of the establishment of a Free Trade. Could this country be made one great free port, the same consequences would follow'.[114] Turning Britain into a general free port was an old idea, as we have seen (above, pp. 51–3), transmitted from the age of Walpole in the writings of Sir Matthew Decker, which were still widely cited, and indeed republished in the 1780s.[115] Shelburne too talked of turning Britain into a free port, as those 'best circumstanced for trade, could not but be gainers by having trade open'.[116] If all Britain were a free port, its position as the entrepôt for European trade to America would be assured.

But the restoration of the American trade by the extension of freedom of trade to the United States was not to be realised. A group of Tory MPs led by

Eden and Sheffield blocked the Intercourse Bill in the House of Commons. They promoted a political-economic vision based on a different attitude to America and a competing understanding of free trade. If Britain admitted American navigation into its Caribbean colonies, Eden charged, its own shipping would soon be pushed out of the carrying trade there with ruinous consequences for naval power.[117] Sheffield conceded the *commercial* advantages of abrogating the navigation acts in America's favour. But the implications for security would be damaging. The navigation laws artificially drew more capital into shipping than would naturally be invested there, allowing Britain to sustain a large merchant marine, which underpinned its naval power.[118] Ultimately, it was to slow America's emergence as a future naval rival that Tories rejected the bill.[119] Long before this, American shipping might allow France and Spain to evade British naval blockades in wartime. Privileging American commerce was the more imprudent, Sheffield argued, because it was unnecessary; American markets would fall to Britain's share anyway. As Sheffield put it, 'The superior state of British manufactures in general does not require other means of monopoly than what their superiority and cheapness will give.'[120] Besides, as we have seen, in his view, America had never been critical to Britain's commercial fortunes. The American Intercourse Bill having failed to pass, and Shelburne's government having fallen, the succeeding Fox–North coalition send David Hartley to Paris to negotiate a commercial treaty with the United States. When it became clear that these talks would not produce a better settlement, the new administration used an Order in Council to reopen trade with America on 2 July 1783, essentially on the basis suggested by Eden and Sheffield.[121]

To some of Shelburne's followers, this devaluing of America was baffling. The politically radical cleric and philosopher Richard Price complained that 'we are pursuing measures which will deprive us of the trade and friendship of a world rapidly increasing and throw it entirely into the scale of *France*'. The shift in thinking was disorienting: 'During the war the cry was that our essential interests depended on keeping the colonies. Now it seems to be discover'd that they are of no use to us.' Meanwhile the French pursued the very policies Price advocated at home, 'offering to take from them duty free that oil which we have prohibited'.[122] As a result, he later complained, 'The trade and friendship of that increasing world, which we might have secured, and from which we might have derived greater advantages than ever, are lost and become the means of adding to the power and increasing the naval force of France.'[123]

Price was responding no doubt partly to the extension of the French free-port system in the Caribbean announced in August 1784. A compromise measure, the edict issued by the naval minister Charles-Eugène-Gabriel de La Croix, marquis de Castries, sought to regularise – the better to control – the expansion of trade between the French islands and what was now the United States. Castries slightly expanded the range of goods that could be traded, established a free port in each of Martinique, Guadeloupe, Saint Lucia, and Tobago, and three in Saint-Domingue, at Le Cap, Port-au-Prince, and Les Cayes-Saint-Louis.[124] The decision sparked a renewed howl of protest from French port interests. Jean-Baptiste Dubuc entered the fray to demand a greater measure of openness. Planters should be allowed to trade sugar and coffee directly for American provisions. French producers derived little protection from prohibitions, he argued, because the cost advantages of American imports were too great to overcome. Moreover, the less they paid for provisions, the larger the surplus planters would have to spend on French manufactured goods and wines.[125] But as critics warned Castries, the United States now presented the same danger to the French colonies as Britain formerly had. If planters were allowed to trade freely with Americans, the production of the colonies would be drawn into American commercial circuits. Americans would market French colonial sugar in Europe and supply planters in turn with provisions and manufactured goods. France would lose economic sovereignty over its colonies.[126]

What may have further perplexed Shelburne's friends is that opponents of free trade with America countered with an alternative vision of freedom of trade. Eden claimed to favour American intercourse on 'very liberal terms', and indeed he and Sheffield were willing to see American goods imported duty-free, so long as they came in British ships. Protectionism, in general, was ill-judged, Sheffield argued, while 'competition is useful, forcing our manufacturers to act fairly, and to work reasonably'.[127] Eden claimed that excessive concessions to America would disrupt an alternative system of freer trade with other European states that might be more advantageous. Under the MFN principle of the Russian commercial treaty, then up for renewal, he pointed out, Britain would have to extend the same concessions to Russian merchants as it had to Americans without being able to claim any reciprocal advantages. Eden wanted a bill to subject American trade to the same duties and regulations as European nations.[128] These suggestions largely aligned with the views of Adam Smith, whom Eden consulted. Smith had 'little anxiety about what becomes of the American commerce. By an equality of treatment to all nations,' he told Eden, 'we might soon open a commerce with the neighbouring nations of Europe infinitely more advantageous.' Americans ought to be treated without special favour, he maintained.[129]

There was no one free-trade doctrine to be rejected or accepted in 1783, but competing understandings, more than one of which could derive support from Smithian political economy. Describing one of these positions as liberal and the other as neo-mercantilist, as John Crowley does in an otherwise incisive analysis, is unhelpful.[130] The ostensibly liberal position was in fact an effort to restore the substance of the old British commercial system. It was based on an overrating of the importance of foreign trade and manufacturing for export in entirely conventional ways, contrary to Smith's insights. Sheffield, Eden, and their allies denied that privileged access to American markets was the key to British prosperity, placed more weight on domestic consumption, and, following Smith, looked to freer trade with continental Europe for export markets. Extending more generous terms to Americans was unnecessary because market forces would lead them to sell their provisions to the Caribbean colonies and to buy British manufacturers in any case.

The prospect and then the actuality of American independence led politicians and officials to conclude that the kind of limited, piecemeal, and strategic deployment of free trade that had always been a feature of policy must become more central in the future to fighting and winning the struggle against other states for wealth and power. In this context, both sides regarded Smith as an authority worth invoking to advance the differing conceptions of free trade they promoted. Of course, as a consultant to ministers since the 1760s, the Scot had long been viewed as a voice worth heeding. What warrants attention is the way the reception of the *Wealth of Nations* was transformed by the turn to freedom of trade at the end of the American War. When first published, Smith's great work attracted little public notice – its author had no expectation that it would be otherwise. This changed with the emergence of free trade as a pressing policy idea in the 1780s. The authority of the book would further increase with the Eden–Rayneval treaty, when Smithian arguments in favour of freedom of trade were invoked by Pitt and others.[131] Furthermore, the prominence of free trade among the book's many arguments was magnified and underscored in this process, shifting the meaning of the text, and beginning the process of Smith's canonisation as the father of free trade for nineteenth-century liberals. What had not yet occurred – what the nineteenth century accomplished – was the transformation of Smith into a doctrinaire exponent of free trade, the metamorphosis of freedom of trade from a strategy into a dogma, and from a multiplicity of disparate proposals into a unitary principle.

Between the 1760s and the 1780s, French and British officials, colonists, merchants, and political economists debated the advantages and drawbacks of freer trade in North America and the Caribbean and worked to make greater commercial openness a reality. Their action was part of a political-economic project by which states used free trade to weaken each other and adjust the balance of power. Though aggrandising and sometimes aggressive, this project was ultimately about changing the basis on which France and Britain would compete, and creating a more stable international order. British officials viewed freedom of trade as a substitute for war and conquest in the 1760s, a position echoed by French officials as they contemplated greater freedom of commerce with British North America. Where this project expressly embraced war, as in the French decision to back the American revolutionaries, this was a conflict intended to check Britain's rise to paramountcy and to establish the conditions that would make more amicable Franco-British relations possible in the future. The Eden–Rayneval treaty of 1786 was the sequel to Vergennes's policy of fighting a war for free trade in 1778. With the exceptional economic space of America no longer a British monopoly, the minister hoped, Britain's bid to engross global trade would be blocked, and France could hope to preserve a balance of power by peaceful commercial means.

The move towards freer trade was bound up with new thinking about how to renovate or replace empires with political frameworks for global commerce that would be cheaper and more profitable for the states that governed them. In the 1760s, freer interimperial trade promised to stimulate the prosperity and reduce the costs of empire. Choiseul dreamed of a de-territorialised empire of trade protected by bases, of expansive French markets in Spanish America without any of the costs of sovereignty, of a commercial empire stimulated by limited openings to American provisions and markets. Britons too in the 1760s envisioned a new form of imperium by which the production of the French and Spanish colonies would be sucked into the British imperial economy without the expense of fighting the Bourbons or annexing their settlements. French officials went a step further in the 1770s, proposing confederations of former colonies tied by commercial links to the mother country. Louis XVI backed the American revolutionaries as a means to replace the British empire in America with a free-trade regime anchored in commercial treaties that would keep the United States open to European trade and prevent a re-establishment of Britain's commercial supremacy. Britons imagined their own alternatives to North American empire: new political frameworks to leave America self-governing but tied to a common market of the English-speaking world; or international free-trade leagues governing commerce in the Americas; or – what actually came to pass – an independent America commercially integrated with Britain by a relatively liberal, if not fully free, trade.

The shift towards a freer trade in the Americas, and between Europe and America, did not follow directly from the triumph of Physiocracy or Scottish political economy. Emerging since the 1750s, these had a significant place in debates about American freedom of trade. The Physiocrats formed an alliance of convenience in the 1760s with Caribbean planter interests and a reforming ministry on the question of relaxing the Exclusif, and helped promote the reform policy over the objection of port interests. But the freer trade adopted in 1767 was neither conceived by Choiseul nor justified administratively in Physiocratic terms. Neither was the French decision to pry open the Thirteen Colonies to free trade in 1778. Vergennes's vision was rooted in a balance-of-power framework. Breaking Britain's commercial monopoly in America would distribute the benefits of American markets more widely, and check the British bid to become a hegemonic state. The Physiocratic position in the debate, to the degree there was one, was taken by Turgot, who argued that forcing Britain to accept American commercial independence would neither advantage France nor weaken Britain in the ways Vergennes supposed. Finally, in British debates about freedom of trade conducted during the American War, the ideas of Adam Smith took on new salience. But they were not the driver of either Shelburne or the Tories' embrace of free trade. It was less novel ideas than the new geopolitical conjuncture stripping Britain of guaranteed markets in America that drove the free-trade debate there.

The problems that urged the adoption of freer trade and the shift away from imperial sovereignty in the Americas exemplify the tensions inherent in capitalism that follow from the attempt to combine two forms of power different in their nature – the coercive-territorial power of sovereignty and the cosmopolitan logic of commerce. When sovereigns sought to territorialise and engross the benefits of trade, to check the borderless logic of commercial networks, merchants evaded state controls, producing endemic smuggling. Resentful colonists sought to break the fetters that checked their profits, and looked about for more satisfactory protectors. Wars erupted to preserve or extend colonial monopolies, leaving debt and taxes in their wake. To the degree they appeared successful, colonial monopolies threatened the balance of power, making the interstate system structurally unstable and conflict-prone. The costs of this equilibrium were high, and the drive for freedom of trade and institutional alternatives to closed commercial empires represented the quest for a cheaper, more stable future. Viewed abstractly, we can see the transformation of the interimperial trading regime in the Americas as a working-out of possibilities that present themselves recurrently in the geopolitics of capitalism. It is not by chance that, over the long run, the effort to build closed economic empires has given way to a world of independent states committed to a relatively free trade.

6

~~~~~~

SECURITY CARTEL
The Franco-British Pursuit of a Permanent Peace in India

After years of war, officials of the French and British India companies on the Coromandel Coast signed a treaty late in 1754 to suspend hostilities between them. For nearly a decade, the companies had clashed in this southeastern part of the Indian subcontinent – first as proxies of their home states, and later as allies of rival Indian princes who struggled for political control in the region. Charles Godeheu, the new governor general of the French settlements in India, and Thomas Saunders, the leading East India Company official in Madras, each promised on behalf of their European masters to recognise the possessions of the other company, to permit a 'free trade' in zones where they had established political control, and to withdraw from the Indian power struggles that had enmeshed them in conflict.[1] A provisional accord, the deal would have to be ratified in London, where for a year and a half directors of the two companies negotiated the terms of a permanent settlement. The French proposed a treaty to exempt the outposts and vessels of both corporations from attack in case of future wars in Europe, to disengage them from Indian politics, and to ally them to resist Indian princes who threatened their settlements or trade. Such an understanding would demilitarise Franco-British commercial competition east of the Cape of Good Hope, draw the two companies into a security cartel to jointly manage their relations with Indian powers, and disentangle them from the geopolitical rivalry of their home governments, which threatened to draw them into conflict again in the future.

These talks were overtaken by the outbreak of the Seven Years' War (1756–63), when the East India Company crushed French forces and, in a separate action, overthrew the nawab of Bengal, laying the foundations of a company-empire in northeast India. In the postwar context of French weakness and British strength, French officials periodically renewed proposals to co-operate.

228

In 1772, the minister of the navy and colonies, Pierre-Étienne Bourgeois de Boynes, proposed an alliance between a prospective new French India Company and its British rival to secure their trade from attack by Indian states and to lay the basis for a permanent Franco-British peace in Asia. This scheme failed to elicit much interest in the British company. But thirteen years later, in the aftermath of the American War, the French Crown chartered a new India company whose merchant projectors intended from the outset that it serve as a junior partner of the East India Company and operate in Bengal under its protection. The agreement went too far for the French foreign minister, Charles Gravier, comte de Vergennes. But the governments went on to sign a convention in 1787 to regulate French commercial access to Bengal, and to enjoin the British company to extend its protection to French merchants.

The initiatives to work out an entente evince an impulse in eighteenth-century capitalism to limit geopolitical conflict by establishing shared political frameworks to exploit and protect extra-European trade. Capitalism, I have argued, is a system in which sovereignty is mobilised to foster the private accumulation of capital, and in which capital in turn bolsters sovereign power. The chartered companies represent a special version of this alliance between commerce and sovereignty. More than mere business enterprises, they wielded sovereign powers and prerogatives to govern and secure the trade of their home nations in Asia. They maintained troops, armed ships, fortified their most important settlements, and, through diplomacy with Indian powers (which ruled the territories where they traded), built a favourable environment for business. The companies secured *firmans* – grants of tax privileges and limited self-government – from the Mughal emperor. They negotiated with regional Mughal officials, and, as the empire declined, with the rulers of successor states who had the power to tax their trade or to favour their rivals. Without the political shelter the companies supplied, company merchants argued, it would be impossible to conduct a profitable trade in India – a claim sometimes couched in racialised or civilisational terms. The 'barbarous' state of Indian politics meant that rulers would inevitably prey on merchants.[2] But preventing foreign sovereigns from taxing traders, or blocking their access to markets, was a structural problem, and as salient in Europe as outside it.

Companies 'internalised' their protection costs. Instead of relying on their home states to supply the military and diplomatic services they required, they produced these in-house. To be sure, they did not bear the full cost of sovereignty, sharing it with the Asian rulers who dominated the zones where they traded – at least until the companies began to emerge as territorial sovereigns in their own right. One of the great advantages of companies, from the perspective of their home governments, was that they organised and secured distant trade at minimum expense to the exchequer. This was what justified their monopoly privileges – super-profits being required to defray the heavy expenses of protection in Asia.[3] The way they handled protection costs was a principal advantage of the India companies, some scholars have argued, indeed the secret of their seventeenth-century success. Controlling and minimising the relative costs of securing trade was the key to profit in long-distance commerce for much of the medieval and early modern period, the economic historian Frederic Lane has suggested.[4] Companies partly displaced the overland Asia–Europe trade and bested the Portuguese in Asia, Niels Steensgaard has argued, because by producing their own protection they acquired it at cost instead of paying a premium to others to supply it.[5]

But internalising protection costs also created vulnerabilities – vulnerabilities that recurrently pushed the companies to collaborate. Outlays for defence could easily exceed profits when companies struggled militarily with each other or with Indian powers. As the Mughal Empire declined, companies, their European overlords, and powerful Indian polities were drawn into a struggle for power and commercial advantage that few would have predicted would turn to European advantage.[6] Facing the danger of Indian military might, an intercompany entente might block either corporation from allying with local rulers or unite both for their common defence. Many Europeans wondered if the commerce of their nationals had any future in a region where the balance of military force seemed so heavily against them. While there was once consensus that an early modern 'military revolution' had conferred a decisive advantage on European troops in Asia, allowing small European or European-trained forces to defeat larger Indian armies, historians increasingly emphasise that Indian states adapted rapidly and that technology and organisation explain only part of the military successes the companies enjoyed.[7] Whether fighting Indian states or other companies, military competition could drive protection costs to dangerous heights. The aspiration to lower them and shelter future profits from geopolitical risk drove company leaders to accommodate European rivals. An intercompany political framework for trade promised to provide security at sharply lower cost than when companies pursued this aim alone or in competition with one another.[8]

Of course there was an alternative to such collaboration. Companies could defray rising protection costs by becoming territorial powers and developing a tax base. Yet, anxious about acquiring new administrative and military burdens, company leaders usually preferred commerce to conquest. Directors in London and Paris recoiled from the expense and risks of territorial empire in the early 1750s. Military action, or the acquisition of rule, might drive up costs and, in extremis, push companies to insolvency. They hoped to negotiate a concert with their European rival to prevent either from moving further in this direction. Some company leaders and many government officials continued to prefer trade over empire even as the East India Company acquired the substance of territorial sovereignty in Bengal, because the tax revenues it obtained did not always cover its protection costs. The company edged towards bankruptcy in the early 1770s, and again at the end of the American War, encumbered by its huge military establishment, the expenses of civil administration, and the threat of war with Indian powers and a jealous French rival.

Faced with rising protection costs, companies either became more state-like or relinquished their sovereign prerogatives to evolve into more fully commercial organisations. If the directors of the East India Company reluctantly took the former path, the French had little choice after 1763 but to pursue the latter. In their search for a regime that would protect commerce in India without consuming its profits, French officials swung inconstantly – often unrealistically – among competing designs. Led by Jacques Necker, in the mid-1760s the Compagnie des Indes sought to pass the costs of sovereignty to the Crown, to remake itself as a trading society exclusively, and to take advantage of informal ties with East India Company employees. The duc de Choiseul, alternately French foreign minister and minister for colonial and naval affairs, dreamed of a new regime in India – a French trade protected by a league of friendly Indian rulers. The political framework for distant trade need not be empire – not a French empire, at least. Allied powers might provide it and bear its costs. This paralleled French thinking on the ideal setting for commerce in Spanish America – an allied ruler, the Spanish king, would bear the costs of sovereignty, while French merchants reaped the rewards. Choiseul's successor, the duc d'Aiguillon, returned to the idea of a Franco-British entente to unite the two nations against Indian threats and to carve out a secure space for French trade. Yet another prospect materialised after the American War, when the British government proposed that, in return for minimising Louis XVI's political pretensions in Bengal, the British company protect French merchants – a free trade under British political domination.

THE SEARCH FOR AN ACCORD IN SOUTHERN INDIA, 1753–55

In July 1752, an officer of the Compagnie des Indes, Pierre-Claude Delaître, proposed that the company negotiate with its British rival to end the military conflict that embroiled them.[9] The war the companies had conducted sporadically in the Carnatic since the mid-1740s had ruined trade, Delaître claimed. It exposed both to manipulation by Indian rulers, and risked teaching Indians European military discipline, which might eventually jeopardise the European presence in Asia. It also created an opening for interlopers such as Prussia's new Emden Company.[10] The companies should agree on the possessions of each, and forever renounce claims against the other. They should extend freedom of trade to one another in all parts of India, and make no new exclusive establishments. They should make common cause in the face of pressure from Indian rulers, while both should cease meddling in regional wars and induce their governments to exempt the vessels and settlements of either from attack in case of wars in Europe.[11] In effect, Delaître proposed an alliance between the companies for their collective security, and to neutralise a vast zone east of the Cape of Good Hope from European geopolitical struggles. In April 1753, following a peace overture from Leadenhall Street, the French sent the company director Pierre Duvelaer to London, assisted by his brother, to negotiate a treaty with the East India Company. The search for peace between the companies illuminates the way in which expensive military conflict, which damaged commerce and threatened the solvency of the companies, could drive a search for a joint political framework for trade in India in place of the competing arrangements of rival companies.

This quest for mutual accommodation was not unprecedented. Neutrality agreements between neighbouring French and British settlements to prevent the extension of European wars to Indian trade had been common in the past.

Europeans had occasionally floated schemes to shift their trade in Asia from an antagonistic model to a condominium, or to neutralise the trade in war.[12] In his 1713 plan for perpetual peace, the abbé de Saint-Pierre suggested that all Europeans, including the India companies, have freedom to trade in Asia under the auspices of a governance body to be established by the European federation he proposed, which would provide security and jointly manage diplomatic relations with Asian powers.[13] John Law toyed with the idea of European trading companies operating co-operatively in Asia.[14] Later, when war appeared imminent between France and Britain in 1744, the Compagnie des Indes proposed an accord to its British rival to turn the whole Indian Ocean region into a neutral zone and to prevent the European conflict from irrupting there. The East India Company refused, and war ensued in the Carnatic.

In this context, the security spending of the French and British India companies ballooned disastrously. Until the mid-1740s, the rivals had mostly managed to avoid clashes, even co-operating on occasion.[15] But when France declared war on Britain in 1744, and conflict spread to Asia, British naval attacks dried up the French company's trade and, in 1746, the French seized Madras (now Chennai), the chief East India Company settlement on the Coromandel Coast. Though the return of peace in Europe formally ended the conflict in India and the French returned Madras, the companies were soon fighting a new proxy war in the Carnatic as allies of competing Indian princes. As the authority of the Mughal Empire waned, successor regimes emerged in various provinces, unleashing struggles to control these territories. The companies risked becoming the playthings of contending Indian princes. Battles between them presented the companies with opportunities to gain by backing the winner and the risk of being shut out if they supported the wrong man.[16] The governor general of the French settlements in India, Joseph-François Dupleix, threw the forces of the company behind the claims of Chanda Sahib and Muzaffar Jang, who sought respectively to be recognised as nawab of the Carnatic and subadar of the Deccan.[17] The British, in turn, backed Muhammad Ali Khan's pretentions in the Carnatic and those of Nasir Jang in Hyderabad. To finance their military assistance, the French won new revenue farming rights in the Carnatic and in the Northern Circars (the northern region of modern Andhra Pradesh)– further threatening the East India Company by acquiring additional political means to check its commerce.[18]

4. Eighteenth-century India

An improvisation at first, Dupleix soon justified his actions as a strategy for the Compagnie des Indes to compete against its larger and more profitable British rival. No India company could support itself in the long run on the profits of trade alone, he told the directors in Paris. The costs to secure and administer its *comptoirs* (trading settlements) were too high. Companies needed territorial revenues like those the Dutch had long ago acquired at Batavia (now Jakarta) to offset these costs. Countering the objection that the British company flourished without such revenues, Dupleix claimed that it was unstable, weighed down by huge debts in India, and sustained only by a gullible investing public. To gain territorial revenues in India would also lessen the export of silver from Europe used to pay for Indian trade goods – a huge advantage to the nation, which needed specie to sustain its own prosperity and to subsidise allies. He informed Paris he aimed to secure an annual revenue of 10 million rupees (roughly 25 million livres), though he had acquired only a million or so by 1753.[19]

The scheme of erecting company-empires in Asia, sustained by tax revenues, was not new. In the 1680s, the East India Company had briefly moved in this direction under the leadership of Josiah Child, but emerged bruised from clashes with the Mughal Empire.[20] In subsequent decades, the company avoided war when it could, though violence or the threat of it remained a tool in negotiating political relationships with Indian powers. It is questionable whether Dupleix really intended to build a company-empire. He had been a successful 'country trader' in the 1740s, investing in intra-Asian trade, as so many of his British counterparts had, and began to pursue political projects only when the Royal Navy closed this option in 1745.[21] P.J. Marshall has compared him to Indian 'portfolio-capitalists' – powerful financial allies of Indian rulers who dominated trade and banking, moved into tax collection, and received perquisites from the princes they served. In this reading, Dupleix sought to diversify the portfolio of the company, not to build an empire.[22] Yet British company servants had to respond to the threat that their rivals, by acquiring political power, would close off their trading opportunities. The Fort St David council (in Cuddalore) feared in 1750 that 'the French aim at excluding us from the Trade of the Coast & by degrees that of India'.[23]

Pressure for a deal to end the proxy wars of the companies in the Carnatic built steadily in Paris and London. Dupleix's wars cost the French company over 20 million livres, and struck directly at its commerce by consuming funds destined to buy goods.[24] The East India Company estimated in 1756 that its annual expenses in India had increased by 60 per cent since the fall of Madras, and that it had spent £500,000 on the conflict with the French.[25] These losses dampened stock prices. The declaration of war with France in 1744 had triggered a sharp decline in the value of company shares; the fall of Madras prompted another slump.[26] The Seven Years' War, when it came, entailed the century's longest period of depressed India stock values. It is telling that the peak share price for the entire period between early 1744 and mid-1766 occurred in June 1753, when a deal with the French seemed imminent. 'For my own part,' wrote one major shareholder of the negotiations with the French, 'I shall not be so fond of my Stock, as I am, if no Treaty be establish'd.'[27]

Shareholders lambasted the directors, who, having skimped on military spending, failed to accept the neutrality agreement the French company proffered in 1744 that would have spared Madras.[28] The former Madras president, William Monson, attacked the direction for its 'ill judged Parsimony, or stupid Neglect, to say no worse'. To keep up the dividend, he charged, the directors failed to fortify Madras adequately or to hire enough troops. The leadership should have accepted the French neutrality agreement: 'What could a Set of Merchants have desired or wished for more, than to carry on their Trade free from any additional Expence or Fear of Danger; at least in those Parts where they were most exposed?'[29] Monson reissued his critique in French translation, perhaps to invite the Compagnie des Indes to renew its offer of terms.[30]

Indeed, that same year the French company weighed a new approach to its rival to secure a treaty of 'perpetual neutrality' between them in India – an initiative driven by shareholder anger, pressure from the French government, and worries for the solvency of the company.[31] The Compagnie des Indes had prospered during the long Franco-British peace of the Fleury years. After 1744, it suffered major losses; its trade dried up; shareholders were pressed to recapitalise the company, and dividends went unpaid, leading to revolt in 1745 and a reorganisation of the direction.[32] Shareholder anger brewed again in the early 1750s, now focused on the actions of Dupleix. Joseph-Philippe Narcis, a syndic of the company whose role it was to represent shareholder views, complained that warfare diverted funds sent to buy merchandise, crippling the company's trade.[33] Falling profits ate up dividends and depressed share values. Rumours of new hostilities triggered slumps in the share price. 'It is said publicly that Pondicherry is invested by the Indians, supported by English in disguise,' wrote one observer from Paris in the summer of 1753, and that 'the shares of the company have fallen by nearly 150 livres and it is not doubted but they will fall further every day. This news furiously alarms the poor share-holders.'[34]

One nightmare scenario was that Indian hostilities would trigger a European war. Could Dupleix be unaware, asked the company director Gabriel Michel, of 'the public outcry against a company of merchants that dares . . . to abandon its trade to give itself over to a spirit of conquest, and does not fear to provoke a rupture with our neighbours?'[35] The contrôleur général Jean-Baptiste de Machault d'Arnouville, the minister with responsibility for the company, had long urged Dupleix to end the conflict.[36] If a war in Europe followed, it would wreck Machault's efforts to stabilise French finances. Even if confined to India, war threatened the solvency of the company, and thereby jeopardised the Paris capital market. 'One cannot desire too much the end of the troubles in India,' he told the foreign minister, adding that he hoped the pacific overtures of the East India Company would be 'followed by a happy success'.[37] Étienne de Silhouette concurred. Louis XV appointed him royal commissioner of the Compagnie des Indies in 1751, giving him responsibility to direct the negotiation with the East India Company. The king's choice fell on Silhouette presumably because, in his person, initiatives to end the ongoing struggle in India would be united with efforts to avert future wars in America. (Recall that Silhouette was one of two commissioners named to resolve boundary disputes in America with the British – see above, p. 178.)

In his dealings with Dupleix, Silhouette gave voice to the commerce-versus-conquest trope we have seen him deploy in other contexts. Late in 1752, he wrote to tell the governor that in Paris 'peace is generally preferred to conquests'. Territorial concessions would only drag the French into internecine Indian struggles. 'We do not wish to become a political power in India,' he insisted, 'we want only a few establishments to aid and protect trade.' Therefore, he told Dupleix, 'No more victories! No more conquests! Lots of merchandise, and some augmentation of the dividend!'[38] The Compagnie des Indes had been an important incubator for this political tradition at least since its founding by John Law, who had affirmed that even successful conquest never paid for a modern commercial monarchy. How much truer was this for a company, which had to finance its political costs from its trade? The one-time company insiders Jean-François Melon and Nicolas Dutot had restated the idea in the 1730s that military conflict subverts the foundations of power by damaging commerce – a claim taken up subsequently by Silhouette, whose father was a major stockholder. The Compagnie des Indes was a key incubator for this vision. Indeed, in both France and Britain companies were sites where new political-economic understandings developed that entered into wider intellectual and political circuits.[39]

The tensions within the commerce-versus-conquest perspective, which we have noted in other contexts, were also on display here. Critics of Dupleix acknowledged the attractions of his strategy. Gabriel Michel admitted that the company's civil and military expenses exceeded its profits. Rich new possessions seemed an attractive way to cover these costs, but 'the difficulty is to hold on to them peacefully'. If the company's behaviour led to a war in Europe this would be ruinous for it and for the state.[40] Even Silhouette conceded that if Dupleix were successful 'the greatest advantages for the power, the wealth and the trade of the company would result'. But given the heightened geopolitical risks it entailed, both of ongoing military costs in India, and the potential for war in Europe, this option had to be rejected. Still, the temptation was great to hold onto some of Dupleix's acquisitions. While Silhouette was anxious to be rid of the trading settlement of Masulipatam (now Machilipatnam), which would be ruinously expensive to fortify, he wanted to retain the neighbouring island of Divy. It would also be good to hold onto tax concessions close to Pondicherry (now Puducherry), though the French should give up Bahour, which was too close to Fort St David and would be a permanent source of tensions.[41] Even Delaître counselled Machault to keep some of the gains of Dupleix.[42] In fact, feelings about Dupleix's projects fluctuated at Versailles and Paris with his military fortunes. Anti-Dupleix sentiment strengthened when word arrived early in 1753 that the French had suffered a major defeat the previous year, when enemy Indian and British forces killed Chanda Sahib and forced a French army to capitulate at Trichinopoly (now Tiruchirappalli). His stock rose when news arrived of a French victory at the fortress of Gingee.

This ambivalence was not shared by the writers linked to the influential intendant of commerce Jacques Vincent de Gournay, who deplored Dupleix's activities. According to François Véron de Forbonnais, the establishments of European nations in India 'would deviate from their original purpose if they were to become conquering'. He expressly rejected Batavia as a model for the French. What the Dutch had done was only possible because they had no competitors for control of the spice trade. In India, where the Compagnie des Indes faced European rivals, the consequences of any attempt to emulate the Dutch must be different, exciting the opposition of competing nations.[43] The political economist Louis-Joseph Plumard de Dangeul concurred, remarking that 'it ill behoves a company of merchants to assume the warrior spirit'.[44]

The alternative strategy proposed by Gournay and seconded by some of the directors was to expand the trade and try to undersell rival companies. If they understood their own interest, director Charles Godeheu wrote, companies would 'try to harm one another only by industry and trade'.[45] Gournay proposed to open the trade to all French merchants while retaining the Compagnie des Indes as a structure to administer the French *comptoirs* and to hold the privileges necessary to sustain commerce. The free trade of private merchants would be greater in volume, he argued, and thus more competitive in price. Discharged of burdensome defence costs it would be more economical than the old monopoly commerce, and these cost advantages would permit French merchants to beat their British and Dutch competitors in European and Levantine re-export markets. Taxes on this expanded commerce would generate enough revenue to fund a security umbrella in the shape of the reformed company, eventually allowing the latter to pay its debts and offer a higher dividend.[46] For his part, Dupleix denied that greater commercial competitiveness could solve the company's problems. Competition among the companies had already depressed prices in Europe, and raised them in India. The European market was limited, and a struggle to undersell rivals would become a race to the bottom. Indeed, the arguments of modern economic historians tend to support this view.[47]

If generally true that commerce rather than empire served the national interest, the maxim could not be applied mechanically, without regard to context. Dupleix and his allies in France argued that war served the interests of the company both by securing a fixed Indian revenue, and thus its long-term solvency, and by improving access to credit in India. There was a direct link between the political prestige enjoyed by the company there and the availability of credit at a reasonable cost. Dupleix's son-in-law and supporter, Jacques d'Eprémesnil, denied that commerce everywhere followed 'invariable principles'.[48] A *mémoire* subsequently written by, or for, Dupleix rebuked Montesquieu and Dangeul for making sweeping generalisations about the India trade. But this stance did not entail a general rejection of political economy. The same *mémoire* invoked Richard Cantillon approvingly to argue that no European power could neglect the trade because the alternative was to buy India goods from their rivals.[49] This was the ideological context in which the French sent negotiators to London to treat for peace and partnership with the East India Company's Secret Committee, the body with responsibility for sensitive political matters.

While a split over the political economy of the India trade existed by 1752 between the directors and the leading Frenchmen on the ground, especially Dupleix and his subordinate Charles-Joseph Patissier, marquis de Bussy, such a divergence is harder to discern in the British camp – at least not among company employees in the Carnatic. Agents of the company there argued that peaceful commerce, not empire-building, would best serve the company's interest. 'All the Rights that We demand or any Europeans ought to have, are a few Settlements with a little Country for their Bounds allotted to them; and a Liberty for a free Trade,' remarked Major Stringer Lawrence, a professional soldier in the company's service in 1754.[50] The directors had long urged 'pacific measures' on its servants.[51] In a draft memorandum composed in August 1751, they wrote of the proxy war with the French that it was 'utterly impossible for a Trading Company to support the Expence of it'.[52] Alexander Hume, a major shareholder, former director, and MP who steered the company's negotiations with the French, saw little advantage to acquiring more territory on the Coromandel Coast or anywhere else. 'We desire no Conquests upon the French in India,' he remarked, 'they would be of no use to Us.'[53] There was no point in controlling the territories from which the company purchased the textiles it exported to Europe, and money spent on arms was lost to trade.

Hume wished to separate trade more fully from 'political' sources of profit or advantage – to reverse any drift towards European empires in India. In language adopted by the company's Secret Committee, which handled politically sensitive matters, he proposed that the two companies should have the right to establish any factories they pleased in the Carnatic or the Deccan, 'provid'd such new Establishments or Factories do not by their Extent, Situation, Revenues or other Profits (excepting Those to be obtain'd by Commerce only) give just Cause of Umbrage to either Company'. In other words, neither company was to develop a tax base, nor was either to fortify or garrison new establishments 'beyond what may be necessary to secure their own Persons & Property'.[54] Neither should they use political means to close off trading opportunities to the other. Nobody imagined it was possible to conduct a trade in India without troops; the key was to find a formula that directed rivalry between the companies mostly onto a commercial terrain – a fight Hume and the London directors reasonably supposed they would win.

Hume's career may have particularly sensitised him to the advantages of a purely commercial orientation. A Scot who got his start as an agent of the Ostend Company, which was based in the Austrian Low Countries, he had managed a profitable trade in Bengal with minimal outlay on troops or fortifications. The small companies, unlike their great-power rivals, fought no wars and depended on the protection of rulers in India, allowing them to limit security costs, if also leaving them vulnerable to political pressures. (In 1729, the British and Dutch companies joined in a military assault on the Ostend Company in Bengal.) After the charter of the company was suspended by Emperor Charles VI in 1731 in return for Dutch and British recognition of the Pragmatic Sanction, permitting the emperor's daughter, Maria-Theresa, to succeed him, the East India Company recruited Hume. He served in the direction during the War of the Austrian Succession, where he saw at first-hand the drawbacks of fighting the French.[55]

Managing the negotiations from behind the scenes in 1753, he took up with alacrity the French proposal to neutralise not only the settlements and trade of the companies in India but their shipping on the high seas. Neutrality could appeal to companies for the same reasons it attracted small, commercially vulnerable polities that used neutrality to shelter their shipping and trade in time of war.[56] These powers occupied the interstitial space between the great commercial states, where neutrals, smugglers, and the smaller chartered companies could sometimes ply a thriving trade – a space that offered some of the inspiration for schemes to mitigate great-power conflict over trade. Neutrality must particularly have appealed to India Company agents invested in the country trade, who had the most to lose from maritime marauding.[57] The Secret Committee took up Hume's arguments in favour of neutrality and urged them on the government.[58] However, while the cabinet approved a neutralisation of settlements in Asia, it refused to extend it to French shipping – wanting to profit from naval superiority in any future conflict.[59] Understandably, the French refused a neutrality that did not cover their vessels.[60]

In general, however, the British government favoured an accord to end the hostilities between the two companies. Prime Minister Henry Pelham and the Southern secretary Robert Darcy, earl of Holderness, as we saw in previous chapters (see pp. 170–1, 182–3), were inclined to the old Walpole line that peace best served Britain's commercial interests. They were keen in the same years to avert conflict with the French in America. The conflict in India threatened to drag the two nations into a war Pelham's government was anxious to avoid. Moreover, British public credit was, to a degree, hostage to the fortunes of the East India Company. London merchants and investors used the shares and bonds of the company to keep trading capital in a semi-liquid form. If the company went bankrupt, it would drag down London capital markets and major mercantile houses with it, something the government could not allow. These were issues to which Hume was sensitive, both as a stockholder, and as one of Pelham's City allies in the management of government credit.[61] Once the neutrality question was decided, the talks focused on ending the fighting in India and preventing future struggles by fixing the possessions of the two companies and committing both to withdraw permanently from Indian politics. The French proposed that the corporations become allies in India.[62] The British suggested instead that each company seek the good offices of the other in case of a dispute with an Indian power.[63]

But there were major obstacles to a settlement. The British wanted recognition for their claimant to be nawab in the Carnatic, Muhammad Ali Khan. He owed the company £250,000 for its military services, which it would never recover if he could not make good on his political pretentions.[64] In a compromise, Duvelaer agreed in May 1754 to allow the Mughal emperor to designate a nawab, but he was overruled by Paris.[65] The French were worried about losing credibility in India.[66] The still more fundamental difficulty was how to divide territories and settlements. Initially, the British proposed that both companies withdraw to their prewar limits. The French refused. If they disavowed Dupleix, they wished nonetheless to salvage from his acquisitions whatever seemed compatible with future peace.[67] For their part, the British worried that the French had not broken with the spirit of the bellicose governor-general.

As the talks dragged on, each company feared the other was playing for time, angling to strengthen its military position. At Silhouette's behest, the French sent 2,000 men to India in 1754 under the leadership of the director Charles Godeheu, who was to replace Dupleix as the leading company official there. On learning of this large force, the British directors demanded a naval squadron from their home government.[68] By the end of 1754, Hume was beginning to doubt that negotiation could resolve the outstanding issues and thought increasingly in terms of military solutions – a second-best option, as an accord with the French appeared increasingly out of reach.[69]

Yet a settlement remained possible. The French company had authorised Godeheu to negotiate a provisional settlement with the servants of the East India Company in the Carnatic, and this he quickly did with his opposite number, Thomas Saunders, the Madras president. The agreement, concluded in the final days of 1754, embodied many of the aspirations articulated by both sides in the preceding years. The two officials agreed to withdraw from the quarrels of Indian princes. During the period of the truce, they were to make common cause against any Indian ally that disturbed the peace. The treaty made a preliminary territorial settlement based on a principle of parity between the companies. Trade was to be 'free' throughout the Carnatic in the sense that neither side would obstruct the commerce of the other.[70]

When word of its signing arrived in Europe, the treaty revived optimism that a permanent agreement was possible. Hume criticised the provisional treaty as 'loose and imperfect', but if revised in the right way it might yet serve as the basis for an agreement.[71] Southern secretary Holderness congratulated Hume on 'the appearance there now is of bringing about an accommodation between the English and French E. I. Comp.ʃ'.[72] Indeed, the treaty appeared to concede the priorities of the East India Company and the British government. If approved in Paris and Versailles, it would withdraw the French company from the kinds of alliances with Indian powers that threatened the commercial position of the British company. Moreover, it seemed implicitly to recognise the East India Company's candidate to be nawab of the Carnatic, while conceding the Deccan to the French candidate.

But just at this moment it became clear that war between French and British forces in America was imminent.[73] Frontier clashes in the Ohio Country in the summer of 1754 had broadened by 1755 into an undeclared war pitting British regulars against French colonial troops and their American Indian allies – what was to become the Seven Years' War. With war approaching, the Godeheu–Saunders deal became a dead letter – a reminder that the fates of the Atlantic World and the Indian Ocean were entangled.[74] As is well known, during the war that followed, the East India Company crushed the French and founded a new territorial empire in Bengal after repelling an attack on Calcutta (now Kolkata) by the nawab of Bengal in 1757. But none of this seemed inevitable in 1755, much less in 1753. The company leaders had sought to avoid imperial control and domination; conquest and commerce were incompatible, they feared. Each company wished to prevent its rival from establishing territorial control in India, but also to avoid this fate itself. The directors had hoped instead to erect a firewall around the India trade to separate it from European geopolitical conflicts, and to return to primarily commercial competition. These ambitious schemes to remake the political framework for European trade in the Indian Ocean were cut short by war in America but re-echoed in the following decades.

A NEW GOVERNANCE REGIME FOR TRADE, 1763–70

The Bengal revolution of 1757 placed the question of empire back at the centre of East India Company politics. A fierce fight erupted in the company about whether to consolidate political control or continue to look to Indian rulers to protect trade. The situation of the Compagnie des Indes was different. While peace would see its settlements restored by the victorious British company, it emerged devastated from the Seven Years' War – heavily burdened by debt, its fortifications razed, trade at a standstill. In its dilapidated postwar condition, more than ever, commerce rather than empire appeared the only viable option. Its leaders sought to pass the costs of security to the Crown where possible, to disengage from internecine Indian struggles, and to avoid conflict with its British rival. Though the 1763 peace guaranteed the French a 'safe, free, and independent' trade in Bengal, the British company would use its power in time to obstruct French access to merchandise and producers.[75] The Compagnie des Indes came to rely on covert co-operation with East India Company employees who used the French to transport their goods and remit their fortunes to Europe. The leading French minister in the 1760s, the duc de Choiseul, deplored this state of affairs. Seeking to balance British commercial power, he prompted the monarchy to throw open the trade to all French merchants.

This opening to free trade was less the fruit of an emergent liberal political economy, as Kenneth Margerison has recognised, than a reflex of the monarchy's search to sustain the India trade in the face of British obstruction without taking on onerous military and political costs.[76] For Choiseul, the ideal was a commerce untrammelled by British interference and protected (at no cost to

French taxpayers) by Indian rulers allied to the French Crown. He could achieve this only through an eventual war to break the power of the East India Company – a struggle to be paid for, and mostly fought, he imagined, by Indians. But first he needed to sideline the Compagnie des Indes as a quasi-independent political actor and to take political relationships with Indian rulers into the hands of the Crown. Freedom of trade in 1769, in the sense of a move away from monopoly, was thus a means to achieve a different – more ambitious – vision of free trade at an opportune moment in the future.

There were resonances between Choiseul's views and those of those directors and servants of the East India Company who greeted ambivalently the expanded political power in Bengal the company acquired with the overthrow of Nawab Siraj ud-Daulah in 1757. Three competing proposals for the government of British trade emerged in the 1760s. The leading metropolitan figure in the company, Laurence Sulivan, and his ally, Henry Vansittart, governor of Bengal between 1760 and 1764, hoped to limit the company's political role and thus its costs. Sulivan warned of the dangers of empire for a trading company. He was prepared, he affirmed in 1761, 'to make Peace upon terms of a general restoration of territory to the Indian Princes, resting satisfied, as became a Merchantile Body, with the protection of Commerce'. He rejected the 'doctrine of Mr. Dupleix', declaring that 'if I could not clearly confute his Reasoning I should wish our Trade to India at an end'.[77] Sulivan wanted to maximise trade and minimise military and administrative expenses. The Company did not pursue annexations in the Carnatic, which it might have, and envisioned that an independent nawab would continue in Bengal as an ally.[78] Three times it refused the *diwani*, the right to collect revenue in Bengal, Bihar, and Orissa.[79]

But Sulivan was to lose control of the company to Robert Clive, the architect of the 1757 revolution, who took a different view of the possibilities of a company-empire in Asia. To Clive, tax revenues in Bengal seemed to offer the prospect not only of meeting all political costs shouldered by the company, and financing its exports from India, but of easing the burden of the national debt. These provinces produced a revenue of £2 million yearly, Clive advised William Pitt – resources that 'might in time be appropriated . . . towards diminishing the heavy load of debt'.[80] This line appealed particularly to George Grenville, prime minister in the mid-1760s, who feared the burden of debt and hoped to squeeze taxes from the empire to lighten its weight.[81] Grenville helped Clive to defeat Sulivan's coalition in the company, and when Clive was subsequently sent to quell renewed unrest in Bengal in 1764 he secured the *diwani* for the company. His was a vision of an empire of tribute in Asia.[82]

A third constituency in the company, composed mostly of British private traders in Bengal and company servants engaged in trade on their own account, sought Crown rule in Bengal and hoped it would deliver freedom of trade there. They argued that the exemption from duties enjoyed by the East India Company should extend to all British trade in the province. Many of these men hoped to see Crown rule extended to Bengal, supplemented by councils to represent the interests of British traders on the ground. Some argued for an expansion of British political power to other regions of India to check the predations of 'Asiatic despots' and extend the British 'empire of liberty'.[83] Such demands resonated with earlier Patriot calls to open Spanish America in 1739, and to check a French bid for a universal monarchy of trade in the 1750s. This group temporarily aligned with Clive, who worried that the company was ill-adapted to rule a large territory, and early tried to interest Pitt in establishing British imperial control.[84] But in most respects Clive's vision was quite different from the free traders – less concerned with commerce, more with fiscal extraction. For his part, Pitt was sceptical of the Crown taking on new imperial responsibilities. After he returned to power in 1766, he secured a contribution to the Treasury of £400,000 annually from the company, but left it in political control east of the Cape. However, this merely suspended discussion of the proper governance regime for British trade in India; the debate would continue for decades, as we will see.

The question of the proper political framework for trade in India was also foremost after the war in the French company. On learning that Jean Law de Lauriston, the new French governor-general, was sailing for India in 1765 with 'five ships full of men, military stores, masons, carpenters', Clive assumed the French would seek new territorial concessions from the subadar of the Deccan, picking up where Dupleix had left off.[85] In fact, Law (a nephew of John Law), had received instructions underscoring the exclusively commercial character of the postwar company, and warning him to stay out of internecine Indian struggles.[86] This stance was an extension of the position adopted by Machault d'Arnouville, Silhouette, and most of the directors of the company from the early 1750s; it also reflected the weak position of the company in the 1760s.

Championing this view was one of its informal leaders in the postwar period, Jacques Necker. A Genevan who had joined the Paris banking house of Thellusson & Vernet in 1750, Necker had become a partner by the end of the Seven Years' War and an influential shareholder in the Compagnie des Indes.[87] The company's past difficulties stemmed, in his view, from bearing the costs of defending French trade in India. If these could be reduced or passed to the Crown, the commerce might yet flourish.[88] In line with this programme, the company passed to the king its sovereignty over the Mascarene Islands – the Île de Bourbon (La Réunion) and the Île de France (Mauritius) – an invitation to a formal French imperial presence in the Indian Ocean, and to the naval protection that might follow.[89] The commercial mission of the company was reiterated. Its power was never to be employed 'for purposes of aggrandisement or of conquest to the detriment of its true spirit of commerce'.[90]

Consistent with Necker's exclusively commercial vision of the company, it became entangled financially with its British rival. Under his leadership, the company financed much of its trade by buying bills of exchange on India payable by Britons who needed to remit money from Bengal. East India Company servants had massive sums to transfer home, while the acquisition of territorial revenues meant, for a time at least, that the company had less need to borrow from its own servants, narrowing this channel for remitting. The Compagnie des Indes could finance its trade by buying bills on India in return for long-dated French bills payable in Europe. The Britons who needed to move money were willing to buy this paper and, by this means, company servants and private traders remitted their profits home by transfers of merchandise for the French market. Clive himself sent £20,000 in this fashion in 1765, and for a time defended the practice.[91] Estimating that 20 million livres (nearly £1 million) in such loans were outstanding in 1769, the British ambassador deplored the fact that the French India trade was financed in this fashion, and wondered 'whether some method may not be found out to deprive the French of this Advantage'.[92] A principal London broker for these operations was the banking house of Bourdieu & Chollet, the London correspondent of Thellusson & Necker in Paris (as the firm came to be known after Isaac Vernet's retirement). It was Necker's place in arranging these transactions that gave him influence in the French company.[93]

For several years after the renewal of French trade, the East India Company adopted an accommodating attitude towards its French rival based on a desire to avoid conflict. Harry Verelst, the leading company official in Bengal from 1767 to 1769, maintained good relations with Jean-Baptiste Chevalier, the French agent in Chandernagore (now Chandannagar), principal *comptoir* of the French. (Chevalier had formerly worked for the British firm of Johnstone, Hay, and Bolts in Dacca.[94]) Verelst even permitted the French to add a defensive wall at Chandernagore with twenty cannons. The Southern secretary William Petty, earl of Shelburne subsequently condemned this concession as contrary to the peace settlement, but permitted it to stand.[95] The directors acquiesced in the sale of 3,000 bags of saltpetre to Pondicherry in 1767, 'As good Harmony with the French will be the means of preventing any disagreeable Altercations in point of Trade.'[96]

But relations deteriorated soon after war began between the East India Company and Hyder Ali, sultan of Mysore in 1767, whom it was widely assumed had French backing, and the British company began in earnest to use its political influence in Bengal to thwart French trade. Choiseul complained that the East India Company denied the Compagnie des Indes the 'freedom necessary for its commerce'. French merchants were subject to great vexations, he claimed: they could not sell their merchandise or buy Indian manufactured goods. The British blocked access to weavers until their own orders were met, often leaving nothing for the French. The British company connived at attacks on French trading posts, notably at Patna, where several employees had been killed. Contrary to all precedent, the servants of the East India Company manipulated the nawab of Bengal to ban French private trade.[97] It was against this background that French authorities moved to suspend the monopoly of the Compagnie des Indes in 1769 and to open a 'free' French trade to India.

The French opening to free trade is often viewed as a victory for the *philosophes*, and certainly the debate elicited by the abrogation of the company's privilege was one of the great set-pieces of enlightened public controversy. But this debate followed rather than led to the suspension of the monopoly. The key work, André Morellet's *Mémoire sur la situation actuelle de la Compagnie des Indes*, had been commissioned by the contrôleur général, Étienne Maynon d'Invau, who supplied the writer with documentation of the company's financial plight.[98] Indeed, Morellet was something of an in-house *philosophe*, a pensioner of the ministry who wrote numerous published and unpublished memoranda for it.[99] The monarchy abrogated the company's privilege in order to compete more effectively against Britain in the Indian Ocean.[100]

Two different and, to a degree, competing logics came into play here, both derived from debates about how freedom of trade might solve the problem of balancing profit with protection costs. In 1755, as we have seen (above, p. 239), Jacques Vincent de Gournay had proposed to open the commerce to all French merchants while retaining the Compagnie des Indes as a structure to govern the French *comptoirs* and to preserve the political relationships with Indian rulers necessary to sustain the trade. The model was likely the establishment in 1750 of a Company of British Merchants Trading to Africa, which received licence fees for the upkeep of forts and garrisons in Africa but was not permitted to engage in the slave trade itself.[101]

For Gournay, freedom of trade meant embracing commercial stratagems in place of military and political weapons in the struggle against the East India Company. A trade to India open to all French merchants would greatly expand the volume of goods shipped back to Europe, he argued, driving down prices. If merchants did not have to bear the costs of defending the trade, they would benefit from a huge cost advantage over their British and Dutch competitors. The taxes they paid on this augmented trade would finance protection for French commerce in Asia in the guise of the reformed company. The Compagnie des Indes would be able to settle its debts and offer its shareholders better dividends.[102]

The free-trade scheme the French monarchy adopted in 1769 was closely modelled on Gournay's, with a twist that points to the Choiseulist agenda it would also serve. As Gournay suggested, Louis XV retained the Compagnie des Indes as the political integument of a private French trade in Asia, the governor of French establishments in India, and the bearer of trade privileges granted in the past by Indian rulers. But it would continue in little more than name. Authority over the French *comptoirs* would lie henceforth with the naval ministry, and company servants in India were to be designated officials of the Crown. Choiseul feared that Britain's dominant position in India tilted the balance of power, and he sought a political structure in Asia that would redress this imbalance.[103] What he had in mind was not French territorial empire. The minister was not interested in extensive possessions *à la Dupleix*, which would be expensive to administer and defend, and which would draw the French into Indian conflicts.[104] The rise of a British company-empire in Bengal had not convinced French officials that a territorial strategy was viable in Asia. The subcontinent was too large and populous, they thought, for any European power long to keep it in subjection. The British were digging their own graves, officials argued, through a destabilising expansionism that must soon elicit Indian resistance.[105] Only a commercial role backed by a minimum of force could have any long-term future.

Instead, Choiseul imagined a freedom of trade underwritten by Indian rulers allied to France as the ideal framework for French commerce. In the event of war with Britain, he planned to attack the East India Company from the Mascarenes in coalition with Indian allies.[106] Once the power of the British company was broken, French trade would prosper under the auspices of these auxiliaries, who would protect French merchants and exempt them from taxes and customs duties. This was the second crucial meaning of free trade for Choiseul. It was to be free in the sense of no longer being obstructed by British chicanery, and because French traders would enjoy access, protection, and low taxes, all without the costs of territorial empire. To cite just one example of this pattern of thinking, in discussions for an alliance proposed by the grand vizier of the Mughal Empire to break the power of the East India Company, Louis XV was offered sovereignty over Bengal but demurred, 'wanting only to reserve the post of Chandernagore and the *comptoirs* which will be recognised as necessary or useful for the exploitation of the trade of the French nation'. The chief aim of the alliance, French officials asserted, was to return Bengal to Mughal sovereignty and to 'render commerce free throughout the empire'. However, French subjects were to enjoy 'an exemption from all duties, tolls, and taxes whatsoever'. Even the British might be suffered to remain as a trading presence, at the option of the Mughal emperor, but must be reduced to the status of merchants, with troop numbers strictly equivalent to the French.[107] French officials in India believed there would be determined opposition to the expulsion of the British from Indian portfolio capitalists who benefited from British business. This powerful class could not be alienated.[108]

To achieve the dream of a free French trade under the auspices of Indian allies, the minister had to bring the *comptoirs* under Crown control: hence the reform of 1769. The insistence of the company that its servants stay out of Indian politics ran contrary to Choiseul's desire to build alliances with Indian powers. The military governor of the Mascarenes, Jean-Daniel Dumas, who sought to exploit Law de Lauriston's political contacts in India, received little co-operation, a fact he attributed to countermanding orders from the company. This 'difference of interests' between the Crown and the company, 'this constraint in the course of public business cannot go on', Dumas insisted. He recommended that the king take direct control of the *comptoirs*.[109] The point was echoed by the abbé de Saint-Estevan, curé of Chandernagore and an ally of Chevalier, who told the naval minister, the duc de Praslin, early in 1769 that the company had no interest in effecting the necessary 'revolution' in India, and that the Crown would need to step in to replace it.[110]

Echoes of Choiseul's Indian Ocean politics appear in Guillaume-Thomas Raynal's celebrated *Histoire philosophique et politique des établissements & du commerce des Européens dans les deux Indes*, first published in 1770 and destined to become one of the bestsellers of the century. The book is often read as an impassioned critique of European colonialism, and indeed there is much to support such a reading in this 'polyphonic' text, penned not only by Raynal himself, but in collaboration with others, most prominently Denis Diderot. But the book also offered well-informed commentary on the global politics of trade, some of it supportive of Choiseul's positions. From 1761 Raynal was the beneficiary of a pension from the foreign ministry. He had access to a wide variety of official documents and met weekly with foreign diplomats who shared other sensitive material with him and may even have written passages of the work.[111] Raynal documented the struggle of rival European states for global trade. He and his collaborators pressed Choiseul's position that only by rallying around France might the nations of Europe check the rise of a British universal monarchy of trade.[112] Diderot, who wrote the sections on India, foresaw the French placing themselves at the head of a coalition to liberate the subcontinent from British domination. He called for the development of the Mascarenes as a bastion to secure French commerce in the East – all themes dear to Choiseul.[113]

But the *Histoire* was in no sense a simple mouthpiece for the minister. It forged an independent line on key matters.[114] While supporting the move of the Crown to take into its hands the protection of French trade in the Indian Ocean, Diderot criticised the decision to wind up the commercial operations of the Compagnie des Indes in 1769. After opening the trade to all subjects, the ministry should have preserved the company as a trading enterprise. Only by pooling capital and information, and limiting competition, could profits be sustained in the India trade, Diderot argued. And this trade had generally been beneficial to Europe, he insisted. If Indian manufactures competed with European ones, competition had nevertheless stimulated import substituting industries like porcelain and printed cottons. Moreover, Asian demand for Spanish silver allowed Europe to sell its textiles in America. The suspension of the monopoly in 1769 had led to the virtual cessation of trade with India, Diderot complained, while only two vessels had been fitted out for China, and these only with government subsidies. Such was the reality of free trade. The *philosophe* rejected the idea of perfect liberty pushed by writers he regarded as doctrinaire, envisioning a hybrid in which companies would continue to do the India trade, but not exclusively, allowing private traders to profit from the many commercial opportunities not exploited by the behemoths.[115]

The *Histoire des deux Indes* represents one of the range of relationships to emerge between ministerial politics and works written for the public. It is formally very different from documents such as Morellet's work on the Compagnie des Indes mentioned above, which was written for the contrôleur général, or Gournay's memorandum on the reform of the company, produced for internal circulation but subsequently published in 1769. Like other key works of the Enlightenment such as Diderot and d'Alembert's celebrated *Encyclopédie* (1751–72), Raynal's work offered multiple, sometimes competing, perspectives, allowing readers with widely different ideas to find fodder for their views, sustaining debate, but ultimately resisting closure or any authoritative message. In this sense, the text was an emblem of the enlightened public sphere as a whole, which, far from trumpeting any single stance, brimmed with controversy and contradiction. That there should be any kind of relationship between such a work and the politics of Choiseul may appear odd. But as a bold forum for debate, apparently responsible only to the public, it may have been a peculiarly effective vehicle to nudge opinion. To be sure, this relationship was contradictory and unstable. For elements within the fragmented old regime state, the *Histoire des deux Indes* was a bridge too far. The book was officially banned in 1774 for its anti-Catholic overtones, though this served only to increase its celebrity.

The position of the *Histoire* in the ecosystem of French high politics and the public sphere appears to have shifted after the fall of Choiseul in 1770. At the end of that year, Louis XV disgraced the minister, along with his cousin Praslin, in part to calm relations with Britain. The two nations had nearly come to blows in a confrontation between Spain and the British over the sovereignty of the Falkland Islands. More broadly, Choiseul's commitment to a Bourbon war of revanche against Britain after 1763 had proven unrealistic in light of the financial sclerosis of the French monarchy. Diderot would continue to sound Choiseulist notes in the second edition published in 1774, which cannot have endeared him to the new ministry. But in its polyphony, the book also took new positions on how to meet the British challenge in India – perhaps in search of resonance with the orientation of Choiseul's successor as foreign minister, Emmanuel-Armand de Richelieu, duc d'Aiguillon.

THE QUEST FOR AN ENTENTE IN THE EARLY 1770S

D'Aiguillon presided over the most overt effort since the 1720s to contain the Franco-British rivalry by reconstituting their European and global relationship on a new political-economic basis. The centrepiece of this initiative, as we have seen (above, p. 61), was to have been a commercial treaty to reopen trade between the two nations on a basis similar to the 1713 commercial treaty of Utrecht. The second strand was a prospective accord to end Franco-British rivalry in India and to establish a condominium there to preserve European commercial access in face of a threatened resurgence of Indian power. The proposed India deal represents a complete overturning of Choiseul's view that Indian rulers might serve to protect a free French trade, and a renewed search for the kind of Franco-British accommodation pursued in the 1750s. Choiseul had fallen because his stance threatened war with Britain at a moment of financial distress for the French monarchy. Louis XV and d'Aiguillon were also worried about threats to peace in Eastern Europe and the Baltic, as we have seen (above, p. 60), and needed an understanding with Britain both to avert the threat of war and to constrain Russian and Prussian expansionism.

D'Aiguillon faced the relatively new regime of Lord North, who had emerged as George III's choice for prime minister in 1770. As already noted (above, p. 61), North and the king were not completely unreceptive to the French search for an understanding. One of the prime minister's first important acts in power had been to intervene personally to prevent a war over the

Falklands. In the emergent partisan politics of the late 1760s, he was a Tory –
concerned about the weight of the national debt, wary of imperial expansion,
and anxious to keep in check Britain's restless American colonists. He also had
to deal, during his first three years in office, with a growing crisis in the East
India Company, which formed the background to d'Aiguillon's hopes for an
entente.

Initial British hopes to use Bengal territorial revenues to stabilise the
finances of the company and the kingdom soon proved illusory. By the late
1760s, it was clear that 'the Company had incurred a net financial loss as a
result of its assumption of the Diwani'.[116] It emerged from the Seven Years'
War the master of Bengal, but in so doing spent more than £8 million.[117] Peace
brought little abatement in military spending. Costs in Bengal alone had
grown from £550,036 in 1764–65 to £1,093,006 by 1770–71, not counting
the huge sums spent to rebuild the Fort William fortifications in Calcutta.[118]
Security and administrative costs threatened to absorb the territorial revenues
and more, especially once the company became embroiled again in wars with
Indian rulers, as it had with the powerful Sultanate of Mysore in 1768.[119]

To compound the problem, the territorial revenues could be remitted only
by buying and exporting goods for sale in Europe. Had the balance been transferred in specie, it would quickly have drained the local economy, ruining
future revenue prospects.[120] As senior company servants in Bengal put it in
1769, 'Your trade from hence may be considered more as a channel for
conveying your revenues to Britain, than as only a mercantile system.'[121] To be
sure, trade grew impressively. The company used its political dominance in
Bengal to impose below-market, monopsonist pricing on producers, and to
squeeze out the trade of competing Europeans.[122] But by 1770 its sales in
Britain had plateaued. Greater imports and competition from smugglers
depressed prices, and by 1772 the company had more than £3 million worth
of unsold goods in its London warehouses. These factors forced it to borrow in
the late 1760s to remain solvent, and in 1772, when a major credit crisis broke
in London, it teetered on the verge of financial collapse.

To exacerbate the financial woes of the company, a fierce critique of its
governance emerged in the early 1770s, fuelled by tales of rapine and plunder
in India, a severe famine in 1769–70, and attacks on the company from
disgruntled servants and private traders.[123] British merchants in Bengal, senior

company servants among them, pressed for a transfer of sovereignty to the Crown (or even back to Indian rulers), and the freer trade they assumed this would entail. Britons engaged in commerce in India on their own account resented company monopolies established in the 1760s over branches of the 'inland trade'.[124] The company had long permitted its servants liberty in their private trade, combining monopoly in the intercontinental commerce with relative freedom in Asia.[125] The new inland trade monopolies violated these precedents. Calls for free trade became tied to criticism of company rule, and claims that all parties would be better off under a different system of governance. This was true, for example, of the senior company servant John Johnstone and his business partner William Bolts. Bolts was expelled from Bengal in 1768 after a conflict with Verelst over private trading rights, and suspicions that he had conspired with the French and the Dutch (recall that Chevalier had once been his employee in Dacca).[126] He published an influential attack on company rule in 1772, *Considerations on India Affairs; Particularly Respecting the Present State of Bengal.*

The ultimate problem for Bolts was company sovereignty: 'those countries will not prosper while the Company continue there the Merchant-sovereign and the Sovereign-merchant', he warned.[127] Only the Crown could supply Bengal with good government and the freedom of trade which alone would restore prosperity. The company's oppressions had ruined the prosperity of its provinces and must eventually excite a revolt that would push the British out of India.[128] Though the company's monopoly on Britain's trade with Asia was not his principal target, Bolts favoured an opening here too. A monopoly company had made sense as a protective framework for trade while Bengal was governed by Indian rulers, but no longer did so 'now that the English are become Sovereigns'. Sympathising with the 'oppressions' suffered by the French, Bolts suggested it might be a good idea 'to encourage as much as possible even the ships of all other European nations to frequent those India ports'.[129] A wider commercial liberty could only favour the prosperity of the province. The attacks of Bolts and other critics were taken up by a parliamentary select committee established in 1772 to investigate the company's misrule.

This was the background to French hopes of a new accommodation with British power in India. East India Company weakness and exposure might increase the attractions of an entente with the French that would insulate it from their political machinations in India and the threat of future attacks from this quarter. D'Aiguillon sought initially to ease tensions by intervening in the spring of 1772 to prevent the sailing of a French squadron to the Mascarenes.[130] The North government also wanted to lower the political temperature in the Indian Ocean. It gave powers to the British naval commander there, Admiral Robert Harland, to resolve Franco-British disputes in consultation with Jean Law de Lauriston. Harland intervened forcefully to censure East India Company treatment of French merchants and to recommend 'conciliating measures between the subjects of the two nations'.[131] The French search for détente with Britain naturally demanded a rethinking of Choiseul's strategy for a war to deliver free trade in India, and this rethinking became entangled with initiatives to establish a new India company.

Almost from the moment the Crown suspended the monopoly of the Compagnie des Indes there was talk either of restoring it or launching a new joint stock. The abbé Joseph-Marie Terray, contrôleur général since 1769, had been a syndic of the old company and let it be known that he meant to revive it.[132] As we have seen (above, p. 252), even such advocates of commercial liberty as Raynal and Diderot believed the trade could not be done profitably without a company. Under the naval minister Pierre-Étienne Bourgeois de Boynes, investors moved to found a new company that would be an entirely commercial operation. The minister and his allies argued that private traders lacked the capital necessary to carry on a successful trade and failed to control competition. In fact, under free trade, commerce with India and China eventually rebounded and surpassed previous peaks by the mid-1770s, so we may surmise that proposals for a new company were an effort to capture some of the emerging profits of the private trade. To secure the position of a prospective monopoly company, Bourgeois de Boynes argued for an alliance with its British rival.

Given how precarious its position had become, Bourgeois de Boynes implied, the British company should welcome French amity. Indeed, it was in the interest of the British to 'join with us in such a way as to contain the jealousy that the Indian princes will always have against any European nation that wishes to carry its views beyond trade'.[133] If the powerful Maratha confederacy invaded Bengal, taxation and trade would quickly dry up; Hyder Ali, sultan of Mysore remained a dangerous enemy of the British, who had refused to support him in a conflict with the Marathas in 1770, despite a defensive alliance. The abbé de Saint-Estevan, whom d'Aiguillon consulted, underlined the vulnerability of the East India Company in the face of spiralling military costs. The British risked following the same trajectory as the French, who had diverted funds from commerce to conquest and were ruined by war.[134] Bourgeois de Boynes and those who shared his views saw in the troubles of the British company an opportunity to remake the political framework for trade in India in ways that recall the proposed treaty of 1753. They called for a defensive alliance between the two companies to check the machinations of Indian powers. The commerce should be neutralised in case of future wars in Europe, and these protections ought to extend to shipping. They even had hopes of a new partition of zones of influence.[135]

A commentary on this initiative is to be found in the revised 1773 edition of the *Histoire des deux Indes*, which, predictably, took more than one stance. Diderot affirmed that an agreement between all European nations would certainly be the best framework in which to carry on the trade in the long run. However, in the current circumstances such an accord would simply play into Britain's hands because it would avert the danger of France leading a confederacy of Indian powers against it. Only a war could restore the 'balance' between them necessary to revive a profitable French India trade. The French stood to become 'the idols of the princes and people of Asia, provided the revolution they initiated proved to them a lesson of moderation'.[136] Thus Diderot reasserted the position of Choiseul – now in the political wilderness, but scheming to return to power. Yet this was not his only or final word on the matter. He had previously lauded the efforts of the North administration to come to terms with the problems of the East India Company and hoped to see an extension of Crown rule, British liberties, and free trade to Bengal. If such were to come to pass, asserted the *Histoire*, 'the friends of mankind . . . will invite you to new conquests'.[137] Here was a position neither Choiseul's nor d'Aiguillon's, but resonant with William Bolts's *Considerations on India Affairs*.

The French initiative for a new entente in India was a non-starter for the East India Company, which had troubles enough to deal with without a resurgence of French political power in Asia. The French reached out informally to Leadenhall Street and to the North ministry in 1772 through the embassy secretary Robert Walpole (another nephew of Sir Robert). Lord Rochford, the

Southern secretary, is supposed to have responded noncommittally.[138] At about the same time, the London banker James Bourdieu proposed an arrangement to the East India Company to knit the fortunes of the prospective French company to its own. This would give the British company a means to remit more of its territorial revenues to Europe, and thereby to help resolve its financial woes. The East India Company could furnish its French rival with bills of exchange on its treasuries in India; the French could use these to finance their buying in Bengal and the Coromandel, and after the sale of East India goods in their home market, they would settle their debts in London.[139] The British directors were uninterested, but such a proposal would resurface in 1785 as Bourdieu sought to broker a collaboration on similar lines between the East India Company and a new French India Company established that year in Paris.

Ultimately, the company proposed by Bourgeois de Boynes in 1772 never got off the ground, though d'Aiguillon approved it and its backers tried to launch the new venture in the spring of 1773.[140] Investors apparently subscribed nearly 28 million livres of a 40-million-livre total capitalisation by March.[141] But in the end, the project came to nothing – perhaps the victim of a turf war between the naval ministry and Terray. In fact, without a deal with the British company, it is difficult to see how the high level of geopolitical risk could justify such an investment. When investors founded the Nouvelle Compagnie des Indes in 1785, they conceived of it from the outset as a collaborative venture with the British.

Instead of brokering a deal with a prospective rival company, North – facing the old problem of costs outrunning profits in the India trade – moved to stabilise the company financially and to gain more control over its political affairs. As the price for a financial bailout of £1.4 million in 1773, the East India Company accepted a Regulating Act that allowed the government to appoint a governor-general and a Supreme Council composed of four councillors to confer on major political decisions in Bengal. (Some ministers wanted British naval officials to assume responsibility for diplomatic relations with Indian rulers and the French, but company leaders fought fiercely against such a loss of control.) This was a half measure, and a far cry from the establishment of Crown government in Bengal, but a serious effort, nonetheless, to check the expansionist tendencies of the company in Bengal, which must be reined in if its financial affairs were ever to stabilise. It would ultimately fail, inviting new measures of government intervention in the 1780s.

Though the directors had never ceased to reiterate that commerce rather than empire must be the basis of their affairs in India, the position of the company as a sovereign in a competitive and unstable region drew it into further expansion.[142] From the perspective of Calcutta, it seemed inadequate simply to guard the province's borders. One temptation was to control buffer regions, such as Awadh on Bengal's exposed northwest frontier. Another was to preserve a balance of power among competing Indian states by propping up some and intervening to check the power of others – to be, in Clive's words, 'the great Ballance Masters'.[143] Either position could draw the presidencies into a forward policy. It was Warren Hastings's policy as governor-general in the 1770s to make protective alliances with Indian states intended to defray the company's security costs by laying them off to allied princes. Company troops would be stationed on their territories, at their expense, to protect them, keep them out of the French interest, and indirectly to secure Bengal. Such protectorates repeatedly drew the company into new wars.

Only a radical remaking of the political order in India would check this slippage towards conquest, argued Philip Francis, a former secretary of William Pitt dispatched by North in 1773 as a member of the new Supreme Council. Francis called for Crown sovereignty in Bengal; the company should return to being a commercial operation only, and get out of the business of taxing and governing. He pressed for the creation of a revived Mughal Empire to protect British trade beyond Bengal – a return to the old order when the costs of territorial sovereignty were borne by Indian rulers. 'The System of maintaining a Country Government was the original Policy of the Company from the first acquisition of their influence in Bengal,' he told the prime minister, and 'to recover the Country we ought to revert, as far as possible, to its ancient political System.' He believed that Bengal could not flourish 'while the neighbouring States are perpetually in arms against each another', and he hoped to establish a confederacy of peaceful states instead, arbitrated by British power.[144] Combined with Crown control in Bengal – and internal free trade – this would restore the prosperity of the province and the fortunes of a company now returned to its proper role as a merely commercial enterprise.[145] Neither Francis nor North saw an accommodation with the French as a necessary component of such a transformed political framework. It would take another round of Franco-British military conflict, and an associated financial crisis in the East India Company, to make British public officials and company leaders feel that France, too, would have to be accommodated if there was to be a stable and less expensive framework for trade in India.

THE NOUVELLE COMPAGNIE DES INDES AND THE SEARCH FOR AN ACCORD IN THE 1780S

During the American War, the East India Company overran the French *comptoirs* and French trade to India virtually ceased. Yet officials anticipated that Britain's defeat in America would permit France to improve its commercial position in Asia. The French foreign minister, the comte de Vergennes, aspired to augment trade without extending the formal imperial presence of the monarchy in Asia, without increasing the costs of protection, and without provoking Britain. In 1784, French investors had proposed a partnership between a new French India Company they hoped to found and its larger British rival. Such an arrangement found favour with the Pitt administration, which acquired greater political control over the East India Company with the 1784 India Act. The leading government figure on Indian affairs, Henry Dundas, backed a relatively free trade in Bengal for competing European companies, and hoped to reach an understanding with Versailles on this basis that would secure the peace. He offered to protect the commerce of the French if they moderated their political pretensions in Bengal. This differed from the proposed accommodations of previous decades, pointing towards the free-trade British Empire of the nineteenth century and towards the kind of unequal Franco-British partnership that sometimes characterised the interimperial relationship during the same period.[146] Vergennes rejected these terms, believing that French victory in America should secure it a more commanding position, but as the pre-revolutionary financial and political crisis unfolded in France his successor negotiated a convention with Britain on similar terms.

This groping towards a Franco-British understanding in India must be situated within the broader context of this geopolitical moment, when Vergennes sought to establish a stable balance of power with Britain, and perhaps future partnership, on the basis of greater freedom of trade. As we saw in the preceding chapter (p. 208), the minister believed the establishment of the United States as a free-trading power would redistribute the profits of American trade and reduce British naval dominance. The balance of power would be adjusted thereby to French advantage. For their part, British officials hoped, by adopting a partially free trade, to recover lost markets in America, while excluding American shipping from the British Caribbean, which would check the rapid growth of American navigation. Both Vergennes and Pitt hoped the Eden–Rayneval treaty of 1786 would foster more amicable future relations. For Vergennes, the trade treaty would conciliate Britain, and bind it to accept the new order by offering it real gains, while allowing France to recover economic parity, or even supremacy, over the long run. Pitt for his part assumed the treaty would benefit Britain more, offering continental markets to compensate for American losses. Greater freedom of trade in Europe and in America would be the foundation of a new order in which the Franco-British rivalry would assume a mostly peaceful, commercial form. A final obstacle to the balance necessary to underpin this order was the British position in Bengal. But in Vergennes's view, the monarchy's finances were far too precarious to fight a second war there for free trade. It was in this context that a deal with the British to protect French commerce in India appeared attractive.

But not everyone in the French ministry saw matters as Vergennes did. Vergennes had emerged as a virtual first minister with the conclusion of the peace, allied to Charles-Alexandre de Calonne, the contrôleur général. Ranged against him were the naval minister Charles-Eugène-Gabriel de La Croix, marquis de Castries, the war minister Phillipe Henri, marquis de Ségur, and the minister of the royal household Louis-Auguste Le Tonnelier, baron de Breteuil. (Calonne's rival, Jacques Necker, was poised in the wings to return as finance minister.)[147] A former syndic of the Compagnie des Indies, where he had been allied with Necker, Castries took a more sanguine view of the possibility for French political revival in India than did Vergennes. When he joined the ministry in 1780, he organised naval and military expeditions intended to attack the British there, the latter commanded by Dupleix's former subordinate, the marquis de Bussy.[148] Castries hoped to accomplish Choiseul's old objective of 'liberating' Indian princes from British tyranny. The French were to make no conquests, but demand only privileges for their trade.[149] Bussy held that France should, in addition, occupy territories to generate revenue to cover civil and military expenses, a position Castries came to support.[150] In the event, he arrived too late to affect the outcome of an ongoing war between the kingdom of Mysore and the East India Company.

Under pressure from Castries and his allies, Vergennes initially pressed Shelburne in the 1782 peace negotiations for a substantial rounding out of French territory, demanding lands around Karikal (now Karaikal) and Pondicherry worth £500,000 (more than 10 million livres) annually. Recall that this was the sum Dupleix estimated would be necessary to cover French administrative and security costs in Asia. The French foreign minister was not opposed to the acquisition of limited territories which might defray civil and military expenses without embroiling the nation in Indian conflicts.[151] But he quickly retreated from the demand for territory in the face of Shelburne's rebuff, settling for a token *arrondissement* worth £30,000 a year.[152] The divisions over foreign policy between Vergennes and his rivals were less over ends than means. All saw Britain as the chief rival, and all were concerned to check British power. Vergennes's commitment to peace with Britain from 1783 was not idealistic. He had chosen war five years earlier, when it seemed clear that the potential gains outweighed the risks. But with America now independent, and the French monarchy financially drained, he believed that peace – and ideally partnership – with the British offered the best prospects for the commercial expansion of France that alone would foster a balance of power. Castries and his allies believed a more confrontational stance, and likely another war, would be necessary to check the British threat.

Vergennes's priority, and what he thought actually practicable, was the 'free, independent, and secure' trade in Bengal that the treaty of Paris twenty years before had promised but failed to deliver. From the late 1760s, as we have seen, French ministries complained that the East India Company used its local power to shut French merchants out of commercial opportunities. While Shelburne held out against an expansion of French political power in India, he guaranteed that French trade there would no longer be obstructed. He intended that the French be treated in Bengal 'upon the same footing of our own subjects', so long as they did not try to extend the vestigial political position they still held there.[153] He envisioned a postwar reform of the East India Company to introduce a greater liberty in the India trade – a freedom, he assured Vergennes's subordinate Rayneval, the French would also enjoy.[154]

'I imagine sooner or later . . . that the commerce must be opened subject to regulations of trade & revenue,' he told the merchant banker and company director Francis Baring. The latter proposed a public buy-out of the charter of the company in return for an 8 per cent annuity to the shareholders.[155] Vergennes interpreted Shelburne's attitude over India as a function of the new balance of forces and, despite his diplomatic partner's fall in 1783, he expected to be able to secure from the British government the conditions for an unobstructed French trade.

Such a trade, most of the French ministers agreed, could best be carried on by a new monopoly company. Calonne's predecessor, the contrôleur général Jean-François Joly de Fleury, in particular, had backed such a venture.[156] As already noted (see above, p. 256), there had been initiatives to re-establish an India company virtually since the suspension of the old corporation's privilege in 1769. A group of merchants previously active in the India trade coalesced in 1784 to establish a new corporation which they envisioned would operate in Bengal as a junior partner of the East India Company. The projectors claimed that commerce could not be pursued profitably there without such an arrangement.[157] In part, the aim was to hedge against geopolitical risk – if the French company were to buy from the East India Company, the wager was, future conflict might be avoided.[158] Moreover, French merchants would not have to struggle against constant harassment. The leaders of the French company and the directors of the East India Company reached an initial accord in 1784 under the auspices of Castries, but Vergennes and Calonne quashed the deal as a pretext to take the negotiation, and the company, into their own hands.[159]

What would come to be called the Nouvelle Compagnie des Indes was established in the spring of 1785. A joint-stock enterprise capitalised at 20 million livres (later raised to 40), the Crown initially granted it a monopoly for seven years to import China and India goods, and to exploit the 'country trade' from India to China, Japan, and the Red Sea. The company was to be a commercial operation only, with the monarchy to retain sovereignty and pay all security costs. As a pacific, commercial venture, the company fitted Vergennes's design to extend French trade without an extension of formal empire, without increasing defence costs, and without antagonising Britain. This was of a piece with the decision to move the administrative capital of the French settlements in India from Pondicherry to Port Louis on Mauritius, signalling an abandonment of territorial ambitions.[160] By securing a monopoly for the company on French trade in the Red Sea, Vergennes also acquired a veto over Castries's plans to reopen a French trade to the Indian Ocean via Suez, which might have stirred up tensions with Britain or Constantinople.[161] Calonne soon allowed a renewal of talks between the Nouvelle Compagnie and the East India Company and they reached an agreement late in 1785. For the following three years, the French company was to buy Bengal goods annually to the value of 40 lakhs of rupees (about 10 million livres) from its nominal rival.[162]

The accord with the French promised to solve several problems at once for the British company and the British government. The first of these was financial. Under the burden of military expenses incurred during recent wars against Mysore, the Marathas, and the French, the East India Company was again under huge financial pressure. In August 1782, the company requested a second bailout from the government, noting that 'little short of a million sterling will rescue the Company's affairs, in the Carnatic in particular, from the impending ruin'.[163] In the latter years of the conflict, it had supported 100,000 men under arms. The territorial revenues being consumed by civil and military expenses, goods for export had to be paid for using bills on England and Ireland at high interest, saddling the company with a debt of £4 million costing upwards of £300,000 a year to service.[164] A critical priority was to lift this burden. The company could only transfer its Bengal revenue to London via trade, but struggled to market an adequate volume of goods.

To Henry Dundas, the obvious solution was to encourage the trade of other European companies. Foreign companies would pay for their purchases in specie, reflating the local money supply, or Britons could finance their purchases, allowing them to settle their debts in Europe – effectively remitting British fortunes home – or, better still, the East India Company could sell these rivals Bengal goods to be disposed of in European markets closed to the company – breaching the protective barriers foreign countries erected to reserve the home market to their own India companies. 'Nothing can be greater insanity,' Dundas told Thomas Townsend, a fellow member of the Board of Control, 'than our being jealous of or adverse to other Nations trading to our asiatick possessions.'[165] The chief intermediary for the arrangement, the banker James Bourdieu, stressed the financial advantages of a deal with the new French company. He promised that 'The amount of the goods thus delivered to the

French in India would, without draining India of its specie . . . bring a clear remittance from France of £500,000 a year.'[166] One of the leading directors, Francis Baring, likewise recognised this as the principal benefit of the French deal. It would enable the East India Company 'to realise circuitously through France 40 Lacks [lakhs of rupees] more of the Indian Territorial Revenues than could have been done through her own Sales'.[167]

The deal promised further economic advantages. It would reduce competition among prospective buyers for goods in Bengal. Under the 1783 treaty, the French had the right to carry on a trade there from their *comptoirs*, but the Nouvelle Compagnie undertook not to exercise it – to buy exclusively from its rival.[168] It emphasised that it would be importing for French consumption only, not for re-export. More importantly, the East India Company would no longer have to compete in the markets of Bengal against its own employees, who since the 1760s had supplied the French with Bengal goods as a means to remit their own fortunes to Europe.

A further advantage of the deal with the French company was that it favoured peace and stability in India – a priority of Dundas. In Parliament, he had savaged the 'frantic military exploits' to which the company's employees had sacrificed 'the improvement of the trade and commerce of the country'.[169] Other critics, too, rejected the company's unchecked expansionism, which had brought it 'to the brink of ruin'.[170] This was part of a broader assault on the whole company regime in India led by Edmund Burke in the form of a parliamentary select committee meeting from 1781 to 1784.[171] A major goal of the India Act passed in 1784 by Pitt's government, based on a blueprint first elaborated by Dundas, was to stop the company from engaging in offensive wars.[172] Though the French political position in India was weak, they retained the power to attack the company by aligning with Indian rulers and encouraging their challenges. The British had been shaken by the military successes of the Marathas and of Mysore. A French naval squadron performed creditably against the Royal Navy, and had Bussy's expedition come two years earlier, it might have wreaked havoc. Moreover, beyond any real danger the French presented, the threat of collusion between them and Indian rulers had served in the past to justify the expansionism of the British company in India against which Dundas set his face.[173]

The deal would cement Franco-British harmony in India, and 'establish a long series of Peace between France & England by removing the most probable cause of future contentions', promised Bourdieu.[174] Tying the commercial fortunes of the two countries together would prevent the French from attacking the political position of Britain in India: 'A French Company purely mercantile, free from any Military establishments, can have no other purpose or occupation, but such as may tend to the benefit of their commerce, which being immediately connected with that of our own, the interest of both will become united & inseparable, & all political jealousies cease.'[175] Given his bank's business in brokering French bills on London, Bourdieu had a long-standing interest in better Franco-British relations. He had been d'Aiguillon's intermediary for a proposed commercial treaty in 1772, as we have seen, while in 1782, at the end of the American War, he offered his services as a peace negotiator (Shelburne chose the Scottish merchant Richard Oswald instead).[176] Dundas believed that if the French were allowed commercial access to Bengal, they would cease to challenge British rule there.[177] He and Pitt heartily approved of the intercompany arrangement.[178]

Though the Nouvelle Compagnie had pursued the British deal with his blessing, Vergennes vetoed the final agreement. Instead of building on the gains of the American War, and demanding the treatment that successful French arms and renewed political prestige should command, the new French company had placed itself in a subordinate position. In signing a non-compete clause, the French negotiator had exceeded his instructions and ceded trading rights secured under the peace of 1783. The kind of trade envisaged under the deal, while advantageous to the company, would not be so to the nation. If the new enterprise planned to acquire all its Bengal goods from the East India Company, Vergennes asked, would it not be better to buy them in London, where they might be exchanged for products of French industry or agriculture?[179] A more attractive alternative, suggested his deputy, Rayneval, would be to form a cartel with the Spanish Company of the Philippines. The Spanish could thereby gain access to Bengal markets, where their capacity to pay in silver would permit the Franco-Spanish partners to engross the clandestine trade with employees of the British company and dominate European markets.[180]

In the end, the failure to reach a deal with the British company turned on fundamental questions concerning the political framework for trade in the East. Vergennes was not willing to concede to Britain the role of protector; he did not believe French trade would be viable in India under such conditions.

There was, moreover, considerable opposition to Dundas's position in the East India Company itself. Warren Hastings spoke for many others when he objected that, under the proposed deal, French trade would profit from the security umbrella of its British rival 'instead of paying for its [own] protection'.[181] The hostility of company authorities in Bengal to French political pretensions would make any deal concluded in Europe difficult to enforce. There may also have been in their opposition a desire on the part of East India Company servants to keep open the French route to remit their private gains back to Europe, which the intercompany agreement would preclude.

But Vergennes's veto had not finished efforts to forge a Franco-British accommodation in India. Both Rayneval and Calonne contemplated a future revision of the failed accord. William Eden, who was in France to negotiate the commercial treaty of 1786, hoped that the French and British companies would work towards 'the harmony and the mutual good of the two Nations'.[182] Initiative for a new understanding was to come from Bengal. There John Macpherson, acting governor-general after the departure of Hastings, sought to work out an accommodation with François de Souillac, the French governor-general, to resolve outstanding disputes over French trading rights in Bengal. Remarking that between 'neighbouring and even rival Nations the advantages of a free Commerce may be mutual and reciprocal', Macpherson sent Lieutenant-Colonel Charles Cathcart to hammer out a deal.[183] If the French could be satisfied commercially in India, Macpherson argued, they would be less likely to upset the political status quo.[184] 'It is our Duty,' he argued, 'in every Respect to encourage the Prosecution of a Commerce which is a tie upon the Military Ambition of France and which above all other Obligations promises Permanency to the Peace of India.'[185] The Souillac–Cathcart treaty of April 1786 was the fruit of this negotiation.[186] But neither the new governor-general sent to replace Hastings, Lord Cornwallis, the directors in London, nor Pitt's Board of Control were satisfied, and Dundas instructed Eden to renegotiate the compact at Versailles.

What Dundas proposed, in effect, was a greater measure of French commercial access in Bengal in return for acceptance of British political control. 'I grudge the French no participation of trade,' he told Eden, 'for I know . . . it will ultimately redound to our advantage, but they must agree to enjoy it under our protection without molesting us in the government of the country.'[187] While such an arrangement had been unacceptable to Vergennes, who died in

February 1787, his successor, Armand Marc, comte de Montmorin, a Vergennes protégé and former ambassador to Spain, embraced it. Facing simultaneous financial and foreign policy crises following Prussia's invasion of the Dutch Republic, Montmorin struggled to keep alive the recent rapprochement with Britain. The result was a convention that promised the French navigation rights on the Ganges, the right to import 200,000 *maunds* of salt annually to Bengal, and to buy 18,000 *maunds* of saltpetre and 3,000 chests of opium at fixed prices. Any number of French trading houses might be established in Bengal, but only the six long-established *comptoirs* would be subject to French political jurisdiction.[188]

The official terms of the convention are less important than the instructions Dundas drafted specifying how the governor-general and Supreme Council were to enforce them. He instructed company officials to cease collecting export duties on the trade of other Europeans to prove 'the sincerity of our desire to afford to them the enjoyment of Trade in our Indian Possessions upon the most extensive and liberal footing'. 'It is our positive order,' he specified, 'that the Subjects of France shall receive the same protection to their Commerce, and the same impartial distribution of justice for the execution of their Contracts, that any British Subject possesses in prosecution of similar Interests.' No authority was to be exercised 'to prevent a fair Competition among the purchasers of every Nation'.[189] The East India Company possessed the sovereign prerogatives of a state in Bengal, providing the political and legal infrastructure necessary for a thriving commercial capitalism. Dundas instructed it to use these powers to afford a level playing field to foreign merchants. He was willing to grant the French a relatively free trade in Bengal, but not to make any concessions on British political control. If France accepted British sovereignty there in return for protection, this might prove the foundation for a 'permanent peace'.[190]

Dundas's vision of interimperial commerce in Bengal was typical of the way eighteenth-century officials understood freedom of trade: as a strategy rather than a principle; grounded in realpolitik rather than rights; in the service of national power and geopolitical harmony rather than the welfare of consumers. Above all, free trade was not the antithesis of protection, but an extension of it – a reconfiguration of the protection regime to admit rather than exclude a rival. In Dundas's words, it meant according the French 'the same protection to their

Commerce . . . that any British Subject possesses'. A comparison with Adam Smith's vision of trade in India is instructive. On India questions, Smith was a latecomer. His most substantial passages on the reform of the East India Company appeared only in the 1784 edition of the *Wealth of Nations* when reform was already imminent – driven in no small measure by Dundas's efforts.[191] Dundas knew and respected Smith, and had consulted him in the past, but their priorities were different. Smith wanted to open the trade to all British merchants, to lower the price of India goods for consumers, and to replace the company as the sovereign in Bengal with Crown government. Dundas was sympathetic to these objectives but opted to work through the company, now subordinated to the Board of Control, and to preserve its monopoly. Remitting the Bengal revenues was at the centre of his concerns. This is why allowing foreign companies to trade in Bengal was more important than permitting British merchants to do so. The former could market goods in European nations closed to the East India Company; the latter could not. (Not for the first time, free trade was to be delivered by a monopoly company – see above, pp. 95.) Though Smith still hoped the Bengal revenues might defray some of the burden of the national debt, he evaded the problem of remitting them. His commitment to natural rights is absent in Dundas's statements, and it is unlikely the minister shared his hope that Europeans might one day find themselves in a less powerful position in Asia.[192] The language of humanity and justice, which pervaded Smith's writing on India, and which dominated public criticism of the East India Company in this period, was not much resorted to by Dundas.[193]

Henry Dundas's vision of a permanent Franco-British peace in India went unrealised in the short term. It was one thing for the British government to guarantee the French freedom from harassment in Bengal, and quite another to get the servants of the East India Company to comply. Moreover, France and Britain would be at war again by 1793, when the British company quickly overran the French settlements – not to be returned until 1816. As few concrete results came from proposals for a Franco-British understanding in India, one might conclude that they are worth little attention. Indeed, there is sometimes a visionary quality to these proposals. European officials failed to grasp that it would be the actions of Indians, and of company servants on the ground, not their aspirations that would determine events.

269

Yet unsuccessful, or even unrealistic, as they might have been, the pattern of efforts to reach such an accord is revealing. It points to a logic inherent in intercompany competition that we have already discerned in relations between European states – an impulse to limit geopolitical conflict, and to create structures to contain it in the future, so that the costs of protecting trade did not swallow its benefits. These initiatives recurred across the century because neither company and neither government was satisfied with arrangements to secure its trade in India. Commerce either continued to be insecure (the French problem) or protection threatened to devour its benefits (the British).

After a brief and ruinous flirtation with Indian territorial empire as a solution to the problem of balancing protection costs and profits, the Compagnie des Indes sought to remake itself as a purely commercial enterprise – to separate commerce from conquest. It hardly had a choice after 1763. Initially its leaders hoped that the company's protection problem could be handled by some combination of Crown sovereignty, avoiding conflict with the East India Company, and collaborating commercially with its employees. Choiseul aspired to something more ambitious, and perhaps quixotic. Indian allies would protect French trade at no cost to French taxpayers after a war to break the power of the East India Company and reduce it to a merely mercantile presence. France did not need an empire on the subcontinent, at least not its own empire, Choiseul believed. His successor, d'Aiguillon, abandoned this vision believing that French trade would be secure only under a deal with the British. This was a prospect the latter were willing to take seriously only after the American War, and another bruising confrontation with Hyder Ali. In the mid-1780s the protection they offered French trade was to take the form either of a junior partnership with the East India Company, or a free trade under the auspices of British sovereignty in Bengal.

Back in the 1750s, the directors of the East India Company had initially preferred an entente with the French to empire-building, but when this accord failed to materialise and events on the ground changed the balance of opportunity and risk, they opted for territorial control in Bengal. Long after the company acquired an empire, government officials and company insiders worried that political costs would vitiate profits. And they were right to do so. The military and administrative expenses of the company almost proved its undoing, necessitating a government bailout in 1773 and renewed assistance at the end of the

American War. There was still talk in the 1780s of reforming the company to return it to its commercial roots. Shelburne, who was linked to Sulivan and was planning a reform of the company when he fell from power in 1783, complained 'that the territorial revenue has diverted the attention of everybody concerned about India from every consideration of commerce'. Fixation on territory carried the further risk of 'drawing us into war both with the country and European powers'.[194] His unofficial secretary, Benjamin Vaughan, compared the company's situation in India unfavourably to European commerce in China, where 'trade is embarrassed neither with wars, forts, nor expense establishments . . . which is solely owing to China being an independent power'. 'Happy would it be for Europe and for India,' he wrote, 'could India become self-governed, under the auspices of her ancient freedom of trade.'[195]

Such invocations of freedom of trade are symptomatic of the debate about the proper political framework for European commerce in India. Every proposed Franco-British entente – almost every design to prevent costs from overbalancing profits – included free trade in some form. Freedom of trade was always about securing better or cheaper protection. In the negotiations between the companies in the 1750s, it meant gaining commercial access to zones where the other company exercised political influence or collected revenue. For Gournay, suspending the monopoly of the French company and opening up the trade was a strategy to compete with the British and the Dutch by shifting protection costs off merchants. For Choiseul in 1769 freedom of trade meant an overthrow of East India Company political power and the establishment of a league of allied Indian states to protect French trade. Among disgruntled East India servants in the 1770s it implied a loosening of company monopolies on the inland trade, tied to the demand for Crown government in Bengal – a change of protection regime. For his part, Dundas wanted the company to protect French trade in Bengal, believing this would keep the peace and facilitate the remission of the territorial revenues. Free trade was about remaking the existing protection regime – it was never an alternative to protection.

The various Franco-British accommodations promised to secure commerce and decrease costs by replacing competing protection-providing arrangements with a single political framework to which both sides assented. This impulse to accommodate the rival and to avoid military conflict points towards a post-1815 model of Franco-British global relations when, it has been argued, a

French 'policy of collaboration with Britain [emerged], to preserve and enhance France's stake in the exploitation of the extra-European world'.[196] It is also suggestive of the political framework for global capitalism that has come to prevail over the last half-century when, instead of fighting to elaborate rival political frameworks for trade beyond their borders, most states buy into a common protection regime. Sovereigns extend to each other's citizens the necessary legal cover for their commerce. A relatively free trade prevails. Protection costs have consequently plummeted – a far more favourable equilibrium than that produced by the clashing protection producers of the past. All other things being equal, capitalists will prefer not to internalise protection costs, and not to establish empires where the expenses of sovereignty always threaten the profits of commerce. Protection has become almost invisible today, but it has not disappeared. In a world of competing states, each invested in the economic fortunes of its subjects or citizens – a capitalist world – it never can.

CONCLUSION

In his 'Letter on the Jealousy of Trade', penned against the background of the 1763 treaty of Paris, Isaac de Pinto, a Dutch-Jewish financier turned man of letters, who had played a small personal role in the peacemaking, dreamed of a world where rivalry for colonial trade would no longer provoke war between leading European states.[1] He proposed 'an intimate alliance' among the 'commercial powers' – Britain, France, Spain, Portugal, and the Dutch Republic – to freeze the current distribution of extra-European resources, 'a solemn and mutual guarantee of colonies, possessions, and commercial privileges'. This accord would also stabilise and pacify Europe. The trading nations, 'acting always in concert', might 'prevent a rupture among the rest' – Prussia, Austria, and Russia, powers he construed as more aggressive because less invested in commerce. Pinto called on the French monarchy to accept British domination of North America and India, and to concentrate instead on exploiting its advantages in fashion manufacturing and wines. These resources were 'another Peru' that France could never lose in war. The costs of reversing the verdict of the Seven Years' War would be far greater than any possible gains, he noted. Besides, Britain would be unable to monopolise the benefits of its expanded empire: France would find markets there too, free of the heavy costs of sovereignty. For their part, the British must concede supremacy in the sugar trade to the French, to the Dutch their quasi-monopoly of spices, and to Spain control of world silver production. A universal monarchy of trade, which Pitt the Elder's most radical supporters seemed bent upon, was unachievable, the very quest for it self-defeating. Pinto hinted at the role free trade might play in a reformed international order. Nominally closed commercial empires could not be so in fact, he argued, noting that France would continue to sell its wines and brandies in Canada, whatever nation was sovereign there.[2] Indeed, as we have seen, freedom of trade emerged and re-emerged as a key solution to the problems of conflict and instability created by the Franco-British rivalry because it might temper jealousy of trade, and create a balance of commercial power.

Pinto's scheme never came to pass, but suggests the kind of solutions to the bane of interstate conflict over commerce that appealed to well-informed observers of European international politics.[3] Nor was it only men of letters who conjectured in this fashion. Officials and politically connected merchants too asked whether the Franco-British duel begun in the quarter-century after the Glorious Revolution, and renewed in the 1740s, could be channelled into less dangerous and costly forms of competition. Many recognised that wars for trade and colonies rarely brought gains that outweighed their costs, even for the victor. In this context, enterprising individuals and networks on both sides contemplated the prospect, raised by Pinto, of agreements between powers to apportion key resources or to promote freedom of trade; of a Franco-British accord to end colonial competition; even of a league of commercial states to govern trade in the Americas and stabilise the turbulent politics of Eastern Europe.

Pinto and the officials, merchants, and thinkers who shared a similar perspective wrestled with a problem intrinsic to a capitalist geopolitics. Capitalism is a system in which sovereignty is induced to foster private capital accumulation, and the increase of private capital indirectly serves the ends of sovereignty. It is predicated on an implicit alliance between two kinds of power – the one network-based, cosmopolitan, and oriented to profit, the other hierarchical, territorial, and specialising in security. This union has always been fraught. Yet, seen in broad perspective, these ill-assorted allies augmented each other's power and reach.

The alliance of states with capital profoundly shaped the development of both. In eighteenth-century Britain and France, the needs of sovereignty dictated that a particular sector – foreign trade – enjoy a status that far outweighed its importance as a source of economic growth. Trade, plus the manufacturing and plantation economy that sustained it, delivered benefits to states that could come from no other source. It created pools of liquid capital available to borrow, and helped expand and sustain the money supply, stimulating the economy and facilitating tax collection. Trade generated foreign balances that bankers could draw upon to pay subsidies to a state's allies. It created taxable flows of goods and enlivened domestic consumption by creating new habits and new consumer desires. The associated navigation trained sailors who could be recruited or pressed into wartime navies.

The extroverted form taken by capitalism in Northwest Europe produced endemic geopolitical conflict. European merchants stretched their networks over much of the globe, they built commercial empires, launched chartered companies, and lobbied for commercial treaties to siphon off the profits of other nations' colonies. They drew sovereign power in their wake to supply the necessary protective framework to preserve and foster capital accumulation overseas. The system bred conflict over commerce. Given the strategic importance of foreign trade, states strove to secure it in places distant from the sovereignty of the home country, and confronted rival states engaged competitively in the same undertaking. Colonies, companies, and commercial treaties, along with the naval power states projected, threatened the commerce of neighbours, or narrowed its scope, generating unremitting low-level conflict, punctuated by violent flare-ups.

The costs of strife created incentives to reshape this system. Wars engendered negative feedbacks. Fought to protect commerce, they could finish by undermining it: through disruptions to shipping and markets, and above all massive and ever growing public debts, which locked heavy taxation into place, threatened to increase interest rates, and nurtured extractive classes at the expense of trade and enterprise. If efforts to protect distant trade could imperil its benefits, similar feedbacks confounded regulatory strategies to secure and territorialise the intrinsically borderless benefits of commerce. When governments closed off or monopolised economic spaces to reserve them for their own merchants, manufacturers, or planters, such closure brought collateral damage – loss of export markets, trade wars, increased smuggling, diminished tax revenue, and an erosion of commercial dynamism. These problems were structural, inherent in a capitalist order where the security and power of states depended on commerce, and in which officials felt compelled to foster trade and to seek to engross its advantages.

As they worked to sustain political frameworks to protect commerce while limiting the costs of conflict, officials, merchants, and men of letters regularly resorted to a 'commerce-versus-conquest' trope in their language. They recognised that a shift had occurred in the nature and foundations of power. An age of commerce had displaced, or was displacing, an age of conquest – a more martial era when soldierly virtues had been more central to acquiring and preserving power. The rise of the Dutch Republic in the seventeenth century, and its defeat of Spain, revealed that commerce had become the principal ground of power. This shift had implications for strategy. War could undermine trade, and thus – even when victorious – erode the basis for future wealth creation and future power. Peace, many affirmed, best fostered the interests of trading states. Commerce might even replace war, or become a substitute for it, a new battleground on which the struggle for ascendancy and security could be fought and won without the inevitable liabilities of military confrontation. Commercial supremacy could constitute a new form of imperium.

Yet there could be no simple choice between commerce and coercion, trade and war. Organised violence – or the threat of it – had been and remained indispensable to protect trade in the spaces between polities, from the predation of foreign sovereigns, in the realm of Asian trade, and on the terrain of empire. It had built European colonies in the Americas and the East Indies and remained necessary to keep rival powers, indigenous peoples, and enslaved labourers in check. War, or the need for an alliance, were often the leaven for advantageous commercial treaties. That fortifications, troops, and armed ships were necessary for trade in India no company director would deny, for all that they urged 'peaceful measures' on their employees. Nor could any trading state long hope to preserve its commerce without a navy to convoy its ships and protect its colonies in wartime. Violence, or its threat, was indispensable. Yet it regularly exceeded the limits of utility and undermined the commerce it was supposed to secure.

The pervasiveness of this commerce-versus-conquest theme in eighteenth-century thinking complicates the idea, prevalent in much classic scholarship on mercantilism, that early modern political-economic ideas and policies led inevitably to conflict and war. There was just one scenario under which war for trade was clearly justified – when it was necessary to stop an over-mighty commercial state from engrossing enough wealth to overturn the balance of power. Despite the fact that their nation was in the ascendant, Britons never stopped worrying that Colbert's project to turn France into a commercial superpower would one day be realised. French officials started to worry about a British universal monarchy of trade as early as 1713, and this anxiety became consuming after 1763. The fear of a rising commercial hegemon spurred conflict in the War of the Spanish Succession, the Anglo-Spanish naval war of 1739, the Seven Years' War, and the American War. There is an irony here, of course, because British pre-eminence, once achieved, would function to keep the peace in the following century.

The high costs of the status quo drove officials, elite merchants, and allied men of letters periodically to try to secure commerce at lower expense and with less conflict. The strategies they employed addressed the structural source of high protection costs – clashing protection regimes – by seeking to replace vying political frameworks for trade with more inclusive arrangements arrived at by agreements with rivals and accommodating their interests. The same means states used to secure exclusive benefits could be re-engineered to be more reciprocal and inclusive. Commercial treaties could be negotiated to extort gains from a rival or to open a relatively balanced and reciprocal trade. The Franco-British commercial treaty of Utrecht (1713), if hardly a model of reciprocity, was designed to end the commercial cold war between Britain and France, not to win it. Companies could build alliances with Asian rulers to win privileges for their own trade and cut out a rival. They could conquer empires of their own and exclude competitors, as Dupleix threatened to do in the 1740s. Or they could make agreements to resist the drift to territorial sovereignty, face the pressures of Indian politics as allies of other companies, and divide up commercial zones of influence to create relative parity, as company leaders proposed to do in the 1750s. Empires could debar rivals from valuable markets, or they could be remade to admit and even protect the trade of others. These were the terms in which Dundas and Pitt approached French commerce in Bengal in the mid-1780s in the interests of reducing Franco-British frictions and stabilising the finances of the East India Company.

To put this in more general terms, there were logics intrinsic to eighteenth-century capitalism that restrained war. Far from being a free or low-cost option to acquire market share, or to engross commercially valuable resources, as implied in some scholarship, violence was appallingly expensive. It disrupted trade, threatened the solvency of chartered companies, and drove up public debt, which menaced future economic vitality. 'War capitalism', while it captures something important about the era, is too sweeping a description of the early modern European political-economic order.[4] As indissociably linked as capitalism and organised violence were, commerce and conquest rarely made happy bedfellows.

The search for means to protect distant trade at a reasonable cost could lead to creative efforts to refashion empires, or to find alternatives to the extension of a nation's own sovereignty to secure trade overseas. Consider the Franco-British rivalry to dominate the strategic Spanish trade to America, which exploited lucrative markets and brought much of the world's silver into circulation. The goal of British and French officials was never to establish territorial control over Spain's colonies. Spain's empire seemed to offer an object lesson in how overseas empire could drain and debilitate a great power. No other European state could bear the costs of conquering Spanish America, or of governing it had they been able to do so. Instead, France, Britain, and the Dutch Republic sought to exploit the trade without taking on the costs of sovereignty. Eventually they agreed to share it, under continued Spanish political control, an arrangement that emerged informally in the seventeenth century, and was institutionalised under the treaty of Utrecht. A closed commercial empire from one perspective, the Spanish monarchy in America was also an international regime that served to contain conflict between the dominant commercial states. The establishment of an independent United States of America should be viewed in a similar light – a point to which I will return.

The trajectory of commercial empire followed a different path in India. There a system of company governance of trade under the aegis of Indian sovereigns gave way to the establishment of an East India Company territorial empire in Bengal. Yet it is worth noting how reluctant many of the leaders of the company and their allies in government were to go down this path. They worried constantly – and justifiably – that tax revenues in India could not offset the huge administrative and security costs of territorial empire. In the 1750s, the British and French companies hoped for a Franco-British concert that would spare each side the burdens of sovereignty. Company leaders tried to reach an accord that would have ended the military struggles between them, and neutralised their shipping and settlements in the event of future Franco-British conflicts. In addition, the French wanted a political partnership with the East India Company to secure their commerce in India from the pressures of regional politics. The companies failed to reach a final deal and, in the course of the Seven Years' War, British company servants in Bengal seized the initiative and overthrew the nawab. This revolution triggered a struggle between Robert Clive, who pursued an extractive empire in India, and Laurence Sulivan, who believed that territorial control would sooner or later bankrupt the company, and proposed instead 'to make Peace upon terms of a general restoration of territory to the Indian Princes'.[5]

Clive and his allies won this showdown, but the concern persisted that the profits of empire could not offset its administrative and security costs. Indeed, by the late 1760s, the expenses of governing and defending an empire in India had outrun profits. In 1773 the company accepted a bailout from the North administration, which came with greater political oversight and the promise that this would check further territorial expansion. A drumbeat of criticism continued through the 1770s and 1780s that the acquisition of empire had not paid – in the words of Philip Francis, that 'they prospered while they were merchants, and they have never prospered since'.[6] A series of administrations sought to limit the further expansion of the company and to lower its political costs in India. It was in this context that accommodations with the French to permanently reduce the risk of renewed Franco-British conflict in Asia period-ically appealed. Allowing some scope for peaceful French trade promised lower protection costs than a model predicated on all-out political competition.

The drive to protect global trade at less expense prompted new ways of imag-ining empire in France too, and in some cases proposals to transcend empire altogether in favour of alternative means to secure foreign trade. After the Seven Years' War, during which Canada had proved unable to check attacks on the commercially valuable French sugar islands, the duc de Choiseul came to favour a relatively de-territorialised empire of commercially valuable enclaves protected by strategic strong points such as the Mascarene Islands or French Guiana – an empire that would generate more profit than it cost to defend. In the 1770s, other French officials proposed a devolution of sovereignty to reduce protection costs. Ministers such as Turgot and senior functionaries such as Louis-Paul Abeille – both former protégés of Jacques Vincent de Gournay – proposed to replace formal French empire in the Caribbean with a loose confederation of former colonies tied to the mother country by links of trade and culture.

Perforce, the French had to reimagine ways to protect their trade in India after 1763, where they now faced an aggrandised East India Company. They seesawed inconsistently among different options. Jacques Necker's Compagnie des Indes sought to remake itself as a purely commercial organisation, to avoid conflict with its powerful British rival, and to turn a profit by co-operating informally with the servants of the British company. For his part, Choiseul looked to a league of Indian allies to protect French trade. He did not envision a French empire because the efforts of Dupleix to build one had been ruinously expensive, and any such effort would expose France to enormous future expenses by entangling it in power struggles between Indian states. Choiseul's hope that Indian sovereigns would foster French trade was akin to Versailles's long-standing aspiration that Spain would protect French commerce in the Americas while French merchants engrossed the profits. Choiseul's design was abandoned by his successor, d'Aiguillon, who returned to the idea that only an entente with the British could secure French trade in India at an acceptable price. This scheme recurred in an altered form in the 1780s when the Nouvelle Compagnie des Indes negotiated a commercial compact with the East India Company to make it a junior partner of the British Leviathan.

A critical scholarly tradition represents the business model of chartered companies as depending on coercion and expropriation.[7] This perspective certainly captures important truths to the extent that these were never just business enterprises but stand-ins for states, which carried with them legal, military, diplomatic, and regulatory powers to govern and protect European trade overseas. In this capacity, deploying or threatening violence was an intrinsic aspect of their functioning. Companies could turn into extractive empires, as the Dutch had in Java and the East India Company did in Bengal. But carrying the costs of their own protection was also a huge burden, and it made companies wary of using force to achieve commercial ends. Because military costs could threaten their solvency, for much of their histories British and French company leaders preferred commerce to conquest (though their employees on the ground sometimes had different ideas). Companies had to navigate an equilibrium between coercion and peaceful trade – a balancing act few were able to sustain. Hardly any survived the century, and those that did received bailouts from their home states.

Numerous projectors who wished to remake conventional mercantilist empires looked to freedom of trade to do so. At the beginning of the century, William Paterson proposed to draw most of the trade of America into Caribbean free ports, rendering the closed commercial empires of the European powers obsolete, and simultaneously creating a global free-trade system guaranteed by British naval power. Not only would this check the danger of France engrossing the trade of Spanish America, he argued, it would found a system of perpetual peace by removing conflict over American commerce as a source of strife between states. Echoes of this scheme can be seen in the Caribbean free ports established in 1766 by the Rockingham administration. One of the architects of the free ports, the Boston-born merchant MP John Huske, hoped that they might one day channel the whole of Spain's American trade into British hands. He represented the free ports as an alternative to the conquests and annexations associated with William Pitt's ascendancy during the Seven Years' War, which had inflated the national debt to alarming levels. Britain might acquire the trade of the Spanish and French colonies without courting military conflict. Later, in the midst of the American War, the Whig political economist James Anderson argued that freedom of trade in the Americas might 'fix the general tranquillity of Europe on a firmer basis'.[8] He looked to a league of maritime states, to which the Bourbon monarchies might be admitted, to permit free trade among the colonies of all the members, excluding only those nations that refused to join. The league should agree to neutralise the Americas in time of war, eliminating colonial conflict there as a source of discord.

Beyond remaking empires, officials bent on containing conflict latched onto freedom of trade to recast political frameworks for commerce in Europe. Freer trade meant relaxing prohibitions or other barriers that closed markets to foreign goods, shipping, or merchants. Because these exclusions and monopolies were often intended – and always felt – to be attacks on a foreign nation motivated by jealousy of its trade, removing them would tend to improve relations. Freer trade, officials, merchants, and writers believed, gave states and nations a common interest in each other's prosperity which would help to keep the peace between them. By benefiting exporters, it created lobbies with an interest in future good relations, and generated tax revenues tied to an open trade, creating mutual benefit if the gains could be balanced. It tended to tie national prosperity to continued peaceful relations.

Such thinking motivated officials to negotiate, or revive, a commercial treaty between France and Britain on several occasions between the 1710s and the 1780s. In 1713, the Tory architect of the commerce treaty, Lord

Bolingbroke, hoped that, once the British people had 'felt the sweet of carrying on a trade to France, under reasonable regulations', the Francophobia long nurtured by Whigs would dissolve, for 'nothing unites like interest'.[9] Every effort to renew the treaty or make a new one occurred during a warming of Franco-British relations – in the early 1750s, the early 1770s, and after the American War. The French foreign minister, the duc d'Aiguillon, hoped in 1772 to sign a new commercial treaty with the North administration, believing that 'if the English found advantage in [the trade] they did with us', this would 'insensibly weaken the animosity they bear toward us, and form a tie that would make the continuation of peace as valuable to them as it is to us'.[10] In the negotiations for the 1786 commercial treaty, the French diplomat Rayneval strongly emphasised the effect 'a more amicable intercourse and connexion must have, in preserving them from such frequent wars'.[11]

Aside from transforming animosity into ties of common interest, freedom of trade was a mechanism to create a balance of wealth – to check the threat that any one state would engross enough commerce to elevate itself above its rivals. Just as exclusions tended to monopolise markets or resources for a single nation, so free trade functioned to distribute the gains of trade more widely. But this would only be so when a trading system was designed to permit rivals to access key markets or resources. When free trade occurred within a single economic bloc benefiting one power to the exclusion of others, it promised not balance but disequilibrium, forcing the excluded to fight or relinquish the prospect of maintaining future parity. We have examined two key instances. In 1700, when Louis XIV's grandson acceded to the Spanish throne, British and Dutch officials believed France would try to establish a free trade in Spain's American empire – a common market of the Catholic world – excluding the Protestant commercial powers. They fought the War of the Spanish Succession in part to prevent this from happening. Later, the tables would be turned. After 1713, and especially after 1763, it seemed to French policymakers that Britain was on the path to a universal monarchy of trade. Its control over the Thirteen Colonies proved especially valuable, and promised to be still more so in the future as the population of these settlements continued its rapid expansion. It was principally to break Britain's exclusive commercial access to America that Louis XVI backed the American revolutionaries and entered the American War in 1778. The drive for free trade was not necessarily pacific, then, though officials hoped that it would subsequently make possible a more stable world by assuring a balance of power.

Diplomats sought to impose a more universal, balanced freedom of trade on these strategically critical regions of the Americas to lay a foundation for an equilibrium of power and future peace. The French treaty with the American rebels was built around the principle that the United States should not extend to Britain any trading privileges that would not automatically apply to France. Moreover, the treaty of amity and commerce (1778) was intended to be the model for future treaties to be signed between the United States and other European nations. In this fashion, the British commercial empire in America would be replaced with a system of free trade that would deny the British the exclusive commercial advantages they had so long enjoyed. The ultimate tendency would be to distribute the gains of trade with this exceptional economic space to all commercial nations, creating a balance of commercial advantage.

Jacques Turgot doubted this strategy, not believing that America had actually been the key to Britain's rise. His views converged with influential British politicians like Lord Sheffield, who argued that American empire had never paid – that it cost more to defend than it had ever delivered in profits, and that it diverted investment and population away from more productive uses at home. Whatever the merits of these views, French hopes that opening America to a general freedom of trade would cut Britain down to size quickly proved illusory. If anything, Britain was strengthened by the loss of America, retaining and expanding its markets there without the expense of administration or defence.

The latter years of the War of the Spanish Succession had seen a similar effort to replace the threat of French commercial domination in Spanish America with a system of freer trade that would give all commercial nations a share of these strategic markets. Nicolas Mesnager, the former merchant and leading French commercial diplomat, designed a system that would permit all European goods access to Spanish America, and allow export of silver from Spain on the payment of a small duty. It was to be organised from Cádiz, designated a free port for this purpose and placed under a kind of international jurisdiction. Spanish officials countered with an alternative scheme – an international chartered company to be divided between Spanish, French, Dutch, and British investors, allowing each of the leading commercial nations an equal share of the profits. British officials, who had originally hoped to engineer an Anglo-Spanish monopoly of the trade, proposed instead that French and British companies exploit the trade from bases in the Pacific. None of these schemes proved acceptable to all the leading powers, and the treaty of Utrecht, while conceding to Britain's South Sea Company a monopoly of the slave trade to Spanish America, institutionalised the American trade on the same basis as before the war, when it was informally a French, Dutch, and British condominium. The treaty formally forbade Spain from conceding any further trading privileges that might threaten the balance of commercial power.

To grasp what free trade meant to officials and merchants in the eighteenth century requires a different understanding of the idea than we may be accustomed to. Freedom of trade was rarely embraced as a general principle or precept. Officials, merchants, and most writers saw it as a strategy, a policy to be adopted in certain contexts but not in others. Thus, for example, the freer trading arrangements envisioned in the Eden–Rayneval commercial treaty were to apply to trade between Britain and France in Europe, but not in their empires. In Bengal, a separate convention negotiated a year later proposed to extend liberties to French trade under the auspices of the East India Company. In the Caribbean, a system of free ports had existed since the 1760s to channel a limited commerce in selected commodities. As this example suggests, such trade was often tied to particular nodes and to defined goods rather than applying comprehensively to the trade between nations, though free ports could be envisioned in more universal terms. (The idea of a general free port was proposed in the 1720s and 1730s, and again in the 1780s, as the framework for Britain's trade with Europe.) If the free port was one key institution for governing a freer trade, the other was the commercial treaty. As these examples suggest, freer trade never entailed a withdrawal of the state from the regulation of trade, but was a liberty created by states, often through agreements with other polities.

Free trade and protection were not antitheses. Officials saw freer trade as a way to moderate the ill effects of forms of economic closure still regarded as necessary, indeed indispensable. Protection often led to trade wars and the loss of export markets when aggrieved trade partners retaliated. Freer trade promised to end such overt conflict, and recover lost markets, but it had to be calibrated so that its benefits outweighed the disadvantages of subjecting domestic producers to harmful competition. Protection diminished tax revenues by reducing flows of trade, or driving them into illicit channels. Freer trade promised to check smuggling and increase tax revenue, while continuing to offer some protection under a more modest tariff. Indeed, as Dupont pointed out in 1786, low duties on legally traded English wares offered better protection than outright prohibitions, which could not actually stem the flow of smuggled goods. A measure of competition could also force a necessary adaptation on domestic producers to prevent them from being eliminated, over the long run, by more efficient foreign manufacturers. Free trade and protection were allied strategies, not irreconcilable opposites.

Free trade was an instrument of commercial realpolitik rather than a means to realise a natural harmony between nations. Not that officials failed to see the potential virtues of market liberty, or could not grasp that nations had absolute advantages in certain areas of production (some, like Charles Davenant, came close to articulating ideas of comparative advantage). Neither were they blind to the benefits of freer trade for consumers; this was an advantage that systematic political-economic theories emphasised from the 1760s. Officials drew on all of these ideas, but never envisioned that an autoregulatory economic sphere would do everything for the best. States remained indispensable to ensure that the gains of liberty were not overbalanced by the losses. Another way to put this is that free trade was not necessarily a liberal idea in the eighteenth century – not, at least, if we understand economic liberals to believe in the virtues of self-regulating markets, natural rights, consumer sovereignty, or natural commercial harmony between peoples. This eighteenth-century illiberalism of free trade is not aberrant. Free trade appealed to policymakers, then and ever since, to the degree that it has seemed the best strategy in the more or less peaceful war of all against all for wealth and security.

Over the span of centuries, something like these eighteenth-century solutions to the problems of governing global commerce have turned out to be the arrangements most favourable to the trade and investment of capitalist nations. In effect, the league of trading powers envisioned by Pinto has become a reality. In the nineteenth century, Britain, France, and other European commercial states implicitly renounced wars among themselves over the spoils of global trade and empire. They accepted the status quo, and carved up or shared out remaining opportunities into zones of influence, as in Africa, East Asia, and the Pacific, or permitted rivals to trade in their empires, as became the British practice. They subjected their colonies to a kind of capitalist pacification that was in no sense peaceful, of course, for its numerous victims, but that rendered much of the globe safe for European investment and trade.[12] For a time, protection became cheap and ubiquitous, and receded as a problem. Already by the high Victorian era the conceptual separation of commerce and violence so central to our own ideological system – and so difficult to articulate in the eighteenth century – was mature enough to elicit Marx's scathing critique.[13]

The problem of protecting distant trade re-emerged abruptly and violently during the First World War, and did not abate again until after 1945, when a new capitalist peace began to take shape, back-stopped by US military power. In the latter half of the century, great trading states profited from the end of formal empire, even if decolonisation had to be forced on them by insurgent colonial subjects. They shed most of the burdens of ruling colonies, distributed the costs of sovereignty to newly independent states, and eventually recovered nearly universal commercial access not only to their former colonies but to those of their rivals. Formal empire is just one potential modality of a capitalist order, and neither a necessary nor an ideal political framework to govern commerce beyond the realm of national sovereignty. With the development of the General Agreement on Tariffs and Trade from 1947 and the eventual birth of the World Trade Organization (WTO) in 1995, a more or less free trade secured by independent sovereign states, associated with one another for this purpose and observing common conventions, has proven another boon to the commercial great powers.

The global order that developed over the past half-century has been so successful from a capitalist perspective that the very problem of protecting distant trade has almost disappeared from view. Protection is invisible to the degree that it is effective and uncontested. It is recognised as an issue only occasionally, and patchily, in the midst of international crises in oil-rich parts of the world, in zones governed by failed states, or when trade disputes flare up between commercial nations. The old model of corporate internalisation of protection costs has re-emerged in weak states where multinational corporations have wrung concession agreements from local authorities allowing them to establish private police and military protection.[14] But corporations benefit far more from the model that prevails over most of the planet, where states supply protection to capital at or below cost.

To be sure, the problem of reciprocity persists in the modern global order – the suspicion that the gains of free trade and the burdens of protection are unfairly distributed. Many of the less affluent states fear, as they did in the eighteenth century, that unlimited free trade will lock them into a status of permanent underdevelopment. Others have taken advantage of free trade and the capitalist peace to hurtle toward prosperity, security, and power – periodically arousing anxiety among their longer-established rivals. Some of the nations that did most to build this global order, and that have benefited most from it, sporadically seek to redraw the rules in their favour – haunted by apprehensions of surging rivals, or the costs of openness. Certain problems are recurrent in a world of competing capitalist states.

The problem of channelling the Franco-British relationship in a more peaceful commercial direction, and thereby stabilising the international order, helped drive innovation in political-economic thought. I read political economy in this period less as a science in formation than as an evolving set of heuristics that mediated the relationship between states and commerce in a world where trade had come to seem a principal basis of power. It was the medium in which merchants could make claims on the state for protection, liberty, or favour – the element in which officials, merchants, and pamphleteers debated how to govern commerce for the public advantage. Historians sometimes see the first half of the eighteenth century as an interlude between two moments of innovation in the history of political economy. The first occurred in the final decades of the seventeenth century. The second unfolded after 1748.[15] In fact, the intervening period constituted a particularly creative phase. Much of that creativity issued from attempts to reimagine or remake the political framework for global trade in ways that would favour stability and peace. Some of this reflection found its way into print in works by Huet, Davenant, Law, Defoe, Melon, and Decker. Much of it is to be found in memoranda or correspondence never circulating widely beyond the ministries or diplomatic networks in which it was written. Individuals like Nicolas Mesnager, William Paterson, and Étienne de Silhouette who published little or nothing, but who had the ear of ministers, surely deserve an important place in the history of political economy. Through their actions and their counsel, they laboured to recast the global framework for trade.

While officials continued to respond innovatively to new political-economic challenges in the second half of the century, in a parallel development, men of letters elaborated new systems of political economy in the public sphere. The problem of pacifying a global political order rent by conflict over trade also helped impel this new political economy. In Britain, David Hume strove to shift the British relationship with France onto a more constructive footing, to end the commercial cold war between the two nations, and check an anti-French animus that drew British leaders into imprudent wars pursued far beyond the point where the gains could outweigh the costs. The public debts Britain had run up in the War of the Austrian Succession alarmed Hume. He deplored such feedbacks from conflict, together with the irrational and wasteful pursuit of empire under Pitt in the ensuing Seven Years' War. Across the Channel, Physiocracy, which evolved and was popularised during the war years, represented a bold effort to establish the peace of Europe on a new foundation by reconstituting France as a great agricultural kingdom, and withdrawing from the struggle with Britain to dominate global commerce and manufacturing. A peace project, Physiocracy also promised to restore French prosperity and power, and to make the French monarchy once again the arbiter of European politics.

The most familiar story historians tell about political economy in the eighteenth century turns on the discovery of the economic as a self-ordering realm. Eighteenth-century thinkers grasped the virtues of a market society, or recognised the power of self-regulating systems, or uncovered the economic limits of modern politics. To be sure, this was a frame of reference that was to have a brilliant future. But as an account of political economy in the eighteenth century it is too narrow. The political regulation of commerce remained a central preoccupation. Trade in the spaces between polities required a political framework to protect it, and enormous effort went into thinking about how such frameworks might be configured to allow nations to compete more effectively, and to master the conflicts generated by a world of rival protection-providers. Free trade should also be understood in these terms – less as a device for market self-regulation than a political mechanism to establish a balance of power.

We misconstrue the world of eighteenth-century political economy in other ways too. The idea of *doux commerce* as usually understood misses the mainstream of political-economic thought. Scholars tyically use *doux commerce* to designate idealistic representations of trade as the source of civility, refinement, and sociable impulses that were supposed to issue in more peaceful relations between peoples. The principal eighteenth-century tradition of thinking about commerce and peace – the one I focus on in this book – was quite different. The main line of analysis represented trade as a surrogate for war, a realm where the inevitable struggle for power between states would be continued. Better that states fight on the terrain of commerce than that they suffer the hazards and expense of military confrontation. This line of thinking constituted a refinement of Colbert's project, not a break with it. Nor did this distinction between idealist and realist visions of *doux commerce* map in any clear way onto a split between men of letters and officials. The realist vision was dominant among both groups, which, in any case, overlapped and interpenetrated.

To be sure, many eighteenth-century *philosophes* saw themselves as speaking truth to power, and this vision has shaped our view of the century. But as an account of reality it is inadequate. Writers adopted a stance of independence, claiming to write for the public, eschewing 'the traditional, humanist model of the philosopher as the private counsellor of kings and ministers, whose advice was given in secret'.[16] But they often were, or became, such counsellors. They grasped the challenges officials faced and this shaped their sense of the problems worth wrestling with. Is it possible to understand the point of Physiocracy outside the political, fiscal, and international difficulties faced by the French monarchy? Sometimes men of letters wrote to advance official initiatives – consider Morellet's works, for example – or to curry favour with ministers. Think Defoe. Sometimes they were officials themselves, or became officials having first established themselves as men of letters. Take David Hume, for example, who served on military and diplomatic missions and was for a time an undersecretary in the Chatham administration; or Adam Smith, who finished his days as a customs commissioner; or Jacques Turgot, a long-time provincial intendant and later minister of the navy and contrôleur général.

Philosophes in office had to adapt their language and their action to the official world – as when the Physiocrat Dupont got behind his superiors' agenda to use the 1786 commercial treaty with Britain to boost the competitiveness of

French manufacturing. The ideas of men of letters were read, respected, and often appropriated by officials. What was usually left behind in these borrowings was the philosophical grounding of the ideas in question – Physiocracy's insistence on the sole productivity of agriculture, for instance, or the rich ethical underpinnings of Scottish political economy.

Philosophes tended to adopt a cosmopolitan stance in their public pronouncements, and this is not to be dismissed as a smokescreen. Yet this too could serve official initiatives. Raynal and Diderot's *Histoire des deux Indes* promoted the idea that France should lead an alliance of Indian states to eject the East India Company from Bengal, an objective that aligned with the geopolitical agenda of Choiseul (though this polyphonic text advanced other competing lines of thinking too). After all, cosmopolitan causes have little chance of being realised unless taken up by great powers, and great powers stand to benefit by wrapping their projects in the high-sounding and generous cause of humanity.

And what of the Franco-British rivalry with which we began, and which has served as the structuring spine of the book? If it is compelling to tell the story of Franco-British relations in the century after 1688 as the tale of a Second Hundred Years' War, it can also be narrated as a sequence of moments when officials, merchants, and men of letters converged around schemes to pacify the relationship, or even to transform it into a partnership. Four such moments emerged over the eighteenth century, the first and last of most significance. In the latter years of the War of the Spanish Succession, as already noted, French and British diplomats discussed ways to open, partition, or share the Spanish-American trade, while the same officials negotiated a commercial treaty to reopen commerce between the two nations in Europe with a view to reducing animosity. A generation later, in the early 1750s, officials talked of reopening cross-Channel trade, and worked to avert future war by resolving imperial boundary disputes in America and ending the conflict that had brewed since the 1740s between the India companies. The third moment came in the early 1770s, when the duc d'Aiguillon broached with Lord North a plan for permanent peace between the two nations in India, and a commercial treaty to normalise Franco-British trade in Europe. Though stillborn, this was a bold effort to transform the relationship by checking conflict over commerce, and was intended to facilitate an entente in which the two powers would pivot to tame the turbulent politics of Eastern Europe. In the event, the American War was necessary to shake the status quo and make possible a new understanding – the fourth moment. After France and the revolutionaries opened America to the trade of Europe, a new French India Company sought to collaborate with its British rival, and the British promised to protect French trade in Bengal. Vergennes negotiated a trade treaty with Britain to permanently re-establish freer trade, mitigate commercial jealousies, and give each nation an interest in the prosperity of its rival. He hoped that an alliance might eventually be possible – a Franco-British duopoly to restrain Russia, Prussia, and Austria.

Across the century, Paris proved a remarkably creative site for reimagining global politics. In the name of the French monarchy or in its interest, officials, merchants, and political economists again and again devised strategies to transform the global order. A recurrent vision was that, after some fundamental remaking of its internal political economy, France would draw its European neighbours towards a more peaceful future in which jealousy of trade had been checked, and where the French monarchy had recovered its natural place as the arbiter of European politics. John Law proposed to withdraw from the bitter competition for Spanish-American markets and silver and build new sources of prosperity in a domestic economy enlivened by paper currency. His disciple Jean-François Melon proposed something similar. In a different mould, the Physiocrats dreamed that, once reoriented to the land, France would draw its neighbours into a peaceful free-trading Europe. French officials and merchants were also fertile in schemes to transform the political framework for trade in places distant from Europe – in India, Spanish America, and North America. Such designs issued rather more often from France than from Britain as the French monarchy struggled to preserve its status and security in an international system where Britain was ascendant. Conversely, the most significant bursts of creative and heterodox British thinking came at the beginning of the century and after Britain's defeat in the American War.

Most of the schemes explored in this book failed. Some never got off the ground. Why, then, take them seriously? First, because this clarifies certain structural underpinnings of the international order that remain otherwise submerged. Any one of these abortive initiatives can seem simply anomalous, but viewed in aggregate they point to pressures operating in a quasi-permanent fashion on decision-making. These pressures were not usually strong enough to be deter-mining, but they impinged continuously on the policymakers of the past and formed part of the reality in which they made choices. Second, to miss the other possible futures people envisioned for their world is to fail to fully grasp their reality. Focusing only on the designs that came to pass risks a Whiggish history in which what happened seems destined to have done so. Finally, the losers of yesterday may become the winners of today or tomorrow: if the champions of a more pacific relationship often failed to channel French and British rivalry into peaceful competition in the eighteenth century, they were more successful after 1815. In the nineteenth century, Franco-British relations were still characterised by remorseless rivalry, but never again by armed conflict.

The formula for the post-Waterloo peace embodied all the elements that eighteenth-century officials and merchants had envisioned, and periodically sought to put into practice. France and Britain moved towards an increasingly free trade, crowned by the Cobden–Chevalier treaty of 1860, which became a basis for the extension of free trade throughout Europe for a time.[17] Both powers recoiled from debt financing on a massive scale, and the British gradu-ally retired the vast public debts run up in the wars of the long eighteenth century.[18] The two nations tacitly agreed to fight no more wars against one another for trade or colonial gains. If struggles over commerce and colonies in distant parts of the world were ubiquitous in the eighteenth century, European states fought not a single such war amongst themselves in the century after 1815, though violence, of course, remained ubiquitous in their relations with non-European peoples.[19] Britain, and to a lesser degree France moved towards open commercial empires, while the extension of the sovereign states system facilitated commercial access for both in former European colonies.[20] France and Britain engaged, to a degree, in an imperialism by concert in dealing with non-European powers, on occasion in Egypt but especially in China.[21] And they coalesced periodically to check the powers of Central and Eastern Europe.

The pacific impulses that gestated in eighteenth-century Franco-British rela-tions have subsequently come to fruition in the relatively pacified, yet still grimly competitive, realm of modern world politics. The path from the eigh-teenth century to the twenty-first in this respect is anything but linear. Yet the story traced here helps explain why the contemporary global order looks the way it does – why geoeconomics has mostly edged out geopolitics; why relatively free trade has come to prevail; why global economic exchange is governed under treaties between sovereign states, preferential trading blocs, and international institutions, rather than under closed commercial empires. To be sure, this is no utopia. Those who worked in the eighteenth century to lay its foundations never imagined it would be. They embraced a politico-commercial realpolitik, not an idealised vision that commerce would create peace. Indeed, to the degree theirs was a peace project, it was founded on a vision of trade as a stand-in for war. In the gap between the surrogate and the real thing – between commerce and conquest – lay the promise of taming the struggle for power, not of extinguishing it.

The relatively pacific equilibrium of today seems unlikely to last. Geoeconomics threatens once again to give way to geopolitics. This happened once before in the late nineteenth century, when British commercial and industrial predominance yielded to a multipolar world of fast-growing trading states. Relative peace between great powers gave way to scrambles for colonies and zones of commercial influence, to arms races and eventually to war. Only the overwhelming economic pre-eminence of the United States after 1945 checked new cycles of instability. Conflict for global markets and resources had been endemic in the eighteenth century, too, when no single power enjoyed a hegemonic position. As in this earlier period, there will be strong incentives in the coming decades to make agreements to limit conflict. But the story explored here suggests how difficult such deals can be to conclude or to keep once the balance of power turns again on the economic fortunes of nations. Admittedly, our situation is different in important ways. Weapons of mass destruction increase the costs and risks of war by orders of magnitude. We also already have an institutional architecture in place to govern global trade and resolve conflicts by negotiation. Most states have signed onto a commercial non-aggression pact in the form of WTO rules. These rules may be unfair, distributing both the burdens of protection and the gains of trade unevenly. But a world where the great trading powers resolve to go it alone is likely to be a good deal harder to live with. We are at a fork in the road. We should face our choices with eyes wide open, fixed firmly on the past.

ENDNOTES

COLLECTIONS AND SERIES

Add MS	Additional Manuscripts [BL]
Ang	Angleterre (England) [AAE]
B⁴	Campagnes (campaigns) [AN – Mar]
C	Chancery [TNA]
C²	Compagnie des Indes [AN]
Ch(H) Papers	Cholmondeley Collection (Houghton) [CUL]
Col	Colonies [AN]
CO	Colonial Office [TNA]
CP	Correspondance politique [AAE]
Eg	Egerton Manuscripts [BL]
Eur	European Manuscripts [BL IOR]
F¹²	Commerce et industrie [AN]
fr	Manuscrits français [BNF]
G⁷	Contrôle général des finances [AN]
H	Administrations locales et comptabilités diverses [AN]
Hardwicke	Hardwicke Papers [NYPL]
IOR	India Office Records [BL]
Mar	Marine [AN]
MD	Mémoires et documents [AAE]
MP	Maurepas Papers [Cornell]
naf	Nouvelles acquisitions françaises [BNF]
Ne(C)	Clumber Collection [UNL]
PC	Calonne Papers [TNA]
PRO 30/8	Papers of William Pitt the Elder [TNA]
SP	State Papers [TNA]
Stuart	Stuart Papers [RA]
T	Private papers [AN]

SERIALS

Parliamentary History	William Cobbett (ed.), *The Parliamentary History of England, from the Earliest Period to the Year 1803*, 36 vols (London, 1806–20).
ODNB	*Oxford Dictionary of National Biography*

NOTE ON THE CALENDAR, MONEY, AND TRANSLATIONS

1. Robert D. Hume, 'The Value of Money in Eighteenth-Century England: Incomes, Prices, Buying Power—and Some Problems in Cultural Economics', *Huntington Library Quarterly* 77, no. 4 (2014): 373–416.
2. Jean Sgard, 'L'Échelle des revenus', *Dix-huitième siècle* 14 (1982): 425–33.

INTRODUCTION

1. J.R. Seeley, *The Expansion of England* (London, 1902 [1883]), 29.
2. Jeremy Black, *Natural and Necessary Enemies: Anglo-French Relations in the Eighteenth Century* (Athens, GA, 1986).
3. These moments fit into a broader story of Franco-British connection and sporadic amity, which historians have begun to explore. See Robin Eagles, *Francophilia in English Society, 1748–1815* (Basingstoke, 2000); Robert Tombs and Isabelle Tombs, *That Sweet Enemy: The French and the British from the Sun King to the Present* (New York, 2007); Renaud Morieux, *The Channel: England, France and the Construction of a Maritime Border in the Eighteenth Century* (Cambridge, 2016); Stephen Conway, *Britain, Ireland, and Continental Europe in the Eighteenth Century: Similarities, Connections, Identities* (Oxford, 2011).
4. Anthony Howe, *Free Trade and Liberal England 1846–1946* (Oxford, 1998); Frank Trentmann, *Free Trade Nation: Commerce, Consumption, and Civil Society in Modern Britain* (Oxford, 2008).
5. Rosa Luxemburg, *The Accumulation of Capital: A Contribution to an Economic Explanation of Imperialism*, trans. Agnes Schwartzschild (London, 1951 [1913]); Vladimir Lenin, *Imperialism: The Highest Stage of Capitalism* (London, 1996 [1917]).
6. Adom Getachew, *Worldmaking after Empire: The Rise and Fall of Self-Determination* (Princeton, 2019), 142–75.
7. For instance, Robert Keohane, *After Hegemony: Cooperation and Discord in the World Political Economy* (Princeton, 1984).
8. For example, David Harvey, *The New Imperialism* (Oxford, 2003).
9. Nancy Fraser, 'Behind Marx's Hidden Abode: For an Expanded Conception of Capitalism', *New Left Review* 86 (2014): 55–72.
10. Max Weber, *General Economic History*, trans. Frank H. Knight (New York, 1927), 337; Immanuel Wallerstein, *World-Systems Analysis: An Introduction* (Durham, NC, 2004), 23–6; Giovanni Arrighi, *The Long Twentieth Century: Money, Power, and the Origins of Our Times* (London, 1994), 11–12, 16; Charles Tilly, 'War Making and State Making as Organized Crime', in *Bringing the State Back In*, ed. Peter B. Evans, Dietrich Rueschemeyer and Theda Skocpol (Cambridge, 1985), 169–91, 172.
11. Giovanni Arrighi, *Adam Smith in Beijing: Lineages of the Twenty-First Century* (London, 2009), 90.
12. Though the degree of this extroversion must not be exaggerated. See Julian Hoppit, *Britain's Political Economies: Parliament and Economic Life, 1660–1800* (Cambridge, 2017), 4–5, 35, 90–101.
13. On wages, see Robert C. Allen, *The British Industrial Revolution in Global Perspective* (Cambridge, 2009), 25–56; on institutions, see Daron Acemoglu, Simon Johnson and James Robinson, 'The Rise of Europe: Atlantic Trade, Institutional Change, and Economic Growth', *American Economic Review* 95, no. 3 (2005): 546–79; on incentives, see Guillaume Daudin, 'Le commerce maritime et la croissance européenne au XVIIIe siècle', in *The Sea in History: The Early Modern World*, ed. Christian Buchet and Gérard Le Bouëdec (London 2017), 9–18; Guillaume Daudin, 'Profits du commerce intercontinental et croissance dans la France du XVIIIe siècle', *Revue économique* 57, no. 3 (2006): 605–13.
14. Timothy Mitchell, 'Fixing the Economy', *Cultural Studies* 12, no. 1 (1998): 82–101.
15. On monetary scarcity, see Christine Desan, *Making Money: Coin, Currency, and the Making of Capitalism* (Oxford, 2014), 254–65; Thomas M. Luckett, 'Crises financières dans la France du XVIIIe siècle', *Revue d'histoire moderne et contemporaine* 43, no. 2 (1996), 266–92; Craig Muldrew, '"Hard Food for Midas": Cash and Its Social Value in Early Modern England', *Past & Present* 170 (2001): 78–120.
16. Daniel A. Baugh, 'Maritime Strength and Atlantic Commerce: The Uses of a "Grand Marine Empire"', in *An Imperial State at War: Britain from 1689 to 1815*, ed. Lawrence Stone (London, 1994), 185–223; Ronald Findlay and Kevin O'Rourke, *Power and Plenty: Trade, War, and the World Economy in the Second Millennium* (Princeton, 2007), 227–62.

17. William H. Sewell Jr, 'The Rise of Capitalism and the Empire of Fashion in Eighteenth-Century France', *Past & Present* 206, no. 1 (2010): 81–120; Michael Sonenscher, *Work and Wages: Natural Law, Politics, and the Eighteenth-Century French Trades* (Cambridge, 1989).
18. Guillaume Daudin, *Commerce et prospérité: La France au XVIIIe siècle* (Paris, 2005).
19. On commodity frontiers, see Jason W. Moore, ' "Amsterdam is Standing on Norway" Part I: The Alchemy of Capital, Empire and Nature in the Diaspora of Silver, 1545–1648', *Journal of Agrarian Change* 10, no. 1 (2010): 33–68, and idem, ' "Amsterdam is Standing on Norway" Part II: The Global North Atlantic in the Ecological Revolution of the Long Seventeenth Century', *Journal of Agrarian Change* 10, no. 2 (2010): 188–227.
20. Robin Blackburn, *The American Crucible: Slavery, Emancipation and Human Rights* (New York, 2011), 113.
21. Ralph A. Austen, 'Monsters of Protocolonial Economic Enterprise: East India Companies and Slave Plantations', *Critical Historical Studies* 4, no. 2 (2017): 139–77. On the broader questions of definition, see John J. Clegg, 'Capitalism and Slavery', *Critical Historical Studies* 2, no. 2 (2015): 281–304.
22. Jan de Vries, *The Industrious Revolution: Consumer Behavior and Household Economy, 1650 to the Present* (Cambridge, 2008).
23. Frank Perlin, 'Proto-Industrialization and Pre-Colonial South Asia', *Past & Present* 98 (1983): 30–95.
24. Kaveh Yazdani, *India, Modernity and the Great Divergence: Mysore and Gujarat (17th to 19th C.)* (Leiden, 2017); Muzaffar Alam and Sanjay Subrahmanyam, 'Exploring the Hinterland: Trade and Politics in the Arcot Nizamat (1700–1732)', in *Politics and Trade in the Indian Ocean World: Essays in Honour of Ashin Das Gupta*, ed. Rudrangshu Mukherjee and Lakshmi Subramanian (Delhi, 1998), 113–64.
25. William J. Ashworth, *The Industrial Revolution: The State, Knowledge and Global Trade* (London, 2017); Patrick O'Brien, 'The Nature and Historical Evolution of an Exceptional Fiscal State and Its Possible Significance for the Precocious Commercialization and Industrialization of the British Economy from Cromwell to Nelson', *Economic History Review* 64, no. 2 (2011): 408–46; Prasannan Parthasarathi, *Why Europe Grew Rich and Asia Did Not: Global Economic Divergence, 1600–1850* (Cambridge, 2011); Peer Vries, *State, Economy and the Great Divergence: Great Britain and China, 1680s–1850s* (London, 2015). On the Great Divergence, see Kenneth Pomeranz, *The Great Divergence: China, Europe, and the Making of the Modern World Economy* (Princeton, 2000).
26. Arrighi, *Long Twentieth Century*, 13.
27. John Darwin, *Unfinished Empire: The Global Expansion of Britain* (New York, 2012), 68–71.
28. Felicia Gottmann and Philip Stern, 'Introduction: Crossing Companies', *Journal of World History* 31, no. 3 (2020): 477–88; Andrew Phillips and J.C. Sharman, *Outsourcing Empire: How Company-States Made the Modern World* (Princeton, 2020), 1–9, 22–65.
29. John Shovlin, 'War and Peace: Trade, International Competition, and Political Economy', in *Mercantilism Reimagined: Political Economy in Early Modern Britain and Its Empire*, ed. Philip J. Stern and Carl Wennerlind (Oxford, 2013), 305–27.
30. Cátia A.P. Atunes and Amelia Polónia (eds), *Beyond Empires: Global, Self-Organizing, Cross-Imperial Networks, 1500–1800* (Leiden, 2016).
31. Corey Tazzara, *The Free Port of Livorno and the Transformation of the Mediterranean World, 1574–1790* (Oxford, 2017); Francesca Trivellato, *The Familiarity of Strangers: The Sephardic Diaspora, Livorno, and Cross-Cultural Trade in the Early Modern Period* (New Haven, 2009).
32. Jan de Vries and A.M. van der Woude, *The First Modern Economy: Success, Failure, and Perseverance of the Dutch Economy, 1500–1815* (Cambridge, 1997), 476–9.
33. First appearing as separate essays between 1941 and 1953, and republished in Frederic C. Lane, *Profits from Power: Readings in Protection Rent and Violence-Controlling Enterprises* (Albany, 1979).
34. Michael Sonenscher, *Before the Deluge: Public Debt, Inequality, and the Intellectual Origins of the French Revolution* (Princeton, 2007).

35. Istvan Hont, *Jealousy of Trade: International Competition and the Nation-State in Historical Perspective* (Cambridge, MA, 2005).
36. Key works in this tradition include Steven L. Kaplan, *Bread, Politics and Political Economy in the Reign of Louis XV*, 2 vols (The Hague, 1976); Jean-Claude Perrot, *Une histoire intellectuelle de l'économie politique, XVIIe–XVIIIe siècle* (Paris, 1992); Judith A. Miller, *Mastering the Market: The State and the Grain Trade in Northern France, 1700–1860* (Cambridge, 1999). Important recent contributions include Hoppit, *Britain's Political Economies*; and Sophus Reinert, *The Academy of Fisticuffs: Political Economy and Commercial Society in Enlightenment Italy* (Cambridge, MA, 2018).
37. See also Antonella Alimento and Koen Stapelbroek (eds), *The Politics of Commercial Treaties in the Eighteenth Century: Balance of Power, Balance of Trade* (Basingstoke, 2017); and Koen Stapelbroek (ed.), *Trade and War: The Neutrality of Commerce in the Inter-State System* (Helsinki, 2011).
38. Keith Michael Baker, *Inventing the French Revolution: Essays on French Political Culture in the Eighteenth Century* (Cambridge, 1990), 19.
39. Hont, *Jealousy of Trade*, 185–266.
40. John Robertson, *The Case for the Enlightenment: Scotland and Naples 1680–1760* (Cambridge, 2005), 37.
41. Henry Noel Brailsford, *War of Steel and Gold: A Study of the Armed Peace* (London, 1918).
42. Eli F. Heckscher, *Mercantilism*, trans. Mendel Shapiro, 2 vols (London, 1955 [1935]), vol. 2, 25; Edmond Silberner, *La guerre dans la pensée économique du XVIe au XVIIIe siècle* (Paris, 1939), 117–18.
43. Here I dissent from one element of Steve Pincus's analysis in his 'Rethinking Mercantilism: Political Economy, the British Empire, and the Atlantic World in the Seventeenth and Eighteenth Centuries', *William and Mary Quarterly*, 3rd series, 69 (2012), 3–34.
44. Jean-Baptiste Colbert, *Lettres, instructions et mémoires de Colbert*, ed. Pierre Clément, 7 vols (Paris, 1861–73), vol. 6, 269.
45. Various aspects of this thinking are explored in Paul Cheney, *Revolutionary Commerce: Globalization and the French Monarchy* (Cambridge, MA, 2010); Laurence Dickey, 'Doux-commerce and Humanitarian Values: Free Trade, Sociability and Universal Benevolence in Eighteenth-Century Thinking', *Grotiana* 22/23 (2001–2): 271–318; Albert O. Hirschman, *The Passions and the Interests: Political Arguments for Capitalism before Its Triumph*, 3rd edn (Princeton, 2013 [1977]); J.G.A. Pocock, *Virtue, Commerce, and History: Essays on Political Thought & History, Chiefly in the Eighteenth Century* (Cambridge, 1985); and Céline Spector, *Montesquieu et l'émergence de l'économie politique* (Paris, 2006), 181–9.
46. Sophus A. Reinert, *Translating Empire: Emulation and the Origins of Political Economy* (Cambridge, MA, 2011).
47. David A. Bell, *The First Total War: Napoleon's Europe and the Birth of Warfare as We Know It* (Boston, 2007), 65–78.
48. Charles-Irénée Castel de Saint-Pierre, *Projet pour rendre la paix perpétuelle en Europe*, 3 vols (Utrecht, 1713–17); Jean-Jacques Rousseau, *Extrait du projet de paix perpétuelle de Monsieur l'abbé de Saint-Pierre* (Amsterdam, 1761); Immanuel Kant, *Zum ewigen Frieden: Ein philosophischer Entwurf* (Königsberg, 1795).
49. Béla Kapossy, Isaac Nakhimovsky, and Richard Whatmore (eds), *Commerce and Peace in the Enlightenment* (Cambridge, 2017).
50. Marc Belissa, *Fraternité universelle et intérêt national (1713–1795): Les cosmopolitiques du droit des gens* (Paris, 1998), 43.
51. Martin Ceadel, *The Origins of War Prevention: The British Peace Movement and International Relations 1730–1854* (Oxford, 1996), 152–8. On the history of peacemaking, see Lucien Bély, *L'art de la paix en Europe: Naissance de la diplomatie moderne XVIe–XVIIIe siècles* (Paris, 2007); Jean-Pierre Bois, *La paix: Histoire politique et militaire, 1435–1878* (Paris, 2012).
52. Phillips and Sharman, *Outsourcing Empire*, 60.
53. In the words of François Véron de Forbonnais, 'the balance of commerce is truly the balance of power': François Véron de Forbonnais, *Élémens du commerce*, 2 vols (Leiden, 1754),

vol. 2, 93–4. See also Antonella Alimento and Koen Stapelbroek, 'Trade and Treaties: Balancing the Interstate System', in *Politics of Commercial Treaties*, ed. idem, 1–75; Ana Crespo Solana, 'The Repercussions of the Treaty of Utrecht for Spanish Colonial Trade and the Struggle to Retain Spanish America', in *New Worlds? Transformations in the Culture of International Relations Around the Peace of Utrecht*, ed. Inken Schmidt-Voges and Ana Crespo Solana (London, 2017), 37–57; Koen Stapelbroek, ' "The Long Peace": Commercial Treaties and the Principles of Global Trade at the Peace of Utrecht', in *The 1713 Peace of Utrecht and its Enduring Effects*, ed. Alfred Soons (Leiden, 2018), 93–119.

54. Paul W. Schroeder, *The Transformation of European Politics 1763–1848* (Oxford, 1994).

55. Contra Giovanni Arrighi, it makes little sense to describe the seventeenth-century Dutch position as hegemonic. Though certainly commercial leaders, they lacked the power to impose a political framework on the trade of others, except in the East Indies. See Arrighi, *Long Twentieth Century*, 44–7.

56. Some are sceptical that Britain ever played such a role. See Patrick K. O'Brien and Geoffrey Allen Pigman, 'Free Trade, British Hegemony and the International Economic Order in the Nineteenth Century', *Review of International Studies* 18, no. 2 (1992): 89–113.

57. Sven Beckert, 'American Danger: United States Empire, Eurafrica, and the Territorialization of Industrial Capitalism, 1870–1950', *American Historical Review* 122, no. 4 (2017): 1,137–70; Adam Tooze, *The Deluge: The Great War, America and the Remaking of the Global Order, 1916–1931* (New York, 2014).

58. See Hont, *Jealousy of Trade*; Jeff Horn, *Economic Development in Early Modern France: The Privilege of Liberty, 1650–1820* (Cambridge, 2015); Tazzara, *Free Port of Livorno*.

59. Cheney, *Revolutionary Commerce*, 172; Simone Meyssonnier, *La balance et l'horloge: La genèse de la pensée libérale en France au XVIIIe siècle* (Montreuil, 1989), 56.

60. David Hancock, *Citizens of the World: London Merchants and the Integration of the British Atlantic Community, 1735–1785* (Cambridge, 1995), 38.

61. James Livesey, 'Free Trade and Empire in the Anglo-Irish Commercial Propositions of 1785', *Journal of British Studies* 52, no. 1 (2013): 103–27.

62. Of course the two realms were not separate, but interpenetrating and symbiotic. See Emily Erikson, *Between Monopoly and Free Trade: The English East India Company, 1600–1757* (Princeton, 2014); Leos Müller, 'Trading with Asia without a Colonial Empire in Asia: Swedish Merchant Networks and Chartered Company Trade, 1760–1790', in *Beyond Empires*, ed. Atunes and Polónia, 253–77; Silvia Marzagalli, 'Was Warfare Necessary for the Functioning of Eighteenth-Century Colonial Systems? Some Reflections on the Necessity of Cross-Imperial and Foreign Trade in the French Case', in *Beyond Empires*, ed. Atunes and Polónia, 253–77; Ana Crespo Solana, 'A Network-Based Merchant Empire: Dutch Trade in the Hispanic Atlantic (1680–1740)', in *Dutch Atlantic Connections, 1680–1800: Linking Empires, Bridging Borders*, ed. Gert Oostindie and Jessica V. Roitman (Leiden, 2014), 139–58.

63. On the general problem of mercantile influence on politics, see Perry Gauci, *Emporium of the World: The Merchants of London, 1660–1800* (London, 2007), 165–200; Daeryoon Kim, 'Political Convention and the Merchant in the Later Eighteenth Century', in *Regulating the British Economy, 1660–1850*, ed. Perry Gauci (Farnham, 2011), 123–37.

64. See Brendan Simms, *Three Victories and a Defeat: The Rise and Fall of the First British Empire, 1714–1783* (New York, 2007).

65. There are exceptions, for instance, Ragnhild Hatton, *War and Peace, 1680–1720* (London, 1969).

66. David Armitage, *Foundations of Modern International Thought* (Cambridge, 2013); Duncan Bell (ed.), *Victorian Visions of Global Order: Empire and International Relations in Nineteenth-Century Political Thought* (Cambridge, 2007).

67. Isaac Nakhimovsky, *The Closed Commercial State: Perpetual Peace and Commercial Society from Rousseau to Fichte* (Princeton, 2011); Stapelbroek (ed.), *Trade and War*; Alimento and Stapelbroek (eds), *Politics of Commercial Treaties*.

68. Hoppit, *Britain's Political Economies*, passim.

69. Julia Adams, *The Familial State: Ruling Families and Merchant Capitalism in Early Modern Europe* (Ithaca, 2007); Robert Fredona and Sophus A. Reinert, 'Leviathan and Kraken: States, Corporations, and Political Economy', *History and Theory* 59, no. 2 (2020): 167–87; Philip J. Stern, '"A Politie of Civill & Military Power": Political Thought and the Late Seventeenth-Century Foundations of the East India Company-State', *Journal of British Studies* 47, no. 2 (2008): 253–83.

1. TRADE TALKS: PEACE, PROTECTION, AND THE RISE OF FREE TRADE

1. François Crouzet, *La guerre économique franco-anglaise au XVIIIe siècle* (Paris, 2008); John V.C. Nye, *War, Wine, and Taxes: The Political Economy of Anglo-French Trade, 1689–1900* (Princeton, 2007).
2. Alimento and Stapelbroek (eds), *Politics of Commercial Treaties*.
3. Hoppit, *Britain's Political Economies*, 216–48, 297–9; Michael Kwass, *Contraband: Louis Mandrin and the Making of a Global Underground* (Cambridge, MA, 2014); Cal Winslow, 'Sussex Smugglers', in *Albion's Fatal Tree: Crime and Society in Eighteenth-Century England*, ed. Douglas Hay et al. (New York, 1975), 119–66.
4. On English wages, see Allen, *British Industrial Revolution*, 25–56.
5. John Cary, *An Essay on the State of England in Relation to Its Trade, Its Poor, and Its Taxes, for Carrying on the Present War Against France* (Bristol, 1695). On Cary's political economy, see Reinert, *Translating Empire*, 73–128. For an overview of ideas about the infinite expansibility of wealth, see Fredrik Albritton Jonsson, 'The Origins of Cornucopianism: A Preliminary Genealogy', *Critical Historical Studies* 1, no. 1 (2014): 151–68. On such ideas in Cary's England, see Carl Wennerlind, *Casualties of Credit: The English Financial Revolution, 1620–1720* (Cambridge, MA, 2011), 44–79.
6. Reinert, *Translating Empire*, passim. See also idem, *Academy of Fisticuffs*.
7. Ha-Joon Chang, *Bad Samaritans: The Myth of Free Trade and the Secret History of Capitalism* (London, 2009); Erik Reinert, *How Rich Countries Got Rich, and Why Poor Countries Stay Poor* (New York, 2008).
8. Hoppit, *Britain's Political Economies*, 13–14; Tim Keirn, 'Monopoly, Economic Thought, and the Royal African Company', in *Early Modern Conceptions of Property*, ed. John Brewer and Susan Staves (London, 1995), 427–66; William A. Pettigrew, *Freedom's Debt: The Royal African Company and the Politics of the Atlantic Slave Trade, 1672–1752* (Chapel Hill, 2013), 35; Abigail L. Swingen, *Competing Visions of Empire: Labor, Slavery, and the Origins of the British Atlantic Empire* (New Haven, 2015), 140–71.
9. Henry Martyn, *Considerations upon the East India Trade* (London, 1701). *The British Merchant* was published as a periodical in 1713 and 1714, and republished by Charles King as *The British Merchant, or Commerce Preserv'd*, 3 vols (London, 1721). Martyn was a principal contributor.
10. Lionel Rothkrug, *The Opposition to Louis XIV: The Political and Social Origins of the French Enlightenment* (Princeton, 1965), 392–416.
11. Horn, *Economic Development*.
12. Lars Magnusson, *The Tradition of Free Trade* (London, 2004), 2–3.
13. Éric Schnakenbourg, 'Les interactions entre commerce et diplomatie au début du xviiie siècle: L'exemple du Traité de commerce franco-anglais de 1713', *Histoire, économie & société* 23, no. 3 (2004): 349–65.
14. Reinert, *Translating Empire*, passim.
15. Alimento and Stapelbroek, 'Trade and Treaties', in *Politics of Commercial Treaties*, ed. idem, 1–75.
16. David Todd, *Free Trade and Its Enemies in France, 1814–1851* (Cambridge, 2015), 1–3.
17. The minister rationalised the French tariff system in 1664, and sharply raised duties in 1667 on about sixty foreign commodities, mostly to protect infant industries. He maintained the charge of 50 sols per *tonneau* on foreign shipping instituted by his predecessor Nicolas

Fouquet to encourage the growth of French navigation. (A *tonneau* is a measure of volume equivalent to 1.44 cubic metres. Fifty sols was equivalent to two and a half livres tournois.) See S. Elzinga, 'Le tariff de Colbert de 1664 et celui de 1667 et leur signification', *Economisch-historisch jaarboek* 15 (1929): 221–73; Charles Woolsey Cole, *Colbert and a Century of French Mercantilism*, 2 vols (Hamden, CT, 1964), vol. 1, 428–36.

18. Moritz Isenmann, '*Égalité, Réciprocité, Souveraineté*: The Role of Commercial Treaties in Colbert's Economic Policy', in *Politics of Commercial Treaties*, ed. Alimento and Stapelbroek, 77–103.

19. Jonathan Barth, 'Reconstructing Mercantilism: Consensus and Conflict in British Imperial Economy in the Seventeenth and Eighteenth Centuries', *William and Mary Quarterly*, 3rd series, 73, no. 2 (2016): 257–90.

20. Charles Woolsey Cole, *French Mercantilism, 1683–1700* (New York, 1943), 14–15, 307–9.

21. Their protégé, François de Callières, negotiated the treaty of Ryswick. On the Colbert clan, see John C. Rule and Ben S. Trotter, *A World of Paper: Louis XIV, Colbert de Torcy, and the Rise of the Information State* (Montreal, 2014), 90–106. On the role of Beauvillier and Chevreuse, see Laurence Pope, *François de Callières: A Political Life* (Dordrecht, 2010); W.T. Morgan, 'Economic Aspects of the Negotiations at Ryswick', *Transactions of the Royal Historical Society* 14 (1931): 225–49.

22. Pierre-Daniel Huet, *Grand trésor historique et politique du florissant commerce des Hollandois, dans tous les états et empires du monde* (The Hague, 1713). The first edition was published in Rouen in 1712; a Paris edition followed in 1714. The book is better known under the title used from 1717, *Mémoires sur le commerce des Hollandois*. A manuscript version can be found at AAE MD Hollande 49 fols 4–147, dated 1694. Numerous other manuscript copies exist. Huet was a client of Colbert, writing another work at the minister's behest which absolved Colbert of much of the blame for past missteps in commercial policy. See Pierre-Daniel Huet, *Histoire du commerce et de la navigation des anciens* (Paris, 1716), preface, 1–3.

23. Huet, *Grand trésor historique*, preface, and 104–5, 111–13.

24. On the 'liberty and protection' motif, see Cheney, *Revolutionary Commerce*, 30–1, 172; Meyssonnier, *La balance et l'horloge*, 33, 56–58, 66; Jean-Pierre Hirsch and Philippe Minard, '"Laissez-nous faire et protégez-nous beaucoup": Pour une histoire des pratiques institutionnelles dans l'industrie française', in *La France n'est-elle pas douée pour l'industrie?*, ed. Louis Bergeron and Patrice Bourdelais (Paris, 1998).

25. David Kammerling Smith, 'Structuring Politics in Early Eighteenth-Century France: The Political Innovations of the French Council of Commerce', *Journal of Modern History* 74, no. 3 (2002): 490–537. At first named the Council of Commerce, the body was renamed the Bureau of Commerce in 1722 and retained this name until the Revolution. See also Thomas J. Schaeper, *The French Council of Commerce 1700–1715: A Study of Mercantilism after Colbert* (Columbus, 1983).

26. Indeed, the key English market for French wines had contracted sharply; as late as the reign of James II, nearly 13 million litres of French wine were imported annually into England: Nye, *War, Wine, and Taxes*, 32–9.

27. For the way regional economic interests, such as the Bordeaux wine industry, could inspire free trade talk, see Moritz Isenmann, 'From Privilege to Economic Law: Vested Interests and the Origins of Free Trade Theory in France (1687–1701)', in *Economic Growth and the Origins of Modern Political Economy: Economic Reasons of State, 1500–2000*, ed. Philipp R. Rössner (New York, 2016), 103–21.

28. See, for instance, Pierre Clément, *Histoire du système protecteur en France depuis le ministère de Colbert jusqu'à la révolution de 1848* (Paris, 1854), 49–58; Philippe Sagnac, 'La politique commerciale de la France avec l'étranger, de la Paix de Ryswyk à la Paix d'Utrecht (1697–1713)', *Revue historique* 104, no. 2 (1910): 265–86; Cole, *French Mercantilism, 1683–1700*, 229–72; Rothkrug, *Opposition to Louis XIV*, 211–32; Schaeper, *French Council of Commerce*, chapter 3; Jean Tarrade, 'Liberté du commerce, individualisme et État: Les conceptions des négociants français au XVIIIe siècle', *Cahiers d'économie politique* 27–8 (1996): 175–91.

29. The thinking of the deputies was radically different, for example, from that of the most prominent critic of Colbert outside the administration of trade: Pierre Le Pesant de Boisguilbert, who rejected Colbertism root and branch. Boisguilbert advanced a system in which agriculture and domestic commerce rather than export manufacturing and foreign trade were the keys to French prosperity, and he rejected the Colbertist fixation on the money supply. A royal official based in Rouen, Boisguilbert was regarded as a crank by the officials he approached. But his *Détail de la France* went through eight editions between 1695 and 1699 and enjoyed seven more in 1707, when its message achieved new resonance by its apparent similarity to the maréchal de Vauban's *Dixme royale*. See Kenneth E. Carpenter, *The Economic Bestsellers before 1850: A Catalogue of an Exhibition Prepared for the History of Economics Society Meeting, May 21–24, 1975, at Baker Library* (Cambridge, MA, 1975), 10–11. On Boisguilbert, see Gilbert Faccarello, *The Foundations of Laissez-Faire: The Economics of Pierre de Boisguilbert* (London, 1999).

30. G.N. Clark, 'War Trade and Trade War, 1701–1713', *Economic History Review* 1, no. 2 (1928): 262–80; Kammerling Smith, 'Structuring Politics', 504–9. Over 4,000 passports were issued to Dutch ships during the war. See J.S. Bromley, 'Le commerce de la France de l'ouest et la guerre maritime (1702–1712)', *Annales du Midi* 65 (1953), 66.

31. AN G⁷ 1695 nos 224, 229, 263, 266, 271, 274, 276. See Éric Schnakenbourg, 'L'indispensable ennemi: Le gouvernement français et le commerce hollandais pendant la guerre de Succession d'Espagne, 1702–1713. Approche politique et diplomatique', *Revue du Nord* 379 (2009): 85–101; David Kammerling Smith, '"Au Bien du Commerce": Economic Discourse and Visions of Society in France', PhD thesis, University of Pennsylvania, 1995, 349–95.

32. BNF fr 8038 fol. 431, [Léon de Rol], 'Mémoire du deputé de Bayonne'.

33. AAE MD Ang 33 fols 4–41, 'Mémoire sur le traité de commerce entre la France et l'Angleterre'.

34. AN G⁷ 1700 pp. 227–8, Nicolas Desmaretz to Nicolas Mesnager, 15 Mar. 1712.

35. 'Préliminaires pour la paix avec la France du 28 mai 1709', in *Mémoires pour servir à l'histoire du XVIIIe siècle, contenant les négociations, traitez, résolutions, et autres documents authentiques concernant les affaires d'État*, ed. Guillaume de Lamberty, 14 vols (The Hague, 1724–40), vol. 5 (1727), 293.

36. AAE CP Hollande 222 fols 153–60, 'Sommaire exposition des differents prejudices que la France souffriroit par la pleine execution des articles preliminaires pour la paix', 5 Mar. 1710. For a similar assessment, see AAE CP Hollande 214 fols 108–9, Mesnager, 'Vues secrètes du mémoire contenant les moyens de conclure la paix avec les États généraux' [1708].

37. AAE CP Hollande 222 fols 152–3, Mesnager to Jean-Baptiste Colbert de Torcy, 5 Mar. 1710.

38. AAE MD Amérique 24 fols 13–75, 'Memoire concernant les colonies, le commerce, et la navigation, pour Messʳˢ les plenipotentiaires du Roy', 2 Jan. 1712. See also Lucien Bély, *Espions et ambassadeurs au temps de Louis XIV* (Paris, 1990), 574.

39. Tory political economy has been characterised as land-focused, in contrast to that of Whigs, which valorised labour. See Steve Pincus, *1688: The First Modern Revolution* (New Haven, 2009), 369–81. To be sure, the Tories viewed themselves as the party of the landed interest and supported schemes, such as land banks, intended to benefit landowners.

40. Ralph Davis, 'English Foreign Trade, 1660–1700', *Economic History Review*, new series, 7, no. 2 (1954): 150–166; idem, *A Commercial Revolution: English Overseas Trade in the Seventeenth and Eighteenth Centuries* (London, 1967), 9–12; idem, *The Rise of the English Shipping Industry in the Seventeenth and Eighteenth Centuries* (London, 1962), 15–16, 23. On London's leading role in this expansion, see Nuala Zahedieh, *The Capital and the Colonies: London and the Atlantic Economy 1660–1700* (Cambridge, 2010).

41. On Tory foreign policy, see Jeremy Black, 'The Tory View of Eighteenth-Century British Foreign Policy', *Historical Journal* 31, no. 2 (1988): 469–77; idem (ed.), *The Tory World: Deep History and the Tory Theme in British Foreign Policy, 1679–2014* (Farnham, 2015);

Shinsuke Satsuma, *Britain and Colonial Maritime War in the Early Eighteenth Century: Silver, Seapower and the Atlantic* (Woodbridge, 2013), 42. After 1688 a pattern developed of Tory patronage of the older joint stocks and Whig support for the claims of the 'separate traders' in Africa and the East India 'interlopers', who sought to prise open Asian trade and founded a new India Company in 1698 under Whig patronage. See Gary Stuart De Krey, *A Fractured Society: The Politics of London in the First Age of Party 1688–1715* (Oxford, 1985), 127–34; Henry Horwitz, 'The East India Trade, the Politicians, and the Constitution: 1769–1702', *Journal of British Studies* 17 (1978): 1–18; Keirn, 'Monopoly, Economic Thought, and the Royal African Company'; Swingen, *Competing Visions of Empire*, 140–71; Robert Walcott, 'The East India Interest in the General Election of 1700–1701', *English Historical Review* 71, no. 279 (1956): 223–39; Steve Pincus and Alice Wolfram, 'A Proactive State? The Land Bank, Investment and Party Politics in the 1690s', in *Regulating the British Economy*, ed. Gauci, 41–62.

43. David Waddell, 'Charles Davenant (1656–1714) – A Biographical Sketch', *Economic History Review*, new series, 11, no. 2 (1958): 279–88; Paula Watson and Perry Gauci, 'Moore, Arthur (c. 1666–1730)', in *History of Parliament: The House of Commons 1690–1715*, ed. D. Hayton, E. Cruickshanks and S. Handley (London, 2002). See also H.T. Dickinson, *Bolingbroke* (London, 1970), 107; and Ian K. Steele, *Politics of Colonial Policy: The Board of Trade in Colonial Administration 1696–1720* (Oxford, 1968), 136–7.

44. Charles Davenant, *An Essay on the East India Trade* (London, 1696), 18. Idem, *New Dialogues upon the Present Posture of Affairs, the Species of Mony, National Debts, Publick Revenues, Bank and East-India Company, and the Trade Now Carried on between France and Holland* (London, 1710), 92.

45. Cheney, *Revolutionary Commerce*, 25.

46. Davenant, *East India Trade*, 26; idem, 'Discourses on the Publick Revenues, and on the Trade of England, Part II', in *Political and Commercial Works of that Celebrated Writer Charles D'avenant*, ed. Charles Whitworth, 5 vols (London, 1771), vol. 1, 116. See also Doohwan Ahn, 'The Anglo-French Treaty of Commerce of 1713: Tory Trade Politics and the Question of Dutch Decline', *History of European Ideas* 26 (2010): 167–80.

47. St John worried that the wartime prohibition of cross-Channel trade, while Franco-Dutch exchange remained open, would lead to the loss of branches of trade to the profit of the Dutch. St John to Drummond, 28 Nov. 1710, in Henry St John, Viscount Bolingbroke, *Letters and Correspondence, Public and Private, of the Right Honourable Henry St John, Lord Visc. Bolingbroke*, ed. Gilbert Parke, 4 vols (London, 1798), vol. 1, 17.

48. BL Add MS 22206 fols 17–18, St John to John Robinson, bishop of Bristol and Thomas Wentworth, earl of Strafford, 16 May 1712. See also BL Add MS 22205 fols 325–6, St John to Bristol and Strafford, 12 Mar. 1712; fols 333–4, Bristol and Strafford to St John, 15 Mar. 1712. On the hostility to the Dutch widespread among English Tories, see Douglas Coombs, *The Conduct of the Dutch: British Opinion and the Dutch Alliance during the War of the Spanish Succession* (The Hague, 1958).

49. 'A Letter to Sir William Windham', in Henry St John, Viscount Bolingbroke, *Works of Lord Bolingbroke*, 4 vols (London, 1967), vol. 1, 121.

50. Bolingbroke to Matthew Prior, 31 May 1713, in Bolingbroke, *Letters and Correspondence*, vol. 4, 153.

51. H.T. Dickinson, 'Politique britannique et luttes de partis dans les négociations du Traité d'Utrecht', in *Le négoce de la paix: Les nations et les traités franco-britanniques, 1713–1802*, ed. Jean-Pierre Jessenne, Renaud Morieux and Pascal Dupuy (Paris, 2008), 15–46, 34.

52. B.R. Mitchell, *British Historical Statistics* (Cambridge, 1988), 600; Peter Mathias and Patrick O'Brien, 'Taxation in Britain and France, 1715–1810: A Comparison of the Social and Economic Incidence of Taxes Collected for the Central Governments', *Journal of European Economic History* 5 (1976), 601–50.

53. Jonathan Swift, *The Conduct of the Allies, and of the Late Ministry, in Beginning and Carrying on the Present War*, 4th edn (London, 1712).

54. Bodl. Eng. MSS Misc. e. 180 fols 4–5, St John to Charles Boyle, earl of Orrery, 9 July 1709. Cited in Dickinson, *Bolingbroke*, 69.

55. Tony Claydon summarises Tory foreign policy positions in 'Toryism and the World in the Later Stuart Era, 1679–1714', in *The Tory World*, ed. Black, 21–32. On party ideology and English foreign policy, see Tony Claydon, *Europe and the Making of England 1660–1760* (Cambridge, 2007).

56. Charles Davenant, *A Report to the Honourable the Commissioners for Putting in Execution the Act, Intitled, An Act, for the Taking, Examining, and Stating the Publick Accounts of the Kingdom* (London, 1712).

57. Davenant, *New Dialogues*, 245.

58. Davenant, *Report to the Commissioners*, 63.

59. *The Mercator; or, Commerce Retrieved, Being Considerations on the State of the British Trade* (30 May 1713).

60. Ibid. See also 2 and 4 June 1713. It appeared thrice weekly from 26 May 1713, its circulation peaking at 14,400 per week (4,800 per issue) just before the Commons vote on 18 June. See Perry Gauci, *The Politics of Trade: The Overseas Merchant in State and Society, 1660–1720* (Oxford, 2001), 243.

61. As late as the 1680s, half of the total value of Brittany's linen production was exported to England. See Jean Quéniart, *La Bretagne au XVIIIe siècle (1675–1789)* (Rennes, 2004), 344–5.

62. Davenant, *East India Trade*, 42–3. See Hont, *Jealousy of Trade*, 59–60.

63. A point Istvan Hont neglects in his lengthy account of Davenant's political economy. See *Jealousy of Trade*, 201–22.

64. Cary, *Essay on the State of England*, 49.

65. Parliament cited this figure when it passed a three-year prohibition of trade with France in 1678. See Margaret Priestley, 'Anglo-French Trade and the "Unfavourable Balance" Controversy, 1660–1685', *Economic History Review*, new series, 4, no. 1 (1951): 37–52. See also Charles-Édouard Levillain, *Vaincre Louis XIV: Angleterre, Hollande, France, histoire d'une relation triangulaire 1665–1688* (Seyssel, 2010).

66. Paul Slack, 'The Politics of Consumption and England's Happiness in the Later Seventeenth Century', *English Historical Review* 122, no. 497 (2007): 609–31.

67. Josiah Child, *A New Discourse of Trade* (London, 1693), 142–9.

68. William Deringer, *Calculated Values: Finance, Politics, and the Quantitative Age* (Cambridge, MA, 2018), 115–52, 115.

69. Lars Magnusson, *The Political Economy of Mercantilism* (Abingdon, 2015), 117–20.

70. Gauci, *Politics of Trade*, 244.

71. Doohwan Ahn, 'Anglo-French Treaty of Utrecht of 1713 Revisited: The Politics of Rivalry and Alliance', in *Politics of Commercial Treaties*, ed. Alimento and Stapelbroek, 125–50; Dickinson, *Bolingbroke*, 107.

72. On the commercial treaty debate, see D.C. Coleman, 'Politics and Economics in the Age of Anne: The Case of the Anglo-French Trade Treaty of 1713', in *Trade, Government and Economy in Pre-Industrial England: Essays Presented to F.J. Fisher*, ed. D.C. Coleman and A.H. John (London, 1976), 187–211; Gauci, *Politics of Trade*, 234–70; Nye, *War, Wine, and Taxes*, 51–3.

73. *British Merchant*, vol. 1, 13–15, 145–6.

74. For Sir Theodore Janssen, 'Exportation of our Woollen Goods to France is so well barr'd against, that there is not the least hope of reaping any Benefit by this Article.' Ibid., 6. See also ibid., 169–70; *British Merchant*, vol. 2, 149.

75. CUL Ch(H) Papers 89/1c1–1c2, 'Notes on the balance of trade'. Some critics even claimed that the woollen industry would be overwhelmed by French imports: *A Collection of Petitions Presented to the Honourable House of Commons against the Trade with France* (London, 1713), 18–19.

76. *British Merchant*, vol. 2, 314–20.

77. 'The Case of the Clothiers', *Collection of Petitions*, 23–4.

78. Lord Halifax declared that every English commercial city should erect a statue to John Methuen, the negotiator of the deal. See A.D. Francis, *The Methuens and Portugal,*

1691–1708 (Cambridge, 1966), 354–5. See also Paul Duguid, 'The Making of Methuen: The Commercial Treaty in the English Imagination', *História: Revista da Faculdade de Letras da Universidade do Porto* 3, no. 4 (2003): 9–36.

79. *Mercator*, 28 and 30 May 1713.
80. Claydon, *Europe and the Making of England*, 203–4. Defoe approached Harley in 1711 about the French trade, 'how it may be opened most to advantage both of the nation and of the revenue': Daniel Defoe to Robert Harley, 13 Feb. 1711, in *Manuscripts of His Grace the Duke of Portland, Preserved at Welbeck Abbey*, 10 vols (London, 1897), vol. 4, 659. See also Peter Earle, 'The Economics of Stability: The Views of Daniel Defoe', in *Trade, Government and Economy in Pre-Industrial England*, ed. Coleman and John, 274–92, 279–80.
81. AAE MD Ang 33 fols 151–3, Mesnager to Desmaretz, 23 Jan. 1713. See also AN G⁷ 1700 pp. 1–6, 9–15, 19, 32–3; also AAE MD Ang 33 fol. 163, 'Extraits d'un mémoire contenant les propositions de l'Angleterre', June 1712.
82. AN G⁷ 1699 fol. 63, Jean Anisson and Jean-Baptiste Fenellon to Desmaretz, 19 July 1713.
83. BL Add MS 22205 fols 333–4, Bristol and Strafford to St John, 15 Mar. 1712; fols 349–51, Bristol to St John, 25 Mar. 1712; Prior to Bolingbroke, 17/28 Dec. 1712, in Bolingbroke, *Letters and Correspondence*, vol. 3, 243–8.
84. Bolingbroke to Prior, 10 Oct. 1712, in ibid., 118.
85. Bolingbroke to Shrewsbury, 30 Jan. 1713, in ibid., 309–13. See also BL Add MS 22206 fols 93–110, and fols 137–8.
86. Walpole warned that nothing would be neglected to force it through Parliament. [Sir Robert Walpole], *A Short History of the Parliament* (London, 1713), 17.
87. Gauci, *Politics of Trade*, 263–4.
88. AAE MD Ang 33 fols 251–60, Nicolas-Louis Le Dran, 'Sur les difficultés qui ont arêté la conclusion et l'exécution du traité de commerce signé à Utrecht entre la France et la Grande Bretagne'; Gauci, *Politics of Trade*, 266.
89. Fenellon, on the other hand, was willing to concede more to reopen the wine trade between his home city of Bordeaux and lost markets in Britain. See AN G⁷ 1704 no. 338.
90. When relations warmed, as under the Regency of Philippe d'Orléans, the idea was renewed as a goodwill gesture though nothing came of this. See Basil Williams, *Stanhope: A Study in Eighteenth-Century War and Diplomacy* (Oxford, 1932), 211; AAE CP Ang 331 fols 158–9, Philippe Néricault Destouches to the abbé Guillaume Dubois, 3 June 1720. There were occasional rumours of new proposals in the two following decades. See, for example, Jeremy Black, *British Foreign Policy in the Age of Walpole* (Edinburgh, 1985), 99.
91. Linda Colley, *In Defiance of Oligarchy: The Tory Party, 1714–60* (Cambridge, 1982).
92. Corey Tazzara, 'Managing Free Trade in Early Modern Europe: Institutions, Information, and the Free Port of Livorno', *Journal of Modern History* 86 (2014): 493–529; Trivellato, *Familiarity of Strangers*, 74–8, 108.
93. Joshua Gee, *The Trade and Navigation of Great-Britain Considered: Shewing that the Surest Way for the Nation to Increase in Riches is to Prevent the Importation of Such Foreign Commodities as May Be Rais'd at Home* (London, 1729), 109–11.
94. Anon., *The Genuine Thoughts of a Merchant* (London, 1733).
95. William Coxe, *Memoirs of the Life and Administration of Sir Robert Walpole, Earl of Orford*, 3 vols (London, 1798), vol. 1, 399.
96. Paul Langford, *The Excise Crisis: Society and Politics in the Age of Walpole* (Oxford, 1975).
97. Justin Du Rivage, *Revolution Against Empire: Taxes, Politics, and the Origins of American Independence* (New Haven, 2017), 38–40, 48–9.
98. [Sir Matthew Decker], *An Essay on the Causes of the Decline of the Foreign Trade, Consequently of the Value of the Lands of Britain, and on the Means to Restore Both* (London, 1744). For Decker's concerns about smuggling as chairman of the East India Company, see K.N. Chaudhuri, *The Trading World of Asia and the English East India Company 1660–1760* (Cambridge, 1978), 392–4.

99. John Russell, duke of Bedford to Willem Anne van Keppel, earl of Albemarle, 3 Aug. 1749, in John Russell, duke of Bedford, *Correspondence of John, Fourth Duke of Bedford*, ed. Lord John Russell, 3 vols (London, 1844–46), vol. 2, 40–4; AAE MD Ang 69 fol. 17, François-Marie Durand to Louis-Philogène Brulart, marquis de Puysieulx, 17 July 1749.

100. AAE MD Ang 69 fol. 5, Antoine-Louis Rouillé, 'Droit de fret imposé en France sur les navires anglois', 6 June 1749.

101. AAE MD Ang 69 fols 151–2, Philibert Trudaine de Montigny to Puysieulx, 27 May 1751.

102. AAE MD Ang 69 fols 207–10, 'Préçis de ce qui s'est passé le 9 et 10 May 1753 dans la Chambre de Communes lors de l'examen en grand committé du Bill pour prevenir plus efficacement l'importation des Batistes et Linons de France'.

103. On Hume's political economy, see Margaret Schabas and Carl Wennerlind, *A Philosopher's Economist: Hume and the Rise of Capitalism* (Chicago, 2020).

104. Duncan Forbes, *Hume's Philosophical Politics* (Cambridge, 1975), 136–9.

105. David Hume, 'Of the Balance of Trade', in idem, *Political Discourses* (Edinburgh, 1752), 79–100, 88.

106. David Hume, 'Of Taxes', in idem, *Political Discourses*, 115–22, and 'Of the Balance of Trade', 98.

107. Isenmann, 'From Privilege to Economic Law', 107.

108. David Hume, 'Of the Balance of Power', in idem, *Political Discourses*.

109. David Hume, 'Of Public Credit', in idem, *Political Discourses*.

110. David Hume, *The Letters of David Hume*, ed. J.Y.T. Grieg, 2 vols (Oxford, 1969), vol. 1, 142–4.

111. David Hume, 'Of the Jealousy of Trade', in idem, *Essays and Treatises on Several Subjects*, 2 vols (Edinburgh, 1764), vol. 1, 365. The essay first appeared in editions dating from late in 1759 or early in 1760. See David Hume, *Letters of David Hume*, ed. Greig, vol. 1, 272, 317.

112. David Hume to William Strahan, 26 Oct. 1775, in Hume, *Letters of David Hume*, ed. Greig, vol. 2, 301.

113. Loïc Charles, 'French "New Politics" and the Dissemination of Hume's Political Discourses on the Continent', in *David Hume's Political Economy*, ed. Margaret Schabas and Carl Wennerlind (London, 2008), 181–202.

114. Ibid.; John Shovlin, 'Hume's *Political Discourses* and the French Luxury Debate', in *David Hume's Political Economy*, ed. Schabas and Wennerlind, 203–22.

115. Jean-François Melon, *Essai politique sur le commerce. Nouvelle édition, augmentée de sept chapitres, & où les lacunes des éditions précédentes sont remplies* (n.p., 1736), 132–3.

116. For this liberal reading of the Gournay circle, see Felicia Gottmann, *Global Trade, Smuggling, and the Making of Economic Liberalism: Asian Textiles in France 1680–1760* (Basingstoke, 2016).

117. Antonella Alimento, 'Beyond the Treaty of Utrecht: Véron de Forbonnais's French Translation of the *British Merchant* (1753)', *History of European Ideas* 40, no. 8 (2014): 1,044–66. On the illiberal dimensions of Gournay's thinking and that of his circle, see Reinert, *Translating Empire*, 146, 164–5, 169–75.

118. For a sense of the range, see John Shovlin, *The Political Economy of Virtue: Luxury, Patriotism, and the Origins of the French Revolution* (Ithaca, 2006), 80–117.

119. Philippe Steiner, 'Wealth and Power: Quesnay's Political Economy of the "Agricultural Kingdom"', *Journal of the History of Economic Thought* 24, no. 1 (2002): 91–110.

120. On tax resistance, see Michael Kwass, *Privilege and the Politics of Taxation in Eighteenth-Century France: Liberté, Egalité, Fiscalité* (Cambridge, 2000), 161–93.

121. Commerce and manufactures were 'sterile'. The value-added conferred by manufacturing covered only labour and production costs, and a profit for the entrepreneur equivalent to interest on his capital. Agriculture, by contrast, paid wage costs, offered a return on the capital of the farmer, and still left a surplus – a 'net product' – embodied in the rent paid to landlords. On Physiocratic doctrine, see Philippe Steiner, *La 'science nouvelle' de*

l'économie politique (Paris, 1998); and Liana Vardi, *The Physiocrats and the World of the Enlightenment* (Cambridge, 2012).

122. Paul-Pierre Le Mercier de La Rivière, 'Mémoire sur la Martinique', 8 September 1762, reproduced in idem, *Le Mercier de La Rivière (1719–1801): Mémoires et textes inédits sur le gouvernement économique des Antilles*, ed. Louis Philippe May (Paris, 1978), 147–8.

123. Steiner, 'Wealth and Power', 103, citing François Quesnay, 'Hommes', in idem, *François Quesnay et la Physiocratie*, 2 vols (Paris, 1958), vol. 2, 525.

124. [Victor Riqueti, marquis de Mirabeau], *L'ami des hommes, ou Traité de la population*, 3 vols (Avignon, 1756), vol. 3, 103. See Nakhimovsky, *Closed Commercial State*, 87–8.

125. On the evolution of Physiocratic theories, see Loïc Charles and Arnaud Orain, 'The Physiocratic Movement: A Revision', in *The Economic Turn: Recasting Political Economy in Enlightenment Europe*, ed. Steven L. Kaplan and Sophus A. Reinert (London, 2019), 35–70.

126. AAE CP Ang suppl. 14 fols 98–9, Emmanuel-Armand de Richelieu, duc d'Aiguillon to Adrien-Louis de Bonnières, comte de Guînes, 27 Nov. 1772. See also Bertrand de Fraguier, 'Le duc d'Aiguillon et l'Angleterre', *Revue d'histoire diplomatique* 26 (1912): 607–27.

127. Marcel Marion, *L'histoire financière de la France depuis 1715*, 6 vols (Paris, 1914–31), vol. 1, 248–79; J.F. Bosher, 'The French Crisis of 1770', *History* 57, no. 189 (1972): 17–30; James C. Riley, *International Government Finance and the Amsterdam Capital Market, 1740–1815* (Cambridge, 1980); François R. Velde and David R. Weir, 'The Financial Market and Government Debt Policy in France, 1746–1793', *Journal of Economic History* 52, no. 1 (1992): 1–39.

128. Bailey Stone, *The Genesis of the French Revolution: A Global-Historical Perspective* (Cambridge, 1994), 46–58.

129. Michael Roberts, 'Great Britain and the Swedish Revolution 1772–3', in idem, *Essays in Swedish History* (London, 1967), 286–347; H.M. Scott, *British Foreign Policy in the Age of the American Revolution* (Oxford, 1990), 181–8.

130. Trivellato, *Familiarity of Strangers*, 115.

131. George III, *The Correspondence of King George the Third from 1760 to December 1783*, ed. Sir John Fortescue, 6 vols (London, 1927–28), vol. 2, 428–9. See also Scott, *British Foreign Policy*, 84–5.

132. AAE CP Ang 500 fol. 336, Guînes to d'Aiguillon, 27 Dec. 1772.

133. AAE CP Ang 500 fols 332–41, Guînes to d'Aiguillon, 27 Dec. 1772.

134. AAE CP Ang suppl. 14 fols 97–100, d'Aiguillon to Guînes, 27 Nov. 1772.

135. AAE CP Ang 500 fol. 276, d'Aiguillon to the abbé Joseph-Marie Terray, 30 Nov. 1772. See also AAE CP Ang suppl. 14 fols 97–100, d'Aiguillon to Guînes, 27 Nov. 1772.

136. AAE CP Ang 501 fols 27–30, Terray to d'Aiguillon, 26 Jan. 1773. D'Aiguillon received broadly similar input from others he consulted. See AAE CP Ang 500 fols 344–51, untitled, Dec. 1772.

137. AAE CP Ang 501 fols 68–9, d'Aiguillon to James Bourdieu, 15 Feb. 1773.

138. Kaplan and Reinert (eds), *Economic Turn*; Gérard Klotz, Philippe Minard and Arnaud Orain (eds), *Les voies de la richesse? La physiocratie en question (1760–1850)* (Rennes, 2017).

139. Kaplan, *Bread, Politics and Political Economy*, vol. 2, chapters 11–13; Georges Weulersse, *La physiocratie à la fin du règne de Louis XV (1770–1774)* (Paris, 1959), 163–205.

140. AAE CP Ang 500 fols 277–83, 'Note', 1 Dec. 1772.

141. AAE CP Ang 500 fols 199–205, Jean-Baptiste Garnier to d'Aiguillon.

142. AAE CP Ang 500 fols 344–51, fol. 350, untitled, Dec. 1772.

143. Josiah Tucker, *The Case of Going to War, for the Sake of Procuring, Enlarging, or Securing of Trade . . .* (London, 1763), 35–6. Tucker claimed that it was he who had sensitised Hume to the problem of jealousy of trade. See BL Add MS 4319 fol. 269, Josiah Tucker to Thomas Birch, 19 May 1760.

144. Adam Smith, *Lectures on Jurisprudence*, ed. R.L. Meek, D.D. Raphael and P.G. Stein (Indianapolis, 1982), 389–93, 512–14.

145. W.R. Scott, 'Adam Smith at Downing Street, 1766–7', *Economic History Review* 6, no. 1 (1935): 79–89. In the North administration, Smith had ties with Solicitor General Alexander Wedderburn and with Henry Dundas, a key government spokesman in the Commons. See Adam Smith, *Correspondence of Adam Smith*, ed. Ernest Campbell Mossner and Ian Simpson Ross (Indianapolis, 1987).

146. Thomas Mortimer, 'France', in *A New and Complete Dictionary of Trade and Commerce: Containing a Distinct Explanation of the General Principles of Commerce*, 2 vols (London, 1766), vol. 2, unpaginated.

147. Gauci, *Politics of Trade*, 270.

148. [Arthur Young], *Political Essays Concerning the Present State of the British Empire* (London, 1772), 486–90.

149. AAE CP Ang 500 fols 249–51, Bourdieu to d'Aiguillon, 20 Nov. 1772. On Glover's role, see also AAE CP Ang 501 fols 121–3, Bourdieu to d'Aiguillon, 2 Mar. 1773.

150. 'Glover, Richard (?1712–1785), of Exchange Alley, London', *History of Parliament: The House of Commons, 1754–1790*, ed. Lewis Namier and John Brooke (London, 1964).

151. Richard Glover, *The Substance of the Evidence Delivered to a Committee of the Honourable House of Commons by the Merchants and Traders of London, Concerned in the Trade to Germany and Holland, and of the Dealers in Foreign Linens* (London, 1774). On Glover's earlier activism in this cause, see P.D.G. Thomas, *British Politics and the Stamp Act Crisis: The First Phase of the American Revolution, 1763–1767* (Oxford, 1975), 55.

152. Roberts, 'Great Britain and the Swedish Revolution', 312–22; Scott, *British Foreign Policy*, 186–8.

153. AAE CP Ang 500 fol. 320, d'Aiguillon to Bourdieu, 19 Dec. 1772.

154. AAE CP Ang 501 fols 73–4, d'Aiguillon to Bourdieu, 15 Feb. 1773; fols 70–2. 'Note pour Monseigneur', 15 Feb. 1773.

155. AAE CP Ang 500 fols 249–51, Bourdieu to d'Aiguillon, 20 Nov. 1772; Ang 501 fols 121–3, Bourdieu to d'Aiguillon, 2 Mar. 1773.

156. *Traité de navigation et de commerce entre la France et la Grande Bretagne* (Paris, 1787).

157. Jeff Horn, *The Path Not Taken: French Industrialization in the Age of Revolution, 1750–1830* (Cambridge, MA, 2006).

158. See Vincent T. Harlow, *The Founding of the Second British Empire 1763–1793*, 2 vols (London, 1952–64), vol. 1, 312–42; and Andrew Stockley, *Britain and France at the Birth of America: The European Powers and the Peace Negotiations of 1782–83* (Exeter, 2001), 74–138.

159. AAE CP Ang 538 fol. 182, Joseph Matthias Gérard de Rayneval to Charles Gravier, comte de Vergennes, 18 Sept. 1782.

160. Rayneval to Vergennes, 24 and 28 Jan. 1783, in *Histoire de la participation de la France à l'établissement des États-Unis d'Amérique. Correspondance diplomatique et documents*, ed. Henri Doniol, 5 vols (Paris, 1886–92), vol. 5, 279, 285.

161. AAE CP Ang 538 fols 179–80, Rayneval to Vergennes, 13 Sept. 1782.

162. Charles Gravier, comte de Vergennes, 'Mémoire de Vergennes à Louis XVI sur la situation politique de la France' (1774), in *Politique de tous les cabinets de l'Europe, pendant les règnes de Louis XV et de Louis XVI*, ed. L.P. Ségur, 3 vols (Paris, 1801), vol. 3, 158. On Vergennes's diplomatic career, see Orville T. Murphy, *Charles Gravier, Comte de Vergennes: French Diplomacy in the Age of Revolution: 1719–1787* (Albany, 1982).

163. WCL Shelburne Papers 87a/159–60, untitled note.

164. Léon Cahen, 'Une nouvelle interprétation du traité franco-anglais de 1786–1787', *Revue historique* 185, no. 2 (1939): 257–85.

165. He had long held that the commerce Britain carried on with Spain curbed British aggression. See Murphy, *Vergennes*, 252.

166. William Eden to Francis Osborne, marquess of Carmarthen, 17 Apr. 1786, in William Eden, *Journal and Correspondence of William Eden, Lord Auckland*, ed. R.J. Eden and G. Hogge, 4 vols (London, 1861–62), vol. 1, 102.

167. In July 1783, Vergennes arranged to have him assigned in equal measure to the ministries of the navy, foreign affairs, and the Contrôle Général. Shortly thereafter he was ennobled,

and in 1786 Vergennes had him appointed a *conseiller d'État*. See Ambrose Saricks, *Pierre Samuel Du Pont de Nemours* (Lawrence, KS, 1965), 76–89.

168. AAE MD Ang 65 fols 3–8, Pierre-Samuel Dupont de Nemours, 'Réflexions sur le bien que peuvent se faire réciproquement la France et l'Angleterre'.

169. AAE CP Ang 552 fol. 351, Vergennes to Jean-Balthasar Adhémar de Grignan, 13 Mar. 1785. On Pitt's Irish trade proposals, see Livesey, 'Free Trade and Empire'.

170. Calonne prohibited certain classes of British goods to get Pitt's attention, absorbed as he was with his Irish trade initiative. See John Ehrman, *The Younger Pitt: The Years of Acclaim* (New York, 1969), 483–4. Yet the Board of Trade viewed lawful commerce as 'so inconsiderable' between the two countries that Britain would suffer little from its total loss. See BL Add MS 34462 fol. 265.

171. *Parliamentary History*, vol. 26, cols 392–4. Fox charged Pitt with naivety for crediting French pretentions to friendship (col. 397). See also [Denis O'Bryen], *A View of the Treaty of Commerce with France*, 2nd edn (London, 1787), 118–20.

172. Such gendered rhetoric was characteristic of Francis. See Linda Colley, 'Gendering the Global: The Political and Imperial Thought of Philip Francis', *Past & Present* 209 (2010): 117–48.

173. Anon., *A Short Vindication of the French Treaty* (London, 1787), 47.

174. William Knox, *Helps to a Right Decision Upon the Merits of the Late Treaty of Commerce with France* (London, 1787), 32–4.

175. Leland J. Bellot, *William Knox: The Life and Thought of an Eighteenth-Century Imperialist* (Austin TX, 1977), 200.

176. Anon., *Short Vindication*, 48.

177. Anon., *The Necessity and Policy of the Commercial Treaty with France, &c. Considered. By Anglicanus* (London, 1787), 59, 61.

178. Knox, *Helps to a Right Decision*, 37.

179. *Parliamentary History*, vol. 26, cols 559–60. Lansdowne wondered privately if Eden's treaty had been 'done upon a system of eternal peace'. Baring NP1.B1, William Petty, marquis of Lansdowne to Francis Baring, 1 Nov. 1786. On Shelburne's interest in European peace in the late 1780s, see Emmanuelle de Champs, *Enlightenment and Utility: Bentham in French, Bentham in France* (Cambridge, 2015), 97–103; Richard Whatmore, 'Shelburne and Perpetual Peace: Small States, Commerce, and International Relations within the Bowood Circle', in *An Enlightenment Statesman in Whig Britain: Lord Shelburne in Context, 1737–1805*, ed. Nigel Aston and Clarissa Campbell Orr (Woodbridge, 2011), 249–73.

180. Failure in Parliament might even bring down the Pitt ministry, which was better disposed to good relations than an opposition administration would be. See Marie Donaghay, 'The Maréchal de Castries and the Anglo-French Commercial Negotiations of 1786–1787', *Historical Journal* 22, no. 2 (1979): 295–312, 311.

181. See notably O'Bryen, *View of the Treaty of Commerce*, 3–5; [Joseph Richardson], *A Complete Investigation of Mr Eden's Treaty, as It May Affect the Commerce, the Revenue, or the General Policy of Great Britain* (London, 1787), 3–11. For analysis of Whig caricature of the treaty, see Pascal Dupuy, 'Image et images des traités', in *Le négoce de la paix*, ed. Jessenne, Morieux and Dupuy, 111–24.

182. Anon., *A Letter from a Manchester Manufacturer to the Right Honourable Charles James Fox, on His Political Opposition to the Commercial Treaty with France* (Manchester, 1787), 13–15; Knox, *Helps to a Right Decision*, 25; Sir Nathanial Wraxall, *A Short Review of the Political State of Great-Britain at the Commencement of the Year One Thousand Seven Hundred and Eighty-Seven* (London, 1787), 49. It is significant in this light that Decker's *Essay on the Causes of the Decline of the Foreign Trade* (1744), which bemoaned the scuttling of the 1713 treaty, was republished in 1787.

183. *Parliamentary History*, vol. 26, cols 402, 406, 410–12, 435, 448–58. See also Richardson, *Complete Investigation of Mr Eden's Treaty*, 27–45.

184. See, for instance, *Parliamentary History*, vol. 26, cols 372, 389, 424. See also Anon., *An Answer to the Woollen Draper's Letter on the French Treaty* (London, 1787), 18. On the

changing status of the Portugal trade, see BL Add MS 34462 fols 1–12, 33–4, 258–65. Pitt was, in fact, open to abrogating the Methuen Treaty in favour of French wines. See Pitt to Eden, 10 May 1786, in Eden, *Journal and Correspondence*, vol. 1, 481–6.

185. Smith, *Lectures on Jurisprudence*, 392.
186. *Parliamentary History*, vol. 26, col. 386. The logic was in line with his Commutation Act, which lowered the duty on tea from 119 per cent to 12.5 per cent, with a view to increasing legal consumption and thus revenue. See W.O. Henderson, 'The Anglo-French Commercial Treaty of 1786', *Economic History Review* 10, no. 1 (1957): 104–12.
187. *Parliamentary History*, vol. 26, col. 389. Also Anon., *Necessity and Policy of the Commercial Treaty*, 44; Anon., *Short Vindication*, 36–9; Baring NP1.B1, Lansdowne to Baring, 11 Nov. 1785.
188. John Hardman, *Overture to Revolution: The 1787 Assembly of Notables and the Crisis of France's Old Regime* (Oxford, 2010), 7–11, 33, 40.
189. AAE MD Ang 65 fols 9–21, Dupont de Nemours, 'Observations sur les motifs particuliers qui peuvent déterminer le traité de commerce'. See also J.F. Bosher, *The Single Duty Project: A Study of the Movement for a French Customs Union in the Eighteenth Century* (London, 1964); Hardman, *Overture to Revolution*, 20–55.
190. BL Add MS 34462 fols 48–51, 69–77.
191. BL Add MS 34462 fols 24–8, 33–4, 48–51, 61–8.
192. Murphy, *Vergennes*, 454–5, 457; Frank Fox, 'Negotiating with the Russians: Ambassador Segur's Mission to Saint-Petersburg, 1784–1789', *French Historical Studies* 7, no. 1 (1971): 47–71. See also AAE MD France 584 fols 93–9, 'Notice biographique sur le comte de Vergennes'.
193. John Ehrman, *The British Government and Commercial Negotiations with Europe, 1783–1793* (Cambridge, 1962).
194. *Parliamentary History*, vol. 26, col. 385. Dundas echoed this view (cols 444–5).
195. Adam Smith, *Additions and Corrections to the First and Second Editions of Dr. Adam Smith's Inquiry into the Nature and Causes of the Wealth of Nations* (n.p., n.d. [1784]), 5. See also idem, *An Inquiry into the Nature and Causes of the Wealth of Nations*, ed. R.H. Campbell, A.S. Skinner, and W.B. Todd, 2 vols (Indianapolis, 1981), vol. 1, 496.
196. Scott, 'Adam Smith at Downing Street'.
197. For a contrary position, seeing Smith's political economy as a defining element in the treaty, see Richard Whatmore, *Against War and Empire: Geneva, Britain and France in the Eighteenth Century* (New Haven, 2012), 181–2, 184.
198. *Parliamentary History*, vol. 26, col. 444.
199. William Eden, *Four Letters to the Earl of Carlisle* (London, 1779); idem, *A Fifth Letter to the Earl of Carlisle* (London, 1780). Eden's thinking is explored at greater length in Chapter 5, in the context of the American War when it first evolved in this direction.
200. Oscar Browning, 'The Treaty of Commerce Between England and France, 1786', *Transactions of the Royal Historical Society*, new series, 2 (1885): 349–64, 358; François Dumas, *Étude sur le traité de commerce de 1786 entre la France et l'Angleterre* (Toulouse, 1904), 59.
201. For references to agricultural primacy, see notably, AAE CP Ang 556 fol. 95, Rayneval, 'Lu au Conseil d'État et approuvé le 21 mai 1786'; and AAE MD Ang 74 fol. 78, Rayneval, 'Réflexions détachées sur notre commerce avec l'Ang^{re}'.
202. Marie Donaghay, 'The Exchange of Products of the Soil and Industrial Goods in the Anglo-French Commercial Treaty of 1786', *Journal of European Economic History* 19 (1990): 377–401, 379, 384. Only a general prohibition on imported hardware might have checked British contraband, which came in through the Low Countries and Germany, but such a drastic measure would damage trade with these valuable markets. AAE MD Ang 74 fols 78, Rayneval, 'Réflexions détachées'. Donaghay demolished the once widely accepted view that the treaty was negotiated on the French side by naive and ill-informed officials who conceded far too much. For the older view, see Camille Bloch, 'Le traité de commerce de 1786 entre la France et l'Angleterre', *Études sur l'histoire économique de la France*,

1760–1789 (Paris, 1900): 239–69, 268; Dumas, *Étude sur le traité de commerce de 1786*. For Donaghay's views, see also idem, 'Calonne and the Anglo-French Commercial Treaty of 1786', *Journal of Modern History* 50, no. 3, supplement (1978): D1,157–84; and idem, 'Textiles and the Anglo-French Commercial Treaty of 1786', *Textile History* 13, no. 2 (1982): 205–24.

203. In Jeff Horn's words, the commercial treaty was meant to 'coerce the French into being more competitive'. See Horn, *Path Not Taken*, 77; Donaghay, 'Calonne and the Anglo-French Commercial Treaty', D1, 158.

204. AAE CP Ang 546 fols 23–54, [Calonne to Vergennes], 'Mémoire', 18 Nov. 1783.

205. TNA PC 1/123/38, 'Travail sur les sucres rafinés, remis par M. Boyetet'.

206. Pierre-Samuel Dupont de Nemours, *Lettre à la Chambre du Commerce de Normandie sur le mémoire qu'elle a publié relativement au traité de commerce avec l'Angleterre* (Rouen, 1788).

207. Hont, *Jealousy of Trade*, 354–88.

208. Most of his memoranda are collected at AAE MD Ang 65.

209. Dupont de Nemours, *Lettre à la Chambre du Commerce*, 75. For Quesnay's critique, see 'Remarques sur l'opinion de l'auteur de l'*Esprit des loix* concernant les colonies', *Journal de l'agriculture, du commerce et des finances* (Apr. 1766), 4–34.

210. According to Fox, 'where France has the advantage (as in wines, brandies, vinegars etc) the advantage is permanent and certain; where we have it (as in cutlery, cotton etc) it is accidental and temporary; they may gain our skill, but we can never gain their soil and climate'. See BL Add MS 47501 fol. 88, Fox to William Cavendish-Bentinck, duke of Portland, 18 Nov. 1786. See also Richardson, *Complete Investigation of Mr Eden's Treaty*, 21–3.

211. In British ministerial propaganda, I found just one mention of lower prices for consumers as an advantage of the treaty. See Anon., *Answer to the Woollen Draper's Letter*, 26.

2. A SYSTEM OF COLLECTIVE RESTRAINT: SPANISH AMERICA, FREEDOM OF TRADE, AND THE PROBLEM OF THE SOUTH SEA COMPANY

1. *Parliamentary History*, vol. 10, col. 771. See Richard Pares, *War and Trade in the West Indies 1739–1763* (Oxford, 1936), 139–40.

2. *Parliamentary History*, vol. 10, col. 772.

3. By a 'regime' I mean a system of governance overlaying the individual sovereignty of states, regulating matters of common concern, institutionalised either formally or informally, and imposing collective restraints on those it encompasses. This term, coined by international relations scholars, has been fruitfully used to describe the Holy Roman Empire in this period. See Andreas Osiander, 'Sovereignty, International Relations, and the Westphalian Myth', *International Organization* 55, no. 2 (2001): 251–87.

4. Ana Crespo Solana, 'A Change of Ideology in Imperial Spain? Spanish Commercial Policy with America and the Change of Dynasty (1648–1740)', in *Ideology and Foreign Policy in Early Modern Europe (1650–1750)*, ed. David Onnekink and Gijs Rommelse (Farnham, 2011), 226–7; Mark A. Thomson, 'Louis XIV and the War of the Spanish Succession', in *William III and Louis XIV*, ed. Ragnhild Hatton and J.S. Bromley (Liverpool, 1968), 140–61.

5. Simms, *Three Victories*.

6. Shovlin, 'War and Peace'.

7. Andrea Finkelstein, *Harmony and the Balance: An Intellectual History of Seventeenth-Century Economic Thought* (Ann Arbor, 2000), 65; Horn, *Economic Development*.

8. Stapelbroek, '"The Long Peace"'.

9. As Newcastle recognised. *Parliamentary History*, vol. 10, cols 772–3.

10. J.G.A. Pocock, *Barbarism and Religion: The Enlightenment of Edward Gibbon 1737–1764* (Cambridge, 1999), 106–14.

11. William Paterson, 'A Proposal to Plant a Colony in Darien; to Protect the Indians against Spain; and to Open the Trade of South America to All Nations', in idem, *The Writings of*

William Paterson, ed. Saxe Bannister, 2nd edn, 3 vols (London, 1859), vol. 1, 115–60; William Paterson to Robert Harley, 31 Jan. 1702, in *Manuscripts of His Grace the Duke of Portland, Preserved at Welbeck Abbey*, 10 vols (London, 1897), vol. 4, 33.

12. Deringer, *Calculated Values*, 81–3, 155.

13. Douglas Watt, *The Price of Scotland: Darien, Union and the Wealth of Nations* (Edinburgh, 2006), 36–45, 91–2, 96–102; David Armitage, 'The Scottish Vision of Empire: Intellectual Origins of the Darien Venture', in *A Union for Empire: Political Thought and the British Union of 1707*, ed. John Robertson (Cambridge, 1995), 97–118.

14. *Manuscripts of His Grace the Duke of Portland*, vol. 4, 18, 28, 33, 43–5, 60, 64, 67–8, 78, 330–1, 396–7. Harley considered employing Paterson as the ministry's chief propagandist before his choice fell on Defoe. See J.A. Downie, *Robert Harley and the Press: Propaganda and Public Opinion in the Age of Swift and Defoe* (Cambridge, 1979), 60.

15. Andrew Forrester, *The Man Who Saw the Future: William Paterson's Vision of Free Trade* (New York, 2004), 24–7.

16. Louis Dermigny, 'Escales, échelles et ports francs au moyen âge et aux temps moderns', in idem, *Les grandes escales* (Brussels, 1974), 521–626; Tazzara, *Free Port of Livorno*.

17. Paterson, 'Proposal to Plant a Colony in Darien', 153.

18. Paterson's vision also owed something to the Hartlib circle of the mid-seventeenth century, whose members were later influential in the Royal Society. They embraced schemes for improvement, touted the possibility of open-ended economic expansion, and were noted advocates of banks and paper money schemes. See Wennerlind, *Casualties of Credit*, 44–79.

19. Trivellato, *Familiarity of Strangers*, 108.

20. Paterson, 'Proposal to Plant a Colony in Darien', 153.

21. Ibid., 148, 155.

22. Ana Crespo Solana, 'The Spanish Colonial Empire in an Age of Transition: Political Discontinuity and Commercial Interests at the Time of the Treaty of Utrecht', in *Peace Was Made Here: The Treaties of Utrecht, Rastatt and Baden, 1713–1714*, ed. Renger de Bruin and Maarten Brinkman (Petersberg, 2013), 42–8; Stanley J. Stein and Barbara H. Stein, *Silver, Trade, and War: Spain and America in the Making of Early Modern Europe* (Baltimore, 2000), 57–67, 65.

23. Ibid., 3–105.

24. An eighth of London's vital woollen export was destined for Cádiz, and about 8 per cent of England's total exports. It was comparably important to the Dutch, and still more significant for French merchants, who controlled about 40 per cent of the trade. Michel Morineau, *Incroyables gazettes et fabuleux métaux: Les retours des trésors américains d'après les gazettes hollandaises (XVIe–XVIIIe siècles)* (Paris, 1985), 265–70.

25. Graciela Márquez, 'Commercial Monopolies and External Trade', in *Cambridge Economic History of Latin America, vol. 1, The Colonial Era and the Short Nineteenth Century*, ed. Victor Bulmer-Thomas, John Coatsworth, and Roberto Cortes-Conde (Cambridge, 2006), 417–20; Leticia Arroyo Abad, Elwyn Davies, and Jan Luiten van Zanden, 'Between Conquest and Independence: Real Wages and Demographic Change in Spanish America, 1530–1820', *Explorations in Economic History* 49 (2012): 149–66; John Tutino, *Making a New World: Founding Capitalism in the Bajío and Spanish North America* (Durham, NC, 2011), 183.

26. Harry E. Cross, 'South American Bullion Production and Exports, 1550–1750', in *Precious Metals in the Later Medieval and Early Modern Worlds*, ed. J.F. Richards (Durham, NC, 1983), 397–423. Precious metals made up nearly four-fifths of Spanish America's exports. See A. García-Baquero González, 'American Gold and Silver in the Eighteenth Century: From Fascination to Accounting', in *Global Connections and Monetary History, 1470–1800*, ed. Dennis O. Flynn, Arturo Giraldez, and Richard von Glahn (Aldershot, 2003), 107–22, 107.

27. Dennis O. Flynn, 'Arbitrage, China, and World Trade in the Early Modern Period', *Journal of the Economic and Social History of the Orient* 38, no. 4 (1995): 429–48.

28. Nuala Zahedieh, 'The Merchants of Port Royal, Jamaica, and the Spanish Contraband Trade, 1655–92', *William and Mary Quarterly*, 3rd series, 43 (1986): 570–93; G.V.

Scammell, ' "A Very Profitable and Advantageous Trade": British Smuggling in the Iberian Americas Circa 1500–1750', *Itinerario* 24, nos 3–4 (2000): 135–72. The Asiento was the only branch of the slave trade in which captives could be exchanged directly for silver. In the cash-strapped Caribbean, slavers had to accept sugar or other commodities in payment. See Cary, *An Essay on the State of England*, 76.

29. Anon., *The Duke of Anjou's Succession Considered, as to Its Legality and Consequences*, 2nd edn (Dublin, 1701), 17–18, 30. For an overview of the commercial stakes of the war, see Aaron A. Olivas, 'Globalizing the War of the Spanish Succession: Conflict, Trade, and Political Alliances in Early Bourbon Spanish America', in *The War of the Spanish Succession: New Perspectives*, ed. Mathias Pohlig and Michael Schaich (Oxford, 2018), 411–30.

30. 'Traité d'alliance entre l'Empereur, le Roi d'Angleterre, & les États Généraux des Provinces Unies', in *Mémoires pour servir à l'histoire du XVIIIe siècle*, ed. Lamberty, vol. 1, 626.

31. Charles Frostin, 'Les Pontchartrain et la pénétration commerciale française en Amérique espagnole (1690–1715)', *Revue historique* 245, no. 2 (1971): 307–36.

32. Henry Kamen, *The War of Succession in Spain 1700–15* (London, 1969), 145–6, 149.

33. Stein and Stein, *Silver, Trade, and War*, 85. See also Morineau, *Incroyables gazettes*.

34. AAE MD France 2018 fols 111–15, 'Mémoire du sieur Mesnager'. On Mesnager's career, see Bély, *Espions et ambassadeurs*, 576–95.

35. Guillaume Hanotin, *Ambassadeur de deux couronnes: Amelot et les Bourbons entre commerce et diplomatie* (Madrid, 2018).

36. Guillaume Hanotin, 'Trade and Men of Trade in the Conduct of Louis XIV's Diplomacy', in *War of the Spanish Succession*, ed. Pohlig and Schaich, 85–100.

37. Kammerling Smith, 'Structuring Politics'; Schaeper, *French Council of Commerce*.

38. Charles Carrière, *Négociants marseillais au XVIIIe siècle: Contribution à l'étude des économies maritimes*, 2 vols (Marseille, 1973), vol. 1, 238–43. One of the first acts of the Bureau was to ask the king to adopt this term for large-scale merchants. The distinction was officially embraced in the tax rolls of the *dixième* of 1710.

39. William Beik, *Absolutism and Society in Seventeenth-Century France: State Power and Provincial Aristocracy in Languedoc* (Cambridge, 1985).

40. Kwass, *Privilege and the Politics of Taxation*.

41. Viewed from yet another perspective, using in Marxist social thought, France did not become a truly capitalist society until the twentieth century, when its predominant peasant class came to be fully integrated into and dependent upon markets for its economic survival and reproduction. See Stephen Miller, 'Peasant Farming in Eighteenth- and Nineteenth-Century France and the Transition to Capitalism Under Charles de Gaulle', in *Case Studies in the Origins of Capitalism*, ed. Xavier Lafrance and Charles Post (London, 2019), 87–109. My view is that capitalism is not a total and coherent system. A nation can be capitalist in some important respects and non-capitalist in others. Take contemporary China, for example. In its integration into global systems of commerce and finance, China is capitalist. But major sectors of its economy and society are not fully integrated into capitalist structures.

42. For the general argument that feudal arrangements proved compatible with a high degree of commercialisation in early modern Europe, see Shami Ghosh, 'Rural Economies and Transitions to Capitalism: Germany and England Compared (*c*. 1200–*c*. 1800)', *Journal of Agrarian Change* 16 (2016): 255–90; Alessandro Stanziani, 'Revisiting Russian Serfdom: Bonded Peasants and Market Dynamics, 1600s–1800s', *International Labor and Working-Class History* 78 (2010), 12–27.

43. On the kind of domestic underdevelopment this arrangement could entail, see Jean-Yves Grenier, *L'économie d'ancien régime: Un monde de l'échange et de l'incertitude* (Paris, 1996).

44. This is the point at which Julia Adams's comparative analysis of France, Britain, and the Dutch Republic breaks down. Although merchants were never fully integrated into the 'familial state' as it evolved in France, the monarchy nevertheless sought to foster trade, and did so with great success in the eighteenth century, as the rapid growth of international and colonial trade demonstrates. See Adams, *Familial State*.

45. E.W. Dahlgren, *Les relations commerciales et maritimes entre la France et les côtes de l'Océan Pacifique: Le commerce de la Mer du Sud jusqu'à la Paix d'Utrecht* (Paris, 1909), 335, 338–9. André Lespagnol, *Messieurs de Saint-Malo: Une élite négociante au temps de Louis XIV* (Rennes, 2011).

46. Carlos Daniel Malamud Rikles, *Cádiz y Saint Malo en el comercio colonial peruano (1698– 1725)* (Cádiz, 1986), 65–7, 80–1, 280; Stein and Stein, *Silver, War, and Trade*, 113.

47. Paul W. Mapp, *The Elusive West and the Contest for Empire, 1713–1763* (Chapel Hill, 2011), 131–2.

48. Guy Rowlands, *Dangerous and Dishonest Men: The International Bankers of Louis XIV's France* (Basingstoke, 2015).

49. James Vernon to George Stepney, 13 Feb. 1702, in James Vernon, *Letters Illustrative of the Reign of William III from 1696 to 1708 Addressed to the Duke of Shrewsbury from James Vernon, Esq., Secretary of State*, ed. G.P.R. James, 3 vols (London, 1841), vol. 3, 176–7.

50. Anon., *The Dangers of Europe, from the Growing Power of France* (London, 1702), 60–2.

51. John Le Wright, *Two Proposals Becoming England at this Juncture to Undertake: One for Securing a Colony in the West Indies . . . and the Other, for Advancing Merchandize, and the Crown Revenue to at Least 40000l. p. An.* (n.p., 1706). For nearly identical arguments, see Anon., *An Account of What Will Do; or, An Equivalent for Thoulon* (London, 1707). See also Anon., *A Letter to Sir William Robinson, in Relation to a Proposal for a Trade to the Spanish West-Indies* (London, 1707); *Observator* (29 Oct. 1707). See also Satsuma, *Britain and Colonial Maritime War*, 86–7.

52. TNA SP 94/76, Stanhope to Hedges, 5 Oct. 1706, unfoliated. A new treaty project expedited in November 1706, which hinted at direct trade, still did not satisfy the general. See Frances Gardiner Davenport (ed.), *European Treaties Bearing on the History of the United States, vol. 3, 1698–1715* (Gloucester, MA, 1967 [1917]), 124–5. It seems possible that Charles did not appreciate the strategic potential of the Spanish-American trade. See Leopold Auer, 'A Habsburg Overseas Empire after 1700? Contemporary Austrian Views on the Colonial Dimension of the Spanish Succession', in *War of the Spanish Succession*, ed. Pohlig and Schaich, 411–30. If so, this would soon change. See Michael Hochedlinger, *Austria's Wars of Emergence, 1683–1797* (London, 2015), 196–7.

53. AAE CP France 173 fols 106–11, 'Traité de commerce fait à Barcelone le 10 juillet 1707'. See Williams, *Stanhope*, 60–1.

54. Josep M. Delgado Ribas, *Dinámicas imperiales (1650–1796): España, América y Europa en el cambio institucional del sistema colonial español* (Barcelona, 2007), 53–4.

55. Robert B. Ekelund and Robert D. Tollison, *Mercantilism as a Rent-Seeking Society: Economic Regulation in Historical Perspective* (College Station, TX, 1982).

56. Niels Steensgaard, *Carracks, Caravans and Companies: The Structural Crisis in the European-Asian Trade in the Early 17th Century* (Lund, 1973); Stern, '"A Politie of Civill & Military Power"'.

57. The pointlessness of conquest was a central theme of Jean-Baptiste Dubos, *Les interêts de l'Angleterre, malentendus dans la guerre présente*, corrected edn (Amsterdam, 1704), 226–38. The English and the Dutch derived more benefit from an America in Spanish hands, he argued, than they could from an English Mexico.

58. Dahlgren, *Relations commerciales*, 575–6; Georges Scelle, *La Traite négrière aux Indes de Castille, contrats et traités d'Assiento*, 2 vols (Paris, 1906), vol. 2, 478–80. See also Alimento and Stapelbroek, 'Trade and Treaties', in *Politics of Commercial Treaties*, ed. idem, 1–75, 20–2.

59. Kamen, *War of Succession*, 158.

60. Despite the hopes invested in it, the Guinea Company was a commercial failure. See Léon Vignols, 'L'Asiento français (1701–1713) et anglais (1713–1750) et le commerce franco-espagnol vers 1700 à 1730', *Revue d'histoire économique et sociale* 17, no. 3/4 (1929): 403–36.

61. AAE CP Hollande 214 fols 31–2, Mesnager, 'Mémoire touchant le commerce de l'Amérique espagnole et les moyens de l'assurer esgallement à touttes les nations de l'Europe', 12 Jan.

1708; CP Hollande 213 fols 102–13, 'Analyse de la négociation de M. Mesnager en Hollande de janvier à février 1708'. See also CP Espagne 179 fol. 265, 'Mémoire du Sr. Mesnager de quelques explications touchant le commerce des Indes qui pourront etre utiles à M. Amelot'.

62. José Manuel Santos Pérez, 'Trade, the Spanish Empire, and the War of the Spanish Succession', in *War of the Spanish Succession*, ed. Pohlig and Schaich, 395–410.

63. Dahlgren, *Relations commerciales*, 498–500; Bély, *Espions et ambassadeurs*, 580.

64. Dahlgren, *Relations commerciales*, 515–18; Kamen, *War of Succession*, 153. Recall that Mesnager had once been a member of this community.

65. AN F^{12} 644, Amelot, 'Mémoire', Apr. 1722; Dahlgren, *Relations commerciales*, 518.

66. Ibid., 520–1.

67. See B.W. Hill, 'The Change of Government and the "Loss of the City", 1710–1711', *Economic History Review* 24, no. 3 (1971): 395–413; and John G. Sperling, *The South Sea Company* (Boston, 1962), 3–5.

68. *An Act for Making Good Deficiencies, and Satisfying the Publick Debts; And for Erecting a Corporation to Carry on a Trade to the South-Seas* (London, 1711), 433.

69. Though Paterson pressed Harley to secure 'two or three cautionary places in South America', he played no role in the establishment of the company, nor was his expansive vision of free trade canvassed. See Paterson to Harley, 4 Sept. 1710, in *Manuscripts of His Grace the Duke of Portland*, vol. 4, 584–5.

70. AAE CP Ang 233 fols 87–9, 'Demandes préliminaires', July 1711.

71. Steve Pincus, 'Addison's Empire: Whig Conceptions of Empire in the Early 18th Century', *Parliamentary History* 31, no. 1 (2012): 99–117; idem, 'Empire and the Treaty of Utrecht (1713)', in *New Worlds?*, ed. Schmidt-Voges and Crespo Solana, 153–75.

72. Francis Hare, *A Letter to a Member of the October-Club: Shewing, that to Yield Spain to the Duke of Anjou by a Peace, Wou'd be the Ruin of Great Britain*, 2nd edn (London, 1711). See also Anon., *Caveat to the Treaters; or, The Modern Schemes of Partition Examin'd* (London, 1711), 51, 55–7.

73. Arthur Maynwaring, *Remarks upon the Present Negotiations of Peace Begun between Britain and France* (London, 1711), 15–16; idem, *A Letter to a High-Churchman, in Answer to a Pamphlet, Intitled, Reasons Why this Nation Should Put a Speedy End to this Expensive War* (London, 1711), 26.

74. Daniel Defoe, *Reasons Why this Nation Ought to Put a Speedy End to this Expensive War* (London, 1711), 45–6. See also BL Add MS 70291 fols 19–20, Daniel Defoe, 'Proposall for a Settlement Upon the Coast of America', 23 July 1711.

75. In Colbert de Torcy's words, Prior explained that the queen 'would not find it at all unsatisfactory that France also obtain from the King of Spain establishments in the South Sea'. See L.G. Wickham Legg, 'Torcy's Account of Matthew Prior's Negotiations at Fontainebleau in July 1711', *English Historical Review* 29, no. 115 (1914): 525–32. In Prior's own recollection of his language: 'I see nothing in this demand . . . that forbids France obtaining some collateral advantage of the same kind from Spain.' See *Manuscripts of His Grace the Duke of Portland*, vol. 5, 38.

76. Herman Moll, *A View of the Coasts, Countrys, & Islands within the Limits of the South Sea Company*, 2nd edn (London, n.d.), 231–2.

77. Wickham Legg, 'Torcy's Account of Matthew Prior's Negotiations', 530.

78. AAE CP Espagne 208 fol. 22, Vendôme to Louis XIV, 6 July 1711.

79. AAE CP Ang 233 fol. 75–82, Antoine Pecquet, 'Mémoire pour répondre aux demandes que les Anglais font avant l'ouverture des conférences pour la paix', 1711.

80. AN G^7 1697, register 'Matières de commerce', fols 280–91, Mesnager, 'Nouveau Plan de Commerce aux Indes Occidentales dans lequel toutes les Nations de l'Europe trouveront un égal traitement et une réelle sûreté de son exécution'. See also AAE CP Ang 233 fols 220–8, Mesnager to Colbert de Torcy, 5 Sept. 1711.

81. AAE CP Ang 235 fol. 312ff., 'Instructions pour le Sr Mesnager', 3 Aug. 1711.

82. AAE CP Ang 233 fols 202–4, Mesnager to Colbert de Torcy, 25 Aug. 1711.

83. The British subsequently dropped the claim for tariff preferences in Spain in face of Dutch fury, but obdurately refused to share the Asiento with them. BL Add MS 22205 fols 353–5, Henry St John to John Robinson, bishop of Bristol and Thomas Wentworth, earl of Strafford, 26 Mar. 1712; fols 373–4, St John to Bristol and Strafford, 8 Apr. 1712; fols 379–81, Bristol and Strafford to St John, 8 Apr. 1712.

84. AAE MD Amérique 24 fols 57–62, 'Mémoire concernant les colonies, le commerce, et la navigation, pour Mess.ʳˢ les plénipotentiaires du Roy', 2 Jan. 1712. See also Dale Miquelon, 'Envisioning the French Empire: Utrecht, 1711–1713', *French Historical Studies* 24, no. 4 (2001): 653–77.

85. AAE MD Ang 33 fols 158–62, Mesnager, 'Mémoire secret', enclosed with idem, Mesnager to Nicolas Desmaretz, 23 Jan. 1713.

86. *Treaty of Peace and Friendship between . . . Princess Anne and . . . Prince Philip the Fifth, the Catholic King of Spain, concluded at Utrecht the 2/13 Day of July, 1713* (London, 1714), art. 8.

87. AAE CP France 352 fols 16–23, [Gérard Lévesque de Champeaux], 'Mémoires utils dans la conjuncture des préliminaires de la paix, d'un futur congrès, et d'une ambassade en France, par raport au Commerce de France', Aug. 1727.

88. Virginia Léon Sanz and Niccolò Guasti, 'The Treaty of Asiento between Spain and Great Britain', in *Politics of Commercial Treaties*, ed. Alimento and Stapelbroek, 151–72.

89. Richard Lodge, 'The Treaty of Seville (1729)', *Transactions of the Royal Historical Society* 16 (1933): 1–43.

90. Vera Lee Brown, 'The South Sea Company and Contraband Trade', *American Historical Review* 31, no. 4 (1926): 662–78.

91. AAE MD France 1990 fols 63–72, Louis Ploumier de la Boulay, 'Mémoire concernant le commerce maritime par rapport aux affaires étrangères'.

92. BNF naf 23085, 'Recueil de différens mémoires, concernant le commerce et la marine marchande et militaire, donnez aux ministres dans les années 1728 et 1729, avec le traité de Séville'. See the memoranda collected at AAE CP Ang 364 in anticipation of the congress.

93. Jean-Frédéric Phélypeaux, comte de Maurepas, 'Mémoire et considérations générales sur le commerce de France, présentés à sa majesté par M. le comte de Maurepas', in idem, *Mémoires du comte de Maurepas, ministre de la marine, &c.* ed. Jean Louis Giraud Soulavie, 3 vols, 2nd edn (Paris, 1792), vol. 3, 237–9. The point is reaffirmed in idem, 'Situation du commerce exterieur du roïaume exposée à Sa Majesté par M. le comte de Maurepas, Secrétaire d'État aïant le departement de la marine dans le conseil roïal du commerce tenu à Versailles le 3 Octobre 1730', reproduced in Maurice Filion, *Maurepas, ministre de Louis XV (1715–1749)* (Montréal, 1967), 160–1.

94. AAE MD France 494 fols 162–84, 'Mémoire sur le parti à prendre pour une alliance'. The text is annotated approvingly by Chauvelin. See also AAE MD France 1990 fols 93–101, 'Commerce du dedans et du dehors du Royaume', and the annotations which reject its suggestion that it was time to throw off the constraints of Utrecht. See also Arthur McCandless Wilson, *French Foreign Policy during the Administration of Cardinal Fleury 1726–1743* (Cambridge, MA, 1936), 56–9.

95. Though Charles VI had failed to secure the Spanish Succession, Austria had made territorial gains, and in its willingness to ally with a revanchist Spain in 1725 seemed ready to throw all Europe into war. See Jeremy Black, 'French Foreign Policy in the Age of Fleury Reassessed', *English Historical Review* 103 (1988): 359–84.

96. Stone, *The Genesis of the French Revolution*, 57. Unlike Stone, I see the position of the eighteenth-century French monarchy as defensive rather than aggrandising, a break from rather than a continuation of seventeenth-century trends.

97. He set out systematically to inform himself in the economic domain, gathering information on trade and manufactures solicited from ambassadors, officials in the Bureau of Commerce and the naval ministry, from merchants, and Compagnie des Indes insiders. See, for example, AAE MD France 1274 fols 106–7, Louis Fagon to Chauvelin, 24 Jan. 1732; fols 119–20, Palerme to Chauvelin, 26 Jan. 1732; AAE MD France 1263 fol. 203, circular, 8 Feb. 1729.

98. Jeremy Black, 'British Neutrality in the War of the Polish Succession, 1733–1735', *International History Review* 8, no. 3 (1986): 345–66.

99. AAE CP France 352 fols 16–23, 'Mémoires utils dans la conjuncture des préliminaires'.

100. Among the leading members were the abbé Henri-Charles Arnauld de Pomponne, who had served in the foreign ministry under his brother-in-law, Jean-Baptiste Colbert de Torcy; Dominique-Claude de Barberie, marquis de Saint-Contest, plenipotentiary to the Congress of Rastatt; and François de Franquetot, duc de Coigny, who sat on the Regency *conseil de guerre* and turned down the Madrid embassy. It was a school for future ambassadors and ministers including the marquis d'Argenson (foreign minister, 1744–47), the comte de Plélo (ambassador to Denmark 1729–34), and the younger Saint-Contest (foreign minister 1751–54). See Nick Childs, *A Political Academy in Paris, 1724–1731: The Entresol and its Members* (Oxford, 2000).

101. Arsenal MS 6193, Jean-Roland Malet, 'Mémoire sur le commerce de l'Amérique', Feb. 1732. On Malet, see Margaret and Richard Bonney, *Jean-Roland Malet: Premier historien des finances de la monarchie française* (Paris, 1993). On his influence with Contrôleur Général Orry, see Jon Demarest Rudd, 'Philibert Orry and France's Contrôle Général, 1730–1745', PhD thesis, Georgetown University, 1988, 194.

102. AAE CP France 352 fols 16–23, 'Mémoires utils dans la conjuncture des préliminaires'.

103. BNF naf 23085, 'Recueil de différens mémoires, concernant le Commerce et la Marine marchande et militaire, donnez aux ministres dans les années 1728 et 1729'.

104. NRO Bradfer-Lawrence MS T3/3/29, Charles Townshend to Horatio Walpole, 24 June 1728.

105. J.H. Plumb, *Sir Robert Walpole: The King's Minister* (Boston, 1961), 189–90.

106. NRO Bradfer-Lawrence MS T3/3/29, Townshend to Horatio Walpole, 24 June 1728.

107. Ibid.

108. Brown, 'South Sea Company and Contraband Trade', 667.

109. NRO Bradfer-Lawrence MS T3/3/29, Townshend to Horatio Walpole, 24 June 1728.

110. BL Add MS 25544, General Court, 16 June 1732 fols 105–6. On Tyrry, see Kevin Terry, *The Terrys of Cork: Merchant Gentry 1180–1644* (Andover, Hampshire, 2013), 108.

111. BL Add MS 25544 fol. 117, 8 Sept. 1732; fol. 118, letter in explanation of the first, 28 Nov. 1732.

112. Sperling, *South Sea Company*, 45.

113. BL Add MS 25545, General Courts, 22 Mar. 1733, 9 and 25 May 1733; BL Add MS 25545 fols 36, 41–2, 'Petition of the Company to George II', 4 July 1734.

114. BL Add MS 25545 fol. 31, General Court, 10 Apr. 1734.

115. George Lyttelton, *Considerations upon the Present State of our Affairs* (London, 1739), 4.

116. Anon., *The Original Series of Wisdom and Policy, Manifested in a Review of Our Foreign Negotiations and Transactions for Several Years Past* (London, 1739). See Philip Woodfine, *Britannia's Glories: The Walpole Ministry and the 1739 War with Spain* (Woodbridge, 1998), 50. Ten British ships were seized by the *guardacostas* in 1731, one in 1732, six in 1733, one in 1734, nine in 1735, one in 1736, and eleven in 1737. See Pares, *War and Trade*, 16.

117. Jean O. McLachlan, *Trade and Peace with Old Spain, 1667–1750: A Study of the Influence of Commerce on Anglo-Spanish Diplomacy in the First Half of the Eighteenth Century* (Cambridge, 1940), 177, n78.

118. [Horatio Walpole], *The Grand Question, Whether War, or No War, with Spain, Impartially Consider'd: In Defence of the Present Measures against Those That Delight in War* (London, 1739), 8.

119. CUL Ch(H) Papers 89/11, [John Crookshanks], 'A View of our Trade with Spain, & of our Annual Imports & Exports in the Following Periods, from the year 1696 to 1729 inclusive, with the different Events Affecting Trade'. On Crookshanks's role as an adviser to Walpole, see Deringer, *Calculated Values*, 163–7. Walpole nominated him secretary to the British commissioners appointed after the treaty of Seville to treat Spanish complaints over illicit trade.

120. CUL Ch(H) Papers 73/80/1–11, 'A View of the depredations and ravages committed by the Spaniards on the British trade and navigation'.
121. Woodfine, *Britannia's Glories*.
122. AAE CP Espagne 449 fols 70–4, 'Projet d'un Traité de Commerce entre la France et l'Espagne', 14 Sept. 1738. See also Pares, *War and Trade*, 136–7.
123. *Parliamentary History*, vol. 11, col. 87 (15 Nov. 1739). Whig visions of conquest in the Caribbean are comprehensively explored in Steve Pincus, 'Patriot Fever: Imperial Political Economy and the Causes of the War of Jenkins Ear', unpublished paper.
124. *Parliamentary History*, vol. 11, cols 16–18 (15 Nov. 1739).
125. [Hugh Hume, Lord Polwarth], *A State of the Rise and Progress of our Disputes with Spain, and the Conduct of Our Ministry Relating Thereto* (London, 1739).
126. BL Add 22677 fols 25–6, James Knight to Newcastle, 20 Nov. 1739.
127. Edward Vernon, *The Genuine Speech of the Truly Honourable Admiral Vernon, to the Sea-Officers* (London, 1741), 10. Cited in Pincus, 'Patriot Fever'.
128. Pares, *War and Trade*, 157.
129. *Parliamentary History*, vol. 10, cols 771–2.
130. Paul Vaucher, *Robert Walpole et la politique de Fleury (1731–1742)* (Paris, 1924), 337–41; Pares, *War and Trade*, 162–4.
131. John Russell, duke of Bedford to Benjamin Keene, undated [June 1749], 26 Oct. 1750, 17 Feb. 1751, in Bedford, *Correspondence*, vol. 2, 30–5, 57–60, 70–3.

3. TO KEEP THE EUROPEAN PEACE: JOHN LAW'S FINANCIAL REVOLUTION AND ITS LEGACY

1. John Law to Philippe d'Orléans, Dec. 1715, in John Law, *Œuvres complètes*, ed. Paul Harsin, 3 vols (Paris, 1934), vol. 2, 262–8. On financial revolution, see P.G.M. Dickson, *The Financial Revolution in England: A Study in the Development of Public Credit, 1688–1756* (London, 1967). Some of the material in this chapter first appeared in a different form as 'Jealousy of Credit: John Law's "System" and the Geopolitics of Financial Revolution', *Journal of Modern History* 88, no. 2 (2016): 275–305.
2. John Brewer, *The Sinews of Power: War, Money and the English State, 1688–1783* (Cambridge, MA, 1988).
3. Law to Orléans, Dec. 1715, in Law, *Œuvres complètes*, vol. 2, 263.
4. On that coalition, see Arnaud Orain, *La politique du merveilleux: Une autre histoire du Système de Law (1695–1795)* (Paris, 2018).
5. Antoin E. Murphy, *John Law: Economic Theorist and Policy-Maker* (Oxford, 1997).
6. See Wennerlind, *Casualties of Credit*.
7. Richard Bonney (ed.), *The Rise of the Fiscal State in Europe* (Oxford, 1999).
8. BM MS 614 (355), Law to M. de Rosemberg, 15 May 1722.
9. Magnusson, *Political Economy of Mercantilism*, 217–18.
10. Desan, *Making Money*, 254–65; Muldrew, ' "Hard Food for Midas" ', 97–8.
11. Occurring with roughly the frequency of modern business downturns, such a crisis was known as a *disette d'argent* in France and a 'shortage of money' in England. See Luckett, 'Crises financières'; B.E. Supple, 'Currency and Commerce in the Early Seventeenth Century', *Economic History Review*, new series, 10, no. 2 (1957): 239–55.
12. Philippe Steiner, 'Circuits, monnaie et balance du commerce', in *Nouvelle histoire de la pensée économique*, ed. Alain Béraud and Gilbert Faccarello, 3 vols (Paris, 1992), vol. 1, 111–21.
13. Murphy, *John Law*, 78–80, 88.
14. Wennerlind, *Casualties of Credit*, 95–122.
15. John Law, 'Proposition pour une banque à Turin' (1712), reproduced (ed. Antoin E. Murphy) in *Économies et sociétés* 25, no. 5 (1991): 13–29, 25.
16. Murphy, *John Law*, 199–200, 233–4.
17. On the financiers, see Daniel Dessert, *Argent, pouvoir et société au Grand Siècle* (Paris, 1984); Guy Rowlands, *The Financial Decline of a Great Power: War, Influence, and Money in Louis*

XIV's France (Oxford, 2012). For Law's views on the financiers, see Murphy, *John Law*, 164–5.

18. Ibid., 194–6.
19. Law to Orléans, in Law, *Œuvres complètes*, vol. 2, 263–4. Law constantly reiterated this claim. See idem, 'Effets que le Système de M. Law a produit sur les espèces dans plusieurs états de l'Europe', in idem, *Œuvres complètes*, vol. 3, 170; and idem, 'Mémoire pour démontrer 1° qu'il est nécessaire d'établir le crédit; 2° qu'il est practicable de l'établir en France quoyque cet établissement aye déjà été entreprise et qu'il aye manqué', in idem, *Œuvres complètes*, vol. 3, 184.
20. John Law, 'Mémoire sur les banques', in idem, *Œuvres complètes*, vol. 2, 305.
21. Law to Orléans, Dec. 1715, in Law, *Œuvres complètes*, vol. 2, 266–7.
22. Herbert Lüthy, *La banque protestante en France de la révocation de l'Édit de Nantes à la Révolution*, 2 vols (Paris, 1959–61), vol. 1, 296–300; Jacob M. Price, *France and the Chesapeake: A History of the French Tobacco Monopoly, 1674–1791, and Its Relationship to the British and American Tobacco Trades*, 2 vols (Ann Arbor, 1973), vol. 1, 217.
23. Orain is surely right that Law himself was less central to the System than most scholars assume. Yet to understand its implications for international politics, I maintain, he remains the key figure. See Orain, *Politique du merveilleux*, passim.
24. AAE MD Amérique 1 fols 301–4, 'Mémoire sur l'établissement d'une compagnie d'occident après la remise du privilège du Sr. Crozat'.
25. AAE MD Amérique 1 fols 317–23, 'Paralele de la Compagnie du Sud d'Angleterre avec la comp. d'Occident qu'on propose d'Establir en France'.
26. Price, *France and the Chesapeake*, vol. 1, 197–212.
27. Law, 'Mémoire sur les banques', *Œuvres complètes*, vol. 2, 307–8.
28. Lüthy, *Banque protestante*, vol. 1, 296–99; and Price, *France and the Chesapeake*, vol. 1, 216.
29. AN G⁷ 1699 fols 8–10, Jean Anisson to Nicolas Desmaretz, 4 Feb. 1713.
30. Lüthy, *Banque protestante*, vol. 1, 302.
31. Law to Orléans, Dec. 1715, *Œuvres complètes*, vol. 2, 266–7. His bank, he argued, 'must render the King and the Kingdom of France master of all the powers of Europe'. See 'Projet d'une nouvelle forme d'asseoir les revenus du Roy (Apr. 1718)', *Œuvres complètes*, vol. 3, 31.
32. John Law, 'Idée générale du nouveau système des finances', in *Œuvres complètes*, vol. 3, 89n. It is likely, Arnaud Orain argues, that Jean Terrasson and Jacques Pannier d'Orgeville had a hand in drafting this manuscript, though the geopolitical thinking seems characteristic of the Scot. See Orain, *Politique du merveilleux*, 126.
33. 'Idée générale du nouveau système', in *Œuvres complètes*, vol. 3, 88n, 88–9.
34. François de Salignac de la Mothe-Fénelon, 'Examen de conscience sur les devoirs de la royauté. Supplément', in idem, *Œuvres*, ed. Jacques Le Brun, 2 vols (Paris, 1983–97), vol. 2, 1,009. Probably composed between 1708 and 1711 this work was first published as 'Sentiments of the Balance of Europe', in *Two Essays on the Ballance of Europe* (London, 1720). On Fénelon's international vision, see Rothkrug, *Opposition to Louis XIV*, 270–1, 279–80, 423–33.
35. François de Salignac de la Mothe-Fénelon, *Les Aventures de Télémaque*, ed. Jacques Le Brun (Paris, 1995 [1699]).
36. Fénelon, 'Examen de conscience. Supplément', 1,003–4. See also Sonenscher, *Before the Deluge*, 109–12.
37. Saint-Pierre, *Projet pour rendre la paix perpétuelle en Europe*. On the climate of ideas concerned with establishing peace in this period, see Bély, *Espions et ambassadeurs*, 696–740; and Hatton, *War and Peace*.
38. See Jean-Pierre Bois, *L'abbé de Saint-Pierre: Entre classicisme et Lumières* (Ceyzérieu, 2017).
39. John Law, 'Observations sur l'utilité de la Banque générale', in *Œuvres complètes*, vol. 3, 10.
40. Rowlands, *Dangerous and Dishonest Men*, 75, 142–3.
41. Half its capital was supposed to be raised in London. The company ultimately collapsed following Spanish attacks on the Darien settlement. See Watt, *Price of Scotland*, 36–45, 91–2, 96–102. On the broader significance of the Darien scheme, see Armitage, 'Scottish Vision of Empire'.

42. Mark A. Thomson, 'Self-Determination and Collective Security as Factors in English and French Foreign Policy, 1689–1718', in *William III and Louis XIV*, ed. Hatton and Bromley, 274–7, 284; Marco Cesa, *Allies Yet Rivals: International Politics in 18th Century Europe* (Stanford, 2010), 119–46.

43. AAE CP Ang 327 fols 209–10, James Stanhope to the abbé Guillaume Dubois, 29 Dec. 1719.

44. Historical Manuscripts Commission, *Calendar of the Stuart Papers Belonging to His Majesty the King*, 7 vols (London, 1902–23), vol. 6, 205, Lt Gen. Dillon to the earl of Mar, 17 Mar. 1718.

45. Louis Wiesener, *Le régent, l'abbé Dubois et les Anglais*, 3 vols (Paris, 1890–99), vol. 2, 296–7, citing a letter from John Dalrymple, earl of Stair, to Stanhope, 24 Oct. 1718.

46. RHCL Law Papers 16.0673, nos 6, 21–5. See also Edgar Faure, *La banqueroute de Law, 17 juillet 1720* (Paris, 1977), 169.

47. On Crawfurd's investments in the System and Law's role in facilitating these, see TNA C 108/417/1, Thomas Crawfurd to Thomas Pitt, Lord Londonderry, 19 Oct. 1718 and 15 Nov. 1717. On Crawfurd's disposition towards Law, see TNA SP 78/168 fols. 147–50, Crawfurd to [Stanhope], 16 July 1720.

48. John Dalrymple, earl of Stair to [Stanhope], 18 Sept. 1719, in *Miscellaneous State Papers, from 1501 to 1726*, 2 vols (London, 1778), vol. 2, 589. There is evidence nonetheless that Stair speculated in French stocks. See John Murray Graham (ed.), *Annals and Correspondence of the Viscount and First and Second Earls of Stair*, 2 vols (Edinburgh, 1875), vol. 2, 151–6; TNA C 108/419/1, Crawfurd to Londonderry, 25 Oct. 1719; and Beinecke Osborn MS 24, François de Neufville, duc de Villeroy to Stair, 7 Apr. 1722.

49. Pitt calculated the value of the investment at £6,000; he concurrently owed Law £4,000. See TNA C 108/419/13. The future Lord Londonderry would later have even larger sums tied up in Law's enterprises. See TNA C 108/423/9, 'Bordereau des effets', 22 May 1721. Londonderry's father ventured £5,000 in Law's company. See C108/415/5, Thomas Pitt Sr to Londonderry, 17 Sept. 1720.

50. See TNA C 108/419/13. Also, Larry Neal, *'I Am Not Master of Events': The Speculations of John Law and Lord Londonderry in the Mississippi and South Sea Bubbles* (New Haven, 2012), 40–54.

51. CKS U1590/A94. On 23 August 1717, Thomas Pitt Sr paid Stanhope £5,000 'for my Daughter's fortune' and transferred a further £8,000 to his daughter to help finance the purchase. On the same date, the younger Pitt loaned Stanhope £2,000. Stanhope's personal fortune was modest. See Williams, *Stanhope*, 269–70.

52. Murphy, *John Law*, 194–6, 201.

53. TNA SP 78/165 fol. 343, Stair to Stanhope, 20 Oct. 1719. Stair was not the only Briton dismayed by Law's success. Stanhope told Dubois that Charles Mordaunt, earl of Peterborough was 'alarmed by the prodigious arrangement of your finances, [and] came here only to incite us to thwart it and to propose to us divers schemes to effect this'. AAE CP Ang 326 fols 84–5, Stanhope to Dubois, 8 Oct. 1719. See also CKS U1590/O145/18, Peterborough to Stanhope, 20 Nov. 1719.

54. BM MS 614 (355), Law to Londonderry, 27 June 1721. For an outline of the South Sea proposal, see John Carswell, *The South Sea Bubble*, rev. edn (Dover, NH, 1993), 85–90; Peter M. Garber, *Famous First Bubbles: The Fundamentals of Early Manias* (Cambridge, MA, 2000), 109–13.

55. Murphy, *John Law*, 205–9.

56. *Mercurius Politicus*, Aug. 1719, 520; *Orphan Reviv'd or Powell's Weekly Journal*, 17 Oct. 1719; *Daily Courant*, 18 Nov. 1719; *Post Boy*, 26 Nov. 1719.

57. Including John Hamilton, Lord Belhaven (probably acting for the prince of Wales); William Chetwynd; Henry Furnese; Archibald Campbell, Lord Islay; Sir John Lambert; and William Sloper. See AAE CP Ang 328 fol. 448, James Craggs to Dubois, 17 Nov. 1719; TNA C 108/419/1; Antoin E. Murphy, *Richard Cantillon: Entrepreneur and Economist* (Oxford, 1986), 142–3; Archibald Campbell, earl of Islay to Henrietta Howard, Sept. 1719 and 16

Jan. 1720, in *Letters to and from Henrietta, afterwards Countess of Suffolk*, ed. J.W. Croker, 2 vols (London, 1824), vol. 1, 42, 45; Carswell, *South Sea Bubble*, 71, 85; TNA C 108/418/17, Stair to Londonderry, 29 Apr. 1720.

58. Larry Neal, *The Rise of Financial Capitalism: International Capital Markets in the Age of Reason* (Cambridge, 1990), 68; Murphy, *John Law*, 207–9.

59. AAE CP Ang 330 fols 39–40, London News, 18 Jan. 1720. Law would eventually expel the South Sea director Sir John Lambert, who was active in Paris raising South Sea subscriptions, and whom Law accused of remitting 20 million livres out of the country. See *The Case of Sir John Lambert, Bart. One of the Late Directors of the South Sea Company* (n.p., n.d).

60. Stair to [Craggs], 11 Dec. 1719, in *Miscellaneous State Papers*, vol. 2, 600–1; Claude Frédéric Lévy, *Capitalistes et pouvoir au siècle des Lumières*, 3 vols (Paris, 1969–80), vol. 3, 224.

61. RA Stuart 45/120, 17 Dec. 1719, included in 45/119, John Erskine, earl of Mar to James Stuart, 29 Dec. 1719.

62. TNA C 108/418/17, Stair to Londonderry, 29 Apr. 1720; TNA C 108/418/24, Londonderry to Bernard Vandergrift, 29 Mar. 1720. On Bernard, see Lüthy, *Banque protestante*, vol. 1, 111–13, 121–2.

63. Bruce G. Carruthers, *City of Capital: Politics and Markets in the English Financial Revolution* (Princeton, 1996), 137–59.

64. TNA SP 78/165 fols 483–4, Crawfurd to Craggs, 29 Nov. 1719.

65. [Daniel Defoe], *The Chimera, or, The French Way of Paying National Debts Laid Open: Being an Impartial Account of the Proceedings in France for Raising a Paper Credit and Settling the Mississipi Stock* (London, 1720). For the date of publication, see *Post Boy*, 2 Jan. 1720. Defoe would go on to defend the South Sea Company even after the collapse of the bubble. See Paula R. Backscheider, *Daniel Defoe: His Life* (Baltimore, 1989), 454–7; and P.N. Furbank and W.R. Owens, *A Political Biography of Daniel Defoe* (London, 2006), 183–5.

66. [John Law], *A Full and Impartial Account of the Company of Mississippi; or of the French-India Company, Projected and Settled by Mr Law* (London, 1720). It was published towards the end of January 1720. See *Post Boy*, 23 Jan. 1720.

67. TNA SP 78/166 fol. 186, Pulteney to [Craggs], 26 Mar. 1720.

68. On William Law's statements, see TNA SP 78/166 fol. 90, Pulteney to Craggs, 20 Dec. 1719; on John Law's remarks, TNA SP 78/166 fol. 98, Pulteney to [Craggs], 6 Jan. 1720.

69. Pulteney also worried that Law sought to usurp the trading privileges Britain had won in Spanish America as part of the peace of Utrecht. TNA SP 78/166 fol. 94, Pulteney to [Craggs], 24 Dec. 1719. Stair echoed these complaints: Stair to Craggs, 3 Jan. 1720, in Murray Graham (ed.), *Annals and Correspondence*, vol. 2, 140; NYPL Hardwicke 50, unfoliated, Stair to [Craggs], 7 Jan. 1720.

70. AAE CP Ang 330 fols 98–9, Dubois to Stanhope, 17 Feb. 1720; Stair to [Craggs], 28 Feb. 1720; Stair to [Craggs], 30 Apr. 1720, in *Miscellaneous State Papers*, vol. 2, 608, 618; AAE CP Ang 330 fol. 116, Dubois to Destouches, 24 Feb. 1720. On other efforts by Law to create friction over Gibraltar, see TNA SP 78/166 fols 191–2, Pulteney to Craggs, 10 Apr. 1720.

71. RA Stuart 45/115, Dillon to James Stuart, 19 Dec. 1719; 47/4, Dillon to James Stuart, 20 May 1720; 47/78, Dillon to James Stuart, 13 June 1720; 46/129, James Stuart to James Butler, duke of Ormonde, 12 May 1720.

72. TNA SP 78/165 fol. 537, Stair to Craggs, 20 Dec. 1719; fols 553–6, Stair to Stanhope, 27 Dec. 1719; fols 583–4, Stair to Craggs, 6 Jan. 1720; fol. 582, Stair to Craggs, 6 Jan. 1720.

73. TNA SP 78/167 fol. 247, Stanhope to François-Louis de Pesme de Saint-Saphorin, 1 Apr. 1720.

74. AAE CP Ang 331 fol. 36, Destouches to Dubois, 22 Apr. 1720.

75. TNA SP 78/168 fol. 148, Crawfurd to [Stanhope], 16 July 1720.

76. TNA SP 78/168 fols 159–60, Sir Robert Sutton to Craggs, 16 July 1720. Law also contacted Craggs, sending him 'two mighty civil Letters'. TNA SP 78/168 fols 392–3, Craggs to Sutton, 25 Aug. 1720.

77. Stair implied such a possibility as early as September 1719. Pulteney voiced the same fear in January. TNA SP 78/166 fol. 98, Pulteney to [Craggs], 6 Jan. 1720. But it was in Apr. 1720 that this became a principal concern.

78. TNA SP 78/166 fol. 191–2, Pulteney to Craggs, 10 Apr. 1720. See also Stair to Stanhope, 12 Apr. 1720, in Murray Graham (ed.), *Annals and Correspondence*, vol. 2, 419–22.

79. The *nouvelles à la main* (manuscript newsletters prepared for wealthy patrons) reported in April that the Compagnie des Indes had already made 100 million livres on British stocks. TNA SP 78/167 fol. 295, Stair to Craggs, 17 Apr. 1720. Also TNA SP 78/166 fol. 196, Pulteney to [Craggs], 23 Apr. 1720. The chevalier de Piossens, writing that same month, stated that Law had purchased £800,000-worth of shares in the South Sea Company at prices between 150 and 160 per cent of par (implying the purchases were made in February 1720). Chevalier de Piossens, *Mémoires de la régence de S.A.R. Mgr. le duc d'Orléans, durant la minorité de Louis XV*, 3 vols (The Hague, 1730), vol. 2, 396–7. See also TNA C 108/418/24, Londonderry to William Law, 23 June 1720; Londonderry to Joseph Gage, 23 June 1720; TNA SP 78/166 fol. 257, Pulteney to Craggs, 6 July 1720. There is no evidence to support the claims that Law speculated in South Sea stock. It is unlikely, in my view, that he did so. But all that was necessary to shake the financial markets was the belief that he or allied French speculators had amassed large holdings of English stocks.

80. TNA SP 78/167 fols 271–2, Stair to Craggs, 12 Apr. 1720. Stair expressed similar fears privately. See TNA C 108/418/17, Stair to Londonderry, 29 Apr. 1720.

81. TNA SP 78/166 fol. 198, Pulteney to Craggs, 29 Apr. 1720.

82. John Law, 'Idée générale du nouveau système', *Œuvres complètes*, vol. 3, 90n.

83. TNA SP 78/166 fols 234–5, Pulteney to Craggs, 11 June 1720.

84. *Ordonnance du Roy, portant que les sujets de Sa Majesté qui ont envoyé des fonds en pays étrangers, seront tenus de les faire revenir dans le royaume dans le temps & sous les peines y marquées, à Paris le 20 juin 1720*. A printed copy can be found at TNA SP 78/168 fol. 109.

85. TNA SP 78/166 fol. 245, Pulteney to Craggs, 23 June 1720.

86. Pulteney reported that 'I am told the Regent at Mr. Law's desire sent to Crozat and Bernard and prayed them to withdraw their effects from England, and that Bernard has said He promised the Regent to bring from thence in a month's time 100 millions of livres in gold; it is given out here that he has gained m/1700 L. st [£1.7 million] in the South Sea & that this was discovered by an intercepted letter.' TNA SP 78/166 fols 286–7, Pulteney to Craggs, 31 July 1720.

87. Neal, *Rise of Financial Capitalism*, 109–10; Garber, *Famous First Bubbles*, 118–20.

88. See Murphy, *John Law*, passim.

89. David Hume, 'Of Public Credit', in idem, *Political Discourses*.

90. Murphy, *John Law*, 320–1. A draft decree authorising the Compagnie des Indes to create 150 million livres' worth of credit instruments circulated in 1723. See Arsenal MS 3857 fols 312–20.

91. BNF fr 21750 fols 4–5, Law to Orléans. Law assured Dubois he would work for Anglo-French friendship, and he made similar representations to the marquis de Lassay. BM MS 614 (355), Law to Dubois, 2 Aug. 1721; Law to Armand-Léon de Madaillan de Lesparre, marquis de Lassay, 12 Mar. 1722.

92. Arsenal MS 4500 fols 137–64, [Jean-François Melon], 'Mémoire fait en May 1724', and fols 269–97, 'Mémoire pour examiner quels sont les contradicteurs de la Compagnie des Indes, pourquoi ils en demandent la suppression, et de quelle utilité cette Compagnie est à l'État'; AAE MD France 1258 fol. 28, Louis de Chammorel, 'Idée d'un moyen pour rétablir la confiance'; AAE MD France 1268 fols 133–44, Arnaud de Silhouette, 'Mémoire Pour le Rétablissement de la Confiance', 1 Jan. 1734; Charles-Irénée de Castel, abbé de Saint-Pierre, 'Mémoire de l'abbé de Saint-Pierre pour l'établissement de banques provinciales', reproduced in *L'abbé de Saint-Pierre, économiste d'après de nouveaux documents inédits*, ed. Paul Harsin (Paris, 1932), 19–33; ADG 1E 1762, [Pierre Faventines], 'Mémoire pour prouver l'utilité d'un credit public, et la manière dont il peut etre etably'; AN G⁷ 728–35, 'A Monseigneur Dodun Controlleur general des finances'; François Barbier, 'Abregé du Sistème ou du Plan Général de Finance et de Commerce', 7 Nov. 1726.

93. AAE MD France 1275 fols 166–71, 'Mémoire du 3 May 1732 pour l'accelleration du rétablissement de la Confiance'; MD France 1284 fols 386–7, 'Réflexions sur la confiance

et circulation de l'Espece', 13 Aug. 1733; MD France 1298 fols 130–3, 'Moyen pour retablir la confiance dans le Royaume'; MD France 1303 fols 323–31, Roux Cressy du Laus, 'Observations sur la Dette Publique', 27 Sept. 1736; fols 332–51, 'Projet de Crédit' (1734); MD France 2019 fols 105–8, 'Sur le defaut de la circulation de l'espece dans le Royaume, sur les causes de ce defaut, et sur les moyens de la rétablir'; fols 109–138, d'Hermainville to Germain-Louis Chauvelin, 12 Mar. 1731; fols 178–80, Étienne Portier, 'Mémoire concernant le bien de l'État et l'avantage du commerce'. Chauvelin considered projects for making use of the Compagnie des Indes to finance the war. See René-Louis de Voyer de Paulmy, marquis d'Argenson, *Journal et mémoires du marquis d'Argenson*, ed. E.J.B. Rathery, 9 vols (Paris, 1859–67), vol. 1, 162.

94. AAE MD France 1268 fols 133–44, Arnaud de Silhouette, 'Mémoire pour le rétablissement de la confiance' (cover letter, dated 1 Jan. 1734, at AAE MD France 1289 fol. 7). See also AAE MD France 516 fols 281–6.

95. Melon, *Essai politique*. I explore Melon's ideas in more depth in the following chapter.

96. Nicolas Dutot, *Réflexions politiques sur les finances, et le commerce*, 2 vols (The Hague, 1738).

97. Beinecke Osborn MS 24, Sarah Churchill, duchess of Marlborough to Stair, 6 June 1737.

98. On excise, see Brewer, *Sinews of Power*, 95–101; on Walpole, Michael John Jubb, 'Fiscal Policy in England in the 1720s and 1730s', PhD thesis, Cambridge University, 1977, 243–4.

99. Du Rivage, *Revolution Against Empire*, 46–8.

100. William Pulteney, *A State of the National Debt* (London, 1727), 46–9; Sir John Barnard, *Reasons for the More Speedy Lessening the National Debt, and Taking Off the Most Burthensome of the Taxes* (London, 1737).

101. Though he kept a close eye on French public finances. See CUL Ch(H) Papers 26/81, 'State of the Revenues of France', 22 May 1735; 26/119, 'Mᵣ Bu[ss]y's Paper about the Revenues'; 26/134, 'État des Revenues de la Couronne de France en divers temps'. Walpole may have had concerns about an attack on the British funds launched by domestic political enemies. See CUL Ch(H) Papers 51/107, 'Scheme to bring down the ministry by a trial of public credit'.

102. Henry St John, Viscount Bolingbroke, 'Some Reflections on the Present State of the Nation, Principally with Regard to her Taxes and her Debts, and on the Causes and Consequences of Them', in idem, *Works of the Late Right Honourable Henry St John, Lord Viscount Bolingbroke*, 5 vols (London, 1754), vol. 3, 161–70. This essay was written in 1749.

103. L.S. Sutherland, 'Samson Gideon and the Reduction of Interest, 1749–50', *Economic History Review* 16, no. 1 (1946): 15–29; Sir John Barnard, *Considerations on the Proposals for Reducing the Interest on the National Debt* (London, 1750).

104. François Véron de Forbonnais, *Le négotiant anglois, ou Traduction libre du livre intitulé: The British Merchant, contenant divers mémoires sur le commerce de l'Angleterre avec la France, le Portugal & l'Espagne*, 2 vols (Dresden, 1753), vol. 1, cx.

105. UNL Ne(C) 946, Thomas Pelham-Holles, duke of Newcastle to Henry Pelham, 12 June 1750.

106. UNL Ne(C) 929, William Bentinck to Pelham, 25 Mar. 1750. The reduction of interest would 'certainly tend to increase his majesty's Weight and influence abroad', agreed Robert Keith, the ambassador to the Habsburg court at Vienna. UNL Ne(C) 930, Robert Keith to Pelham, 26 Mar. 1750.

107. Anon., *The Necessity of Lowering Interest and Continuing Taxes, Demonstrated. In a Letter to G.B.* (London, 1750), 9–10.

108. Anon., *Essays, I. On the public debt. II. On paper-money, banking, &c. III. On frugality* (London, 1755), 8–11; Patrick Murray, Lord Elibank, *An Inquiry into the Original and Consequences of the Publick Debt* (1754). See Julian Hoppit, 'Attitudes to Credit in Britain, 1680–1790', *Historical Journal* 33, no. 2 (1990): 305–22.

109. Hume, 'Of Public Credit'.

110. NYPL Hardwicke 75, John Page to Newcastle, 10 Sept. 1754.

111. BL Add MS 32737 fols 97–9, Page to Newcastle, 10 Oct. 1754.

112. Elise S. Brezis, 'Foreign Capital Flows in the Century of Britain's Industrial Revolution: New Estimates, Controlled Conjectures', *Economic History Review*, new series, 48, no. 1 (1995): 46–67; Philip T. Hoffman, Gilles Postel-Vinay, and Jean-Laurent Rosenthal, *Priceless Markets: The Political Economy of Credit in Paris, 1660–1870* (Chicago, 2000), 169.

113. Isaac de Pinto, *An Essay on Circulation and Credit, in Four Parts; and A Letter on the Jealousy of Commerce*, trans. S. Baggs (London, 1774), 75–6.

114. David Stasavage, *Public Debt and the Birth of the Democratic State: France and Great Britain, 1688–1789* (Cambridge, 2003), 96. In the samples of French state loans analysed in Hoffman, Rosenthal, and Postel-Vinay, *Priceless Markets*, 169, the 1750–69 decades represent the nadir for foreign investment, with just 1 per cent of funds loaned to the state coming from abroad as against 12 per cent in the 1730–49 period, and 18 per cent between 1770 and 1789. But this decadal periodisation may not capture the critical turning points in the flow of foreign capital into French funds. The attractions of French public credit collapsed in the late 1750s, but confidence in the French funds appears to have been high in the early 1750s.

115. BL Eg 3456 fol. 287, William Mildmay to Holderness, 8 Nov. 1752.

116. See TNA PRO 30/8/85 fols 40–7, Thellusson, Necker & Co. to Gerard and Joshua Van Neck, 2 Dec. 1757. See also Lüthy, *Banque protestante*, vol. 2, 218–19.

117. Arsenal MS 4591 fols 1–210, 'Abrégé des mémoires pour l'établissement du crédit public'; also BNF naf 4295 fols 1–177.

118. Scores of public credit proposals sent to contrôleur général Boullongne in 1757 and 1758 are summarised in BNF fr 14097, 'Projets de finances, présentés dans l'année 1757 à 1758 & observations par M. D. F***'. Some of these propose schemes in the mould of Law. See particularly nos 1, 32, 41, 77, 86, and 99.

119. Simone Meyssonnier (ed.), *Traités sur le commerce de Josiah Child, suivis des Remarques de Jacques Vincent de Gournay* (Paris, 2008 [1754]), 162.

120. See, for example, AAE CP Ang, suppl. 11 fols 276–9, 'États des revenues et des dettes de la Grande Bretagne'; BNF fr 11150 fols 1–327, 'Mémoire sur les finances'; AAE MD France 1351 fols 73–80, 'Finances'; BNF Joly de Fleury 319 fols 242–4, 'Mémoire'; AN H 713, Antoine-Louis Lefebvre de Caumartin to Étienne de Silhouette, 27 and 31 Aug. 1759. See also Joël Félix, 'Comprendre l'opposition parlementaire: Le parlement de Paris face aux réformes de Silhouette (1759)', *Parlement(s), Revue d'histoire politique* 15 (2011): 31–43.

121. François-Joachim de Pierre, abbé de Bernis to Louis XV, 4 June 1758, in François-Joachim de Pierre, cardinal de Bernis, *Mémoires et lettres de François-Joachim de Pierre, cardinal de Bernis (1715–1758)*, ed. Frédéric Masson, 2 vols (Paris, 1903), vol. 2, 429.

122. Intentions Silhouette had to disavow. *Réponse de M. le Contrôleur général à M. le Premier Président de la Chambre des Comptes, lorsqu'il y est venu prêter serment* (n.p., n.d. [1759]). On the rumours, see Jean-Edmond Barbier, *Chronique de la régence et du règne de Louis XV (1718–1763)*, 8 vols (Paris, 1866), vol. 7, 140. On Silhouette's ministry, see Arnaud Orain, 'Soutenir la guerre et réformer la fiscalité: Silhouette et Forbonnais au Contrôle général des finances (1759)', *French Historical Studies* 36, no. 3 (2013), 417–47.

123. AAE CP Ang 412 fol. 193, [Étienne de Silhouette to Jean-Jacques Amelot], 10 July 1741.

124. AN Mar B⁴ 82 fols 4–10, 'Extrait concernant une Invasion en Angleterre tiré d'un mémoire fait au mois de 9ᵇʳᵉ 1755'.

125. BL Add MS 32861 fol. 493, Philip Yorke, earl of Hardwicke to Newcastle, 29 Dec. 1755. William Pitt evoked the prospect that, following a French landing, 'the noble, artificial, yet vulnerable fabric of public credit should crumble in their hands'. Cited in Richard Pares, 'American versus Continental Warfare, 1739-63', *English Historical Review* 51, no. 203 (1936): 429–65, 441.

126. BL Add MS 32890 fol. 217, Page to Newcastle, 20 Apr. 1759. The mere threat of invasion, Newcastle feared, would make it impossible to float new loans in 1759. BL Add MS 32895 fol. 246, Newcastle to Joseph Yorke, 2 Sept. 1759.

127. AAE MD Ang 54 fols 59–61, 'Mémoire sur l'utilité et la possibilité d'une descente en Angleterre', Jan. 1759; fols 93–8, 'Projet de descente en Angleterre', 16 May 1759; AN Mar B⁴ 82 fols 20–4, 'Mémoire sur l'invasion projetteé en France contre la grande Bretagne, et sur les moyens que l'on suppose aux anglois pour l'empecher', 14 Aug. 1759. Étienne-François de Stainville, duc de Choiseul, architect of French strategy in the 1760s, was fascinated with this notion. See, for example, BL Add MS 36798 fols 83–7, Hans Stanley to William Pitt, 23 June 1761. The Franco-Spanish invasion of England planned for 1779 was supposed to destroy British public credit. See A. Temple Patterson, *The Other Armada: The Franco-Spanish Attempt to Invade Britain in 1779* (Manchester, 1960), 5–6, 11, 14.

128. On this collapse, see Daniel Baugh, *The Global Seven Years War, 1754–1763: Britain and France in a Great Power Contest* (New York, 2011), 447–52.

129. John L. Bullion, ' "To Know This Is the True Essential Business of a King": The Prince of Wales and the Study of Public Finance, 1755–1760', *Albion: A Quarterly Journal Concerned with British Studies* 18, no. 3 (1986): 429–54.

130. BL Add MS 38334 fols 236–8, Charles Jenkinson, 'Observations on the money faculties of the State. 1762'.

131. *The Monitor, or the British Freeholder* 376 (Oct. 2, 1762). See James Vaughn, *The Politics of Empire at the Accession of George III: The East India Company and the Crisis and Transformation of Britain's Imperial State* (New Haven, 2019), 64–5.

132. George Bubb Dodington to William, Lord Talbot, 4 Oct. 1760, in George Bubb Dodington, *The Political Journal of George Bubb Dodington*, ed. John Carswell and Lewis Arnold Dralle (Oxford, 1965), 392. See also Eliga H. Gould, *The Persistence of Empire: British Political Culture in the Age of the American Revolution* (Chapel Hill, 2000), 102–3.

133. [Edward Richardson], 'A Letter to a Gentleman in the City', *St James Chronicle* (7–9 Sept. 1762). On the success of this so-called 'Wandsworth Letter', see John Brewer, *Party Ideology and Popular Politics at the Accession of George III* (Cambridge, 1976), 223.

134. Anon., *A Letter to the Right Honourable the Earl of B***, on a Late Important Resignation, and Its Probable Consequences*, 2nd edn (London, 1761), 23–4.

135. TNA PRO 30/50/48 fols 45–6, 73, Richard Neville to Charles Jenkinson, 2 Dec. 1762.

136. Doddington to Talbot, 4 Oct. 1760, in Doddington, *Political Journal*, 394–5.

137. Thomas Whately, *Considerations on the Trade and Finances of this Kingdom, and on the Measures of Administration, with Respect to those Great National Objects since the Conclusion of the Peace* (London, 1766), 3–4, 11–13. See also Du Rivage, *Revolution Against Empire*, 104.

138. UNL Ne(C) 149/1–4, Pelham to Newcastle, 23 Sept. [4 Oct.] 1748.

139. Mitchell, *British Historical Statistics*, 601.

140. Whatmore, 'Shelburne and Perpetual Peace'.

141. P. Coquelle, *L'alliance franco-hollandaise contre l'Angleterre 1735–1788* (Paris, 1902), 43, 254; Riley, *International Government Finance*, 174–5.

142. See, for example, BL Add MS 36802 fols 18–19, John Stuart, Lord Mountstuart to Wills Hill, earl of Hillsborough, 18 Dec. 1779.

143. Lüthy, *Banque protestante*, vol. 2, 464–519; J. C. Riley, 'Dutch Investment in France, 1781–1787', *Journal of Economic History* 33, no. 4 (1973): 732–60; Riley, *International Government Finance*, 95, 107, 174–5.

144. Richard B. Morris, *The Peacemakers: The Great Powers and American Independence* (New York, 1965), 94.

145. Jacques Necker, *De l'administration des finances de la France*, 3 vols (n.p., 1784), vol. 3, chapter 34.

146. Jacques Necker, *Compte rendu au roi, par M. Necker, directeur général des Finances* (Paris, 1781); Lüthy, *Banque protestante*, vol. 2, 369–70; Riley, *International Government Finance*, 175. J.F. Bosher, *French Finances 1770–1795: From Business to Bureaucracy* (Cambridge, 1970), 149–50, 160–2.

147. Lüthy, *Banque protestante*, vol. 2, 389–438; Lucy S. Sutherland, *The East India Company in Eighteenth-Century Politics* (Oxford, 1962), 143, 210. See also L.M. Cullen, 'Luthy's *La*

Banque Protestante: A Reassessment', *Bulletin du centre d'histoire des espaces atlantiques,* new series, 5 (1990): 228–63, 239–40.

148. BNF Joly de Fleury 1434 fols 131–8, 'Discours d'un actionnaire à la première assemblée générale des intéressés à la Caisse d'escompte, le 26 juin 1776'.

149. [Isaac Panchaud], *Réflexions sur l'état actuel du crédit public de l'Angleterre et de la France* (n.p., 1781). On Panchaud's links with the minister, see BNF Joly de Fleury 1436 fol. 124, Jean-François Joly de Fleury to Isaac Panchaud, 7 Jan. 1782. On Shelburne's concerns, WCL Shelburne Papers 72/424, Francis Baring to William Petty, earl of Shelburne, 24 Sept. 1782; Baring NP1.B1, Shelburne to Francis Baring, 5 Nov. 1782; Baring DEP 193.17.1, Baring to Shelburne, 18 Dec. 1782.

150. Hardman, *Overture to Revolution,* 26.

151. Arrighi, *Long Twentieth Century,* 13–14.

152. Kant, *Zum ewigen Frieden.*

153. Wennerlind, *Casualties of Credit,* 95–122.

4. AN ELUSIVE BALANCE: THE LONG PEACE AND THE PROBLEM OF UNEVEN DEVELOPMENT

1. See T.G.A. Le Goff, 'How to Finance an Eighteenth-Century War', in *Crises, Revolutions and Self-Sustained Growth: Essays in European Fiscal History, 1130–1830,* ed. W.M. Ormrod, Margaret Bonney and Richard Bonney (Stamford, 1999), 377–413, 388.

2. Jubb, 'Fiscal Policy in England'.

3. See James Pritchard, *In Search of Empire: The French in the Americas, 1670–1730* (Cambridge, 2004), 403.

4. With its much smaller population, Britain remained well ahead in per-capita terms. For the figures, see Daudin, *Commerce et prospérité,* 173–209.

5. For 'adulterated mercantilism', see Kathleen Wilson, 'Empire of Virtue: The Imperial Project and Hanoverian Culture *c.* 1720–1785', in *An Imperial State at War: Britain from 1689 to 1815,* ed. Lawrence Stone (London, 1994), 128–64. Wilson has been the most influential exponent of this view. See Kathleen Wilson, 'Empire, Trade and Popular Politics in Mid-Hanoverian Britain: The Case of Admiral Vernon', *Past & Present,* 121 (1988): 74–109; and eadem, *The Sense of the People: Politics, Culture, and Imperialism in England, 1715–1785* (Cambridge, 1995), 137–205. See also Vaughn, *Politics of Empire,* 50–87.

6. The split between these classes went back deep into the seventeenth century, and it had always been the less privileged merchants who favoured an aggressive policy in the Atlantic. Robert Brenner, *Merchants and Revolution: Commercial Change, Political Conflict, and London's Overseas Traders, 1550–1653* (London, 2003).

7. *Parliamentary History,* vol. 11, cols 231–2. See also Black, *British Foreign Policy in the Age of Walpole,* 112. See also CUL Ch(H) Papers 73/30, 'The Interest of Great Britain's Going into the War Consider'd'.

8. BL Add MS 9131 fols 251–71, Horatio Walpole, 'Considerations Relating to the Navigation and Commerce of Great Britain in America, with Respect to the Treatys with Spain, and the Depredations Committed by the Guarda Costas', 23 Jan. 1738.

9. CUL Ch(H) Papers 73/43, 'Several Letters to a Friend Concerning the Present War and the Fruits We Might Expect from a Peace Could it Be Soon Restored'.

10. [Daniel Defoe], *The Advantages of Peace and Commerce, with some Remarks on the East-India Trade* (London, 1729), 1.

11. Lawrence Dickey, 'Power, Commerce and Natural Law in Daniel Defoe's Political Writings 1698–1707', in *A Union for Empire: Political Thought and the British Union of 1707,* ed. John Robertson (Cambridge, 1995), 63–96.

12. Defoe, *Advantages of Peace and Commerce,* 24.

13. Ibid., 20–4. The point is pursued at greater length in [Daniel Defoe], *Peace and Trade, War and Taxes: Or, The Irreparable Damage of our Trade in Case of War. In a Letter to the Craftsman* (London, 1729).

14. Defoe, *Advantages of Peace and Commerce*, 37.
15. [Daniel Defoe], *A Plan of the English Commerce, being a Compleat Prospect of the Trade of this Nation, as Well the Home Trade as the Foreign* (London, 1728), 332.
16. Defoe, *Advantages of Peace and Commerce*, 7.
17. Ibid., 6.
18. Backscheider, *Daniel Defoe*, 511. Key elements in Defoe's corpus include *The Compleat English Tradesman* (1726), the *General History of Discoveries and Improvements* (1726), *Plan of the English Commerce* (1728), *Atlas Maritimus and Commercialis* (1728), and *An Humble Proposal to the People of England, for the Encrease of Their Trade, and Encouragement of Their Manufactures* (1729).
19. Defoe, *Peace and Trade*, passim.
20. Vaucher, *Robert Walpole et la politique de Fleury*, 296–302.
21. *Common Sense* 81 (19 Aug. 1738). Cited in Pincus, 'Patriot Fever', 42.
22. *Gentleman's Magazine* 9 (Jan. 1739), 34.
23. BL Add MS 32800 fol. 23, Thomas Pelham-Holles, duke of Newcastle to James, Earl Waldegrave, 5 Jan. 1739.
24. *Craftsman* 701 (15 Dec. 1739). Étienne de Silhouette commented on Wyndham and Pulteney's admiration of Fleury, especially the augmentation of French seaborne trade. AAE CP Ang 405 fol. 286, Silhouette to Jean-Jacques Amelot de Chaillou, 26 Nov. 1739.
25. Robert Harris, *Politics and the Nation: Britain in the Mid-Eighteenth Century* (Oxford, 2002), 118.
26. John Campbell, duke of Argyll, *The D--- of A-----e's letter to the Right Honourable Sir ****** *******, Upon the Present Intended Expeditions* (London, 1740), 11–13.
27. Ralph Davis, 'English Foreign Trade, 1700–1774', *Economic History Review*, new series, 15, no. 2 (1962): 285–303.
28. Vaucher, *Robert Walpole et la politique de Fleury*, 300.
29. Anon., *The Golden Fleece: Or, the Trade, Interest and Well-Being of Great Britain Considered* (n.p., n.d. [1736?]); CUL Ch(H) Papers 73/66, 'A supplemental proposal to the Golden Fleece'.
30. Cited in Jeremy Black, *Trade, Empire and British Foreign Policy, 1689–1815: The Politics of a Commercial State* (London, 2007), 23.
31. On Patriot fears for Georgia, see Pincus, 'Patriot Fever'. On the deerskin trade, Kathryn E. Holland Braund, *Deerskins & Duffels: The Creek Indian Trade with Anglo-America, 1685–1815* (Lincoln, NE, 1993), 31–9; on the Chickasaw War, Jacob F. Lee, *Masters of the Middle Waters: Indian Nations and Colonial Ambitions Along the Mississippi* (Cambridge, MA, 2019), 108–9.
32. Crouzet, *La guerre économique*, 105. See also Paul Cheney, *Cul de Sac: Patrimony, Capitalism, and Slavery in French Saint-Domingue* (Chicago, 2017), 4.
33. Moore, ' "Amsterdam is Standing on Norway" Part II'.
34. Cheney, *Cul de Sac*, 56–7.
35. The Jamaican industry would grow only a little less slowly than its French rival in the second half of the century, but this growth was sustained by the domestic market in Britain. French producers retained a comfortable advantage in the price at which they offered sugar on European markets. See Crouzet, *La guerre économique*, 103–7; Robert Paul Thomas, 'The Sugar Colonies of the Old Empire: Profit or Loss for Great Britain?', *Economic History Review* 21, no. 1 (1968): 30–45, 37.
36. Anon., *The Importance of the Sugar Colonies to Britain Stated, and Some Objections Against the Sugar Colony Bill Answer'd* (London, 1731), 9.
37. Ibid., 7.
38. William Wood, *A Survey of Trade in Four Parts* (London, 1719), 149.
39. Bladen married a Caribbean heiress in 1728 and had extensive interests in the sugar islands. See Rory T. Cornish, 'Bladen, Martin (1680–1746)', *ODNB*.
40. Melon's book went through numerous French editions and was translated into half a dozen European languages. See Carpenter, *Economic Bestsellers before 1850*, 11. On Melon's work,

see Cheney, *Revolutionary Commerce*, 38–43; Hont, *Jealousy of Trade*, 28–30, 35; idem, 'The Early Enlightenment Debate on Commerce and Luxury', in *The Cambridge History of Eighteenth-Century Political Thought*, ed. Mark Goldie and Robert Wokler (Cambridge, 2006); Robertson, *Case for the Enlightenment*, 343; Sonenscher, *Before the Deluge*, 111–12.

41. Hirschman, *Passions and the Interests*, 79–80.

42. Reinert, *Translating Empire*, 139–42; Anoush Fraser Terjanian, *Commerce and Its Discontents in Eighteenth-Century French Political Thought* (Cambridge, 2013), 14–15. While they recognise the tensions in Montesquieu's ideas on commerce and peace, Claude Morilhat and Céline Spector opt for a more optimistic reading. See Claude Morilhat, *Montesquieu: Politique et richesse* (Paris, 1996), 85; Spector, *Montesquieu et l'émergence de l'économie politique*, 181–9.

43. John Law, 'Idée générale du nouveau système', in idem, *Œuvres complètes*, vol. 3, 88n, 88–9.

44. Charles de Secondat, baron de Montesquieu, 'Réflexions sur la monarchie universelle en Europe', in idem, *Œuvres complètes de Montesquieu*, 18 vols (Oxford, 1998–2012), vol. 2, 319–64.

45. Jean-François Melon, *Essai politique sur le commerce* (n.p., 1734), 1–5, 11. See also Reinert, *Translating Empire*, 20.

46. De Vries, *Industrious Revolution*; Daniel Roche, *A History of Everyday Things: The Birth of Consumption in France, 1600–1800* (Cambridge, 2000).

47. Melon, *Essai politique* (1734), 80.

48. Ibid., 177, 25–56.

49. Ibid., 262.

50. '[T]here are in his work so many other good things, that these observations will never be able to do him any harm'. Dutot, *Réflexions politiques*, vol. 1, x. Melon was aware of Dutot's critique as early as 1735 and encouraged him to elaborate it. See François Velde, 'The Life and Times of Nicolas Dutot', *Journal of the History of Economic Thought* 34, no. 1 (2012): 67–107. Much of the work is taken up with showing in an empirically exhaustive way that variations in the currency always caused harm.

51. D'Argenson, *Journal et mémoires*, vol. 1, 162.

52. AAE MD France 1303 fols 242–53, [René-Louis de Voyer de Paulmy, marquis d'Argenson], 'Lettre sur la circulation, le crédit public et la consommation à M. M** auteur de l'Essai politique sur le commerce, imprimé en 1736'. See also René-Louis de Voyer de Paulmy, marquis d'Argenson, *Considérations sur le gouvernement: A Critical Edition, with Other Political Texts*, ed. Andrew Jainchill (Liverpool, 2019), 53–5, 247–59.

53. BUP Fonds d'Argenson P12, René-Louis de Voyer de Paulmy, marquis d'Argenson, 'Mémoire contre les abus de la taille arbitraire présenté au cardinal de Fleury, en décembre 1731'. Reproduced in idem, *Considérations sur le gouvernement*, 237–46.

54. D'Argenson, 'Essai de l'exercice du tribunal européen par la France pour la pacification universelle. Appliqué au temps courant', in idem, *Considérations sur le gouvernement*, 227–35. See also Belissa, *Fraternité universelle et intérêt national*, 120–1.

55. Robertson, *Case for the Enlightenment*, 36. For some of Melon's memoranda written in the 1720s, see Jean-François Melon, *Opere 1*, ed. Onofrio Nicastro and Severina Perona, 2 vols (Pisa, 1983).

56. *Catalogue des livres de la bibliothèque de feu messire Germain-Louis Chauvelin* (Paris, 1762), 103.

57. AAE MD France 418 fols 218–34, 'Vües sur les affaires générales', approved by the king in council, 19 Oct. 1736. See also AAE MD France 1303 fols 46–51, Chauvelin, 'Sur la Reforme', May 1736. Chauvelin could be bellicose – he actively sought war with Austria in 1733. But revisionist scholarship rejects the idea that he differed greatly in aggressiveness from Fleury. See Alix Bréban, 'Chauvelin', in *Dictionnaire des ministres des Affaires étrangères*, ed. Lucien Bély (Paris, 2005), 141. No less a pacifist than the abbé de Saint-Pierre claimed that, at the time of his disgrace in 1737, Chauvelin had a design for European peace. See Charles-Irénée de Castel, abbé de Saint-Pierre, *Political Annals by the Late Celebrated Charles Irenée Castel, Abbot of Saint-Pierre*, 2 vols (London, n.d.), vol. 2, 294. On the development of

Chauvelin's foreign policy, see Lucien Bély, 'Schoepflin et Chauvelin, l'historien et le ministre: Étude comparative de deux visions des relations internationales', in *Strasbourg, Schoepflin et l'Europe au XVIIIe siècle*, ed. Bernard Vogler and Jürgen Voss (Strasbourg, 1996), 225–42.

58. 'Essai politique sur le commerce. Nouvelle édition, augmentée de sept chapitres', *Journal des sçavans* (Aug. 1736): 496–507. On the *Journal des sçavans* see Raymond Birn, 'Le *Journal des Savants* sous l'Ancien Régime', *Journal des savants* (1965): 15–35. The editor of the journal worked under the director of the Book Trade, Antoine-Louis Rouillé, who answered to Chauvelin, d'Aguesseau and Fleury. See Yves Combeau, *Le comte d'Argenson, 1696–1764: Ministre de Louis XV* (Paris, 1999), 90. This is the more remarkable considering that Melon had criticised the preoccupation with Austrian power that drove the War of the Polish Succession, which he saw as a throwback to the era of Richelieu and Mazarin. See Melon, *Essai politique* (1734), 39. Here I take a rather different view of Melon's essay than Robin J. Ives, who regards Melon's decision to publish his views as subversive. See R.J. Ives, 'Political Publicity and Political Economy in Eighteenth-Century France', *French History* 17, no. 1 (2003): 1–18, 5.

59. Velde, 'Life and Times of Nicolas Dutot'.

60. Joseph Pâris-Duverney and François-Michel-Chrétien Deschamps, *Examen du livre intitulé Réflexions politiques sur les finances et le commerce*, 2 vols (The Hague and Paris, 1740), vol. 2, 445; Nicolas Dutot, *Réflexions politiques sur les finances et le commerce*, ed. Paul Harsin, 2 vols (Liège and Paris, 1935), vol. 2, 310 (transcription of Arsenal MS 4059).

61. AAE CP Ang 406 fols 166–7, Louis-Dominique de Cambis to Amelot, 31 Dec. 1739. The work was translated as *Political Reflections upon the Finances and Commerce of France; Shewing the Causes which Formerly Obstructed the Advancement of her Trade; on How Much Better Footing it Stands Now than it Did Under Lewis XIV, with Several Expedients for Raising it Still to a Greater Height* (London, 1739).

62. Arsenal MS 4745 fols 89–90, Dutot to [comte d'Argenson], 31 Dec. 1739. On d'Argenson's ministerial prospects, see Combeau, *Comte d'Argenson*, 79–84.

63. BUP Fonds d'Argenson P60/1/6, copy of a letter from Nicolas Dutot to [Simon Mérard?], 10 Jan. 1740. Dutot invited d'Argenson to get a copy of this letter from Mérard. See Arsenal MS 4745 fols 89–90, Dutot to [d'Argenson], 31 Dec. 1739.

64. BUP Fonds d'Argenson P19, [Nicolas Dutot], 'Réflexions Politiques sur les finances et le commerce. Tome III. Dans lequel on repond a l'Examen des deux premiers volumes' (a slightly different manuscript copy of this work was published by Paul Harsin in 1935, cited above); idem, 'Manuscrits interesans sur tout ce qui s'est passé depuis la creation de la banque jusqua la decadence du Sisteme . . .', published as Nicolas Dutot, *Histoire du Système de John Law (1716–1720)*, ed. Antoin E. Murphy (Paris, 2000).

65. Including a manuscript translation of Petty's *Political Arithmetick*, plus a partial translation of Davenant's *Discourses on the Publick Revenues and on the Trade of England*. BUP Fonds d'Argenson P60/9/2/2, 'Arithmetique Politique . . . par le chevalier Guillaume Petty'; P60/9/3/1 'Concernant le Credit, et la Maniere de le Retablir'. See also P60/9/1/7, 'Remarques sur les forces et les richesses presentes de la Grande Bretagne'; P60/9/1/8, 'Angleterre. Son Etenduë', 'Credit d'angleterre en 1730'; P60/9/1/13, 'État present de l'Angleterre'; P60/1/23, 'Calculs Politiques tendants à montrer l'État actuel de la Puissance ou des Forces et des Richesse de l'Angleterre', and 'Mémoire de l'état present de l'Angleterre'.

66. He criticises the English aspiration to monopolise the commerce of the world. France might as readily do so, he argues, but this is a 'mad ambition', and he opposes to it the vision of reciprocal trade alluded to in this remark. See Melon, *Essai politique* (1736), 357.

67. Ibid., 164.

68. Ibid., 131–2.

69. Melon, *Essai politique* (1734), 11–12.

70. On the links between Melon and Montesquieu, see Louis Desgraves, *Chronologie critique de la vie et des œuvres de Montesquieu* (Paris, 1998), 244–5, 248, 251.

71. Montesquieu, 'Réflexions sur la monarchie universelle'. See also Cheney, *Revolutionary Commerce*, 58.

72. The broader French and European debate about whether poor countries could leverage their low wages to catch up with and surpass rich countries is analysed in Istvan Hont, 'The "Rich Country–Poor Country" Debate Revisited: The Irish Origins and French Reception of the Hume Paradox', in *David Hume's Political Economy*, ed. Schabas and Wennerlind, 243–323.

73. Dutot, *Réflexions politiques*, vol. 2, 403–4. Dutot had been a cashier of the Compagnie des Indes under the System. See Antoin E. Murphy, 'The Enigmatic Monsieur Du Tot', in *Studies in the History of French Political Economy: From Bodin to Walras*, ed. Gilbert Faccarello (London, 1998), 57–77; and Velde, 'Life and Times of Nicolas Dutot'.

74. AAE CP Ang 405 fols 394–9, Silhouette to Cardinal André-Hercule Fleury, 31 Dec. 1739. This had been a long-standing conviction of Silhouette. See AAE CP Ang 383 fols 5–10, Silhouette to Chauvelin, 1 Jan. 1734. For other evidence of Silhouette promoting Dutot's views, see Arsenal MS 4745 fols 89–90, Dutot to unidentified, 31 Dec. 1739.

75. Peter R. Campbell, *Power and Politics in Old Regime France 1720–1745* (London, 1996), 170.

76. Robert Harris, *A Patriot Press: National Politics and the London Press in the 1740s* (Oxford, 1993), 9. See also Baugh, 'Maritime Strength and Atlantic Commerce', 210–11; Gould, *Persistence of Empire*, 39–40.

77. Fournier was the director of the tobacco department of the United General Farms. He was also, from 1744, a sub-farmer of excise and stamp duties and would go on to become a Farmer General in 1755. See Thierry Claeys, *Dictionnaire biographique des financiers en France au XVIIIe siècle*, 2 vols (Paris, 2009), vol. 1, 889.

78. Gerard was the older brother of Joshua van Neck, whom we encountered in Chapter 3 (see p. 136).

79. Hancock, *Citizens of the World*, 36–7; Margarette Lincoln, *Trading in War: London's Maritime World in the Age of Cook and Nelson* (New Haven, 2018), 66–78.

80. Brewer, *Sinews of Power*, 197–8.

81. Peter Temin and Hans-Joachim Voth, 'Credit Rationing and Crowding Out during the Industrial Revolution: Evidence from Hoare's Bank, 1702–1862', *Explorations in Economic History* 42, no. 3 (2005): 325–48. The legal interest rate was capped at 5 per cent, but the government offered higher rates, effectively, by offering discounts. For example, subscribers might pay £800 for £1,000-worth of consols sold at 5-per-cent interest, offering a real interest rate of 6.25 per cent.

82. [Sir Matthew Decker], *Serious Considerations on the Several High Duties Which the Nation in General (As Well as Its Trade in Particular) Labours under* (London, 1743); idem, *Essay on the Causes of the Decline of the Foreign Trade*. Decker's ideas are explored in Chapter 1.

83. Harris, *Politics and the Nation*, 126.

84. Price, *France and the Chesapeake*.

85. Such a network can be traced in the papers of Pierre Faventines, ADG 1E 1762–1830.

86. P.J. Cain and A.G. Hopkins, 'Gentlemanly Capitalism and British Expansion Overseas I: The Old Colonial System', *Economic History Review*, 2nd series, 39, no. 4 (1986): 501–25.

87. Though their interest could sometimes incline them to war. The South Sea Company directors rejected the convention Walpole had negotiated with Spain to head off conflict in 1739. In 1744 the chairman of the East India Company, Henry Gough, refused a neutrality agreement proffered by the Compagnie des Indes that might have prevented the spread of the European war to India (see Chapter 6, p. 236). In 1756 William Baker, a leading figure in the Hudson's Bay Company, favoured war, a conflict from which the company might hope to gain. See P.W. Kingsford, 'A London Merchant: Sir William Baker', *History Today* 21 (1971): 338–48.

88. Price, *France and the Chesapeake*, vol. 1, 541–3; Sutherland, 'Samson Gideon', 22; Charles Wilson, *Anglo-Dutch Commerce & Finance in the Eighteenth Century* (Cambridge, 1941), 111.

89. Lewis B. Namier, *The Structure of Politics at the Accession of George III*, 2 vols (London, 1929), vol. 1, 69.

90. Gustav Otruba, 'Die Bedeutung englischer Subsidien und Antizipationen für die Finanzen Österreichs 1701 bis 1748', *Vierteljahrschrift für Sozial- und Wirtschaftsgeschichte* 51, no. 2 (1964): 192–234.

91. Lespagnol, *Messieurs de Saint-Malo*, 230.

92. Guillaume Daudin, 'Profitability of Slave and Long-Distance Trading in Context: The Case of Eighteenth-Century France', *Journal of Economic History* 64, no. 1 (2004): 144–71; Silvia Marzagalli, *Bordeaux et les États-Unis, 1776–1815: Politique et stratégies négociantes dans la genèse d'un réseau commercial* (Geneva, 2015); James C. Riley, *The Seven Years War and the Old Regime in France: The Economic and Financial Toll* (Princeton, 1986). On planters, see Cheney, *Cul de Sac*, 108–9.

93. George T. Matthews, *The Royal General Farms in Eighteenth-Century France* (New York, 1958), 252.

94. Le Goff, 'How to Finance an Eighteenth-Century War', 387.

95. BNF fr 12224 fol. 247, Étienne de Silhouette, 'Sur l'importance du tabac, sur le moyen d'en établir des plantations dans les colonies françoises et sur la facilité d'y reussir et de supplanter les anglois dans cette branche de commerce, 1739'.

96. Price, *France and the Chesapeake*, vol. 1, 383–4, 568–71.

97. The foreign ministry viewed Fournier as Orry's choice for the mission and Fournier himself described Orry as his protector. See AAE CP Ang 421 fols 9–10, François de Bussy to the abbé Jean-Ignace de La Ville, 17 Apr. 1745; fols 11–12, [Bussy] to La Ville, 18 Apr. 1745; fols 57–60, Fournier to La Ville, 18 June 1745. Newcastle too regarded him as the contrôleur général's man. See Newcastle to Philip Stanhope, earl of Chesterfield, 30 Nov. 1745, in *Private Correspondence of Chesterfield and Newcastle, 1744–46*, ed. Sir Richard Lodge (London, 1930), 96.

   On Orry's opposition to the war, see AAE MD France 504 fols 241–6, 'Mémoire sur les conjonctures presentes de l'Europe'. See also Evelyn Georgette Cruickshanks, 'Factions at the Court of Louis XV and the Succession to Cardinal Fleury (1737–1745)', PhD thesis, University of London, 1956, 266–7, 270, 387; and Rudd, 'Philibert Orry', 439–40.

98. D'Argenson, *Journal et mémoires*, vol. 3, 341–52.

99. Rudd, 'Philibert Orry', 472–7.

100. Reed Browning, *The War of the Austrian Succession* (New York, 1993), 298; John W. Wilkes, *A Whig in Power: The Political Career of Henry Pelham* (Chicago, 1964), 115–29.

101. Chesterfield to Newcastle, 25 Nov. 1745, in *Correspondence of Chesterfield and Newcastle*, 85–90; Philip Woodfine, 'Stanhope, William, first earl of Harrington (1683?–1756)', *ODNB*.

102. For evidence of his pacific thinking in 1745, see *Correspondence of Chesterfield and Newcastle*, 85–6, 90–1. For his embrace of a war policy in 1746, see Browning, *War of the Austrian Succession*, 279–82.

103. Henry Pelham to Robert Trevor, 11 Dec. 1745, in *Memoirs of the Administration of the Right Honourable Henry Pelham*, ed. William Coxe, 2 vols (London, 1829), vol. 1, 282–4. Bedford led a push in the spring and summer of 1746 to send a major expedition against Canada, a policy about which Pelham was not enthusiastic. See Wilkes, *A Whig in Power*, 135–6. See also Richard Harding, 'The Expedition to Lorient, 1746', in *The Age of Sail: The International Annual of the Historic Sailing Ship*, ed. N. Tracy (London, 2002), 34–54.

104. Charles-Philippe d'Albert, duc de Luynes, *Mémoires du duc de Luynes sur la cour de Louis XV (1735–1758)*, ed. L. Dussieux and E. Soulié, 17 vols (Paris, 1860–65), vol. 7, 136.

105. Rohan Butler, *Choiseul*, vol. 1, *Father and Son, 1719–1754* (Oxford, 1980), 723, 732.

106. These tendencies were reflected in the government, a coalition of forces originally loyal to Walpole with others from opposition ranks. John B. Owen, *The Rise of the Pelhams* (London, 1957).

107. Daniel A. Baugh, 'Withdrawing from Europe: Anglo-French Maritime Geopolitics, 1750–1800', *International History Review* 20, no. 1 (1998): 1–32.

108. For the *doux commerce* reading, see Catherine Larrère, *L'invention de l'économie au XVIIIe siècle: Du droit naturel à la physiocratie* (Paris, 1992), 135–72. For a critique, see Arnault Skornicki, *L'économiste, la cour et la patrie: L'économie politique dans la France des Lumières* (Paris, 2011), 123–38.

109. Jean-Frédéric Phélypeaux, comte de Maurepas, 'Mémoire et considérations générales sur le commerce de France', in idem, *Mémoires du comte de Maurepas, ministre de la marine, &c.*, ed. Jean-Louis Soulavie, 2nd edn (Paris, 1792), 242.

110. Jean-Frédéric Phélypeaux, comte de Maurepas, 'Mémoire sur la marine et le commerce', (late 1745), reproduced in Maurice Filion, *Maurepas, ministre de Louis XV (1715–1749)* (Montreal, 1967), 61–82.

111. Daniel A. Baugh, *British Naval Administration in the Age of Walpole* (Princeton, 1965), 245–7.

112. Henri Legohérel, *Les trésorier généraux de la marine (1517–1788)* (Paris, 1965), table facing 180. Maurepas requested a construction budget of 20 million livres for 1744 and 1745 but received only half this sum. See also Cornell MP 14/38, 'Memoire sur l'estat actuel de la marine, et sur les arrangements à prendre pour le service de l'année 1745'.

113. In 1746 against thirty-five French ships of the line (forty guns or more), the British had eighty-nine. See Jonathan R. Dull, *The Age of the Ship of the Line: The British & French Navies, 1650–1815* (Lincoln, NE, 2009), 51, 89.

114. Compare with the figures for the Spanish and colonial trades in 'Situation du commerce exterieur du roïaume' (1730), reproduced in Filion, *Maurepas*, 157–72.

115. See Robert Chamboredon and Danielle Bertrand-Fabre, 'De la "marchandise" à la magistrature: L'ascension des Fornier de Clausonne au siècle des Lumières, sous la Révolution et l'Empire', *Annales historiques de la Révolution française* 258 (1984): 479–94.

116. Cornell MP 15/14, 'Reflexions sur les moyens de sauver le debris du commerce'. Cover letter found at Cornell MP 5/51, François Fournier to Maurepas, 15 Jan. 1746.

117. Cornell MP 14/36, 'Memoire pour faire connoître la situation actuelle du commerce maritime'. Cover letter, Cornell MP 4/45, Fournier to Maurepas, 19 Oct. 1745. Marseillais merchant Jean-Baptiste Bonnet agreed. Cornell MP 14/34, Jean-Baptiste Bonnet, 'Mémoire' (1745).

118. Cornell MP 15/17, [Pierre-André d'Héguerty], 'Projet pour renouveler le gouvernement de la Grande Bretagne', [Oct. 1745].

119. Gabriel Bonnot de Mably, *Le droit public de l'Europe, fondé sur les traitez conclus jusqu'en l'année 1740*, 2 vols (The Hague, 1746), vol. 2, 243–7. Consistent with this position, Mably was prepared for Spain to confirm the Asiento to the English and concede rights to navigate in the Caribbean. AAE MD France 516 fols 258–65, Gabriel Bonnot de Mably, 'Réflexions sur les intérêts de la France dans la conjoncture présente', 22 Sept. 1746.

120. By 1748, the British had taken twenty-three French naval vessels, and twenty-seven others were unfit for service, leaving Maurepas with only thirty or so ships of motley sizes, just nine actually at sea. André Picciola, *Le comte de Maurepas: Versailles et l'Europe à la fin de l'Ancien Régime* (Paris, 1999), 352. British Patriots continued to press for attacks on French colonies, and the Admiralty equipped a major expedition to take Quebec in 1746. It was diverted to a failed raid on the Breton port of Lorient, but the writing was on the wall for the French empire. Harding, 'Expedition to Lorient, 1746'. The establishment of a western squadron in the late stages of the war completed the stranglehold on French trade. Cruising permanently in the crossroads of north–south European trade, and trans-Atlantic shipping routes, the Royal Navy imposed a virtual blockade on French commerce. See Michael Duffy, 'The Establishment of the Western Squadron as the Linchpin of British Naval Strategy', in *Parameters of British Naval Power 1650–1850*, ed. Michael Duffy (Exeter, 1992), 60–81. In May 1747 the British intercepted two major convoys for a loss of eighty merchant ships, and the near annihilation of an accompanying naval squadron, while in October six French ships of the line were sunk or taken when the British attacked another convoy. Dull, *Age of the Ship of the Line*, 60. Maurepas suspended convoying in 1748 and shipping losses spiked, with colonial trade suffering an especially severe drop. See François Crouzet,' La conjoncture bordelaise', in *Histoire de Bordeaux au XVIIIe siècle*, ed. François-Georges Pariset (Bordeaux, 1968), 191–323, 298–9.

121. Jan Glete, *Navies and Nations: Warships, Navies and State Building in Europe and America, 1500–1860*, 2 vols (Stockholm, 1993), vol. 1, 265–6.

122. James Pritchard, *Louis XV's Navy 1748–1762: A Study of Organization and Administration* (Kingston, 1987). On the disgrace, see Picciola, *Comte de Maurepas*, 357–72.

123. Pinto, *An Essay on Circulation and Credit*, 230.

124. Harris, *Politics and the Nation*, 119.

125. Dull, *Age of the Ship of the Line*, 68.

126. William G. Whitely, 'The Principio Company', *Pennsylvania Magazine of History and Biography* 11, no. 1 (1887): 63–8, 63.

127. Lyttelton, *Considerations upon the Present State of our Affairs*, 3.

128. Steve Pincus, *The Heart of the Declaration: The Founders' Case for an Activist Government* (New Haven, 2016), 35.

129. Davis, 'English Foreign Trade, 1700–1774'; T.H. Breen, 'An Empire of Goods: The Anglicization of Colonial America, 1690–1776', *Journal of British Studies* 25, no. 4 (1986): 467–99; Jacob M. Price, 'Who Cared about the Colonies? The Impact of the Thirteen Colonies on British Society and Politics, *circa* 1714–1775', in *Strangers within the Realm: Cultural Margins of the First British Empire*, ed. Bernard Bailyn and Philip D. Morgan (Chapel Hill, 1991), 395–436.

130. A claim made indefatigably by Americans. See, for example, [Benjamin Franklin], *The Interest of Great Britain Considered, with Regard to her Colonies, and the Acquisitions of Canada and Guadaloupe. To which are Added, Observations Concerning the Increase of Mankind, Peopling of Countries, &c.* (London, 1760).

131. It is possible that he had met Bolingbroke during the latter's exile in France between 1715 and 1725. He stayed with him early in 1734. See AAE CP Ang 383 fol. 215. Also D.J. Fletcher, 'The Fortunes of Bolingbroke in France in the Eighteenth Century', *Studies on Voltaire and the Eighteenth Century* 47 (1966): 207–32, 219. On Silhouette's work for the tobacco monopoly, see Price, *France and the Chesapeake*, vol. 1, 342.

132. Ibid., 540. He also translated works by Pope and Warburton.

133. AAE CP Ang 412 fols 167–9, Silhouette to Amelot, 26 June 1741; CP Ang 414 fols 7–10, Silhouette to Fleury, 1 Jan. 1742.

134. A vice-admiral in the navy, he had been acting governor of New France in the late stages of the War of the Austrian Succession. As the nephew of Michel Bégon, a former royal intendant at Quebec, he had deep ties to the colony, cemented by marriage into the family of a former governor. Étienne Taillemite, 'Barrin de La Galissonière, Roland-Michel, marquis de La Galissonière', in *Dictionary of Canadian Biography* (Toronto, 1966).

135. François Ternat, *Partager le monde: Rivalités impériales franco-britanniques 1748–1756* (Paris, 2015).

136. Butler, *Choiseul*, 1,058.

137. Takumi Tsuda (ed.), *Mémoires et lettres de Vincent de Gournay* (Tokyo, 1993), xi–xiii.

138. Charles, 'French "New Politics"'.

139. Orain, 'Soutenir la guerre et réformer la fiscalité'.

140. AAE MD Ang 46 fols 45–88, 'Observations sur les finances, la navigation & le commerce de l'Angleterre'. See also BNF fr 12162.

141. To be sure, he credits institutional factors also: wise laws regulating trade in the interests of the metropole, and above all the navigation acts, which he saw as the foundation of England's extensive merchant shipping and thus of its powerful navy. But he devotes far less attention to these factors than to England's American commerce. See Cheney, *Revolutionary Commerce*, 45–7.

142. [Georges-Marie Butel-Dumont], *Histoire et commerce des colonies angloises, dans l'Amérique septentrionale* (London, 1755), 1.

143. For his views on tobacco, see BNF fr 12224 fols 241–64, 'Sur l'importance du tabac, sur le moyen d'en établir des plantations dans les colonies françaises et de supplanter les Anglois dans cette branche de commerce'.

144. Loïc Charles, 'Le cercle de Gournay: Usages culturels et pratiques savantes', in *Le cercle de Vincent de Gournay: savoirs économiques et pratiques administratives en France au milieu du XVIIIe siècle*, ed. Loïc Charles, Frédéric Lefebvre, and Christine Théré (Paris, 2011), 63–88.

145. Antonella Alimento, 'Entre animosité nationale et rivalité d'émulation: La position de Véron de Forbonnais face à la competition anglaise', in *Governare il mondo: l'economia come linguaggio della politica nell'Europa del Settecento*, ed. Manuela Albertone (Milan, 2009), 125–48, 126, 136–7.

146. Indeed, the increase in French naval spending won by Maurepas would prove grossly inadequate to protect French commerce in the Atlantic. There was budgetary crisis once again in the navy by the mid-1750s. See Pares, 'American versus Continental Warfare', 451.

147. AAE MD Amérique 24 fols 110–38, 'Mémoire sur les colonies de la France dans l'Amérique septentrionale'. The memoir is often attributed to La Galissonière alone, but an earlier draft in the archives of the naval and colonial ministry indicates that it was written jointly with Silhouette, and indeed the strategic vision owes much to the latter's 1747 memorandum. See AN Col C11A 96 fol. 175.

148. Such prescriptions reflect the local knowledge and the military perspective of La Galissonière, but Silhouette accepted them as an extension of his own position. Nine years later, when asked if it was worthwhile to try to hold on to Canada, he endorsed the mémoire of 1750 as the best treatment of Canada's strategic significance. AAE MD Amérique 24, 'Premier mémoire où l'on traite la question, s'il convient ou non d'abandonner le Canada'. The cover letter identifying Silhouette as the author is at AAE CP Ang 442 fol. 33, dated 8 Feb. 1759.

There is a second, less prominent position outlined in the famous La Galissonière–Silhouette memorandum that envisions the transformation of French North America into a great agricultural empire, a perspective attributable to the marquis who was a noted agricultural improver. See Fredrik Albritton Jonsson, 'Rival Ecologies of Global Commerce: Adam Smith and the Natural Historians', *American Historical Review* 115, no. 5 (2010): 1,342–63, 1,344.

149. Eric Hinderaker, *Elusive Empires: Constructing Colonialism in the Ohio Valley, 1673–1800* (Cambridge, 1997), 32–45.

150. Philippe de Flassan, *Histoire générale et raisonnée de la diplomatie française*, 2nd edn, 7 vols (Paris, 1811), vol. 6, 14–16.

151. See AAE MD Ang 46 fols 45–88, 'Observations sur les finances, la navigation & le commerce de l'Angleterre'. Gournay agreed. See Antonella Alimento, 'Competition, True Patriotism and Colonial Interest: Forbonnais' Vision of Neutrality and Trade', in *Trade and War*, ed. Stapelbroek, 61–94, 69.

152. Cornell MP 15/38, untitled memorandum, June 1746, reproduced in Tsuda (ed.), *Mémoires et lettres de Vincent de Gournay*, 3–12. On the politics of navigation acts, see also Marc Belissa, 'What Trade for a Republican People? French Revolutionary Debates about Commercial Treaties (1792–1799)', in *Politics of Commercial Treaties*, ed. Alimento and Stapelbroek, 421–38.

153. These remarks are reproduced in Jacques-Claude-Marie Vincent de Gournay, *Traités sur le commerce de Josiah Child avec les remarques inédites de Vincent de Gournay*, ed. Takumi Tsuda (Tokyo, 1983), passim.

154. [Jacques-Claude-Marie Vincent de Gournay], *Traités sur le commerce et sur les avantages qui résultent de la réduction de l'interest de l'argent* (Amsterdam, 1754). See Alimento, 'Competition, True Patriotism and Colonial Interest', 73–4.

155. François Véron de Forbonnais, *Essai sur l'admission des navires neutres dans nos colonies* (Paris, 1756); idem, 'Réflexions sur la nécessité de comprendre l'étude du commerce et des finances dans celle de la politique', in *Considérations sur les finances d'Espagne*, 2nd edn (Dresden, 1755), separately paginated, 68–9. See also Alimento, 'Entre animosité nationale et rivalité d'émulation', 146–7.

156. Louis-Joseph Plumard de Dangeul, *Examen de la conduite de la Grande-Bretagne à l'égard de la Hollande, depuis la naissance de la République jusqu'à présent* (Paris, 1756). Alimento, 'Competition, True Patriotism and Colonial Interest', 64–5.

157. See John A. Schutz, 'Imperialism in Massachusetts during the Governorship of William Shirley, 1741–1756', *Huntington Library Quarterly* 23, no. 3 (1960): 217–36.

158. ERO Mildmay Papers D/DM/O1/41, William Shirley, 'Remarks on the Importance of the Province of Nova Scotia'.

159. William Shirley to Newcastle, 29 Oct. 1745, in William Shirley, *Correspondence of William Shirley, Governor of Massachusetts*, ed. Charles Henry Lincoln, 2 vols (New York, 1912), vol. 1, 284–5. See also Gould, *Persistence of Empire*, 63–4.

160. Newcastle, by contrast, was both more pessimistic about French intentions and more willing to confront what he perceived as French aggression in America and India. He was influenced by the belligerent George Montague-Dunk, earl of Halifax, and by Shirley, whose appointment to the boundary commission Newcastle arranged. The revocation of the latter's commission in 1752 suggests that the more pacific position was at least temporarily in the ascendant.

161. For example, William Mildmay, *The Laws and Policy of England, Relating to Trade, Examined by the Maxims and Principles of Trade in General; and by the Laws and Policy of Other Trading Nations* (London, 1765). He had begun to write memoranda on trade in the 1730s when his benefactor, Benjamin Mildmay, Earl Fitzwalter, was first lord of trade. See ERO Mildmay Papers D/DM/O1/19.

162. WCL Mildmay Papers 3, William Mildmay to Benjamin Fitzwalter, 13 Feb. 1754.

163. WCL Mildmay Papers 3, Mildmay to Fitzwalter, 15 Dec. 1751; BL Eg 3456 fol. 134, Mildmay to Holderness, 22 Jan./2 Feb. 1752.

164. 'Under such a constitution', he wrote, 'I think it is impossible they should arrive at any superiority over us either in their trade or marine'. BL Eg 3456 fols 254–5, Mildmay to Holderness, 30 June 1752. On the broad meaning of the term 'constitution' in eighteenth-century political economic thought, see above, p. 43.

165. WCL Mildmay Papers 3, Mildmay to Fitzwalter, 16 Jan. 1754.

166. BL Eg 3456 fol. 203, Mildmay to Holderness, 3 May 1752. For one such proposal, see Lawrence Henry Gipson, 'A French Project for Victory Short of a Declaration of War, 1755', *Canadian Historical Review* 26, no. 4 (1945): 361–71.

167. Coxe (ed.), *Memoirs of Henry Pelham*, vol. 2, 435.

168. Forbonnais, *Élemens du commerce*, vol. 1, 359–61, 366–7. Forbonnais was in possession of a range of memoranda on the boundary questions. Alimento, 'Competition, True Patriotism and Colonial Interest', 72, citing Gabriel Fleury, *François Véron de Fortbonnais: Sa famille, sa vie, ses actes, ses œuvres 1722–1800* (Mamers and Le Mans, 1915). On the importance of neutralised buffer zones to the peace plans of both sides, see Ternat, *Partager le monde*, 419–26.

169. AAE CP Ang suppl. 11 fols 264–5, Silhouette to Antoine-Louis Rouillé, 5 Dec. 1755. A draft of Hardwicke's sympathetic but non-committal reply can be found at BL Add MS 35870 fol. 257. On the separate van Neck peace overture, see BL Add MS 32861 fols 118–19, Thomas Walpole to Horatio Walpole, 28 Nov. 1755; BL Add MS 32862 fol. 279, unidentified to Newcastle, 29 Jan. 1756. See also François-Joachim de Pierre, cardinal de Bernis, *Mémoires du cardinal de Bernis*, ed. Philippe Bonnet (Paris, 1980), 158–60.

170. AAE CP Ang suppl. 11 fols 165–90, 'Mémoire sur les moyens de prévenir la guerre et de parvenir à une conciliation avec l'Angleterre'. This memorandum is attributed to Jean-Louis Favier, but an earlier draft of the same document exists written by Silhouette. See AN Mar B⁴ 47 fols 214–32 (8 Feb. 1755).

171. AAE MD Ang 52 fols 103–12, Adrien-Maurice, duc de Noailles, 'Mémoire sur la conjoncture présente', 15 Feb. 1755.

172. Harris, *Politics and the Nation*, passim; Vaughn, *Politics of Empire*, 58–69.

173. *The Monitor, or the British Freeholder* 220 (6 Oct. 1759).

174. BL Add MS 32923 fols 123–8, Hardwicke to Newcastle, 16 May 1761.

175. Hardwicke to Newcastle, 18 Apr. 1761, in Philip Chesney Yorke, *The Life and Correspondence of Philip Yorke, Earl of Hardwicke*, 3 vols (London, 1913), vol. 3, 317.

176. John Russell, duke of Bedford to John Stuart, earl of Bute, 13 June 1761, in Bedford, *Correspondence*, vol. 3, 17.

177. BL Add MS 4319 fol. 271, Josiah Tucker to Thomas Birch, 2 Nov. 1761.

178. BL Add MS 4326 B fols 64–7, Tucker to Birch, 1 Sept. 1755; BL Add. MS 4319 fol. 260, Tucker to Birch, 30 Nov. 1756; fol. 271, Tucker to Birch, 2 Nov. 1761.

179. Josiah Tucker, *Four Letters on Important National Subjects Addressed to the Right Honourable the Earl of Shelburne* (Dublin, 1783), 1.

180. Tucker, *Case of Going to War*, 40, 37n. See also Nancy F. Koehn, *The Power of Commerce: Economy and Governance in the First British Empire* (Ithaca, 1994), 149–84.

181. *Monitor* 381 (6 Nov. 1762); 382 (27 Nov. 1762). See also Marie Peters, *Pitt and Popularity: The Patriot Minister and London Opinion during the Seven Years' War* (Oxford, 1980), 164–5.

182. A case can be made for Pitt's opportunism where matters of empire were concerned. However, about his desire to permanently reduce Bourbon power there can be no doubt. See Marie Peters, 'The Myth of William Pitt, Earl of Chatham, Great Imperialist, Part I: Pitt and Imperial Expansion 1738–1763', *Journal of Imperial and Commonwealth History* 21, no. 1 (1993): 31–74.

183. The words are those of Edward Richardson, in a key statement representing the views of Bute, 'A Letter to a Gentleman in the City', *St James Chronicle* (7–9 Sept. 1762).

184. *Parliamentary History*, vol. 15, cols 1,251–6.

5. MADE IN AMERICA: FREE TRADE AND THE CRISIS OF EMPIRE

1. Thomas Tod, *Observations on American Independency* (n.p., 1779), 8.

2. Jack P. Greene, *Evaluating Empire and Confronting Colonialism in Eighteenth-Century Britain* (Cambridge, 2013), 90, 299–300.

3. Pernille Røge, *Economistes and the Reinvention of Empire: France in the Americas and Africa, c. 1750–1802* (Cambridge, 2019).

4. Horn, *Economic Development*, passim, and 108–10 for Dunkirk free port.

5. Thomas M. Truxes, *Defying Empire: Trading with the Enemy in Colonial New York* (New Haven, 2008).

6. Alan Karras, 'Transgressive Exchange: Circumventing Eighteenth-Century Atlantic Commercial Restrictions, *or* The Discount of Monte Christi', in *Seascapes: Maritime Histories, Littoral Cultures, and Transoceanic Exchanges*, ed. Jerry H. Bentley, R. Bridenthal, and Kären Wigen (Honolulu, 2007), 121–34.

7. François-Joseph Ruggiu, 'Falling into Oblivion? Canada and the French Monarchy, 1759–1783', in *Revisiting 1759: The Conquest of Canada in Historical Perspective*, ed. Phillip Buckner and John G. Reid (Toronto, 2012), 70–94. Paul W. Mapp analyses the shift in Choiseul's attitude towards Louisiana in *Elusive West and the Contest for Empire*, 359–86.

8. Marion F. Godfroy, *Kourou, 1763: Le dernier rêve de l'Amérique française* (Paris, 2011); Emma Rothschild, 'A Horrible Tragedy in the French Atlantic', *Past & Present* 192 (2006): 67–108.

9. François-Joseph Ruggiu, 'India and the Reshaping of the French Colonial Policy (1759–1789)', *Itinerario* 35, no. 2 (2011): 25–43, 29.

10. Jean Tarrade, *Le commerce colonial de la France à la fin de l'Ancien Régime, l'évolution du régime de 'l'Exclusif' de 1763 à 1789*, 2 vols (Paris, 1972), vol. 1, 229. This recalls the vision of colonies that appealed to French policymakers in 1713. Indeed there was a long-standing tension between strategic and commercial visions of French Empire overseas. See Miquelon, 'Envisioning the French Empire'.

11. Catherine M. Desbarats, 'France in North America: The Net Burden of Empire during the First Half of the Eighteenth Century', *French History* 11 (1997): 1–28.

12. AAE CP Espagne 532 fols 455–73, Pierre-Paul, marquis d'Ossun to Étienne-François de Stainville, duc de Choiseul, 29 June 1761; BNF fr 10766 fols 141–68, the abbé Augustin de Béliardi, 'Mémoire pour l'Espagne'. See also John Fraser Ramsey, *Anglo-French Relations 1763–1770: A Study of Choiseul's Foreign Policy* (Berkeley, 1939), 149–50.

13. BNF fr 10768 fols 491–517, Augustin de Béliardi, 'Mémoire des principales places de commerce'; and fols 152–7, 'Quelques réflexions sur différentes branches du commerce de la France et de l'Espagne'. See Antonella Alimento, 'Raynal, Accarias de Sérionne et le Pacte de Famille', in *Autour de l'abbé Raynal: genèse et enjeux politiques de l'Histoire des deux Indes*, ed. Antonella Alimento and Gianluigi Goggi (Ferney-Voltaire, 2018), 33–45.

14. Monique Cottret, *Choiseul: L'obsession du pouvoir* (Paris, 2018), 235–68.

15. On the structural consequences of war for the plantation economy, see Cheney, *Cul de Sac*, 105–29.
16. There was no demand for molasses in France, while colonial rum was excluded to protect metropolitan distillers. Tarrade, *Commerce colonial*, vol. 1, 167–83.
17. Trevor Burnard and John Garrigus, *The Plantation Machine: Atlantic Capitalism in French Saint-Domingue and British Jamaica* (Philadelphia, 2016), 87–90.
18. Røge, *Economistes and the Reinvention of Empire*, 119, 121–2, 125.
19. AN F^{12} 105(2) fols 59–78, Jean-Baptiste Dubuc, 'Mémoire sur l'étendu & les bornes des loix prohibitives du commerce étranger dans nos colonies'. See also Tarrade, *Commerce colonial*, vol. 1, 241–2.
20. Paul-Pierre Le Mercier de La Rivière, 'Mémoire sur la Martinique', 8 Sept. 1762, reproduced in idem, *Le Mercier de La Rivière*, 104–54. The intendant's inflexibility quickly gave way on the ground to an embrace of trade with foreigners; he was subsequently cashiered for an indulgence of foreign slavers deemed to be excessive.
21. [Victor Riqueti, marquis de Mirabeau and François Quesnay], *Philosophie rurale, ou Économie générale et politique de l'agriculture*, 3 vols (Amsterdam, 1763), vol. 3, 223–42. See also Pernille Røge, 'A Natural Order of Empire: The Physiocratic Vision of Colonial France after the Seven Years' War', in *The Political Economy of Empire in the Early Modern World*, ed. Sophus Reinert and Pernille Røge (Basingstoke, 2013), 32–52.
22. Røge, *Economistes and the Reinvention of Empire*, 88–102.
23. Ibid., 79.
24. Ibid., 122.
25. Mirabeau and Quesnay, *Philosophie rurale*, vol. 3, 223–42.
26. Cheney, *Revolutionary Commerce*, 177–83.
27. Tarrade, *Commerce colonial*, vol. 1, 275. See [Jean-Baptiste Dubuc], 'Mémoire sur l'étendu & les bornes des loix prohibitives du commerce étranger dans nos colonies', *Journal de l'agriculture, du commerce et des finances* (Dec. 1765), 87–122. Quesnay laid out the orthodox Physiocratic position in his 'Remarques sur l'opinion de l'auteur de *l'Esprit des loix* concernant les colonies', *Journal de l'agriculture, du commerce et des finances* (Apr. 1766), 4–34.
28. Tarrade, *Commerce colonial*, vol. 1, 199–200.
29. [Guillaume-Thomas Raynal], *Histoire philosophique et politique des établissements & du commerce des Européens dans les deux Indes*, 6 vols (Amsterdam, 1770), vol. 5, 167–70.
30. Frances Armytage, *The Free Port System in the British West Indies: A Study in Commercial Policy, 1766–1822* (London, 1953).
31. See T.G. Burnard, '"Prodigious Riches": The Wealth of Jamaica before the American Revolution', *Economic History Review* 54, no. 3 (2001), 511–12. Adrian J. Pearce, *British Trade with Spanish America 1763–1808* (Liverpool, 2007), 52–69 disputes the extent of this decline.
32. By slashing the existing duty on this trade and strictly enforcing measures against contraband, he hoped to better protect the British sugar islands and to increase revenues on the import of foreign molasses into the American colonies. See Allen S. Johnson, 'The Passage of the Sugar Act', *William and Mary Quarterly* 16, no. 4 (1959): 507–14.
33. Allan Christelow, 'Contraband Trade between Jamaica and the Spanish Main, and the Free Port Act of 1766', *Hispanic American Historical Review* 22, no. 2 (1942): 309–43.
34. Koehn, *The Power of Commerce*, 193–6.
35. Jack M. Sosin, *Agents and Merchants: British Colonial Policy and the Origins of the American Revolution, 1763–1775* (Lincoln, NE, 1765), 67–8.
36. Indeed, the planter interest had to be bribed to go as far as it did with a lessening of the duties paid by British-produced sugar imported to North America. See Paul Langford, *The First Rockingham Administration 1765–1766* (Oxford, 1973), 10–26.
37. Edmund Burke, *Observations on a Late State of the Nation*, 2nd edn (London, 1769), 127–8. On Burke's role and thinking at this moment, see Richard Bourke, *Empire and Revolution: The Political Life of Edmund Burke* (Princeton, 2015), 310–12; and P.J. Marshall, *Edmund Burke and the British Empire in the West Indies: Wealth, Power, and Slavery* (Oxford, 2019), 105–24.

38. John Huske to Charles Townshend, 9 Apr. 1767. Cited in 'Huske, John (1724–73)', *History of Parliament: The House of Commons 1754–1790*, ed. L. Namier and J. Brooke (London, 1964).

39. Charles Lloyd to Charles Jenkinson, 24 Aug. 1765, in *The Jenkinson Papers, 1760–1766*, ed. Ninetta S. Jucker (London, 1949), 380–1.

40. BL Add MS 33030 fols 318–23, [John Huske], 'Observations on the Trade of Great Britain to her American Colonies' [Oct. 1765]; TNA CO 5/66 fol. 123, Huske to Henry Seymour Conway, 27 Oct. 1765. There was also support for a wider extension of interimperial trade in the new American possessions acquired in 1763. Governor George Johnstone of West Florida in particular saw the future of his colony in trade with Spanish America, and pressed for a free port there. Pearce, *British Trade with Spanish America*, 41, 59.

41. Edmund Burke to Charles O'Hara, 1 Mar. 1766, in Edmund Burke, *The Correspondence of Edmund Burke*, ed. Thomas W. Copeland, 10 vols (Cambridge & Chicago, 1958–1978), vol. 1, 239–40.

42. Burke, *Observations on a Late State of the Nation*, 128.

43. Barlow Trecothick to John Hancock, 13 June 1766, reproduced in 'London Merchants on the Stamp Act Repeal', *Proceedings of the Massachusetts Historical Society*, 3rd series, 55 (1921–22): 220–3.

44. Burke, *Observations on a Late State of the Nation*, 127–30.

45. Armytage, *Free Port System*, 28–51.

46. Gee, *Trade and Navigation of Great-Britain Considered*, 22.

47. Marshall, *Edmund Burke*, 106–7, 116, 122.

48. It may be significant in this regard that Pitt and his loyal supporter, William Beckford, strongly opposed the free ports. See Sosin, *Agents and Merchants*, 83–4. On Beckford, see Perry Gauci, *William Beckford: First Prime Minister of the London Empire* (New Haven, 2013).

49. TNA CO 110/2 fol. 1, Campbell Dalrymple to Charles Wyndham, earl of Egremont, 6 Dec. 1761; Bodl. MS North b. 6 fols 120–3, Dalrymple to John Stuart, earl of Bute, 2 June 1762. On wartime Sint Eustatius, see Willem Klooster and Gert Oostindie, *Realm Between Empires: The Second Dutch Atlantic, 1680–1815* (Ithaca, 2018), 53.

50. BL Add MS 38200 fols 260–4, 261, Dalrymple to Bute, 27 Feb. 1763.

51. BL Add MS 33030 fols 318–23, 319, Huske, 'Observations'. As another commentator would later put it, the goal of the free ports was that 'we might enjoy to the extent of the trade all the advantages of the foreign colonies without being exposed to the expense of establishing or protecting them'. BL Add MS 38345 fols 208–13, 209, Thomas Irving, 'Observations of the Trade Carried on between the British West Indies and the Spanish Colonies'.

52. BL Add MS 33030 fols 318–23, 321, 'Observations'.

53. Marshall, *Edmund Burke*, 122.

54. William Knox, *Three Tracts Respecting the Conversion and Instruction of the Free Indians and Negro Slaves in the Colonies* (London, 1768), 19. Cited in Marshall, *Edmund Burke*, 122.

55. Christopher L. Brown, 'Empire without Slaves: British Concepts of Emancipation in the Age of the American Revolution', *William and Mary Quarterly* 56, no. 2 (1999): 273–306.

56. Nicolas Baudeau, *Idées d'un citoyen sur la puissance du roi et le commerce de la nation dans l'Orient* (Amsterdam, 1763).

57. *Éphémérides du citoyen* (29 Sept.–10 Oct. 1766).

58. Here I follow the analysis in Røge, *Economistes and the Reinvention of Empire*, 72–4, 83–102. On Physiocratic arguments against slavery, see also Caroline Oudin-Bastide and Philippe Steiner, *Calcul et morale: Coûts de l'esclavage et valeur de l'émancipation (XVIIIe–XIXe siècle)* (Paris, 2015), and Madeleine Dobie, *Trading Places: Colonization and Slavery in Eighteenth-Century French Culture* (Ithaca, 2010), 224–30.

59. From an article in the English papers of 16 April 1766 translated by the French naval ministry, and cited in Tarrade, *Commerce colonial*, vol. 1, 297.

60. Tarrade, *Commerce colonial*, vol. 1, 317–20. The fall of Praslin and Choiseul in 1770 did not alter this new orientation (vol. 1, 373–4).

61. TNA CO 137/64 fol. 264, Commander Forrest to lords of the Admiralty, 8 Oct. 1769. Cited in Dorothy Goebel, 'The "New England Trade" and the French West Indies, 1763–1774: A Study in Trade Policies', *William and Mary Quarterly* 20, no. 3 (1963): 331–72, 371.

62. Étienne-François de Stainville, duc de Choiseul, 'Mémoire présenté à Louis XV par le duc de Choiseul', in André Soulange-Bodin, *La diplomatie de Louis XV et le Pacte de Famille* (Paris, 1894), 251; Tarrade, *Commerce colonial*, vol. 1, 229.

63. Jonathan R. Dull, *The French Navy and American Independence: A Study of Arms and Diplomacy, 1774–1787* (Princeton, 1975), 6–7.

64. AAE CP Ang 485 fols 185–92, Louis-Marie Florent, comte du Châtelet to Choiseul, 28 Jan. 1769; fols 233–4, Choiseul to Châtelet, 31 Jan. 1769; fols 303–4, Choiseul to Châtelet, 6 Feb. 1769; AAE CP Ang 486 fols 83–4, Choiseul to Châtelet, 14 Mar. 1769.

65. AAE CP Ang 484 fols 282–5. The quotation is from a summary of Abeille's *mémoire* probably written by Jean-Ignace de la Ville, 31 Dec. 1769 [fol. 281].

66. Gilbert Chinard, *The Treaties of 1778 and Allied Documents* (Baltimore, 1928).

67. Benjamin Frankin to Joseph Priestley, 7 July 1775, in Benjamin Franklin, *Works of Benjamin Franklin*, ed. John Bigelow, 12 vols (New York, 1904), vol. 7, 81. Cited in Felix Gilbert, *To the Farewell Address: Ideas of Early American Foreign Policy* (Princeton, 1961), 48.

68. Vernon G. Sester, *The Commercial Reciprocity Policy of the United States, 1774–1829* (Philadelphia, 1937), 13–18; John Crowley, *The Privileges of Independence: Neomercantilism and the American Revolution* (Baltimore, 1993), 57–60.

69. Charles Gravier, comte de Vergennes to Armand Marc, comte de Montmorin, 20 June 1778, in *Histoire de la participation de la France à l'établissement des États-Unis d'Amérique. Correspondance diplomatique et documents*, ed. Henri Doniol, 5 vols (Paris, 1886–92), vol. 3, 140.

70. Crowley, *Privileges of Independence*, 50–62. See also Larry Sawers, 'The Navigation Acts Revisited', *Economic History Review* 45, no. 2 (1992): 262–84; and Eliga Gould, 'War by Other Means: Mercantilism and Free Trade in the Age of the American Revolution', in *American Capitalism: New Histories*, ed. Sven Beckert and Christine Desan (New York, 2018), 285–302.

71. Doniol (ed.), *Histoire de la participation*, vol. 1, 275–6.

72. 'Réflexions sur la situation actuelle des colonies anglaises, et sur la conduite qu'il convient à la France de tenir à leur égard', in ibid., 244. See also Dull, *French Navy and American Independence*, 37–8.

73. 'Mémoire communiqué au Roi le 23 juillet 1777 et approuvé le même jour par Sa Majté', in *Histoire de la participation*, ed. Doniol, vol. 2, 463.

74. Jean-François Labourdette, *Vergennes: Ministre principal de Louis XVI* (Paris, 1990), 262. The principle of neutral rights was routinely equated with freedom of trade. See, for example, Franklin to the president of Congress, 9 Aug. 1780, in *Revolutionary Diplomatic Correspondence of the United States*, ed. Francis Wharton, 5 vols (Washington, 1889), vol. 4, 24.

75. Marzagalli, 'Was Warfare Necessary'.

76. AAE CP Suède 270 fols 149–50, Vergennes to the chevalier de Sainte-Croix, 6 Apr. 1779. Cited in Éric Schnakenbourg, 'From "Hostile Infection" to "Free Ship, Free Goods": Changes in French Neutral Trade Legislation (1689–1778)', in *Trade and War*, ed. Stapelbroek, 95–113. See also Éric Schnakenbourg, *Entre la guerre et la paix: Neutralité et relations internationales XVIIe–XVIIIe siècles* (Rennes, 2013). Vergennes's aide, Joseph Mathias Gérard de Rayneval, would later publish a fully elaborated defence of freedom of the seas, *De la liberté des mers*, 2 vols (Paris, 1811).

77. *Règlement concernant la navigation des bâtiments neutres en temps de guerre* (26 July 1778).

78. On the subsequent importance of American neutrality to French maritime trade, see Marzagalli, *Bordeaux et les États-Unis*.

79. Jonathan R. Dull, *A Diplomatic History of the American Revolution* (New Haven, 1985), 128–9; Isabel de Madariaga, *Britain, Russia and the Armed Neutrality of 1780: Sir James Harris's Mission to St Petersburg during the American Revolution* (New Haven, 1962), 172–3.

80. Anne-Robert-Jacques Turgot, 'Réflexions rédigées à l'occasion d'un Mémoire remis par de Vergennes au Roi sur la manière dont la France et l'Espagne doivent envisager les suites de la querelle entre la Grande-Bretagne et ses colonies', in *Œuvres de Turgot et documents le concernant*, ed. Gustave Schelle, 5 vols (Paris, 1913–23), vol. 5, 384–420.

81. Doniol (ed.), *Histoire de la participation*, vol. 1, 586. Cited in Manuel Covo, 'Commerce, empire et révolutions dans le monde atlantique: La colonie française de Saint-Domingue entre métropole et États-Unis (*ca.* 1778–*ca.* 1804)', PhD thesis, École des Hautes Études en Sciences Sociales, 2013, 89.

82. Whatmore, *Against War and Empire*, 142–3.

83. Hardman, *Overture to Revolution*; Munro Price, *Preserving the Monarchy: The Comte de Vergennes, 1774–1787* (Cambridge, 1995).

84. Paul Cheney, 'A False Dawn for Enlightenment Cosmopolitanism? Franco-American Trade during the American War of Independence', *William and Mary Quarterly*, 3rd series, 58, no. 3 (2006): 463–88.

85. Part of a larger reckoning with the implications of American independence for Britain's position in the world. On this theme, see Gould, *Persistence of Empire*, 181–214; and Eliga H. Gould, 'American Independence and Britain's Counter-Revolution', *Past & Present* 154 (1997): 107–41.

86. Smith, *Wealth of Nations*, vol. 2, 622–5. See David Stevens, 'Adam Smith and the Colonial Disturbances', in *Essays on Adam Smith*, ed. Andrew S. Skinner and Thomas Wilson (Oxford, 1975), 202–17.

87. He put it most forcefully in a letter a few years later: 'The real futility of all distant dominions, of which the defence is necessarily most expensive, and which contribute nothing, either by revenue or military force, to the general defence of the empire, and very little even to their own particular defence, is, I think, the subject upon which the public prejudices of Europe require most to be set right.' Adam Smith to John Sinclair of Ulbster, 14 Oct. 1782, in Smith, *Correspondence*, 262.

88. Adam Smith, 'Smith's Thoughts on the State of the Contest with America, February 1778', in idem, *Correspondence*, 377–85. Original in WCL Wedderburn Papers 2/8.

89. Charles R. Ritcheson, *British Politics and the American Revolution* (Norman, 1954), 258–78, 284; Andrew Jackson O'Shaughnessy, *The Men Who Lost America: British Leadership, the American Revolution, and the Fate of the Empire* (New Haven, 2013), 61–4.

90. 'Instructions by King George III to his Commissioners to Treat with the North American Colonies', *Manuscripts of the Earl of Carlisle* (London, 1897), 322–32.

91. *Parliamentary History*, vol. 19, cols 1,022–3. See also H.T. Dickinson, 'The Failure of Conciliation: Britain and the American Colonies 1763–1783', *Kyoto Economic Review* 79, no. 2 (2010): 2–20, 5.

92. *Parliamentary History*, vol. 19, cols 850–2. Here the distinction Jack Greene proposes between a language of liberty and commerce, favoured by the opposition, and a language of state power and imperial grandeur, used by the North administration and its supporters, seems to break down. See Greene, *Evaluating Empire*, 91–111.

93. [John Almon], *A Plan or Articles of Perpetual Union, Commerce, and Friendship between Great-Britain and her American Colonies* (London, 1780), 25, 58.

94. William Eden, *Four Letters to the Earl of Carlisle*, 2nd edn (London, 1779), 48–9. See Leonard J. Sadosky, 'Reimagining the British Empire and America in an Age of Revolution: The Case of William Eden', in *Old World, New World: America and Europe in the Age of Jefferson*, ed. Leonard J. Sadosky, Peter Nicolaisen, Peter S. Onuf and Andrew J. O'Shaughnessy (Charlottesville, 2010), 83–104, 92–3.

95. William Eden, *A Fifth Letter to the Earl of Carlisle* (London, 1780).

96. Adam Smith to William Eden, 3 Jan. 1780, in Smith, *Correspondence*, 244–6.

97. On the ethical underpinnings of Smith's political economy, see Donald Winch, 'Adam Smith: Scottish Moral Philosopher as Political Economist', *Historical Journal* 35, no. 1 (1992): 91–113.

98. Anon., *Address to the Rulers of the State in which their Conduct and Measures, the Principles and Abilities of their Opponents, and the Real Interest of England, with Regard to America and her Natural Enemies, are Freely Canvassed* (London, 1778), 33. See also Anon., *The Cabinet Conference, or Tears of Ministry* (London, 1779), 14.

99. Hugh Elliott to Eden, 28 Mar. 1778, in *B.F. Stevens's Facsimiles of Manuscripts in European Archives Relating to America, 1773–1783*, ed. Benjamin Franklin Stevens, 25 vols (London, 1889–95), vol. 4, 410.

100. James Anderson, *The Interest of Great Britain with Regard to her American Colonies Considered. To which is Added an Appendix, Containing the Outlines of a Plan for a General Pacification* (London, 1782), separately paginated appendix. See also Greene, *Evaluating Empire*, 296–7.

101. Anderson, *Interest of Great Britain*, 110, 120–1.

102. Fredrik Albritton Jonsson, *Enlightenment's Frontier: The Scottish Highlands and the Origins of Environmentalism* (New Haven, 2013), 102–9.

103. George Chalmers, *An Estimate of the Comparative Strength of Great-Britain during the Present and Four Preceding Reigns* (London, 1786 [1782]), 204–5. See also Crowley, *Privileges of Independence*, 346.

104. John Baker Holroyd, earl of Sheffield, *Observations on the Commerce of the American States*, 6th edn (London, 1784).

105. Harlow, *Founding of the Second British Empire*, vol. 1, 200ff; Whatmore, 'Shelburne and Perpetual Peace'; Nigel Aston, 'Francophilia and Political Failure: Lord Shelburne and Anglo-French Interactions, *c.* 1760–1789', *European History Quarterly* 47, no. 4 (2017): 613–33; Anthony Howe, 'Restoring Free Trade: The British Experience, 1776–1873', in *The Political Economy of British Historical Experience, 1688–1914*, ed. Donald Winch and Patrick K. O'Brien (Oxford, 2002), 193–213.

106. André Morellet, *Mémoires inédits de l'abbé Morellet*, 2 vols (Paris, 1823), vol. 1, 221–2; idem, *Lettres de l'abbé Morellet à Lord Shelburne, depuis marquis de Lansdowne, 1772–1803* (Paris 1898).

107. See also C.R. Ritcheson, 'The Earl of Shelburne and Peace with America, 1782–1783: Vision and Reality', *International History Review* 5, no. 3 (1983): 322–45.

108. Pownall was not a follower of Pitt as such. He was regarded as an independent and owed his re-election to Parliament in 1774 to the patronage of Lord North, with whom he was expected to vote. But he broke with North after Saratoga, calling for the return of William Pitt the Elder to the ministry.

109. Thomas Pownall, *A Letter from Governor Pownall to Adam Smith* (London, 1776).

110. [Thomas Pownall], *A Memorial Most Humbly Addressed to the Sovereigns of Europe, on the Present State of Affairs, between the Old and New World* (London, 1780), 78–9, 92–7, 109–17. The pamphlet was successful beyond Pownall's hopes and quickly ran to several editions and two French translations, one arranged by John Adams. See John A. Schutz, *Thomas Pownall, British Defender of American Liberty: A Study in Anglo American Relations in the Eighteenth Century* (Glendale, 1951), 261–2.

111. Pownall's pamphlet received some notice in the press. See *Monthly Review* (Aug. 1780), 104–8; *Edinburgh Magazine* (14 Sept. 1780), 321–4; *Westminster Magazine* (Feb. 1781), 97–8; *Critical Review* (Mar. 1781), 229. The work appears to have wrought a striking change in John Adams's thinking about the commercial implications of American independence. Adams sent a long summary of Pownall's argument to Congress in April 1780. He subsequently published an expurgated version of Pownall's text in English and in French, playing down the degree to which a free-trading America would require an institutionalised European response, but emphasising Pownall's argument that American commercial independence would force a free-trade revolution. See John Adams, *A Translation of the Memorial to the Sovereigns of Europe Upon the Present State of Affairs, between the Old and the New World, into Common Sense and Intelligible English* (London, 1781); idem, *Pensées sur la révolution de l'Amérique-Unie, extraites de l'ouvrage anglois,*

intitulé Mémoire, adressé aux souverains de l'Europe, sur l'état présent des affaires de l'ancien et du nouveau-monde (Amsterdam, 1780). The same arguments appeared in Adams's 'Letters from a Distinguished American', subsequently published in 1782. See John Adams, *Letters from a Distinguished American: Twelve Essays by John Adams on American Foreign Policy, 1780*, ed. James H. Hutson (Washington, 1978). The letters were originally published in a London newspaper, *Parker's General Advertiser and Morning Intelligencer*, between 23 Aug. and 26 Dec. 1782. Pownall's thesis shaped the whole of Adams's subsequent thinking about the position of America in the European states system. See 'Editorial Note', in John Adams, *Papers of John Adams*, ed. Gregg L. Lint et al., 18 vols (Cambridge MA, 1996), vol. 9, 157–64.

112. Edward Payne, on behalf of the Committee of American Merchants, 'Observations on the Trade, which Before the Late War Subsisted Between Great Britain and that Part of America Now Composing the United States with Such Regulations as Appear Proper to be Adopted for the Recovery and Retention of a Considerable Part of that Commerce', 22 July 1783, reproduced in Edmund C. Burnett, 'Observations of London Merchants on American Trade, 1783', *American Historical Review* 18, no. 4 (1913): 769–80.

113. Brian Edwards, *Thoughts on the Late Proceedings of Government Respecting the Trade of the West India Islands with the United States of North America* (London, 1783). See Andrew J. O'Shaughnessy, 'The Formation of a Commercial Lobby: The West India Interest, British Colonial Policy and the American Revolution', *Historical Journal* 40, no. 1 (1997), 94–5.

114. Richard Champion, *Considerations on the Present Situation of Great Britain and the United States of America, with a View to their Future Commercial Connexions*, 2nd edn (London, 1784), 212.

115. [Sir Matthew Decker], *Sir Matthew Decker's Essay on the Causes of the Decline of the Foreign Trade, Its Effects on the Value of Land, and the Means to Restore Both* (London, n.d. [1787]).

116. Benjamin Vaughan to Franklin, 25 Feb. 1783, in Benjamin Franklin, *Papers of Benjamin Franklin*, ed. Ellen R. Cohn et al., 43 vols to date, vol. 39 (New Haven, 2008), 213.

117. *Parliamentary History*, vol. 23, col. 604.

118. Sheffield, *Observations on the Commerce of the American States*, 295–7.

119. Stephen Conway, *The British Isles and the War of American Independence* (Oxford, 2000), 327.

120. Sheffield, *Observations on the Commerce of the American States*, 300.

121. It banned American vessels from carrying provisions to the West Indies. But many staple American products were allowed duty-free entry, or admission under nominal duties. American goods imported in American vessels to Britain were exempt from aliens' duty.

122. Richard Price to William Petty, marquis of Lansdowne (formerly earl of Shelburne), 29 Oct. 1785, in Richard Price, *Correspondence of Richard Price*, ed. D.O. Thomas, 3 vols (Durham, NC, 1991), vol. 2, 318.

123. Price to Lansdowne, 29 Nov. 1785, in ibid., 323–4.

124. Tarrade, *Commerce colonial*, vol. 2, 539, 545–7; Frederick L. Nussbaum, 'The French Colonial Arret of 1784', *South Atlantic Quarterly* 27 (1928): 62–78.

125. [Jean-Baptiste Dubuc], *Le pour et le contre sur un objet de grande discorde et d'importance majeure: Convient-t-il à l'administration de céder part, ou de rien céder aux étrangers dans le commerce de la métropole avec ses colonies?* (London, 1784).

126. Covo, 'Commerce, empire et révolutions dans le monde atlantique', 120–42.

127. Sheffield, *Observations on the Commerce of the American States*, 286–7.

128. *Parliamentary History*, vol. 23, cols 602–8, 642–3; see also Edmund Jenings to John Adams, 14 Mar. 1783, in John Adams, *Papers of John Adams*, vol. 14, 331.

129. Smith to Eden, 1 Dec. 1783, in Smith, *Correspondence*, 271–2. Smith favoured free trade between the British Caribbean colonies and the United States, however, on the grounds that the West Indies needed American provisions more than the Americans needed their rum and sugar.

130. John E. Crowley, 'Neo-Mercantilism and *The Wealth of Nations*: British Commercial Policy after the American Revolution', *Historical Journal* 33, no. 2 (1990): 339–60. Also unhelpful

is Charles Ritcheson's assumption that the choice lay between 'free trade theory' (implicitly identified with Smith's ideas) and a pragmatic mercantilism. This analytic framework makes it difficult to grasp what was new in this ideological moment and assumes that free trade must be understood as a systematic intellectual theory coming from outside the policy world. See Charles R. Ritcheson, 'Britain's Peacemakers 1782–1783: "To an Astonishing Degree Unfit for the Task"?', in *Peace and the Peacemakers: The Treaty of 1783*, ed. Ronald Hoffman and Peter J. Albert (Charlottesville, 1986), 70–100.

131. Richard F. Teichgraeber, III, ' "Less Abused than I Had Reason to Expect": The Reception of *The Wealth of Nations* in Britain, 1776–90', *Historical Journal* 30, no. 2 (1987): 337–66.

6. SECURITY CARTEL: THE FRANCO-BRITISH PURSUIT OF A PERMANENT PEACE IN INDIA

1. BL Add MS 32856 fols 279–89, Copy of the Saunders–Godeheu treaty, 31 Dec. 1754. See also BL Eg 3487 fols 278–9; and BL IOR I/1/4 'Articles for a Provisional Treaty'.
2. Chaudhuri, *Trading World of Asia*, 113, 121; Indrani Ray, 'Some Aspects of the French Presence in Bengal: 1731–40', in *The French East India Company and the Trade of the Indian Ocean*, ed. Lakshmi Subramaniam (New Delhi, 1999).
3. Philip J. Stern, 'Limited Liabilities: The Corporation and the Political Economy of Protection in the British Empire', in *Protection and Empire: A Global History*, ed. Lauren Benton, Adam Clulow, and Bain Attwood (Cambridge, 2017), 114–31.
4. Frederic C. Lane, 'Economic Consequences of Organized Violence', *Journal of Economic History* 18, no. 4 (1958): 401–17; idem, *Profits from Power*.
5. Steensgaard, *Carracks, Caravans and Companies*. The merits of this argument are analysed and reaffirmed by Andrew Phillips and J.C. Sharman, *International Order in Diversity: War, Trade and Rule in the Indian Ocean* (Cambridge, 2015), 117–35.
6. John Darwin, *After Tamerlane: The Rise and Fall of Global Empires, 1400–2000* (London, 2008), 163; J.C. Sharman, *Empires of the Weak: The Real Story of European Expansion and the Creation of the New World Order* (Princeton, 2019), 65–98; Sanjay Subrahmanyam, 'Dreaming an Indo-Persian Empire in South Asia, 1740–1800', in idem, *Mughals and Franks: Explorations in Connected History* (Oxford, 2005), 173–209.
7. Randolf G.S. Cooper, *The Anglo-Maratha Campaigns and the Contest for India: The Struggle for Control of the South Asian Military Economy* (Cambridge, 2003); Kaushik Roy, *War, Culture and Society in Early Modern South Asia, 1740–1849* (Abingdon, 2011). For the older argument on the consequences of the military revolution, see Geoffrey Parker, *The Military Revolution: Military Innovation and the Rise of the West, 1500–1800* (Cambridge, 1988).
8. The lack of a governance regime to keep such political costs low was a major source of the high overhead costs plaguing the companies identified by Jan de Vries. See Jan de Vries, 'The Limits of Globalization in the Early Modern World', *Economic History Review* 63, no. 3 (2010): 710–33.
9. AN Col C² 38 fols 74–81, [Pierre-Claude Delaître], 'Mémoire sur les inconvénients pour les trois Compagnies françoise, angloise et hollandoise de leur mésintelligence dans l'Inde, sur les avantages communs à ces trois Comp.ᵉˢ qui resulteroient de leur union', 30 July 1752. Some of the material in this section first appeared in a different form as 'Securing Asian Trade: Treaty Negotiations between the French and English East India Companies, 1753–1755', in *Politics of Commercial Treaties*, ed. Alimento and Stapelbroek, 267–93.
10. See Florian Schui, 'Prussia's "Trans-Oceanic Moment": The Creation of the Prussian Asiatic Trade Company in 1750', *Historical Journal* 49, no. 1 (2006): 143–60.
11. The idea of joint action in their dealings with Indian rulers had been mooted by Dupleix, then the leading French official in Bengal. See Ray, 'Some Aspects of the French Presence in Bengal', 136.
12. Rupali Mishra, *A Business of State: Commerce, Politics, and the Birth of the East India Company* (Cambridge, MA, 2018), 209–41.

13. Saint-Pierre, *Projet pour rendre la paix perpétuelle en Europe*, vol. 2, 264–9.
14. John Law, 'Réponse aux deux lettres, sur le Nouveau Système des Finances', in idem, *Œuvres complètes*, ed. Paul Harsin, 3 vols (Paris, 1934), vol. 3, 115.
15. See, for example, BL IOR E/1/22 fol. 160; E/1/24 fol. 157; E/1/25 fols 94, 163–4.
16. P.J. Marshall, 'The British in Asia: Trade to Dominion, 1700–1765', in *The Oxford History of the British Empire*, vol. 2, *The Eighteenth Century* (Oxford, 1998), 487–507.
17. Philippe Haudrère, *La Compagnie française des Indes au XVIIIe siècle*, 2nd edn, 2 vols (Paris, 2005), vol. 2, 730–7.
18. G.J. Bryant, *The Emergence of British Power in India, 1600–1784: A Grand Strategic Interpretation* (Woodbridge, 2013), 62.
19. AAE MD Asie 4 fols 44–62, 'Mémoire de M. Dupleix sur les Compagnies de Commerce', 16 Oct. 1753. Dupleix had long entertained doubts about the financial stability of the British company. See Ananda Ranga Pillai, *The Private Diary of Ananda Ranga Pillai*, ed. and trans. J. Frederick Price and R. Rangachari, 2 vols (Madras, 1904–7), vol. 2, 81.
20. Chaudhuri, *Trading World of Asia*, 115–16.
21. Catherine Manning, *Fortunes à Faire: The French in Asian Trade, 1718–48* (Aldershot, 1996).
22. Gregory Mole, 'L'économie politique de Joseph Dupleix: Commerce, autorité, et deuxième guerre carnatique, 1751–1754', *Outre-Mers, Revue d'histoire* 103, no. 388–89 (2015): 81–98, 86, citing P.J. Marshall, 'Introduction', in idem, *The Eighteenth Century in Indian History: Evolution or Revolution?* (Oxford, 2003), 25–6. For 'portfolio capitalists' see Sanjay Subrahmanyam and C.A. Bayly, 'Portfolio Capitalists and the Political Economy of Early Modern India', *Indian Economic and Social History Review* 25, no. 4 (1988): 401–24.
23. BL IOR E/4/5, Fort Saint David president and council to General Court, 12 Feb. 1750.
24. Alfred Martineau, *Dupleix et l'Inde française*, 5 vols (Paris, 1920), vol. 3, 26.
25. BL Eg 3487 fols 185–6, Secret Committee of the East India Company to Robert Darcy, earl of Holderness, 21 Dec. 1756.
26. John Castaing, *Course of the Exchange* (published from January 1698 through to the end of the eighteenth century); online at European State Finance Database, www.esfdb.org/Table.aspx?resourceid=11710 (accessed 28 Aug. 2020).
27. BL Eg 3484 fols 45–50.
28. The proposal had been vetoed by Henry Gough, the dominant figure in the English company, who hoped to attack French shipping in the Indian Ocean. See BL Add MS 35906 fols 180–1.
29. [William Monson], *A Letter to a Proprietor of the East-India Company* (London, 1750), 18, 26. See also Anon., *Some Thoughts on the Present Trade to India, by a Merchant of London* (London, 1754).
30. [William Monson], *Lettre écrite à un actionnaire de la Compagnie des Indes Orientales d'Angleterre* (London, 1750).
31. AAE MD Asie 12 fol. 228, 'Sur le Projet d'un Traitté de Neut.ᵉ perp.ˡˡᵉ entre les Comp.ⁱᵉˢ des Indes de France et d'Ang.ʳᵉ', Oct. 1750.
32. Haudrère, *Compagnie française des Indes*, vol. 1, 126–7. Crouzet, *La guerre économique*, 320–7.
33. AN Col C² 44 fols 48–60.
34. ERO Mildmay Papers D/DM/O1/27, unidentified to William Mildmay, 17 July 1753.
35. BNF naf 9150 fols 22–3, Gabriel Michel to Joseph-François Dupleix, 21 Jan. 1754.
36. BNF naf 9150 fols 7–8, Jean-Baptiste de Machault d'Arnouville to Dupleix, 19 Jan. 1753.
37. AAE CP Ang 436 fol. 7, Machault d'Arnouville to François-Dominique de Barberie, marquis de Saint-Contest, 1 Mar. 1753.
38. BNF naf 9150 fols 266–7, Étienne de Silhouette to Dupleix, 13 Sept. 1752.
39. William A. Pettigrew, 'Political Economy', in *The Corporation as a Protagonist in Global History*, c. *1550–1750*, ed. William A. Pettigrew and David Veevers (Leiden, 2019), 43–67; John Shovlin, 'Commerce, not Conquest: Political Economic Thought in the French Indies Company, 1719–1769', in *New Perspectives on the History of Political Economy*, ed. Robert

Fredona and Sophus A. Reinert (Cham, 2018), 171–202; Philip J. Stern, 'Companies: Monopoly, Sovereignty, and the East Indies', in *Mercantilism Reimagined*, ed. Stern and Wennerlind, 177–95.

40. BNF naf 9150 fols 24–5, Michel to Dupleix, 14 Aug. 1754.
41. AN Col C² 39 fols 88–102, Silhouette, 'Mémoire sur les affaires de l'Inde', July 1753.
42. Haudrère, *Compagnie française des Indes*, vol. 1, 744–5.
43. See Forbonnais, *Élémens du commerce*, vol. 1, 355.
44. [Louis-Joseph Plumard de Dangeul], *Remarques sur les avantages et les désavantages de la France et de la Grande Bretagne, par rapport au commerce, & aux autres sources de la puissance des États*, 3rd edn (Paris, 1754), 237.
45. Charles Godeheu, *Lettre de M. Godeheu à M. Dupleix; mémoire à consulter, et consultation; piéces justificatives, et extraits de quelques lettres de M. Godeheu à M. Saunders* (Paris, 1760), 15.
46. Jacques-Claude-Marie Vincent de Gournay, 'Observations sur le rapport fait à M. le Contrôleur-Général, par M. de S.*** le 26 juin 1755, sur l'état de la Compagnie des Indes', published in André Morellet, *Mémoire sur la situation actuelle de la Compagnie des Indes* (n.p., 1769), x–xxiv.
47. De Vries, 'Limits of Globalization', 724.
48. Cited in Mole, 'Économie politique de Joseph Dupleix', 89.
49. Anon., *Mémoire pour le sieur Dupleix contre la Compagnie des Indes* (Paris, 1759), 208, citing Richard Cantillon, *Essai sur la nature du commerce en général, traduit de l'anglois* (London, 1755), 308, 317.
50. Stringer Lawrence to Thomas Saunders and Fort St George Council, 17 Mar. 1754, in *Records of Fort St George. Diary and Consultation Book, Military Department, 1754*, ed. Henry Dodwell (Madras, 1911), 67.
51. P.J. Marshall, 'British Expansion in India in the Eighteenth Century: A Historical Revision', in idem, *Trade and Conquest: Studies on the Rise of British Dominance in India* (Aldershot, 1993), 28–43, 30–1.
52. BL IOR E/3/121, General Court to the president and council at Fort St David, 23 Aug. 1751. The sentence was removed from the final draft, replaced with the more encouraging promise to send 'such a Force' as would enable the council 'to act upon the Defensive at least'.
53. BL Eg 3484 fols 45–50.
54. BL Eg 3486 fols 119–20, draft proposal for a revised fifth article. See also fol. 121, Alexander Hume to Holderness, 30 Oct. 1754.
55. BL Add MS 73965 fols 27–8, John Drummond to Horatio Walpole, 12 Aug. 1737.
56. Schnakenbourg, *Entre la guerre et la paix*; Stapelbroek (ed.), *Trade and War*.
57. Holden Furber, *Rival Empires of Trade in the Orient 1600–1800* (Minneapolis, 1976), 147.
58. In the duke of Newcastle's words, 'our Directors now press the neutrality extremely'. BL Eg 3484 fol. 17, minute of a cabinet meeting, 30 May 1753. See also UNL Ne(C) 1497, Thomas Pelham-Holles, duke of Newcastle to Joseph Yorke, 14 Sept. 1753.
59. BL Eg 3484 fols 34–5, Newcastle to Yorke, 26 June 1753; fols 43–5, Secret Committee to Newcastle, 18 July 1753; fols 74–5, Newcastle to Yorke, 14 Sept. 1753. AAE CP Ang 436 fols 193–6, Gaston-Pierre de Lévis, duc de Mirepoix to Machault d'Arnouville, 8 June 1753.
60. BL Eg 3484 fols 27–9, copy of a letter to Pierre Duvelaer, 16 June 1753.
61. BL Add MS 33055 fols 265–8, 'Memorandum relating to Mr H[ume]', 10 Dec. 1760.
62. BL Eg 3484 fol. 59, 'Extrait des articles d'un projet de neutralité envoyé par M. Duvelaer, le 23 May 1753 avec des observations par le Comité Secret de la Compagnie des Indes de France'.
63. BL Eg 3484 fols 122–3, 'Heads of Articles', 26 Oct. 1753.
64. Bryant, *Emergence of British Power in India*, 69
65. AN Col C² 41 fols 114–15, Duvelaer to the directors of the Compagnie des Indes, 2 May 1754.

66. BL Add MS 33031 fols 155–70, 'Mémoire sur les projets de convention entre les Compagnies des Indes de France & d'Angleterre', 4 Feb. 1754; also, AN COL C² 41 fols 3–28.

67. BL IOR I/1/4, 'Narrative of what formerly passed towards effecting an Accommodation between the English and French Companies in the East Indies'. AN Col C² 39 fol. 97, Silhouette, 'Mémoire sur les affaires de l'Inde'. BL Eg 3484 fols 280–4, Machault d'Arnouville to Mirepoix, 11 Mar. 1754.

68. BL Eg 3484 fols 70–2, Court of Directors to Holderness, 14 Sept. 1753; fol. 98, minutes of a cabinet meeting, 27 Sept. 1753; AAE CP Ang 437 fols 25–6, Mirepoix to Saint-Contest, 17 Jan. 1754; BL Eg 3484 fol. 136, minute of the council, 17 Jan. 1754.

69. BL Eg 3486 fol. 193, Hume to Holderness, 1 Dec. 1754; fols 210–13, 'Plan humbly offered for the Support of the British Possessions Trade & Privilidges in the East Indies'. Hume soon brought the Secret Committee around to this position. BL Eg 3487 fol. 46, Hume to Holderness, 18 Mar. 1755; fol. 52, Secret Committee to Holderness, 20 Mar. 1755.

70. BL Add MS 32856 fols 279–89, copy of the Saunders–Godeheu treaty, 31 Dec. 1754. See also Ternat, *Partager le monde*, 424–6.

71. BL Eg 3487 fol. 72, Hume to Holderness, 8 June 1755; fols 76–7, Hume to Holderness, 26 June 1755.

72. BL Eg 3487 fols 112–13, Holderness to Hume, 11 July 1755.

73. BL Eg 3487 fol. 83, Secret Committee to Holderness, 27 June 1755; BL Add MS 32856 fol. 113, Roger Drake to Newcastle, 22 June 1755; BL Eg 3487 fols 134–5, Secret Committee to Henry Fox, 18 Aug. 1756.

74. BL Eg 3487 fols 116–17, Secret Committee to Sir Thomas Robinson, 30 July 1755.

75. Lucy Sutherland, 'The East India Company and the Peace of Paris', *English Historical Review* 62, no. 243 (1947): 179–90.

76. Kenneth Margerison, 'Commercial Liberty, French National Power, and the Indies Trade after the Seven Years' War', *Historical Reflections/Réflexions Historiques* 35 (2009): 52–73.

77. BL IOR H/808 fols 186–8, Laurence Sulivan to William Pitt, 27 July 1761. See also James Gordon Parker, 'The Directors of the East India Company, 1754–1790', PhD thesis, Edinburgh University, 1977, 379–80, 382.

78. Marshall, 'British Expansion in India', 36, 40.

79. Vaughn, *Politics of Empire*, 96–8.

80. Robert Clive to William Pitt, 7 Jan. 1759, in *Correspondence of William Pitt, Earl of Chatham*, ed. John Henry Pringle and William Stanhope Taylor, 4 vols (London, 1838–40), vol. 1, 387–92. He had raised this assessment to £2.5 million by 1767. See Thomas Whately to George Grenville, 22 July 1767, in *The Grenville Papers: Being the Correspondence of Richard Grenville, Earl Temple, K.G., and the Right Hon. George Grenville, their Friends and Contemporaries*, ed. William James Smith, 4 vols (London, 1852–53), vol. 4, 95. The king, too, saw Bengal as a critical resource in dealing with the debt. George III, *Correspondence*, vol. 1, 424.

81. H.V. Bowen, *Revenue & Reform: The Indian Problem in British Politics 1757–1773* (Cambridge, 1991), 22, 51.

82. Vaughn, *Politics of Empire*, 103–5.

83. Ibid., 100–1. There is some overlap, but not a perfect correspondence, between these forces and those analysed in Robert Travers, 'Ideology and British Expansion in Bengal, 1757–72', *Journal of Imperial and Commonwealth History* 33, no. 1 (2005): 7–27.

84. 'So large a sovereignty may possibly be an object too extensive for a mercantile company', he wrote, 'and it is to be feared they are not of themselves able, without the nation's assistance, to maintain so wide a dominion.' Clive to Pitt, 7 Jan. 1759, in *Correspondence of William Pitt*, vol. 1, 387–92.

85. Clive to George Grenville, 5 Jan. 1765, in *Grenville Papers*, ed. Smith, vol. 3, 1–2.

86. AN Col C² 48 fols 3–23.

87. Robert D. Harris, *Necker: Reform Statesman of the Ancien Régime* (Berkeley, 1979), 5–6.

88. AN Col C² 47 fols 53–60, 'Discours de M. Necker, banquier' (1764).

89. Kenneth Margerison, 'The Shareholders' Revolt at the Compagnie des Indes: Commerce and Political Culture in Old Regime France', *French History* 20, no. 1 (2006): 25–51. On the history of the French colony, see Megan Vaughan, *Creating the Creole Island: Slavery in Eighteenth-Century Mauritius* (Durham, NC, 2005).

90. AN Col C² 51 fol. 62, 'Prospectus des statuts et règlements concernant la Compagnie des Indes de France'.

91. P.J. Marshall, *East Indian Fortunes: The British in Bengal in the Eighteenth Century* (Oxford, 1976), 226; NYPL Hardwicke 76/29, 'Extract of a Letter from the President and Select Committee at Fort William in Bengal to the Court of Directors of the East India Company dated the 5th and 9th December 1766'. Clive was later to criticise the practice. See BL IOR Eur G37/51/2 fols 209–10, Clive to David André, 3 Feb. 1768.

92. TNA SP 78/277/79 fols 211–12, Simon, Earl Harcourt to Thomas Thynne, Viscount Weymouth, 28 Mar. 1769.

93. Herbert Lüthy, 'Necker et la Compagnie des Indes', *Annales. Economies, Sociétés, Civilisations* 15, no. 5 (1960): 852–81. Other London banking houses were involved, notably that of John and Francis Fatio, David André, and Sir John Lambert. See BL IOR Eur G37/49/2 fols 5–8, John David Fatio to Clive, 17 Nov. 1767; fols 35–6, George Clive to Robert Clive, 21 Nov. 1767; fols 48–9, John Walsh to Robert Clive, 23 Nov. 1767; Eur G37/59/4 fol. 20, Sir John Lambert to Messrs Gosling and Clive, 9 Apr. 1770.

94. Marshall, *East Indian Fortunes*, 121.

95. WCL Shelburne Papers 99a/89–94, William Petty, earl of Shelburne to EIC directors, 27 Jan. 1768. See also Bowen, *Revenue & Reform*, 74.

96. N.K. Sinha (ed.), *Fort William–India House Correspondence*, 21 vols (New Delhi, 1949), vol. 5, 19.

97. TNA SP 78/278/62, Memorial delivered by Louis-Marie Florent, comte du Châtelet. These charges were well founded. See R. Mukherjee, 'The Last Commercial Frontier: French and English Presence in South Eastern Bengal and Beyond', *Indian Historical Review* 34 (2007): 167–86.

98. André Morellet, *Mémoire sur la situation actuelle de la Compagnie des Indes* (n.p., 1769).

99. André Morellet, *Mémoires de l'abbé Morellet de l'Académie française, sur le dix⊠huitième siècle et sur la Révolution*, ed. Jean⊠Pierre Guicciardi (Paris, 1988), 191–3.

100. Margerison, 'Commercial Liberty, French National Power'.

101. Discussed in a work by Gournay's protégé Plumard de Dangeul. See Plumard de Dangeul, *Remarques sur les avantages et les désavantages*, 230–2.

102. Gournay, 'Observations sur le rapport fait à M. le Contrôleur-Général', x–xxiv.

103. On Choiseul's general position, see Sudipta Das, *Myths and Realities of French Imperialism in India, 1763–1783* (New York, 1992), 130–2; Kenneth Margerison, 'French Visions of Empire: Contesting British Power in India after the Seven Years War', *English Historical Review* 130, no. 544 (2015): 583–612.

104. Ruggiu, 'India and the Reshaping of the French Colonial Policy'.

105. AAE CP Ang 482 fol. 232, Chatelet to [Choiseul], 23 Oct. 1768; AN Col C² 246 fols 4–8, César-Gabriel de Choiseul, duc de Praslin, *Mémoire* read to the Royal Council, 1 July 1770.

106. Das, *Myths and Realities*, 133–4; François Dutacq, 'La politique de revanche du duc de Choiseul au lendemain du traité de Paris', *Ministère de l'instruction publique et des Beaux-Arts. Bulletin de la section de géographie* 40 (1925), 45–62. See also WCL Shelburne Papers 99a/423–76, a French plan dating to 1767 to attack the East India Company from the Mascarenes, stolen from the minister of the navy's office.

107. AN Col C² 246 fols 42–5. See also Das, *Myths and Realities*, 140–1.

108. Jean Law de Lauriston, *État politique de l'Inde en 1777*, ed. Alfred Martineau (Paris, 1913), 110–12. For the background to such claims, see Catherine B. Asher and Cynthia Talbot, *India Before Europe* (Cambridge, 2006), 281–4.

109. Dumas to Praslin, 2 Aug. 1768. Cited in Dutacq, 'Politique de revanche', 62.

110. TNA SP 78/283 fols 68–81, the abbé de Saint-Estevan to [Praslin], 1 Jan. 1769. Enclosed in SP 78/283/28, Harcourt to Weymouth, 13 Aug. 1771. See also AN Col C² 246 fols 4–5, Praslin, Mémoire, 1 July 1770.

111. Antonella Alimento and Gianluigi Goggi, 'Introduction. L'abbé Raynal avant l'*Histoire des deux Indes*: L'ouverture d'un chantier', in *Autour de l'abbé Raynal: Genèse et enjeux politiques de l'Histoire des deux Indes*, ed. idem (Ferney-Voltaire, 2018), 7–15, 7–8; Michèle Duchet, *Anthropologie et histoire au siècle des Lumières: Buffon, Voltaire, Rousseau, Helvétius, Diderot* (Paris, 1971), 129–36; Gianluigi Goggi, 'Quelques remarques sur la collaboration de Diderot à la première édition de l'*Histoire des deux Indes*', in *Lectures de Raynal: L'Histoire des deux Indes en Europe et en Amérique au XVIIIe siècle*, ed. Hans-Jürgen Lüsebrink and Manfred Tietz (Oxford, 1991), 17–52.

112. The *Histoire des deux Indes* also took up Choiseulist themes in its discussion of the appropriate political-economic strategy for the Spanish Empire and its relationship with France. Alimento, 'Raynal, Accarias de Sérionne et le Pacte de Famille'.

113. Raynal, *Histoire des deux Indes* (1770), vol. 1, 379, 383–4; vol. 2, 137–43. See Anthony Strugnell, 'The *Histoire des deux Indes* and the Debate on the British in India', *SVEC* 7 (2003): 240–4. On Choiseul and the Mascarenes, see Ruggiu, 'India and the Reshaping of the French Colonial Policy', 29; Vaughan, *Creating the Creole Island*, 68–71.

114. Kenta Ohji argues that Raynal was closely aligned with Jacques Necker, and that the *Histoire* regularly echoed the latter's views. This may account for some of the divergence from a straight Choiseulist line. See Kenta Ohji, 'Raynal, Necker et la Compagnie des Indes: Quelques aspects inconnus de la genèse et de l'évolution de l'*Histoire des deux Indes*', in *Raynal et ses réseaux*, ed. Gilles Bancarel (Paris, 2011), 105–81.

115. Raynal, *Histoire des deux Indes* (1770), vol. 2, 283–91.

116. Bowen, *Revenue & Reform*, 118.

117. NYPL Hardwicke Papers 76, George Oldmixon, 'States of the Expences incurred by the East India Company at their several Settlements & Factories, on account of the Wars & Disturbances in the East Indies, from 1754 to 1766', 5 Feb. 1767.

118. Bowen, *Revenue & Reform*, 117.

119. A similar story could be told about the VOC. In the words of Jan de Vries, 'the costs of protecting and administering its territories appear always to have exceeded revenues'. See De Vries, 'Limits of Globalization', 727. De Vries overstates the benefits to the East India Company of the move to extraction. Here Bowen is a better guide.

120. Bowen, *Revenue & Reform*, 13, 15.

121. H.V. Bowen, 'British India, 1765–1813: The Metropolitan Context', in *Oxford History of the British Empire*, vol. 2, ed. Marshall, 530–51, 535.

122. Om Prakash, *European Commercial Enterprise in Pre-Colonial India* (Cambridge, 1998), 347–8.

123. Bowen, *Revenue & Reform*, 118, 121.

124. On these monopolies, see P.J. Marshall, *The Making and Unmaking of Empires: Britain, India, and America c. 1750–1783* (Oxford, 2005), 251. The idea that the company stamped a Smithian vision of free trade on Bengali marketplaces, as Sudipta Sen suggests, may be more appropriate to a later period of company rule. See Sudipta Sen, *Empire of Free Trade: The East India Company and the Making of the Colonial Marketplace* (Philadelphia, 1998).

125. Erikson, *Between Monopoly and Free Trade*.

126. H.V. Bowen, 'Bolts, William (1739–1808)', *ODNB*.

127. William Bolts, *Considerations on India Affairs; Particularly Respecting the Present State of Bengal and Its Dependencies* (London, 1772), vii. See Emma Rothschild, *The Inner Life of Empires: An Eighteenth-Century History* (Princeton, 2011), 146–8.

128. Nor could any framework better secure Bengal against French machinations than Crown sovereignty, Bolts argued. 'It is a fact well known abroad', he remarked, 'that the late minister of France, the Duke de Choiseul, gave up as totally overset, all his schemes regarding the East Indies, upon his first hearing a report, current in the year 1768, that the

Crown of Great Britain was going to take into its hands the government of the territorial possessions held by the English East India Company. It was the only thing the French then dreaded; it is the thing which they now most wish to see delayed, till they have an opportunity of striking a *coup d'éclat* in those regions.' Bolts, *Considerations on India Affairs*, 223–4.

129. Ibid., 71–2, 218.

130. Nicholas Tracy, 'Parry of a Threat to India, 1768–1774', *Mariner's Mirror* 59 (1973): 35–48, 43.

131. BL IOR I/1/5 p. 182, Robert Harland to Josias Du Pré and the Fort St George Council, 5 Oct. 1772; IOR I/1/7 pp. 565–68, Fort William Secret Consultations, 23 Dec. 1771, extract of a letter from Sir Robert Harland; pp. 605–12, Harland to the Fort William Council, 29 May 1774.

132. Tarrade, *Commerce colonial*, vol. 1, 374.

133. AAE MD Asie 15 fols 458–62, Pierre-Étienne Bourgeois de Boynes to Emmanuel-Armand de Richelieu, duc d'Aiguillon, 6 May 1772. On the need for a company, see also AAE MD Asie 5 fols 40–50, 'Réflexions sur un projet d'établissement d'une Compagnie des Indes'; fols 54–66, 'Mémoire', Aug. 1773.

134. AAE MD Asie 15 fols 508–11, untitled, 19 Aug. 1772. A copy at AN Col C² 164 identifies the author as Saint-Estevan.

135. AAE MD Asie 4 fols 82–9, 'Projet d'une Ligue offensive et déffensive, entre les françois et les anglois au dela du Cap de Bonne Esperance et d'un traité de partage entre les deux Nations pour les Cotes de Coromandel, Dorixa, et le Bengal'; AAE MD Asie 7 fols 22–45, 'Projet politique d'arrangement dans l'Inde entre les François et les Anglois. Avantages aux deux nations'; AN Col C² 164, 'Projet politique d'arrangement dans l'Inde entre les françois et les anglois'.

136. Guillaume-Thomas Raynal, *A Philosophical and Political History of the Settlements and Trade of the Europeans in the East and West Indies*, trans. J. Justamond (London, 1776), vol. 1, 158–60. The argument for a general neutrality is reiterated in ibid., vol. 2, 320.

137. Ibid., vol. 1, 381. See also Strugnell, '*Histoire des deux Indes* and the Debate on the British in India'.

138. AN Col C² 164, 'Mémoire'.

139. AAE CP Ang 500 fols 258–60, James Bourdieu to d'Aiguillon, 24 Nov. 1772.

140. AAE MD Asie 15 fol. 476, d'Aiguillon to Bourgeois de Boynes, 18 May 1772; fols 512–13, Jacques Necker to d'Aiguillon, 2 Sept. 1772.

141. TNA SP 78/287 fols 58–60, Horace St Paul to William Henry van Nassau van Zuylestein, earl of Rochford, 17 Feb. 1773; fol. 93, St Paul to Rochford, 3 Mar. 1773.

142. On the continuing resonance of the commerce-versus-conquest theme, see Bowen, 'British India, 1765–1813', 534.

143. Cited in Bryant, *Emergence of British Power in India*, 223. See also Marshall, *Making and Unmaking of Empires*, 254.

144. BL IOR Francis MSS no. 36, 433–8, Philip Francis to Frederick, Lord North, 21 Nov. 1775. Reproduced in Sophia Weitzman, *Warren Hastings and Philip Francis* (Manchester, 1929), 241–5. See also Ranajit Guha, *A Rule of Property for Bengal: An Essay on the Idea of Permanent Settlement* (New Delhi, 1981), 143–50. As Robert Travers has argued, a distinctively Whig respect for ancient constitutions marked Francis's perspective. This extended to his vision of Indian politics beyond Bengal. See Robert Travers, *Ideology and Empire in Eighteenth-Century India: The British in Bengal* (Cambridge, 2007), 141–80.

145. After his return to England in 1781, Francis continued to press, as an MP, for a radical remaking of the political framework for trade in India. The company had never benefited from the *diwani*, he argued, because of the military and administrative costs it entailed: 'they prospered while they were merchants, and they have never prospered since'. *Parliamentary History*, vol. 28, col. 1,183; see also *Parliamentary History*, vol. 30, cols 688–9.

146. David Todd, 'A French Imperial Meridian, 1814–1870', *Past & Present* 210 (2011): 155–86, 156.

147. Hardman, *Overture to Revolution*, 7–8.
148. Tarrade, *Commerce colonial*, vol. 1, 483–91; idem, 'Le Maréchal de Castries et la politique française dans l'océan Indien à la fin de l'Ancien Régime', in *Révolution française et océan Indien: Prémices, paroxysmes, héritages et déviances*, ed. Claude Wanquet and Benoît Jullien (Paris, 1996), 39–48; Philippe Haudrère, *Les Français dans l'océan Indien* (Rennes, 2014), 287–95.
149. BNF naf 9433 fol. 64.
150. S.P. Sen, *The French in India 1763–1816* (Calcutta, 1958), 304.
151. The size of the territories discussed in the advice he received was far smaller than the demands made in 1782. AAE CP Ang 537 fols 234–9, Claude Antoine Valdec de Lessarts, 'Notes sur l'Inde relativement au futur traité de paix'; fols 285–90, Jean-Marie de Bruny, 'Mémoire sur la paix prochaine'; CP Ang 539 fols 79–80, 'Idées sur le rétablissement de nos colonies dans l'Inde'; fols 81–3, 'Observations sur les Indes orientales par rapport aux conditions du traité de paix'.
152. Harlow, *Founding of the Second British Empire*, vol. 1, 330–1, 364–84.
153. WCL Shelburne Papers 71/299–303, William Petty, earl of Shelburne to Alleyne Fitzherbert, 21 Oct. 1782.
154. WCL Shelburne Papers 71/505–15, Shelburne to Joseph Mathias Gérard de Rayneval, 13 Nov. 1782.
155. Baring NP1.B1, Shelburne to Francis Baring, 25 Nov. 1783. See also Baring DEP 193.17.1, Baring to Shelburne, 30 Nov. 1783. Shelburne had solicited reform proposals from company insiders early in 1783. See NLI MS 15,978 George Johnstone to Thomas Orde, 12 Jan. 1783, and Orde to Johnstone, 17 Jan. 1783.
156. AAE MD Asie 7 fol. 424, Jean-François Joly de Fleury to Charles Gravier de Vergennes, 12 Feb. 1783.
157. AN T/38/1–2 no. 548, 'Exposé des services que M. James Bourdieu et sa maison de Londres ont rendues, avant, et durant la négociation du Traité entre les deux Compagnies des Indes de France et d'Angleterre'; AAE MD Asie 5 fols 152–69, 'Observations des administrateurs de la Compagnie des Indes [et] remarques par M. de Rayneval'.
158. As first envisioned, an accord would confer protection on vessels in case of renewed conflict. BL Add MS 34466 fols 80–1, 'Bases des arrangements de commerce que la Compagnie des Indes de France désireroit prendre avec la Compagnie des Indes Angloise'. See also TNA PRO 30/8/360 fols 163–5.
159. Elizabeth Helen Cross, 'The French East India Company and the Politics of Commerce in the Revolutionary Era', PhD thesis, Harvard University, 2017, 113–14.
160. Mike Rapport, '"Complaints Lost in the Wind" – French India and the Crisis of the Absolute Monarchy: A Global Dimension?', in *The Crisis of the Absolute Monarchy: France from Old Regime to Revolution*, ed. Julian Swann and Joël Félix (Oxford, 2013), 223–43, 223–4.
161. Cross, 'French East India Company', 131–2. Frederick L. Nussbaum, 'The Formation of the New East India Company of Calonne', *American Historical Review* 38, no. 3 (1933): 475–97, 492–93.
162. BL Add MS 34466 fols 94–104, 94, 'Heads of Articles as the Basis of a Treaty and Agreement between the English and French East India Companies'.
163. NLI MS 15,976, Henry Fletcher, Nathaniel Smith, and John Harrison to Shelburne, 29 Aug. 1782.
164. WCL Shelburne Papers 87b/228–35, 'Advantageous Prospects to Great Britain & the East India Company from the Present Peace', Jan. 1783. See also H.V. Bowen, *The Business of Empire: The East India Company and Imperial Britain, 1756–1833* (Cambridge, 2005), 226–7; Sutherland, *East India Company*, 375.
165. WCL Melville Papers, Henry Dundas to Thomas Townsend, 30 Nov. 1786. See also BL Add MS 58914 fol. 12, Dundas to William Grenville, Sept. 1786.
166. TNA PRO 30/8/360 fols 150–7, 152, 'Proposals for a Negotiation between the English & French East India companies presented to Government and the Directors of the English East India Company by Messrs Bourdieu, Chollet & Bourdieu'.

167. BL Add MS 34466 fols 121–3, 'Observations of Francis Baring upon Mr Hasting's Paper of Sentiments relative to the proposed treaty to be entered into with the French East India Company'.

168. Add MS 34466 fols 89–91, Minutes of a secret court, 28 Sept. 1785.

169. *The Parliamentary Register; or, History of the Proceedings and Debates of the House of Commons*, 45 vols (London, 1780–1796), vol. 7, 29–35.

170. J.Z. Holwell, *An Address to the Proprietors of East India Stock* (London, 1783), 54.

171. Greene, *Evaluating Empire*, 305–17.

172. Sutherland, *East India Company*, 391–2, 409.

173. Conway, *British Isles and the War of American Independence*, 331; Marshall, *Making and Unmaking of Empires*, 369–70.

174. TNA PRO 30/8/360 fols 156–7, 'Proposals for a Negotiation'. The French negotiator, Périer, emphasised that an accord would end all frictions. Add MS 34466 fols 83–4, Périer to the Secret Committee, 17 Aug. 1785.

175. TNA PRO 30/8/360 fols 156–7, 'Proposals for a Negotiation'; AN T/38/1–2 no. 548, 'Exposé des services'.

176. Henry Laurens to Bourdieu, 26 Dec. 1782, in Henry Laurens, *The Papers of Henry Laurens*, vol. 16, ed. David R. Chesnutt and C. James Taylor (Columbia, SC, 2003), 104–6. On Oswald, a wealthy and well-connected trader, see Hancock, *Citizens of the World*, 61–9.

177. Michael Fry, *The Dundas Despotism* (Edinburgh, 1992), 125.

178. Dundas described it as 'a very favourite measure of mine'. WCL Melville Papers, Dundas to Townsend, 5 Nov. [1785]. 'With regard to the French Treaty', he told Baring, 'you know I always was, and still am a great friend to the principle of it.' Baring Archive NP1.C 23, Dundas to Baring, 25 Oct. 1785. On Pitt's favourable attitude, see Baring NP1.C24, Pitt to Baring, date obscured, 1785; BL Add MS 34466 fol. 196, Sydney, Pitt and Walsingham to the East India Co., 4 Nov. 1785.

179. TNA PC 1/123/18 (i), Vergennes to Calonne, 'Notes relative aux arrangements de commerce à faire avec l'Angleterre'; PC 1/123/18 (ii), Vergennes to Calonne, 10 Dec. 1785; AAE MD Asie 5 fols 152–69, 'Observations des administrateurs'.

180. AAE MD Asie 5 fols 170–6, Rayneval, untitled, Jan. 1786.

181. BL Add MS 34466 fols 118–120, 'Extract of a letter from Warren Hastings Esq. to Laurence Sulivan Esq. with his sentiments upon the proposed arrangement to be entered into with the French East India Company'.

182. BL Add MS 34421 fol. 358, William Eden to Rayneval, 28 June 1786; Add MS 34422 fol. 15, Eden to Rayneval, 5 Aug. 1786.

183. John Macpherson to François de Souillac, 26 Jan. 1786, in *Fort St George Consultations*, vol. 113A, 15 Aug. 1786. Cited in G.C. Bolton and B.E. Kennedy, 'William Eden and the Treaty of Mauritius, 1786–7', *Historical Journal* 16, no. 4 (1973): 681–96, 687. See also BL IOR I/1/6 no. 5, Cathcart's instructions from Macpherson and the council, 31 Jan. 1786.

184. Kennedy and Bolton, 'William Eden and the Treaty of Mauritius', 687.

185. Bengal Foreign Branch, Foreign Proceedings, 9 Mar. 1786, cited in Kennedy and Bolton, 'William Eden and the Treaty of Mauritius', 688. See also BL Add MS 34466 fols 138–62, 'Correspondence, instructions, *etc.* relative to a mission of Lieut. Col. Charles Cathcart from the Governor General and Council to the Vicomte de Souillac, French Governor General', 31 Jan.–4 Feb. 1786.

186. BL Add MS 34466 fols 282–8, 'Provisional Convention', 30 Apr. 1786.

187. BL Add MS 34422 fol. 353, Dundas to Eden, 28 Sept. 1786.

188. BL IOR I/1/6 no. 16, 'The Convention between His Britannick Majesty & the Most Christian King, signed at Versailles the 31 August 1787'.

189. Ibid. no. 19, 'To the Governor General & Council at Fort William'.

190. Ibid. no. 16, 'Draft instructions to Mr Eden to conclude the Treaty with the Court of France'.

191. Smith backed the failed India bill proposed by Charles James Fox, which Dundas opposed. See Adam Smith to William Eden, 1 Dec. 1783, in Smith, *Correspondence*, 272. On the

relevant additions in 1784 see idem, *Additions and Corrections*, 47–50, 65–79. Smith's general view seems to have been close to that of Bolts. See Emma Rothschild, 'Adam Smith in the British Empire', in *Empire and Modern Political Thought*, ed. Sankar Muthu (Cambridge, 2012), 184–98.

192. On this dimension of Smith's thinking, see Sankar Muthu, 'Adam Smith's Critique of International Trading Companies: Theorizing 'Globalization' in the Age of Enlightenment', *Political Theory* 36, no. 2 (2008): 185–212.

193. On the language of justice and humanity, and the emergence of a critique of empire framed in these terms by the early 1780s, see Greene, *Evaluating Empire*, xii, 156–99, 296–361.

194. Shelburne to Morellet, 7 Apr. 1788. Cited in Edmond George Petty-Fitzmaurice, baron Fitzmaurice, *Life of William, Earl of Shelburne*, 3 vols (London, 1875–1876), vol. 3, 477–8. Sulivan sat as an MP in Shelburne's interest. See Lucy Sutherland, 'Lord Shelburne and East India Company Politics, 1766–9', *English Historical Review* 49, no. 195 (1934): 450–86.

195. [Benjamin Vaughan], *New and Old Principles of Trade Compared; or A Treatise on the Principles of Commerce between Nations* (London, 1788), viii–ix.

196. Todd, 'A French Imperial Meridian', 156. See also idem, *A Velvet Empire: French Informal Imperialism in the Nineteenth Century* (Princeton, 2021).

CONCLUSION

1. On his role in the negotiations, see Ets Haim 48 A 19, 'Mémoire provisoire sur la part que Mr. Is. de Pinto a eu à la signature du traité définitif de la paix de Fontainebleau'.

2. First published as part of Pinto's *Traité de la circulation et du crédit, contenant une analyse raisonnée des fonds d'Angleterre* (Amsterdam, 1771), the work previously circulated in manuscript. Philip Francis published an English translation in 1774 as *An Essay on Circulation and Credit, in Four Parts; and A Letter on the Jealousy of Commerce* (London, 1774), from which the quotations are drawn. On Pinto's biography, see José Luís Cardoso and António de Vasconcelos Nogueira, 'Isaac de Pinto (1717–1787): An Enlightened Economist and Financier', *History of Political Economy* 37, no. 2 (2005): 263–92; and Richard H. Popkin, 'Hume and Isaac de Pinto', *Texas Studies in Literature and Language* 12, no. 3 (1970): 417–30.

3. Koen Stapelbroek, 'From Jealousy of Trade to the Neutrality of Finance: Isaac de Pinto's "System" of Luxury and Perpetual Peace', in *Commerce and Peace in the Enlightenment*, ed. Kapossy, Nakhimovsky, and Whatmore, 78–109.

4. Sven Beckert, *Empire of Cotton: A Global History* (New York, 2014), 29–55.

5. BL IOR H/808 fols 186–8, Laurence Sulivan to William Pitt, 27 July 1761.

6. *Parliamentary History*, vol. 28, col. 1,183.

7. For a prominent recent example, see Beckert, *Empire of Cotton*, 37–8.

8. James Anderson, *The Interest of Great Britain with Regard to Her American Colonies Considered. To which is Added an Appendix, Containing the Outlines of a Plan for a General Pacification* (London, 1782), separately paginated appendix.

9. Bolingbroke to Matthew Prior, 31 May 1713, in Bolingbroke, *Letters and Correspondence*, vol. 4, 153.

10. AAE CP Ang 500 fol. 276, d'Aiguillon to abbé Joseph-Marie Terray, 30 Nov. 1772. See also AAE CP Ang suppl. 14 fols 97–100, d'Aiguillon to Guînes, 27 Nov. 1772.

11. William Eden to Francis Osborne, marquess of Carmarthen, 17 Apr. 1786, in Eden, *Journal and Correspondance*, vol. 1, 102.

12. Beckert, *Empire of Cotton*, 279–80.

13. Karl Marx, *Capital*, trans. Ben Fowkes, 3 vols (London, 1990 [1867]), vol. 1, 916.

14. Fredona and Reinert, 'Leviathan and Kraken', 179–81.

15. On the seventeenth-century moment, see, for example, Joyce Appleby, *Economic Thought and Ideology in Seventeenth-Century England* (Princeton, 1978); Faccarello, *Foundations of Laissez-Faire*; Wennerlind, *Casualties of Credit*.

16. Robertson, *Case for the Enlightenment*, 36.
17. Paul Bairoch, 'European Trade Policy, 1815–1914', in *Cambridge Economic History of Europe*, vol. 8, *The Industrial Economies: The Development of Economic and Social Policies*, ed. Peter Mathias and Sidney Pollard (Cambridge, 1989), 1–137; Peter T. Marsh, *Bargaining on Europe: Britain and the First Common Market 1860–1892* (New Haven, 1999); Nye, *War, Wine, and Taxes*.
18. Philip Harling and Peter Mandler, 'From "Fiscal-Military" State to Laissez-Faire, 1760–1850', *Journal of British Studies* 32, no. 1 (1993): 44–70.
19. Schroeder, *Transformation of European Politics*.
20. P.J. Cain and A.G. Hopkins, *British Imperialism 1688–2000* (Harlow, 2001).
21. Todd, 'French Imperial Meridian'; idem, *Velvet Empire*.

SELECT BIBLIOGRAPHY

Ahn, Doohwan. 'The Anglo-French Treaty of Commerce of 1713: Tory Trade Politics and the Question of Dutch Decline', *History of European Ideas* 26, no. 2 (2010): 167–80.

Alimento, Antonella and Gianluigi Goggi (eds). *Autour de l'abbé Raynal: Genèse et enjeux politiques de l'*Histoire des deux Indes. Ferney-Voltaire, 2018.

Alimento, Antonella and Koen Stapelbroek (eds). *The Politics of Commercial Treaties in the Eighteenth Century: Balance of Power, Balance of Trade.* Basingstoke, 2017.

Armitage, David. *Foundations of Modern International Thought.* Cambridge, 2013.

Arrighi, Giovanni. *The Long Twentieth Century: Money, Power, and the Origins of Our Times.* London, 1994.

Aston, Nigel and Clarissa Campbell Orr (eds). *An Enlightenment Statesman in Whig Britain: Lord Shelburne in Context, 1737–1805.* Woodbridge, 2011.

Atunes, Cátia A.P. and Amelia Polónia (eds). *Beyond Empires: Global, Self-Organizing, Cross-Imperial Networks, 1500–1800.* Leiden, 2016.

Barth, Jonathan. 'Reconstructing Mercantilism: Consensus and Conflict in British Imperial Economy in the Seventeenth and Eighteenth Centuries', *William and Mary Quarterly* 73, no. 2 (2016): 257–90.

Baugh, Daniel A. 'Maritime Strength and Atlantic Commerce: The Uses of a "Grand Marine Empire"'. in *An Imperial State at War: Britain from 1689 to 1815*, ed. Lawrence Stone. London, 1994.

— 'Withdrawing from Europe: Anglo-French Maritime Geopolitics, 1750–1800', *International History Review* 20, no. 1 (1998): 1–32.

Beckert, Sven. *Empire of Cotton: A Global History.* New York, 2014.

Belissa, Marc. *Fraternité universelle et intérêt national (1713–1795): Les cosmopolitiques du droit des gens.* Paris, 1998.

Bély, Lucien. *L'art de la paix en Europe: Naissance de la diplomatie moderne XVIe–XVIIIe siècles.* Paris, 2007.

Black, Jeremy. *Natural and Necessary Enemies: Anglo-French Relations in the Eighteenth Century.* Athens, GA, 1986.

— *Trade, Empire and British Foreign Policy, 1689–1815: The Politics of a Commercial State.* London, 2007.

Bois, Jean-Pierre. *L'abbé de Saint-Pierre: Entre classicisme et Lumières.* Ceyzérieu, 2017.

Bourke, Richard. *Empire and Revolution: The Political Life of Edmund Burke.* Princeton, 2015.

Bowen, H.V. *The Business of Empire: The East India Company and Imperial Britain, 1756–1833.* Cambridge, 2005.

Brewer, John. *The Sinews of Power: War, Money and the English State, 1688–1783.* Cambridge, MA, 1988.

Ceadel, Martin. *The Origins of War Prevention: The British Peace Movement and International Relations 1730–1854.* Oxford, 1996.

Charles, Loïc, Frédéric Lefebvre, and Christine Théré (eds). *Le cercle de Vincent de Gournay: Savoirs économiques et pratiques administratives en France au milieu du XVIIIe siècle.* Paris, 2011.

Charles, Loïc and Christine Théré. 'The Writing Workshop of François Quesnay and the Making of Physiocracy', *History of Political Economy* 40, no. 1 (2008): 1–42.

Chaudhuri, K.N. *The Trading World of Asia and the English East India Company 1660–1760*. Cambridge, 1978.

Cheney, Paul. *Cul de Sac: Patrimony, Capitalism, and Slavery in French Saint-Domingue*. Chicago, 2017.

— *Revolutionary Commerce: Globalization and the French Monarchy*. Cambridge, MA, 2010.

Conway, Stephen. *Britain, Ireland, and Continental Europe in the Eighteenth Century: Similarities, Connections, Identities*. Oxford, 2011.

Crouzet, François. *La guerre économique franco-anglaise au XVIIIe siècle*. Paris, 2008.

Crowley, John E. *The Privileges of Independence: Neomercantilism and the American Revolution*. Baltimore, 1993.

Darwin, John. *After Tamerlane: The Rise and Fall of Global Empires, 1400–2000*. London, 2008.

Das, Sudipta. *Myths and Realities of French Imperialism in India, 1763–1783*. New York, 1992.

Daudin, Guillaume. *Commerce et prospérité: La France au XVIIIe siècle*, 2nd edn. Paris, 2005.

De Vries, Jan. *The Industrious Revolution: Consumer Behavior and Household Economy, 1650 to the Present*. Cambridge, 2008.

Delgado Ribas, Josep M. *Dinámicas imperiales (1650–1796): España, América y Europa en el cambio institucional del sistema colonial español*. Barcelona, 2007.

Deringer, William. *Calculated Values: Finance, Politics, and the Quantitative Age*. Cambridge, MA, 2018.

Desan, Christine. *Making Money: Coin, Currency, and the Making of Capitalism*. Oxford, 2014.

Donaghay, Marie. 'Calonne and the Anglo-French Commercial Treaty of 1786'. *Journal of Modern History* 50, no. 3, supplement (1978): D1,157–84.

Dull, Jonathan R. *The French Navy and American Independence: A Study of Arms and Diplomacy, 1774–1787*. Princeton, 1975.

Ehrman, John. *The British Government and Commercial Negotiations with Europe, 1783–1793*. Cambridge, 1962.

Erikson, Emily. *Between Monopoly and Free Trade: The English East India Company, 1600–1757*. Princeton, 2014.

Fraser, Nancy. 'Behind Marx's Hidden Abode: For an Expanded Conception of Capitalism'. *New Left Review* 86 (2014): 55–72.

Fredona, Robert, and Sophus A. Reinert. 'Leviathan and Kraken: States, Corporations, and Political Economy'. *History and Theory* 59, no. 2 (2020): 167–87.

Gauci, Perry. *The Politics of Trade: The Overseas Merchant in State and Society, 1660–1720*. Oxford, 2001.

Gauci, Perry (ed.). *Regulating the British Economy, 1660–1850*. Farnham, 2011.

Genet, Jean-Philippe, and François-Joseph Ruggiu (eds). *Les idées passent-elles la Manche? Savoirs, représentations, pratiques (France–Angleterre, Xe–XXe siècles)*. Paris, 2007.

Gottmann, Felicia. 'French-Asian Connections: The Compagnie des Indes, France's Eastern Trade, and New Directions in Historical Scholarship'. *Historical Journal* 52, no. 2 (2013): 537–52.

— *Global Trade, Smuggling, and the Making of Economic Liberalism: Asian Textiles in France 1680–1760*. Basingstoke, 2016.

Gould, Eliga. 'War by Other Means: Mercantilism and Free Trade in the Age of the American Revolution', in *American Capitalism: New Histories*, ed. Sven Beckert and Christine Desan, 285–302. New York, 2018.

Greene, Jack P. *Evaluating Empire and Confronting Colonialism in Eighteenth-Century Britain*. Cambridge, 2013.

Hancock, David. *Citizens of the World: London Merchants and the Integration of the British Atlantic Community, 1735–1785*. Cambridge, 1995.

Hanotin, Guillaume. *Ambassadeur de deux couronnes: Amelot et les Bourbons entre commerce et diplomatie*. Madrid, 2018.

Harlow, Vincent T. *The Founding of the Second British Empire 1763–1793*, 2 vols. London, 1952–64.

Harris, Robert. *Politics and the Nation: Britain in the Mid-Eighteenth Century*. Oxford, 2002.

Haudrère, Philippe. *La Compagnie française des Indes au XVIIIe siècle*, 2nd edn, 2 vols. Paris, 2005.

Heckscher, Eli F. *Mercantilism*, trans. Mendel Shapiro, 2 vols. London, 1955.

Hirsch, Jean-Pierre and Philippe Minard. ' "Laissez-nous faire et protégez-nous beaucoup": Pour une histoire des pratiques institutionnelles dans l'industrie française, XVIIIe-XIXe siècles', in *La France n'est-elle pas douée pour l'industrie?*, ed. Louis Bergeron and Patrice Bourdelais, 135–58. Paris, 1998.

Hirschman, Albert O. *The Passions and the Interests: Political Arguments for Capitalism before Its Triumph*, 3rd edn. Princeton, 2013.

Hont, Istvan, *Jealousy of Trade: International Competition and the Nation-State in Historical Perspective*. Cambridge, MA, 2005.

Hoppit, Julian. *Britain's Political Economies: Parliament and Economic Life, 1660–1800*. Cambridge, 2017.

Horn, Jeff. *Economic Development in Early Modern France: The Privilege of Liberty, 1650–1820*. Cambridge, 2015.

— *The Path Not Taken: French Industrialization in the Age of Revolution, 1750–1830*. Cambridge, MA, 2006.

Isenmann, Moritz. 'From Privilege to Economic Law: Vested Interests and the Origins of Free Trade Theory in France (1687–1701)', in *Economic Growth and the Origins of Modern Political Economy: Economic Reasons of State, 1500–2000*, ed. Philipp R. Rössner, 103–21. New York, 2016.

Jessenne, Jean-Pierre, Renaud Morieux, and Pascal Dupuy (eds). *Le négoce de la paix: Les nations et les traités franco-britanniques, 1713–1802*. Paris, 2008.

Kaplan, Steven L. and Sophus A. Reinert. *The Economic Turn: Recasting Political Economy in Enlightenment Europe*. London, 2019.

Kapossy, Béla, Isaac Nakhimovsky, and Richard Whatmore (eds). *Commerce and Peace in the Enlightenment*. Cambridge, 2017.

Kwass, Michael. *Contraband: Louis Mandrin and the Making of a Global Underground*. Cambridge, MA, 2014.

Lane, Frederic C. *Profits from Power: Readings in Protection Rent and Violence-Controlling Enterprises*. Albany, 1979.

Lespagnol, André. *Messieurs de Saint-Malo: Une élite négociante au temps de Louis XIV*. Rennes, 2011.

Lincoln, Margarette. *Trading in War: London's Maritime World in the Age of Cook and Nelson*. New Haven and London, 2018.

Livesey, James. 'Free Trade and Empire in the Anglo-Irish Commercial Propositions of 1785'. *Journal of British Studies* 52, no. 1 (2013): 103–27.

Lüthy, Herbert. *La banque protestante en France de la révocation de l'Édit de Nantes à la Révolution*, 2 vols. Paris, 1959–61.

Lynd, Staughton and David Waldstreicher. 'Free Trade, Sovereignty, and Slavery: Toward an Economic Interpretation of American Independence'. *William and Mary Quarterly* 68, no. 4 (2011): 597–630.

Magnusson, Lars. *The Political Economy of Mercantilism*. New York, 2015.

— *The Tradition of Free Trade*. New York, 2004.

Mapp, Paul W. *The Elusive West and the Contest for Empire, 1713–1763*. Chapel Hill, 2011.

Margerison, Kenneth. 'Commercial Liberty, French National Power, and the Indies Trade after the Seven Years' War'. *Historical Reflections/Réflexions Historiques* 35 (2009): 52–73.

— 'French Visions of Empire: Contesting British Power in India after the Seven Years War'. *English Historical Review* 130, no. 544 (2015): 583–612.

Marshall, P.J. *Edmund Burke and the British Empire in the West Indies: Wealth, Power, and Slavery*. Oxford, 2019.

— *The Making and Unmaking of Empires: Britain, India, and America* c. *1750–1783*. Oxford, 2005.

Marzagalli, Silvia. *Bordeaux et les États-Unis, 1776–1815: Politique et stratégies négociantes dans la genèse d'un réseau commercial.* Geneva, 2015.

Meyssonnier, Simone. *La balance et l'horloge: La genèse de la pensée libérale en France au XVIIIe siècle.* Montreuil, 1989.

Morieux, Renaud. *The Channel: England, France and the Construction of a Maritime Border in the Eighteenth Century.* Cambridge, 2016.

Muldrew, Craig. ' "Hard Food for Midas": Cash and Its Social Value in Early Modern England'. *Past & Present* 170 (2001): 78–120.

Murphy, Antoin E. *John Law: Economic Theorist and Policy-Maker.* Oxford, 1997.

Murphy, Orville T. *Charles Gravier, Comte de Vergennes: French Diplomacy in the Age of Revolution, 1719–1787.* Albany, 1982.

Muthu, Sankar. 'Adam Smith's Critique of International Trading Companies: Theorizing "Globalization" in the Age of Enlightenment'. *Political Theory* 36, no. 2 (2008): 185–212.

Nakhimovsky, Isaac. *The Closed Commercial State: Perpetual Peace and Commercial Society from Rousseau to Fichte.* Princeton, 2011.

Neal, Larry. *'I Am Not Master of Events': The Speculations of John Law and Lord Londonderry in the Mississippi and South Sea Bubbles.* New Haven, 2012.

Nye, John V.C. *War, Wine, and Taxes: The Political Economy of Anglo-French Trade, 1689–1900.* Princeton, 2007.

Orain, Arnaud. *La politique du merveilleux: Une autre histoire du Système de Law (1695–1795).* Paris, 2018.

— 'Soutenir la guerre et réformer la fiscalité: Silhouette et Forbonnais au Contrôle général des finances (1759)'. *French Historical Studies* 36, no. 3 (2013): 417–47.

Pares, Richard. *War and Trade in the West Indies 1739–1763.* Oxford, 1936.

Peters, Marie. *Pitt and Popularity: The Patriot Minister and London Opinion during the Seven Years' War.* Oxford Press, 1980.

Phillips, Andrew and J.C. Sharman. *Outsourcing Empire: How Company-States Made the Modern World.* Princeton, 2020.

Pincus, Steve. *1688: The First Modern Revolution.* New Haven, 2009.

— 'Addison's Empire: Whig Conceptions of Empire in the Early 18th Century'. *Parliamentary History* 31, no. 1 (2012): 99–117.

— *The Heart of the Declaration: The Founders' Case for an Activist Government.* New Haven, 2016.

— 'Rethinking Mercantilism: Political Economy, the British Empire, and the Atlantic World in the Seventeenth and Eighteenth Centuries'. *William and Mary Quarterly*, 3rd series, 69 (2012): 3–34.

Pocock, J.G.A. *Barbarism and Religion: The Enlightenments of Edward Gibbon 1737–1764.* Cambridge, 1999.

— *Virtue, Commerce, and History: Essays on Political Thought & History, Chiefly in the Eighteenth Century.* Cambridge, 1985.

Pohlig, Mathias and Michael Schaich (eds). *The War of the Spanish Succession: New Perspectives.* Oxford, 2018.

Price, Jacob M. *France and the Chesapeake: A History of the French Tobacco Monopoly, 1674–1791, and Its Relationship to the British and American Tobacco Trades,* 2 vols. Ann Arbor, 1973.

Reinert, Sophus A. *Translating Empire: Emulation and the Origins of Political Economy.* Cambridge, MA, 2011.

Riley, James C. *The Seven Years War and the Old Regime in France: The Economic and Financial Toll.* Princeton, 1986.

Ritcheson, C.R. 'The Earl of Shelburne and Peace with America, 1782–1783: Vision and Reality'. *International History Review* 5, no. 3 (1983): 322–45.

Robertson, John. *The Case for the Enlightenment: Scotland and Naples 1680–1760.* Cambridge, 2005.

Robertson, John (ed.). *A Union for Empire: Political Thought and the British Union of 1707.* Cambridge, 1995.

Røge, Pernille. *Economistes and the Reinvention of Empire: France in the Americas and Africa,* c. *1750–1802.* Cambridge, 2019.

Rössner, Philipp Robinson. 'Heckscher Reloaded? Mercantilism, the State, and Europe's Transition to Industrialization, 1600–1900'. *Historical Journal* 58, no. 2 (2015): 663–83.

Rothkrug, Lionel. *The Opposition to Louis XIV: The Political and Social Origins of the French Enlightenment.* Princeton, 1965.

Rothschild, Emma. 'Adam Smith in the British Empire', in *Empire and Modern Political Thought,* ed. Sankar Muthu, 184–98. Cambridge, 2012.

— *The Inner Life of Empires: An Eighteenth-Century History.* Princeton, 2011.

Rowlands, Guy. *The Financial Decline of a Great Power: War, Influence, and Money in Louis XIV's France.* Oxford, 2012.

Ruggiu, François-Joseph. 'India and the Reshaping of the French Colonial Policy (1759–1789)'. *Itinerario* 35, no. 2 (2011): 25–43.

— 'Falling into Oblivion? Canada and the French Monarchy, 1759–1783', in *Revisiting 1759: The Conquest of Canada in Historical Perspective,* ed. Phillip Buckner and John G. Reid, 69–94. Toronto, 2012.

Rule, John C. and Ben S. Trotter. *A World of Paper: Louis XIV, Colbert de Torcy, and the Rise of the Information State.* Montreal, 2014.

Satsuma, Shinsuke. *Britain and Colonial Maritime War in the Early Eighteenth Century: Silver, Seapower and the Atlantic.* Woodbridge, 2013.

Schabas, Margaret and Carl Wennerlind. *A Philosopher's Economist: Hume and the Rise of Capitalism.* Chicago, 2020.

Schabas, Margaret and Carl Wennerlind (eds). *David Hume's Political Economy.* London, 2008.

Schnakenbourg, Éric. *Entre la guerre et la paix: Neutralité et relations internationales XVIIe– XVIIIe siècles.* Rennes, 2013.

— 'Les interactions entre commerce et diplomatie au début du XVIIIe siècle: L'exemple du Traité de commerce franco-anglais de 1713'. *Histoire, économie & société* 23 (2004): 349–65.

Scott, H.M. *British Foreign Policy in the Age of the American Revolution.* Oxford, 1990.

Silberner, Edmond. *La guerre dans la pensée économique du XVIe au XVIIIe siècle.* Paris, 1939.

Simms, Brendan. *Three Victories and a Defeat: The Rise and Fall of the First British Empire, 1714– 1783.* New York, 2007.

Skornicki, Arnault. *L'économiste, la cour et la patrie: L'économie politique dans la France des Lumières.* Paris, 2011.

Smith, David Kammerling. 'Structuring Politics in Early Eighteenth-Century France: The Political Innovations of the French Council of Commerce'. *Journal of Modern History* 74, no. 3 (2002): 490–537.

Soll, Jacob. *The Information Master: Jean-Baptiste Colbert's Secret State Intelligence System.* Ann Arbor, 2009.

Sonenscher, Michael. *Before the Deluge: Public Debt, Inequality, and the Intellectual Origins of the French Revolution.* Princeton, 2007.

Spector, Céline. *Montesquieu et l'émergence de l'économie politique.* Paris, 2006.

Stapelbroek, Koen. '"The Long Peace": Commercial Treaties and the Principles of Global Trade at the Peace of Utrecht', in *The 1713 Peace of Utrecht and its Enduring Effects,* ed. Alfred Soons, 93–119. Leiden, 2018.

Stapelbroek, Koen (ed.). *Trade and War: The Neutrality of Commerce in the Inter-State System.* Helsinki, 2011.

Steiner, Philippe. 'Circuits, monnaie et balance du commerce', in *Nouvelle histoire de la pensée économique,* ed. Alain Béraud and Gilbert Faccarello, vol. 1, 111–21. Paris, 1992.

— 'Wealth and Power: Quesnay's Political Economy of the "Agricultural Kingdom"'. *Journal of the History of Economic Thought* 24, no. 1 (2002): 91–110.

Stern, Philip J. *The Company-State: Corporate Sovereignty and the Early Modern Foundations of the British Empire in India.* Oxford, 2011.

— 'Limited Liabilities: The Corporation and the Political Economy of Protection in the British Empire', in *Protection and Empire: A Global History*, ed. Lauren Benton, Adam Clulow, and Bain Attwood, 93–113. Cambridge, 2017.

Stern, Philip J. and Carl Wennerlind. *Mercantilism Reimagined: Political Economy in Early Modern Britain and its Empire*. Oxford, 2013.

Stockley, Andrew. *Britain and France at the Birth of America: The European Powers and the Peace Negotiations of 1782–83*. Exeter, 2001.

Sutherland, Lucy S. *The East India Company in Eighteenth-Century Politics*. Oxford, 1962.

Tarrade, Jean. *Le commerce colonial de la France à la fin de l'Ancien Régime: L'évolution du régime de 'l'Exclusif' de 1763 à 1789*, 2 vols. Paris, 1972.

Tazzara, Corey. *The Free Port of Livorno and the Transformation of the Mediterranean World, 1574–1790*. Oxford, 2017.

Teichgraeber, Richard F., III. ' "Less Abused than I Had Reason to Expect": The Reception of the Wealth of Nations in Britain, 1776–90'. *Historical Journal* 30, no. 2 (1987): 337–66.

Terjanian, Anoush Fraser. *Commerce and Its Discontents in Eighteenth-Century French Political Thought*. Cambridge, 2013.

Ternat, François. *Partager le monde: Rivalités impériales franco-britanniques 1748–1756*. Paris, 2015.

Tilly, Charles. 'War Making and State Making as Organized Crime', in *Bringing the State Back In*, ed. Peter B. Evans, Dietrich Rueschemeyer, and Theda Skocpol, 169–91. Cambridge, 1985.

Todd, David. *Free Trade and Its Enemies in France, 1814–1851*. Cambridge, 2015.

— *A Velvet Empire: French Informal Imperialism in the Nineteenth Century*. Princeton, 2021.

Tombs, Isabelle and Robert Tombs. *That Sweet Enemy: The French and the British from the Sun King to the Present*. New York, 2007.

Travers, Robert. *Ideology and Empire in Eighteenth-Century India: The British in Bengal*. Cambridge, 2007.

Trivellato, Francesca. *The Familiarity of Strangers: The Sephardic Diaspora, Livorno, and Cross-Cultural Trade in the Early Modern Period*. New Haven, 2009.

Vaughn, James. *The Politics of Empire at the Accession of George III: The East India Company and the Crisis and Transformation of Britain's Imperial State*. New Haven, 2019.

Wennerlind, Carl. *Casualties of Credit: The English Financial Revolution, 1620–1720*. Cambridge, MA, 2011.

Whatmore, Richard. *Against War and Empire: Geneva, Britain, and France in the Eighteenth Century*. New Haven, 2012.

Wilson, Kathleen. 'Empire, Trade and Popular Politics in Mid-Hanoverian Britain: The Case of Admiral Vernon'. *Past & Present* 121 (1988): 74–109.

ACKNOWLEDGEMENTS

In the years it took to research and write this book, I came to understand that history is really a collaborative enterprise. The book could not have been written without the labour of many other scholars on whose work I build – some of them writing decades ago. It has also benefited immeasurably from the criticism and advice of numerous colleagues and friends, and the support of individuals and institutions. I would like to acknowledge the early assistance and encouragement of Loïc Charles, Katherine Fleming, Colin Jones, Tony Judt, Emma Rothschild, Christine Théré, and Larry Wolff. My thanks to the Minda de Gunzburg Center for European Studies at Harvard University, and the Institut National d'Études Démographiques in Paris, which hosted me in the earliest stages of the project. Thanks also to the National Endowment for the Humanities, which made possible a fellowship year at a key moment in the drafting, and to New York University for permitting time away from teaching to finish the manuscript. I am fortunate to work with brilliant and supportive colleagues in the History Department at NYU. Special thanks to Karl Appuhn, Guy Ortolano, and Andrew Sartori, who read and commented on parts of the manuscript, to Liz Ellis and Stephen Gross for reading suggestions, and to Barbara Weinstein, who supported my research at a critical moment as department chair.

The most gratifying aspect of scholarly work is the conversation it generates with others. Over the years, I have profited from discussions with Antonella Alimento, David Armitage, Lauren Benton, Alex Bick, Rafe Blaufarb, Paul Cheney, Stephen Conway, Manuel Covo, Elizabeth Cross, Oliver Cussen, Will Derringer, Jean-François Dunyach, François Furstenberg, Jan Goldstein, Felicia Gottmann, David Singh Grewal, David Hancock, Istvan Hont, Jeff Horn, Daniel Hulsebosch, Andrew Jainchill, Maya Jasanoff, Fredrik Albritton Jonsson,

ACKNOWLEDGEMENTS

Thomas Kaiser, Michael Kwass, Mary Lewis, James Livesey, Gabe Paquette, Steve Pincus, Sanjay Reddy, Sophus Reinert, Pernille Røge, Sophia Rosenfeld, Éric Schnakenbourg, William Sewell, Arnault Skornicki, David Kammerling Smith, Michael Sonenscher, Koen Stapelbroek, Philip Stern, Fidel Tavárez, Anoush Terjanian, Christine Théré, Richard Tuck, James Vaughn, Carl Wennerlind, and Owen White.

My warm thanks also to the editorial team at Yale University Press who improved the book in so many ways: especially Jacob Blandy, Rachael Lonsdale, Marika Lysandrou, and above all Heather McCallum, who saw value in the project from our first conversation. I am grateful to Bill Nelson for preparing the maps. Sincere thanks also to the anonymous readers who evaluated the manuscript for the press and offered valuable advice for revision.

I have shared chapters with too many seminars and workshops to name individually, but for their kind invitations to present, and their gracious hospitality, I particularly thank Antonella Alimento, David Bell, Megan Black, Loïc Charles, Paul Cohen, Robert Fredona, Perry Gauci, Martin Giraudeau, Michael Griffin, Carla Hesse, Michael Kwass, Simon Macdonald, Philippe Minard, Isaac Nakhimovsky, Arnaud Orain, Steve Pincus, François-Joseph Ruggiu, Jonathan Sheehan, Koen Stapelbroek, and Charles Walton. I am especially grateful to Sophus Reinert who organised a workshop around the manuscript at Harvard Business School, and to the participants in that event who offered such great advice. Special thanks to Carl Wennerlind, who has patiently listened to me talk about this project for a decade, and who read the penultimate manuscript with his customary generosity and intelligence.

This would have been a lonely enterprise, and my life a great deal poorer, without the tolerance, teasing, and laughter of my children, Aoife and Nicolas, and the grace and generosity of my wife Kristel Smentek. I cannot thank them enough. My ultimate debt is to my parents, Frank and Collette Shovlin, who gave me everything I needed for the journey and always trusted me to find my way. The book is dedicated to them.

INDEX